MW00535351

Hegelianism

Hegelianism

The Path Toward Dialectical Humanism, 1805–1841

John Edward Toews

Department of History
University of Washington

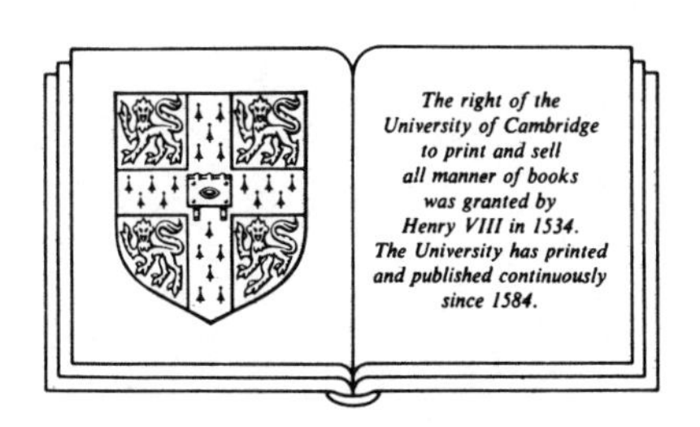

Cambridge University Press

Cambridge
London New York New Rochelle
Melbourne Sydney

Published by the Press Syndicate of the University of Cambridge
The Pitt Building, Trumpington Street, Cambridge CB2 1RP
32 East 57th Street, New York, NY 10022, USA
10 Stamford Road, Oakleigh, Melbourne 3166, Australia

© Cambridge University Press 1980

First published 1980
First paperback edition 1985
Reprinted 1985

Printed in the United States of America

Library of Congress Cataloging in Publication Data
Toews, John Edward.
Hegelianism.
Bibliography: p.
Includes index.
1. Hegel, Georg Wilhelm Friedrich, 1770–1831
– Influence. 2. Humanism – History. I. Title.
B2948.T63 193 80–16370
ISBN 0 521 23048 9 hard covers
ISBN 0 521 31636 7 paperback

IN MEMORY OF MY FATHER
JOHN ARON TOEWS
1912–1979

We are seeking in knowledge of the past the same thing which we are seeking in knowledge of contemporary men, above all the fundamental attitudes of individuals and human groups with respect to values, the community and the universe. If knowledge of history has any practical importance for us, it is because we learn from it about men, who, in different circumstances and with different means, for the most part inapplicable in our own time, fought for values and ideals which were similar, identical, or opposed to those of today; and this makes us conscious of belonging to a totality which transcends us, which we support in the present and which men who come after us will continue to support in the future.

– Lucien Goldmann

Contents

Preface

This book grew out of a doctoral dissertation entitled "The Innocence of the Self: Cultural Disinheritance and Cultural Liberation in the Thought and Experience of the Young Germans and Young Hegelians," which was completed under the direction of H. Stuart Hughes at Harvard University in 1973. In contrast to the usual pattern of development, the process of rethinking and revision has produced a book both shorter and narrower in scope than the original dissertation. My attempt to achieve a systematic comprehension of the evolution of experience and thought from the young Hegel to the radical Left Hegelians of the 1840s transformed what had been an introductory chapter into a full-scale historical study of the early phases of Hegelian ideology and the Hegelian school. This new focus on origins, on the ideological and experiential presuppositions of the radical stances of the 1840s, was obviously influenced by the historical disappointments and disillusionments experienced by members of my generation during the 1970s. What had begun as a sympathetic rehabilitation of utopian hopes for a cultural revolution that would integrate the socially and psychically emancipated self into a nonrepressive community or "civilization without discontents" (and thus "actualize" the dreams of art and philosophy) gradually turned into a disabused investigation of the recurring, apparently intractable, dilemmas of human emancipation as conceived within the categories of the dialectical tradition. The present volume constitutes the first part of this redefined project. A sequel will trace the disintegration and transformations of Hegelian humanism through the crisis years of the 1840s, and I eventually hope to complete the revision of my original project with a separate study of contemporaneous, homologous developments in literature and art.

During the long and difficult years between the inception and completion of this study, I have been intellectually and morally sustained by teachers, colleagues, students, and friends who possessed enough faith to encourage and support me in going my own way. H. Stuart Hughes remained amazingly tolerant and supportive as I stubbornly expanded my project beyond the reasonable scope of a doctoral dissertation. My colleagues in the History Department at Columbia University shielded me from professional disaster when I appeared determined to perish rather than publish and insisted on reworking and reconceptualizing my study from the ground up. Joe Lawrence, David Luft, Eleanor Toews, and John Traficonte know the extent of my spiritual indebtedness and how little of it I can hope to repay. In a more mundane sense the completion of this study was made possible by generous grants from the Canada Council and the Council for Research in the Social Sciences of Columbia University, and by the efficient and intelligent services of librarians at the Bayerische Staatsbibliothek; the Schiller National-Museum; and the university libraries at Tübingen, Munich, Harvard, and Columbia. The final stages of revision were greatly aided by the trenchant but supportive criticism of George Armstrong Kelly and Jerrold Seigel. Julia and Jonathan made certain that I never forgot that a book is, after all, just a book.

J.E.T.

Introduction: the Hegelian project in ideological perspective

This study is intended as a contribution to the contemporary understanding and inner appropriation of modern European cultural and intellectual history on two distinct, but intimately connected and overlapping, levels. It can be read, first of all, as a contribution to the early history of Hegelianism, as an attempt at a systematic description and comprehensive, contextual reconstruction of the historical genesis, appropriation, inner division, and first fundamental transformation of what was certainly one of the most significant and influential of the many competing *Weltanschauungen,* philosophical "faiths," or cultural ideologies (British philosophic radicalism and French Saint-Simonianism are obvious parallel phenomena) that replaced traditional Christian or Jewish religion in the minds and hearts of many European intellectuals in the first half of the nineteenth century. But the thematic focus of this particular historical reconstruction of Hegelianism – the transition from "the actualization of the absolute" to the "self-actualization of man," from the incarnation of the transcendent in the immanent to the self-production of man's immanent essence in concrete historical existence – also connects this study to a more general problem that transcends the specific experiences and perspectives of academic schools and intellectual cliques in pre-1848 Germany and has constituted a major factor in the social and intellectual history of the western world for at least the last three centuries: the protracted, often agonizing, sometimes exhilarating, disintegration of the experienced vitality and viability of religious and metaphysical faith, of belief in the objective reality of a transcendent foundation of personal identity and communal integration.

It has often been claimed – from both elegiac and prophetic perspectives – that the decomposition of Hegel's "synthesis" of the transcendent and the immanent in the 1840s marked a radical turning point in western man's experience and self-consciousness: the recognition of his transcendental "homelessness" and commitment to the necessity or at least possibility of a completely immanent, natural, and/or historical actualization of human redemption.[1] The experiential origins of this study as well lie in the peculiarly modern oscillation between hope and despair regarding the problem of secular redemption, of the immanent historical actualization of human autonomy and community. For both external and internal reasons, however, the analysis of the historical development of Hegelianism in this book does not extend (except in the brief sketch of the Epilogue) to the crisis of the mid-1840s from which emerged the complementary, yet antagonistic, "resolutions" of Marxism and Existentialism, but concludes with what may appear to be a preliminary, transitional stage in the disintegration and transformation of Hegelianism – the Left Hegelian humanism articulated in the critical writings of Strauss, Bauer, and Feuerbach between 1835 and 1841. But this does not mean that this book should be read as a somewhat lengthy preparation for an absent conclusion, except insofar as all histories must necessarily be read as fragments of an incomplete story. It is relatively easy to write the story of Hegelianism if one is convinced that it is informed by a teleological development toward a convincing resolution or conclusion in Marx, Kierkegaard, or Stirner and Nietzsche, or that it can be judged and dismissed from some external standpoint as a bizarre curiosity or dangerous delusion.[2] The basic premises from which this investigation proceeds, however, are a conviction of the human and historical significance of the Hegelian project, and a belief in the inconclusive and incomplete character of its trajectory.

These premises undergird the decision to undertake a comprehensive and systematic analysis of early Hegelianism and to conclude this particular history in 1841. Once the teleological straitjacket of "Hegel to Marx" or "Hegel to Nietzsche" is removed from the history of Hegelianism, those forgotten Hegelians apparently left behind or overcome by the inexorable process of historical evolution gain a new status: They have to be taken seriously. It is truly amazing, considering the amount of intellectual energy that has been expended on the investigation of Hegel, Feuerbach, Marx, and their interrelationships, how little effort has been devoted to the analysis of the Hegelianism of the 1820s and 1830s.[3] Misleading and simply wrong conceptions of the origin and nature of the divisions of the Hegelian school have been repeated over and over again in the most scholarly works. Moreover, a reconstruction of the comprehensive scope of early Hegelianism is more than simply a matter of rehabilitating the historically forgotten or correcting tired clichés. It is directly relevant to the interpretation of the intellectual stances of more familiar figures. For example, the belief that the problem of transition from theory to practice first arose around 1840 and marked a new departure in the Hegelian tradition is clearly based on ignorance of earlier developments. The problematic relationship between thought and being, consciousness and existence, critical theory and revolutionary practice is one of the recurring dilemmas of the Hegelian and, more broadly, the dialectical tradition: a dilemma that has been reconstituted in different form at each stage of its development and is still, of course, being constantly reformulated in Marxist and Existentialist thought. [4] An investigation of the genesis of the first major reformulation of this problematic – its anthropological "reduction" or "inversion" in Left Hegelian humanism – need not, therefore, be considered a mere prolegomena to the main event, but can stand on its own as an analysis of the nature and experiential determinants of a dilemma that is still with us. Furthermore, the humanist inversion of Hegelian metaphysics first clearly brought to light the constituent elements of the theory/practice problematic of the dialectical tradition within an immanent framework, within a situation in which the dialectical unification of subject and object, consciousness and existence, had been deprived of its transcendent foundation, or, from a different perspective, liberated from its transcendent illusion.

As a disabused, disillusioned investigation of a major phase and turning point in the history of disillusionment and demystification, this study conforms to the general methodological principles of "ideological" analysis. Such a stance would seem only fitting and proper for an analysis of the intellectual tradition that played such a predominant role in formulating the concept of ideology and inaugurating the methods of ideological criticism, but it does require some preliminary clarification.[5] Hegelian philosophy has been treated throughout this study as a subjectively coherent system of ideas, beliefs, and assumptions whose "subjective coherence" was rooted in a particular configuration of psychological, social, and historical experience. The focus, therefore, is on the relationship between thought and thinkers, ideas and experience, rather than on a comparative or developmental situating of Hegelian thought in relation to earlier or later systems of thought, or on a judgment of Hegelian thought according to allegedly objective criteria of rational coherence and empirical verifiability. The ideological approach does not, of course, necessitate a reduction of the thought of Hegel and his disciples and heirs to a merely passive reflection of their personal experiences and particular historical world. Hegelian thought should be viewed as an act of both self-comprehension and self-transcendence. It was a world view not in the sense of a view of the world as externally given to the observing and reflecting subject, but in the sense of a comprehension of the world as lived and actively experienced by the subject. Moreover, Hegelian thought claimed to transcend the particularity of the individual, subjectively experienced world by incorporating this particularity into the systematic totality of human experience and, even more ambitiously, into the self-sufficient structure of unconditioned, "absolute" being.

The particular character of Hegelian philosophy as an ideology is perhaps most clearly revealed if it is interpreted as a titanic attempt to reconstruct a convincing consciousness of cultural integration, of communal and "religious" or "absolute" identity in a historical context in which traditional modes of integration had lost their experiential viability. That the social and religious, communal and "ontological," dimensions of the self's integration into the universal were inextricably connected was a fundamental presupposition of Hegel's philosophy and one of the most problematic aspects of his legacy to his students and disciples. Throughout this work, I will be constantly concerned with the particular ways in which both the identity of and tensions between the communal and ontological dimensions ("politics" and "religion") of cultural integration and cultural disinheritance defined the experience of Hegelians and determined the evolution of Hegelianism. In fact, the adjective "cultural" in phrases like "cultural integration," "cultural disinheritance," and "cultural ideology" is generally used in this study as an abbreviated way of referring to both dimensions of the self's relation to its world of experience and its efforts to establish a satisfactory identity. "Cultural integration" designates the process in which the self experiences and comprehends its "true" identity through incorporation into a sociohistorical community and connection to some ultimate or absolute ground of being; "cultural disinheritance" refers to the experienced breakdown of this process; and "cultural ideology" is defined as a system of ideas and beliefs that attempts self-consciously to reconstruct the connection between self and world on both levels.

At the very outset of his academic career, Hegel himself defined the historical role of philosophy as a cultural ideology. "When the power of unification has disappeared from the life of man," he wrote in his first published book, "when opposites have lost their living relationship and reciprocity and gained autonomy, the need for philosophy arises." The task of philosophy was to resolve the crisis of "bifurcation (*Entzweiung*)" that characterized all levels of personal, social, and religious life, to provide man with a self-conscious comprehension of the unity in experience that would allow him to feel "at home" in the world.[6] Despite the notorious difficulty of his writings, Hegel never conceived of a philosophy as an esoteric discipline for professional thinkers, but viewed his writing and teaching as directly relevant to the most acutely felt and universally experienced existential needs and interests of man. Moreover, both the questions out of which his philosophy arose and the solution it offered were consciously defined in terms of man's personal and collective needs and interests in a particular historical situation: It was "absurd" to imagine that philosophy could "transcend its contemporary world."[7] Yet Hegel's recognition of the ideological nature of philosophy was severely circumscribed. Although he admitted that the truth of philosophy was limited by the horizons of its "age," he was not willing or able to admit the legitimacy of divergent "truths" within one age. He was convinced that his philosophy was philosophy per se for his time, that it was not "Hegel's system" but simply "truth" in the form of a completely articulated, "scientific" system. Moreover, this claim was grounded in the conviction that the truth of his philosophy was not simply a human truth, but a comprehension of the embodiment of the absolute in the human. In the development of Hegelianism after Hegel the scope of ideological self-criticism was broadened as Hegel's claim regarding knowledge of absolute spirit was "unveiled" as an illusion. But even Hegel's Left Hegelian critics believed that Hegelian philosophy had embodied the truth, in a universal human sense, of *its* time. It was only on this basis that they could claim that the critical inversion of Hegelian thought was synonymous with an epochal transition to a new form of human existence and consciousness. In this study, however, the ideological mode of analysis has been pushed farther than either Hegel or his immediate heirs were willing to apply it to themselves, and an attempt has been made to provide a systematic reconstruction of the particular configuration of social and historical experience that constituted the matrix of Hegelianism.

The problem of defining the "experiential matrix" of the genesis and evolution of Hegelianism has been approached from four different angles. First, an attempt has been made to specify the social and institutional determinants that defined the horizons of the problem of cultural integration for members of the university-educated, professional civil service class in the Protestant areas of Germany during the late eighteenth and early nineteenth centuries. Second, the impact of social and demographic changes and specific political events on the character and composition of this "educated estate" and on the experience and thought of particular groups within it (especially the academics) has been examined. Third, divergences in individual psychobiographical development, especially as they relate to the formation of generational groupings, have been described in terms of their significance for the emergence, appropriation, and interpretation of Hegelian philosophy within the educated estate at different stages in its historical evolution. Finally, a number of attempts have been made, especially in Chapters 2, 3, and 7, to illuminate the sociohistorical roots and implications of the viewpoints of Hegel and his disciples by placing them within the comparative context of alternative, competing ideological responses to a shared historical experience.

All of the methods of ideological analysis used in this study, however, have been subordinated to, or incorporated within, a chronological framework. This book was conceived and written as a historical account of the emergence, appropriation, and transformation of a specific cultural ideology, as a work of intellectual history, not as an essay in philosophical criticism or as a psychological or sociological case study. The three major divisions of the book thus constitute chapters of a "story," although they remain fragmentary chapters of an incomplete story reconstructed from a particular personal, cultural, and historical perspective.

In Part I, I have tried to show how Hegel's mature philosophical position emerged as a response to the experiences and hopes of his historical generation and to describe its character and implications in terms of his own definition of the historical role of philosophy as a means to cultural integration. Because so much has been written on Hegel and so much is obviously left out of my account, some clarification of my focus and criteria of selection in this section may be useful. The genesis and significance of Hegel's philosophical position is analyzed here not as an impersonal comprehension or objective response to the revolutionary transformations of his era, but as a comprehension and response conditioned by the experience of, and perspective on, the world particular to Hegel as a member of a specific historical generation within a specific social group within a specific sociopolitical and cultural system. Hegel's mature philosophy constituted a remarkable attempt to grasp and articulate his experiential world as a completely coherent totality, to absorb the last remnants of "otherness" in the transparency of self-conscious knowledge. The task of "filling in" the background to the evolution of the Hegelian movement, therefore, cannot be performed adequately by simply summarizing Hegel's system (as if such a summary were a simple task!). Only when Hegel's philosophy has been placed in context, when the general structure of his philosophical viewpoint has been reconstructed as a particular response to a generational experience conditioned by the social perspective of the intellectual elite in Protestant Germany, is it possible to understand the impact of his thought on students and disciples whose historical and sociocultural perspectives and experiences often differed in significant ways from those of their teacher and master.

The task of situating Hegel's philosophy in its experiential matrix has been approached through an analysis of the major stages of his development. The first chapter tries to show how the historical problematic that provided the framework for the intellectual itineraries of Hegel and his generational contemporaries – the apparent contradiction between autonomy and "wholeness," between subjective freedom and communal and ontological integration – emerged out of the social and cultural tensions of late eighteenth-century Germany. Chapter 2 reconstructs the parallel developments of the members of the Hegelian generation through the crisis of the 1790s, as they tried to resolve the dichotomies of their inheritance in the light of the eschatological hopes aroused by the French Revolution, and culminates in a description of the Romantic ideology of cultural renovation that emerged during the last years of the decade. The aim of this chapter is to delineate the historical roots and purposes of the philosophy of "absolute" identity. Chapter 3 is devoted to an analysis of how Hegel's mature articulation of the philosophy of the absolute differentiated itself from the Romantic ideology and was connected to a particular type of cultural reform and reconstruction in the years after 1800. The focus in this chapter is on the historical context of Hegel's notorious reconciliation of Reason and reality and its relationship to the contemporary development of Romanticism into the cultural philosophy of the Historical School and, more particularly, of Hegel's rival at the University of Berlin, Friedrich Schleiermacher. Throughout Part I the emphasis is not on the detailed explication and critical analysis of Hegelian texts, but on the general delineation, within a comparative context, of the nature and sociocultural roots and implications of Hegel's particular resolution of the historical crisis of bifurcation.

Part II describes the complex transformation of Hegel's philosophy into the ideology of a Hegelian "school" or "movement." As far as I know, it constitutes the first attempt to provide a systematic description of the reception of Hegel's philosophy by sympathizers and disciples during his own lifetime. The aim of this description, however, is not just to fill one of the countless gaps in our historical knowledge, but to uncover the experiential and intellectual origins of the conflicts that divided Hegelians into opposing factions in the 1830s and 1840s. My investigations have revealed that significant divergences in the interpretation of the relationship between Hegel's conception of cultural integration and the concrete actuality of contemporary German sociopolitical and religious life emerged during the formative years of the Hegelian school and evolved into recognizable accommodationist, reformist, and "revolutionary" positions during the 1820s. By examining the thought and experience of representative individual Hegelians, I have tried to show how these divergences were connected to differing patterns of sociohistorical experience. Before Hegel's death, however, the differences among his disciples remained differences within Hegelianism; they were contained and relativized by a common commitment to Hegel's basic philosophical presuppositions and methodological principles. The historical actualization of absolute Reason, the incarnation of the infinite spirit in the world, whether it was defined as a completed process, a partially completed process, or a future goal, was conceived as synonymous with the actualization of man's essence as a free and rational being.

Part III is devoted to a comprehensive investigation and reconstruction of the division of the Hegelian school and the emergence of a new Hegelian Left during the 1830s. Its aim is to clarify the nature and development, and describe the experiential origins, of the transition from divergences within a common framework of philosophical presuppositions to fundamental disagreements about the meaning and ultimately the validity of these presuppositions. In the writings that Strauss, Bauer, and Feuerbach published between 1835 and 1841 the inherited Hegelian project of the historical actualization and comprehension of the self-relating, self-sufficient totality of absolute spirit was redefined in completely immanent, human terms as man's self-actualization and self-comprehension of his own universal essence. This humanistic "reduction" or transformation of the Hegelian absolute placed the new Left Hegelians in opposition to all other Hegelian factions, but it was still conceived as a "positive" reduction that simply unveiled and appropriated the "real" human content of Hegel's metaphysical mystifications. The project of secular historical redemption, of the ultimate identification of essence and existence, subject and object, theory and practice, was retained, and the inherent dilemmas of that project soon reemerged in new form. The Epilogue gives a brief sketch of the historical fate of Left Hegelian humanism as it encountered the political and social changes of the 1840s – the consolidation of the new principles of immanent dialectical development into the ideology of a radical "movement," the impotence and ultimate shattering of this movement in its battle with the established order, and the subsequent process of disillusionment and self-criticism out of which emerged new formulations of the Hegelian project, and new forms of its inner contradictions.

Throughout this historical account of the Hegelian project, I have made every effort to eschew hasty judgments concerning the historical or philosophical inadequacy of specific positions and have tried to give my protagonists a more sympathetic hearing or reading than they have usually received in previous accounts. My primary aim has been to comprehend how a particular configuration of aims and problems emerged from a particular configuration of historical experience and thus, indirectly and tentatively, to shed a little light on the roots of both a despair and a hope that are still very much with us.

1

Philosophy and cultural integration: Hegel in context

1

The origins of the Hegelian project: tensions in the father's world

In the fall of 1788, Hegel, who had just passed his eighteenth birthday, left his parental home in Stuttgart in order to begin a five-year program of theological study at the Protestant Seminary (*Stift*) in Tübingen. By going to Tübingen he was acting in conformity with the long-standing wishes of his father, and following the traditional avenue toward becoming a man of importance in his father's world. During the years at home and school in which the young Hegel was being prepared for his future vocation as a spiritual leader in the traditional culture of Old Württemberg (Altwürttemberg), however, this world was characterized by increasing political, social, and cultural tensions. Contrary to his father's hopes and expectations, Hegel's experience at Tübingen led not to a personal identification with the vocation that had been chosen for him, but to a radical disinheritance and commitment to liberation from the whole cultural world that had provided that vocation with meaning and importance. Hegel would later describe this crisis in terms of a universal revolution in man's cultural development, but the manner in which he perceived the general transformation was conditioned by the conceptual and experiential framework he brought to it from his own particular past in the *ancien régime.* When his father died in 1799, Hegel used his inheritance to finance the beginning of the academic career and philosophical vocation that defined his cultural identity for a new age.[1] But it was more than just this material legacy that Hegel brought from the old world into the new. He also carried within him an inheritance of social experience and cultural values that was transformed, but never extinguished, in his later development.

A reconstruction of the cultural inheritance that Hegel absorbed during the years of childhood and adolescence can best begin with a description of the social world into which he was born. Hegel's father was an administrative official in the ducal bureaucracy, a secretary and later counselor in the Chamber of Accounts. He was not, as has often been claimed, a petty functionary, but an important career bureaucrat who was able to buy a house in Stuttgart's "rich suburb" in 1776.[2] These facts locate Hegel's childhood and youth in the world of a particular social stratum in eighteenth-century German society, a stratum whose definition evades both the modern categories of economic class and the traditional categories of privileged corporation. It was a group whose social status was determined by the professional qualifications and political and cultural functions of its individual members. In a narrow sense it could be described as a state-service class, a class that would include the three subgroups of the judicial and administrative bureaucracy, the ecclesiastical hierarchy of the established Protestant state churches, and the teachers and professors in the state-controlled schools and universities. Individual merit expressed in the attainment of certain professional qualifications, usually a university degree, rather than corporate privilege or economic wealth, was, at least in principle, the basis for entry into this stratum. The historical process in which feudal forms of inherited and electoral office were gradually replaced by a professional salaried bureaucracy was, of course, not unique to Germany. It coincided with the general emergence of the sovereign territorial state out of the feudal monarchies and empire of the medieval period. In Germany, as elsewhere, the professional bureaucracy evolved as the executive agency of princely ambition to destroy or at least inhibit the traditional political powers of aristocratic and municipal corporations and to control the human and financial resources required for the construction of a powerful centralized state.[3]

As functionaries of the dynastic sovereign, members of the professional stratum represented political centralization versus provincial and local autonomy, rational organization and efficient regulation of economic activity for the common welfare versus the customary rights and inherited privileges of the traditional estates, public law versus private law. In modern terminology one might describe them as agents of modernization or rationalization. In this sense they formed a part of a larger and more amorphous group within eighteenth-century society that Mack Walker has aptly described as the "movers and doers." This group included members of the "free" professions – journalists, writers, medical doctors, and lawyers in private practice – as well as an embryonic capitalist bourgeoisie – the merchants, retailers, bankers, and manufacturers whose economic activity extended beyond the confines of the legal restrictions and customary usages of the local market. What these groups shared with the professional stratum was an emancipation from the corporate ties and local horizons of the nobles and peasants in the countryside and the tradition-ridden burghers of the towns and cities. The geographic and social mobility that characterized the experience of these modern elements in the social order was reflected in social attitudes and perceptions that emphasized individual initiative, self-discipline and achievement, and rational detachment from, and active manipulation of, a world whose concrete totality could be divided into uniform abstract parts and ordered according to universal categories.[4]

What is most striking about the social structure of eighteenth-century Germany is the overwhelming preponderance of the professionally educated state-service class within the modern sector of society. The impact of capitalist modes of production and market relationships on the social structure was still very limited, and economic activity that did transcend the bounds of the traditional agrarian and guild economy tended to be regulated and encouraged by, and thus to depend on, the state and its functionaries. The primary avenue for upward social mobility was not so much entrepreneurial ability as professional education. It was above all the university, as Walker has commented, that "was Germany's place for mixing and changing."[5] The universities were state-controlled institutions, staffed by civil servants, whose main function was the recruitment and training of the state-service class. Intellectual life in eighteenth-century Germany was dominated by the universities, and the universities were integrally connected to the state in its role as the primary agent of modernization and rationalization. The social and cultural tensions between traditional and modern elements in the German *ancien régime* thus often appeared indistinguishable from the political tensions between the state and the incorporated estates.[6]

This schematic and dualistic model is useful as an introductory conceptualization of the evolving tensions within the German *ancien régime,* but it can also be misleading, especially for defining the political role and social location of the professional stratum during the last three decades of the eighteenth century. Even the most ambitiously absolutist of German princes never aimed at a total dissolution of the corporate structure of traditional society. As members of the aristocratic estate within the Holy Roman Empire, the German territorial princes tended to identify themselves socially with the landed aristocracy within their own states. Moreover, the continuing social and economic power of traditional elements in the society, the absence of any significant indigenous capitalist bourgeoisie as a social base for wide-reaching reforms, placed definite practical limits on political centralization and economic rationalization or liberalization. By the middle of the eighteenth century a compromise, sometimes approaching the nature of a fusion, had been reached between state and society, modernity and traditionalism. The corporate structure of traditional society was not destroyed, but was functionally defined and administratively regulated within the overarching authority of the state. This marriage of the old and new was expressed in the gradual transformation of the state-service class into a relatively autonomous, legally defined "general estate" whose self-defined purpose was to mediate between the claims of universal rational law and particular social privilege in the name of the general welfare.[7]

The Prussian experience is usually presented as the most striking and historically important example of this development. In Prussia the process of reconciliation between state and society took the particular form of the absorption of the landed aristocracy into the state-service class. Defeated in their attempts to resist the centralizing policies of the Prussian kings and their bureaucratic servants, the landed nobles regained much of their former social and political power by joining the state-service stratum and gradually coming to dominate it. In Hans Rosenberg's words, "the partially dispossessed began to dispossess their parvenue dispossessors."[8] The compromise between state and society expressed in the formation of an "oligarchy" allying the professional bourgeoisie with the traditional aristocracy was clearly articulated in the codification of Prussian law in the *Allgemeine Landrecht* between 1781 and 1794. Most of the privileges of the traditional estates were reaffirmed, but they were systematically codified according to general, rational principles; given a functional rather than a customary basis; and relativized within the broader context of the general welfare of the state. The rights and privileges of the "general estate" of state servants were written into law. These included exemption from most taxes, from patrimonial or local justice, and from military service. The relative autonomy of this "state estate" was expressed in the institutionalization of standardized civil service examinations and legal security of tenure for most offices.[9] The general pattern of sociopolitical development that culminated in the compromises of Prussia's *Allgemeine Landrecht* was also evident in other German states, including Württemberg, which on the surface seemed very unlike Prussia.

Three major historical factors contributed to the peculiarly individual character of the relationship between state and society in Altwürttemberg. The first was the absence of an aristocratic estate. During the political and social upheavals of the early sixteenth century, the local landed nobility had freed themselves from subjection to the duke and become imperial knights (immediate subjects of the emperor), leaving the duke as the only landed aristocrat in the duchy.

Other nobles in Württemberg- who held positions at the court or in the military - were "foreigners" appointed by the duke and without local feudal rights and privileges. The estates represented in the territorial diet (Landtag) consisted almost entirely (fifteen "prelates" represented the church) of the corporate *Bürgertum* of the villages, towns, and cities, and were thus relatively homogeneous in their social and legal status. As a result the political tension between prince and estates overlapped almost completely with the social and cultural tension between burgher and aristocrat. But this should not be confused with a conflict between traditional aristocracy and modern "bourgeoisie." As in other German states, the estates in Württemberg represented traditional privileged corporations that opposed the rationalizing policies of the sovereign authority in the name of local autonomy and inherited customs and rights.[10]

The second peculiarity of Württemberg's development during the old regime was the ability of the territorial estates to maintain their political powers and rights through the era of princely absolutism between 1650 and 1750. The dualistic constitutional structure established in 1514, in which control over taxation, financial administration, and even military and foreign affairs was shared between duke and Landtag, was sustained throughout the *ancien régime* and reaffirmed, after fifteen years of litigation and conflict, in the Hereditary Settlement (*Erbvergleich*) of 1770, the year of Hegel's birth.[11] This remarkable continuity in Württemberg's political development was due in part to the extravagance, inefficiency, and political ineptness of those dukes who had entertained absolutist ambitions, but also to the Landtag's ability to sustain a unified and vital role as the political representative of a *bürgerlich* and Protestant society threatened by rulers who were not only aristocratic, but also, after 1733, Catholic. Moreover, the Württemberg Diet was able to exploit the imperial constitutional structure and the European power balance of which it was an integral part in its battles with the duke. The treaty of 1770 was negotiated through an appeal to the Imperial Aulic Council in Vienna, and the rights of the diet were guaranteed by the Protestant rulers of Denmark, Prussia, and England.

The dualistic political structure in which power was shared between princes and estates was not unique to Württemberg. What was unique in the Württemberg experience was that this dualism was maintained at the central level of government in the form of a constitutional dualism between prince and Landtag. The full Landtag, however, met only very rarely, during times of extreme crisis and constitutional confrontation. The day-to-day and year-to-year workings of Württemberg's constitutional dualism were carried out in negotiations between the Landtag's standing committees and ducal bureaucrats.[12] This oligarchical government by professional bureaucrats and Landtag committees was not very different from the oligarchical rule instituted by the marriage of bureaucracy and aristocracy in Prussia. Moreover, in Prussia, as in Württemberg and throughout Germany, the traditional corporations maintained almost exclusive control over the spheres of local government.

The final factor that defined the particular character of Altwürttemberg was the remarkable autonomy and social and political power of the established Protestant church. During the Reformation the properties and feudal rights of the Catholic church were not sold, distributed, or absorbed into the ducal domains, but taken over by the new Protestant establishment. As a result the church controlled about one-third of the land in the duchy and had an independent income large enough to finance its ecclesiastical and educational activities. In Württemberg as in all Protestant German principalities, the church administration was legally subordinate to the prince's central administrative council, but in Württemberg the special rights and privileges of ecclesiastical property were defined by the constitutional compact of 1514 and thus dependent on the political ability of the Landtag to defend the terms of that compact. Despite repeated attempts by dukes to absorb ecclesiastical finances and administration into the ducal bureaucracy, the intimate connection of the church with the Landtag and the rights of the privileged estates allowed it to retain its special position as a kind of state within the state until the dissolution of the traditional order in 1806.[13] In contrast to developments in the other German Protestant states, where the eighteenth century witnessed an increasing subjection of the church to the state and a decline of the prestige of ecclesiastical office in relation to the lay sectors of the state-service class, the Württemberg clergy retained its sociopolitical independence and also its cultural role as the spiritual elite of the ruling oligarchy.

The unusual aspects of Württemberg's social, political, and ecclesiastical structure were reflected in the composition and outlook of its professional stratum. The absence of a local aristocracy saved the professional *Bürgertum* from some of the social and cultural tensions evident in other areas of Germany. Hegel's father did not have to worry about barriers of birth, special privilege, and aristocratic pretensions to social superiority in preparing his son for a position of leadership in his society. But the social and religious homogeneity of the professional class led to a distinct sense of separation from the world of the court and, together with the constitutional powers of the Landtag in the duchy's administration and the alliance between the church and the traditional estates, produced extensive connections between the professional elite and the political leaders of the traditional corporations. In Württemberg as elsewhere in Germany, the professional estate tended to see itself as the representative of a "state of laws (*Rechtsstaat*)" rather than as an arm of personal power, but in Württemberg this *Rechtsstaat* was embodied in the traditional constitution to which every state servant had to swear an oath of allegiance. The relative independence of the bureaucracy vis-à-vis the duke was evident in its system of recruitment. Most Württemberg bureaucrats were not educated in state-controlled universities, but trained in their profession through a system of apprenticeship within the bureaucracy itself. The dukes, of course, continually attempted to staff the bureaucracy with dependent and loyal servants, but their attempts were stymied by constitutional prohibitions on the appointment of foreigners, by the collegial organization of the administration (even under the most favorable circumstances the dukes found it impossible to maintain a majority of their own men in any bureaucratic body), and by the apprenticeship system of recruitment. The quasi-independent status of the bureaucracy was also strengthened by the fact that almost a third of its members were employed in the administration of church lands and property and paid out of church funds.[14]

The church also played a prominent role in determining the character of Württemberg's professional stratum in another respect. Until the 1770s the entire educational system of the duchy was administered by the church council in Stuttgart. On its higher levels (above the elementary Latin schools) this system was primarily geared toward the training of a clerical elite. Four of the five intermediate schools were boarding schools specifically designed to train candidates for the *Stift*. The other, the Stuttgart Gymnasium that Hegel attended, was slightly more diverse in its emphasis, but more than 50 percent of its graduates also pursued theological vocations. Higher education in Württemberg was virtually synonymous with theological training. Theologians were an important segment of the intellectual elite throughout Germany, but in Württemberg the clergy completely dominated the intellectual and cultural life of the society. Even teachers of nontheological subjects in the schools and authors of nontheological writings were almost exclusively theologically trained.[15]

An exclusive focus on the unique characteristics of Württemberg's professional stratum, however, can easily lead to misconceptions. This is especially true if its self-definition as the representative of a unified society vis-á-vis an aristocratic ruler is accepted at face value. As in other areas of Germany, the social experience and consciousness of the Württemberg professional stratum was clearly differentiated from the experience and consciousness of the burghers of the traditional estates. The social status of both clerics and bureaucrats was based on their individual achievements and their functional role within the totality of the society, rather than on inherited privilege and a traditionally defined place within a local community; the horizons of their "home" were the boundaries of the duchy, not the walls of a specific town.[16] The political alliance between the professional and the traditional burghers in Württemberg was in fact quite tenuous, filled with implicit tensions, and dependent on the particular historical circumstances that created their common opposition to the court. Aside from close ties to the few leading families who dominated the Landtag committees, the professional stratum established social alliances not with the "hometowners," but with two other groups whose activities and consciousness also extended beyond the borders of local communities – the patriciates of larger urban centers, primarily Stuttgart and a few neighboring imperial cities, and the bankers, merchants, and manufacturers whose activity was not confined to local markets or restricted by municipal guilds. Together these groups constituted the *Ehrbarkeit* or "notables" of the duchy. But the predominance of the professional stratum within this ruling elite made it virtually indistinguishable from the *Ehrbarkeit* as a whole.

The Württemberg *Ehrbarkeit* was a small and exclusive oligarchy. Although entry into the *Ehrbarkeit* was open, in principle, to anyone who acquired the necessary professional training, by the eighteenth century nepotism was widespread and self-recruitment often the rule rather than the exception.[17] Hölderlin's father obtained a university degree, but he still held the same administrative office in the ecclesiastical bureaucracy as Hölderlin's grandfather.[18] The genealogical trees of Hegel and Schelling show an almost unbroken succession of church officials and bureaucrats going back to the sixteenth century.[19] Constant intermarriage for over two centuries had also given the *Ehrbarkeit* the appearance of a large kinship group. It was not as astounding a historical coincidence as it may at first appear that Hegel was related not only through personal friendship but also through kinship to Schelling and Hölderlin.[20] Social mobility within the *Ehrbarkeit* was extensive, both horizontally between functional groups and vertically between status groups, but social mobility between the *Ehrbarkeit* and the burghers and peasants of the traditional estates, though legally possible, was extremely limited, and decreased throughout the eighteenth century. The position of the *Ehrbarkeit* as a kind of self-contained and self-recruiting patriciate of the duchy as a whole was even evident in the speech of its members: They spoke a form of Swabian German that was recognizably different from the various local dialects of the duchy.[21]

The Swabian accent that Hegel retained until his death was thus a constant reminder not only of his geographical origins but also of his social roots in the Württemberg *Ehrbarkeit.* Although entry into this elite was not theoretically his birthright, everything in his early experience, beginning with Latin instruction from his mother at the age of three, prepared him to conceive the eventual attainment of a position of cultural leadership as virtually inevitable. Like the other members of the galaxy of intellectual giants - Schelling, Hölderlin, Schleiermacher, the Humboldts, the Schlegels, Niebuhr, and Novalis - born between the years of 1767 and 1775 into the upper echelons of Germany's professional stratum, Hegel naturally saw himself as a member of a cultural elite that represented the general welfare of the society and was responsible for the articulation and purveyance of cultural values. When Hegel first began to define his cultural vocation for himself during the 1780s, however, the legitimacy of this spiritual elite and its ability to perform its self-conceived task were being called into question. In response to this historical situation, Hegel followed the lead of some of his older contemporaries in an attempt to reformulate the role and tasks of the spiritual elite in ways that differed markedly from the traditional religious cultural ideology of the Württemberg *Ehrbarkeit.*

Throughout the first three-quarters of the eighteenth century the Württemberg *Ehrbarkeit* had retained a remarkably homogeneous cultural ideology. This homogeneity was related both to the internal composition of the professional stratum and to its relationship to the court and traditional society. As an exclusively nonaristocratic group whose intellectual leadership was virtually monopolized by its ecclesiastical component, the Württemberg *Ehrbarkeit* remained remarkably closed to the neo-classical humanism that developed as the idealized cultural expression of the marriage of professional bourgeoisie and aristocracy in the lay sectors of the ruling elites in other Protestant areas of Germany.[22] In Württemberg classical studies generally retained their traditional place as a subordinate and preparatory element of a theological education and a Protestant world view.[23] The cultural "backwardness" that many eighteenth-century observers discerned in Württemberg's intellectual life was also evident in another area - the absence of any significant tradition of metaphysical rationalism and the slow and weak penetration of the secular, practical, and rational ethos of the

German Enlightenment or *Aufklärung* into the consciousness of the professional stratum. The absence of a significant group of lay intellectuals may have contributed to this immunity to secular and rational values but does not explain it completely. In other Protestant states theologians absorbed the new intellectual currents and were often the leaders and spokesmen of the *Aufklärung*, rather than its opponents.[24] In eighteenth-century Germany rationalism and the *Aufklärung* were intimately connected to the consolidation of a centralized state and the process of modernization and liberalization from "above" through enlightened absolutism, and thus opposed to the interests and values of the traditional estates.[25] In Württemberg, of course, the interests of the *Ehrbarkeit* were closely connected to those of the traditional estates.

The distinctive social, political, and cultural position of the *Ehrbarkeit* was clearly articulated in its political philosophy and theological viewpoint. As late as the constitutional conflicts of the 1760s the political thought of the *Ehrbarkeit* was characterized by a tendency to merge the conception of the general welfare of the "people (*Volk*)" with a defense of the traditional constitution. The general will of the society, which the *Ehrbarkeit* claimed to embody, was perceived not as a rational unity imposed from above but as a consciousness of communal solidarity, a Württemberg "patriotism" arising from a shared cultural experience.[26] The theological outlook of the *Ehrbarkeit* was integrally related to this social and political stance. In his classic study of German pietism, Albrecht Ritschl saw the peculiarity of Württemberg Protestantism in the "convergence of oppositional patriotism on the basis of the territorial constitution with a pietistic religious consciousness."[27] Although his judgment must be qualified in the light of recent scholarship, it does point to the crucial issue in defining the cultural ideology of the *Ehrbarkeit* – the role of pietism within the theological world view of the established church.

Pietism as a general religious reform movement based on the direct inner relationship of the believer to Christ through an experience of spiritual rebirth, on the brotherhood of the reborn in an invisible community of the saints, and on the necessity of saintly living as a sign of personal salvation did not, of course, originate in Württemberg and was not confined within its borders. What was distinctive about Württemberg's evolution was the absorption of the theological, ecclesiological, and moral attitudes of pietism into the theology, institutions, and practice of the established Lutheran church. As a hierarchically organized and centralized church establishment, the Württemberg clergy retained much of the traditional Lutheran emphasis on obedience to authority and conformity to orthodox doctrine. As the spiritual leaders of a Protestant community in its conflicts with a Catholic court, however, the clergy tended to perceive the church as the organizational structure of a community of believers that had a special and direct relationship to the divine and was involved in the conflicts of a sacred history that would culminate in an eschatological fulfillment.[28] The dominant cultural ideology of the Württemberg *Ehrbarkeit* during most of the eighteenth century was thus a distinctive synthesis of orthodox Lutheranism and pietism. By the 1780s, however, this synthesis was obviously disintegrating. Although Schelling and Hölderlin absorbed significant pietistic influences during their youth, Hegel apparently did not.[29] The disintegration of the unified religious world view of the *Ehrbarkeit* expressed in this diversity was conditioned by a change in the historical circumstances that had originally led to its construction.

The most obvious indication of this change was a shift in the attitudes and policies of the reigning duke. After the *Erbvergleich* of 1770, Duke Karl Eugen made a determined effort to overcome the opposition of the Landtag by cooperating with its committees and conforming to the terms of the traditional constitution. Instead of playing the role of a provincial Louis XIV, he now presented himself as an enlightened servant of the general welfare. By assuming this role, the duke seemed both to ally himself with the *Ehrbarkeit* and to threaten its autonomy by usurping its cultural function. The latter aspect was expressed most clearly in the transformation of the Karlsschule in Stuttgart from a military school into a full-fledged university during the early 1780s. The Karlsschule broke the *Ehrbarkeit's* monopoly of professional education and the church's monopoly of intellectual life. Its teaching was dominated by the administrative ethos of state service and the secular outlook of the *Aufklärung.*[30]

The *Ehrbarkeit* did not respond to the shift in ducal policy in a unified fashion. Some of its members, especially in the upper echelons of the bureaucracy, allied themselves with the duke, redefined their cultural function in terms of state service, and became proponents of enlightened administrative reform. Others, especially in the upper echelons of the ecclesiastical hierarchy, withdrew to a defensive conservative position that opposed any reform of the "Old Law (*Altes Recht*)" and the intrusion of the *Aufklärung* into Württemberg's traditional religious culture. Although there is no direct documentation of the response of Hegel's father to the new situation, his ambitions for his sons indicate a certain indecisiveness. By sending Hegel to the *Stift* he conformed to the traditional values of the *Ehrbarkeit,* but by sending his younger son to the Karlsschule to be educated as a military officer he seemed to display an implicit approval of the shift in ducal policy. Moreover, his position in the financial administration placed him within that part of the bureaucracy most noted for its support of the duke and his attempts at economic and financial reform.[31] By the time Hegel entered the Stuttgart Gymnasium, however, it was clear that the traditional solidarity of the *Ehrbarkeit* was dissolving. In the last decades of the century there was increasing evidence of conflict within its ranks, not only between the bureaucracy and the church, but also between opposing parties within the bureaucracy and the church.[32]

At the same time that the *Ehrbarkeit* was experiencing the disconcerting impact of a changing relationship to the duke, its legitimacy as a cultural and political elite was being threatened from "below." The 1780s witnessed the emergence of a number of separatist pietist movements led by itinerant self-styled religious prophets and supported by discontented groups of artisans and peasants.[33] These signs of a popular religious rebellion against the established church, moreover, coincided with an increasingly widespread and vocal criticism of the *Ehrbarkeit's* oligarchical exclusiveness and its consequent inability to represent the general welfare of the society. After 1780 the social and political discontents of both liberal publicists and popular petitioners were directed more often at the *Ehrbarkeit* than at the court.[34]

Both the division within the ranks of the professional stratum and the attacks on its political and cultural legitimacy as a ruling elite were also evident in the other Protestant states in Germany and were expressions of general tensions within the political and social structure of the *ancien régime.*[35] The most easily quantifiable source of these tensions was the remarkable surge in population growth during the last half of the eighteenth century. In many areas of Germany, including the already densely populated Württemberg, population almost doubled during the eighteenth century.[36] Although there was no German Malthus, pauperization among the lower classes in both the cities and countryside by the 1780s and 1790s brought forth pessimistic warnings from publicists and rulers.[37] In Württemberg the problems of overpopulation were made evident by a disturbing increase in emigration.[38] Rapid population growth was transformed into a problem of overpopulation, however, because of its specific social and political context. The alliance between state and traditional estates expressed in Prussia's *Allgemeine Landrecht* as well as Württemberg's dualistic constitution resulted in a social and political rigidity that made any fundamental social or economic reforms virtually impossible. The ways in which the Prussian political and military system was integrally related to a protection of the traditional social and economic position of the landed aristocracy and prevented a liberalization of the agrarian structure in response to both rural pauperization and agricultural commercialization have been the subject of extensive scholarly analysis.[39] A similar situation, however, also developed in the apparently very different social order of Württemberg. Attempts by the duke and his administrators to embark on even a limited policy of economic liberalization were stymied by the entrenched interests and constitutionally protected privileges of the "hometowners." The traditional elements in the *Ehrbarkeit,* moreover, would not support any reforms that threatened their political power and autonomy by increasing the duke's financial resources.[40] This inability of the existing political system to deal with the problems of economic and social dislocation undermined the legitimacy of the ruling oligarchies.

The general problems of overpopulation and social dislocation that changed the relationship between the professional, educated estate and the rest of German society were also evident within its own ranks. Despite the rapid population increase, the number of bureaucratic, ecclesiastical, and pedagogical positions available for university graduates remained stable or even declined during the course of the eighteenth century. By the 1780s the professional elite was acutely aware of the problem of an excess production of university graduates and responded by imposing more stringent requirements for university study and state appointments and in general closing off the already limited avenues of entry into its ranks from the peasant and artisan classes. In Württemberg a special decree was passed in 1788 that simply refused admission to the *Stift* to any students whose fathers were not members of the *Ehrbarkeit.*[41] Such measures aggravated popular discontent with the oligarchical exclusiveness of the professional stratum, but did not allay the discontents and frustrations of the younger generations of the university educated. By the end of the century the period of waiting in miserably paid and socially humiliating tutorial or apprentice positions between graduation and fully salaried offices often extended to a decade or more.[42] Hegel's, Schelling's, Hölderlin's, and Schleiermacher's experience of this aspect of the crisis of the German old regime during the 1790s undoubtedly contributed to their general feeling of cultural alienation, though it is not a complete explanation.

The problem of finding suitable employment and vocational satisfaction among the younger members of the educated estate was also aggravated by the tendency to equate upward mobility through individual achievement exclusively with entry into the professional stratum and by the minimal career possibilities that existed for educated young men outside the church and state bureaucracies. The last quarter of the eighteenth century witnessed a remarkable growth in the number of intellectuals who tried to make a living as independent writers and journalists. As even extremely productive writers like Friedrich Schlegel and Ludwig Tieck of Hegel's generation were to discover, however, the German publishing market could not sustain this tremendous increase in writers and writings. There was, as W. H. Bruford has pointed out, "something very like an intellectual proletariat" among writers and journalists by the end of the century.[43] The enthusiasm with which many German intellectuals greeted the possibility of revolutionary change during the 1790s, therefore, had a concrete historical basis in the social dislocation, fragmentation, and loss of cultural legitimacy of the professional stratum, developments that were directly related to, and a part of, the general tensions within the social, political, and cultural order of the German *ancien régime.*[44]

The extant documentation for a reconstruction of Hegel's experience of and response to the crisis of the *ancien régime* begins with the diary entries, reading excerpts, and essays from his last four years at the Stuttgart Gymnasium. During his years at the gymnasium (1777–88), the conflict between the new enlightened policies of Duke Karl Eugen and the traditional outlook of the *Ehrbarkeit* was reflected in a battle over curricular reform.[45] In this situation of tension and transition, Hegel clearly made a choice for the new against the old, and when he began self-consciously to formulate his cultural outlook and define his vocation he did so in the intellectual framework of the *Aufklärung* rather than the pietistic Lutheranism of his ancestors. At the same time, however, he revealed an acute sensitivity toward the tensions and problems that arose during the transition from traditional to more enlightened, modern forms of cultural consciousness and organization. This self-awareness was clearly evident in an essay on the history of Greek religion that Hegel composed in 1787.

The two-stage pattern of evolution in Greek religious history, Hegel claimed, was common to all historical religions and thus directly relevant to the present situation. The first stage was defined as "an original state of nature" in which men perceived the "Godhead" as an "almighty being who ruled them and all things in an arbitrary fashion." During the intellectual "ignorance" of cultural "childhood" all knowledge remained confined to manipulation of sensuous images by the imagination, and the powers responsible for human fortune and misfortune were personified as deities with a "sensible shape and an individual name." In the sphere of ethics the stage of cultural childhood was characterized by fear, impotence, and subjection to external authority. The achievement of earthly happiness was tied to gaining the favor of supernatural beings through superstitious rituals, material sacrifices, and blind obedience to authoritarian commands. In Hegel's view this ethical and religious standpoint was integrally related to a political and cultural system in which fathers and tribal chieftains "held power over their subjects absolutely at their pleasure" and a cunning priestly class manipulated popular fears and ignorance for its own benefit and power.

The childhood stage of cultural development began to disintegrate when the nation attained a level of cultivation (*Bildung*) that allowed an intellectual elite to discover and articulate a more "enlightened and sublime" conception of the Godhead as a benign, rational, and providential power that "gives to every man sufficient means and power to achieve happiness and has so ordered the nature of things that true happiness is achieved through wisdom and moral goodness." This enlightened, rational religion of the philosophers of the Greek *Aufklärung,* however, had failed to achieve cultural hegemony. The ignorant masses (*Pöbel*) remained immune to the dignity and beauty of critical self-knowledge and the ethical directives of a "purer religion." Moreover, the philosophers themselves soon abandoned their cultural vocation of moral education as they focused their concern on the construction of opposing speculative systems about the nature of ultimate reality and "other things incomprehensible to man" and thus lost sight of their common ethical viewpoint and historical task.[46]

Hegel was obviously convinced that his own age, like classical Greece, was characterized by a division between a superstitious, barbaric, *Pöbel* and an educated elite in the process of formulating more enlightened conceptions of human autonomy and ethical obligation.[47] The failures of the Greek philosophers thus provided contemporary *Aufklärer* with some important historical lessons. First, it was imperative to close the gap between the masses and the intellectual elite through a systematic program of cultural education. This task was fraught with dangers, because historical experience seemed to indicate that traditional religion was the "strongest bridle" for popular passions, but Hegel generally expressed confidence that a state-supported enlightenment imposed from "above," grounded in an interpretation of Christianity as an embodiment of the universal religion of reason, could create a community of rational citizens.[48] Secondly, the Greek experience revealed the need to avoid conflicts based on speculations about matters in which man could attain no certain knowledge. Constant rational criticism of all unquestioned presuppositions would produce an atmosphere of humane tolerance regarding ultimate questions and allow the intellectual elite to focus its energies on the actualization of the ethical and social goals that everyone shared.[49]

Hegel's youthful commitment to the moral, rational, and pedagogical ideals of the *Aufklärung* was not superficial or ephemeral, but remained an important component of the cultural outlook he would evolve in later years. Already during his gymnasium years, however, he was aware of the limitations of the Enlightenment program for cultural reform and expressed some doubts about the progressive nature of the historical transition from sensuous knowledge and natural community to self-critical rationality and individual autonomy. Like so many of his contemporaries, Hegel formulated these doubts through a comparison of the artificiality and fragmentation of modern rational culture with the vital "wholeness" expressed in Greek art and literature.

In a comparative study of ancient and modern poets written in 1788, Hegel defined the primary characteristics of Greek literature as simplicity and originality. Both traits arose from the "natural," unreflective consciousness of the ancient poets and dramatists. The Greek writers had simply described the objects and sensations of immediate, direct experience "without separating the manifold elements within [them] that reflective understanding can distinguish and without dissecting what lies hidden." The content and form of their works was original in the sense that it emerged directly from concrete individual experience. In contrast, Hegel judged the works of modern poets as both artificially reflective – concerned with the subtleties of style and explanations of hidden motivations and causes – and derivative – based on the accumulated knowledge of years of "book learning."

These differences, Hegel contended, were directly connected to differences in the historico-cultural milieux of writers in the two eras. In ancient Greece the poet's own experience was simply one form, and individual modification, of the collective experience of his cultural community. The myths and images he used in his art were a part of everyone's consciousness. Thus although his art was more concrete and original than that of the modern poet, it was also more universal in its appeal. In contrast to the modern situation, the Greek poet and his audience shared a common life and consciousness. The modern poet gleaned his materials from an esoteric intellectual culture and expressed his vision in an artificial language and eclectic mythology that were not accessible to the majority of his contemporaries. Moreover, he considered his own individual experience as separate from that of his audience and worried self-consciously about the problem of communication. Both the unity of experience and presentation and the unity of poet and people had been lost in contemporary culture.[50]

Hegel obviously felt that this loss was significant. It was directly related to his own growing uneasiness about his cultural vocation and identity. The development of self-conscious, critical rationality and recognition of the universal laws that transcended the diversity of individual experience had liberated at least some men from the limitations of the sensuous imagination and the authority of irrational myth and unquestioned dogma. At the same time, however, it had alienated them from the immediacy of concrete experience and the community of their fellow men. Could this abstract, esoteric culture of the educated elite become the foundation of a new form of vitality and communal solidarity? Or was the world view of the *Aufklärung* simply one pole of a cultural dualism that could be resolved only through elevation to a more all-encompassing perspective?

At this point, Hegel made no attempt to resolve the dilemma, but simply presented it as the historically given situation. His simple, relatively serene, and straightforward presentation of the conflict between self-conscious autonomy and communal integration, between universal rational values and the concrete totality of immediate experience, seems radically removed from some of the more dramatically expressed inner conflicts of some of his contemporaries. In 1788 the variety of individual experiences and of forms in which those experiences were expressed made it extremely difficult to discern the similarity in the fundamental conflicts that the members of Hegel's generation brought with them into the 1790s. It was only after the crystallizing experience of historical change and revolutionary possibility that their individual experiences of the tensions in their fathers' world were recognized as the shared starting point for the construction of a world of their own.

2

Revolution and Romanticism: the generational context of Hegel's ideology of cultural integration

"It is surely not difficult to see that our time is a time of birth and transition to a new period," Hegel wrote in 1807. "Spirit has broken with the world as it has hitherto existed and with the old ways of thinking, and is about to let all this sink into the past; it is at work giving itself a new form."[1] When Hegel made this claim he had already differentiated his own conception of the "new form" of "spirit" from the cultural perspectives of other members of his generation and reduced their positions to limited "Moments" in the transition from the old to the new world. The unique aspects of Hegel's viewpoint that eventually led to the formation of a distinctive Hegelian school, however, only gradually emerged in the years between 1802 and 1807 as a particular variant of a more general intellectual transformation. The basic intellectual framework in which Hegel conceived the process of cultural revolution and the vocation of the intellectual was shared by the other prominent intellectuals of his generation – Schelling, Hölderlin, Schleiermacher, the Schlegels, the Humboldts, Novalis, Tieck, and Niebuhr – and this common framework was the product of the shared experience of an epochal break during the 1790s with "the world as it has hitherto existed, and with the old ways of thinking."

The formative experience of Hegel's generation can be divided into two phases. The first, lasting until about 1796, was dominated by the experience of inner liberation from, and critical opposition to, the political and religious forms of the old regime. It was a period of discipleship in which the task of cultural transformation was largely defined in terms of the actualization of ethical ideals – rational autonomy and Hellenic "wholeness" – inherited from older mentors. Disillusionment with the project of actualization and a concomitant critical distancing from the intellectual inheritance led into the second phase, spanning the years between 1796 and 1802. This period was characterized by generational solidarity and creative ideological con struction and synthesis. The apparent contradictions of rational autonomy and empirical necessity were reconciled in an ontological vision of the dynamic identity of subject and object in the self-differentiating totality of the "absolute." The new vision was programmatically formulated in literature as Romanticism and in philosophy as "speculative" or "absolute" idealism, and prophetically connected to the historical progression of mankind toward both an imminent and an immanent actualization of freedom and unity.

The French Revolution had a decisive impact on the intellectual development of Hegel's generation. At precisely that juncture in their personal histories - their years of university study and professional apprenticeship - when they were being educated and socialized into their future roles as moral and spiritual leaders in their culture, the news from France presented the historical possibility of a radical transformation of "the whole previous constitution of the world."[2] The events in Paris gained universal significance as signs of an epochal historical confrontation that directly affected their own lives and vocational commitments. The necessity of accommodation or resignation to the restricted horizons of their fathers' world dissolved with the opening up of new historical possibilities. A new consciousness of liberation from the past was displayed, first of all, in a general unwillingness to conform to traditional career patterns and the discipline of an educational process tied to these career patterns. Although Hegel did not follow the example of some of his fellow students, who abandoned their studies for direct participation in revolutionary activity, he did quarrel with his father over his desire to change his career from theology to law and displayed a noticeable lack of enthusiasm for the traditional program of study offered at the *Stift*.[3] Similar vocational crises and filial rebellions can be found in the personal histories of other members of his generation during the early 1790s.[4] There is nothing particularly unique or startling about such a youthful generational rebellion, but for the members of the Hegelian generation this stage in personal development had a peculiar, decisive significance, because they identified their personal crises with the historical crisis of European culture and connected the possibility of a satisfactory resolution to the hopes for a collective historical transformation aroused by the French Revolution.

The specific articulation of this connection had two aspects. It was expressed, first of all, in an identification with the movement for civil and political liberation, both in France and in Germany. The onset of the war between France and the German princes in 1792 brought the confrontation with the politics of the old regime to a head, because the possibility of a liberal revolution at home now seemed inextricably tied to a military victory of the French. Schelling translated the Marseillaise for the benefit of his fellow students, Hegel exchanged revolutionary mottoes in autograph books with French students at the *Stift,* and Hölderlin asked his sister to "Pray for the French, the defenders of the Rights of Man," in their battle against the German princes.[5] Such expressions of sympathy for political revolution, however, were from the very beginning of the revolution connected to a conception of a more general and fundamental transformation of the principles of ethical life and cultural organization. Years later, Hegel would describe the impact of the revolution as a "glorious mental dawn," a time when "a spiritual enthusiasm reverberated through the world" because of a general belief that "the reconciliation between the secular and the divine was now accomplished."[6] This widespread initial "spiritual enthusiasm" gradually disintegrated as the revolution in France moved into the period of war, dictatorship, and terror. But disappointment with the actual direction of historical developments during the mid-1790s did not lead the members of Hegel's generation to share the general disillusionment of many of their older contemporaries and repudiate the eschatological hopes the revolution had initially aroused. In fact it was precisely the failure of the revolution to actualize these hopes that provided them with their own particular historical purpose and cultural identity: to become the historical midwives of a world in which "the reconciliation of the secular and the divine" would finally be accomplished.

It was the construction of their cultural identity on the premise of the historical necessity of radical cultural transformation that distinguished members of Hegel's generation from their older contemporaries. In their correspondence of 1794–5, Hegel, Hölderlin, and Schelling described themselves as members of an "invisible church" committed to the historical actualization of the Kantian ideals of "reason and freedom," to the creation of the "Kingdom of God" on earth. "The Kingdom of God must come," Hegel wrote to Schelling, "and may our hands not lie idle in our laps."[7] Such eschatological hopes, in both their religious and their secularized forms, were a prominent element in the German intellectual tradition, and the conviction that the actualization of these hopes demanded a transformation of the communal ethos through a process of cultural education (*Bildung*) also seemed to reaffirm the traditional role of the German intellectual as the spiritual and ethical "tutor" of his society. The formative impact of historical change and revolutionary possibility, however, had infused the eschatological hopes with the sense of historical necessity and the pedagogical role with practical urgency.

Although the members of Hegel's generation absorbed the particular political impulse of the French Revolution into what they considered to be a more fundamental "revolution of the mind," they continued to maintain that political liberation was a necessary part of cultural transformation. The claim of the protagonist of Hölderlin's *Hyperion* expressed their position succinctly: "The new union of spirits cannot live in the air, the sacred theocracy of the beautiful must dwell in a free state and that state must have a life on earth and that place we will surely conquer."[8] In 1795, Hegel reminded Schelling that the subjection of man to the arbitrary authority of a supernatural God in traditional Christianity was inseparable from the political authoritarianism of the old regime, both as its expression and as its justification. By destroying the "halos" surrounding the "heads of the oppressors and Gods of this earth," he insisted, "philosophers will demonstrate the dignity of man and people will learn to feel it and will not just ask for their rights but make them their own."[9] Novalis wrote to Schlegel that the achievement of genuine spiritual autonomy was not possible without a "Bartholomew's Eve" for "despotism and dungeons."[10]

The political concerns of Hegel's generation in the years before 1796 were focused on the act of liberation, rather than on the positive political and social structures of a genuine ethical community. Hegel claimed that articulation of the new communal ethos in the form of a "people's religion" would have to ensure that "all the needs of life – the public affairs of the state – are tied in with it," but the content of these "public affairs" was simply described as "freedom."[11] Political revolution was seen as the instrument for the creation of a community of self-legislating moral subjects who would not require the coercive control of political government. As Niebuhr insisted to his skeptical father in 1794, the destruction of the old structures of political authority was to lead not to new forms of coercion, but to the creation of a human community in which "all human government would cease and reason alone would rule."[12]

In preparing themselves for the role of bringing about a cultural liberation that would make political authority superfluous, the members of Hegel's generation were forced to grapple with three major issues. The first was the need to construct a metaphysical guarantee for the claim that man could and should structure his world according to the dictates of his autonomous rationality and that he was not hindered in his freedom by any "external" – natural, historical, or supernatural – power. The search for an ontological basis of absolute human autonomy, however, soon merged into another issue, which could most simply be described as the problem of "mediation." How could the actualization of man's essence as an autonomous subject be reconciled with the revolutionary task of creating an integrated ethical community in the sphere of concrete natural and historical existence? Finally, both of these theoretical issues were tied to the practical problem of bridging the gap between the visionary ideals of the intellectuals and the collective desires and consciousness of the "people," the need to construct concrete religious forms and images that could function as both the public expression and the popular pedagogical instrument of the new communal ethos.

"From the Kantian system and its ultimate perfection," Hegel claimed in 1795, "I expect a revolution in Germany that will proceed from principles that are already present and demand to be generally worked out and applied to all previous knowledge."[13] This view was widely shared among Hegel's contemporaries. Despite the apparent technical difficulty of Kant's philosophical treatises, his works were quickly hailed throughout Germany as revolutionary manifestos of the liberation of the self as knower from passive subordination to impressions from the external world and the liberation of the self as ethical actor from the chains of an externally given or imposed (heteronomous) morality. Kant seemed to provide a philosophical basis for the revolutionary desire to structure the external world according to the universal laws of human reason and to establish an ethical community, a "Kingdom of Ends" in which man obeyed only self-imposed laws. Hölderlin described the Königsberg sage as "the Moses of our nation who leads it out of its Egyptian inertia."[14] But if Kant had brilliantly fulfilled the role of a liberator from slavery, the entry into Canaan required a Joshua able to undertake the "perfection" and "application" of Kantian principles. "With Kant came the dawn," Schelling wrote; "why be surprised that a little mist remained here and there in the swampy valleys while the highest mountains already stood in the sunlight?"[15] Much of the apparently esoteric philosophical criticism and experimentation that constituted such a prominent aspect of the thinking and writing of Hegel, Schleiermacher, Schlegel, Novalis, and Schelling during the mid-1790s becomes historically understandable if viewed as a series of attempts to clear away the remaining "mists" in the Kantian system, to perfect the Kantian system in the light of their own experience of historical change and their own chosen vocations as leaders of their people into a new Canaan.

The implicit criticism of Kant articulated in the demand for a perfection and clarification of his principles was not as peripheral or minor as it may first have seemed to his youthful disciples. In fact, it focused directly on the unresolved dualism that characterized Kant's entire philosophy. Kant had begun his revolution in philosophy by making a radical distinction between the realm of phenomena that could be apodictically or scientifically known because all rational minds structured the manifold of experience in the same way, and the realm of noumena or "things-in-themselves" that man could never experience and thus not know in a scientific sense, but that could be postulated as "Ideas" of pure reason (God, the immortal subject, the totality of the universe) through inference from the internal workings of the rational mind. This dichotomy was repeated in Kant's ethics in the apparently unbridgeable chasm between the autonomous rational self that freely determined the will according to the universal laws of pure reason and the empirical, historical, instinctual self that remained bound by the necessary laws governing the world of phenomena. The movement to perfect Kant during the 1790s aimed at resolving these dichotomies by expanding the sphere of knowledge to encompass the constitutive Ideas of the universe and by demonstrating the power of the autonomous subject over the phenomenal world. Such resolutions were felt to be urgently needed because Kant's residual dualism seemed to deny his own principle of autonomy and open the door to both a fatalistic acceptance of the gap between man's essential nature and his historical existence and a renewed belief in a transcendent world whose existence was "proven" by man's practical need for it. Hegel and Schelling were acutely aware of such misuse of Kant by the orthodox theologians at Tübingen. "All possible dogmas," Schelling wrote to his friend in 1795, "have already been designated as postulates of practical reason."[16]

The philosopher generally acknowledged as the leader of the movement to revise Kantian principles in response to the hopes aroused by the French Revolution was Johann Gottlieb Fichte. Fichte himself was clearly aware of the revolutionary significance of his perfection of Kantian principle in a "system of liberty" that freed man from the "chains of the thing-in-itself" just as the political revolution had liberated him from "external chains."[17] His system of liberty involved two major departures from Kant's positions. Liberation from the inhibiting "otherness" of the thing-in-itself was achieved through an inflation of Kant's theory of knowledge into a monistic subjective idealism. According to Fichte the subjective, transcendental ego not only structured the manifold of experience into an ordered world, but actually "posited" the phenomenal world in the process of its own self-determination. Insofar as the individual subject recognized his essence in the totally self-sufficient subjectivity of the absolute ego, all limitations on human knowledge were overcome. For Fichte, moreover, this perfection of Kant's epistemology was integrally related to a rejection of the separation between knowledge and ethics. The self-knowing subject of Fichte's epistemology was identical with the self-actualizing ethical subject that asserted its freedom from all external conditioning as it recognized the world as its own creation. Schelling claimed that Fichte's standpoint during the mid-1790s had overcome Kant's dichotomies in a "higher" system that was "neither theoretical nor practical alone, but, as it were, both."[18]

The "religious" quest for an ontological ground for the liberated subject was at least as powerful a factor in the general "Fichtomania" of the 1790s as the desire to liberate the ego from external influence. Schlegel described the motivation of his philosophical studies as "the hot thirst for immortality, the yearning for God," and praised Fichte for his ability to bring religion back into philosophy without repudiating the principle of autonomy.[19] The transformation of Kant through Fichte and the interpretation of Fichte in a religious sense, however, was most clearly revealed in Schelling's early writings. In an enthusiastic letter to Hegel in 1795 he claimed that Fichte's doctrine of the absolute ego provided both a guarantee for man's essential autonomy and a redemptive reconciliation between the divine and the human, for "God is nothing but the absolute ego."[20] Moreover, Schelling believed that knowledge of, and thus identification with, the infinite self-sufficient subjectivity of the absolute ego was not simply a product of logical inference, as Fichte seemed to imply, but attainable in the unmediated experience of intellectual intuition, when "under the form of immutability we perceive the eternal in us."[21]

The central problem in Fichte's doctrine of the absolute ego, however, soon became evident to Schelling, that is, "the resolution of the antagonism between the pure and empirically determined ego."[22] The individual self was determined and limited by the "nonego" of natural and historical existence; its essence, however, was complete, self-sufficient freedom. Man's ethical task was to actualize this essence, to overcome natural and historical determination. "Be absolute, identical with yourself," was Schelling's reformulation of the Categorical Imperative.[23] "Strive therefore to become absolutely free," he insisted, "strive to subordinate every heteronomous power to your autonomy, strive to extend your freedom to absolute unlimited power."[24] The result seemed to be a conception of earthly existence as an endless, and hopeless, striving to overcome the condition of existence, that is, finitude. As a philosophical basis for the negation of the political, religious, and ethical heteronomy of the old regime, Fichte's principle of absolute subjective freedom was attractive and compelling, but it was virtually impossible to conceive of the actual historical creation of an ethical community within his philosophical categories. As Novalis and Hölderlin were among the first to see, in Fichte's intellectual framework, self-actualization could be completed only outside nature and history.[25]

It was this particular concern, not only to perfect Kant's principle of autonomy in a monistic system, but also to integrate this principle in a convincing fashion with the concrete realities of historical and natural existence, that predominated in the early fragmentary and unpublished writings of Schleiermacher and Hegel. If the ethic of rational self-determination was to become the collective ethos of an immanent historical community, a present, experiential reality for all men rather than a transcendent ideal or otherworldly hope of an invisible church or sect of philosophers, it would have to be connected to the concrete natural and social needs and desires of finite, existing human beings. For both Schleiermacher and Hegel the task of actualizing the Kantian ethic centered on the problem of giving it a religious form and on the relationship between such a Kantian religion and the actual historical development of Christianity. If Christ had originally taught "not a virtue grounded on authority . . . but a free virtue springing from man's own being," as Hegel claimed,[26] was the development of Christianity into a religion of "positivity," in which man renounced his essential freedom, subordinated his will to external authority, and sought compensation for earthly misery in an otherworldly realm, simply an aberration or corruption produced by particular historical conditions? Or was the dualism and heteronomy of historical Christianity connected to inherent problems in the very nature of the Kantian ethic that had been defined as its universal essence? The fragmentary character of Hegel's and Schleiermacher's writings between 1793 and 1796 revealed their inability to discover a satisfactory resolution of these problems in the framework in which they were posed and led to crises of confidence concerning their historical vocations as leaders of cultural transformation.[27]

As Hegel and his generational contemporaries grappled with the dilemmas imposed by the demand for the historical actualization of Kant's Kingdom of Ends, a historical archetype of their goal – the identity of individual and communal will, of natural inclination and moral duty, in the classical Greek polis – was a constant presence in their consciousness. The general ideal of Hellenic "wholeness" was an inheritance from the neoclassicism of the eighteenth century, but the members of Hegel's generation reinterpreted this ideal in terms of their own particular historical experience and tasks, focusing on the sociohistorical matrix of the self-sufficient wholeness of the Greek personality and the beauty of Greek art.[28] There was a new historical focus and historical distance in this generation's Graecomania. The Greeks were perceived no longer as an absolute model for the task of individual cultivation toward the universal humanity of "world citizenship," but as a historically situated "natural" paradigm of communal integration. Because the identity of individual and communal will, of inclination and duty, in the polis had been completely spontaneous or natural, the Greeks, as Hegel noted, had not required a Kantian educator: "They neither learned nor taught a moral system, but evinced by their actions the moral maxims which they could call their own."[29] But it was precisely the "natural" character of Greek life and culture that made a simple restoration of the classical polis historically impossible. The actualization of the Hellenic ideal of communal integration in the modern world was possible only if this ideal could be stripped of its natural forms and reconstructed on the basis of self-conscious rational autonomy, if it could survive the incorporation of the truth of subjectivity – the necessary transcendence of any particular finite determination by the autonomous ego – which was the fruit of postclassical, Christian, and modern history.

Just as the members of Hegel's generation looked to Fichte for guidance in their perfection of Kant's principle of autonomy, so they looked to Fichte's contemporary and colleague at Jena, Friedrich Schiller, for guidance in their attempts to resolve the tensions between modern subjectivity and the Hellenic ideal. Schiller not only provided a classic formulation of the contrast between Greek harmony and the bifurcations of modern experience and consciousness that had achieved philosophical clarity in the Kantian antinomies; he also, expecially in his *Letters on the Aesthetic Education of Man,* seemed to provide a possible resolution of the Kantian antinomies and thus an opening toward the reconstitution of Hellenic wholeness in the modern world. Yet Schiller's claim that the realm of aesthetic experience and creativity constituted the crucial mediating, unifying link between the polarities of reason and inclination, morals and nature, activity and passivity, freedom and necessity, form and matter, the state and the individual, the intellectual and the people, and so on, although initially greeted as a pathbreaking insight by most members of Hegel's generation, was soon perceived as an inadequate basis for this generation's peculiar historical aspirations and mission. For Schiller conceived the synthetic power of "Beauty" or "living shape" as a necessary postulate that reason constructed on a priori "transcendental grounds" in order to fulfill the idea of "humanity." Although he did present his conception as a response to the present historical situation of cultural bifurcation, that response itself was not "historical" but grounded in a definition of the universal essence of humanity. Thus, Schiller's viewpoint could not provide an adequate metaphysical or historical basis for the revolutionary demand to actualize the Kingdom of God on earth. In fact, Schiller insisted that the unity of opposites in the "realm of aesthetic appearance" remained an ideal that could not be "realized in actuality" but existed only in the few select conventicles of a "pure church" or "pure republic" of beautiful souls.[30]

By 1796 the leading members of Hegel's generation were convinced that the attempts by their intellectual mentors both to perfect the emancipatory consciousness articulated in Kant and the French Revolution and to resolve the contradictions raised by the demand for absolute autonomy were not a satisfactory resolution of their own revolutionary demands for the actualization of freedom and unity in a modern polis. Their mutual recognition of shared problems and aspirations was made evident in their increasing interpersonal relations and geographical concentration in Frankfurt, Jena, and Berlin and was exemplified in articulate form in a remarkable document, entitled "The Oldest System-Program of German Idealism," which has been attributed at various times to Hölderlin, Schelling, and Hegel.[31] This fragmentary sketch of a program for cultural transformation had three major aspects. First, the basic premise on which the demand for total cultural transformation was grounded was defined as the identity of metaphysics and ethics. The self-conscious recognition and philosophical demonstration that man was essentially "an absolutely free being" and that as a free being or autonomous subject he was identical with the absolute creative power of the universe, dissolved the inhibiting "otherness" or externality of mechanistically determined nature, coercive politics (the state as "machine"), and supernatural divinity, and thus opened the way to the creation of an immanent community of free spirits, a unified republic of self-legislating subjects, who did "not need to seek for God or immortality *outside of themselves.*" This Fichtean manifesto, however, was followed by what one could call a "Schillerian" paragraph. The identity of the "good" and the "true" in the unified totality of the universe was defined as the idea of "beauty" that could be grasped only in an "aesthetic act." The "philosophy of the spirit" was described as an "aesthetic philosophy," and literature or art

(*Poesie*) was given back its original dignity as the "teacher of mankind." Finally, the particular historical aspirations of Hegel's own generation came to the fore in the claim that the vision or Idea of freedom and totality must take on public, popular, sensuous form as a new mythology or religion: "Mythology must become philosophical in order to make the people rational, and philosophy must become mythological in order to make the philosophers sensuous." The completion of this task of cultural liberation and education would usher in the earthly millenium: "Then eternal unity will reign among us . . . No power shall any longer be suppressed. Then will reign universal freedom and the equality of spirits!"

The concluding sentence of this program revealed that the central problem in this generation's self-chosen historical mission – the collective actualization of the ideal identity of freedom and unity – still remained unresolved: "A higher spirit sent from heaven will found this new religion among us; it will be the last, greatest work of mankind."[32] Within a few years, however, Hegel, Schelling, and Hölderlin, as well as their north German contemporaries Schlegel, Schleiermacher, Novalis, and Tieck, were confident that they themselves were ready to fulfill the role of the "higher spirit" and become the "messias in pluralis" of the earthly millenium.[33] This collective appropriation of the messianic mantle was based not on any practical success in founding a new religion or educating the people, but on a new conception or visualization of the problem, on a transcendence of the inherited intellectual framework that had made the task of unifying and actualizing the ideals of autonomy and wholeness inherently contradictory. The tendency to describe the achieved vision in terms of the reciprocal interdependence and ultimate identity of abstract polarities, like idealism and realism, subject and object, spirit and nature, infinite and finite, eternity and time, individual and universal, may drive the modern reader to distraction. But the use of interchangeable abstract oppositions that might refer to the epistemological relationship between knower and known, the religious relationship between man and God, the metaphysical relationship between particular and universal, the social relationship between self and society, or the psychological relationship between reason and instinct is revealing as well as disconcerting. It was an expression of having achieved a breakthrough to a fundamentally new vision, of having attained a standpoint that would make possible a reformulation and resolution of all the major problems of human existence.

The easiest way to begin an explication and explanation of the new framework of perception and knowledge is on the level of the greatest philosophical abstraction. As was noted above, by 1796, Hegel and his generational contemporaries had become dissatisfied with the conception of the relationship between the autonomous subject and the objective empirical world as it had been developed from Kant through Fichte. For Fichte, the empirical world (the nonego) was essentially derivative, posited by the ego as a means for the practical assertion and self-conscious recognition of its moral autonomy. Within the world of concrete human experience, conflict between the subject and its other was endemic. The finite determinateness of natural and historical being was overcome only by stripping it of all substantiality. Freedom became actual only when life dissolved. The keystone of the new framework was the claim that the relationship between subjective freedom and objective determination was one of primal identity, reciprocal interdependence, and self-relating totality. The "absolute identity" that was at the center of the new vision was actually a combination of two identities: the primal, undifferentiated, indeterminate unity of subject and object and the identity of this "One" with the manifold of natural and historical determination. Schlegel and Schleiermacher simply referred to the absolute as "the universe."[34] In 1801, Schelling stated: "The absolute identity is not the cause of the universe, but the universe itself. And the universe is everything that is."[35] Hegel described the absolute as the "union of union and non-union" in "infinite life."[36]

The "discovery" of the absolute as a dynamic totality in which all the oppositions of existence were grounded and ultimately reconciled was the core of the generational *Weltanschauung* that has come to be called Early Romanticism (*Frühromantik*). The Romantic absolute, however, should not be conceived as simply an abstractly posited, external, or transcendental solution to the dilemmas of historical experience, as a "miraculous" escape from the inherent contradictions of life and thought.[37] The experiential origins of the construction or discovery of the absolute lay in the revolutionary aspirations of a generation that refused to resign itself to the apparent necessity of a bifurcated world in which the ideals of autonomy and unity would remain eternally opposed to the existential, natural, and social reality of fragmentation and particularized determination. The very nature of the Romantic absolute expressed its function as a guarantee and demonstration that the concrete actualization of a unified community of free self-legislating subjects was historically imminent and historically necessary.

The new orientation of what we may now call the Romantic generation was expressed on the most general level in its conception of the relationships among religion, philosophy, and art. Religion was no longer reduced to the status of applied, public morals but presented as the sphere of the direct experience of the primal identity of "One" and "All" in the absolute, as, in Schlegel's words, "the center of everything else, always the first and the ultimate, the absolutely original."[38] In 1800, Hegel claimed that the "partial character of the living being is transcended in religion; finite life rises to infinite life."[39] The classic formulation of the Romantic conception of religion, however, was clearly Schleiermacher's *On Religion: Speeches to Its Cultured Despisers,* in which religion was both separated from, and made the primal source of, philosophy, art, and ethics in its character as "the immediate consciousness of the universal existence of all things in and through the eternal" and as "life in the infinite nature of the whole, in the One and the All."[40]

This conception of religion as the direct experience of the "union of union and non-union" in the infinite life, the "living totality" of the absolute, entailed a new focus on the ontological or theological content of the historical forms of religious experience, and especially of Christianity. Most of the Early Romantics were convinced that the content of Christian faith – its trinitarian theology, the doctrines of the incarnation, resurrection, and Holy Spirit – was, at least implicitly, identical with their own conception of the absolute as a dynamic movement from undifferentiated identity to the differentiated totality of the "living whole." But the tensions between the absolute content of Christianity, and its particular historical manifestations remained a problem, and a source of some disagreement. Schleiermacher saw himself as a religious "reformer" giving voice to the historical emergence of the perfected, authentic appropriation of Christianity's absolute content.[41] Schlegel and Novalis, at least for a time, however, thought that the transition from traditional Christian to Romantic conceptions of religious experience was radical enough to justify revolutionary phraseology. Schlegel's own ambiguity about the relationship between religious reform and the foundation of a new religion was made evident in the comparison of his own historical mission to that of both Luther and Mohammed.[42]

In the new world view that emerged in the writings of the Early Romantics during the late 1790s, philosophy and art were defined as the complementary modes, theoretical and practical, subjective and objective, ideal and real, in which the religious experience of absolute identity was self-consciously appropriated and articulated. Although both Schlegel and Novalis experimented in an aphoristic fashion with the construction of a philosophy of the absolute, it was Schelling who gave the most systematic and influential form to the Early Romantics' philosophical aspirations. In a series of rapidly produced books published in the late 1790s, Schelling focused on the "objective" pole of absolute knowledge and constructed a system of nature as a dynamic, teleological organism struggling upward from the inanimate to the animate and culminating in man. Although nature constituted the objective side of the ultimate identity of subject and object in the absolute, it was also a subject–object unity within itself, a unified self-developing totality animated by the "world soul."[43] The aim of Schelling's philosophical project was made evident in 1800–1 when he added a "system of transcendental idealism," or philosophy of the self-knowing subject, to his philosophy of nature and insisted that both poles of knowledge were ultimately identical, that nature and mind were equally self-revelations or "potencies" of the absolute.[44] The goal of philosophical knowledge was not to assert the absolute supremacy of the subject over the object, of mind over nature, but to reconcile these polarities in the totality that encompassed them both. Although Schelling admitted that the "essential identity" of the real and the ideal could not be philosophically demonstrated, he insisted that this identity was presupposed in every claim to knowledge, even knowledge of the most limited, particular kind, and could be "shown" in the possibility of fully "translating" the ideal into the real and the real into the ideal.[45] Moreover, Schelling claimed that the identity of the real and ideal was also revealed through the embodiment of this identity in art, for art was "the genuine and universal organon" of the absolute.[46]

Schelling's definition of art as the expression of the absolute identity in the form of the real, the concrete particular, provides a succinct summary of the theory of Romantic *Poesie* (a term that encompassed both the act and the product of aesthetic creation) that Novalis and the Schlegels developed during the late 1790s. In his *Dialogue on Poetry,* Schlegel defined *Poesie* as the creative reproduction of the self-actualizing and self-revealing activity of the absolute in the concrete determinations of nature and history. As historical embodiments of the eternal divine act of self-creation, artists were the mediators between the divine and the human, the "Christs" of their cultures.[47] The peculiarity of the new Romantic *Poesie* was that it raised the act of aesthetic creation to self-awareness. It was both "poetry" and "poetry of poetry," uniting the self-transcending irony and restless "agility" of modern subjectivity with the chaotic multiplicity of concrete determination in the form of a living, self-relating totality.[48] Schlegel's program for a new art culminated in a demand for the creation of a new mythology, a new Bible, which would be "the most artful of all works of art" and "encompass all the others." This modern mythology would organize the progressive revelation of the absolute in the world history of *Poesie* into a systematic totality and thus constitute the one great "infinite poem" in which all of the particular creations of individual artists would find "a matrix, a sky, a living atmosphere."[49]

It would be misleading to confine the Romantic "revolution" of the late 1790s to a reorientation of perspectives on religion, philosophy, art, and their interrelationships. In fact, the whole point of the redefinition of the absolute as a union of union and nonunion was to provide an ontological basis for the creation of a positive, immanent community in which man's subjective autonomy was not in endless conflict with, but actualized and recognized itself in, the concrete particularity of natural and social being. The human essence was conceived no longer as absolute autonomy that could be actualized only through a subjugation and ultimate destruction of concrete being, but as a manifestation and unique "modification" of the infinite life, the "living whole," of the absolute. Self-realization entailed not a ceaseless striving to conform to an abstract "ought," but the development and revelation of the self's unique potentialities and capacities as a concrete existing being. In 1800, Schleiermacher described as his "highest intuition" the discovery that "each man is meant to represent humanity in his own way, combining its elements uniquely so that it may reveal itself in every mode, and so that all that can issue from its womb may be made actual in the fulness of space and time."[50] As the incarnation of the One in the All, as the living totality of the universe, the absolute itself was an "individual," a concrete universal.[51] By actualizing his own unique individual powers, therefore, man reproduced the divine act of self-production and expressed his identity with the absolute.

The Romantic ethic of individuality was an ethic of reconciliation rather than conflict and domination, of communion rather than separation and duality. The natural and historical particularity of the empirical self was perceived no longer as the "other" against which the autonomy of the transcendental ego defined itself, but as the medium in which subjective freedom became actual and revealed its nature. It was precisely through the development of his individuality that man affirmed his essence as a communal and universal being. In social interaction and communication men gave concrete existence to their unique individual capacities and at the same time came to a mutual recognition of their common participation in the fellowship of divine life. The "communion" of individualities in a "living whole" was often described as the triumph of the ethic of love over the Kantian ethic of duty. " 'Love has conquered' does not mean the same as 'duty has conquered,' i.e. subdued its enemies; it means that love has overcome hostility," Hegel wrote in 1799, and he insisted that this "cancellation of lordship in the restoration of the living bond, of that spirit of mutual love," was "the highest freedom."[52] Yet Hegel, like the other members of his generation, was acutely aware that the ideal of fellowship in a common life would remain historically impotent unless it could be given positive form in the objective institutions and laws of a state.[53]

Schelling, Schleiermacher, Novalis, and Schlegel were all convinced that the ethical ideal of self-realization through reconciliation with, rather than domination of, the "other," through the mutual recognition and affirmation of embodied subjectivities or individualities as participants in a common "infinite" life, could not be actualized in an invisible church but must necessarily achieve historical incarnation in the objective, empirical relationships of a real human community, a "state." Schelling described this state as an "absolute organism," as "the immediate and visible image of absolute life," as "the external organism of a freely achieved harmony between necessity and freedom."[54] Schleiermacher also repudiated this generation's earlier conception of the state as a coercive mechanism opposed to human autonomy and now defined it as "the greatest achievement of human art, by which man should be raised to the highest level of which he is capable."[55] Schelling's and Schleiermacher's discussions of the state as the positive form of human autonomy and communal life, like those of Novalis and Schlegel, remained confined to sweeping generalizations and prophetic utterances about the necessary synthesis of unity and individuality, of the One and the All in an organic totality.[56] Of all the members of this generation, it was clearly Hegel who revealed the greatest concern for the specificities of social and political life and the need to discern the actualization of the absolute in the differentiated and complex structures of man's economic activities, social relations, and political institutions. Whereas Schelling focused his attention on the study of natural science in the years between 1797 and 1801, Hegel devoted much of his time to the investigation of political economy, history, and constitutional theory, and his interests were continually aroused by signs of political and social transformation.[57] In an investigation of the German Imperial Constitution that Hegel did not publish during his lifetime, he tried to show how the identity of the "sacrosanct" principles of "freedom" and "unity" could emerge from the present disintegration of the traditional state and be given objective institutional form in a constitutional monarchy.[58] Novalis also wrote of the future organic state as a synthesis of republican and monarchical forms, but Hegel provided a much more detailed analysis of the way in which a transformation of the old federation of feudal estates into a unified system of constitutional representation based on legal equality would mediate between the right of the individual to control his own life and the necessity for a unified sovereign will, and produce a "free and unregimented" devotion to the common welfare.[59]

In the introduction to his essay on the German constitution, Hegel described his aim as "promoting the understanding of what is," as an introduction to "the habit of trying to recognize necessity and to think it."[60] This did not mean that he wanted to encourage a passive acquiescence to the given; he wished simply to insist that just as the present disintegration was a necessary consequence of historical evolution, so a new form of communal integration would emerge from the historical resolution of the inherent self-contradictions of existing reality and not from the arbitrary imposition of an abstract utopian "ought" on the "is." In this conviction that the actualization of freedom and unity, the construction of a genuine ethical community, a modern polis, was the immanent telos of historical development, Hegel gave expression to the final, and perhaps most distinctive, element in the cultural ideology of Early Romanticism. "The symmetry and organization of history teaches us that mankind, during its existence and development, genuinely was and became an individual, a person," Schlegel claimed. "In this great personality of mankind, God became man."[61] Moreover, in the period of modern history inaugurated by the French Revolution, the necessary goal of history became the object of self-conscious activity; the progressive incarnation of God in man became an act of self-divinization embodied in "the revolutionary desire to realize the Kingdom of God on earth."[62] In a similar vein, Novalis insisted that the actualization of the millenium was a "historical necessity," and Schelling described the purpose of history as "the realization of an objective order of freedom" in which human autonomy was reconciled with "universal necessity."[63]

It should be remembered that the Romantic absolute was conceived not as a transcendent One but as the One embodied in the differentiated determinations of the All and thus actualized as a dynamic totality, a "living whole." The critical point in this dynamic ontology, in this vision of the spiral movement of being from undifferentiated unity through separation, division, and particularization to the union of union and nonunion in totality, was, of course, the moment of both return and elevation to the final, higher unity, the achieved reconciliation of the One and the All. But this process of return and elevation was precisely the meaning and goal of human history; the redemption of the world, the reconciliation of God and man, the "return of all things" to the

Godhead, was made actual and thus fulfilled through man's active objectification and recognition of his own divine nature in the secular collective education (*Bildung*) of world history. The temporal Moments of man's development therefore mirrored, reproduced, and made actual and objective the differentiated inner structure of the absolute as a dynamic totality. Thus, Schelling could describe history as the "eternal poem of the divine mind" and Schlegel could define the living totality of Romantic art as the articulation of the historical stages in the history of art as one unified vision.[64]

The self-actualization and revelation of the absolute in the developmental structure of human activity and experience was evident first of all in the pattern of individual biography, the circular or spiral pilgrimage of the psyche. In 1799, Hegel described the "circle of man's development" in this fashion:

Everything lives in the Godhead, every living thing is its child, but the child carries the unity, the connection, the concord with the entire harmony, undisturbed though undeveloped, in itself. It begins with faith in gods outside itself, with fear, until through its actions it has isolated and separated itself more and more; but then it returns through associations to the original unity which now is developed, self-produced, and sensed as a unity. The child now knows God, i.e. the spirit of God is present in the child, issues from its restrictions, annuls the modification, and restores the whole. God, the Son, the Holy Spirit![65]

But Hegel was also quite aware that the final "restoration of the whole" as a fully "developed" and "self-produced" unity, as the revelation of God in the Holy Spirit, must take the collective form of a secular church, a genuine presence of the absolute in the objective forms of man's ethical life. When Humboldt, in 1797, claimed that "man must necessarily make his way from the character-unity that belongs solely to the imagination and inner sensation, through a one-sided development of his individual capacities, to a fully rounded maturity through Reason," he was not referring to individual man but to the collective mankind of world history.[66]

The specific historical content that individual members of the Early Romantic generation put into this framework of history as the actualization of the absolute, as a redemptive process from simple unity to developed, self-produced totality, was not always the same, especially because the triadic spiral of historical evolution was reconstituted in different form at each state of development. Thus, Novalis's *Christendom or Europe* (1799), which confined itself to Christian culture, presented the original golden age of unity as the highly developed stage of early medieval Christendom, whereas Schelling, from a longer perspective, sought the original unity in a vanished civilization existing before recorded history.[67] All the members of the Early Romantic generation, however, were convinced that the present age constituted an epochal turning point in human history, the point in which the reciprocal poles of the absolute totality – God and man, spirit and nature, subject and object – had reached a state of extreme, pure antagonism whose resolution would necessarily bring about the second golden age of achieved, developed harmony. A true understanding of the present thus revealed the meaning of the past and the future. To grasp the poles of the present in their reciprocal relations was to view history from the standpoint of its totality. In his *Dialogue on Poetry,* Schlegel wrote:

It seems to me that he who could understand the age – that is, those great principles of general rejuvenation and of eternal revolution – would be able to succeed in grasping the poles of mankind, to know and to recognize the activity of the first men as well as the nature of the Golden Age which is to come. Then the empty chatter would stop and man would become conscious of what he is: he would understand the earth and the sun.[68]

Schelling insisted that it was precisely because the "modern world" was destined to create "a higher, truly comprehensive unity" that "all oppositions must be made manifest."[69] The genuine man of the present was thus a "backward-looking prophet"[70] for whom the absolute in its temporally differentiated totality became an eternal now.

Despite differences in individual emphasis, therefore, I believe that one can reconstruct what amounts to a shared cultural ideology among the major poets and thinkers of Hegel's generation at the turn of the century. The experiential center of this generational ideology was the identification of the nature and resolution of individual identity crises with the collective process of cultural crisis and transformation. For the Early Romantics, self-understanding was identified with comprehension of the world and of the actualization of the absolute in the world. The consciousness of generational identity as a "messias in pluralis" of a new epoch in world history was expressed in the social solidarity of the Romantic groupings at Jena and Berlin during the late 1790s. In the years after 1800 this solidarity rapidly disintegrated. The personal squabbles and disagreements through which this disintegration was made manifest were an expression of a fundamental differentiation of perspectives and commitments that occurred during the process of systematically working out the implications of the Early Romantic ideology and relating that ideology to the various historical attempts at cultural reconstruction in Germany during the first two decades of the nineteenth century.

3

The reconciliation of Reason and reality: Hegel's differentiation from Romanticism

Although the ideology of cultural renovation formulated by the Romantic generation at the turn of the century articulated a vision of the identity of the ideal and real, nature and mind, being and becoming, the absolute and the concrete determinations of nature and history, it could still be described as "abstract" or "ideal" in relation to the prevailing historical actuality of social and cultural fragmentation. This chapter focuses on the evolving relationship of the Romantic vision of absolute identity to the historical changes that occurred in Germany under the impact of Napoleonic conquest and occupation, the wars of liberation, and the consolidation of a post-Napoleonic order (the "Restoration") after 1815. As individual members of the Romantic generation tried to connect their vision of eschatological fulfillment to the changing historical actuality after 1800, that vision itself underwent a process of revision and differentiation. In terms of the theme of this study the developments that culminated in the opposing cultural stances of Hegel and the Historical School during the 1820s are of particular significance. For purposes of historical perspective, however, these positions should be viewed within the broader spectrum of the various responses of the Romantic generation to historical developments after 1800.

Two general distinctions may help to clarify the differentiation in patterns of response. First, one should make a distinction between those thinkers who were able to connect their hopes for the historical incarnation of the absolute to the actual historical developments of the period and those who were unable to forge such connections, lost confidence in the historical possibility of an immanent millenium, and gradually disassociated their vision of absolute, self-sufficient being from the limited, finite realm of natural and historical existence. The major exemplars of the latter type of response are Tieck and Schelling.[1] In order to clarify the particular position of Hegel and members of the Historical School, especially Schleiermacher, within the former type of response, however, a further distinction must be made.

There were three major patterns of political and social reform and reconstruction in the lands of the disintegrating German Empire during the first decade of the nineteenth century. The first and most inclusive pattern might be described as a socially liberalizing and politically centralizing bureaucratic "statism." In those south German states, like Bavaria, Baden, and Württemberg, whose borders had been extended by Napoleon's territorial reorganization after 1803, the overwhelming focus of the movement for inner reform was on the political integration of new lands and the abrogation of the traditional privileges and liberties of the corporate bodies of the old regime. This pattern was also very evident in Prussia, but Prussia had been mutilated and humiliated by military defeat. Reform and reorganization were directed against the Napoleonic hegemony rather than under its aegis. Administrative rationalization was complemented by popular mobilization; the desire for centralized control was balanced by the need to arouse active commitment to the defense of the state and cultural community against the foreign invader. The third pattern was connected to the second in its anti-Napoleonic animus, but differed from it in its definition of the Germanic community to be defended against French imperialism as an idealized model of traditional feudal society, Catholic culture, and imperial political organization. This restorationist response was present to some degree in Prussia and the smaller German states, but its spiritual center was obviously Vienna.[2]

The threefold pattern of political and cultural response to Napoleonic imperialism provided the matrix for the major differentiations in the Romantic ideology as it was connected to historical actuality in the years after 1800. After the dissolution of the old empire and the defeat of Prussia and Austria in 1805–6, Hegel went to Bavaria to work as a newspaper editor and then gymnasium director under the administration of the bureaucratic reformer Maximilian von Montgelas; Schleiermacher and Humboldt chose to become active participants in the Prussian reform movement; and Schlegel moved to Vienna to work as a publicist for the revival of the Holy Roman Empire. Such geographic localizations, however, though they may indicate general trends, are obviously oversimplifications. The intellectual itineraries of Hegel and Schleiermacher reveal that the tendency to seek a reactionary, restorationist solution to the problem of cultural integration was not confined to Austria. Moreover, their constant struggle to reaffirm and validate their original faith in the historical actualization of the absolute indicates that Schelling's and Tieck's separation of the ontological and sociohistorical spheres remained a continuous temptation, which had to be continuously overcome.

The years between 1801 and 1807 were decisive for the development of Hegel's distinctive revision and reformulation of the cultural ideology of Early Romanticism. In 1800 he had still shared the Romantic view that comprehension of the absolute transcended the capacities of rational thought, although he did express dissatisfaction with the relegation of this task to religious faith or aesthetic intuition and was acutely aware of the consequences - the misery of self-division and alienation from the world - of the Romantic failure to construct convincing mediations between the absolute and concrete existence.[3] When he finally resolved his prolonged vocational identity crisis and committed himself to an academic career in the winter of 1800-1 he was convinced that the millenial ideals of his youth would have to be transformed "into reflective form, into a system," and that it was necessary to "find a way back to intervention in the life of men."[4] Hegel's first publications as lecturer in philosophy at Jena indicated the general direction he would take in fulfilling these tasks and resolving the dilemmas of his generation. He redefined the absolute as the dynamic self-embodiment of Reason rather than the self-expression of infinite life and insisted that philosophy rather than religion or art was the ultimate medium in which the absolute achieved complete self-transparency and through which the reconciliation of the autonomous subject with nature, society, and God was finally accomplished.

The theoretical basis for this new confidence in the capabilities of philosophy was Hegel's reformulation of the Kantian distinction between understanding (*Verstand*) and Reason (*Vernunft*). He continued to define the activity of understanding or "isolated reflection" in terms of the analytic separation, delimitation, organization, and fixation of phenomena, as an activity that presupposed and was inextricably bound to a bifurcated world that set abstract universality against concrete particularity, the inner freedom of the subject against the external necessity of objective natural and historical existence; but he now claimed that the vision of finite existence as a modification or self-expression of infinite life, the experience of totality that transcended the world of fixed oppositions and isolated finite entities constituted by the understanding, could be conceptually grasped and rationally articulated. The finite perspective of the rational subject set over against a world of disparate, externally related objects did not define the limitations of rational comprehension but constituted a limited stage or Moment within the all-encompassing, infinite activity of speculative thought or Reason. The task formerly left to aesthetic intuition or religious feeling was thus included within an expanded vision of philosophy and man's rational capacities. The inner logic of reflective rationality itself produced a negation and "sublimation of such oppositions as have become fixed" and a rational, conceptual comprehension that "every individual entity has meaning and significance only in its relation to the whole." This did not imply, however, that speculative Reason was "against opposition or limitation in general," for "bifurcation" was a "necessary factor in a life that forms itself through eternal opposing." The absolute comprehended in the act of speculative thought would not be "absolute" if it left the differentiation, separation, and antagonism of the world of finite being outside itself. It did not dissolve the world of the understanding but simply denied its "fixation." The unity articulated in the conceptual structure of speculative philosophy was a totality of the "highest vitality," a reconciliation that encompassed the "highest separation."[5]

Two aspects of the new philosophical perspective that Hegel gradually developed during his years at Jena deserve special emphasis. The first is his identification of thought and being. Hegel defined ultimate reality as the activity of an infinite rational subject that gave itself determination, embodied or actualized itself, in the creation and articulation of a universe, and thus came to know itself as the infinite individual, the concrete totality, as absolute self-consciousness or absolute spirit. The structure of speculative thinking or Reason – the necessary, dialectical self-movement of the "concept" from the abstract, unmediated, and implicit to the concrete, fully mediated, and explicit – was thus identical with the structure of ultimate reality or "Being." The systematic comprehension and reconstruction of the self-development of the categories of thinking in a speculative logic thus also provided a fully determinate, completely mediated, "absolute" knowledge of ultimate reality or God.[6] This fusion of logic and ontology allowed Hegel to construct a conception of the reconciliation between man and God, between the finite and the infinite spirit, that affirmed rather than denied man's essential nature as a free, rational, self-conscious being. In the activity of speculative comprehension, in the elevation to the fully transparent universe of the rational concept, man was finally free of the "other" and completely "at home." At the same time, however, he became an organ, vehicle, or "modification" of the absolute. Absolute spirit could fully actualize itself and thus come to know itself only through a medium that corresponded to its own nature, that is, self-conscious rational being, or spirit. Man's comprehension of the structure of his own rational activity was not only a knowledge of God, but also God's knowledge of himself. In the activity of speculative self-comprehension, therefore, man not only achieved absolute knowledge but became a modification of infinite "Being," a completely transparent vessel of the divine. This must all seem extremely abstract. But the whole point of this rational ontology in Hegel's view was that it provided a foundation for overcoming the bifurcation between the rational subject and its natural and historical existence. Like many of his Romantic contemporaries, Hegel continued to insist that the absolute embodied and thus revealed itself in the natural and historical world, but he also claimed that this embodiment and revelation was a necessary logical process, the self-explication of the structure of Reason. The totality of nature and history, however, could be comprehended as a rational totality and articulated in the form of a scientific system of concepts only when all of the determinations of Reason had been actualized. The absolute knowledge of speculative Reason, Hegel stated in 1807, was simply "history comprehended."[7] The Moments that comprised the dynamic totality of ultimate reality and the process of speculative knowing were also the necessary Moments or stages in the life history of individual men and the collective history of mankind. In *The Phenomenology of the Spirit* the comprehension of the identity of identity and nonidentity was revealed as the culmination of the whole process of human cultural development, the necessary outcome of the dialectical progression, the negation and "supersession" of the shapes of human experience and consciousness. "The beginning of the new spirit," Hegel claimed, "is the product of a far-reaching transformation in the manifold forms of culture; it is the goal of an immensely tangled path and an equally immense amount of exertion and toil."[8] Hegel's rational ontology disclosed the logical necessity in this tangled path and thus allowed the individual to comprehend the meaning and purpose of his concrete, finite existence within the infinite dynamic totality of absolute spirit.

The significance of Hegel's revision of the Early Romantic ideology became evident in his changing relationship to Schelling. When Hegel began his philosophical career he presented himself as the proponent and defender of the general standpoint of the philosophy of absolute identity as it had been developed, albeit in rather sketchy form, by Schelling. His critical writings focused on the inadequacies of the two mutually negating and thus finite poles of Enlightenment thought, the standpoints of empiricism ("pure being") and subjective idealism ("pure thinking"), and especially the latter, in its most self-aware and systematic form in the philosophies of Kant and Fichte. In the works of Kant and Fichte, Hegel claimed, Reason was reduced to mere *Verstand* and thus forced to acknowledge its own "nothingness" by "placing that which is better than it in a *faith outside and above* itself, as a *beyond.*"[9] Schelling had apparently overcome the bifurcation of Enlightenment consciousness, and rescued philosophy from its subordination to religious faith, by comprehending and articulating the identity of thinking and being in the absolute. Between 1803 and 1806, however, Hegel gradually became convinced that Schelling's philosophy could not fulfill its own claims, that its conception of the absolute remained an indeterminate, empty, purely formal intellectual "intuition." As such it remained esoteric and not rationally comprehensible. In fact, Hegel claimed that Schelling's standpoint left the absolute in a "beyond" where it could function only as a means toward "edification" and an object of "yearning." If the philosophical comprehension of the absolute was to become the foundation of a new cultural integration, however, it would have to be fully articulated in the details of its development, the Moments of its self-actualization in both nature and history.[10]

The social and political theory that Hegel developed in his published essays and unpublished lectures during the Jena years was inextricably connected to the gradual shift in his metaphysical standpoint. In 1802–3 he concentrated his efforts on the critique of the fixated dichotomy between subjective autonomy and the necessary structure of objective social and political relationships in the thought of the Enlightenment, and on a general description of the way in which the Romantic ideal of the identity of individual and society in the concrete freedom of "ethical life" was actualized through the necessary historical stages of mankind's struggle for mutual recognition in the development of language, economic activity, social relationships, and political institutions.[11] As Hegel struggled to give systematic conceptual form to the meaning of the actuality of ethical life under the conditions produced by the emancipation of the autonomous individual from the bonds of corporate privilege and hierarchical political authority, however, the distinctive aspects of his standpoint soon became evident. First, he displayed an acute understanding of, and concern for, the contradiction between individual freedom and the subordination to the blind necessity or impersonal fate of the systematic interdependencies of economic and social life that emerged through the pursuit of private interests in modern or "bourgeois" society. Second, he placed an overwhelming emphasis on the state proper, on law, administration, and constitutional structures, as the sphere in which the conflicts of bourgeois society were reconciled and the will of the individual was integrated with the general will of the community. The conception of the state that Hegel developed after 1803 had two fundamental features. As the basis of rational law and administration, the state gave systematic, comprehensible form to the interdependencies of economic and social life, allowing the individual to understand the relationship between private interest and the general welfare. At the same time, however, the political institutions in which the bourgeois with civil rights and duties was transformed into a citizen with political rights and duties made it possible for the individual actually to will the universal will of the community as his own will, to identify his own subjective freedom with the universality of the social "substance" of which he was a part. The final distinctive aspect of Hegel's sociopolitical theory arose from his concern about the problematic relationship between bourgeois society and the rational state: the need for a convincing structure of "mediations" that would prevent the reemergence of the dichotomy between individual and general will. During the first decade of the nineteenth century, Hegel's conception of the mediating links between state and society had not yet attained the architectural complexity and completeness expressed in his writings after 1815, but the focus on the role of functional classes or modernized "estates," and especially on the rational administrative rule and ethical leadership of the universal class – the educated estate of civil servants – was already present in embryonic form.[12]

During his Jena years, therefore, Hegel gradually became convinced that the "natural" ethical life of the Greek polis was in the process of being reconstituted in self-conscious, completely articulated, and systematic form in the immensely differentiated and complex identity of identity and nonidentity in the modern state. This new communal integration was not simply an ideal, an "ought," to which the contemporary world was to conform, but the culminating truth of man's actual historical development, the necessary result of the progressive incarnation of Reason in historical time and place. Yet during the first decade of the nineteenth century the specific meaning of Hegel's insistence that the absolute was present in the determinate forms of contemporary historical actuality was not always obvious. Many of his statements indicate that his conception of the actuality of ethical life in the modern state was a projection of tendencies evident in Napoleonic politics and their effect on Germany rather than a comprehension of a completed process. In July 1808 he spoke of a "new world" arising in the Bavarian reform movement and added that he had "hoped for this for a long time."[13] This orientation toward the future, however, also made Hegel's conception of the relationship between the realm of absolute spirit – the self-comprehension of the absolute in art, religion, and finally philosophy – and the sphere of objective spirit or practical Reason – the actualization of the absolute in communal life – somewhat ambiguous. Sometimes it seemed that the self-transparency of the absolute in philosophical speculation was the basis for a practical transformation of the world, rather than vice versa. "Daily I become more convinced that theoretical work achieves more in the world than practical work," Hegel wrote to Niethammer on October 28, 1808. "Once the realm of representation (*Vorstellung*) is revolutionized, actuality cannot hold out."[14]

Schleiermacher's elaboration of the Early Romantic cultural ideology in the years after 1800 revealed significant parallels and contrasts to the pattern of Hegel's development. Like Hegel, Schleiermacher resolved his vocational crisis by taking up an academic career, accepting a position at the University of Halle in 1804; and, like Hegel, he connected this decision to both a need to elaborate more systematically his youthful ideals and a desire to return to a more active relationship with his historical environment. His wide-ranging investigations of the unity of natural, social, and spiritual life in the developing actualization of the "idea of culture" paralleled Hegel's contemporary concern with the definition of "ethical life" within the complex structures of the postrevolutionary world.[15] Moreover, Schleiermacher continued to maintain that the ultimate identity of the individual self and the absolute was intrinsically connected, both as "basis" and "expression," to the natural and social determinations of concrete historical existence. In his dramatic dialogue *Christmas Eve*, published in 1805, the reconciliation of man and God through the appropriation of the idea of the Christian incarnation was presented as evolving out of, and giving meaning to, the natural sociability of family life, the interaction of autonomous individuals in "free society," and participation in the rituals and institutions of the ecclesiastical community.[16]

Two crucial differences between the viewpoints of Hegel and Schleiermacher, however, soon became obvious. First, Schleiermacher continued to insist that the absolute identity could not be rationally comprehended or articulated in a totally transparent system of concepts. The polarities of subject and object in reflective thought and of individual and general will in communal life were reconciled by recognizing their origins in the self-differentiation of the absolute, but this presupposed unity could only be intuited or "felt," not rationally comprehended. In fact, Schleiermacher claimed that the reconciliation of finite and infinite, universal and particular, in the concrete universality of "individuality" – whether the individuality in question was a person, a historical epoch, a cultural community, or a work of art – was essentially unknowable and could only be "divined" through a progressive series of hermeneutical studies. Schleiermacher's second major divergence from Hegel's standpoint concerned his conception of the structure of mediation between the various Moments of the absolute. In Schleiermacher's writings the self-movement of the absolute became an organic, evolutionary process. The reciprocal negativities of the stage of reflection were described as a dialogue, the conflicts of civil society became the "free sociability" of the mutual exchange of goods and ideas. The ultimate stages of religious "grace" and ethical community seemed to develop almost "naturally" out of the concrete natural and social relationships of individuals.[17]

The growing divergence between Hegel's and Schleiermacher's viewpoints was clearly expressed in their attitudes toward the contemporary issues of reform and reconstruction and in their responses to political events between 1805 and 1814. Whereas Hegel believed that the rational structure of the modern state was the sphere in which the conflicts of bourgeois society were reconciled and the ideal of ethical life finally actualized, Schleiermacher saw the state simply as the external organizational form of the organic communality of a people (*Volk*) sharing the same language and cultural traditions. The function of the state, in Schleiermacher's view, was to preserve, protect, and encourage the free self-development and self-expression of the various "individualities" - individual persons, families, voluntary associations, occupational corporations, schools, and churches - that constituted the larger "individuality" of the national community. The locus of communal integration, the actuality of ethical life, was the community itself, not the state. From this perspective, Napoleon appeared as a foreign despot intent on destroying the Protestant and German individuality of Prussia. When Napoleon shut down the University of Halle after his victory at Jena, Schleiermacher went to Berlin to join a secret organization of "Patriots" who hoped to overthrow Napoleon's European empire through a regeneration of the power and vitality of the German national community under the leadership of the Prussian state. Schleiermacher perceived the opposition to Napoleon as a defense of "German freedom" and "German character," as a battle for the very essence of German ethical life.[18] But he also realized that the actualization of an authentic German-Protestant-Prussian ethical community would not be accomplished simply by a military defeat of Napoleon's armies. His patriotic sermons would have little impact unless the divided and passive subjects of the old regime were transformed into an active, emancipated citizenry with a genuine experience and consciousness of participation in a common destiny. External freedom implied internal reform, and by 1810, Schleiermacher had become an active participant, as advisor to Wilhelm von Humboldt and Baron von Stein, in the bureaucratically led movement to reform the social, political, educational, and religious structure of Prussia.[19]

In stark contrast to Schleiermacher, Hegel welcomed Napoleon's victories as a triumph of the principle of modern rational politics over the irrational and obsolete social and political forms of the old regime. The "great political scientist" from Paris would finally teach Germans, by force if necessary, how to organize a "free monarchy" on the basis of universal law and a rational administrative and constitutional structure.[20] The reconstruction of German law and politics instituted by Napoleon or under his aegis represented the triumph of the principles of 1789. In Germany, however, the catastrophic sequel of 1794 would be avoided, because in Germany the external constitution of modern politics would be combined with, and completed by, the self-conscious appropriation of man's spiritual autonomy and identity with the absolute, a process embodied in the Protestant tradition and comprehended in the philosophy of speculative idealism. Like so many of his later disciples, Hegel conceived the contemporary cultural revolution as a fusion of French politics and German religion and philosophy.[21] The "new world" that was the object of Hegel's hopes as he became involved in the Bavarian reform movement had a universal, or at least European, dimension; it was not simply a regeneration of Germany's peculiar cultural "individuality." Hegel therefore did not share the enthusiastic involvement of most Romantic thinkers, including Schleiermacher and Humboldt, in the wars of national liberation of 1813. When Nürnberg was "liberated," Hegel wrote: "Several hundred thousand Cossacks, Bashkirs and Prussian Patriots have seized the city."[22] While Schleiermacher preached nationalistic sermons to the volunteer brigades and even participated in their military training exercises, Hegel discouraged his students from volunteering to join a barbarian horde whose aims, he felt, were the defeat of the political principles of reason and freedom as well as the foreign invader. Much more than Schleiermacher or Humboldt, Hegel saw that the emphasis on the liberation of the "organic" national community could easily lead to a regressive fixation on premodern forms of social and political organization. He would rather have had no popular participation in government at all than see it used as a means to overthrow the legal, social, and political reforms that Napoleon had brought to Germany.[23]

The growing divergence of Hegel's and Schleiermacher's cultural stances during the Napoleonic era can be related in a general way to the different patterns of domestic reform in Prussia and the south German states. The oversimplified nature of this geographic localization, however, was made evident by the conflict between the bureaucratic factions led by Prince Karl August von Hardenberg and Baron Karl von Stein within the Prussian reform movement. After 1810, Hardenberg's emphasis on rational administration and legal and economic reforms imposed from "above" increasingly dominated the reform movement. There were two primary reasons for this shift away from Stein's ideals of popular participation and national mobilization. First, the principle of self-government soon became irreconcilable with a successful institutionalization of liberal legal and economic reforms. The conservative forces of the old regime retained sufficient social power and vitality to control the institutions of self-government and thus stymied liberal reforms that threatened their privileged position. Moreover, that segment of society – students, professors, and journalists – who desired a national mobilization of a liberated citizenry were vociferous enough to strike fear into the hearts of traditionalists (especially the king, who retained ultimate political power), but not economically or socially powerful enough to provide the reformers with a significant base for a "democratic" attack on the old order. The second reason was that after 1814, Prussia was faced with a problem similar to that of the south German states a decade earlier: consolidation of a patchwork of newly acquired territories with different institutions and traditions. The first political priority thus became administrative centralization and rational integration.[24]

As a result of these factors, the conception of German–Prussian cultural renovation represented by Humboldt and Schleiermacher gradually declined in influence. It was opposed both by bureaucrats concerned with political integration and the imposition of liberal economic reforms and by conservative elements in the aristocracy and at the court who feared the democratic threat of popular self-government. Humboldt fell from power in 1819 because of his opposition to Hardenberg's dictatorial methods in the state council of ministers and because of his agitation for a political constitution that would provide for a "representation" of the people in the form of a system of modernized estates (based on social function) with significant legislative and executive power.[25] Schleiermacher had already been forced to resign his position on the commission for educational reform in 1814. His writings were censored and he was prevented from lecturing on political matters at the university.[26]

When Hegel accepted an invitation to become professor of philosophy at the University of Berlin in 1818, he soon became embroiled in the tensions within the Prussian bureaucratic elite. He came to Berlin from Heidelberg, where for two years he had displayed his sympathy for rational administrative reform and opposition to the nationalist populism of the student movement (the *Burschenschaften*) and its Romantic mentors. His invitation came from Baron von Altenstein, a member of Hardenberg's "party," who had been appointed minister of religious and educational affairs in 1817. Years later the historian Heinrich Leo claimed that Altenstein and Hardenberg had called Hegel to Berlin in order to establish a power base at the university in opposition to Schleiermacher and his friends.[27] Hegel himself was clearly attracted by the prospect of political and cultural influence that the chair at Berlin brought with it, but there was also an inner affinity of viewpoint between Hegel and the Hardenberg-Altenstein party of bureaucratic reformers. Altenstein praised Hegel's ability to transform the immature emotional enthusiasms and subjective fantasies of youth into a disciplined rationality and objectivity, their populist nationalism into a devoted service to the state.[28] Hegel in turn hailed the reformed Prussian state as an example of a state that had attained world-historical stature by making the political actualization of Reason its inner purpose and essence.[29]

The tensions within the bureaucracy were thus reflected in the academic sphere. In later years the historian Leopold von Ranke remembered his student days at the University of Berlin during the 1820s as a time when the faculty was divided into two conflicting schools of thought: "Two parties stood opposed to one another, the philosophical and the historical, both represented . . . by great personalities."[30] The "philosophical" party seemed relatively easy to define; it was unified by a common allegiance to Hegel's philosophy and consisted of disciples. The "Historical School" was less unified and more difficult to define. It consisted of a "spiritual aristocracy" – Schleiermacher, Humboldt, the historian Niebuhr, the legal philosophers Savigny and Eichhorn, the philologists Bopp, Lachmann, and Böckh – unified by a shared experience of the Romantic revolution, the early phases of the reform movement, and the national "awakening" of 1813. As Hegelian influence at the university increased, the members of the Historical School entrenched themselves in the Royal Prussian Academy of Sciences, from which they excluded Hegel. In response, Hegel and his disciples set up a Hegelian "counter-academy" in 1826, the Society for Scientific Criticism, whose journal engaged in continuous polemics against the positions of the Historical School.[31]

During Hegel's first years at Berlin a number of controversies hardened the lines between the two schools. In 1819 the Prussian government agreed to support the program of repression (the Carlsbad Decrees) formulated by Metternich after the assassination of the playright August Kotzebue by the nationalistic student Karl Sand. What this meant in practice was a much stricter censorship of all publications with political content and the creation of special commissions with power to investigate and prosecute members of the university communities. Schleiermacher was one of the victims of these repressive measures. Between 1819 and 1824 he was subjected to intermittent investigation and harassment because of his loyalty to the national and liberal aims of the "Liberation" of 1813 and because of his sympathy for the student movement which grew out of that experience.[32] Moreover, three of his close friends – his Berlin colleague Christian De Wette, his brother-in-law Ernst Moritz Arndt, and the Jena philosopher J. J. Fries – were dismissed from their academic positions. Hegel, however, justified the repressive action against nationalistic students and their professorial mentors as a necessary and progressive defense of modern rational politics against the assaults of irrational demagogues and feudal reactionaries.[33]

From the perspective of the Historical School, Hegel's attack on the victims of political persecution appeared as a self-seeking accommodation to political repression. For Hegel, however, the political conflicts of 1819–20 concerned matters of fundamental principle. Schleiermacher viewed the Carlsbad Decrees as an attack on the corporate freedoms of the self-governing individualities that constituted the organism of the cultural community. Hegel, on the other hand, insisted that the state had the right, in principle, to impose its will (the general will) on any particular corporate body, including the university. Isolated abuses of this power did not affect the validity of the general principle.[34] The same principle was at stake in a second controversy that divided Hegel and Schleiermacher during the 1820s – the battle over ecclesiastical reform. Hegel and his disciples opposed Schleiermacher's conception of a unified, but decentralized and self-governing, "people's" church and supported centralized bureaucratic control of the liturgy and institutional structure of the Protestant state church.[35]

Throughout his polemical battles with the Historical School during the 1820s, Hegel remained loyal to the conception of the modern state as the actualization of ethical life that he had developed during his years in Jena. In his *Philosophy of Right,* written immediately after his arrival in Berlin and published in 1820, he defined the incarnate rationality of the modern state:

The state is the actuality of concrete freedom. But concrete freedom consists in this, that personal individuality and its particular interests not only achieve their complete development and gain explicit recognition for their right (as they do in the sphere of the family and civil society), but, for one thing, they also pass over of their own accord into the interest of the universal, and, for another thing, they know and will the universal; they even recognize it as their own substantive mind; they take it as their end and aim and are active in its pursuit... The principle of modern states has prodigious strength and depth because it allows the principle of subjectivity to progress to its culmination in the extreme of self-subsistent personal particularity, and yet at the same time brings it back to the substantive unity and so maintains this unity in the principle of subjectivity itself.[36]

By 1821, however, one significant element in Hegel's political perspective *had* changed. He now insisted that the unity of "subject" and "substance" in the ethical life of modern politics had in fact been historically actualized, at least in general outline if not in every detail, in the reformed Prussian state. The orientation toward the future and concomitant active and creative role of philosophical comprehension that had characterized his position during the Napoleonic era had disappeared. Philosophy was confined to the comprehension of completed practice: "It appears only when actuality is already there cut and dried after its process of formation has been completed."[37] Yet Hegel clearly believed that the actualization of Reason in the Prussian reform movement was tenuous and fragile, threatened by both populist national demagoguery and atavistic traditionalism. It was with the defense of incarnate Reason against irrational feeling and subjection to historical "positivity" that he was concerned. This position did not, of course, imply a radical disavowal of either communal feeling or historical tradition. It was precisely the intricate rational architecture of the modern state that gave objective content to the communal feeling of identity and a comprehended, systematic unity to historical tradition.[38]

Hegel focused his criticism on the writings of members of the Historical School during the 1820s because he was convinced that their ontological and methodological principles condemned them to remain ensconced in the fixated bifurcation of subjective feeling (politically expressed in populist nationalism) and passive subjection to impenetrable objective "facts" (politically expressed in regressive traditionalism). In his Berlin Inaugural Address of 1818 he insisted that the methodological stance of the Historical School necessarily led to the subjective fantasies of intuitive divination and the impotence and superficiality of passive empiricism. The only way out of this impasse was a resurgence of confidence in the power of man's rational capacities: "Man cannot think highly enough of the greatness and power of the spirit: the hidden essence of the universe has no power in itself which can resist the courage of rational comprehension, it must reveal itself, display its riches and depths, and allow their enjoyment."[39] In 1822, Hegel penned an especially vicious attack on Schleiermacher's conception of the identity of self and absolute experienced in religious feeling. He described it as a regression to an animalistic (*tierische*) viewpoint that reduced the identity of man and God in self-conscious spirit to the dependence of a faithful dog on its master.[40]

It is not difficult to see why Schleiermacher considered Hegel's attack unworthy of reply.[41] In the very work that Hegel criticized in 1822, Schleiermacher had clearly reiterated that his conception of religious "piety" or feeling of absolute dependence marked an elevation to a unity within differentiation, incorporating both the self-conscious individuality of the stage of reflective bifurcation and the original stage of unmediated, "natural" identity with the absolute.[42] Moreover, in the previous year, Schleiermacher himself had attacked proponents of a neo-pietistic conservatism for their emphasis on blind emotional faith and unthinking submission to the positive dogmas of traditional orthodoxy and the literal "factual" truth of the biblical narrative.[43] If Hegel was guilty of misrepresentation in his criticism of Schleiermacher, however, Schleiermacher and other members of the Historical School were equally guilty in their reduction of Hegel's conception of Reason to the reflective *Verstand* of the prereligious stage of consciousness and being.[44] This process of mutual misrepresentation informed the conflicts of the two schools of thought on every level. Each accused the other of falling back into the bifurcations that the Early Romantic ideology of the absolute and its historical incarnation in ethical life had originally tried to resolve. The differences between the models of cultural integration developed by Schleiermacher and Hegel in the two decades after 1800, however, were actually differences of emphasis within the common framework they had achieved during the late 1790s. The polemical battles of the 1820s tended to obscure this essential unity of outlook.

In conclusion it may be useful to summarize both the common perspective and the divergent emphases of their cultural stances. In the sphere of sociopolitical or communal relationships, both Schleiermacher and Hegel constructed a model of integration in which the subjective autonomy of the individual was conceived as fully actualized through the process of identification with the historical "substance" of the communal totality of which he was a part. For both, the premise for the creation of a modern ethical community was an affirmation of the liberal individualism heralded by the *Aufklärung* and expressed in the

French Revolution. In their clear support of free market relationships, the sanctity of private property, and equality under the law, Hegel and Schleiermacher can be seen as ideologues of the "bourgeois" revolution in Germany.[45] They perceived and responded to this revolution, however, from the particular perspective of the educated professional stratum, the bourgeoisie of *Bildung* rather than *Besitz.* The emancipated egos of civil society were to be integrated into an ethical community that transcended the merely mechanical harmonization of individual interests through a process of moral and theoretical cultivation in which identification with the ethical substance of communal relationships would emerge as the culminating fulfillment and actualization of the subjective will of the individual. This process of communal integration was directed by the educated estate, the crucial mediating link between the old and the new order.[46]

Both Schleiermacher and Hegel believed that their vision of ethical community had attained historical reality - albeit imperfectly - in the Prussian reform movement. Their social and political theory was not revolutionary or oriented toward the future, but it cannot be reduced to a simple justification of the existing order. To their students in the 1820s they purveyed a conception of communal integration that had triumphed in principle but that required a continuing commitment to the process of education to be fully realized in detail. Ranke described the 1820s as "halcyon years," as a period of relative social and political stability when the reconciling visions of the scholar and philosopher reigned supreme.[47] The image is revealing, for it conveys the impression of a temporary, threatened calm in the eye of a storm. The educated estate perceived itself as a universal class that embodied a new general historical experience and consciousness of communal integration, but its vision and experience remained confined to a small elite. During the Restoration its claims to universality and cultural hegemony were threatened not so much by the discontents of a liberal bourgeoisie as by the restorationist demands of traditional social groups. Even Prussia's "bureaucratic absolutism" was never really absolute.[48] By 1822 it had become obvious that the extent to which society could be transformed from "above" by reform-minded bureaucrats was severely restricted by the unbroken political power of the traditional aristocracy, not only at the local and provincial levels, but also at the center of government, through its favored position at the court.[49] In the south German states a similar situation prevailed, as administrative reformers were stymied by the ability of the traditional corporate bodies to protect their ancient rights and privileges.[50] Moreover, as the Carlsbad Decrees made only too obvious, nowhere in Germany was the intellectual elite powerful enough to protect even its own domain of educational institutions and the printed word from the arbitrary interference of special investigating committees and censorship boards. The ideology of accomplished communal integration articulated in the writings and lectures of Schleiermacher and Hegel was the ideology of an intellectual elite of a professional class in a position of precarious, threatened, and artificial dominance.

The factional conflicts within the Prussian bureaucracy and the reflection of these conflicts in the theoretical polemics of the academic elite represented differences of emphasis within the general perspective of the educated state-service class, but as the vehemence of these conflicts revealed, such differences in emphasis could have significant implications. For Schleiermacher and Humboldt the primary role of the state and its professional servants was to provide the institutional framework for a spontaneous or "natural" self-expression and evolution of the unique organic individuality of the cultural community. For Hegel, however, the state was not just an instrument for the emancipation and protection of the ethical substance of a "people," but "the actuality of concrete freedom." It was only in the explicitly articulated structure of law and political institutions that the self-conscious individual could overcome his alienation from the community, recognize its ethical substance as the objective actuality of his own spiritual essence, and will the communal will as his own rational will. Because of his acute insight into the radical conflicts that necessarily arose from the structure of bourgeois society, Hegel did not share the Historical School's faith in the spontaneous evolution of ethical life in the organic communality of a "people." In the modern world, communal integration demanded the rigorous and laborious supersession of natural, emotional ties and subjective desires and the self-conscious, clear-eyed recognition of rational necessity. Hegel's educational philosophy expressed a similar constrast to the views of Schleiermacher and Humboldt. The transition from the "first paradise" of "natural humanity" to the "higher" modern "paradise of the human spirit" was not a process of "natural" growth but a severe and rigorous discipline of negation and supersession, a product of "labor and sweat."[51]

The pattern of differentiation within a shared perspective was also evident in the conceptions of ontological identity that Hegel and Schleiermacher constructed out of their historical experience. Both rejected the dualism of man and God, the immanent and the transcendent, embodied in the traditional teachings of orthodox Christianity. The reconciliation of finite and infinite being, of the individual self and the absolute, was conceived as the fulfillment, rather than the transcendence, of human experience in the world, as an experiential reality in the here and now. For Schleiermacher the incarnation of the infinite in the finite was revealed in the religious feeling of dependence on the absolute that was the necessary presupposition of all human being and consciousness. Hegel claimed that man could achieve a satisfactory and completely transparent identity with the absolute only in the activity of speculative thought. Both, however, viewed their own conceptions of ontological identity as the fulfillment of the redemptive promise of Christian faith and the culminating comprehension of Christian history. "Christian faith-propositions are conceptions of religious states set forth in speech," Schleiermacher wrote in *The Christian Faith,* summarizing his conviction that his theological constructions were merely systematic conceptual articulations of the actual religious experience of the Christian community of his age and culture.[52] Hegel also insisted that the content of his philosophical speculation was identical with the content of Christian faith, but he was convinced that the forms of religious consciousness were inadequate to their absolute content. The ultimate reconciliation of man and God was achieved only when religious consciousness comprehended itself in the activity of absolute knowledge. In philosophical comprehension the subjectivity of feeling and faith was superseded by the objectivity of rational knowledge, and the "positivity" of religious symbols and representations dissolved in the comprehension of the "positive" as a Moment in the self-transparent structure of Reason, of "the self-thinking Idea, the truth aware of itself."[53] The supersession of religious faith by "universal knowledge and cultivation," Hegel believed, was not a denial of religion, but the ultimate actualization of its content. "Our universities and schools are our churches," he wrote to Niethammer in 1816.[54]

Finally, Schleiermacher and Hegel agreed that the spheres of religious consciousness, described in terms either of pious feeling or of rational knowledge, and social being, described in terms of the ethical life either of the "people" or of the state, were inseparable aspects, reciprocal poles, of a unified totality – the self-differentiated unity of the absolute. The twofold aspect of this identity within difference was clearly formulated in a succinct passage of Hegel's 1830 *Encyclopedia.* "Genuine" religious consciousness, that is, the identity of infinite and finite spirit in speculative thought, "issued from ethical life"; it was simply ethical life elevated to thought, "become aware of the free universality of its concrete essence (*Wesen*)." The ultimate identity of the divine and the human could thus emerge only when the absolute had fully realized and revealed itself in the practical realm of concrete social existence, in the rational structure of the modern state. At the same time, however, Hegel insisted that a genuine, self-aware religious consciousness was the *basis* of ethical life. The experience of a completely satisfactory communal identity, the identity of the individual and social will, was possible only if the structure of communal relationships was comprehended as a manifestation and actualization of the absolute. It was thus "folly" to believe in the possibility of the creation of a genuine ethical community without a transformation of religious consciousness.[55]

Because both Schleiermacher and Hegel believed that the absolute had attained empirical historical actuality in the structures of ethical life that emerged from the Prussian reform movement, their viewpoint might be described as an "actualized eschatology."[56] But this "actualized eschatology" had a distinctive form. The empirical form and content of contemporary ethical life was not simply equated with the Kingdom of God, with the identity of the divine and the human per se. Ethical life remained an "objectification," a "manifestation" of the absolute in the world of finite appearance. The eschatological fulfillment of the "eternal now" was achieved only when the historical particularity and therefore finitude of ethical life was "divined" or philosophically comprehended *as* the actuality of the absolute. It was this complex identity in difference of the absolute and the historical, religious consciousness and ethical life, Reason and reality, that constituted the problematic nature of the ideological legacy that Hegel and Schleiermacher passed on to their students during the 1820s. In the years after 1800 they had both connected the historical actualization of the Romantic vision of the immanent absolute, of "natural supernaturalism,"[57] to the particular forms of sociopolitical and cultural transformation of their own age and culture, thus leaving their conceptions of ontological and communal identity peculiarly vulnerable to the judgment of sociohistorical development. During the Restoration, at least in Prussia, Hegel's particular conception of the actualized absolute appeared on the verge of triumphing over its competitors and achieving a convincing historical validation. As we shall see in the next section, however, the historical appropriation of Hegel's ideology of cultural integration by increasing numbers of Hegelian converts also revealed the tenuous and ambiguous character of his reconciliations and the historically relative experiential validity, and thus therapeutic power, of his "truth."

II

The historical appropriation of the absolute: unity and diversity in the Hegelian school, 1805–1831

4

Hegel and Hegelianism: disciples and sympathizers in the formation of the Hegelian school

In 1807, Hegel claimed that "the individual needs public acceptance to prove the truth of what is as yet his solitary concern; he needs to see how the conviction that is as yet particular becomes general." When Hegel made this claim he was confident that his "particular" view of the nature and historical role of philosophy would become "general," that his subjective conviction would attain the historical verification of public acceptance. "We must have the conviction," he wrote, "that it is of the nature of truth to prevail when its time has come and that truth appears only when its time has come – and thus never appears too early, and never finds the public that is not ready for it."[1] The emergence of a Hegelian "movement" or "school" in the years after 1816 appeared to confirm Hegel's belief that his truth was more than a solitary, subjective conviction. It is obvious, however, that the historical verification of Hegel's viewpoint through public acceptance was severely limited in scope. Although his truth may have prevailed among a significant number of students and academics and a few public officials, primarily in Prussia, it certainly never became the "property of all."[2] Even within the confines of the Hegelian school, moreover, the appropriation of Hegel's truth took such a variety of forms that the identity of the individual and the universal, the subjective and the objective, often seemed very tenuous indeed. The transition from the particular to the general, which Hegel had so confidently prophesied in 1807, proved to be a much more complex and problematic process than he had imagined.

Although Hegel did eventually experience the gratification of public recognition during his lifetime, to some extent his truth did appear "too early." It found its public not in the period of dislocation and transformation in which it was conceived, but in the period of political and cultural consolidation after 1815. Connected to this delay in public response was the significant fact that Hegel (unlike Schelling) did not find his audience among members of his own historical generation. The vast majority of Hegelians were considerably younger than Hegel (he himself described his relationship to his disciples in generational terms in 1826),[3] and only one – the theologian Karl Daub (1765–1836) – could be described as his generational contemporary. The configuration of historical experience that led most Hegelians to Hegel was thus different from that which conditioned the original construction of his position. But it would be misleading to transform this distinction into a radical and simplistic dualism between Hegel and his school. First, there were significant differences in experience and outlook among the disciples themselves. Secondly, there were obvious, shared patterns of experience and outlook that made it possible for master and disciples to see themselves as representatives of a distinctive cultural stance within the ideological conflicts of their age. The divergence within unity of Hegelianism became divisive disunity only after Hegel's death.

The problematic relationship between Hegel and his disciples is best approached through Hegel's own conception of the kind of public response that would constitute a historical verification of his truth. As Hegel differentiated himself from Schelling and the other Romantics during his years at Jena, he became increasingly convinced that it was "the concrete experience of how far one can go with them" that determined the truth of philosophical systems:

> Blindly the disciples work out their implications, but the texture becomes thinner and thinner, until they are finally shocked at the transparency of their spiderweb. Before they are aware of it the system has melted like ice in front of them and runs through their fingers like quicksilver. They simply do not possess it anymore, and whoever looks into the hand with which they offered their wisdom sees nothing but the empty hand and moves on with contempt.[4]

By 1807, Hegel believed that such a historical judgment on Schelling's version of speculative idealism was imminent – not because it had promised too much, but because it had failed to fulfill its promise of absolute reconciliation. It had ignored the "demand for detailed knowledge and the otherwise generally accepted claim that the whole can be grasped only by those who have worked through the parts." Instead of producing an "accomplished community of consciousness" based on an objective systematic science "capable of being appropriated by all self-conscious Reason," Schelling's philosophy had spawned a flock of self-styled "geniuses" and "high priests" who presented their subjective intuitions of the absolute to the public in the form of esoteric myths or a few abstract principles repeated over and over like a religious catechism.[5] The historical impact of such forms of philosophical edification, Hegel claimed, could only be superficial and ephemeral. They could not withstand the test of historical reality. He thought he spoke for the authentic public (the public "instinct," he called it on one occasion)[6] when he insisted that catechisms and myths were no longer viable means of cultural integration. Contemporary men might temporarily seek the emotional solidarity of a lost *Gemeinschaft* in sectarian devotion to a charismatic "genius" or the solace of a lost faith in subjection to a new myth, but the realities of the historical world in which they lived would inevitably produce a disillusionment with such regressive therapies. In the differentiated complexity of the postrevolutionary world, communal and ontological integration could be maintained only on the basis of self-conscious freedom and rational knowledge.[7]

For Hegel, therefore, the creation of a Hegelian sect based on a common faith in an esoteric philosophical "revelation" or worship of his personal "genius" would not constitute an adequate historical verification of his truth. What he sought was public acceptance in a wider sense – official recognition of his system as the coherent articulation of the implicit practical consciousness of his age and culture. Already in 1807, Hegel sketched a plan for a national journal of scientific criticism that would express the collective effort of an academy of sciences and be universally recognized as the final "objective" judge in all areas of intellectual production. The plan was revived in 1819 and eventually became the model for the Hegelian journal that began publication in 1827.[8] The desire for official and institutionalized recognition from "above" rather than popular recognition of his personal genius from "below" was also evident in Hegel's activity as an academic politician. He was always less interested in rallying students to his personal banner than in controlling appointments and influencing institutional and curricular changes in such a way that his philosophy would no longer appear as his personal philosophy at all, but simply as the accepted framework of all scientific work.[9]

Because Hegel conceived of his philosophy as the objective or universal self-consciousness of his age, he did not expect the historical validation of his truth to be restricted to the experience of an academic clique or philosophical school. In 1826, Varnhagen von Ense noted that Hegel was unlike other philosophers in that he did not aim merely at founding a "sect" or "school," but at training an activist party or "faction" that would take on a directive, organizing role, and thus achieve "external significance" in political and cultural institutions. But it is important to emphasize that Hegel conceived this directive group as an "organic" elite that raised the collective practice of its community to self-consciousness.[10] The aim of philosophical education was self-comprehension, the recognition of the structure of Reason in the actuality of concrete historical experience. Those who appropriated the Hegelian truth were expected not to separate themselves from the general community and devote themselves to philosophizing, but to reenter the world of concrete human activity with a consciousness that would give vitality and purpose to their particular vocations. Philosophy, Hegel insisted, was a propadeutic science; it prepared men for a life of concrete freedom; it should not lead to withdrawal from the world or to attempts to impose an abstract "ought" on the world.[11] If the impact of his philosophy was simply to create an academic elite who attained existential satisfaction in pure philosophical activity, the historical validity of his system was obviously called into question. When Hegel took on the role of vocational counselor, his first advice to students was always to choose a "practical" career, and if they insisted on becoming teachers or academics, philosophy was the last specialization he would recommend.[12] To be sure, a number of individuals could legitimately choose to take up academic careers, but the historical verification of his truth would depend not merely on the existence of such an intellectual elite, but on its ability to fulfill its mediating, educative function, on its effectiveness in providing a convincing comprehension (for the total community) of the present as the actuality of the absolute.

The actual historical appropriation of Hegel's philosophy, of course, did not conform to his expectations. Even at the height of his influence, Hegelianism remained one of a number of competing ideologies within the German intellectual elite. During his early years in Berlin, Hegel himself experienced moments of pessimism in which he admitted to his students that the reconciliations achieved in his philosophy were still without "external universality" and that the "servants" of philosophy would, for a time at least, "compose an isolated priestly class, which may not walk together with the world and must protect the possession of the truth."[13] Moreover, the "servants" of philosophy were not always united among themselves. Even Hegelians who considered themselves mere "organs" of Hegel's truth necessarily appropriated this truth in the light of their own diverse personal and historical experiences. The history of Hegelianism as distinct from the history of Hegel's own philosophical development does not begin with the explicit conflicts among different Hegelian parties in the 1830s but with the original appropriation of Hegel's philosophy by his first followers and sympathizers during his own lifetime. In a strict sense, of course, one could claim that there were as many versions of Hegelianism as there were Hegelians,[14] but respect for such individuality must be tempered by recognition of general, conceptualizable stages in the evolution of

Hegelianism; discernible patterns of inner differentiation in the school; and most of all, the unity within diversity that made it possible to distinguish Hegelians from proponents of other cultural ideologies during the Restoration.

As Hegel prepared to reenter the academic world in the summer of 1816, he was acutely aware that his particular conviction regarding the nature of philosophy and its cultural role had not yet become general, and thus still remained a "subjective judgment."[15] At the same time, however, he thought that the public had not been given an adequate opportunity to respond to his truth. His system had not undergone the test of historical experience and been found inadequate; it had simply not been tested.[16] The years of academic teaching at Jena were dismissed as a time of apprenticeship, as the years of a "beginner" who had been awkwardly chained to his lecture notes and who had not yet "worked himself through to clarity" in his philosophical position.[17] Hegel obviously thought that his experience as a journalist and gymnasium professor between 1807 and 1816 had greatly increased his ability to communicate his position clearly and succinctly. During these years, however, his audience had been severely restricted by his isolation from the centers of intellectual life, especially the major institutions of public education. As he commented in September 1816, a chair at a major university was an "almost indispensable condition" for gaining a significant audience for a philosophical position in Germany.[18] Finally, Hegel could argue, with apparent justification, that it would be unfair to judge the historical truth of his philosophy before the major part of his system was published. The final volume of the *Science of Logic* was published only in 1816 and the overview of the whole system, the *Encyclopedia of the Philosophical Sciences,* did not appear in print until the summer of 1817.

The arguments Hegel used to explain his lack of historical impact before 1816 deserve closer scrutiny. First, it is not at all clear that his ability to communicate his position to the average uninitiated member of the educated public improved radically between 1805 and 1816. Hegel retained his reputation for obscurity of thought and awkwardness of expression throughout his lifetime.[19] The barriers an individual had to overcome in order to appropriate Hegel's message were not of the kind that could be easily demolished by improvements in the technical aspects of oral or written communication. In 1830, as in 1805, arguments over Hegel's comprehensibility tended to be arguments between insiders and outsiders, disciples and opponents. Already during the Jena years, Hegel's supporters claimed that criticisms of his oral delivery were based on the "prejudices" of minds closed to the content of his message.[20] For the insiders, Hegel's halting, almost tortuous lecturing style became an integral part of the content of his message. Before their very eyes they witnessed the struggle of the concept as it worked to overcome the unmediated otherness of the concrete particulars of experience and finally came to comprehend itself as a self-determined unity.[21] What changed over the years was not so much Hegel's style of communication as the willingness of students and readers to display the "ardor and perseverance" that could transform the struggle for comprehensibility into a daily "Damascus experience,"[22] a spiritual victory over the restricted, fragmented, alienated perceptions of the finite individual consciousness. It would also be misleading to claim that the public needed to see the whole of Hegel's system before it could make a historical judgment of the truth of his viewpoint. For many of Hegel's students in the 1820s it was the *Phenomenology*, rather than the *Encyclopedia* or even the *Logic*, that opened the gates to absolute knowledge; and the *Phenomenology*, of course, had been available since 1807.

Finally, the significance of Hegel's relative isolation from the centers of intellectual influence as a *cause* of his lack of impact is also not immediately clear. We do know that Hegel made every effort to avoid intellectual "exile" in a provincial town or university. As Jena rapidly lost its position of cultural leadership after 1803, Hegel tried desperately to join the emigrants from Jena at the new centers of the German "spiritual" avant-garde in Heidelberg and Munich. He was eager to be at the center of the intellectual revolution that would accompany the political and social changes stimulated by the Napoleonic hegemony in Germany.[23] Hegel was correct in his belief that the "spiritual" avant-garde had shifted its locus from Jena to Heidelberg and Munich, but he was wrong in believing that it was ready to accept his philosophical position. There were individual, particular reasons, reasons that had little or nothing to do with his philosophical viewpoint, which prevented Hegel from becoming a professor of philosophy at Heidelberg in 1806 or the editor of a journal of scientific philosophical criticism in Munich in 1808; but there was also a basic incompatibility between Hegel's views and the second phase of the Romantic movement that dominated the cultural viewpoint of these centers after 1805. Hegel remained in provincial obscurity largely because he was out of step with the times. His judgment of all forms of Romantic philosophizing as historically bankrupt had been premature. Between 1805 and 1815 it was precisely those thinkers whom Hegel had relegated to historical obsolescence – Romantic "nature" philosophers and social thinkers like Schelling, Franz von Baader (1765–1841), Henrik Steffens (1773–

1845), Friedrich Schlegel, Schleiermacher, Josef Görres (1776–1848), G. H. von Schubert (1780–1860), Karl Windischmann (1775–1839), Ernst Moritz Arndt (1769–1860), and their slightly younger students and disciples – who dominated German intellectual life and whose truths were "verified" by public acceptance. Hegel's relative isolation before 1816 was not so much a cause as an expression of the public indifference to his mode of philosophy.

The lack of response to Hegel's philosophy before 1816 raises some interesting questions about the basis of the response after 1816. Did the events of the postwar era finally accomplish the disillusionment with edifying and regressive resolutions of the cultural crisis that Hegel had expected much earlier? Did individuals come to Hegel "on the rebound" from Schelling and other Romantic philosophers? But the period before 1816 is also significant for an analysis of Hegelianism in a more direct sense. Hegel was able to sustain his confidence in the historical truth of his philosophy during the years of isolation in part because he was not totally isolated. Although apparently swamped by the wave of national and religious emotion that provided such fertile soil for Romantic modes of thought, Hegel's viewpoint did make some impact on his contemporaries before 1816. This impact took two main forms: the beginnings of a committed discipleship among a handful of students who appropriated the Hegelian philosophical standpoint as their own world view, and the more diffuse growth of his reputation and influence among diverse groups and individuals who might best be called "sympathizers," those who were attracted for various reasons to particular facets of the Hegelian viewpoint but never committed themselves to the system as a general world view.

The first group of disciples emerged during Hegel's last two years at Jena. By the summer of 1805 a small but enthusiastic band of Hegelians formed the continuous core of Hegel's classes. The membership of this group probably did not extend much beyond the six names that are known to us: Hermann Suthmeyer (1784–1824), Christian G. Zellmann (1785–1806), Georg Andreas Gabler (1786–1853), Peter Gabriel van Ghert (1782–1852), Karl Friedrich Bachmann (1785–1855), and Christian F. Lange (n.d.).[24] Under the dynamic leadership of Suthmeyer, a theology student from the Bremen area, the group took on the character of both a religious sect and a personality cult. By his "genuine disciples," Hegel was worshipped as a prophetic philosophical "genius" of the kind he criticized so severely in his writings. Even his most trivial words and actions were viewed with an "almost superstitious" awe. The consciousness of these original Hegelians was dominated by the apparent collapse of the traditional order in the face of the Napoleonic onslaught in 1805 and 1806. In Hegel's philosophy they found an interpretation of this epochal historical transition that promised a new life arising out of the death of the old. The "total spiritual revolution" that Hegel's philosophy initiated in their personal lives, the salvation from the "night of ignorance and doubt" and elevation to the consciousness of unity with the universal spirit, was understood as the prefiguration of a radical collective cultural transformation.[25] The sense of historical expectancy so dominant in the mood of the group reflected Hegel's own sense of an imminent, qualitative "leap" of the spirit during these years.[26]

In 1812, Hegel wrote to Ghert that he still retained fond memories of the "beautiful times of vital enthusiasm for philosophy" that he had experienced with his Jena students.[27] Hegel did take a keen interest in his students' intellectual and spiritual development during these years. He gave individual tutorial aid to Ghert, a Flemish Catholic who had some difficulty handling a new language and a new philosophy at the same time, and his genuine interest and concern for the sickly and impoverished Zellmann is evident from his letters.[28] At the same time, however, it is clear that Hegel did not perceive himself as the leader of this tiny philosophical sect, or consider their enthusiastic discipleship an important sign of public influence. Although he did try, on at least one occasion, to interpret their personal adulation as an indication of respect for his "science" rather than his personal genius, he displayed, already in Jena, an attitude of benevolent detachment, of ironic distance, from the more emotional expressions of discipleship.[29]

Hegel's fond memories of his students in Jena were probably kept alive by the virtual absence of any kind of discipleship in the following decade. Although he had a few very devoted students at the gymnasium in Nürnberg, their intellectual immaturity would make it very dubious to classify them as "Hegelians."[30] Moreover, while the emergence of new Hegelians virtually stopped, the Hegelianism of the Jena group seemed in imminent danger of disappearing altogether. Zellmann, the most brilliant of the Jena students, and Hegel's obvious favorite, died of tuberculosis in 1806. Lange and Suthmeyer, the two theology students, vanished into the world of the village pastorate without making any noticeable impact on public life. Gabler's continued loyalty was also a silent one for more than twenty years.[31] Only Ghert and Bachmann made an effort to bring their Hegelian convictions to public notice in the years between 1805 and 1816.

In the years immediately following Hegel's departure from Jena it appeared that Bachmann would become his first major disciple in the German academic community. Bachmann stayed on in Jena as a lecturer in the philosophical faculty and in 1810 published an extremely enthusiastic review of the *Phenomenology* in which both Hegel's superiority to Schelling and his contemporary historical relevance were given strong emphasis. By transforming the poetic insights of the Romantic philosophers into the durable, rigorous, "masculine" form of a scientific system, Bachmann claimed, Hegel had inaugurated a new era in philosophy and human cultural development. Bachmann clearly expected that the Hegelian revolution would not be confined to philosophy. "Completely penetrated by the truth of the system," he wrote, "I have made participation in its realization in a more practical way the goal of my life; for we philosophize for our compatriots, for the fatherland and for the state." A new kind of practice "must emerge" from the "science of the spirit," he insisted, "philosophy must have a vital impact on action."[32] In a work that Bachmann published a year later, this emphasis on the need to move from theory to practice was even more pronounced. Philosophy was relegated to the realm of "mere" knowledge, a limited stage in man's process of divinization. "Knowledge elevates man to a contemplation of God," Bachmann stated, "but only through moral action does he actually become divine."[33]

Bachmann's conception of the Hegelian system as a reconciliation in thought that had still to be accomplished in practice was not easy to harmonize with the Hegelian doctrine of the dialectical unity of Reason and reality, thought and being. Hegel himself, though gratified by the enthusiasm of the review, noted that Bachmann had not penetrated very deeply into his method.[34] Bachmann, however, became more and more convinced that Hegel's philosophy could not provide the therapeutic reconciliation that it promised. By 1816 he was ready to place Hegel in the historical stage of unresolved bifurcation between thought and life, the intellectual elite and the *Volk*. Impressed by what he described as the "wonderful sympathy" that united all Germans during the wars of liberation, Bachmann denied that the presence of the universal in communal feeling or religious faith could ever be fully appropriated in thought or expressed in logical concepts. There was an ultimately irrational content in the ethical communality of the *Volk* that could never be fully articulated in the self-conscious rationality of the state, and an irreducible "otherness" to the absolute experienced in religious feeling that philosophical concepts could not mediate or comprehend. Hegel's attempt to grasp the totality of life in a scientific system was now seen as a futile and arrogant denial of the fact that the evolution of the divine in history was always a step ahead of human comprehension.[35] Bachmann increasingly placed his hopes for cultural regeneration in the awakening of a new ethical and religious feeling that would transcend the limitations of present philosophical comprehension.[36]

During the 1820s, Bachmann explicitly formulated his disagreement with Hegel as a rejection of the identity of logic and metaphysics. Logic, he claimed, was restricted to a description of the purely formal, a priori categories of thinking; it remained in the realm of abstraction, of the universal without concrete content.[37] The "real" could never be contained within the structure of logical concepts; it could be approached only in the "higher" realms of aesthetic intuition, religious contemplation, and ethical activity. After 1827, Bachmann was joined in this criticism of Hegel's identification of thought and being by a group of young philosophers, theologians, and literati who also demanded a progressive development of philosophy "beyond" Hegel's allegedly "abstract" system.[38] For Hegelians, however, this demand that philosophy should transcend the realm of "mere" logic and move toward an authentic recognition of the concrete universal in new forms of aesthetic and religious consciousness represented a misunderstanding of Hegel's position and a regression to philosophical stances that Hegel had overcome. Those who had not broken through to a comprehension of the real as the actuality of Reason were labeled renegades or "pseudo-Hegelians" and ejected from the school.[39]

Ghert was one of the first to notice that Bachmann had become a renegade. The continuous emphasis on the "heart" rather than the "head" as a source of insight, the mysterious prophetic utterances about the emergence of a new era of religious faith – these, in Ghert's view, were clear signs of a basic lack of philosophical courage and perseverance.[40] Ghert himself never wavered in his loyalty to his master. In fact, precisely during the years in which Bachmann's Hegelianism disintegrated under the historical impact of national and religious feeling, Ghert's Hegelianism became more intense and confident. This steadfastness was connected to Ghert's particular perspective on the events of 1810–15. After his return to the Low Countries he held a number of important administrative appointments and supported a rational reform of the educational system and church–state relations against the opposition of traditional privileged groups and demagogic manipulators of mass emotion.[41] In 1816 he invited Hegel to come to Louvain to help him transform the traditional Catholic clergy into a modern cultural elite loyal to Hegelian principles, and during the 1820s he was instrumental in the formation of a Dutch branch of the Hegelian school.[42]

In 1816, however, Hegelianism in the Netherlands was still restricted to the person of Ghert. In Germany, after the defection of Bachmann,

Hegelianism appeared to have vanished altogether. The offers Hegel received from three major universities in the summer of 1816 may thus seem particularly surprising. But academic appointments are not usually made by the disciples of the appointed or in response to a groundswell of popularity. They are more often the product of personal connections and general acceptability, and in 1816, Hegel seems to have possessed both. The *breadth* of support he received among the academics in faculty senates and the ministers in state bureaucracies is expecially striking. Although few of his sympathizers had actually read his work with any care, there was general agreement that his systematic rigor, vast erudition, and general "sobriety" or "realism" were just what German academic philosophy needed in the postwar era.[43] Moreover, Hegel was the only speculative philosopher who had made a serious attempt to work through the speculative principles in an important area of traditional philosophical teaching – the science of logic. As long as Hegel's philosophical position and its implications were only vaguely or poorly understood he was able to gain sympathetic support from intellectuals of divergent viewpoints. For the genuine disciple the scientific form and the absolute content of Hegel's philosophy were inseparable. The sympathizers, however, tended to emphasize one aspect at the expense of the other.

In 1816, despite the vehement criticism of Romantic subjectivity in the preface to the *Phenomenology,* Hegel still had many sympathizers among the academic Romantics. Many of Schelling's students and disciples perceived Hegel's deviation after 1807 as additions, revisions, and "perfections" of a shared position rather than as a radical step in a new direction. Already at Jena, Hegel's viewpoint gained the admiration of two talented students of Schelling – C. G. W. Kastner (1783–1857) and F. J. Schelver (1778–1832) – who felt that Schelling's description of the relationship between the absolute unity and its manifestations could use a little more scientific rigor in order to be usefully applied to their specialized fields of botany and chemistry.[44] Schelling himself first tended to interpret Hegel's emphasis on scientific rigor as simply an expression of a personal idiosyncracy. He wrote to his disciple Schubert in 1809 that Hegel was "a pure exemplar of inward and outward prose" who "must be considered saintly in our overly poetic times."[45] But to another disciple, Karl Windischmann, Schelling commented: "It would be very wrong . . . to let him get away with the manner in which he wants to make a general standard out of what is in accord with and granted to his own individual nature."[46] In 1816 the view of Hegel as a peculiarly "prosaic" and "sober" philosopher of a poetic and intoxicated Romantic generation, who had given Schelling's speculations greater scientific rigor and developed them more fully in the areas of logic and social and historical philosophy, seems to have been quite common. Hegel's candidacy for an academic chair was supported in Berlin by noted Romantics like Schleiermacher, the aesthetic philosopher K. W. F. Solger (1780–1819), and the speculative theologian Philipp Marheineke, and in Heidelberg by two of Schelling's most important academic disciples, Daub and the historian of ancient myth, Friedrich Creuzer (1771–1858).[47]

Hegel's relationship to disciples of Schelling and other Romantic philosophers is best exemplified in his relationship to Windischmann. This Catholic medical doctor, practitioner of mesmeristic cures, and poetic historian had been one of those Schellingians whom Hegel had criticized most severely for concocting confused imaginative visions where scientific knowledge was required.[48] In 1809, however, Windischmann had published a favorable review of the *Phenomenology,* and in a letter to Hegel even effusively stated that "the study of your system of science has convinced me that this work will some day, when the time of understanding arrives, be seen as the elementary book of the emancipation of man, as the key to the new gospel that Lessing prophesied."[49] Hegel was gratified by Windischmann's praise and did not press the obvious differences that still separated them. Windischmann, who was engaged in the study of occult forces in the natural world, was eager to discover a more scientific basis for his speculative theories, but he did not follow Hegel into the identification of thought and being, the premise on which Hegel's scientific method was constructed. Like another contemporary philosopher of nature who was favorably impressed by the *Phenomenology,* Erich von Berger (1772–1821),[50] Windischmann continued to conceive of the absolute as something separate from the movement of logical categories that described its structure. It was this residue of unmediated transcendence that lay at the basis of Windischmann's almost mystical Catholic piety.[51] Not until the 1820s did Windischmann begin to recognize that he and Hegel were not in complete agreement. Hegel himself, however, did not encourage this recognition. In 1823 he wrote to Windischmann that their disagreements were trivial when placed beside the fact that they were "companions in arms" who had attained the "common ground" of the "speculative standpoint."[52]

In February 1816, Karl Daub, another such "companion in arms," grouped Hegel, Schelling, Schubert, Baader, and Steffens together as the leaders of the speculative revolution that had overcome the unresolved dichotomies in the "critical-transcendental idealism" of Kant and Fichte.[53] But Hegel's anomalous position in this group was already evident in the fact that he also found many sympathizers precisely among those "critical-transcendental" idealists whom Daub had placed in the opposing camp. In fact, Hegel's closest friends and most influential supporters during the Nürnberg years were individuals like H. E. G. Paulus (1761–1851), Isaak von Sinclair (1775–1815), Immanuel Niethammer (1766–1848), and Nikolaus von Thaden (1770–1848), whose intellectual outlook had been formed by the philosophies of Kant, Reinhold, and Fichte during the 1790s and who viewed the "identity philosophy" of the Romantics with extreme suspicion. For such thinkers, Hegel's "sober" scientific method and criticism of the mystical tendencies in Romanticism were not personal idiosyncracies but essential facets of his philosophy. The significant differences that separated their own viewpoint from Hegel's became clear to many of them only as the political implications of Hegel's philosophy of identity became evident during the postwar years. Paulus and Thaden were severely critical of Hegel's identification of the historically real with the philosophically ideal in the *Philosophy of Right.*[54] Even Niethammer, one of Hegel's oldest and closest friends, commented that Hegel would soon change his position regarding the rationality of the real if he had the opportunity "to see these ruling rationalities face to face."[55] For the critical idealists the unity of the rational and the real remained an ethical ideal, a goal of moral striving and a basis for moral judgment, not the absolute spirit's self-comprehension of its own revelation and actualization in the natural and cultural world.

Confusion regarding Hegel's particular position in the spectrum of German idealism never completely disappeared during the Restoration, and divergent tendencies within the school sometimes came very close to reconstituting the "overcome" viewpoints of Fichte or Schelling; but as the number of committed Hegelians increased after 1816 and Hegel's distinctive philosophical positions were more clearly defined in the polemical battles that Hegelians waged against their competitors, the sympathetic support Hegel had received from proponents of the Romantic and critical idealist positions gradually disintegrated. Hegel's rise to a position of cultural eminence after 1815 was undoubtedly connected to the general sympathy and respect he received from important representatives of those major intellectual currents – neoclassical humanism, critical idealism, and Romanticism – that had constituted important stages in his own development and that he had tried to incorporate as Moments within his mature system. But the development of a distinctive Hegelian movement or school was based on the recognition of, and commitment to, precisely those elements in Hegel's viewpoint that differentiated it from other intellectual currents and defined it as an alternative to ideologies that seemed to become less and less convincing and historically viable after 1815. The historical emergence of Hegelianism as the ideology of a recognizable intellectual school during Hegel's lifetime was a gradual and complex process and is best understood if it is divided into two phases.

During the years of postwar conflict, reconstruction, and consolidation between 1816 and 1823, an increasingly significant number of students and academics recognized that hidden within the apparent obscurities of Hegel's philosophical prose was a distinctive and convincing answer to their quest for a satisfactory communal and religious identity. Even those students who were not particularly philosophically inclined and could barely struggle through the *Logic* were made aware that Hegel claimed to have discovered the actualization of ethical life in the laws and political constitutions of the postrevolutionary, "modern" state rather than in the irrational communality of the *Volk* or the traditional structures of social privilege and political authority, and that he presented the self-comprehending activity of thought, rather than aesthetic vision or religious faith, as the only satisfactory way to attain religious peace or reconciliation with God.[56] Recognition of the political and religious implications of Hegel's philosophy did not, of course, necessarily lead to a Hegelian conversion. As Hegel became more relevant, he also became more controversial. In 1816, Hegel congratulated his students on their good fortune at living in a time when they could devote their energies to the pursuit of truth unbothered by the stormy conflicts that had marked his own generation's years of maturation.[57] But the conflicts of the Napoleonic era did not cease suddenly in 1815, and Hegel's first disciples were often more interested in finding solutions to pressing contemporary issues than in the pursuit of truth for its own sake. Most of the early published expressions of Hegelianism were not scholarly treatises but political and cultural manifestos, personal confessions, visionary prophecies, and essays attempting to apply Hegel's viewpoint to immediate concerns. The first signs of a more academic, scholarly form of Hegelianism did not appear until 1822, and they heralded a general, though never complete, transformation of the combative early Hegelian movement into an academic school.

The developmental phases and inner differentiation of Hegelianism cannot be understood solely on the basis of a separation between political and theological or religious Hegelianism. All Hegelians viewed politics, the objective spirit, within the context of religion and philosophy, the absolute spirit. Yet significant differences of emphasis, focus, and particular concern on this issue cannot be denied. As Karl Rosenkranz noted in 1844, the Hegelianism of the immediate postwar era was characterized by an overwhelming emphasis on Hegel's political thought.[58] The most committed and active early Hegelians were disillusioned prophets of national regeneration like Johannes Schulze (1786–1869); veterans of the wars of liberation like Leopold Henning (1791–1866) and Friedrich C. Förster (1791–1868); leaders of the *Burschenschaften* like Friedrich W. Carové (1789–1852), Heinrich Leo (1799–1878), and Gustav Asverus (1798–1843); and half-emancipated Jews seeking social and political integration like Eduard Gans (1797–1839), Moses Moser (1796–1838), and Immanuel Wohlwill (1799–1847). The formative significance of postwar political conflicts in the Hegelian conversions of these individuals remained evident in their focus on the ethical–communal dimension of Hegel's thought after 1823.

As the overt conflicts of the postwar years subsided in the mid-1820s there was a gradual shift in emphasis from politics to art, religion, and philosophy within the Hegelian school. The younger generation that crowded into the classrooms of Hegel and his older disciples during the 1820s was more concerned with the relationship between faith and knowledge, between Christian religious culture and modern "scientific" consciousness, than with the debate over whether *Volk* or state was the locus of communal integration. This emphasis was not entirely new. A significant number of early Hegelians, including the academic theologians Karl Daub and Philipp Marheineke and their students Isaak Rust (1796–1862), Hermann Hinrichs (1794–1861), and Christian Kapp (1798–1874), had concentrated their attention on the religion/philosophy relationship. What *was* new was that in the younger generation the major divergences in defining the historical significance and cultural role of Hegelian philosophy were expressed through disagreements concerning the identity and nonidentity of religion and philosophy. The emergence of this new focus of concern within Hegelianism occurred in the context of two other major changes that marked the transition to the second phase of the school's evolution during the Restoration – consolidation and expansion.

The consolidation of Hegelianism was expressed, first of all, in the organization of Hegelians into a relatively unified school with a single organ of public expression. The character of this unification – the creation of an academic society centered in Berlin – represented the ascent of Prussian academicians to a position of obvious dominance within Hegelianism. Nonacademics, non-Prussians, and even non-Hegelians were welcomed into the Society for Scientific Criticism (only Hegel's most vociferous opponents were excluded), but the society and its journal were clearly dominated and controlled by Hegelian academics at the University of Berlin.[59] Nonacademic Hegelians like Carové or Rust and academic Hegelians who were not in close contact with the Berliners, like Christian Kapp in Erlangen, Julius Abegg (1796–1868) in Breslau, or Karl Friedrich Ferdinand Sietze in Königsberg, were relegated to positions of relative isolation on the fringes of the school, remaining outside that inner circle which defined the character of Hegelianism for the contemporary public. Autonomous expressions of particular viewpoints of different groups of Hegelians, like the journals edited by Förster in 1821 and the Jewish Hegelians in 1822, did not reappear within the Hegelian school until after the divisions of the 1830s. Although the Hegelian school was never the disciplined army that some of its opponents made it out to be, there was a definite hierarchical element in its composition. The generation of students who attended the University of Berlin in the mid and late 1820s encountered what one might justifiably call a Hegelian "establishment," consisting of Hegel, Schulze, Marheineke, Henning, and to a lesser extent Gans and Förster, whose approval and support were necessary for acceptance into the inner "magic circle"[60] of the school and, in an increasing number of cases, for appointments or promotions within the Prussian educational system.

The inner consolidation of Hegelianism into an academic school centered in Berlin was intimately connected to the external consolidation of the ties among Hegelianism, the Prussian Kultusministerium, and the Berlin literary and cultural elites. Altenstein and Schulze had reestablished firm control over the Kultusministerium by 1823–4 (after a period of conservative interference that followed the Carlsbad Decrees of 1819) and were thenceforth, within the limitations of their budget and the diplomatic compromises required to placate their opponents, able to express their ideological sympathies in the making of university and gymnasium appointments. By 1826 a student might easily have been motivated to become a Hegelian for purely practical, careerist reasons.[61] Moreover, the influence of Hegelianism in Berlin was not confined to the university. The sympathy and support of patrons of literature and the arts like the Varnhagens, the Veits, and the Mendelssohns and influential cultural critics and journalists like Förster and Moritz Saphir (1795–1858) made Hegelianism an extremely important, if not completely dominating, presence in the Berlin literary world and general cultural scene.[62]

The final aspect of Hegelian consolidation during the last half of the 1820s was ideological. As long as the "school" consisted of scattered individual thinkers and relatively isolated groups, consciousness of an orthodox interpretation against which individual viewpoints might be judged could not easily develop. This situation changed as the school attained a measure of organizational unity and established itself as an academic power in Berlin. A conservative accommodationist interpretation of the relationship between Hegelian philosophy and the existing religious and political order, best exemplified in the viewpoints of Marheineke, Henning, and Schulze, increasingly came to be considered the orthodox interpretation. Hegel himself encouraged this development by excessively praising mediocre but safely uncritical thinkers like Gabler and Karl Friedrich Göschel (1784-1861) and thus elevating them to the undeserved status of spokesmen for the Hegelian position.[63]

The attempt to define a particular interpretation of Hegel's reconciliation of Reason and reality as orthodox, however, had only limited success. By 1830 it was quite obvious that the process of consolidation had produced its own negation. As the Hegelian school became more unified, cemented its ties to the Prussian state, and increased its academic power and influence, its membership expanded enormously, producing centrifugal tendencies that worked against the process of consolidation. Some of the new converts, like Göschel, Kasimir Conradi (1784-1849), and Johann F. G. Eiselen (1785-1865), were generational contemporaries of older members of the school like Marheineke and Schulze and had shared their experience of the Napoleonic wars and postwar conflicts, but the vast majority were members of the generation born in the first decade of the century, who had missed the crucial formative historical experiences of the older Hegelians. In Berlin the major spokesmen for this group in the last half of the decade were a number of young lecturers at the university: Karl Ludwig Michelet (1801-93), Heinrich Gustav Hotho (1802-73), Heinrich Theodor Rötscher (1802-71), Karl Friedrich Werder (1806-93), Ferdinand Benary (1805-80), and Agathon Benary (1807-61). This group of aspiring academics, however, was surrounded by a whole host of Hegelian gymnasium professors, independent intellectuals, and students, some of whom - I will mention only Johann E. Erdmann (1805-92), Max Stirner (1806-56), Wilhelm Vatke (1806-82), and Bruno Bauer (1808-82) - were destined to play major roles in the future history of the school.

As the Hegelian school absorbed members of a new generation with formative cultural experiences that differed not only from those of Hegel but also from those of his earliest disciples, it also expanded geographically beyond the confines of Berlin and Prussia. Before 1827-8, Hegelianism outside Berlin was represented by scattered individuals like Daub in Heidelberg, Hinrichs in Breslau (1824–6) and Halle (1826 ff.), Kapp in Erlangen, and Gabler in Bayreuth. During the last years of the decade, however, distinct groups of Hegelians emerged outside Berlin. Halle, whose large university and prestigious pedagogical institutes provided excellent career opportunities, became the major outpost of Hegelianism in Prussia. In 1828, Leo, Johann Georg Mussmann (1798–1833), Eiselen, Karl Rosenkranz (1805–79), and Theodor Echtermeyer (1805–44) joined Hinrichs to form the core of an influential Hegelian contingent that was soon producing its own converts, like Arnold Ruge (1802–80), Friedrich Richter (1807–56), Julius Schaller (1810–68), and Moritz Besser (1806–?). Kapp's isolation in Erlangen was broken by the arrival of Rust in 1827 and Ludwig Feuerbach (1804–72) a year later. The main center of south German Hegelianism, however, was destined to be, not Erlangen, but Tübingen. The evolution of a distinctive Swabian Hegelianism still lay in the future, but by 1830 a small group of students at the Tübingen seminary – which included David Friedrich Strauss (1808–74) and Friedrich Theodor Vischer (1807–87) – had already laid the basis for a southern branch of the Hegelian school.

The appropriation of Hegelianism by members of different historical generations living in different political and cultural environments naturally exacerbated existing tensions and produced new conflicts within the Hegelian school. But Hegelians remained convinced that there was an essential core of Hegelianism that they all shared. What was this core? What made obvious differences in experience and viewpoint among Hegelians appear trivial in comparison to differences between Hegelians and non-Hegelians? Some indication of the appropriate categories in which an answer to these questions must be phrased can be found in the orations delivered at Hegel's funeral by two members of the Berlin Hegelian establishment – Marheineke and Förster.

"Let the dead bury the dead," Förster proclaimed at Hegel's graveside; "to us belongs the living; he who, having thrown off his earthly chains, celebrates his transfiguration."[64] Marheineke also placed the burial of Hegel's earthly remains in the context of the immortal life of his spirit, which "still lives and will live forever in his writings and his countless admirers and students."[65] In fact, Marheineke claimed that the departure of the empirical, individual Hegel allowed his eternal spirit to be appropriated by his followers in "a purer fashion than before." "Emancipated from all sensual appearance," Hegel was now "no longer susceptible to misinterpretation," but "transfigured in the hearts and spirits of all who recognized his eternal worth." The analogy that lay behind statements like this must have been obvious to Marheineke's audience, but to prevent any misunderstanding he made the comparison specific:

> In a fashion similar to our savior, whose name he always honored in his thought and activity, and in whose divine teaching he recognized the most profound essence of the human spirit, and who as the son of God gave himself over to suffering and death in order to return to his community eternally as spirit, he also has now returned to his true home and through death has penetrated through to resurrection and glory.[66]

Hegel's Christ-like resurrection and transfiguration in the community of his disciples, Marheineke stated, was grounded in his ability to elevate himself to the realm of spiritual immortality within his own earthly existence. Hegel had been able "to emancipate himself from the ego and its selfish desires, from all appearance and vanity . . . and out of the death of this life had been spiritually reborn and resurrected." The philosophical comprehension of the self-development of the absolute spirit within the "passing appearances of life in nature and history" was also an elevation to a state of spiritual "being." The comprehension of the infinite was synonymous with an attainment of infinity. This was the existential meaning of the Hegelian doctrine of the unity of knowing and being, reason and reality, logic and metaphysics. For both Marheineke and Förster, the Hegelian system was not just a set of philosophical propositions that could be learned and affirmed like a catechism but a "Kingdom of eternal reality and truth" in which Hegel and his disciples lived in a state of achieved immortality.[67] By providing philosophical knowledge, Hegel also provided personal salvation. "Was it not he," Förster asked, "who reconciled the discontented with the manifold confusions of life in that he taught us really to know Jesus Christ? . . . Was it not he through whom the weary and heavy-laden learned to love this world even in misfortune?" The obvious answer to these rhetorical questions was: "Yes, he was for us a mediator, savior, and liberator from every care and need, for he saved us from the bonds of madness and selfish egoism."[68]

Although one must make allowances for exaggerated rhetoric because of the context of these statements, the funeral orations delivered by Marheineke and Förster do provide an important insight into the nature of Hegelianism during the 1820s. The school was perceived by its members as a spiritual community of individuals who had attained a state of being and knowledge that elevated them above the merely finite standpoint of the perceptions, cares, and desires of the particular empirical ego. To enter the school, to become an authentic Hegelian, a person had to undergo an existential transformation, a philosophical "rebirth." Hegel himself had stated that "the free spirit exists only as twice-born" and had described his own breakthrough to the scientific comprehension of the absolute as the resolution of a crisis of intellectual doubt and personal identity.[69] For his disciples it was precisely this philosophical second birth that defined what it meant to become a Hegelian. As Göschel stated in 1829, the elevation to philosophical knowledge was a process analogous to religious conversion:

It is the same with philosophy. Or does it not also have a point that cannot be learned, not coerced or externally appropriated, or more specifically, that cannot be transferred from one person to another? And is this point not precisely the vital point? We may comprehend a complete system with our understanding, teach and learn philosophy, and yet lack the standpoint that gives light and truth to what has been learned. The philosopher must also celebrate his day of pentecost. Without a second birth no one can rise from the sphere of natural understanding to the speculative heights of the living concept. That famous bridge that leads in one sudden leap from the limited horizons of the psychological sphere to the philosophical circle of light must be crossed by everyone.[70]

Göschel and the other members of the Hegelian school were convinced that in the Hegelian system they had discovered the bridge that led from the finite to the infinite. "Only in the system itself," Christian Kapp wrote to Hegel in 1823, "can salvation be found."[71]

In 1835, at a time when the signs of irreconcilable division were becoming evident in the school, Karl Rosenkranz attempted to define the "vital point" that had been the source of the unity and common purpose among Hegelians during the 1820s. The shared sense of exaltation and enthusiasm possessed by Hegelians, he claimed, was based on

the consciousness that man's spirit was not in essence different from the divine spirit . . . that man on this earth was not abandoned by God in a corner of the universe as a creature of little value, but was taken up into the world-creating bosom of the heavenly father as his own child and image.

The state of "blessedness" that traditional religion had relegated to a life after death could be achieved through philosophical thinking in the "here and now." It was this experience, not only of having discerned the presence of the infinite within the finite appearances of everyday experience, but of actually living in the infinite in one's earthly life, that "aroused a shudder of the most sublime emotion . . . A joyful earnest rapture came over many . . . and ennobled their life anew."[72]

The intoxicating exhilaration of perceiving and experiencing the world as a vessel of absolute spirit was already evident among the first group of Hegelian converts at Jena in 1805–6,[73] and is expressed in the letters and autobiographical accounts of many members of the school. When Rosenkranz, Michelet, Ruge, Strauss, Feuerbach, and Vischer reconstructed their life histories in later years, the Hegelian conversion emerged as the fundamental turning point of their spiritual developments, the transition between two radically different modes of existence.[74] Kapp claimed that the Hegelian rebirth was analogous to the turning point in man's collective history represented by the incarnation of the divine in Jesus Christ.[75] In a thinly disguised autobiographical novel published in 1835, Heinrich Hotho made the Hegelian conversion the nodal point of his protagonist's spiritual pilgrimage:

> Inwardly exhausted and spiritually dead, without hope and without faith, I threw myself into the arms of philosophy and she alone embraced me with generous consoling grace. I can no longer describe the specific stages of this process – the emotionally moving days of learning and striving, the glimmerings of the first comprehension, the expanses that opened up to me . . . the riches that flowed toward me daily without interruption, until I was overcome by an unhoped-for blessedness – but the remembrance of this happiness still rests in my soul with the echo of an attained peace, as when doubters are delighted when, forgetting all earthly dissensions, they suddenly feel themselves elevated to a pure heavenly activity. Hardly a year had passed and I discovered myself again as a totally new person.[76]

As one might well imagine, many young converts to Hegelianism had a great deal of difficulty articulating and explaining their new standpoint to family and friends. In 1830, Wilhelm Vatke wrote to his brother;

> You will think I am insane when I tell you that I see God face to face, but it is true. The transcendent has become immanent, man himself is a point of light in the infinite light and like recognizes like. Because I myself am all essence (*Wesenheit*) I can know all essence, and insofar as I rest in the great heart of God I am blessed here and now. Oh, if I could only describe to you how blessed I am.[77]

When Michelet tried to describe his newfound blessedness to his skeptical father, he was forced to explain how the apparently finite activity of philosophical analysis could produce such a state of spiritual exaltation. The redemptive power of Hegelian science, Michelet stated, was based on its ability to transcend the limited standpoint of "finite existence." It was "a science that exalts man and teaches him his highest calling" because it elevated the individual to a state of complete identification with the divine spirit. In the activity of philosophical comprehension man "carries the consciousness of God within himself," Michelet insisted, and "is thus elevated above the limitations of the world and lives eternally in the realm of truth."[78]

The significance and implications of the Hegelian "second birth" can be clarified by separating out three of its major elements. In his retrospective analysis of 1835, Rosenkranz noted that the denial of the natural desires and self-centered intellectual perspective of the individual ego was a crucial element in the Hegelian conversion. "One wanted to rid oneself of all selfish egoism," he claimed; "Hegel's emphasis on . . . the universal, the objective, made individuality, the particular subjectivity, a matter of indifference."[79] The fervor with which Hegelians attacked the "sins" of egotism and sensuality often rivaled that of their pietistic contemporaries. "If you do not feel that which elevates the thinking spirit of our times," wrote Christian Kapp, ". . . then neither God nor the saints can help you, for you are buried in the living flesh and no sound of trumpets will awaken you from your damnation as long as you desire to remain what you are."[80]

Heinrich Hotho noted that the Hegelians' insistence that existential fulfillment could "be found only in the universal that is to fill each and regulate each according to the same laws" appeared to deny the subjective autonomy of the "modern personality."[81] But this traditional emphasis on the submergence of the subjective individual in the objective universal was deceptive. For the Hegelians defined the universal, the absolute objective "substance," as an absolute "subject." In the activity of philosophical comprehension, the individual recognized his own essence in the infinite activity of the absolute subject. The Hegelian conversion experience liberated the individual from the merely individual subjectivity in which self-consciousness was defined as consciousness of the particular empirical self and opposed to the universal and objective, and elevated him to the state of unity with the absolute subject in which self-consciousness was synonymous with consciousness of the universal, objective, infinite substance. Insofar as a person's "individuality" did not correspond to his "essence" as an autonomous subject, insofar as it represented only his finite particular "appearance," Michelet wrote to his father, it had to "die." But a person's authentic individuality as a self-conscious, free subject was not denied by the Hegelian conversion. It was simply recognized and grasped as an "expression of the divine spirit."[82]

For Hegelians the achievement of unity with the absolute was not the result of an act of "grace," not something "given" to man, but the result of his own free activity as a thinking subject. A conversion experience that transformed the finite ego into a purified "vessel" of the divine was not, of course, unique to Hegelians. What was unique in their experience was the form in which this conversion was accomplished. Only after he had undergone "the absolute discipline and cultivation of consciousness" under Hegel's tutelage, Heinrich Stieglitz (1801–49) wrote to Hegel in 1827, did his "awakened heart begin to live its authentic life in the fullness of thought."[83] "Every human being who desires to attain his highest calling," Carové stated, "must study philosophy," for it was only in the act of philosophical comprehension that "Reason became conscious of itself as all being in its necessary development, so that instead of being overcome by the overwhelming mass of finite experience, man could integrate himself into this experience as a living member, and having given himself his own wings, peacefully face the power of storms."[84]

For Hegelians, of course, "thinking" was defined not as abstract ratiocination or momentary flashes of insight, but as the systematic comprehension of the real. The elevation to the "blessed" consciousness of unity with the absolute spirit was at the same time a reconciliation with the previously alien world of natural and historical phenomena, which was now understood from the inside, "objectively," as the reality of Reason. The Hegelian conversion did not transport the individual from the finite relationships of the empirical world (*Diesseits*) into an infinite unity in the beyond (*Jenseits*), but culminated in the reconciling recognition that the spirit was actual and present in the world. It was this conviction that lay behind the Hegelians' common claim that they possessed an irrefutable method for attaining absolute, objective truth in every area of scholarly research. To organize the empirical materials in a given area of study according to Hegelian categories was not to impose a subjective meaning on the naked facts, but to reveal the true, objective dialectical structure and unity of the real. "All the sciences are transparent and illuminated for me," Vatke claimed; "I know what history wants, I know how art is formed, how religion creates itself."[85] The Hegelian perspective, Michelet insisted, was the only standpoint from which objective knowledge could be achieved, "because in it the finite self-consciousness has elevated itself to the absolute spirit; in scientific endeavor it produces out of itself an adequate description of infinite Reason, of the subject matter as it really is in itself."[86]

These three elements – the negation of the standpoint of the empirical individual ego, the identification with the absolute spirit in the activity of philosophical comprehension, and the reconciling recognition of the natural and historical–cultural world as the spatial and temporal reality of Reason – comprised the essential core of what it meant to be a Hegelian. But all Hegelians were not in agreement concerning the historical implications of their shared conversion experience. Variations within the school were articulated in terms of differing judgments of the present stage in the actualization of Reason and divergent interpretations of the historical meaning of the reconciliation of Reason and reality. Did the existing political community and religious forms express the completed actualization of Reason in the historical world? If not, if the perfected reality of Reason and the existing historical world were still in a state of dynamic tension, what kind of change was required before man would be able to recognize his political and cultural environment as the authentic actualization of his own universal nature as a free, self-conscious, "spiritual" being? Would minor reforms suffice, or was a radical transformation of the existing order necessary? Individual Hegelians answered such questions according to their own particular historical experiences, and their answers converged and diverged as those experiences converged and diverged.

5

Hegelian politics during the Restoration: accommodation, critique, and historical transcendence

We now have monks of Atheism, whom Mr. Voltaire, because he was an obstinate Deist, would have broiled alive. I must admit that this music does not appeal to me, but it does not frighten me either, for I have stood behind the Maestro while he composed. To be sure, he composed with indistinct and elaborately adorned notes – so that not everyone could decipher them. Occasionally I observed how he anxiously looked about in fear that he might have been understood. He liked me very much because he was convinced that I would not betray him; I even thought him servile at that time. Once, when I expressed displeasure with the phrase 'Everything that is, is rational,' he smiled strangely and said, "One could also read it as 'everything which is rational must be.'" He quickly looked about, but soon regained his composure.

. . . for Hegel was a man of character. And though, like Schelling, he bestowed on the existing order of church and state some all too dubious vindications, he did so for a state that, in theory at least, does homage to the principle of progress, and for a church that regards the principle of free inquiry as its vital element.

I could easily prophecy which songs would one day be whistled and trilled in Germany, for I was present at the hatching of the birds that later intoned the new music. I saw how Hegel, with his almost comically serious countenance, sat like a brood-hen on the fatal eggs, and I heard his cackling.[1]

These three brief characterizations of Hegel from the pen of the poet Heinrich Heine, in spite of their comical exaggerations, apparent contradictions, and mixed metaphors, provide a succinct and subtle introduction to the complex, multidimensional problem of defining the relationship between Hegel and his "time," and more particularly, that between Hegel's political philosophy and the Prussian state of the Restoration. In fact, most subsequent scholarly contributions to the rather virulent debate over this problem might have profited from a more serious consideration of the poet's insights.

In the first passage quoted, Heine makes what may seem to be an obvious point, but one that has only very recently been appropriated by academic Hegelian scholarship as an important "discovery," that is, that in order to make a proper judgment of Hegel's political position it is useful, even necessary, to distinguish between the personal "servility," or tendency to accommodate existing authority, that was evident in Hegel's response to the political repression initiated by the Carlsbad Decrees of 1819, and the essentially "liberal" and "progressive" substance of his political philosophy.[2] That Hegel should have appeared "servile" to Heine during the years immediately following the publication of the *Philosophy of Right* in 1820 is not surprising. In the tense political atmosphere of 1820–1, Hegel's notorious phrase about the identity of Reason and actuality was immediately interpreted (not only by the *Völkisch* nationalists and democratic radicals, but by most of the moderate-liberal "progressive" elements in the German intellectual community) as a philosophical justification of the recently instituted political repression.[3] Although such an interpretation was, as the Hegelian Eduard Gans correctly pointed out in 1833, based on a "misunderstanding and false exegesis"[4] of the Hegelian text, Hegel himself had contributed to this misunderstanding to a not inconsiderable degree by failing to provide adequate or obvious guidelines for the interpretation of some of his more cryptic and ambiguous phrases and by attacking some of the recent victims of repression with excessive ardor. In 1821, Hegel described himself as a "fearful, anxious person" who desired "peace" above all.[5] It was this fear of persecution and desire for peace that led him to modify and mystify some of his positions in 1820. But he still thought that anyone who read his work with any care would realize that he had not identified himself with the repressors, and he was deeply hurt by the general response his work aroused.[6] It is fitting that a master of irony like Heine should have been the first to perceive the ironical aspect of the popular image of Hegel as the anointed philosopher of the German Restoration. For the deceptive phrases and personal polemics from which this image was constructed had their experiential source in a fear of persecution, not a respect or love for the persecutors. It was during the time when Hegel was most pessimistic about bridging the gap between empirical existence and the philosphical Idea that he appeared to identify them most completely.

The image of Hegel as an essentially progressive, liberal thinker half hidden behind the cloak of a fearful conformist is more subtle than many later portrayals, but it remains an oversimplification. A new dimension is added to the portrait by Heine's recognition that even the true Hegel, the authentic "man of character," construed his political philosophy as a comprehension of the postrevolutionary state, and that his primary model for this modern state of actualized Reason was –

Prussia. The Prussia comprehended in Hegel's political philosophy, however, was not the Prussia of the reactionary repressions of 1819–20 but a "progressive" state – the Prussia of Stein, Hardenberg, and Humboldt, the Prussia of the Reform Era. Unlike many later liberal apologists for Hegel,[7] however, Heine was only too well aware that the Prussia of the 1820s was no longer the Prussia of 1807–19, that the Prussia Hegel comprehended could not be simply identified with the Prussia in which Hegel lived, for the latter was inwardly divided between progressive principle and a somewhat less than progressive practice. Heine's basic perception that Restoration Prussia was inwardly divided points to the implicit critical elements in Hegel's reconciliation of Reason and actuality. Which, or more aptly "whose," Prussia did his philosophy comprehend? More particularly, which generational or social groups recognized their "home" in Hegel's modern state?

Beneath the "servile" and "critical" aspects of Hegel's political stance, Heine finally discerned a third, revolutionary dimension. Hegel's political philosophy could be fully comprehended only as a Moment within the totality of his system, and the principles of this system, Heine was convinced, had historical implications that transcended the stage of objective spirit conceptualized in Hegel's social and political theory. The form of ethical community actualized in the particular form of the modern state was sublated (*aufgehoben*) in the world-historical process of cultural development, and this evolution of the "world spirit" was in turn sublated in the universal self-comprehending, self-determining activity of the absolute spirit.[8] The revolutionary potential implicit in the dialectical tensions between the objective and absolute spirit in Hegel's system was usually described by Heine in terms of Hegel's conception of religion. In his role as a "monk of Atheism," Hegel had comprehended both the death of the old transcendent father-God and his resurrection as the Holy Spirit immanent in the process of human historical development. Heine's recognition of the revolutionary millenarian dimension in Hegel's identification of Reason and actuality was based on his own personal experiences with Hegelianism during the 1820s. He could so "easily prophesy" the cultural radicalism of the Young Hegelians of the 1830s and 1840s because the seeds of this radicalism were already present during the Restoration.[9]

The historical significance, context, and interrelationship of the three dimensions of Hegelian politics – accommodation, critique, and historical transcendence – were most clearly revealed in the emergence and increasing differentiation of the political Hegelianism of Hegel's disciples during the 1820s. The individual Hegelians whom I have chosen for particular analysis are Johannes Schulze, Leopold Henning,

Friedrich Christoph Förster, Eduard Gans, Heinrich Leo, and Friedrich Wilhelm Carové. This particular group has been selected for three major reasons. First, they were all converted to the Hegelian position during the period of transition from reform to Restoration between 1817 and 1823, and their writings reveal the complex nature of the relationship between Hegelian philosophy and the political experience of the educated estate during this crucial period. Secondly, although they believed, like all Hegelians, that the communal dimension of human experience could be fully grasped only as a Moment within Hegel's total system, their activity and intellectual production was specifically focused on the major problem of Hegel's political thought: the historical emergence of the modern state as the ultimate form of ethical community. Aside from Hegel's own writings and lectures, their works were the most significant and influential expression of political Hegelianism during the Restoration. It should be noted, moreover, that Hegel himself did not lecture on the philosophy of law and politics between 1824 and 1831, but delegated this task to his followers Henning and Gans.[10] Finally, unlike younger, more famous, Hegelians who were still students during the mid- and late- 1820s, all the individuals in this group had completed their studies by the early 1820s and held influential positions and/or wrote major works during the Restoration. Henning, Leo, and Gans had attained the rank of associate professor at the University of Berlin by 1826, and Gans and Leo were promoted to full professorships before the end of the decade. This academic trio also filled the most important positions on the editorial staff of the Hegelian *Jahrbücher*. Förster and Carové exercised their considerable literary and journalistic talents in bringing their interpretation of the Hegelian message to the educated public outside the university. Schulze, the administrative aide for higher education in Altenstein's Kultusministerium, was the primary link between the Hegelian school and the Prussian government. These six Hegelian disciples thus played key roles in both the creation of the Hegelian school and the articulation and dissemination of political Hegelianism during the 1820s. But by the second half of the decade it had become obvious, to borrow Heine's metaphor, that they were no longer singing in harmony; the three dimensions that Heine had discerned in Hegel's political stance had become three alternative positions.

THE EXPERIENTIAL MATRIX OF POLITICAL HEGELIANISM

When Hegel began teaching at the University of Heidelberg in the fall of 1816 he was confident that the historical moment for the validation of his philosophy had come. Not only was he finally ready, at the age of forty-six, to present his complete system of philosophy to his students and readers, but he also believed that the postwar generation of students was ready to respond to his message. In his inaugural lecture he noted that during the previous decades of revolution, war, reform, and liberation the "world spirit" had turned "outward" to practical activity; political interests had absorbed all human energies and his contemporaries had become "dumb" to the voice of "pure science" and philosophical comprehension. But now that the practical task of saving the substance of the German cultural and political community from external domination and internal disintegration had been accomplished, the time had come for the spirit to "return to itself," to comprehend the results of its actions and construct a world in its own element, "a free rational world of the spirit."[11] As a memorandum that Hegel had prepared for the Prussian university authorities a few months earlier revealed, he believed that this activity of self-comprehension was of great political and cultural importance. The years of upheaval, reconstruction, and liberation had been accompanied by new forms of communal and religious consciousness, but these forms were not adequate to the historical actuality they had helped to produce. "Though recent times have revived the tendency toward solid content, higher ideas, and religion," Hegel wrote, "yet the forms of feeling, fantasy, and confused concepts are unsatisfactory for this content, indeed more unsatisfactory than ever."[12] It was the inevitable feeling of dissatisfaction and disillusionment aroused by this tension between the subjective forms of "feeling, fantasy, and confused concepts" and the objective "content" of a rational ethical community actualized in the reformed and reconstructed postwar German states, Hegel believed, that would lead his contemporaries to undertake the difficult, but ultimately therapeutic, labor of philosophical comprehension.

For those individuals who did become Hegelians, Hegel's analysis proved basically correct; the immediate experiential matrix for the emergence of political Hegelianism was the disillusionment created by the conflict between postwar historical realities and the visions of cultural regeneration spawned by the reform and liberation movements before 1815. The simple pattern of disillusionment and conversion, however, is complicated by a significant variety (even among our selected subjects) in the ideological positions that preceded individual Hegelian conversions. An adequate understanding of the origins of political Hegelianism requires an extension of the experiential matrix into a three-stage process: (1) a disinheritance or liberation from the traditional cultural and political world; (2) an identification with alternative visions of cultural regeneration and communal integration; and (3) a disillusionment with these "subjective" conceptions in response to the political developments after 1815.

For Schulze, Henning, Förster, and Leo, the disintegration of their fathers' world was experienced more as a disinheritance than as an emancipation. Their fathers were members of the administrative (Schulze), military (Henning), and ecclesiastical (Förster, Leo) branches of the professional state-service "estate" in the tiny Protestant principalities bordering Prussia in north and central Germany, and they were all placed on the educational path that was to lead them back into their fathers' world very early in their lives.[13] A university education had traditionally entailed a temporary emancipation from family ties and local horizons and an initiation into the wider context of the German cultural community, but for Schulze, Henning, Förster, and Leo the divorce from "home" became permanent. For it was during their years of educational preparation for traditional vocations within the professional estate that the cultural context in which those vocations made sense began to disintegrate around them. Unlike the members of Hegel's generation, whose divorce from the traditional order was accompanied by a fervent commitment to the vision of general human emancipation from the yoke of authority and privilege, Schulze, Henning, Förster, and Leo experienced the crumbling of their fathers' world as the product of external aggression, as a violent conquest by the armies of a foreign despot. Although they recognized that the victory of the aggressor was made possible by the impotence and moral bankruptcy of the victim, they could not embrace the agent of deserved death and destruction as the source of new life and cultural resurrection.

In their search for an alternative to the historically obsolete values of their fathers' world and the alien values of the foreign invader, Schulze, Henning, Förster, and Leo all eventually committed themselves to what could be generally described as a Romantic ideology of national cultural regeneration. This Romantic nationalism, however, was never a unified, monolithic ideology; it contained significant inner differentiations and went through definite phases of historical development. Schulze, Henning and Förster, and Leo committed themselves to this ideology at three different stages of its evolution and expressed their commitments, in theory and action, in significantly different ways.

Schulze, the oldest member of the group, encountered the Romantic vision during the earliest phase of its connection to the nationalist cause

– in the classrooms of Schleiermacher, the philologist Friedrich Wolf (1759–1824), and the philosopher Henrik Steffens at Halle in 1805–6. By the time he took up his first teaching position at the Weimar Gymnasium in 1808 he had defined his vocation as pedagogue, preacher, and prophet of a German cultural regeneration. Together with Franz Passow (1786–1833) he tried to make the study of Greek language and literature relevant to the contemporary situation by emphasizing the communal content of the Hellenic ideal of self-sufficient beauty. If Germans were to become modern Greeks, however, they would first have to become authentic Germans. This required not only the appropriation of a purified linguistic heritage, which embodied the values of Germanic culture, but also a resurgence of religious faith in the divine basis of communal identity.[14] In the patriotic lay sermons Schulze published in 1810–11 this new faith was defined in terms of the Romantic breakthrough to an experience of the immanent absolute.[15] Both Schulze's pedagogical Graecomania and his quasi-religious sermonizing focused on the ethical task of inspiring a consciousness of communal solidarity among his contemporaries. That the envisioned *Volksgemeinschaft* would take a political form was implied, but never specified in detail.

The military campaigns of 1813 naturally aroused Schulze's enthusiasm. Although the Hessian authorities (he had moved to Hanau in 1812) rejected his request to join the volunteers, he did encourage many of his students to enlist and preached patriotic sermons to the troops as they set out on their anti-Napoleonic crusade.[16] But Schulze also warned that the nationalist exaltation of 1813 would soon dissolve unless it became the inspiration for wide-ranging domestic reforms that would create "a fortress of faith and love that would remain unshaken by the shifting winds of time."[17] The "reborn Hessians" whom Schulze had eulogized in 1813 remained indifferent to his pleas for domestic reform, however, and in 1815 he joined the Prussian administration as director of educational reorganization and reform in the Rhenish provinces. A brief friendship with the nationalist publicist Josef Görres in 1815–16 temporarily refurbished his faith in the possibility of a spontaneous national revival through liberation of the *Volk* from traditional political authority, but daily experiences with this *Volk* in his administrative work soon led him to take a less optimistic position. The hoped-for *Volksgemeinschaft* could become a reality only through a gradual, arduous process of disciplined education. When Görres attacked the government for its failure to fulfill the promise of constitutional rule, Schulze refused to support him. By 1818 the movement for national reform had divided into opposing camps of populists and bureaucrats, and Schulze, though somewhat reluctantly, chose the side of the bureaucrats.[18]

In 1818 this choice placed Schulze in opposition to Henning and Förster. Although Henning and Förster had been introduced to the ethical-cultural form of Romantic nationalism during their university studies between 1809 and 1812, their decisive commitment to the ideal of Germanic *Volksgemeinschaft* occurred during the politicization of that ideal between 1813 and 1815. Henning, whose father was killed fighting with Napoleon against the Austrians in 1809, was forced to make a decision in 1812, when he was called for service in the Gotha regiments during Napoleon's Russian campaign. He chose exile over service to Napoleon and rejoined his regiment only when it switched to the side of the "liberators" in 1814.[19] Förster was rescued from aimless studies and a depressing tutorial position by the Prussian call for volunteers in 1812. He immediately rushed to Breslau to join the Lützow brigade and, with his friend Theodor Körner, greeted the rediscovered unity of prince and people in numerous patriotic poems and war songs.[20] For both Henning and Förster the fraternal democracy of the nationalist volunteers became the model for a postwar reconstruction of Germany. Their disillusionment began in 1815 when the Congress of Vienna showed little interest in German unification and the German princes even less in liberal constitutional reform.[21] Like Schulze, they reacted to these disappointments by transferring their hopes for domestic reconstruction to the Prussian reform movement. Both chose Prussia as their home when they returned to civilian life – Henning as a legal secretary in the judicial bureaucracy and Förster as lecturer in modern history at the Royal Academy of Military Engineers and Artillery Officers in Berlin.

Unlike Schulze, however, both Förster and Henning entered Prussian service convinced that 1813 had marked a decisive historical turning point not only in the external circumstances of German politics but in the inner evolution of German communal life. The traditional relationships of authority and obedience between an absolutist state and a society of bureaucratically administered and disciplined subjects had been made historically obsolete by the emergence of the people as an autonomous, progressive, and unifying power. The experience of 1813, Förster claimed, had to be sustained as "the torch that will light our way through the stormy night of the present and illuminate the darkness of the future" because it revealed the possibility of an authentic ethical community in which traditional leaders recognized that their power was sustained by the energy and unity of the people and the people recognized the expression of their own will in the actions of their leaders.[22] This concern for maintaining the wartime association between governments and people led Henning and Förster to focus their postwar activity on the constitutional issue. They supported Görres's attempts to mobilize public opinion in favor of a rapid fulfillment of the Prussian king's promise that "a representation of the people is to be formed,"[23] and identified themselves with the leaders of the national student fraternities who attacked the postwar political leadership for betraying the principles of 1813. Such activity placed Henning and Förster in opposition not only to the defenders of the old regime, but also to bureaucratic liberals who, in Niebuhr's famous phrase, believed that "freedom depends much more on administration than on a constitution."[24] In the summer of 1818, Förster's vehement attacks on the reactionary "court party," whom he blamed for the delay in constitutional reform, resulted in his dismissal from his teaching position.[25] Henning would also eventually pay for his agitation for constitutional reform with a seven-week jail sentence and months of harassment by the Prussian police.[26] By the time Hegel arrived in Berlin in the fall of 1818, Henning and Förster had seen their ideal of a German *Volksgemeinschaft,* which had seemed so real in the exalted atmosphere of 1813, gradually turn into a chimera; they were ready to rethink their ideological commitments.

In the years between 1815 and 1818, Förster's and Henning's faith that postwar political reconstruction would give historical actuality to the consciousness of national solidarity aroused by the war of 1813 was sustained by widespread commitment to their ideal among the younger generation of gymnasium and university students. In fact, the consciousness and activity of this new generation of the educated classes, rather than any mass consciousness or political movement outside the traditional elites, was the actual historical referent for the myth of the *Volksgemeinschaft.* Heinrich Leo was a leading member of this generation. Although he was introduced to Romantic nationalism by Schulze while he was still a young boy, his views attained the form of self-conscious commitment in 1815–16 under the guidance of a gymnasium professor who had returned from the campaign of 1813 with an ideology both more virulently Germanic and more radically populist than that espoused by Schulze, Henning, or Förster. The historical models Leo was inspired to emulate and recreate were not the Greek polis or the Roman republic but the warrior community of the ancient Teutons (*Alt-Germanen*) and the Christian–German empire of the Middle Ages. By the time Leo enrolled at the University of Breslau in 1816, he was a committed Germanomaniac (*Deutschtümler*) who treated the words of the notorious apostle of Teutonic virtue Friedrich Ludwig Jahn as the "gospel" of a new historical dispensation.[27] The cultural and racial chauvinism of Jahn's gospel was combined with a social radicalism that differentiated the vitality and moral purity of the *Volk* who "traveled by foot" from the corrupt impotence of "the social classes who ride in carriages."[28] The uncompromising moralism of this Germanic ideology gave a distinctly sectarian character to the student subculture of reborn Teutons that set the tone in the student fraternities of the postwar years. Leo and his friends dressed in ancient Teutonic costume and kept themselves apart from Jews, foreigners, and philistines. They saw themselves as the vanguard of a new culture, inspired and sustained by identification with an ancient communal tradition and uncorrupted by the self-serving materialism of their fathers' generation.[29]

For a few years, Leo and his fellow reborn Teutons believed that a new order of freedom and unity would arise spontaneously from the impact of the younger generation's ethical commitments. This optimistic idealism reached its culmination at the Wartburg festival of October 1817, which Leo later described as the "May-day" of his generation.[30] The euphoria produced by this demonstration of unity by the *Burschenschaften* and their intellectual mentors, however, was of short duration. As it became obvious that the old order would not simply collapse under the pressure of moral indictment, the *Burschenschaften* split into opposing factions. The majority looked for a gradual realization of their aspirations through an inner transformation of existing institutions as the new generation attained positions of power and influence. A significant minority, however, turned to more direct forms of political action. Leo's development between 1818 and 1820 was marked by successive commitments to the most extreme forms of both positions.

Although Leo, like Henning and Förster, participated in the agitation for liberal, representative constitutions in the German states in 1817–18, his political thinking took a more radical direction when he fell under the spell of Karl Follen, the self-styled Robespierre of the student movement, in the spring and summer of 1818. For almost a year, Leo was absorbed by the task of realizing Follen's vision of a democratic, centralized German republic whose free and equal citizens would be bound together by a revitalized and reformed civic Christianity. Leo was among the inner circle of "unconditionals" who, having purified themselves of all corrupting association with the existing order, were prepared to engage in whatever actions were necessary to bring about the revolutionary emancipation of the people. Only in the aftermath of the Kotzebue assassination (a deed inspired by Follen's principles) did Leo come to realize the completely utopian character of Follen's political program. Public reaction to Sand's deed revealed not only the strength of existing authorities, but also the complete indifference of the *Volk* to the activities of its self-appointed liberators.[31]

Leo's response to this experience, like his earlier commitment to revolutionary activism, took an extreme form. A new ideological "conversion" not only drove the "revolutionary devil" out of his soul but transformed him into a fervent proponent of a feudal-Christian restorationism that aimed at expunging all liberal and modern, rational tendencies from German culture.[32] When Leo began his academic career as a lecturer in history at Erlangen in 1820, he insisted that the creation of a genuine Germanic community depended on a restoration of medieval corporatism. In the hierarchically structured organism of traditional estates, Leo claimed, each individual experienced his life as an "individualized manifestation" of the totality; the general will of the communal organism was experienced not as an abstract external force but as the implicit power that "moved" each individual. Against this conception of "organic" communality Leo set the modern principle of the "abstract" centralized state in which the relationship between individual and general will was nothing more than the imposition of an abstract identity on uniform, isolated units, each locked in the prison of its own ego and capable of acting only according to selfish utilitarian motives.[33] The relationship between these two paradigms of communal organization was presented not as a historical process, but in absolute moral terms. "The absolute unity of the state," Leo claimed, was "a groundless, shallow doctrine that originated in brains without spirit and sinfully blasphemed the principle of life." The "system of equality" was described as "the political devil of all ages."[34]

Leo's conversion to the feudal restorationism purveyed by the most conservative representatives of Romantic historicism thus merely reproduced the dilemmas he had sought to escape. Follen's revolutionary utopia had been replaced by an equally utopian vision of historical regression to the medieval past. The gap between consciousness and contemporary reality remained almost as wide as before, and by 1821, Leo was complaining about his sense of "isolation" among the reactionary circles in the "desert of Erlangen."[35] Ironically, his commitment to the principle of "life" had associated him with reactionary groups who were defending institutions and cultural forms that had lost their historical vitality and removed him from the actual center of activity within his own age. In the summer of 1822, Leo decided once again to rethink his relationship to his age and his cultural environment, and like Schulze, Förster, and Henning, he was led by this process to Prussia, Berlin, and Hegel.

That Leo's intense search for an ideology of communal integration that would connect the subjective vision of an ethical community of reborn Teutons to the objective realities of the postwar situation should eventually lead him in the direction already taken by such teachers and mentors of his generation as Schulze, Henning, and Förster is not particularly surprising. Although Leo's commitments to both the revolutionary and the reactionary extremes of Romantic nationalism placed him first to the left and then to the right of his three contemporaries, the situation that produced his extremism and his disconcerting shifts in political position – the continually widening gap between the vision of national community and historical reality – was shared by them all. But that Leo's resolution of his dilemma should place him in the same philosophical camp as Friedrich Wilhelm Carové and Eduard Gans does seem surprising, for the formative historical experiences of Gans and Carové appear to diverge rather sharply from those of Leo, Schulze, Henning, and Förster. Closer analysis, however, reveals significant parallels within the apparent divergences and can provide additional insight into the general structure of the experiential matrix of political Hegelianism.

Carové was a Rhenish Catholic whose father's career as a *Hofrat* at the court of the archbishop elector of Trier had been cut short by the French invasion, occupation, and annexation of the left bank of the Rhine. For almost a decade the Carovés lived the uncertain, rootless life of refugees, and they established permanent residence in Coblenz (now a part of the French state) only after the consolidation of Napoleonic power in 1801.[36] Carové thus completed his education and made his original vocational commitments within the environment of Napoleonic France. He received a law degree from the French Université in 1809 and between 1809 and 1812 began what promised to be a highly successful career in the French civil service at the appellate court in Trier. Despite his French background, French education, and service in the French administration, however, Carové did not identify himself completely with the regime that had destroyed and then replaced his father's world. Though he had little sympathy for defenders of the old regime and welcomed the legal and administrative reforms instituted by the French government, he did resent attempts to impose French cultural hegemony on the conquered German population, and he was drawn to the Romantic cultural nationalism of his German contemporaries. In 1813 he resigned his post in Trier and took a job as customs administrator on the North Sea coast, which allowed him enough free time to write Romantic poetry and engage in historical research in medieval German art, literature, and popular culture.[37] In 1814 he returned to the Rhineland in the entourage of the Prussian governor-general, but he soon left this position to pursue his studies of medieval German literature and culture at the University of Heidelberg. His literary reputation, political experience, and maturity helped him to rise rapidly to a position of leadership among the war veterans and students who formed the patriotic reading societies and *Burschenschaften* of the postwar years.[38]

The Romantic nationalism articulated in Carové's early "Teutonic" writings was influenced by his particular perspective on the Napoleonic era. Although he idealized the Germanic culture of the early Middle Ages as a "beautiful and exalted springtime" when simple religious piety and natural communal feeling had not yet been corrupted by papal despotism and French rationalism, he did not believe that this "beloved homeland" could be restored. Just as the individual's experience of childhood innocence and maternal love was inevitably transformed into a mental image to which the adult ego could relate only with unfulfilled longing, so the childhood of a culture was inevitably transformed into a "magic, distant land" through the process of historical evolution. Although one might discover faint traces of unreflective piety and natural communal feeling in isolated rural villages, the historical consciousness that had created Gothic cathedrals and *Nibelungenlieder* existed only as a "spiritual ideal" in the minds of poets and scholars.[39] Carové's lyrical poetry clearly articulated his belief that absorption in the Old German ideal was a regressive escape into an unrecoverable individual and collective past. Imaginary recreations of the lost world of individual and cultural childhood could not dissolve the realities of modern society and individual self-consciousness. The pain of alienation always returned, the remembered joys of springtime inevitably gave way to autumnal laments.[40]

Carové thus perceived the contradiction between subjective ideals and objective realities as an expression of a general crisis in European cultural development produced by the emancipation of the individual from traditional social bonds and the creation of objective, rational social and political relationships. It was not simply moral corruption, or foreign invasion, or political betrayal that had destroyed the reality of a community of love and faith and transformed it into a subjective ideal; contemporary man had been disinherited from his "beloved homeland" through a necessary process of historical development and maturation. Carové thus did not have to wait for the events of 1818 and

1819 to recognize the futility of political attempts to recreate the past. If the generation of the disinherited was to find a new home, it would be not a home for children, but a home for liberated, self-conscious, individual adults. Carové's longing for such a home was as intense as that of any member of his generation, but his background and experience made it impossible for him to recognize this home in the chauvinistic and regressive nationalism of so many of his contemporaries. He was among the first converts to Hegel's philosophy at Heidelberg, and for a number of years this decision involved him in constant and often virulent conflict with the likes of Förster, Henning, and Leo.

Carové's growing opposition to the ideology of Romantic nationalism during the postwar years was shared by Eduard Gans, but Gans came to this position by a different route. At the same time as returning war veterans and patriotic students were joining together in organizations that expressed their new consciousness of national community, a few members of their historical generation with a rather different cultural experience formed their own discussion group in Berlin. In the fall of 1816, Gans, who had just registered as a student in the law faculty, Moses Moser, a self-educated philosopher and bank clerk, and Immanuel Wohlwill, a gymnasium student, began to meet together to discuss Plato's *Dialogues* and other philosophical and literary classics. Within a year this casual reading group had grown into an organized Scientific Circle of about twenty members that met regularly for the presentation and discussion of papers and lectures.[41] All members of the group were Jewish, and the majority were university students born, like Gans, Moser, and Wohlwill, during the mid- or late 1790s. The ethnic and generational homogeneity of the group expressed the particular historical experience that separated its members both from their non-Jewish contemporaries and from older members of their own "nation." The crucial, differentiating factor in this experience was the civil emancipation of the Jews during the reforms of the Napoleonic period. For young Jews just entering the formative years of higher education and vocational choice, this event marked a decisive break with the narrow confines of their fathers' world and opened up the exhilarating possibility (although the Prussian Edict of Emancipation was disturbingly vague on this point)[42] of a free choice of vocation within the larger community of German and European culture.

In Gans's case the feeling of alienation from his original home in preemancipation Jewish culture was particularly pronounced. His father, the son of a religiously orthodox and politically conservative "court agent" in Hanover, had already taken a major step toward assimilation when he married into the Marcuse family in 1795 and thus entered the legally privileged, wealthy Jewish aristocracy of bankers and merchants in Berlin. But even the enlightened, reformed Judaism of this Jewish elite seems to have had only a superficial impact on Gans's early development. After 1805 his family was often away from Berlin, as his father became involved in increasingly speculative financial ventures as an agent for war payments to the French and as a provisioner for the German armies. Although the elder Gans enjoyed the special favor and support of Hardenberg, he left his family only debts and unresolved lawsuits when he died in Prague in 1813. The Marcuse family wanted Gans to pursue a career in banking or commerce so that he could liquidate his father's debts, but Gans had no intention of entering the postemancipation world with such a burden from the past. By the time Gans began his studies at the University of Berlin he was intent on pursuing an academic career and finding a vocational identity that transcended the horizons of the Jewish community.[43]

The intellectual production of the Scientific Circle that Gans helped organize in 1816-17 expressed this feeling of liberation from the confines of a cultural ghetto. Papers and lectures were given on all aspects of European literature, philosophy, history, and politics; very few were devoted to specifically Jewish themes.[44] Within a few years, however, this sense of participation in the universal culture of modern Europe had begun to fade. In 1819 the circle reconstituted itself as the Society for the Amelioration of the Condition of the Jews in the German Federation, and in 1821 it attained legal recognition as the Association (*Verein*) for the Culture and Science of Judaism.[45] This new focus on Jewish experience and cultural identity was a response to the resurgence of anti-Semitic activity and ideology during the postwar years. Within the university communities these anti-Semitic prejudices found strong support in the Christian-German ideology purveyed both by conservative Romantics in the Historical School and by the Teutonic radicals of the *Burschenschaften.*[46] Alienated from both the traditional Jewish culture they had left behind and the Christian-German values of the broader culture they had hoped to join, members of this generation of Jewish intellectuals were caught in what one scholar has called a "rebellious dilemma" that forced them to reconsider their Jewish identity, their desire for assimilation, and the relationship between the two.[47]

It did not take long for Gans to become embroiled in controversies with both the conservative and the populist versions of the Romantic nationalism that sought to define the German cultural community in a manner that would exclude his participation. After a number of minor skirmishes, matters came to a head in 1817 when one of the populist nationalists at the University of Berlin, the historian Friedrich Rühs, published an article attacking Gans's father's financial transactions during the war as an example of unpatriotic Jewish usury. Gans replied to the article by denouncing the author as a "political charlatan" who had concocted a personal libel out of vulgar anti-Semitic prejudice and primitive patriotic moralism. His father's financial dealings, Gans claimed, had conformed strictly to the letter of the law and the objective conditions of the existing financial market. Against Rühs's conception of communal ethics as an inner identification with the subjectively defined moral substance of a particular historical nationality, Gans set the rational ideal of formal adherence to objective laws that applied equally to all individuals in the society.[48] In opposition to the pressures of the Christian-German revival in his immediate environment, therefore, Gans continued to defend the conception of a secular state based on universal rational principles that he saw embodied in the ideals and activities of the Prussian reform movement. Even the defeat of Napoleon in 1813, he would later claim, had been possible only because liberal bureaucratic reformers, like Hardenberg, had appropriated the French ideals of freedom and reason and turned them against the Napoleonic despotism.[49] In his search for an academic mentor who shared this perspective, Gans eventually went to Heidelberg in the fall of 1818 to study under the legal scholar who had gained a national reputation as a defender of Jewish emancipation and as the most eloquent opponent of the narrow nationalism and conservative historicism of the Historical School: Anton Friedrich Julius Thibaut (1771–1840).

Thibaut's emphasis on the universal principles contained within the positive laws of particular cultural systems and on the active reforming role of the jurist as a constructor of systematic codes that conformed to these principles as closely as possible provided Gans with a theoretical and historical framework for his opposition to the exclusive cultural nationalism and passive traditionalism of the Historical School.[50] The two scholarly monographs Gans published in rapid succession after his graduation in the spring of 1819 clearly revealed Thibaut's influence; both were historical studies of aspects of Roman civil law that tried to illuminate the general principles contained in the apparent confusions and contradictions of positive law.[51] Gans had hoped that these monographs would launch his academic career at the University of Berlin. But Karl Friedrich von Savigny and his colleagues in the Historical School were quick to recognize the opposition to their own views in Gans's first work and rejected his application for the privilege of lecturing in their faculty.[52] Gans responded with a vehement critique of the control of the legal profession by a closed "guild" or "party" whose leaders acted as if they were infallible popes with the right to ordain only those scholars, regardless of their intellectual ability, who adhered strictly to orthodox doctrine.[53]

Gans was well aware, however, that his difficulties in gaining an appointment were not due merely to his scholarly disagreements with leading members of the faculty. The letter from the faculty to the ministry that advised against Gans's appointment closed with the statement: "In conclusion we would venture to point out that we do not know if Dr. Gans, who stems from a well-known Jewish family, has personally converted to the Christian faith, and whether, therefore, there may not be an obstacle to his appointment to a position of public service from this side as well." After a second application had also been rejected, Gans wrote to Altenstein, "I belong to that unfortunate class of men who are hated because they are uneducated and who are persecuted because they educate themselves."[54]

The frustration of Gans's attempts at cultural assimilation forced him to take a second look at the ideological commitments that had buttressed his political hopes and academic ambitions during the immediate postwar years. His conception of a society of free self-determining individuals bound together in common commitment to the universal values of a secular, rational, humanistic culture seemed increasingly to contradict his concrete historical experience as a Jew in a Christian and German cultural environment; it had become "an abstract ideal in hostile opposition to reality."[55] Like his non-Jewish contemporaries who joined the "magic circle" of Hegel's disciples during the early 1820s, Gans was drawn toward Hegel by the need to resolve the frustrating, debilitating dichotomy between a subjective vision of communal integration and the social and political reality of postwar Germany.

The general patterns in the experiential matrix of political Hegelianism should by now have become fairly clear. All six of our subjects experienced the events of the era of French domination, domestic reform, and national liberation as a radical break with the political and cultural world of their fathers. Their feeling of historical discontinuity was undoubtedly magnified beyond that of many of their contemporaries by the fact that the particular social, ethnic, and political worlds into which they had been born were so radically affected by the changes of this period. The deaths of the fathers of Gans, Leo, Henning, and Förster during these years only added to their feeling of radical historical dislocation. This common experience of a decisive historical break with the past helps to explain why all of them committed themselves to ideologies of political and cultural reconstruction with such emotional intensity. They sought not merely a piecemeal, limited reform of existing institutions but the creation of a new moral and cultural world in which they would feel at home. Their faith in the imminent historical realization of their various visions of communal integration was grounded in an idealization and absolutization of particular components in the conflict of historical forces produced by the period of reform and liberation. During the postwar period these idealizations failed the test of historical reality and produced a crisis of disillusionment that Hegel would eventually resolve by helping them recognize the fulfillment of their desires and the objective content of their subjective feelings in the philosophically comprehended substance of contemporary historical reality. However, the significant differences in historical experience and perspective within the general pattern of the path to Hegel that were left behind in the common commitment to Hegelianism soon reemerged as variations in the interpretation of the historical significance and meaning of the Hegelian resolution.

FROM CONVERSION TO ACCOMMODATION

In 1815, Schulze, Henning, and Förster had all attached their hopes for German political and cultural reconstruction to the activities and aims of the academic, bureaucratic, and military leaders of the Prussian reform movement. By the time Hegel arrived in Berlin in the fall of 1818, however, the increasingly evident inability of the Prussian reformers to actualize the dreams of freedom and unity inspired by the national liberation had led all three to reconsider and reassess both their relationship to the Prussian state and their commitment to the world view of Romantic nationalism that provided the historical and philosophical framework for their previous conviction of cultural vocation and ethical calling. It was the ideological crisis produced by this experience of historical disillusionment that sent Schulze, Förster, and Henning back to school between 1820 and 1821. Although they had all completed their university educations before the war, they attended Hegel's lectures and studied his philosophy with an intense concentration and methodical seriousness that revealed their deeply felt need for a new intellectual orientation. Even Schulze, despite his high official rank and busy schedule, attended all of Hegel's lectures on a regular daily basis for a two-year period, reworked and puzzled through his extensive notes, and discussed particular difficulties and ambiguities with Hegel himself in long evening walks.[56] Such commitment to the "labor of the concept" brought its reward in an elevation to a philosophical perspective that seemed to provide a satisfactory resolution of the frustrating, debilitating contradictions between subjective vision and objective reality. This philosophical or ideological "conversion" provided the basis for a positive evaluation of the general evolution of contemporary or "modern" politics in Prussia and in western Europe, but it did not immediately or necessarily produce a complete reconciliation with the particular, empirical political situation in Prussia around 1820. By the late 1820s, Schulze, Förster, and Henning had become pillars of the accommodationist Hegelian "establishment" in Berlin, but this development from conversion to accommodation was a result of their particular experience as Hegelians rather than a consequence of their Hegelianism per se.

During the Restoration, Schulze devoted his energies almost exclusively to the practical tasks of administering and reorganizing Prussia's system of higher education. Because he wrote so little, his personal and exemplary importance in the formation of the Hegelian school has been ignored by intellectual historians; but it was Schulze's conversion to Hegelianism between 1818 and 1821 that helped produce the particular circumstances and most clearly revealed the general historical trends out of which the special relationship between a significant segment of the Hegelian school and the Prussian state emerged during the 1820s. One might even say that it was the close personal friendship, practical cooperation, and intellectual agreement between Schulze and Hegel that was the concrete reality behind the theoretical reconciliation of philosophy and the Prussian state during the Restoration. Schulze found in Hegel's system historical and metaphysical justification and significance for his practical activity.[57] Hegel, in turn, perceived the particular historical realization of his philosophical ideas in Schulze's activity as an educational bureaucrat. While Schulze attended Hegel's lectures, Hegel presided over the examination board Schulze had set up to test the qualifications of new gymnasium teachers. For the majority of Prussian Hegelians (who were either academics or students preparing themselves for academic careers), Schulze represented the power and policy of the state in the area that most immediately and personally affected their own lives: appointments and promotions in the educational system. Although Baron von Altenstein, the minister of education, religion, and cultural affairs, retained the right of final decisions in such matters, he rarely, if ever, acted in opposition to Schulze's advice.[58] But Schulze attained such a position of power and influence only because his shift in viewpoint under Hegelian influence corresponded to a general shift in the character and aims of those reform-minded bureaucrats in the Prussian administration who survived the conservative reaction of 1818–20.

Although this transformation of the reform movement has often been described simply as the failure of the reform movement itself, it was actually a complex process of adaptation to the historical realities of the postwar years. What failed was the impulse for a bureaucratically led but still genuinely populist transformation of Prussian political culture and institutions represented by intellectuals like Schleiermacher and Humboldt. By 1819 it had become evident that the reformers could not sustain or justify their attempt to liberalize Prussian society and create a unified community of autonomous state citizens by representing themselves as spokesmen for a popular communal consciousness and liberators of an aroused popular will. The *Volk,* in fact, had proven to be either indifferent or hostile to both socioeconomic liberalization and political integration. A political community of equal autonomous citizens would not emerge from a simple liberation of the "natural" communal will from artificially imposed restrictions; a disciplined, systematic process of education and socialization was required in order, first, to liberate the individual from the historically obsolete communal bonds of legal privilege and blind obedience to inherited custom and, second, to reintegrate this liberated individual into a truly universal community on the basis of self-conscious knowledge. Hegel, of course, had formulated this conception of communal integration long before he arrived in Prussia. What happened in the early 1820s was that his views found a ready public in a significant segment of the Prussian civil service and educated elite.[59]

The alliance between Hegelian philosophy and the Prussian administration did not evolve smoothly, however, and was never complete. The conservative reaction after the Carlsbad Decrees was directed not only against the conception of a *Volksgemeinschaft* purveyed by Romantic nationalists but also against the Hegelian conception of communal integration in a modern, centralized rational state. It was not really until 1824 that Hegel, Schulze, and Altenstein could feel assured that their viewpoint was in harmony with the actual historical evolution of Prussian politics and culture. But this triumph was tenuous and gained only at the cost of significant compromise. Because the bureaucratic reformers could not justify their activity or maintain their power on the basis of a popular mandate, they were forced to compromise with existing political and social powers – the arbitrary authority of the monarch, the social and political privileges of the aristocracy – in order to survive. At the same time, the essential structures of a modern social, legal, and political order that had been salvaged through this compromise had to be defended against that significant segment of the bureaucratic and academic elite that still identified the reality of communal integration with either traditional or emotional conceptions of a peculiarly Germanic *Volksgemeinschaft.* The precarious domination of the bureaucratic proponents of communal integration through self-conscious acceptance of the rational structure of the modern state collapsed in the 1830s and 1840s. But during the mid- and late 1820s it sustained the conviction of leaders of the Hegelian establishment, like Schulze, that reason and freedom had attained historical actualization in the contemporary Prussian state.

It is not surprising, therefore, that Schulze described his conversion to Hegel's philosophical standpoint as a process of self- and cultural comprehension.[60] Hegel's philosophy gave unity and coherence to Schulze's practical activity and provided the basis for a principled attack on his Romantic opponents. Schulze differentiated his educational viewpoint from that of his Romantic critics in three important ways.[61] First, he insisted that the whole educational system be centralized and unified under state control. Secondly, he claimed that the curriculum in secondary and higher education should encompass the totality of knowledge in both a systematic and a historical sense. Finally, he conceived the educational process as a rigorous, disciplined, systematic conversion of subjective, individual feeling and opinion into objective, universal knowledge. The Romantic attempts to nurture the individuality of subjective genius or inspire emulation of past forms of communal solidarity merely expressed the alienation and homelessness they hoped to cure. For Schulze communal integration and socialization into the complex rational organization of the modern state had become synonymous, and by 1825 he made no distinction between this "modern state" and contemporary Prussia.

Although Förster and Henning were in essential agreement with Schulze by 1825, their original conversions to the Hegelian standpoint were more dramatic than Schulze's because their disillusionment at the failure of the popular movement for national unity and liberal constitutional reform was more intense and their persecution under the conservative reaction more severe. When Ernst Förster arrived in Berlin in April 1819, still full of the Teutonic enthusiasm for a popular national regeneration that he had absorbed at Jena, he found his older brother strangely transformed. Friedrich's former commitment to the ideology of Romantic nationalism preached by Schleiermacher, Fries, and other mentors of the *Burschenschaften* had changed to a contemptuous criticism of their inability to break out of the circle of their subjective fantasies and comprehend the objective truth about God, man, and history. He now claimed that he had found "the perfected solution of his highest scholarly goals, a satisfactory direction for his practical life, and the complete and total truth" in Hegel's philosophy.[62] Moreover, Ernst Förster soon discovered that the "majority of his friends" were similarly changed.[63] Even Henning, who as recently as the fall of 1818 had journeyed to Jena to renew his contacts with the proponents of populist nationalism, had become so committed to the Hegelian standpoint that he had decided to take up a career as a teacher of philosophy and, in preparation for this task, had begun to offer informal repetition sections on Hegel's logic and metaphysics for students who experienced difficulty in comprehending the master's lectures.[64]

Ernst Förster was soon forced to recognize that this ideological transformation of his former comrades could not be explained simply as a practical accommodation to the recently imposed reactionary policies of the Prussian administration. In fact, the majority of Hegel's most vociferous disciples were placed under arrest by the political police during the summer of 1819.[65] The Berlin Hegelians clearly believed not that Hegel had taught them to resign themselves to external necessity or to betray their former political ideals, but that he had initiated them into a realm of absolute knowledge and total freedom that represented a fulfillment rather than a denial of their former hopes. From Ernst Förster's perspective such convictions could be explained only as a debilitating surrender to the seductive abstractions of Hegel's dialectical logic. Hegel had led them to believe that their thoughts were more real than the concrete experience of national brotherhood, the immediate feeling of dependence on the divine, or the irresistible demands of conscience. They could claim that Reason and reality were identical only because they had abandoned the real world for a world of illusory transcendence.[66] From the Hegelians' perspective, however, it was people like Ernst Förster who remained ensconced in subjective "abstractions" and transcendent illusions that prevented an objective comprehension of contemporary historical reality.

In 1821, Friedrich Förster and Henning articulated their own conceptions of the Hegelian conversion and its political implications in the pages of the short-lived, little-known *Neue Berliner Monatsschrift für Philosophie, Geschichte, Literatur und Kunst.* This journal was introduced to the public by Förster, its unofficial editor, as a "Protestant" journal that would "ally itself completely with the spirit of the Prussian government,"[67] but most contemporaries viewed it as an aggressive, polemical, proselytizing organ of the new Hegelian "party" in Berlin. Although the message purveyed by Henning and Förster was one of reconciliation with the "present" and the "real," this contemporary reality was defined within the context of a dynamic historical development. The events of the revolutionary and Napoleonic era, they insisted, had introduced a radically new stage of historical development that made traditional forms of thought and belief obsolete. The present, Henning claimed, was "separated from the past in an essential way, not merely by degrees, but in its very character,"[68] and Förster hailed the present as the era of the "resurrection of the spirit" in which a "world judgment" of previous forms of politics, art, religion, and philosophy had already begun.[69] The stated allegiance to Protestantism and the "spirit of the Prussian government" can be understood only within the context of this conviction of epochal historical transformation.

The particular brand of Protestantism espoused by Henning and Förster in 1820–1 was opposed not only to the Catholicism of Romantics like Friedrich Schlegel and Adam Müller, which tried "to force a world that has finally attained maturity back into the cradle," but to all forms of religious faith.[70] Religion itself, as a mode of consciousness characterized by the subject's surrender of its freedom to an arbitrary transcendent authority and dependence on emotional states, was historically regressive. Modern man, who had finally recognized his own essence as a thinking being, could be satisfied only with a truth that he could affirm as his own and left the consolations of religious faith to the weak, cowardly, and immature.[71] "Only the comprehending activity of thought," Henning insisted, "assures the absolute reconciliation of the spirit with itself and with the world which is set over against it, which, insofar as it is comprehended, ceases to appear as something external to the comprehending spirit."[72] The Christian promise of salvation was thus fulfilled in Hegel's philosophy. "Only in thought," Förster wrote, "is the realm of truth also the realm of freedom, for here spirit determines itself freely, it rediscovers itself in the other, in the objective world and in the God that faith represents as a transcendent being. Nowhere does it face anything alien, nowhere does it encounter limitation."[73] In these early essays, written in the euphoric state of recent conversion, the Hegelian doctrine of the identity of content in religion and philosophy was submerged in the epochal consciousness of the historical implications of the difference in form. The completion of the Protestant tradition in the scientific self-knowledge of Hegelian philosophy marked the boundary between an era of unfreedom and alienation and one of freedom and reconciliation.

For both Henning and Förster the focal point of the Hegelian reconciliation of Reason and reality was politics. Man could grasp the absolute because the absolute had revealed itself in the world, but this "presence of the spirit," Henning claimed, was "the state insofar as its particular content, which is there in the will of the individual, is elevated to the form of thought, i.e., universality, and as such is willed and known."[74] The Hegelian conversions of Henning and Förster thus produced radical shifts in their political viewpoints. In a biography of Marshall Blücher published in 1821, Förster described the Germanic ideology of the 1813 volunteers as a reactionary political stance, a defense of "serfs and slaves" against the representatives of the rational freedom of constitutional monarchism.[75] Henning also now saw the reality of freedom not in the emotional solidarity of national fraternity but in the structures of a legal and political system in which "the relationships of man to man and to things that effect other men" were elevated to the level of rational universality, so that the individual could self-consciously will the common will as his own.[76]

It was this conception of the modern state as the systematically articulated structure of Reason and freedom that, Förster and Henning believed, had animated the "spirit of the Prussian government" in the reforms of the eighteenth century and the Napoleonic period. But in 1821, Förster and Henning were not in complete agreement on the question whether the existing Prussian regime represented a completed actualization of the spirit of freedom and Reason. Henning had virtually identified the existing political order with the Hegelian modern state by 1821. He related all demands for continued reform to a failure of philosophical comprehension. The proper task of the Hegelian disciple was not the practical one of working for the actualization of Reason in the contemporary world – that task was already accomplished – but the theoretical, scholarly one of demonstrating the presence of the spirit in every sphere of empirical existence.[77] The vast body of factual material accumulated by the "positive sciences" was to be penetrated by the dialectical method until it had completely lost its alien character and could be recognized as the objective expression of the progressive self-determination of absolute spirit. Henning's critical energies were directed primarily against the unphilosophical empirical methods of the Historical School of law, which could produce, at best, only a feeling of the "external" historical necessity of inherited customs, traditions, and laws. But "the living obey only the living, not the dead," Henning insisted; so the methods of the Historical School led inevitably to a rebellion of the free subject against a world of impenetrable facticity that it could not recognize as the expression of its own will. At the same time, however, Henning described the conservative historicists' desire to "inculcate a respect for the real and the given" as "praiseworthy."[78] The Hegelian philosophical method simply revealed the empirically given as the spiritually necessary and thus reconciled the alienated individual subject with the existing historical community.

The message of achieved reconciliation that Henning purveyed to his contemporaries expressed his own successful accommodation with the existing Prussian regime. After completing his doctoral dissertation in the summer of 1820 he was able to obtain permission to pursue an academic career at the University of Berlin. His lectures made no pretense of originality; they simply "reproduced" the Hegelian system in a popular, but uncritical and dogmatic, fashion.[79] In the years between 1821 and 1824, when Hegel's philosophy was still struggling for recognition and acceptance, Henning's defense of the Hegelian method retained some of the vitality and fervor of a polemical battle against the misconceptions of reigning ideologies. After his promotion to an associate professorship in 1825, however, his constantly reiterated claim that the purpose of philosophy was simply to provide a "scientific conviction" that "that which should be also *is*" appeared more and more as a self-satisfied justification of his accommodation to the existing order. The "presently existing, real, positive system of laws," he insisted, was nothing less than the perfected "Kingdom of the Spirit on earth."[80] Although many students found Henning's exposition of the Hegelian position clearer than Hegel's own, they also eventually found it bland, rhetorical, and ultimately unconvincing.[81] Henning's reconciliations were achieved too easily; the dynamic, negative, critical moment of the Hegelian dialectic was submerged in the dogmatic affirmation of an achieved peace.

For Förster the process of accommodation was more difficult. Unlike Henning, he was refused permission to take up an academic career, and he also experienced the pressures of Prussian censorship in his role as the editor of the *Neue Berliner Monatsschrift*.[82] This tension with the existing Prussian regime was expressed in his interpretation of the reconciliation of Reason and reality. Although Förster did perceive a progressive actualization of Reason in the evolution of the modern Prussian state he did not agree with Henning that this evolution had been successfully completed. In fact, he used the principle of Prussia's political development, especially as it was manifested in the policies of Frederick the Great, as a means for an implicit criticism of the existing regime.[83] He also gave Hegel's philosophical reconciliation an activist future orientation. A "Sonnet to Hegel" in the first issue of the journal ended with the prophetic proclamation: "The World Spirit must actualize itself in the world,"[84] and the last issue closed with an admonition to his readers to devote themselves, not to comprehension of the "spirit as present," but to the practical transformation of the idea of free, rational community into a historical reality.[85]

Förster's opposition to the existing regime, however, was considerably mitigated when Altenstein and Schulze succeeded in appointing him to a prestigious editorial position on the staff of the official Prussian state newspaper in 1823. By the late 1820s he was popularly known as the "court demagogue (*Hofdemagog*)" because of his fervent, often belligerent, defense of the Prussian bureaucratic monarchy as the actualization of the ethical community he had formerly sought in the popular consciousness of the *Volk.*[86] In 1826, at Hegel's birthday celebration, Förster praised Hegel for helping him recognize that the communal "home" he had sought so long was already there in the present, real world of the Prussian state.[87] Like Henning, Förster rejected all demands for political reform as expressions of a subjectively distorted perspective on reality, and like Henning he defined the task of the Hegelian disciple as "protecting, proclaiming and consolidating" Hegel's philosophy.[88] For Förster, Henning, and Schulze, the political task of creating a vital community of reborn Germans had been transformed into a pedagogical task of teaching their contemporaries to recognize the reality of that community in the existing state.

This tendency to interpret Hegel's political philosophy as an uncritical justification of the status quo was evident among many, perhaps the majority of Hegelian political scientists and legal philosophers in the years between 1822–3 and 1831. In conformity with Henning's definition of the Hegelian vocation of philosophical therapy, these conservative Hegelians focused their intellectual energies on the philosophical penetration of the given facts in their discipline. They attempted to grasp the historical particularities of past stages in the development of human association as necessary Moments in the self-development of the spirit,[89] or to comprehend the present stage of communal organization in all of its seemingly arbitrary empirical diversity as the objective expression of the unified totality of all the Moments of development in a fully articulated system.[90] The process of communal integration was conceived purely as an act of theoretical comprehension in which the empirically given was recognized as the spiritually necessary. This accommodationist stance attained its most extreme and enthusiastic expression in a notorious book by the Königsberg Hegelian Karl Friedrich Ferdinand Sietze in which the Prussian state was described as "a gigantic harp tuned in the garden of God in order to lead the world chorale" and the Prussian General Legal Code (*Allgemeine Landrecht*) was given divine status as the political constitution of the millenial

Kingdom of God.[91] The Hegelian establishment greeted this book with embarrassed silence, perhaps because it differed more in style than in substance with their own equation of the Prussian status quo with the actualized realm of the spirit.

FROM CONVERSION TO HISTORICAL CRITIQUE

Heinrich Leo and Eduard Gans were not able or willing to accommodate themselves quite as easily or completely to the Prussian status quo of the 1820s as many of their contemporaries in the Hegelian school. Their writings revealed a persistent conviction of continuing historical tension between the perfected actualization of ethical community in the universalized or "rational" legal and political relationships of the modern state and the empirical realities of the existing regime. From their perspective the Hegelian system provided not a reconciling comprehension of an achieved peace, but a critical standpoint for historical orientation within the ongoing dialectical conflicts of the present. It would be an exaggeration, however, to describe either Leo or Gans as an alienated critic of Restoration Prussia or an isolated outsider on the fringe of the Hegelian school. Their opposition to the existing order was moderate, reform-oriented, and basically "loyal"; their disagreements with other Hegelians were not considered fundamental and did not evolve into explicit conflict until the 1830s. By that time, however, the disagreement between Gans and Leo was more significant than their common opposition to the accommodationists. For their apparent agreement within the general stance of a critical "liberal" Hegelianism during the 1820s proved to be ephemeral, formal, and misleading, hiding fundamental divergences in both the personal and historical grounds of their criticism and the social and political content of their "liberalism."

The differences between critical and accommodationist Hegelianism and between the divergent versions of critical Hegelianism espoused by Leo and Gans did not develop into open conflicts during the Restoration because of the overwhelming emphasis within the Hegelian school on the more significant differences that separated all Hegelians from their non-Hegelian contemporaries. The critical, polemical component of Leo's and Gans's writings during the 1820s was devoted almost exclusively to unveiling the historically regressive and thus philosophically inadequate, one-sided character of the world views of Hegel's academic opponents – the "abstract" rationalists who remained loyal to the Enlightenment tradition, the populist Germanic nationalists produced by the national liberation, and above all, the conservative

Romantics of the Historical School. Both Leo and Gans gained academic recognition in the mid-1820s as belligerent and articulate defenders of the Hegelian method in controversies with leading representatives of the Historical School in their respective disciplines, Ranke and Savigny. It was their skill as Hegelian apologists and their importance as academic representatives of Hegel's position in disciplines dominated by members of the Historical School that brought Leo and Gans the attention, favor, and support of Hegel, Schulze, and Altenstein; and the same factors were instrumental in their appointments and rapid promotions within the Prussian university system. No one appeared to notice that their defense of Hegel implicitly contained a specific, critical interpretation of the Hegelian doctrine of the realization of Reason in history.

Leo came to Berlin in the fall of 1822 determined to end his estrangement from the dynamic forces of contemporary historical development, an estrangement that his antirevolutionary conversion to the ideology of the Historical School had not cured, but simply made more acute. After a year in Hegel's classroom, Leo claimed that he had finally found a resolution of his dilemma. In 1824 he published a totally revised version of his earlier historical study in which the decline of natural or "sensual" communal unity during the battle between empire and papacy was described as a necessary stage in the "progress toward the highest goal of the spirit and human culture."[92] The "angel of death and destruction" was also an "angel of life"; the self-division of the original unity into the contradictory powers of the "world" and the "spirit" eventually produced a "higher elevation of the people" to a "necessary, inner, eternal" unity. But this higher stage, the "ultimate creation of the spirit," was the "state, in the sense in which the word is used in modern times," that is, a political community based on universal norms and the self-conscious freedom of individuals who could rationally comprehend and will these norms as their own.[93]

During the next few years, Leo's historical research and writing continued to focus primarily on a description of the emergence of rational and systematically centralized social and political systems during the late Middle Ages and Renaissance as manifestations of a necessary stage in the evolution of the human spirit to a higher, self-consciously grasped, universal form of community and culture. His historical interests, his philosophical perspective, and his personal ambitions almost inevitably brought him into conflict with his young rival at the University of Berlin, Leopold Ranke. Leo initiated the conflict in 1826 with a critique of Ranke's claim that Machiavelli's political thought could be understood only as a practical response to a unique combination of historical circumstances. Such a limited and superficial concentration on the historically unique and the empirically particular, Leo stated, could not penetrate to Machiavelli's general perception of the structure of human relationships and thus failed to comprehend his world-historical significance as a representative of the epochal transition in the development of the spirit from feudal particularity to centralized monarchy, from the sensuous immediacy of feeling and faith to the self-conscious freedom and amoral objectivity of reflective rationality.[94] In 1827 and 1828, Leo developed these specific criticisms into a general critique of the empirical methods and backward-looking historical perspective of the Historical School. Only in the act of philosophical comprehension, in "thinking activity," Leo claimed, could the historian penetrate through the external arbitrariness of Ranke's "naked" facts and grasp the dynamic unity of the spirit in the Moments of its necessary development toward complete historical actualization. "The process of the spirit," he claimed, "is the process of history and this process is the *truth* and the only *truth*."[95]

But Leo, unlike Schulze, Henning, and Förster, did not think that this process of the spirit had attained its ultimate goal in the contemporary forms of social and political life. His Hegelian conversion had convinced him that the historical disintegration of "natural" forms of *Volkgemeinschaft* by the forces of political centralization and socioeconomic rationalization was spiritually necessary, but only as a limited, negative stage in the process toward a more perfect, universal form of communal integration. His own age, he felt, was still divided by conflicts of the negative stage. "When one speaks of our age," he wrote in 1827, "one must speak of an age of spiritual ferment, an age torn apart by contradictions, an age in which previous divisions between nations have gradually lost their sharp contours and significance and in which inner, spiritual contradictions emerge within the individual nations." But in such an age it was impossible to speak of reconciliation with the given or the "real"; one had to "declare oneself" for "one side or the other," for whichever side one believed "should *now* attain dominion." To accept a certain form of communal association as a necessary stage of man's spiritual development did not mean that one had to accept this form as necessary for the present. Leo's own declaration, however, was formulated in purely negative terms, as a "decisive hatred for everything that even slightly resembles theocracy and hierarchy."[96]

What Leo meant by "theocracy and hierarchy" was clarified to some extent in his *Lectures on the History of the Jewish State,* published in 1828. A hierarchical state was defined as a form of human association in which every aspect of life was systematically and uniformly regulated according to a single abstract principle. It was fanatically intolerant, allowing no room for autonomous individual development or the creation of alternative forms of communal association.[97] Although Leo believed that the most highly developed historical forms of hierarchical organization, the theocratic systems of the ancient Levitical state and the medieval Catholic church, had fulfilled a necessary and progressive historical function, he also presented them to his contemporaries as examples of "how a people ought not to live."[98] Ranke thought Leo's *Lectures* should be classified as a political polemic rather than an attempt at historical understanding,[99] and Leo himself clearly perceived the book as a tract for his times.[100] What concerned him most was the contemporary resurgence of theocratic forms of hierarchy in the Catholic church and among pietistic Fundamentalists within the Protestant church, and, more significantly, the emergence of modern, secular forms of hierarchical domination in revolutionary republican ideology and the centralizing, leveling policies of bureaucratic government.

Leo's criticism of bureaucratic government most clearly revealed the sources of his discontent with the present stage of historical development. Bureaucratic absolutism, he claimed, did not differ "in the slightest degree" from Jacobinism. Both represented attempts to impose an external, abstract, "mechanical" unity on society. Their historical success was inextricably connected to the transformation of a highly differentiated social organism composed of relatively autonomous associations and institutions into an undifferentiated, atomized mass or "rabble (*Pöbel*)."[101] The greatest threat to man's progress toward a self-consciously affirmed, ethical community was not the rapidly fading power of traditional feudal corporations, but the leveling tendencies of bureaucratic centralization and socioeconomic liberalization. Leo's continuing commitment to the Hegelian conception of dynamic historical progress toward the actualization of human freedom was increasingly and paradoxically expressed in 1829 and 1830 in a defense of the traditional freedoms of local and professional corporate bodies threatened by bureaucratic centralization. Unlike Schulze, he virulently opposed any extension of state control over the universities and viewed the existing bureaucracy not as the embodiment of Reason, but as a "hierarchy" whose desire to transform the pedagogical process into an instrument of political integration tended to stifle the spiritual vitality and freedom required for further historical development. The core of the Prussian reform movement in Leo's view was the attempt to reconstruct the autonomy of city and provincial governments on the basis of individual freedom rather than traditional privilege. The Prussia to which he swore his loyalty was more the Prussia of Stein's reform program – the revitalization and modernization of an organic society composed of corporate "individualities" – than the rational bureaucratic state of Hardenberg.[102]

Leo's critical Hegelianism, his focus on the dynamic conflicts that characterized the evolution of the spirit in his own age, thus had conservative roots. His defense of spiritual liberty and individual vitality against the threat of bureaucratic despotism was connected to a historical idealization of the period of dynamic tension that marked the transition from the medieval to the modern era.[103] What Leo feared and opposed was the one-sided reduction of these tensions through a victory of the "principle of mechanical unity and peace, which rejects every opposition as something vile."[104] The historical actualization of the union of individuality and universality in the modern state would be accomplished only if the tendency toward centralization and rationalization was resisted. Unlike Schulze, Henning, and Förster, Leo interpreted Hegelian theory as the basis for an active commitment to the historical actualization of what should be, or more precisely and immediately, for a stubborn resistance to what ought not to be.

Leo's particular interpretation of the contemporary relevance of Hegel's political and historical philosophy emerged out of his own personal experience of the Restoration. During his first years in Berlin it seemed that he was destined to follow Henning and Förster on the path toward accommodation. After his appointment to an associate professorship in 1825 he finally cut his shoulder-length hair and abandoned the Teutonic costume he had worn since his high-school days. His engagement to one of Altenstein's nieces opened the doors to the salons of the Berlin cultural aristocracy, and his close friendship with Henning, Schulze, and Gans brought him into the inner circles of the Hegelian academic establishment. In 1826 he was elected secretary of the historical-philological division of the Hegelian Society for Scientific Criticism. That significant tensions persisted beneath this external conformity, however, became evident in the fall of 1827, when Leo suddenly packed his bags and fled to the "clear mountain air" of his old haunts in Jena without prior consultation with Altenstein, his Hegelian colleagues, or his fiancée.[105] His academic appointment had been without salary, so that he was forced to spend up to six hours a day at the menial, humiliating, and exhausting tasks of a librarian's assistant. He felt that his "individualistic spirit" was being stifled by his situation in Berlin, that the development of his intellectual capabilities and the fulfillment of his academic ambitions were being frustrated by petty bureaucratic interference based on unwarranted suspicions about his political past. Moreover, Leo also felt ill at ease in the social circles into which his engagement and academic connections had suddenly thrust him. Acutely conscious of his poverty and lack of social graces, he suffered from the constant humiliation of being made to feel an inferiority that his "righteous pride" could not accept.[106] Leo insisted that his flight from Berlin was the only alternative to "spiritual death,"[107] but after a few months in the company of his old comrades from the *Burschenschaft* days he realized that he was not prepared to sever his connections with the Prussian state and make his home in some petty principality left behind by the process of historical development. He reiterated his loyalty to both Prussia and Hegel, and in 1828, Schulze and Altenstein found a new, fully salaried position for him at the University of Halle.

Leo's flight from, and subsequent return to, Prussia expressed in dramatic fashion the combination of alienation and accommodation that characterized his relationship to the existing order and that was articulated in the critical Hegelianism of his historical writings and reviews. Gans, whose relationship to the Prussian regime manifested a similar tension, also contemplated emigration on at least two occasions during the 1820s. His chosen destinations, however, were the United States and Paris, the spiritual homes of the liberal revolution, rather than Jena, the spiritual home of the *Burschenschaften* – a difference that revealed the fundamental divergence between the sources of his own alienation and the roots of Leo's discontents.

The earliest evidence of Gans's conversion to Hegelianism is contained in his annual presidential addresses to the Association for the Science and Culture of Judaism in 1821, 1822, and 1823.[108] Following the lead of Moser and Wohlwill, Gans first appropriated and presented the Hegelian reconciliation of Reason and reality as a resolution of the problems of Jewish cultural identity in the postemancipation era. Philosophical or "scientific" comprehension of the historical reality of Jewish culture within the context of the "millenial labor of the rational spirit that reveals itself in world history,"[109] Gans claimed, would dissolve the barriers that separated Christians and Jews, the European world from the Jewish world. Like Wohlwill,[110] Gans defined the "idea" actualized in Jewish cultural development as "unconditional unity in the all," but unlike Wohlwill and like Leo, he insisted that the self-comprehension of Jewish culture as an abstract unity, as a "unity without differentiation," revealed its limitations, its one-sidedness in relation to the final goal of human history: the actualization of the idea of "a manifold variety whose unity lies only in totality."[111] To comprehend one's own identity as a Jew thus led to the recognition of the need for "humanization in a higher sense," for an elevation from the particularity of Jewish culture to the universality of human culture. Gans insisted that this universality was present and actual in contemporary European culture and the modern state. "We have a fatherland and can enjoy it," he proclaimed. "We are citizens of a wise state, subjects of a beneficent ruler and we can be happy for this." The task of the younger generation of both externally and inwardly emancipated Jews was to convince other members of the Jewish community that the "homeland of their yearning" had become a historical reality. The consciousness of this pedagogical vocation in the "brotherly solidarity" of the Association represented nothing less than the "dawn of the messianic age of which the prophets speak."[112]

Gans constantly emphasized that this messianic age was an age of integration, of reconciliation. The thinkers of the Enlightenment, like Moses Mendelssohn, had defined emancipation in merely negative terms, as the emancipation of the rational individual subject from the fetters of historical tradition and arbitrary authority. The comprehension of the present age, however, offered a positive freedom. "That which is truly liberated, that which is authentically autonomous," Gans claimed, "celebrates its emancipation by once again integrating itself, by returning to the substance from which it had freed itself." Rational consciousness no longer stood in opposition to "the appearances of life, always ready to dominate or condemn them," but recognized these appearances as its "home," just as the appearances found their "justification and significance in it." Those particular historical appearances in the political, social, and religious life of both Jewish and European culture that were tied to the traditional order of faith, privilege, and authority, Gans believed, would not be able to withstand the inexorable convergence of Reason and reality. If consciousness "cannot penetrate a particular appearance, if it cannot know itself in it," he stated, "then a death sentence is simultaneously pronounced on this appearance; it is not real, but its existence is merely ephemeral, temporary, empty."[113]

By the fall and winter of 1822–3, however, Gans had become frustrated and discouraged by the stubborn resistance of existing "appearances" to the death sentences that had been pronounced on them. Both the leaders and the masses of the Jewish community in Berlin and elsewhere in Germany ignored or rejected his call to seek the promised land through a process of self-comprehension and integration into the universal spirit of European culture. In his final address to the society, on May 4, 1823, Gans expressed both resentment and disgust at the persistent unwillingness of his Jewish contemporaries to see beyond the particular, immediate issues of cultural survival and personal welfare.[114] At the same time, the frustration of Gans's personal efforts to achieve, not only in theory but also in reality, the kind of cultural integration he demanded from the whole Jewish community clearly indicated that the historical actualization of the idea of "manifold variety that finds its unity only in the totality" was still far from complete in German culture and, more particularly, in the Prussian state. In the spring of 1822, Gans described the free choice of a career as a central component in the realization of this idea:

> This is European man's good fortune and significance – that in the various estates of civil society he may freely choose his own and that through his own estate he feels his relationship to all the other estates in society. Take this freedom away and you have also taken away the foundations and concept of this society.[115]

In August of the same year, Gans's freedom to choose his own estate was severely restricted by a royal ordinance that finally clarified the ambiguous clause of the Edict of 1812 in a way that excluded members of the Jewish faith from careers in university teaching, public administration, and any other areas involving direct or indirect participation in the sovereign activity of the state.[116]

The combination of the Prussian ordinance and the apparent failure of the movement for inner reform of Jewish culture produced an acute and prolonged crisis of homelessness in Gans and other leading members of the Association. For a few months they seriously considered the possibility of a radical utopian resolution of their dilemma. They would pursue their collective calling as a messianic vanguard by leading an emigration of inwardly liberated Jews to the United States, where they could construct the free "homeland" of their dreams on an island in the Niagara River or on the banks of the Mississippi.[117] When these plans for a collective solution collapsed, each member was left with the task of working out an individual solution to their common problem. Moser and Wohlwill chose to maintain a precarious cultural identity as reformist members of the Jewish community. Their exclusion from the existing order made them increasingly critical of the Hegelian emphasis on the reconciling power of philosophical comprehension, and they looked to a future religious transformation for the historical actualization of Hegel's vision of a universal ethical community.[118]

Gans, however, refused to admit that the frustration of his academic ambitions and the disintegration of his messianic hope for an imminent integration of Judaism into European culture demonstrated an essential contradiction between his philosophical ideals and contemporary historical reality. He continued to prepare himself for an academic vocation in the service of Hegelian *Wissenschaft,* and in the fall of 1823 he published the first volume of a massive historical study of the law of inheritance that reiterated his belief in the validity of Hegel's comprehension of the present as the actuality of Reason. Through the intensive study of Hegel's philosophy he had "experienced for the first time the illuminating light of day after stumbling around in the dark"; his frustrating feelings of alienation from the present had been cured by a reconciling comprehension of "divine Reason" as the "substance of both past and present," by his initiation into the "higher blessedness" of "becoming conscious of the necessity of the concept."[119] The particular governmental policies that excluded Gans as a Jew from full participation in the existing state, and the academic ideologies that justified such policies, were not perceived as authentic manifestations of the contemporary stage of historical development, but as ephemeral appearances of a bygone age, the last futile spasms of a dying world. It was not Hegel and the Hegelians who were alienated from the present stage of political development, but Savigny and other members of the Historical School who refused to recognize that the systematic articulation of rational law was the ethical substance of the modern state.[120] Gans's polemics against both the methodological principles and the political viewpoint of the Historical School were particularly virulent, but the actual content of his criticism was essentially an elaboration of positions already taken by Hegel and Henning.[121] Gans's work was very favorably received by Hegel and Schulze,[122] and, despite his lack of academic credentials, he was accepted as an important member of the Hegelian school. When Victor Cousin arrived in Berlin in the winter of 1824–5, Hegel delegated to Gans the task of initiating the French philosopher into the Hegelian science of law and politics.[123]

The intellectual support and encouragement that Gans received from Hegel and Schulze was flattering, but it had little practical value in furthering his academic career as long as he refused to submit to Christian baptism. The most his Hegelian allies could do for him was ensure that he received the two-year stipend for travel and research that Hardenberg had promised him in 1822. Hardenberg had intended this stipend to provide an opportunity for Gans to prepare himself for a scholarly career abroad, and when Gans finally left for Paris in the spring 1825, many of his friends and relations thought that he would never return. On the way to France, Gans stopped briefly in Göttingen to visit Heine and apparently gave the impression that he would never "crawl to the cross."[124] After a few months in France, however, Gans had changed his mind. The religious and political situations in France and Germany, he discovered, were not radically different, but manifested a remarkably similar pattern of conflict between appearance and reality, between the past and the present. In France as in Germany, the principles of individual freedom, rational law, and the secular state were opposed by powerful reactionary groups who wanted to turn the clock back to the prerevolutionary period. Like Leo, Gans came to realize that the political and cultural conflicts of his age could not be reduced to the opposition between nations or national principles. Moreover, the longer Gans stayed in Paris the more he was forced to recognize the extent to which his cultural viewpoint had been formed by the German literary and philosophical tradition. Although he could identify himself politically with French constitutional liberals like Constant and Royer-Collard, he clearly felt more at home in the company of other Germans living in, or traveling through, Paris. Finally, personal contacts with prominent Germans in Paris opened up opportunities for intellectual fame and influence in Germany that made the temptation to convert almost irresistible. The prestigious south German publisher Baron von Cotta offered to take on the final volumes of Gans's scholarly work on inheritance law and showed a keen interest in the plan for a Hegelian journal presented to him by Gans and another Hegelian in temporary exile, Heinrich Hotho.[125] By the fall of 1825, Gans's head was filled with projects he hoped to undertake on his return to Germany. He finally decided to make the necessary compromise, and on December 12, 1825, he was baptized into the Christian faith.

For Gans this "conversion" was a purely external and formal act. Like other Hegelians he interpreted Hegel's philosophical system as a self-comprehension of the absolute content of Christian religion.[126] But he also insisted that philosophical comprehension of the universal content of the Christian faith had made that faith superfluous and relegated it, together with Jewish religion, to the dustbin of history. In 1822 he had claimed that commitment to the Hegelian conception of modern culture was "antireligious" in the sense that it consigned religion to the private, subjective sphere of particular individual choice. "On God, immortality etc.," he claimed, "only philosophy can provide us with adequate knowledge, and in accordance with this knowledge everyone may construct his own subjective religion."[127] The fact that he was eventually required to express his adherence to a particular, historically limited form of the Christian religion in order to pursue his vocation simply revealed the gap that still existed between appearance and reality in contemporary culture. He did not see his conversion as an accommodation to a hostile "reality," but as a conformity to appearances that were in clear contradiction with the essential principles of the state that required it. As Gans himself noted, the state was not in the least concerned with his actual religious beliefs.[128]

The conformity to appearances brought its promised rewards. In March 1826, shortly after his return to Germany, Gans received an associate professorship in the faculty of law, and within three years he was promoted to a full professorship despite the virulent protests of Savigny and other members of the faculty. But Gans could not easily forget the act of hypocrisy that had been required to open the doors to academic success and cultural acceptance. He remained acutely aware of the gap that still existed between the "reality" of the reformed Prussian state and some of its particular institutions and policies. This critical consciousness was expressed in both his conception of the relationship between the Hegelian school and the existing regime and his particular interpretations of Hegel's political and historical theory.

During 1826 and 1827 much of Gans's time was spent on organizational activity within the Hegelian school. With Hegel's enthusiastic support he worked tirelessly for the creation of a critical journal edited by a Hegelian "academy." When this academy was finally established in July 1826 as the Society for Scientific Criticism, Gans was elected its first chairman and placed in charge of drawing up its statutes and editorial policy. In contrast to Hegel, Gans clearly envisioned the Hegelian academy as an autonomous organization of intellectuals that would articulate the consciousness of the most progressive elements in the German republic of letters, rather than as an official, subsidized institution of the Prussian state. Judgments of intellectual productions submitted for review, as well as of the reviews themselves, were to be made collectively, according to strict parliamentary procedure. By the spring of 1828, however, Gans's projected Hegelian parliament had degenerated into a bureaucratic editorial committee that compromised the principles of autonomy and universality by soliciting and receiving financial support from the Prussian government. In response to these developments, Gans relinquished his chairmanship to the more conservative Henning and shifted his efforts to present a critical interpretation of the historical significance of Hegelian philosophy to his role as an academic teacher.[129]

Although his continuous attacks on the political perspective of the Historical School contained implicit judgments of the contemporary political situation and embroiled him in numerous conflicts with his colleagues, Gans did not address himself specifically to the problems of modern politics and contemporary history until the winter semester of 1827–8, when he took over Hegel's lecture course on the philosophy of law. In the summer of 1828 he tried to reach a wider audience with an "open" or public course on political history since the French Revolution. Unlike Hegel, Gans was a popular, eloquent, and passionate lecturer who consciously tried to "fire up" his students and arouse their commitment to a specific political perspective.[130] He was so successful in this role of political professor that the Prussian government forced him to cancel his public lectures and restrict himself to traditional academic subjects. It was even rumored that the crown prince had complained to Altenstein that Gans was turning his students into revolutionary republicans.[131] This complaint, if it was ever made, was surely an exaggeration, but Gans's conflict with the authorities in 1829 and 1830 clearly was connected to the fact that he presented Hegel's political philosophy not as a reconciling comprehension of the existing regime, but as the basis for a critical differentiation of the essential and the arbitrary, the rational and the irrational, within the established political order.

Like Leo, Gans insisted that the Hegelian doctrine of the identity of the real and the rational should be interpreted in a dynamic, critical fashion. To understand Hegel's viewpoint properly, one had to recognize that "reality" was "opposed to appearance; appearance is arbitrary; the reality in the appearance is that which has intelligibility, that to which the Idea is connected." To say that the rational was real and the real rational, Gans claimed, was simply to say "that the rational has the power to realize itself."[132] Only if Hegel's position was understood from this perspective, as the comprehension of a dynamic historical process in which mere appearances were forced to submit to the power of Reason, could the Hegelian reconciliation with reality be differentiated from the Historical School's passive submission to the external necessity of the empirically given. But though Gans defended his Hegelian orthodoxy and introduced his lectures as simply an explication and reproduction of Hegel's *Philosophy of Right,* he obviously felt that Hegel himself had included more of the arbitrary appearances of the present in his definition of reality than was demanded by his own principles. Gans's critical Hegelianism thus also involved an implicit and moderate, but still clearly discernible, critique of Hegel's political theory.

Although Gans's divergence from Hegel became much more obvious after 1830, it was already evident in the 1820s in three areas. First, Gans's description of the structure of bourgeois or "civil" society was more unambiguously liberal than Hegel's. In part this was a matter of emphasis; Gans stressed individual freedom and choice more strongly than Hegel in his discussion of socioeconomic class and the organization of the business classes into corporations.[133] But his divergence became more specific when he described the relationship between social groupings and political representation. Unlike Hegel, he thought that the election of political representatives by corporate bodies was merely an interim solution for a culturally backward society where few individuals had the requisite knowledge for participation in public affairs. It was more in keeping with the general culture of modern times for representatives to be elected by the individuals of a particular district.[134] Like Leo, Gans placed special emphasis on the necessity for individual freedom within the ethical community of the modern state. But for Leo this freedom was tied to the autonomy of traditional corporate bodies, whereas Gans stressed the need to limit the power of corporations over the individual.

In his discussion of the constitutional structure of the state, moreover, Gans devoted a whole section to a topic Hegel did not mention at all: the "opposition." In Gans's view the existence of a constitutionally recognized political opposition within the chamber of deputies was a "necessary" element in the structure of the modern state. The opposition represented the principle of negation and thus dynamic progress in the rational structure of state; a state without an opposition would inevitably decline into a condition of historical inertia.[135] Leo had sought this dynamic element in the tension between the autonomous associations of society and the state; Gans placed it within the structure of the state itself.

The tendency to view the Hegelian doctrine of the state within the context of progressive historical change was evident throughout Gans's work. He often treated elements of social and political structure that Hegel had justified as philosophically necessary as historically relative "appearances" that could be justified only temporarily, for pragmatic reasons. Moreover, Gans placed his description of the structure of the state between two long historical sections: an introductory history of the evolution of political theory (totally absent in Hegel's text) and a greatly expanded discussion of the necessary submergence of the individual state in the ongoing process of world history, the "highest power of reality."[136]

The stage in world history that pronounced the judgment of a "higher reality" on all contemporary states, Gans claimed, was the actualization of freedom and unity heralded by the French Revolution. "All other histories ceased with the coming of the French Revolution," he told his students in 1828; "only its effects on the other states need to be considered."[137] In a conversation in the spring of 1830, Gans paired the revolution with the beginning of Christianity as the two great "epochal" events that forged the "unity of all nations." Although the principle of the revolution – that "simply on the basis of his quality as a human being everyone is called to enjoy civil, political, and religious freedom" – was the "reality" of contemporary history, it had not yet found complete actualization in historical appearances. The history of the revolution had not yet reached completion, and Gans predicted the imminent collapse of those Restoration regimes throughout Europe that were attempting to hold back the irresistible, necessary process of historical development.[138] Unlike Hegel or Leo, Gans welcomed the European revolutions of 1830. But he did not see them as a sign of the historical breakthrough to a new level of "reality." He merely hoped that they would destroy the last vestiges of those "appearances" that remained in contradiction to the reality already comprehended by Hegel's philosophy. This moderate "reformist" stance differentiated him from another Hegelian who welcomed the end of the Restoration: Friedrich Wilhelm Carové.

FROM CONVERSION TO HISTORICAL TRANSCENDENCE

At the time of Carové's conversion to Hegelianism, in the spring of 1817, the relationship between Hegel's concept of the modern, rational state and the reality of the postreform Prussian state had not yet become an issue of contention or even discussion. From the very beginning, Carové conceived the historical significance of Hegel's philosophy in general and his political theory in particular in universal and dynamic terms, as the conceptualization of a new and ultimate stage of human development in which "self-conscious Reason" was "arising triumphantly and gloriously" from the "ashes of the past" and was about to attain its final goal of complete historical realization.[139] The task of his own generation was to become the midwife of this new age, to become the agent of Reason's realization. The postwar student unions, he claimed, would accomplish their aim of cultural regeneration only if they allowed the principle of self-conscious Reason "unlimited dominion" in the creation of their organization and the definition of their program. If the *Burschenschaft* transformed itself into a community of actualized Reason it could become the vanguard of Reason's actualization in the German nation. By reconciling itself with the spiritual necessity of the present stage in historical development, it could become the agent of historical change.[140]

Carové's proposals for a transformation of the *Burschenschaft* into a vanguard of the new culture of self-conscious Reason focused on what he considered to be the three major elements in the educational process of cultural integration. The first was the emancipation of the individual from "external necessity," both from the natural "coercion" of his drives and feelings and from the historical or cultural authority of traditional political, social, and religious institutions and beliefs. The *Burschenschaft* should encourage the "purely personal development of youth" toward a "knowledge of his free, divine nature," and its organization should recognize each individual member as a free, self-determined spiritual being who was "limited by nothing except the limitations he sets for himself."[141] What this meant in practical terms was that the *Burschenschaft* should refuse to recognize differences in ethnic or national origin, religious belief, social class, physical prowess, or regional political loyalty as a basis for either exclusion from the organization or a differentiation of rights within the organization. It was Carové's insistence that Jews and foreigners should be allowed to become full participating members of the *Burschenschaft,* or more particularly, that the designation of individuals as Jews or foreigners had no place in an association of free and rational beings, which aroused the greatest opposition from the Romantic nationalists.[142] For Carové, however, the recognition that an individual's dignity and worth, and thus his rights, were based on that universal quality - self-conscious autonomy - which defined him as a man was the necessary prerequisite for the integration of the individual into a truly universal culture on both communal and ontological levels.

The central focus of Carové's analysis of the process of communal integration or "national and civic education" was the concept of law. "Law," he insisted, was "the soul of political and social life."[143] The relationships between individual *Burschen* should be clearly defined by a code of universally applicable rational laws. Conflicts between members could not be resolved by the traditional method of dueling, which left justice under the arbitrary control of chance or physical prowess, but only by the objective application of the universal to the particular in rational, open judicial procedure. To define the unity of the community in terms of the "superficial monkey-love"[144] of nationalist feeling, moreover, was also to reduce the universal to the particularities of sensuous existence. A truly universal community could exist only where all members recognized their universal essence as rational, autonomous beings in the laws that governed their association. Such a community of actualized Reason, however, was ultimately grounded in a consciousness of ontological identity attained through elevation to the "free kingdom of thought, where everything finite melts away, and only the eternal and the true has a place."[145]

One of the leading supporters of Carové's "universalist" program, Theodor von Kobbe (1798-1854), later admitted that Hegel's "philosophical science of law, his doctrine of the state as the actualized ethical idea . . . entered into the consciousness of only a few." But these few, he claimed, were also the "best minds" and were able, "almost involuntarily," to "impose their perceptions on the rest" by convincing them "that one must first learn a great deal before one can reform the world."[146] The impact of the Hegelian faction in the *Burschenschaft,* however, was confined almost exclusively to Heidelberg. In Jena and Giessen, Carové was vilified as a betrayer of the nationalist cause and his program was soundly defeated at the national congress of the student unions at Jena in the fall of 1818.[147] Despite such setbacks, Carové remained convinced that historical events would soon demonstrate the validity of Hegel's comprehension of the contemporary age. In the spring of 1819 he interpreted the Kotzebue assassination as a sign of the imminent historical triumph of a "heaven of actualized freedom and peace." Kotzebue and Sand, he claimed, were representative figures, embodying the empirical individual egoism of the *Aufklärung* and the indeterminate feeling of total communal and religious integration of postwar Romantic nationalism. The murder of Kotzebue and Sand's subsequent suicide revealed that "the two extremes of the contradiction that determines the movement of the present age have developed their tension beyond the breaking point, and both, because of their one-sidedness, gone aground." The obvious historical bankruptcy of these conflicting cultural ideologies must force contemporary man to recognize the historical necessity of the Hegelian conception of the identity of individual freedom and communal integration in the differentiated totality, the concrete universal, of the modern state.[148]

At the time of the Kotzebue assassination, Carové was in Berlin. He has followed Hegel to the Prussian capital in the fall of 1818 with the hope of pursuing his chosen vocation as a midwife of the new age of "actualized freedom and peace" within the context of the Prussian educational system. Conservative opposition to his application for an academic position, however, proved stronger than Hegel's support, and after one semester as an unsalaried lecturer at Breslau he was forced to abandon his hopes for an academic career.[149] In the summer of 1820 he returned to the Rhineland to begin a lifelong career as an independent writer and journalist.

Carové was denied an appointment in the Prussian academic system because he refused to accommodate himself to the existing political order. He made no attempt to disguise or revise his dynamic future-oriented interpretation of Hegel's reconciliation of Reason and reality. Hegel's historical accomplishment, Carové wrote to Altenstein in July 1819, was that he had completed the reconciliation of Reason and reality, thought and being, on the level of pure science or speculative thought. The task that remained for his disciples was to apply the "power of the achieved concept" to "real life."[150] Philosophy was to turn away from pure speculation, which had attained its ultimate perfection and completion in Hegel's philosophy, and become a critical theory of reality. But Carové also clearly expected that critical theory would become the basis for historical practice. The application of Hegel's concept of the modern state to existing politics revealed, he claimed in 1820, that "the true relationship of the citizen to the state and the state to the citizen," a relationship in which the "individual perceived his pure and innermost essence in the universal" and the state found the "source of its vitality" in the "protection and sanctification" of the free self-determination of its citizens, still awaited its "full recognition and complete realization." The task of the present generation was not merely theoretical but practical: to bring the Hegelian philosophical concept of the state "out of the realm of thought and into the historical world," to "construct," not merely comprehend, "free, rational states."[151]

Between his conversion to Hegelianism in 1817 and his departure from Prussia and academic life in 1820, therefore, Carové articulated a form of critical Hegelianism much like the positions developed later by Gans and Leo. Like Gans and Leo he interpreted the identity of Reason and reality as an ongoing process that necessitated a differentiation between the historical triumph of a new political principle, which Hegel had comprehended, and the continuing existence of historical phenomena or appearances that were in contradiction with that principle and that still needed to be penetrated and transformed by self-conscious Reason. Even after Carové had become a "free-floating" intellectual, an itinerant, cosmopolitan publicist without permanent ties to any particular state, or even national culture, his writings displayed significant parallels with those of his Prussian contemporaries. Like Gans he continued to emphasize the need for further development of civic and political emancipation from the bonds of traditional forms of association and looked to France and the United States for models and inspiration in his discussion of individual rights and political institutions. Although this emphasis placed him definitely to the left of Leo, he did share Leo's concern about the resurgence of "hierarchy and theocracy" in the contemporary era. In 1826–7 he published a massive critical study of the Roman Catholic Church in which the evils of an abstract unity imposed on society and culture by a theocratic hierarchy were attacked with a zeal and "decisive hatred" that Leo could only have approved.[152] Nevertheless, it is also clear that the evolution of Carové's cultural viewpoint took a definite turn in a new direction after 1820. His commitment to the task of constructing "free, rational states" was gradually absorbed into a larger and more momentous historical task: "the constitution of the Kingdom of God on this earth."[153]

Carové's new consciousness of cultural calling was connected to a revised conception of the significance of the present stage in man's historical evolution. The longer he was separated from the academic world of the Berlin Hegelians the more he became convinced that their belief in an achieved historical reconciliation was an illusion. The present age was characterized by the development of the opposition between freedom and unity, between the demand for rational self-determination and the equally legitimate demand for self-surrender to the whole, to its most extreme form; it was an age of self-destructive bifurcation (*Zerrissenheit*) that could be compared only to the period preceding the establishment of Christianity. The radicalization of Carové's critical judgment of the self-defeating contradictions of the present, however, was paralleled by a radicalization of his hopes for the future. "The more profound the bifurcation," he claimed, "the more powerful also becomes the need for peace."[154] The fires of destruction were also fires of purification, preparing mankind for a blessedness as total and absolute as its present suffering. Carové's experience of homelessness in the present thus produced an increasingly utopian orientation toward the future.

The shift in Carové's historical perspective was clearly expressed in his conception of the three stages of communal integration. The original and most primitive form of ethical community was defined as the natural, or "unmediated," integration of individuals into a particular "people (*Volk*)" on the basis of race, contiguous habitation, language, custom, and shared historical experiences. The emancipation of the self-conscious individual from dependence on the naturally "given," however, necessitated the development of a higher form of ethical community – the state. The natural, and thus "contingent," unity of the *Volk* was transformed into a rational, and thus "necessary," unity in a two-stage process: the creation of a system of universal norms that regulated the relationships between the emancipated individuals in "civil society" and the creation of a "constitution" or system of political institutions that allowed each individual to recognize these universal norms as the expression of his own will. But for Carové the political state did not represent the highest form of ethical community. It remained a "particular" community, in conflict with other states, and more importantly, Carové claimed that it remained merely "a higher form of mechanism."[155] The ultimate actualization of the ideal of an ethical community in which the free self-conscious spirit would feel entirely at home demanded the absorption of the political state into the "association of humanity in a divine, fraternal community," into the ethical community of a universal "church."[156] It was Carové's definition of the "church" as the highest form of ethical community and the final goal of man's historical development that most distinguished his writings of the 1820s from his earlier work, and also differentiated his position most clearly from the outlook of critical Hegelians like Leo and Gans.

Gans and Leo had emphasized that every particular objectification of the spirit in a political community was subject to the higher judgment of world history. What Carové claimed, in effect, was that the judgment of history was about to create a form of ethical community that transcended the limitations of the state altogether. The final goal of history, Carové claimed, was the complete self-revelation of God through the "development, actualization, harmonization and satisfaction of man's divine faculties, capacities, and powers."[157] But the reconciliation of God and man through the divinization of man could not be accomplished within a single individual or a particular state; only mankind as a totality, as an inwardly differentiated, universal community, could constitute the Kingdom of God in this earth.

Carové conceived the breakthrough to a universal human community primarily, or at least in the first instance, as a transformation of consciousness, as a product of cultural education. Man could attain the blessedness of feeling completely at home in the world only if the revelations of the divine in the human – the "true," the "beautiful," and the "good" – were recognized as the products of his free self-determination, as authentic expressions of his own universal nature as a divine being.[158] The task of the intellectual as midwife for the new age was therefore twofold: He must bring all authentic expressions of the human spirit into the realm of public consciousness, and he must comprehend these expressions within the context of the harmonious totality of the human. Carové himself devoted a great deal of his energy during the 1820s to the task of bringing developments in French religion and philosophy to public consciousness in Germany and revealing their connection to German developments.[159] His personal attempts to raise the level of mutual understanding between the French and the Germans, however, constituted only a small part of what he hoped to see accomplished: the creation of a unified, worldwide public consciousness that would allow every individual to comprehend the whole variety of human expression as a revelation of his own "divine faculties, capacities and powers."

But universal knowledge was only one of the pillars of the future association of all men in a fraternal community; the other was love. Comprehension of the unity of the divine spirit in the differentiated totality of human expression, Carové claimed, would also transform man's feeling and will; it would arouse a "free love for humanity" and motivate man to make this love universally effective.[160] The fusion of Reason and love into a new, universal religion of humanity, he noted, had already found expression in a number of ecumenical sects and charitable organizations. Such groups, he claimed, were the "most beautiful blossoms on the highest twig of the old tree of humanity,"[161] and portended the imminent emergence of a new historical era in which all men would be united with each other and with the divine, not only in thought, but also in love and deed, in an actually constituted "Kingdom of God on this earth."

In later years, Carové admitted that his writings during the 1820s diverged from the Hegelian standpoint in "many essential points."[162] Although he never explicitly criticized Hegel, the determining factor in these divergences is not difficult to discern. Carové implicitly rejected Hegel's claim that man's final and absolute reconciliation with the divine was accomplished in the act of philosophical comprehension, in the transformation of the content of political and religious experience into the form of the philosophical concept. Instead he saw this absolute reconciliation as an ideal prefiguration of a new content that was to be made actual in man's communal and religious life. Hegel's absolute spirit was thus understood as a critical transcendence of the existing forms of objective spirit and a prophetic vision of an "absolute" objectification of the spirit in the world.

By 1828, Ludwig Feuerbach had arrived at a cultural stance very similar to that of Carové. But Feuerbach, unlike Carové, was acutely aware of the philosophical problems involved in the transformation of the absolute identity of the finite and infinite from a comprehended practice into the basis of a future practice. These difficulties were most clearly expressed in Hegel's conception of the relationship between his philosophy and the evolution and historical fulfillment of Christian culture.

6

Christian religion and Hegelian philosophy during the Restoration: accommodation, critique, and historical transcendence

THE APPROPRIATION OF HEGEL'S PHILOSOPHY OF RELIGION BY THE "OLD" HEGELIANS

In the introduction to his *Lectures on the Philosophy of Religion,* Hegel claimed that his speculative philosophical elevation of religious faith and dogmas to the sphere of rational knowledge and truths did not constitute an attempt to instill a new religion into the minds of those who were without faith, but simply provided a conceptual understanding of the religious faith that the members of his audience already possessed.[1] But Hegel also insisted that the religious form of the relationship between man and the divine was no longer satisfactory for modern consciousness. "The spirit of the time," he wrote in 1822, "has developed to a stage where *thinking,* and the way of looking at things that goes together with thinking, has become an *imperative condition* for consciousness in defining what it shall admit and recognize as true." If contemporary man was to attain assurance of salvation, the blessedness of immortality, the content of his former faith would have to take the form of philosophical truth:

> The absolute content of religion is essentially here and now for spirit. Consequently, it is . . . only in the speculative knowledge of that content that spirit, which requires something more than simple faith, can find a truth that is freely accessible to it here and now and that alone is capable of satisfying its eternal need, namely, to think, and so to endow the infinite content of religion with its infinite form.[2]

What was the historical significance of this doctrine of the identity of content and difference of form in religion and philosophy? Had philosophy *replaced* religion as the modern way of attaining ontological security, or had it merely secured the traditional faith by demonstrating its absolute truth? In his later years, Hegel often seemed to favor the latter view, emphasizing the identity of content over the difference in form, and thus affirmed the Christian apologetics of the theological wing among his older disciples.

In 1816, Daub and Marheineke were the major academic representatives of the "speculative standpoint" in German Protestant theology.[3] They were thus generally sympathetic to Hegel's philosophical aims, but during the first years of their direct personal contact with Hegel (1816 to 1820) they remained loyal to Schelling's conception of the absolute as an undifferentiated ground of all being that could be known only through the act of inner intellectual intuition or contemplation in which the absolute "revealed" itself to consciousness. For more than a decade they had both been engaged in attempts to reconstruct and fortify the Christian conception of the relationship between man and God on this basis. The fact that both Daub and Marheineke became Hegelians at the beginning of the 1820s seemed to validate Hegel's belief that the test of historical experience would demonstrate the superiority of his philosophical science over the vague intuitions of Schelling and his disciples. But the discipleship of Daub and Marheineke was also gratifying in other respects. As academic theologians in major universities and influential ecclesiastical bureaucrats, they increased Hegel's impact both on students and in public life. Many members of the Hegelian school were first introduced to Hegel in their classrooms. It was not always clear, however, that the philosophical theologies purveyed by Daub and Marheineke were completely compatible with Hegel's philosophical position or even in agreement with each other. Both the shared and the individual divergences from Hegel's standpoint evident in the writings of Daub and Marheineke focused on central issues in the interpretation of Hegel's doctrine of absolute spirit and can be related to the common and individual past experiences and ideological commitments that the two theologians carried with them into the final, Hegelian phase of their development.

The fifteen-year age difference between Daub and Marheineke had a significant impact on the difference in their intellectual developments. Daub's formative years, his period of university study and first ideological commitments, overlapped with the revolutionary 1790s. Like the young Hegel, Daub had committed himself to the collective historical realization of the Kantian ideal of a rational and moral religion that would affirm the autonomy and unity of all men as self-legislating members of a Kingdom of Ends. Daub's social origins in the impoverished strata of the urban artisanate may have given special impetus to his radical espousal of the Kantian ideals of autonomy. His first book, a volume of ethical "sermons" based on Kantian principles, defined the content of Christian religion in exclusively ethical terms.

Christianity was "no more and no less than the religion of the pure heart," he claimed. The historical significance of Christ was that he provided a model of ethical perfection. The doctrine of immortality was described as a necessary postulate of practical reason, an expression of man's moral nature.[4] The book was considered heretical enough to justify Daub's dismissal from a lectureship in the theological faculty at Marburg in 1794.

When Daub returned to academic life two years later as a professor of theology at Heidelberg, his hopes for a cultural revolution based on Kantian principles had begun to subside, and like so many of his contemporaries, he began to explore the ways in which the Kantian ideals of autonomy and universality might be reconciled with the concrete historical particularities of personal and collective existence. After an ultimately unsuccessful and, as he himself conceded, "misconceived" attempt actually to "deduce" the particular historical dogmas and ethical teachings of Christianity from Kantian principles,[5] he was forced to realize that the Kantian principles themselves were in contradiction to the very concept of a positive historical religion and thus also to Christianity. What was required for a reconstruction and reformation of Christianity in the postrevolutionary world was a redefinition of the religious reconciliation between God and man, the incarnation of the divine Logos in the world, in the form of a self-validating universal truth. The historical reality of the Christian reconciliation of God and man could be accepted by modern consciousness only if it was demonstrated to be spiritually necessary. By 1806, Daub thought he had found the basis for such a reconstruction and reformation of Christianity in Schelling's philosophy of absolute identity.[6]

Although Marheineke's initiation into the advanced study of Christian theology at Göttingen between 1798 and 1802 was directed by a Kantian rationalist of Daub's generation,[7] his first publications revealed that the dominant influences on the formation of his theological viewpoint came from Schleiermacher and Schelling rather than Kant. His first volume of sermons, published in 1805, was clearly modeled on Schleiermacher's *Speeches.* The sublime "feeling" of unity with the absolute ground of all being was described as the essence of religious experience and consciousness. This feeling could be aroused through a contemplation of the incarnation of the divine in the particular as it was expressed in aesthetic symbols or self-transcending ethical acts, and it produced a total regeneration of the self. The instrumental rationality and hedonistic materialism of the finite empirical ego (the "sickness" of the age) was left behind and the individual recognized his true calling – to make himself into a work of art, an individualized expression of the divine unity. The biblical accounts of Christ's birth, death, and resurrection gained a new, vital, present significance as aesthetic representations of the universal truths of religious consciousness.[8] In his more scholarly works the young Marheineke tried to apply this Romantic conception of religious experience to the collective history of the Christian church. The ethical and dogmatic systems as well as the institutional arrangements and ritualistic practices of particular Christian eras and communities were described as secondary elaborations or objectifications of a shared religious experience.[9]

Unlike Daub, or Hegel, Marheineke does not seem to have had a very intense experience of the contradictions or polarities that the Romantic vision of absolute identity tried to reconcile. From the very beginning of his intellectual development he perceived the crisis of bifurcation from the standpoint of its resolution. His writings purveyed not a sense of inner struggle, but a consciousness of achieved peace. In contrast to Daub's convoluted and obscure prose, Marheineke's writing was characterized by a surface clarity in which difficult problems often seemed to be skirted by an elegant phrase or rhetorical declamation. Daub appeared to his contemporaries as a man of exceptional moral courage and intellectual honesty who was involved in a constant struggle to overcome his individual subjectivity and become an objective organ of divine truth.[10] Marheineke, in contrast, impressed both his enemies and his allies as a man who was completely confident that he possessed the truth and could treat those who were still struggling in the vale of doubt with an irritating condescension. Among Berlin students, Marheineke was popularly known as "Don Philipp" or "The Cardinal."[11] Part of this difference might be traced to differences in social background: Marheineke's roots were in the wealthy merchant patriciate of the city of Hildesheim. But the transformation of a natural sense of cultural superiority into a supreme historical confidence that he possessed the answer to the cultural crisis of the age was also determined by an intellectual development in which the solutions were received before the depth of the problems had been fully explored.

When Marheineke joined Daub in Heidelberg in 1807 their differences seemed relatively trivial in comparison to their common commitment to the task of constructing a new philosophical basis for Christian culture in the modern world. Daub concentrated his efforts on the preliminary process of clarifying the general principle that would allow the truth of the positive dogmas and ethical teaching of biblical revelation and Christian tradition to be objectively validated by the philosophical knowledge attained through the speculative method of intellectual intuition. Daub did not claim that Schelling's philosophical method could function as the basis for a new religious consciousness. What it did provide was a secure and objective foundation for the reconciliation between the divine and the human given in biblical revelation, expounded in Christian dogma, and appropriated through religious faith.[12] The task of the speculative theologian was very much an "apologetic" one. He was to comprehend the materials of Christian dogma as a systematic representation of the self-movement of the absolute, as a self-comprehending totality that was the demonstration of its own truth and did not need to be buttressed by the external support of supernatural authority or factual historical truth, both of which were subject to the corrosive skepticism of modern rationality and critical scholarship.[13] But Daub found it easier to outline a program for speculative theology than to carry it out. The particular representations of Christian doctrine and facts of Christian history were not as easily transposed into the form of self-validating philosophical truth as he had hoped.[14]

While Daub struggled with the problems of bridging the gap between the idea of absolute identity and the particular forms in which it allegedly found historical expression, Marheineke continued his studies of the relationship between the Christian Idea and its various historical embodiments in different confessional communities or "parties." His analysis of the "symbol systems" or Ideas of previous religious communities obviously had a contemporary purpose. Like Daub, Marheineke thought that a new era in Christian culture was imminent, that he was living in a period of "reformation," and that a new form for the appropriation of Christian truth must be created. Contemporary man could not recognize the character of his religious experience in confessions of faith, rituals, and divine revelations that could not be comprehended as self-validating truths. The task of theologians and church leaders was to articulate the basic teachings of Christianity in a form that would allow modern man to grasp them as objective expressions of their experience of identification with the ground of all being.[15] After Marheineke moved to Berlin in 1811 and became involved in both the reconstruction of the Prussian educational and ecclesiastical system and the religious awakening that accompanied the wars of liberation, he became convinced that the historical moment for a reconstitution of the Christian "Symbolic" had arrived.[16] Without any of the doubts and hesitations that had kept Daub from completing his project, Marheineke quickly set to work and wrote a systematic speculative interpretation of the Christian doctrines of Father, Son, and Holy Spirit as Moments in the self-movement of the absolute. He expressed complete confidence that the content of the message of reconciliation in the Bible, the tradition of the church, and speculative philosophy was the same.[17]

By the time Marheineke completed his speculative reconstruction of Christian teaching in 1819, Daub had begun to have serious doubts about the ability of Schelling's philosophical method to fulfill the theological task he and Marheineke had hoped it would. In a massive two-volume study of the nature of evil, published in 1816 and 1818, Daub appeared to reject the possibility of a philosophical reconciliation of the absolute unity of the One with the world of particularized finite existence in space and time. Evil was defined as the principle of unmediated or unreconciled particularity; it found expression in the stubborn resistance of the finite ego to absorption in the infinite unity of divine spirit. The origin of this absolute particularity, personified in the Devil, could not be explained as a necessary manifestation of the absolute; its source must lie in an autonomous power that opposed the divine unity and goodness of God. The existence of evil was an ultimately inexplicable "miracle" that could be overcome only by the equally miraculous intervention of divine grace.[18] But Daub was clearly dissatisfied with this dualistic perception, which placed the reality of the reconciliation achieved in Christian faith beyond the reach of philosophical comprehension. For a number of years he devoted all of his energies to a systematic study of Hegel's *Phenomenology* and *Logic*, in the hope of finding a solution to his dilemma.

Daub described his conversion to Hegel's position as the product of an intense and lengthy inner struggle.[19] As late as January 1819, Richard Rothe claimed that Daub was ready to reject Hegel's philosophy because it relegated religion "to nothing more than a stage, albeit a necessary stage, in the evolution of the self-comprehending spirit, a stage in which this spirit has not attained the true concept of itself, which is first possible for it in philosophy."[20] But this judgment was premature. While Rothe himself turned his back on speculative philosophy and sought a secure foundation for his faith in the neoorthodox Protestant fundamentalism that emerged simultaneously with Hegelianism in the postwar period, Daub was eventually convinced that the Hegelian "science" provided a secure grounding for the truths of the Christian faith. In Hegel's rational ontology the evil of absolute particularity was comprehended as the necessary Moment of negation in the dialectical totality of the absolute; the miracle of redemption became the necessary, comprehensible truth of dialectical mediation. By the summer of 1820, Daub was explicating Hegel's works in his classes and had rejected his earlier works as products of a "prescientific" consciousness.[21] But even though Daub portrayed Hegel's philosophy throughout the 1820s as an authentic comprehension of the truth of the Christian revelation, his own titanic personal struggle to grasp the particular as a Moment in the self-development of the absolute was never completely successful. He did not publish any major work during the Restoration, and the reviews and essays that he did publish were restricted to the critical analysis of theological standpoints that remained mired in the subjective "opinion" of prescientific ratiocination and feeling.[22] After 1827, Daub relied on Marheineke's Hegelian dogmatic as a textbook for his own lectures.

In Marheineke's case the transition from Schelling to Hegel had proceeded much more smoothly; it developed as a gradual clarification and increasingly rigorous articulation of already held convictions rather than as a radical transformation that demanded a rejection of his earlier writings. Like Daub, Marheineke had reached a standpoint in 1819 which rejected Schleiermacher's claim that a durable conviction of reconciliation with God could be grounded on a "subjective" feeling of dependence on the absolute. A more objective, secure basis for religious assurance, a conviction based on self-conscious knowledge, was required in the modern world. In his Schellingian dogmatic of 1819, Marheineke stated that such knowledge could be attained through the speculative process of intellectual contemplation or intuition, although he did admit that this knowledge could never be totally satisfactory. A residue of ungrasped "immediacy," an element of transcendent mystery, remained in man's knowledge of God.[23] For Marheineke the Hegelian method made possible the elimination of this final source of subjective uncertainty; the revelation of God's nature and plan of salvation, the absolute truth of the reconciliation of the divine and the human, could now be fully comprehended and articulated in an objective system of universal truth; the content of faith could now be completely appropriated in thought.[24] Marheineke's shift from Schelling to Hegel was also influenced by his involvement in the reorganization and unification of the Prussian Protestant church in the postwar period. He had been an early opponent of Schleiermacher's conception of a "people's church," insisting both on the right of the state to determine the external institutional arrangements of the church and on the necessity for a unified doctrine and liturgy, or *Symbolik,* constructed for, and imposed on, the church by the intellectual elite of theologians who had comprehended the present developmental stage of Christian consciousness.[25] Hegel's claim that theology could become a system of scientific truth appeared to provide philosophical justification for these positions.

It was Marheineke who provided the most succinct and popular formulation of the relationship between faith and knowledge, religion and philosophy, within the Hegelian school during the Restoration. This formulation was based on a rather schematic application of Hegel's distinction between "representation (*Vorstellung*)" and "concept (*Begriff*)" to the historical and dogmatic materials of Christian theology. In the Christian religion the absolute truth, the dynamic unification of the divine and the human in history, was presented or "revealed" in the form of concrete images, historical narratives, or doctrinal statements about supernatural beings and transcendent relationships. These images, historical narratives, and statements were now defined as "representations" of the absolute in the form of the particular. The truth appeared to man as something "other," as a message from outside himself, which he was then asked to accept and appropriate in faith. In Hegel's philosophy these representations were understood *as representations,* as objectifications of the dynamic self-developing unity of spirit, not as factual descriptions of external supernatural events or transcendent beings. The dependence and thus alienation of faith was transformed into the freedom and thus reconciliation of knowledge. For example, the Christian doctrines concerning the end times, the last judgment and final union of the blessed in heaven, could now be comprehended as representations of spiritual truths.[26] Heaven was not some future state in a transcendent realm but a present consciousness of identity with the infinite. As Hegel had stated, "The absolute content of religion is essentially here and now for spirit."

Marheineke was convinced that the Hegelian transformation of representation into concept, faith into knowledge, did not threaten the viability of the Christian faith or the existing church, but provided the basis for their revitalization. Unlike the critical rationalism of the Enlightenment, Hegelian philosophy did not challenge the truth of Christian dogma or biblical history, nor did it assail the validity of the salvation gained through faith. What it did accomplish was to change the form in which the old truths were demonstrated and the old salvation appropriated. Marheineke seemed to interpret this change as a change that affected only the human side of the human-divine relationship. The reconciliation between God and man had been completely given, revealed, in the incarnation of Christ.[27] The historical development of human consciousness toward more and more adequate means of appropriating this reconciliation added nothing to the absolute. Hegel's conception of the absolute as a self-developing, self-comprehending process, a process in which the absolute came to know itself only by becoming "for itself" in history, was thus virtually ignored in Marheineke's work.[28]

In Marheineke's view the unity of content in Christian religion and Hegelian philosophy was clearly more important than the difference in form. In this sense he was clearly more "orthodox" than Hegel himself. In the *Phenomenology*, and even in the more conservative *Lectures on the Philosophy of Religion* (which Marheineke edited), Hegel had emphasized the historical deficiencies of the representational form, the self-alienating character of the stage in spiritual development in which the infinite and the finite, God and man, faced each other as separate powers.[29] The philosophical comprehension of Christian "truth" was thus a product of the tremendous historical struggle in which this separation was overcome. For Hegel the contradiction between form and content in Christian culture constituted the crisis of bifurcation that his philosophy had set out to resolve. In Marheineke's writings the critical, negative Moment that marked the transition from representation to concept, the death of God that preceded his resurrection as spirit, was given very little emphasis. The doctrine of the reconciliation of faith and reason, religion and philosophy, became the basis for an uncritical affirmation of the truth of the Christian representations. Marheineke experienced no difficulty in reconciling his Hegelian convictions with his vocation as a Christian theologian, preacher, and churchman. In his academic lectures and scholarly writings he translated the Christian representations into conceptual form; in his sermons and popular religious writings he continued to use the traditional language of the representation.[30] He perceived his actions not as a hypocritical conformity to appearances, but as an authentic expression of his conviction that religious faith and Hegelian philosophy were merely different froms of appropriating the same Christian truth.

Marheineke's and Daub's tendency to interpret the Hegelian philosophy of religion as a modern form of Christian apologetics was developed to its conservative extreme by Göschel, Conradi, and Rust. Göschel was a superior court judge in Naumburg and the lay leader of a local pietist conventicle.[31] The primary aim of his writings was to show that the postwar religious awakening and the development of Hegel's science of absolute spirit were mutually supportive elements in a general regeneration of biblical Christianity. The "speculative spirit," he claimed, was aroused in "the subject [only] when it endures in prayer and faith and seeks consolation for its despair in the Scriptures, the word of God."[32] The "life and truth" of "philosophical concepts" were based on "their identity with the words of God, of which they are a translation."[33] Though Göschel advised his fellow pietists to find a secure foundation for their subjective beliefs in the philosophical comprehension of Christian revelation, he warned his fellow Hegelians not to stray too far from their task of merely "translating" the divine word. "Speculative philosophy would gain in light and determination," he claimed, if it would "tie itself more decisively to the Bible."[34]

The Christian apologetics of Conradi and Rust focused more particularly on a reconstruction of the historical evolution of religious consciousness to its perfect and absolute expression in Christian revelation and faith.[35] Although Hegel's philosophy had provided them with the conceptual tools required to demonstrate the "absolute" content of the Christian religion, they clearly did not think that philosophical science was in any way a higher or more advanced form of appropriating Christian truth than the form of religious faith. The difference between philosophy and religion, Rust claimed, was rooted in the necessary distinction between the practical or ethical and the theoretical dimensions of human experience. Like other Hegelians, Rust believed that absolute spirit revealed itself and actualized itself in stages of self-development and self-comprehension, but in his view these stages were characterized by a parallel evolution in both religion and philosophy, not by a development from faith to knowledge or religion to philosophy. Hegelian philosophy articulated man's final and complete reconciliation with God on the intellectual or theoretical level. But the "practical" reconciliation achieved by the orthodox Christian believer was just as complete and perfect in its own sphere as the philosophical reconciliation, and it was clear from the sequence of Rust's chapters (religion followed philosophy in each stage of development) that he did not consider theory a higher level of human experience than practice. "Faith has the same assurance and conviction," he wrote, "the same power and vitality as knowledge."[36] Christian faith and Christian knowledge (Hegelian philosophy) were two necessary and complementary aspects of the final stage of human culture. In faith as much as in knowledge the spirit recognized itself in "indestructible unity with everything true and eternal," but this conviction was gained in religion through activity, by proving what had been accepted in faith as true through moral action in the historical world.[37] The unity between God and man was demonstrated in practice rather than in thought.

Both Conradi and Rust were Protestant pastors who had studied theology under Karl Daub.[38] Their daily contact with Christian believers who had neither the leisure nor the training to engage in the conceptual labor of translating the truths of religious experience into the truths of philosophical knowledge undoubtedly contributed to their emphasis on the equal validity of faith and knowledge as means of appropriating the Christian message. The academic Hegelians who reviewed their works in the *Jahrbücher* gently chided Rust and Conradi for their undialectical conception of the relationship between faith and knowledge.[39] But more than mere misunderstanding was involved here. When Rust entered the academic world in 1827 he became as adamant as any other Hegelian in his demand that theology should take the form of a systematic rational science and transform the truths of the traditional Christian faith into the universal truths of Reason.[40] The dialectical *Aufhebung* of faith into knowledge in the realm of theology, however, did not resolve the problem raised by his earlier work. How was the knowledge of the academic theologians to be related to the faith of the people? How was the triumph of Reason in the academic world connected to the collective evolution of the cultural community, and particularly the church? Conservative "Hegelian Christians" like Daub, Marheineke, Göschel, Conradi, and Rust tried to resolve such questions by placing an overwhelming emphasis on the identity of content rather than difference of form between Christian religion and Hegelian philosophy, and thus stripping Hegel's philosophy of religion of most of its critical, dynamic, historical qualities. Like their political counterparts, Schulze, Henning, and Förster, they focused their critical energies on the analytical dissection of the philosophical limitations and historical obsolescence of opposing theoretical viewpoints, not on the tension between theory and practice, Reason and reality.

Although this conservative, accommodationist interpretation of Hegel's conception of the identity of faith and Reason, religion and philosophy, became the dominant, "orthodox" interpretation within the Hegelian school during the 1820s, and thus provided the intellectual starting point for the emergence of divergent viewpoints among members of the younger generation, two little-read books published in 1822 and 1823 by Hinrichs and Kapp gave early indication of the basis of future conflicts. Both Hinrichs and Kapp were sons of Protestant pastors and had begun their university studies as theological students.[41] Both transferred to the philosophical faculty, however, in the wake of their Hegelian conversions. This change in vocational choice expressed their inner convictions that philosophy had replaced theology as a means to attain knowledge of, and thus reconciliation with, God in the modern world.

Before his absorption in philosophy, Hinrichs wrote to Hegel, he had possessed a firm, unquestioning faith in the truth of the Christian religion for "the simple reason that mankind could not have deceived itself on this issue." The first effect of philosophical study was to rob him of this simple faith and produce a crisis of "self-division" and "extreme doubt." He persisted in his studies only because of Hegel's promise that the ontological security he had formerly possessed in faith would eventually be restored to him "in the element of knowledge." "I often said to myself," he wrote, "that if I cannot grasp that which is given as absolute truth in the form of the representation in Christianity through the pure form of knowledge (in which the Idea is its own form) in Hegelian philosophy, then I will reject the latter completely." He did not reject Hegelian philosophy because he eventually became convinced that it constituted the "highest creation of Christendom."[42]

Like his friend and mentor Karl Daub, however, Hinrichs had a great deal of difficulty working out and articulating his convictions in the form of a systematic scholarly demonstration. Even Hegel found his book on the "philosophical grounding of religion through science"[43] too obscure to follow in detail, and Karl Rosenkranz doubted if more than a dozen people had struggled through its turgid and abstract exposition of the development of Christian truth from religious representation to philosophical concept.[44] This very incomprehensibility, however, may have been to Hinrichs's advantage in his application for an academic appointment in Prussia. Hegel had originally been concerned about the orthodoxy of the book, but nobody understood it well enough to discern the possible heresy in a study that, despite its constant reiteration of the claim that religion and philosophy expressed the same absolute truth in different forms, placed a great deal more emphasis on the difference in form than the works of Marheineke, Daub, or Göschel. Although Hinrichs contended that Hegel's philosophical science merely made explicit the truth of absolute spirit that was implicitly "given" in Christian revelation, this making explicit was described as the completion and fulfillment of the Christian promise of reconciliation, as the final resolution of the alienation between man and God and thus also of the self-alienation of the absolute. It was not only the human subject who finally elevated himself to identity with the absolute in scientific thought; God himself actualized and comprehended himself as the absolute only in the act of mediation through which his "otherness" in relation to man was overcome.[45]

The difficulty that Hinrichs experienced in communicating his conception, as Hegel himself noted, was caused by his inability to connect his internal description or reconstruction of the self-movement of the absolute idea with the concrete actuality of this development in nature and history.[46] Readers who were not already converts to the speculative standpoint could find no point of entry into Hinrichs's completely closed world of philosophical abstractions. This was not merely a problem of style or skill in communication; it expressed a significant element in Hinrichs's reception and interpretation of Hegel's philosophy. For Hinrichs the philosophical reconciliation achieved in Hegel's system was not presented or really understood as a comprehension of the actuality of the absolute in history. Hinrichs's extreme poverty as a lecturer in Heidelberg and his intellectual isolation as a Hegelian at Breslau and Halle between 1822 and 1828 encouraged him to see himself as a misunderstood, persecuted emissary from an intellectual realm that was radically separated from its cultural environment.[47] Although he continued explicitly to affirm the Hegelian doctrine of the identity of Reason and reality, his writings, as Daub and Rosenkranz noted, implicitly expressed their separation.[48] In 1826, Hinrichs published an introduction to Hegelian logic that attempted to show how Hegel's concrete logic developed out of the categories of traditional Aristotelian logic.[49] The book revealed no consciousness that Hegel had already provided such an introduction in the *Phenomenology* and that he had formulated this introduction in the form of a *history* of the forms of consciousness. For Hinrichs, Hegel's identity of Reason and reality was not a "history comprehended" but an abstract truth that still needed to be brought into some kind of satisfactory relationship with the world of everyday experience.

During the period in which Hegel was helping Hinrichs revise his study of religion and philosophy so that it would not give offense to the pious and thus hinder his academic career, Kapp was busily composing a book on a similar theme with little concern for its academic consequences (it was published anonymously) and with more than a little intention of giving offense to his contemporaries. His book was almost as unreadable as Hinrichs's first effort, but for different reasons. It was an almost totally unorganized collection of aphorisms and fragmentary historical essays written during the four-year period of travel and self-education that separated Kapp's conversion to Hegel in Berlin in 1819 from his first academic appointment at Erlangen in 1823.

Like Hinrichs, Kapp interpreted Hegel's philosophy as the culmination of Christian culture. "In the scientific comprehension of the concrete idea," he stated, "science reveals itself as the highest self-consciousness of Christianity."[50] In contrast to Hinrichs, however, Kapp emphasized that the comprehension of the truth of the Christian revelation in scientific, conceptual form was made possible by the long labor of historical actualization in which the Christian Idea became "concrete," in which the implicit truth contained in Christian revelation became the "authentic reality of spirit on earth," the "real heaven" of the state.[51] Religion and philosophy, representational and conceptual forms of consciousness, were expressions of different stages in the historical process. Once the Christian Idea had become the concrete reality of man's life on earth, representational or religious forms of consciousness, which expressed the separation of the universal and the concrete, were obsolete, in contradiction to the present stage of spiritual development. Kapp's insistence that scientific knowledge had *replaced* traditional religious faith as a means for attaining personal salvation was evident in his tendency to describe Hegelian philosophy as a "new covenant" between the divine and the human.[52] Salvation in the modern world was defined as self-conscious recognition of the reality of the spirit in the modern state and thus actual participation in the "real heaven." Only philosophy could provide such a redemptive comprehension of reality; to close one's eyes to the truth of science was to live in a state of "sin," stubbornly to refuse entry into the actualized Kingdom of God.[53]

Kapp did not believe that the Hegelian system articulated a cultural ideal that was yet to be historically realized. He repeatedly insisted that the political discontents of both radicals and conservatives were products of theoretical misconceptions.[54] The modern state was the historical actualization of the Christian incarnation, the reality of the resurrected Christ, and merely needed to be recognized as such. At the same time, however, Kapp's work was animated by a prophetic urgency. "Our time is a time of judgment and resurrection," he claimed. Science had "come into the world not in order to establish peace, but rather to ignite a fire in the name of the Lord."[55] For Kapp the distinction between the representational and scientific forms of conceiving the truth was so radical that the transition from one to the other constituted an epochal moment in human history. In 1839, Ludwig Feuerbach praised Kapp's early writings as the first expression of a recognition within the Hegelian school of the "sublime destiny of science" as a "world-reforming power" that declared the historical bankruptcy of all traditional forms of religious consciousness.[56]

During the 1820s, however, Kapp's work had little impact on the Hegelian school. And even Feuerbach discovered the historical significance of Kapp's radical distinction between religion and philosophy only after he himself had arrived at a similar position. Hinrichs's hapless abstractions were also not judged in historical terms, but seen as the product of a personal idiosyncracy. It was only among the younger Hegelians who came to intellectual maturity at the end of the decade that the problematic nature of the use of Hegelian philosophy for

Christian apologetics became explicit and led to significant divergences of interpretation within the school. The development of these divergences is most clearly revealed in the experience and thought of Karl Rosenkranz, David Friedrich Strauss, and Ludwig Feuerbach.

KARL ROSENKRANZ AND THE RECONSTITUTION OF THE IDENTITY OF RELIGION AND PHILOSOPHY

When Karl Rosenkranz published his autobiography in 1873 he described the major theme of the first twenty-eight years of his life as his gradual and difficult emancipation from the "labyrinthian mazes of Romanticism." He claimed that he had lived through both "the good and the bad sides of the Romanticism of the times" and had devoted himself to its "aberrations" with a "fervor that would have been worthy of a better cause." His "terrible struggle" with the communal, aesthetic, and especially theological or religious dimensions of the Romantic world view had been resolved only when he attained the "freedom of philosophy" under Hegel's guidance. It was his appropriation of the scientific systematic knowledge of the absolute as a resolution of the debilitating bifurcations of Romantic consciousness, he stated, that constituted the "essentially significant" aspect of his life history.[57] This claim had two distinct meanings. First, it expressed Rosenkranz's conviction that his own particular struggles with Romanticism during the Restoration were in some sense paradigmatic, that they embodied the general experience of his generation and expressed an epochal transition in western Christian culture. But Rosenkranz's claim also implied that the "essentially significant" period of his life *ended* with the overcoming of Romantic alienation in his Hegelian conversion. He was acutely conscious of the fact that his period of creative, dynamic intellectual development had reached its conclusion during the early 1830s.[58] The remainder of his life was devoted to the exegesis, popularization, reproduction, defense, and modest modification and revision of the philosophical position and cultural stance he had attained in his youth. Rosenkranz also liked to think that this aspect of his experience was paradigmatic, that the epigonal role was the historical fate of his generation.[59] But this claim was clearly a defensive response to some of his fellow Hegelians' rejection of the epigonal role. By the time of Hegel's death it was already evident that Rosenkranz's cultural stance was representative not of his whole generation within the Hegelian school, but of only one group – the new accommodationists – within that generation.

I have used the term "new accommodationists" because it would be misleading to see Rosenkranz simply as a carrier or purveyor within the new generation of the positions formulated by older accommodationists like Daub, Marheineke, and Göschel. Like other members of his generation, Rosenkranz was acutely aware of the historical significance of the differences between the religious and philosophical forms of appropriating the absolute truth. It was only after struggling with, and perhaps suppressing significant doubts about, the absolute identity of religion and philosophy that he was able to reconstitute the accommodationist position in what he believed was a convincing manner. In fact, Rosenkranz later admitted that some of his "toughest battles" with his own "consciousness" occurred after his Hegelian conversion, as he tried to sustain and justify his new perspective against recurring doubts.[60] It was only after these doubts had been overcome that he could finally feel totally emancipated from the seductions of Romanticism.

The Romantic world view was not, of course, the starting point of Rosenkranz's intellectual development. He had "fallen only gradually into Romanticism" after being raised in a "thoroughly rationalistic fashion."[61] Like his fellow Prussian Hegelians Michelet and Hotho, Rosenkranz grew up in a community of French-speaking Calvinists who had emigrated to Prussia during the eighteenth century.[62] His father, the son of a rural linen weaver in Mecklenburg, had been recruited into the Prussian army as a teenager. After almost twenty years of military service he had been rewarded with a bureaucratic post in the lower echelons of the Prussian tax administration near Magdeburg. In 1799, when he was already past forty, he married the young daughter of one of the leaders of the Walloon community that had settled in a suburb of Magdeburg during the reign of Frederick the Great. As a loyal Prussian bureaucrat and veteran of the Frederician campaigns, Rosenkranz's father experienced little difficulty in feeling at home in the community of Calvinist brewers, lumber merchants, and skilled craftsmen who idolized "old Fritz" and conceived their communal identity primarily in terms of their relationship to the state, rather than to traditionally privileged local or social groups. Like virtually all the Prussian Hegelians of his generation, Rosenkranz was born into a social and cultural group that was not a part of the traditional corporate society and whose identity, survival, and welfare was primarily determined by, and bound up with, the policies and administrative practices of the centralized bureaucratic state.[63] The cultural viewpoint that young Rosenkranz absorbed from his father, grandfather, uncles, and local pastor was that of the enlightened, state-dependent, eighteenth-century Prussian bourgeoisie. In the religious sphere it was expressed in an undogmatic Protestantism that supported the principle of religious toleration, emphasized the universal rational and moral content of Christian teaching, and opposed "superstition" and "priestly domination." In the political sphere it supported the Enlightenment ideal of a state of rational, universal law against both feudal privilege and arbitrary personal despotism.[64] The philosophical correlate of this cultural stance was Kant's critical idealism, and the one academic in Rosenkranz's family, an uncle who taught mathematics at the Military Academy in Berlin, was, in fact, a loyal Kantian.[65]

Rosenkranz experienced his first doubts about the historical viability of his cultural inheritance when his father's world began to show signs of crumbling during the Napoleonic period. In 1812 he witnessed the demolition of his home when the whole Walloon suburb was razed by French military engineers. The social displacement caused by this event, together with the general political instability of the French occupation, a short-lived puppet regime, and the liberation wars, produced a feeling of cultural dislocation that allowed the emerging nationalistic and pietistic movements to make significant inroads into the traditional Prussian state loyalty and rational Protestantism of the Walloon community. Within Rosenkranz's own family a conflict developed between the older father, who maintained his loyalty to the traditional views, and the younger mother, who became totally absorbed in the mystical piety of the religious awakening.[66]

Rosenkranz himself was torn in both directions. His father controlled the external aspects of his education. In 1816 he was taken out of the Walloon School – in opposition to the wishes of his mother, who had planned a theological vocation for her son – and placed in the state grammar school, where his father hoped he would prepare himself for a "practical" career in business or state service. Rosenkranz seemed quite willing to fulfill his father's ambitions and devoted himself to his studies with a self-disciplined concentration and ambitious desire for success worthy of his Calvinist heritage. In 1818 he was able to transfer to the local gymnasium, a major step in the established path of upward social mobility into the Prussian professional elite. Though his external successes gratified his father's ambitions, however, his inner life was dominated by his mother. In his "heart" he claimed, he shared his mother's pious religiosity and prayed to her personal god with "utmost fervor."[67] During his gymnasium years this "maternal" side of his existence, the inner longing for a redemptive absorption into some kind of all-encompassing unity, found an ideological focus in his enthusiastic immersion in the Teutonic Romanticism purveyed by a young professor of medieval German literature who had fought with the Lützow volunteers.

In contrast to the older Romantic nationalists, however, Rosenkranz experienced the Teutonic cultural ideal not as a goal of practical political activity but as a literary image of cultural integration and personal fulfillment that merged almost imperceptibly with adolescent sexual yearnings, nostalgic visions of childhood innocence and maternal love, and religious visions of a mystical absorption in the divine. "I wavered unhappily," Rosenkranz wrote, "between the soft pressure of a warm maiden's hand and the ecstatic vision of the heavenly Sophia."[68] The transformation of the hopes for cultural regeneration into a mystical *Schwärmerei,* Rosenkranz claimed, was due to the political conditions that marked his generation's adolescence:

> There reigned in Magdeburg at that time, as in so many other places, an intense ferment that did not know exactly what it wanted. The wars of liberation were over, the *Burschenschaft* that had dreamed of a German emperor was persecuted by the police; the most effeminate kind of sentimentality became rampant.[69]

A lengthy illness brought on by the death of his mother and paternal pressure to make some kind of practical vocational decision finally motivated Rosenkranz to seek some escape from the hopeless longing of his adolescent Romanticism. Attempts to transform his inner pain into poetic form had led him to appreciate the virtues of Goethean "objectivity" and "resignation," but he did not have the talent or the leisure to pursue a career as a *Dichter.* In the summer of 1824 he matriculated at the University of Berlin with the aim of transforming his subjective "obsessions" into a professional career of philological scholarship.

Rosenkranz's desire to overcome the "effeminate sentimentality" of Romantic subjectivity made him receptive to the aim of Hegel's philosophy, but his first contact with Hegelianism at Berlin was disappointing. Because of Hegel's reputation for difficulty and obscurity, Rosenkranz enrolled in Henning's introductory course on the Hegelian system. Although extensive reading in classical and Romantic philosophy had prepared him for many aspects of the speculative viewpoint, he simply could not accept or fully comprehend the Hegelian doctrine of the identity of being and knowing. Henning's description of the self-development of the concept in Hegel's logic seemed completely formal and abstract to him. The claim that this dialectical self-movement of the process of thought was the self determination of the divine substance itself remained unconvincing. Rosenkranz experienced no contact with "divine being" in his abstract speculations and continued to "thirst" for "life and love."[70] Henning's lectures aroused his interest in speculative philosophy and theology, but he turned elsewhere for a satisfactory resolution of the contradictions of human experience – to the visionary philosophy of nature purveyed by Schelling's disciple Henrik Steffens and, above all, to the theology of Schleiermacher. By the spring of 1825, Rosenkranz had become a committed "Schleiermacherian," and at the beginning of the summer semester he transferred into the theological faculty.

Because a Schleiermacherian phase was an important stage in the path toward Hegelianism for so many members of the school, it is important to define exactly what attracted Rosenkranz to, and eventually alienated him from, Schleiermacher's position. What Rosenkranz and other Hegelians found in Schleiermacher's theology was not very different in content from what they later found in Hegel's philosophy. Rosenkranz described the Schleiermacherian position as an "absolute mysticism" in which all the phenomena of natural and historical existence were perceived and experienced as dynamically evolving individualized forms of the ultimately mysterious, divine "life source (*Lebensquell*)."[71] The intuitive divination of the presence of the One in the All allowed the individual self to recognize, to "feel," its own connection to the divine. To recognize this presence of the infinite within the individual self, to discover the "genius" of one's individuality and actualize it in the world, was the purpose of human existence. For Rosenkranz, Schleiermacher's theology of "feeling" revealed the reality of the union of the infinite and finite and produced a state of "grace" in which immortality, or identity with the absolute, became a present experiential condition rather than a future or transcendent goal. "Authentic mystics," he claimed, were the "real optimists," because they had attained the redemptive knowledge of "the reconciliation of heaven and earth."[72]

The Schleiermacherian resolution, however, proved to be ephemeral. Within a year, Rosenkranz had come to realize that what he had perceived as a solution was really only a replication of his former Romantic dilemma. The state of "grace" attained through the method of "absolute mysticism" was only temporary, a brief moment of visionary ecstasy produced by the contemplation of art or the wonders of nature. The reconciliation of the individual with the divine, the identity of finite and infinite, was only a subjective feeling; the feeling passed and the pain returned. "The suffering that Schleiermacher had aroused in me," Rosenkranz wrote, "originated primarily in the fact that I wanted to gain absolute assurance of God's grace." But such assurance, such objective conviction, could not be attained through fleeting emotional experiences and subjective visions. As soon as the individual tried to give objective form to his inner experience he fell into a "superstitious" belief in the reality of symbolic representations and regressed to the self-alienating consciousness of traditional Christian faith. Rosenkranz's Schleiermacherian phase was, in fact, marked by a regression to the pietistic religiosity he had shared with his mother when he was a young teenager. What he desired was a "personal relationship" to the actual objective source of his subjective states that would allow him to break out of the Romantic circle of narcissistic infatuation with the subjective states themselves.[73]

The recognition that Schleiermacher's theology was just another cul de sac in the Romantic labyrinth stimulated Rosenkranz to return to the study of Hegelian philosophy. He attended Hinrichs's lectures on Hegelian aesthetics at Halle in the fall of 1826 and Daub's lectures on Hegelian philosophy of religion in the summer of 1827. He systematically worked his way through the *Phenomenology* and *Science of Logic.* This willingness to undertake the labor of the concept was finally rewarded by the hoped-for breakthrough to philosophical comprehension. His "whole past," he claimed, was "swept away" as he transcended the limited finite standpoint of the "empirical person" and attained the "totally new ground" of absolute spirit. He became a "new person" with a "totally new perspective" on nature, history, and his own "individuality and past." His previous ephemeral feelings of being absorbed into the infinite while still in the here and now were transformed into a conviction based on scientific knowledge of the identity of the human and the divine spirit. The world that constituted the hell of "otherness" for the Romantic ego locked in its narcissistic subjectivity became the spiritual home of the transformed self. "I could no longer doubt," he wrote, "that the absolute revealed itself in nature and history."[74]

Rosenkranz's Hegelian conversion was the culmination of a religious quest for salvation. He viewed Hegel's philosophy as the fulfillment of the Christian promise that the truth would make man free, and as a comprehension of the Christian revelation that the divine and the human were reconciled through the actualization of spirit in the world.[75] But even though the absolute content of Hegelian philosophy was in a sense already "given" in the representations of Christian revelation, Rosenkranz insisted that the "content itself" was "perfected" only when it had given itself "appropriate form."[76] That he viewed Hegel's philosophy as more than a mere means for securing the traditional faith, more than a form of Christian apologetics, was already evident from the fact that he transferred from the theological to the philosophical faculty after his Hegelian conversion. His interests remained focused on religious questions, but he now dealt with these questions from the standpoint of their philosophical and historical resolution. In 1827 he briefly considered the possibility of expressing his new viewpoint in literary form and constructed a project for a philosophical novel in which the self-development of the Christian Idea would be portrayed as the objective content of an individual's personal dialectical evolution toward the peace of "absolute reconciliation."[77] He abandoned this project, however, as he became increasingly convinced that the actualization of spirit in the world of human experience could more easily and convincingly be portrayed in terms of a philosophically comprehended history of Christian culture. In 1828, Rosenkranz joined Leo and Hinrichs on the faculty of the University of Halle, and his first attempts to express his new perspective on the relationship between the Christian religion and modern scientific consciousness took the form of scholarly treatises on the history of medieval German literature.

Rosenkranz's studies of the literary forms that expressed the "metamorphosis of the spiritual Idea in the Middle Ages"[78] had a twofold purpose. He hoped, first of all, to make a contribution to the creation of a German national consciousness by reconciling his contemporaries with an important aspect of their historical heritage. "History is spirit giving itself being," he stated, "and thus everything in it hangs together in the most intimate manner." The task of "inner historiography" was to grasp the apparently arbitrary disconnected facts of "external" history as manifestations of the necessary stages or Moments in the self-development and self-actualization of spirit,[79] to show that "in history the external is in itself (*an sich*) also the internal."[80] The past lost its alien character and became "authentically present" as man elevated himself to the standpoint of spirit and "remembered" the religious, political, and aesthetic forms of the past as the product of its own previous creative activity, as self-objectifications.[81] At the same time, however, Rosenkranz was clearly concerned with demonstrating – and this was the second aspect of his purpose – that a rememberance of the Christian–Germanic Middle Ages as a Moment within the dynamic totality of absolute spirit would lead to a recognition of the necessary historical limitations of that Moment. The Middle Ages were merely the first stage in the three-stage process whereby the absolute content of the Christian revelation had found its appropriate form and made itself actual in the historical world. Rosenkranz thus rejected any attempts to revive the political or religious forms of medieval life as absolute norms for contemporary consciousness or activity.[82] To comprehend the past was at the same time to strip the past of its power over the present.

For Rosenkranz the historical limitations of the cultural forms of medieval Christendom were most clearly expressed in the two predominant characteristics of its religious consciousness: heteronomy and dualism. The absolute content of the Christian truth was perceived as an external revelation "given" to man by a transcendent authority, not as the inner self-affirming truth of his own identity with the divine as a free spiritual being. The form of religious consciousness – the dependent relationship of faith and blind obedience – was thus in contradiction with the content of religious consciousness – the absolute autonomy of spirit. Moreover, the actualization of the content of the Christian revelation, the final reconciliation of God and man, was relegated to a future, otherworldly heaven. The transcendent and the immanent, the spiritual and the earthly, the heavenly and the worldly, the divine and the human, were conceived as radically separate spheres, rather than Moments of a dialectical unity.[83] These contradictions within the "unhappy consciousness" of medieval Christianity were overcome only by the historical emancipation of the finite individual from the external religious and political authority that denied his freedom and right to earthly enjoyment, and, finally, by the reappropriation of the Christian truth of absolute reconciliation as the highest expression of human freedom and this-wordly blessedness. Like Kapp, Rosenkranz contended that this reappropriation of Christian truth in the modern world was possible only because this truth had become actual in the "rational home" of the social and political relationships of the modern state.[84] The modern Christianity of Goethe and Hegel was expressed in a knowledge and presentation of the actual, rather than in "representations" of the transcendent.[85]

But what exactly was the relationship between this modern Christianity of Goethe and Hegel and the "representations" of the traditional faith? Could the consciousness of unity with the infinite in the "here and now" really be reconciled with the religious representation of that unity in an otherworldly future? Rosenkranz was forced to face these questions, which he had avoided in his historical works, when he was confronted by the radical answers of his friend, pupil, and disciple Friedrich Richter in 1829–30. Richter claimed that there was a vast difference between Hegelian Christianity and the traditional faith. It was impossible to claim that immortality was a present condition, that heaven and hell were mental states, and still affirm the truth of orthodox dogmas that asserted exactly the opposite. Hegel's philosophy was not a comprehension of the existing religious consciousness of the Christian church but a prophetic vision of a new religious consciousness. Richter demanded that Rosenkranz expose the equivocations of theologians like Marheineke and join him in proclaiming the dawn of a new religious era.[86] Rosenkranz was extremely troubled by this encounter with Richter. He had to admit that he was not an "orthodox Christian"[87] in the sense in which orthodoxy was defined by the confessions of the existing Protestant churches, but he refused to make a public break and become the Melancthon (to Richter's Luther) of a new religious reformation. He dismissed Richter's prophetic activism as a product of psychological instability and insisted that the problem of the relationship between the religious representation and the philosophical concept was extremely complex and required more scientific study. In fact, Rosenkranz stated that the whole issue should be left in the realm of academic discussion and not related to the larger problem of general cultural change at all.[88] It was only after this conscious separation of philosophical theology from the contemporary historical evolution of religious consciousness that Rosenkranz felt that he could reconstitute the Hegelian reconciliation between religious faith and philosophical knowledge.

Rosenkranz fortified himself for this task with two preliminary critiques of the major opponents of the Hegelian position. The doubts about the absolute truth of the Christian faith that were raised by the critical rationalists of the Enlightenment could be turned back by demonstrating that their criticisms were directed at the representational form rather than the absolute content of the traditional Christian faith. Their viewpoint was thus relegated to the status of a legitimate but limited stage in the development toward an appropriation of the religious truth in the higher form of the concept.[89] The Romantic theology of Schleiermacher, on the other hand, was rejected not because it denied the truth of the faith, but because it tried to ground this truth on the uncertain evidence of subjective states and individual feelings.[90] The truth could be demonstrated only in the form of a scientific system that simply reproduced the "self-movement" of the absolute "substance" itself.[91] In his *Encyclopedia of the Theological Sciences,* Rosenkranz tried to show that Christian theology could be reconstructed as just such a system of scientific truth, and was thus completely identical with Hegel's philosophy.

Rosenkranz's Hegelian theology was divided into three major parts. In the first part, entitled "speculative theology," the Idea of the absolute or Christian religion was developed, completely independently from its empirical content, as "the absolute self-knowledge of religion," as "the evolution of the simple and eternal concepts that are contained in the relationship of God to man and man to God."[92] Following the lead set by Marheineke, Rosenkranz tried to demonstrate the truth of the basic Christian doctrines by describing them as Moments in the logical explication of the idea of the union of God and man in absolute spirit. This purely speculative section was followed by "historical theology" in which the empirical materials of Christian history, from the Bible to modern Protestantism, were comprehended as the objectification of the Christian Idea in the finite world of space and time. Finally, Rosenkranz presented "practical theology" as the third and final stage in the system of the theological sciences. In the contemporary institutions and activities of the church the absolute Idea of the Christian religion was to be comprehended and articulated as the highest stage in the empirical, historical evolution of Christian history. But Rosenkranz did not really attempt to demonstrate that the present actuality of Christian religion was the perfected expression of the Christian Idea in the particular historical form of the religious representation. In fact, his last section, as one critic has noted, remained fragmentary and constituted a statement of principle rather than a convincing historical demonstration.[93] Rosenkranz's reconstitution of the accommodation theory, therefore, took on the character of an abstract assertion and mirrored his own continuing doubts about the total identity in content of the representations of faith and the conceptual truths of philosophy.

David Friedrich Strauss was the first Hegelian to point out the weaknesses in Rosenkranz's philosophical theology. According to Strauss, Rosenkranz had made a fundamental mistake in the way he conceived the relationship between speculative and historical theology. "Speculative theology is not related to the historical simply in the fashion of essence to appearance," he claimed, "but as the concept to being (*Sein*) and appearance, and therefore essentially presupposes being and appearance."[94] For Strauss, Rosenkranz's reconciliation of the absolute Idea and the historical development of Christianity was too artificial, too easy. Instead of attempting to comprehend the actual process of historical development, he deduced the truth of history from the concept. The representations of biblical Scripture, church dogma, and ecclesiastical tradition, Strauss claimed, must be subjected to careful historical criticism before they could be brought into harmony with philosophical truth. This emphasis expressed Strauss's own experience of the historical tension between the representations of the orthodox faith purveyed by the contemporary Protestant church and the philosophical truth of Hegelian philosophy.

Christian religion and Hegelian philosophy

STRAUSS AND THE HISTORICAL TENSION BETWEEN REPRESENTATION AND CONCEPT

In November 1831, less than a week before Hegel's unexpected death, Strauss made his first and only personal call on the thinker whose philosophy had become the center of his intellectual and spiritual life. Hegel was extremely pleased to meet this brilliant young member of a new generation in the theological elite of the Württemberg *Ehrbarkeit* and pumped Strauss for information about the contemporary state of the educational, political, and ecclesiastical system that had played such an important role in his own development. "Regarding Tübingen," Strauss reported to his friend Christian Märklin, "he said that he had heard that malevolent and to some extent malicious conceptions about his philosophy reigned there; the adage, he said with a smile, that a prophet is without honor in his own country is also appropriate in this instance."[95] The very presence of Strauss in Hegel's study, of course, suggested that this judgment was a little premature. Hegel was to be honored as a prophet in his own country. It is doubtful, however, that he would have been entirely pleased by the manner in which that honor was expressed. For it was Strauss who first transformed the divergences within Hegelianism into open conflicts and thus initiated the historical disintegration of the Hegelian reconciliation of religion and philosophy. The tensions that eventually produced this result were already present in his consciousness as he sat before Hegel in 1831.

Strauss's intellectual development during the formative years of his late teens and early twenties, like that of Rosenkranz, was dominated by his absorption in, and eventual emancipation from, the various forms of the Romantic seduction. Moreover, Strauss's experience was so similar to that of his classmates and eventual fellow Hegelians Märklin, Vischer, and Gustav Binder that he felt justified in writing the biography of Märklin as a collective biography.[96] This group of young seminarians, educated from the age of fourteen for a career in the service of the Württemberg church, had not, any more than Rosenkranz, imbibed the world view of Romanticism at their mothers' knees; nor was the source of this view, despite what some Swabian patriots might claim, the beauties of the local landscape. Although they did not completely lack intellectual mentors among their teachers and older contemporaries, their commitment to Romanticism marked a significant historical break with the cultural ideology of their parents and the established church in whose service they were supposed to find their cultural vocations and communal identities.

The starting point of Strauss's intellectual development might best be described as a compromise between an orthodox biblical Protestantism and the moralistic and rational outlook of the bourgeois elite of the Württemberg oligarchy. On the theological level this compromise was expressed in the "rational supernaturalism" of the "older" Tübingen school, in which the truths of Christian dogma and biblical history were supported by rational explanations and arguments drawn from Kant's ethical philosophy.[97] The fathers of Märklin, Vischer, and Binder were all representatives of this theological position. In his later years, Strauss often praised the practical, ethical emphasis of the older Tübingen theology, especially as it found political expression in the form of a moderate constitutional liberalism.[98] These were retrospective judgments. When Strauss and his friends came into contact with the traditional theology of the *Ehrbarkeit* in the preparatory "monastic" school at Blaubeuren and the seminary at Tübingen, their response was almost totally negative, and they turned elsewhere for a world view that might still their longing for "spiritual peace."

In Württemberg, as elsewhere in Germany, the decline in the binding power of the cultural ideology of the bourgeois elites was connected to the dislocating impact of the period of French occupation, war, and postwar economic difficulty and political conflict. Vischer experienced this dislocation in a very direct and personal fashion when his father died in 1814 after contracting typhoid fever in a military hospital. His mother was forced to move in with relatives in Stuttgart, and Vischer claimed that poverty rather than religious conviction was the primary motivation in his choice of a theological career.[99] In Märklin's case it was the political expansion and centralization of Württemberg during the Napoleonic and postwar era that determined the initial consciousness of historical change and cultural disinheritance. The transfer of Märklin's father from the quiet village of Maulbronn in Old Württemberg to the bustling market town of Heilbronn in the newly acquired territories, Strauss claimed, was a crucial factor in Märklin's gradual emancipation from the confined perspectives of the traditional ecclesiastical oligarchy.[100] Strauss's own early experience was also dominated by the effects of political and economic change. His father was a merchant and retailer in Ludwigsburg who supplied imported spices and teas to the royal court. The flooding of the German market with low-priced English goods after 1815, the transfer of the royal residence from Ludwigsburg to Stuttgart in 1816, and the miscalculations of Strauss's father, who refused to liquidate his inventory in the hope that prices would rise and business improve, led to a situation of near bankruptcy in the family firm.[101] These financial difficulties affected Strauss most directly through the tensions they created between his parents. When the family business began to falter, his father was subjected to continuous nagging criticism by his wife. In response, he withdrew more and more into a private world and, according to Strauss, sought compensation for his external frustrations in an "absolute faith" in the "atoning death of Christ, to whose power of saving man from sin he surrendered himself."[102] While his father found a modicum of psychological peace in religious piety, Strauss's mother took over the duties of home and business. Strauss invariably sided with his mother in these parental conflicts, perhaps because he felt himself to be so much like his father. When his father died in 1841, Strauss confessed that he had often acted like a "dualistic manichean being" in his attempts to deny all traces of his father's "seed" and to see himself solely as his mother's offspring.[103] What he meant by this paternal "seed" was the longing for transcendence, the desire to escape the here and now and find peace in a world "beyond." This tendency was clearly evident in his first immersion in Romanticism during his last years at Blaubeuren and first years at Tübingen.

Like their generational contemporaries in northern Germany, Strauss and his classmates first encountered Romanticism in the politically oriented form in which it was popularized by the postwar nationalistic movement. Some, like Vischer, tried to sustain the active, political impulse of Romantic nationalism. Strauss, however, sought compensation for his adolescent feelings of homelessness in the imaginative world of Romantic art. When his class entered the *Stift* in 1825 this internalization of the Romantic vision had become dominant. As both Strauss and Vischer noted, the "reign of terror" instituted by the political police in Tübingen made any form of political activism impossible and, as in Rosenkranz's Magdeburg, created an atmosphere in which the sentimental and mystical forms of Romanticism were able to flourish.[104] In his first year at the *Stift,* Strauss joined a circle of young poets who sought the beautiful in "the mystical and miraculous, in the musical echoes of inarticulate infinite feelings and the dissolution of all solid forms of the visible world in the delirium of the imagination."[105] Philosophy and theology gained Strauss's attention only when he realized his own lack of poetic talent and discovered an intellectual articulation of the content of his "waking dreams" in the philosophical theology of Jakob Böhme, Franz von Baader, and Schelling.

This second phase of Strauss's journey through the Romantic labyrinth lasted until the spring of 1828. The general spread of mystical tendencies among the younger seminarians was noted with concern by members of the faculty and the ecclesiastical council in Stuttgart, and Strauss's essays and practice sermons in 1827–8 were continually criticized for their complete dependence on Schelling's philosophy and insistence that the experience of the absolute's direct presence in the act of intellectual intuition was a more adequate foundation for Christian faith than the authority of the Bible.[106] The mystical enthusiasms of Strauss and his classmates were encouraged by one of Schelling's disciples – the philosopher C. A. Eschenmayer – who taught at the University of Tübingen. Eschenmayer introduced his band of youthful believers to the wonders of animal magnetism, clairvoyance, somnambulism, and other occult phenomena that demonstrated the presence of the spirit in the "night side" of nature. In 1827, Strauss made a pilgrimage to the home of the poet and mesmerist Justinus Kerner in order to meet the famous "Seeress of Prevost." His contact with this woman was a shattering experience. "As I gave her my hand," he claimed, "I felt as if the floor had been pulled out from under me and I was sinking into a bottomless void."[107] Convinced that he had made direct contact with the supernatural world and actually "heard the spirit," Strauss now possessed "such a rigorous supernatural faith as only the prophets or apostles had possessed before." "The miraculous," he claimed, "was no longer something for which we yearned, but became our living present . . . the element in which we moved."[108]

For Strauss and his classmates, as for Rosenkranz, however, this "absolute mysticism" did not prove powerful enough to withstand the test of time. The ecstatic experiences became fewer and fainter and the search for a more durable and objective foundation for ontological security more pronounced. The shift to a "new spiritual ground from which the land of clairvoyance, magic, and spiritual sympathy . . . had to appear as though placed on its head" was mediated through a study of Schleiermacher's writings.[109] That Strauss and his friends, unlike Rosenkranz, experienced Schleiermacher as a demystifier, as a critical scholar who relegated their previous belief in the supernatural to the status of an immature, self-alienated stage of consciousness, was due in large part to the fact that they first encountered Schleiermacher in the classroom of Ferdinand Christian Baur (1792–1860).

Baur was one of the two professors who guided Strauss's class through the years of preparatory school at Blaubeuren between 1821 and 1825. During these years he worked out his own position in opposition to the reigning "natural supernaturalism" and in 1824–5 published a massive study of the ancient religions in which he applied Schelling's conceptions of myth and symbol and Schleiermacher's conception of religious experience to the historical evolution of religious consciousness.[110] Baur maintained a critical distance from his Romantic mentors, however, and emphasized the need for a more objective and methodical comprehension of the evolving relationship between finite and infinite being in religious history.[111] Although he shared his ideas and ideals with his young students at Blaubeuren, they were not fully appropriated by Strauss's class until they began a systematic study of Christian history and theology under his guidance in 1828–9. For Strauss, as for Rosenkranz, disillusionment with the subjectivity of the Romantic standpoint was a prerequisite for the laborious appropriation of a more scholarly and "scientific" resolution of the problems of religious consciousness.[112]

Both Baur and his students eventually resolved what they perceived as basic contradictions in the Romantic viewpoint by moving on to Hegel. In this case, however, the students preceded their teacher. Stimulated by the lectures of a teaching fellow who had studied under Marheineke, Strauss, Binder, and Märklin began to meet in a weekly study group on Hegel's *Phenomenology* in the summer of 1829. The zeal and earnestness that they brought to their study of Hegel revealed how ready they were for his solution to the disease of Romantic subjectivity. Within a few months they had become converts, convinced that they had attained the standpoint of absolute knowledge that resolved the contradictions of Romantic consciousness.[113] This conversion also resolved a very practical question for Strauss and his friends, for the Hegelian doctrine of the identity of content and difference of form in religion and philosophy appeared to provide a means of reconciling their inner convictions with their chosen careers as clerics and theologians.[114]

The impact of Hegelian conversion as a justification for cultural accommodation was most striking in Strauss's case. He threw himself into his studies with a new enthusiasm and graduated at the top of his class in 1830. His essays and sermons no longer brought reprimands from the faculty. In the homiletics examination of 1830, which was given by one of the most conservative theologians at the *Stift,* Strauss received special commendation for his simple, orthodox, and clearly conceptualized sermons.[115] In June of the same year he was chosen by the faculty to preach a sermon at the tricentennial celebration of the Confession of Augsburg. Hegel had helped him find both inner spiritual peace and acceptance in his cultural environment.

The year after Strauss's graduation from Tübingen was a year of apprenticeship in his chosen vocation as minister of the church and Christian theologian. For eight months (until the end of May 1831) he held the position of assistant vicar in Klein Ingersheim, a small village parish with approximately four hundred members. The head vicar was old and sickly; so Strauss took over most of the pastoral duties: preaching on Sunday mornings, teaching catechism classes, and giving a course in religious instruction in the local Latin school. In June 1831 he was transferred to the lower seminary or *Klosterschule* at Maulbronn, where he worked as a teaching fellow during the summer semester. The duties of both positions were not particularly time-consuming, and Strauss found free time to continue his studies in philosophy and theology. He subscribed to the *Jahrbücher für wissenschaftliche Kritik* and worked his way through Hegel's *Logic*. In November 1830 he cheerfully informed Märklin that he had become adept as an alchemist at transforming Being into Nothing, and Nothing back into Being.[116]

During the winter of 1830–1, Strauss was engaged in the process of testing the validity of the Hegelian conception of the identity of content in the different forms of *Vorstellung* and *Begriff* on two levels. In his practical activity as the vicar of a village congregation he was forced to ask himself if his own philosophical Christianity was really compatible with the traditional faith of his parishioners. Could he preach and teach in the language of the religious *Vorstellung* with an honest conviction that such activity merely represented the expression of his inner philosophical convictions in a different form? This practical question was inextricably connected to a theoretical, theological problem. As Strauss expanded his knowledge of Hegel's philosophy during the winter of 1830–1, he became increasingly skeptical of its compatibility with the dogmas of the established Protestant church. By the spring of 1831 obvious tensions had arisen within the Hegelian identity.

The relationship between his own Hegelian theology and the traditional faith of his parishioners does not seem to have bothered Strauss during the first months at Klein Ingersheim. In November he wrote to Märklin, who was in a similar position, that his congregation treated him with friendliness and respect and that he felt quite content in his new position.[117] The sermon he delivered on November 21, 1830, revealed no signs of Hegelian speculation, but was couched in the "representational" language of traditional Christian piety.[118] It was Märklin who first raised the question of the possible hypocrisy and dishonesty involved in delivering such sermons. Strauss tried to assure Märklin that he need have no conscience scruples about preaching in the language of orthodox faith. But the reasons he gave for this view revealed that the identity of the speculative philosophical truth of the intellectual and the representational truth of the ordinary Christian was not unproblematical in his own mind.

Strauss accepted Märklin's view that the difference between *Vorstellung* and *Begriff* was not merely a difference in language, in expression; it also represented a significant difference in understanding, knowledge, consciousness. But this division, Strauss claimed, must be accepted as a "historical necessity." They were living in a time when a small segment of the population had advanced beyond the general community in its understanding of the Christian truth. But this did not mean that the members of this intellectual elite should break off their connections with that general community. Such a response would be nothing less than an "arrogant act of excommunication." As servants and teachers of the historical Christian community they could not simply abandon their duties or throw the common folk into confusion and despair by demanding that the latter accept the philosophical version of the Christian truth. A retreat to the orthodox faith on their own part was also impossible. There was only one rational response to the situation: to continue to speak to the common people in the language they could understand. One might also hope for a gradual increase in the general level of understanding, but Strauss warned Märklin that the individual could not take upon himself the responsibility of reforming the communal consciousness. One must conform to "the nature of things, the course of events, the spirit of the times," and for Strauss this clearly meant that "the individual servant of the church cannot arbitrarily undertake the reform of the representational form of religion into the concept, but must wait for the church and in the meantime teach according to its representation."[119]

A few months later, Strauss was more optimistic about the possibilities of overcoming the division between the intellectual or "cleric (*der Geistliche*)" and his congregation. "We can see that the people, generally considered, are undeniably involved in a movement from the mere representation to the concept," he wrote to Märklin in February 1831. The task of the intellectual elite in such a situation was to "further this development of popular religion toward the elements of the concept." They could do this by "allowing the concept to shine through the representation as much as possible, and translating those representations that the people were ready to grasp in spiritual terms into ideas."[120] A month later he gave even more specific advice to another of his former classmates, Gustav Binder:

> We intellectuals, who at least have the duty of bringing the people closer to the conceptual stage of religion, can drop those representations that the people no longer need (the devil, etc.), but in the case of those that the people cannot live without (eschatology, etc.), we should allow the conceptual meaning to shine through the representation as much as possible.[121]

Throughout this whole discussion with his friends, however, Strauss continued to insist on the intellectual's duty to conform to the general consciousness of the Christian community. The demand for absolute honesty and integrity vis-à-vis the church was a sign of self-indulgence and arrogance. But there was certainly also a good deal of arrogance, or at least a consciousness of intellectual superiority, in Strauss's position. Both he and Märklin identified the Christianity of faith and the language of representation with either a former historical period or the uneducated popular consciousness – in any case, with a "lower" form of understanding. It is thus understandable that Strauss did not think that the compromise between philosophical understanding and the traditional faith, which was a historical necessity in relationship to the general Christian community, was a necessity in the realm of theological interpretation. Within the intellectual elite the battle for the dominance of the *Begriff* should be fought with complete integrity.[122] It was on this theological level that Strauss's growing discontent with the Hegelian reconciliation of concept and representation was most evident in the winter of 1830–1.

Strauss first expressed this discontent in a letter to Ludwig Georgii on January 1, 1831. The only theology that he found satisfactory, he claimed, was one with philosophical content, and the only satisfactory philosophical content was that provided in Hegel's philosophy. Existing attempts to "grasp" the theology of the established Protestant church as philosophical truth, such as Marheineke's, however, Strauss found "highly imperfect." The contradictions within the representational form were not honestly analyzed, and thus the construction of the identity was deceptively easy. The task of proving the identity between the dogmas of faith and the truths of philosophy had not yet been successfully accomplished. Moreover, Strauss was convinced that such a "proof" would involve a much greater emphasis on the stage of negation of traditional dogma, on the destructive criticism that preceded the elevation to unity in the concept.[123] In the spring of 1831, Strauss received an opportunity to expound his conception of the manner in which the representations of Christian dogma could be transformed or grasped through the philosophical concept in an essay required of all young vicars of the Württemberg church who had not yet been assigned to permanent positions. Strauss's paper, entitled "The Doctrine of the Return of All Things in Its Religious-Historical Development," was written in April and May 1831 and was to serve as his doctoral dissertation in October of the same year.[124]

Although Strauss's dissertation was only thirty pages long, his topic was formidably all encompassing. His main aim was to describe the historical development of the idea of the "return of all things" from the religions of ancient India to contemporary Hegelian philosophy. Moreover, he equated this idea with the general doctrine of eschatological fulfillment. And finally, he defined the eschatological problem as the basic content of religion. "Religion," he claimed, was in its "most general sense" the "relation posited (*gesetzt*) in consciousness between the divine and the human, the finite and the infinite." This relationship was one of opposed, contradictory principles, and the task that all religions set themselves was to overcome this contradiction. The aim of religion was thus to bring man back to his original or primal unity with the Godhead.[125]

Strauss's description of the historical development of this basic religious doctrine had two fundamental characteristics. First of all, he claimed to discern a "most gratifying progress" in man's understanding of the relationship between the divine and the human, the finite and infinite. The religious consciousness of man had become progressively "richer and more concrete."[126] In the ancient religions the resolution of the contradictions between the divine and human had been conceived in terms of a subordination of one principle to the other. In Christianity, however, an attempt was made to describe the ultimate unity as a unity within differentiation, as a unity in which the reality of both the human and the divine was affirmed. Strauss viewed this progress essentially as a progress in understanding, in knowledge. Religious consciousness was conceived in basically cognitive terms, as a lower form of philosophy. Strauss did not try to make a distinction between religious experience and philosophical comprehension, and thus he excluded, virtually by definition, the possibility of religious faith and philosophical knowledge existing in the same person at the same time.

The second salient characteristic of Strauss's analysis was closely related to this view of religious development as a progress in knowledge. The evolution of man's knowledge of eschatological fulfillment was a process in which a transcendent, objectified, representational viewpoint was transformed into an immanent, subjectively appropriated, and conceptually expressed viewpoint. From the standpoint of traditional faith, eschatological fulfillment was seen as a transcendent, future state. From the standpoint of modern philosophical understanding, eschatological fulfillment was an immanent present condition. The resolution of the contradictions within the religious consciousness was grasped within present earthly existence, not postponed to some heavenly future.[127]

The attempt to describe the whole history of mankind's religious development from this perspective in thirty pages naturally led to a cursory survey based largely on a few secondary sources. Strauss's dependence on a few works of Hegel and Baur and his generally slipshod scholarship have recently been emphasized.[128] It was only when Strauss arrived at Schleiermacher's modern discussion of the eschatological problem that he engaged in a systematic analysis of primary source material. Schleiermacher's position was important to Strauss because it contained both of the major eschatological viewpoints of his own time in an unresolved tension. In some passages, Schleiermacher appeared to hold the view that the union of the divine and the human was a present condition revealed in the state of pious feeling. Because this experience of achieved eternity did not have the assurance of absolute knowledge, however, Schleiermacher often reverted to the orthodox Christian eschatology of a personal heavenly immortality after death.[129]

The dualism in Schleiermacher's theology, however, was resolved in Hegel's philosophy. The contradictions between the finite and infinite that characterized the experience of religious feeling were overcome in the elevation to philosophical knowledge. Hegel's philosophy, Strauss claimed, "is the return of all things."[130] The dissertation concluded with the statement that "modern Christian philosophy overcomes the contradictions of existence without postponement or hypotheses, and does not point to a reconciled future beyond the contradictory present, but recognizes the allegedly contradictory present as itself without contradiction."[131]

It is important to note that Strauss did not see the content of the philosophical reconciliation as simply a different form of the reconciliation already achieved in religious consciousness. "Hegel denies, and rightly so," Strauss claimed, "that religion itself can already provide the spirit with a present resolution of the contradictions of its pious consciousness."[132] Strauss thus stressed the necessity of moving from the representational consciousness of religion to the philosophical *Begriff*. To remain in the old forms of understanding was the sign of a "lazy reason," which hoped to escape from the responsibility of resolving the contradictions of existence within the present life.[133] This transition from the epistemological stage of representation to that of the concept was crucial in Strauss's view because of its ethical implications. In traditional Christian faith, evil was objectified as an evil being, and the process of judgment was made into an external event that divided the saved and the damned. The religious intolerance that caused so much division and conflict in the world was thus a corollary of the religious mode of conceiving the problem of evil.[134] But such major differences between the two viewpoints were very difficult to reconcile with the fundamental position that religion and philosophy merely differed in form and not in essential content. It was thus not surprising that

Strauss wrote to Märklin on May 31, 1831, that they should spend the next year in Berlin in order to "be initiated in the mysteries of science (*Wissenschaft*)." The Hegelian identity had to be rethought and reworked. This task could not be delayed. If they attempted to postpone the resolution of the tensions in their theological positions for another year, it might have become "too late," not only in terms of their career responsibilities, Strauss asserted, "but for our lives, my friend."[135] Ludwig Feuerbach, who had made a pilgrimage to Berlin in 1824 for similar reasons, might have advised Strauss, on the basis of his own experience, that it was already "too late" to reconstruct the Hegelian reconciliation of Christian religion and modern philosophy.

LUDWIG FEUERBACH AND THE HISTORICAL TRANSCENDENCE OF CHRISTIAN CULTURE

In contrast to Rosenkranz and Strauss, Ludwig Feuerbach experienced the conversion to Hegel's philosophical viewpoint as a radical break with both the form and the content of Christian religion and culture. For Feuerbach the speculative comprehension of the inner spiritual meaning of the representational forms of Christian dogma and history was at the same time a comprehension of the historical limitations, the philosophical, existential, and cultural inadequacies, of the Christian world view. Hegel's philosophy was interpreted not as the final, "highest" stage of Christian culture, as the self-comprehending completion of the historical process initiated by the Christian incarnation, but as a breakthrough to a new understanding and experience of man, nature, and God, as the prophetic conceptualization of a new period of human development, of a post-Christian cultural era. Why did Feuerbach appropriate the Hegelian message in this fashion? What were the theoretical and practical consequences of such an appropriation? These two questions will function as guidelines in our attempt to reconstruct the particular character of Feuerbach's Hegelianism during the 1820s.

In 1840, when Feuerbach jotted down a few reflections on the role the "relationship to Hegel" had played in his intellectual evolution, he noted that it was "a great error" to date the beginnings of the "characteristic essence" of a thinker from the time of his university studies. "The birth certificate precedes matriculation, man is a member of the human community before he becomes a member of a university," he claimed. "How can one then ignore this past?"[136] It is only in recent years, however, that serious attempts have been made to follow Feuerbach's advice and uncover the formative experiences that influenced the character of his philosophical commitments during his university years. Moreover, these studies of the presuppositions of Feuerbach's Hegel reception have focused almost exclusively on the definition of the teenage religious experience that Feuerbach claimed gave the first "decisive direction" to his life.[137] But Feuerbach also noted that his youthful religiosity should not be equated with the inheritance of cultural values he had absorbed from his family, teachers, and social milieu; it had originated in a subjective "need" for a "certain something (*einem Etwas*)" that his environment was unable to provide.[138] The starting point of Feuerbach's intellectual development, the fundamental presupposition of his eventual conversion to Hegelianism, was his disillusionment with and emancipation from the cultural world in which he had become a member on the basis of his birth certificate. For his birth in the "dog days" of late July 1804, as the fourth son of a Protestant professor of jurisprudence at the Catholic Bavarian University of Landshut, made him a member not only of the universal "community of humanity" but also of a particular family, generation, social grouping, and historical community that delimited the boundaries of his "human" experience and the nature of his cultural inheritance.

For Feuerbach the first, most decisive, and most powerful incarnation of this cultural inheritance was his own father. In order to adopt Hegel as his "second father"[139] he had first to free himself from not only the personal domination but also the cultural outlook of his first father. This emancipation was a lengthy, difficult, and conflict-ridden process, for Feuerbach's father was not the kind of man who would allow himself to be displaced, or relegated to the position of a historical anachronism, without a fierce battle. (Paul Johann) Anselm von Feuerbach (1775–1833) was one of the most brilliant and passionate (his friends called him Vesuvius) representatives of the rational humanism and ethical idealism that characterized the academic and bureaucratic reformers of the Napoleonic era.[140] His intellectual outlook had been formed by the Kantianism taught by Reinhold and the young Fichte at Jena during the early 1790s, and in his first writings he had applied this outlook to problems of criminology and legal reform with a dazzlingly precocious intellectual penetration and ethical fervor that brought him almost immediate national recognition and numerous academic offers. When he accepted an invitation from Landshut in 1803 he became the first north German Protestant intellectual to throw in his lot with the Bavarian reform administration of Count Maximilian von Montgelas. By the fall of 1805 he had moved his growing family into the royal residence in Munich, where they resided for eight years while he completed a pathbreaking revision and codification of the Bavarian penal code. Although Anselm Feuerbach was knighted for his services, his passionate advocacy of civil equality and political liberalism had made his position at the Bavarian court extremely precarious by the time the new code was promulgated in 1813. Like so many other liberal reformers, he fell victim to the combined powers of ecclesiastical and aristocratic conservatism and political authoritarianism in the post-Napoleonic period. In 1814 he was removed from the center of political influence by "prómotion" to the vice-presidency of the appellate court in Bamberg. But he would not resign himself to historical irrelevance and continued to oppose vehemently the political and religious forces whose apparent triumph he could see only as a historical regression.[141] During Ludwig's teenage years, Anselm Feuerbach's public activity was especially focused on a defense of the traditions and institutions of liberal Protestantism in Bavaria against both the hegemonial ambitions of a resurgent Catholic church and the inward "corruption" of an obscurantist and populist pietism purveyed by "awakened" preachers within the Protestant community.[142]

What did it mean for Ludwig Feuerbach to be the son of this particular father? In the most general social terms it meant, first of all, that he considered his eventual membership in the German academic-bureaucratic elite as his birthright and inevitable fate. There seemed to be no question that he and his four brothers would attend gymnasium and university and then take up academic, bureaucratic, or perhaps ecclesiastical careers. Their struggles to find satisfactory personal and cultural identities took place within the horizons of the world of the traditional educated estate. The perception of this world that Feuerbach gained through his early experiences, however, was both peculiarly abstract and narrowly personal. Anselm Feuerbach was a Protestant "foreigner" without family ties or traditional roots in Bavaria. Moreover, during the first thirteen years of Ludwig's life his family changed its place of residence four times. The sense of financial security and social superiority that Feuerbach inherited as the son of a man of importance was offset by the feeling of rootlessness that he experienced as the son of an itinerant intellectual whose communal ties were peculiarly ideal and general, finding concrete expression primarily in a cosmopolitan circle of like-minded intellectuals scattered throughout the intellectual centers of Germany. These factors may help to explain why Feuerbach's early social and cultural experience was defined so exclusively by his relationship to the members of his own family. His primary companions from his own generation throughout his childhood and youth were his own brothers; his major, and virtually exclusive, cultural role model from the older generation was his father. In Feuerbach's experience the postwar tension between different historical generations within the German educated estate was indistinguishable from the personal tension between father and son.

Although the tensions in the Feuerbach family were a reflection of more general cultural changes, they were also exacerbated by a number of personal factors. As Anselm Feuerbach's public influence declined in the years after 1813, he became increasingly concerned that his ethical principles and cultural stance should at least not be betrayed by his own sons. He watched over their educational development with an overbearing concern and was quite willing to use all of his considerable powers of persuasion to keep them free of the various forms of the Romantic "disease": excessive indulgence in psychological self-reflection, cynical withdrawal from life's practical tasks and duties, surrender to the illusory consolations of mystical metaphysics or superstitious religion.[143] The sons admired their father and sought his approval for their intellectual commitments and career choices, but they could not help resenting his rejection of the validity of their own experiences and his desire to make them over in his own image. Two of Ludwig's older brothers, following the general tendency within their own generation, had displayed a deep interest in the new Romantic trends in theology and natural science, but they were unable to withstand their father's opposition and unwilling to risk his disapproval and the possibility of disinheritance. Both eventually abandoned their original career choices and surrendered to the paternal will.[144]

As in the experiences of Rosenkranz and Strauss, the tension between father and son in the Feuerbach family was complicated by parental conflict. In 1813, Anselm Feuerbach had begun a serious affair with Nanette Brunner, the wife of one of his closest friends. In 1815 she bore him a son and in 1816 the Feuerbachs agreed on a formal separation. When Anselm Feuerbach was appointed president of the appellate court in Ansbach in 1817, he established a new household with his mistress and left his wife and daughters in Bamberg. Ludwig and two of his brothers were moved into an apartment near their father's residence so that he could continue to supervise their education. This division of the family lasted until 1822, after Nanette Brunner's death. Feuerbach's letters to his mother from this period reveal how deeply his emotional life was affected by the long separation from his mother and sisters. "Oh, how often I have dreamed about you," he wrote in October 1818. "Dear Mother, who knows how it will all turn out?"[145] He made some touchingly childish attempts to reconcile his parents and visited his mother as often as possible. Although Feuerbach's emotional sympathies were clearly on the side of his mother, he did not turn against his father. Whatever hostility and aggression he might have felt was repressed, partly out of fear of his father's wrath,[146] but also because of the ambivalence of his own emotions.[147] It was in the search for a satisfactory resolution of these conflicts and insecurities that Feuerbach turned to religious faith.

The religious stage in Feuerbach's early development can be broken down into two distinct phases. The first phase was characterized by a simple, fervent faith in a benevolent father God who responded to the sincere prayers of his children and had revealed his will in the inspired texts of the Bible. The phrase "Whatever God does is for the best" is repeated like a refrain in Feuerbach's letters to his mother.[148] He clearly found consolation in the conviction that his family's tribulations had a providential significance that would ultimately be revealed. Behind the dubious passions and wrathful countenance of the earthly father, Feuerbach saw the inscrutable but benevolent will of the heavenly father. It was not a mystical spirit of unity with the divine that defined the direction of Feuerbach's early religious experience but a filial trust in and devotion to the service of this "higher" father.[149] All available evidence indicates that Feuerbach committed himself to his religious calling with intense seriousness and incredible zeal. He studied the biblical texts so assiduously that a report of his gymnasium instructor claimed that his knowledge was comparable to that of "many pastors."[150] "The Bible is the book of books and our most precious possession," he wrote to his mother, "for only the Bible can make us happy, blessed, and at peace with ourselves."[151] Feuerbach had every right to point out to his detractors during the 1840s that his criticism of Christianity was not merely based on external knowledge gained through books, but rooted in his own personal experience: he had first known religion as an object of "praxis" before it became an object of theory for him.[152]

The second phase of Feuerbach's youthful religious period was characterized by an increasing tendency to reflect critically on the meaning and basis of his faith, to move toward what he called a "thinking religiosity."[153] During his last two years at the gymnasium his interest in the speculative comprehension of the philosophical truth of Christian dogma had been aroused by the comments of his religion teacher, Theodor Lehmus (1777–1837), who was an enthusiastic proponent of the philosophical theology of Karl Daub. [154] Feuerbach's own earliest forays into speculative interpretation were understandably crude and aroused the skepticism of his schoolmates and critical warnings about the dangers of "mysticism" from some of his teachers.[155] But he persisted in his efforts, and during the year of private study that divided his graduation from the gymnasium and his matriculation in the theological faculty at Heidelberg in 1823, he worked his way carefully through the theological works of Herder, Hamann, Novalis, and Jakob Böhme.[156]

Although Feuerbach's teenage religiosity can be interpreted as a response to the tensions and insecurities of his family situation, it was also in conformity with general trends within his cultural environment. In fact, there is some evidence that his piety was part of a broader immersion in the Christian–German ideology of the patriotic student organizations of the postwar era. He was a member of the Turnverein in Ansbach and he wore the distinctive Old German costume and hairstyle recommended by Jahn. In 1820, Feuerbach and one of his brothers made a pilgrimage to the grave of the "brave" Karl Sand in Mannheim. Some of the grass they tore up from the grave to save as a souvenir of Sand's heroic deed was, interestingly enough, sent to their mother, because, as Feuerbach commented, she shared their love and admiration for this German youth.[157] As late as the fall of 1823, Feuerbach described the religious faith and communal patriotism of the medieval Germans as expressions of a "golden age" that he associated with the wish-fulfilling dreams and fairy tales of childhood and the harmonious beauty of nature. On this occasion as well, these associations were connected to his emotional identification with his mother. The letter in which he described them was sent to her with the admonition that she let no one else read it.[158]

The estrangement from his father implicitly expressed in Feuerbach's religious faith, Old German enthusiasms, and emotional identification with his mother did not become an explicit conflict until after Feuerbach left home in the summer of 1823. On June 16 of that year, Anselm Feuerbach could still write to his son: "You are the kind of person who does not need to hide anything from his father, and a better friend than your father you will not find anywhere."[159] That Feuerbach was in fact able to hide his disagreements with his father for such a long time was due to Anselm Feuerbach's tendency to see the significance of the student movement in terms of his own opposition to the reactionary policies of the German states after 1815 and his interpretation of Feuerbach's "thinking religiosity" as synonymous with his own opposition to the Fundamentalism and superstitious mysticism of the pietist awakening. He agreed to his son's choice of Heidelberg as a place of study because he thought that Ludwig would absorb his own rational and ethical interpretation of Christian doctrine and history there under the tutelage of his personal friend, the Kantian theologian and church historian H. E. G. Paulus.[160] Feuerbach had chosen

Heidelberg, however, in order to continue his initiation into speculative philosophical theology under the guidance of Karl Daub.

By the end of his first semester at Heidelberg, Feuerbach had mustered up enough courage to "alienate" his father and end the dissimulation that had veiled their disagreements. He articulated his filial rebellion in the form of a radical, polemically aggressive assault on the character and viewpoint of the man his father had chosen as the model for a theological vocation. No student seriously devoted to the search for truth, he claimed, could afford to waste his time studying Paulus's vulgar, trivial, and stupid interpretations of Christian doctrine and history. His forced and artificial attempts to provide a naturalistic explanation for every statement in the biblical texts differed from the vulgar opinions expressed in any local tavern only in their "hairsplitting pedantry." All Paulus could offer his students was a frail web of subjective sophistry, a set of arbitrary hypotheses that revealed a total inability to penetrate to the spiritual core of the Christian message. Feuerbach realized that this attack might seem pretentious and arrogant, even "blasphemous," coming as it did from the pen of a *homo novus* in the "state of the academy." But such criticism of his right to an independent judgment, Feuerbach asserted, in a scarcely veiled aggressive assault on his father's projected response, could be made only by those who considered the university a "penitentiary" in which every professor must be treated as a pope on a throne, even if that throne were nothing more than a chamber pot.

Feuerbach's contemptuous denigration of Paulus was complemented by an enthusiastic portrayal of the "magnificent, brilliant Daub" as an alternative vocational model. Unlike Paulus, Daub did not try to impose his arbitrary, personal, subjective opinions on the material or on his students. He was not a "mystic," as both his shallow rationalist critics and narrow-minded orthodox detractors claimed; for he hated the "obscure representational method and indeterminate speculative feelings of the mystic" with a mortal passion. Daub had subordinated his individual personality, his subjective needs and desires, so completely to the objective necessity of truth that he had become a pure organ of "science." In his lectures he "allowed everything to develop out of itself in the clear sunshine of reason." In Feuerbach's view, Daub's self-transcending objectivity provided the only satisfactory model for an academic vocation. The "essence of the academy," its inner purpose and ultimate justification, Feuerbach claimed, was to incarnate the "absolute unity of knowledge with itself in all its relationships, of life with itself, and of both knowledge and life with each other." This goal could be realized only if all members of the university community, both professors and students, subjected their individual opinions to the authority of "science (*Wissenschaft*)." This authority was implicitly present in each person in the form of an "intellectual conscience." The role of the professors was simply to elevate the "immediate" knowledge of their students to the level of self-conscious science. Feuerbach was obviously convinced that Daub had performed this mediating function in his own life. When Feuerbach pronounced judgment on the inadequacies of the subjective rationalism of Paulus and his father, he saw himself not as a rebellious son, or a personal disciple of a particular professor, but as the spokesman for "science" and "reason."[161]

It was through Daub's lectures, Feuerbach claimed, that he was liberated from the limited viewpoint of individual subjectivity and introduced to the "concrete science" in which man "found the eternal, substantial form of his life, truth and reality," in the self-comprehending activity of absolute Reason.[162] But Daub's version of the Hegelian philosophy of identity was unable to satisfy completely "the longing of [Feuerbach's] soul for truth, that is, for decisiveness, unconditionality."[163] After his first semester in Heidelberg, Feuerbach described himself as a "polyp who still wavers in his development between the free total life of knowledge and the merely vegetative life of unconscious representation and opinions,"[164] and after his second semester he still suffered from an "unhappy, indecisive, inwardly divided state of mind."[165] The more he immersed himself in the speculative standpoint the less convincing he found Daub's claim that the content of Christian faith and that of Hegelian science were identical. Was the Hegelian concept of *Vernunft* simply a comprehension of the benevolent heavenly father to whom he had prayed as a teenager, was his new knowledge simply his old faith finally understood? Wasn't his earlier faith an integral component of that "subjectivity" from which speculative science had liberated him? Daub was quite ready to admit that in the final analysis he could not demonstrate the identity of Reason and faith in which he believed and which was the presupposition of his own theological endeavours. He encouraged Feuerbach to seek a resolution under the tutelage of Hegel himself. By the beginning of the spring semester in 1824, Feuerbach was in Berlin.

Feuerbach traveled to Berlin with the hope and expectation that he would experience an epiphany that would end his indecision and inner division. He was not disappointed. A few weeks after his arrival he could report that much of what had seemed obscure, contradictory, arbitrary, or disconnected in Daub's presentation of the speculative viewpoint had been clarified and developed in its "necessity and inner connection" in Hegel's lectures.[166] At the end of his first semester he claimed that the few short months of direct contact with Hegel had "the significance of an eternity" for him and constituted the "turning point" of his "whole life."[167] Through Hegel he had come to "self- and world-consciousness"; his "heart and head" had been "placed back in their proper relationship," and he finally recognized what he "should do" and what he "wanted to do."[168] Berlin had become "the Bethlehem of a new world" for him, the place of his spiritual second birth and entry into the "Kingdom of the Millenium."[169]

For Feuerbach the philosophical understanding that defined his entry into the Kingdom of the Millenium also marked the first step in his emancipation from Christian theology. With the help of the "heavy cross of the concept" and the "thunder and lightning of the dialectic" he had come to realize that Christian dogma could attain the status of rigorous scientific truth only if it was presented as the "divine drama" of "the inner process of God's self-development from the primal ground of abstract essence to the concrete form of self-consciousness, in short, as the logic of God." In the Bible, and thus also in Christian theology that presupposed the absolute validity of the biblical revelation, the Christian "truth" was expressed in the inadequate, unscientific form of a particular historical revelation of a series of external relations among God, men, and nature. This unscientific representational form corresponded to the limited perspective of the "finite consciousness" that had been transcended in Hegel's comprehension of the totality as the dialectical self-development of infinite Reason.[170] Feuerbach thus resolved the apparent contradictions between the theological and scientific or philosophical viewpoints by relegating the former to the status of a limited developmental stage within the all-encompassing perspective of the latter. By the middle of his second semester at Berlin, Feuerbach had drawn the personal consequences of this "dissolution" of the limited theological perspective in the absolute perspective of philosophical science.[171] He abandoned his theological vocation and decided to commit himself to a career in the service of philosophy.

Feuerbach did not claim that his change in vocational choice was a necessary consequence of the historical emergence of the Hegelian speculative science. Other Hegelians, like Daub, might legitimately devote themselves to the important task of mediating between the limited perspectives of a particular discipline like Christian theology and the absolute knowledge of philosophy. His own choice was based on a personal inability to separate his ontological identity from his cultural vocation. He had originally devoted himself to the theological vocation, not just as a congenial career, but as "the form-giving determination of his existence." By the winter of 1824–5, however, theology had ceased to provide him with "the daily bread, the necessary spiritual sustenance" for a meaningful existence. "Palestine," he claimed, "is too narrow for me; I must, I must move out into the wide world, and only philosophy carries it on her shoulders."[172] His "limitless and unconditional" desire to "encompass and devour" everything – God, man, and nature – "not only as an empirical aggregate but as a systematic totality" could be fulfilled only by philosophy. Feuerbach was clearly convinced that he had to abandon his theological career in order to remain faithful to the religious calling that had first led him to theology. For it was only through scientific comprehension of the totality that contemporary man could find the "spiritual satisfaction" his forefathers had secured through religious faith. "Philosophy extends to me the apples of immortality," Feuerbach claimed, "and assures me of the enjoyment of an eternally present blessedness, a harmony with myself." In an important sense, therefore, Feuerbach *did* place theology and philosophy in stark opposition. It was philosophy that defined the criteria of truth, the terms of redemption, the nature of the absolute. Insofar as theology continued to lay claim to these functions it was incompatible with philosophy and deserved destruction, as an outgrown husk of the human spirit. Feuerbach's decision to switch from theology to philosophy was not merely a choice for a particular career; it signified his commitment to a "new world" in which philosophy was defined as man's highest calling and philosophical knowledge expressed man's highest form of "being."[173]

The total character of Feuerbach's commitment to his new vocation was clearly evident in his personal life-style. The ascetic self-discipline and self-denial that had characterized Feuerbach's service to the God of Christian theology was carried over into his new service to the absolute of Hegelian science. In order to become a transparent organ of objective knowledge, in order to attain the status of "absolute, universal man," the philosopher was required to transcend his individual subjective opinions, to deny the diverting, distorting influence of his concrete sensuous desires.[174] The only method of entering the elite circle of immortal philosophers who had attained such self-transcending universality and objectivity was to undertake the labor of the concept, and Feuerbach devoted himself to this labor with such zeal that Daub felt it necessary to remind him that the philosopher's proper stance toward the everyday world of empirical existence was resignation, not contempt.[175] In Berlin, as in Heidelberg, Feuerbach lived almost exclusively in the world of the library, study, and lecture hall. The "work-house" atmosphere at the University of Berlin, he claimed, suited him perfectly. He lived alone, avoided social gatherings, and did not form any close personal friendships, not even among his fellow Hegelians. His empirical individual existence was so totally absorbed in his studies that he did not even suffer from the usual self-conscious hypochondria of the lonely scholar.[176] The desire to transcend the merely "subjective" standpoint was also evident in Feuerbach's political perspective. When he arrived in Berlin in April 1824 he was immediately placed under police investigation because of unwarranted suspicions that he belonged to one of the conspiratorial wings of the *Burschenschaft.* This "regrettable incident" was, Feuerbach claimed, "purely fortuitous" and did not affect his admiration for the "rational, legal freedom" provided by the Prussian state. His former sympathy for the Old German ideology had vanished. He now found it "right and proper" that the state should discipline and control students who continued to demand the realization of such "fanciful whims."[177]

Feuerbach's father was outraged by the actions of the Prussian government in the "regrettable incident" that his son treated with such equanimity, but he was even more upset by the effect of Hegelian philosophy on his son's mental health. When Feuerbach finally informed his father of his decision to become a philosopher (almost two months after he had broken the news to Daub), he pleaded for sympathetic understanding and support:

> Father! Do not turn away angrily from your son; do not refuse your consent. Allow me to enter with joy into the new land that I have conquered under the sweat of my brow, the land in which I am confident I can accomplish something, in which I have the complete conviction of having found satisfaction and peace.[178]

This plea fell on deaf ears. Anselm Feuerbach contemptuously dismissed his son's Hegelian convictions as self-deluding fantasies. The "new land" Ludwig had entered was no "Canaan" of absolute scientific knowledge, but simply the artificially systematized, scientifically dressed up, private world of Hegel's conjectures and subjective opinions on matters in which no genuine knowledge was possible. Although he could not prevent his son from pursuing his "self-chosen fate," he refused to give his consent to such a foolish surrender to the illusions of Hegelian metaphysics. "Do what you want," he wrote, "but do not blame your father in the future when you come to regret your choice." The anger and bitterness with which Anselm Feuerbach responded to his son's Hegelian conversion and choice of a philosophical career was clearly tied to a deep feeling of filial betrayal. The "confusions" of his two older sons, Karl and Anselm, had already caused him more misery than any father should be expected to bear. "And now you, even you, my son Ludwig," he lamented, "from whom I expected so much joy!"[179]

As Feuerbach's father had anticipated, his intense disappointment and opposition did not divert his son from his "self-chosen fate." During the summer semester of 1825 and the winter semester of 1825–6, Feuerbach devoted his intellectual energies almost exclusively to the task of inwardly appropriating the speculative science of the absolute. When financial circumstances[180] forced him to return to Bavaria in the spring of 1826, he was confident that the task of appropriation had been completed. "I am now finished with Hegel," he noted; "with the exception of the Aesthetics, I have attended all of Hegel's lectures, and even heard his Logic twice."[181] Direct personal contact with Hegel himself became superfluous once he had made the Hegelian standpoint his own. As Feuerbach worked on his doctoral dissertation and *Habilitationsschrift* in Ansbach and Erlangen between 1826 and 1828, he did not perceive his intellectual standpoint as that of a "formal" Hegelian or a "Hegelian of the letter." He was not a mere philologist exegizing the Hegelian texts, but a true philosopher, an "organ" of the objective, universal Reason that had found its most perfect and profound contemporary articulation in Hegel's books and lectures.[182] Once Feuerbach was back home in Ansbach his claim that he was an "essential, ideal" Hegelian whose ultimate commitment was to Reason, speculative science, and philosophy per se, rather than to the person of Hegel and the particular words of the Hegelian texts, appears to have mollified his father's anger. Anselm Feuerbach became increasingly reconciled to his son's emancipation from his own tutelage once he was convinced that filial dependence had not simply been replaced by an uncritical surrender to the personal visions of Hegel's philosophy. After reading Ludwig's dissertation he even asserted that it revealed the mind of a "great thinker" who possessed a "more than sufficient portion of philosophical courage and high-spirited self-confidence," qualities that might very well transform Ludwig's "self-chosen fate" into a promising academic career.[183]

The critical component in Feuerbach's Hegelianism that aroused his father's respect and lay behind his own distinction between "formal" and "essential" Hegelianism was first articulated in the form of three "doubts (*Zweifel*)" that Feuerbach jotted down in his notebooks in the winter of 1827–8.[184] These "doubts" about the adequacy of Hegel's particular conception or formulation of the relationship between speculative philosophy and religion, between philosophical comprehension and the present and future, and between thought and being or logic and nature were published by Feuerbach only in 1846, after his break with Hegel, and there has been considerable controversy over their historical authenticity.[185] The tendency of later scholars to doubt Feuerbach's claim that he had major doubts about the Hegelian position in 1827–8, however, has been based on the assumption that an acceptance of the veracity of Feuerbach's statements would necessarily lead to the conclusion that Feuerbach "broke" with Hegel almost immediately after leaving Berlin. But such an assumption is unwarranted. Feuerbach did not think his doubts were inconsistent with an "essential" Hegelianism. His criticisms were internal criticisms, based on what he thought were the fundamental assumptions and methodological principles of the Hegelian system. His doubts defined the character of his Hegelianism, the nature of his philosophical conversion, and were not inconsistent with his other writings in the period between 1828 and 1830: his long letter to Hegel in 1828; his dissertation, "Of Reason, One, Universal and Infinite"; and his *Thoughts on Death and Immortality,* which was published anonymously in the spring of 1830. The authenticity of Feuerbach's "doubts" is demonstrated by the fact that they provided the major themes of his writings during this period; they gave his discipleship a significance and purpose that went beyond the epigonal task of mere exegesis of the Hegelian texts.

It should come as no surprise that one of Feuerbach's three "doubts" focused on the question, How is philosophy related to religion?[186] This question had been at the center of Feuerbach's intellectual concerns since his earliest contact with the speculative theology of Lehmus and Daub. By 1828 he had become convinced that the inner divisiveness that had prompted his abandonment of theology for philosophy was connected to an ambiguity with the Hegelian position itself. Hegel had insisted on the agreement between the content of speculative science and the teachings of Christian religion, but he had at the same time relegated religion to a limited "stage in the development of spirit."[187] In a letter to Hegel written in November 1828, a letter that began with an effusive declaration of continuing discipleship, Feuerbach dared to question both of Hegel's apparently contradictory conceptions of the relationship between philosophy and religion. The attempt to comprehend Christianity as the "perfect and absolute religion," he claimed, was destined to fail. The teachings and symbols of the Christian religion did not contain the truth of Reason as a self-comprehending totality in representational form, but articulated the viewpoint of the subjective and dualistic philosophies that had reigned in western culture from the time of the decline of ancient civilization to the contemporary speculative revolution. "Christianity," Feuerbach insisted, "is nothing more than the religion of the pure self, of the person as the only spirit that is, and is thus merely the antithesis of the ancient world." In contrast to Hegelian philosophy, Christianity left those aspects of reality that constituted the "other" for the subjective ego – "nature, the world, and spirit" – uncomprehended and thus unredeemed.[188] The perception of this radical and obvious difference in "content" between Christianity and Hegelian philosophy led Feuerbach to suggest a more general revision of the Hegelian conception of the relationship between philosophy and religion. Religion should be conceived not as a "stage" in the development toward philosophical comprehension, but as the "immediate presence" in concrete collective human life of a determinate philosophical viewpoint. Philosophical transformations were the "ground and root" of religious transformations. All religions were simply cultural expressions, expansions into "appearance," incarnations in "existence (*Dasein*)" of modes of philosophical thought.[189] In this sense an authentic religious expression of Hegel's philosophical viewpoint did not yet exist.

Although the claim that Christianity was the religious expression of the philosophical principle of subjective egoism was implicit in the philosophical analysis of Feuerbach's dissertation, it was fully developed and explicated only in the discussion of the doctrine of the immortality of the soul that provided the focus for his *Thoughts.* In the ancient world, Feuerbach claimed, immortality was conceived and experienced in a totally immanent fashion. The individual Greek or Roman achieved his immortal, universal "essence" through identification with his historical community, his "state" and his "people," and thus did not feel any need to denigrate the concrete limitations of terrestial existence and construct or posit the ideal of an autonomous, essential self that transcended the determinations of communal life. It was only with the disintegration of the classical Greek and Roman communities and the triumph of Christian culture that the idea of a personal immortality of the soul beyond the temporal and spatial conditions of earthly life became "a universal article of faith and doctrine." During the Catholic Middle Ages, however, the belief in individual immortality was not the decisive characteristic of Christian consciousness; the medieval Christian experienced the realization of his essence (i.e., salvation) as an elevation and incorporation into the "holy community of the faithful," into the "real, supersensual order" of the church. The human essence had been spiritualized, differentiated from the merely natural and social existence of the individual, but it remained communal, experientially present, and thus, at least to a certain extent, "real." The implicit individualism in the Christian doctrines of personal immortality and a personal transcendent God became the explicit and dominant characteristic of Christian culture only in the "modern" period. Since the Reformation, Feuerbach claimed, Christianity had increasingly revealed itself as a religious viewpoint in which "the person as person, and therefore the single human individual for himself and in his individuality, was recognized as divine and infinite." The rational individualism, ethical idealism, and deism of the *Aufklärung* were for Feuerbach, not the antithesis of Christian culture, but its authentic expression.[190] The cultural standpoint that he so vehemently attacked as the "Christian" religion of the "pure self" was revealed, in this schematic historical sketch, as indistinguishable from the world view of his own father. In the Kantian "rationalism" and "moralism" of his father's generation the doctrine of personal immortality became the decisive principle of Christian consciousness, unveiling the subjective egoism implicit in the Christian representations that portrayed the absolute in personal terms.

The historical incarnation of the Christian principle of subjective egoism in contemporary culture, Feuerbach argued, was made clearly evident by the fact that it had become the presupposition that defined the boundaries of human experience, the unexamined a priori according to which contemporary men constituted their world. By presupposing that "pure naked personality" was the infinite and divine essence of man, a radical disjuncture was created between man's essence and existence. As a concrete existing individual, man was forced to recognize that his "I," his "personality" or subjectivity, was not "pure" or absolute, but necessarily limited and conditioned by natural and sociohistorical reality. He could perceive his essence no longer as a realizable present possibility but only as a transcendent ideal attainable in the "higher" reality of a future life in the "beyond." This bifurcation of human experience into a meaningless immanent existence and an empty or ideal transcendent essence had obvious ethical implications. The moral obligation to determine one's actions in accordance with the unconditional dictates of the "pure self," the absolute subject, was impossible to fulfill. The very natural and sociohistorical conditions that defined human existence made virtue or perfection an unattainable ideal. The conditions of concrete life, of actual existence in the here and now, were defined as faults, as inadequacies, as sin. In the Christian moral universe, man was guilty simply because he existed. Finally, Feuerbach thought the triumph of Christian culture was expressed in the general skepticism concerning man's ability to attain a reconciling comprehension of nature, mankind or spirit, and God. Because the categories of essence, reality, universality, unity, and infinitude were attached to the pure self, the subjective ego, the totality of the world outside this ego was perceived as a shadowy, unreal, impenetrable, meaningless series of "others." But the self without the "other" was simply an act of negation. Human existence within Christian culture was characterized by a double emptiness, a "double nothing," a subject without substance and a substance without meaning. It was out of this dual impoverishment that Christian man created the ideal transcendent world of the absolute subject that he hoped to enter once his travail in "reality" was completed.[191]

For Feuerbach, therefore, the fundamental presuppositions of Christian culture were in direct opposition to the viewpoint of Hegel's philosophy. Christianity denied the real presence of the universal in nature and history; it was a cultural expression of the bifurcation of the world into subject and object that Hegel's philosophy had overcome. The speculative revolution in philosophy did not articulate the inner truth of Christian faith, but pronounced historical judgment on the "double nothing" of the Christian philosophy of subjective individualism.

Feuerbach's conception of the relationship between philosophy and religion as a relationship between pure thought or the Idea and its "realization (*Verwirklichung*)" and "secularization (*Verweltlichung*)" in the world of historical "appearance" and "existence" allowed him to provide his Hegelianism with a future-oriented historical significance. The philosophical task of grasping all of "reality" (God, nature, and spirit) as the dynamic totality of self-comprehending Reason had been completed in Hegel's works. The task that still remained was "to found a Kingdom, the Kingdom of the Idea," to bring the Idea down from "the heaven of its colorless purity, untainted brilliance, blessedness, and unity with itself" and transform it into a "universal, world-historical, manifest point of view," to make the absolute philosophy into an absolute religion "of the reality of the Idea and existent Reason."[192] Feuerbach did not conceive his calling as that of a mere epigone, an exegete of the Hegelian texts, but as that of an active participant in the creative, dynamic development of the "world spirit" that would bring about "a new basis of things, a new history, a second creation."[193] "Our contemporary age," he wrote in the *Thoughts,* "is the keystone (*Schlusstein*) of one great period of humanity and the starting point of a new spiritual life." The Hegelian system was transformed from a comprehension of past history, of concern only to a restricted academic "school," to a prophetic vision of the future, of concern of all "humanity."[194]

The imminent epochal cultural change from Christendom to the Kingdom of the Idea was defined by Feuerbach as a revolution in consciousness, as a radical transformation of the basic presuppositions or categories that define man's perception of himself, nature, culture, and God. The realm in which the Idea needed to be realized was the subjective consciousness of those (the clear majority) whose conception of the world was still determined by the "Christian" standpoint of the individual ego or the "pure self." Mere popularization or the translation of Hegelian concepts into "pictures" and "signs," Feuerbach claimed, would not bring about the desired transformation of consciousness. What was required was a critical application of the Hegelian viewpoint to previous conceptions of "time, death, transcendence, immanence, the ego, the individual, the person and . . . God, etc." Critical theory applied to the various "perceptual modes (*Anschauungsweisen*)" of Christian culture was the only valid path to practical change. It seemed "obvious" to Feuerbach that

> when the ego, the self (together with the infinite number of things connected with it), as the absolutely secure, as the universal and determining principle of the world . . . is overcome through knowledge, it will disappear from perception by itself, that the self will cease to be what it was previously; indeed, that it will die.[195]

The "essential being (*wesentliche Sein*) of an individual," he insisted, was the "mode of his thinking" for

> his mode of feeling, sensation, and action, the rest of his being in general, depends on and is determined by his thought. The way in which thinking represents the world is also the way the world is for it, and how and what the world is for thinking, it is also in itself.[196]

The revolutionary task of philosophy after Hegel was to change the world by changing the concrete individual's subjective perception of the world.

In his dissertation, Feuerbach applied the Hegelian viewpoint to the general problem of the relationship between man's individual concrete or sensuous existence and his universal, infinite, and divine essence. Insofar as man was merely a sensuous being, a perceiving and feeling body, he remained locked in the circle of his individuality. The immediacy of sensuous perception and of feelings like joy and suffering, Feuerbach claimed, could not be communicated to others. Even within the realm of sensuous immediacy and particularity, however, Feuerbach discerned signs of man's ultimate unity: "There exists in man an irresistible and indestructible drive toward unity with the other from whom he is separated by nature. He seeks the other, he needs him, he is driven by a mysterious life-force to love him; yes, he cannot even exist without the other."[197] The natural drive toward unity, however, could attain realization only when the limitations of concrete individuality and sensuous estrangement were overcome through the shared structures of thought and language. "Insofar as I think," Feuerbach asserted, "I cease to be an individual, for thought and universality are one and the same."[198] Individuals who, as sensuous beings, were as impenetrable to one another as solid bodies became transparent to one another in thought. In every act of thought the individual realized his universal essence, existed as a "species being (*Gattungswesen*)," as universal man. "The essence of man is the same as the absolute unity of humanity," Feuerbach stated, "but this essence consists in thinking; therefore in thinking I elevate myself to absolute unity with all men."[199]

The constantly reiterated theme of Feuerbach's dissertation was the actual presence of infinite Reason, the incarnation of the "pure Logos" in man insofar as he was engaged in the activity of thinking, that is, insofar as he was a "spiritual" or cultural being. Man was not born with Reason; thinking activity was not a mere attribute or faculty of the individual. An individual person could never realize his essence, become a thinking being, on his own. Thinking was synonymous with the elimination of individuality, with absorption into the already existing universality of the species.[200] The great sin of "self-consciousness" or subjective egoism was the denial of the objective universality of Reason; it "broke" the unity of mankind by defining rational thought as a mere attribute of the individual ego.[201] From the perspective of subjective egoism the essence of man was understood not as the real and present unity of all men in the infinite totality of Reason, but as an abstract concept, an idealized absolute ego set over against the fragmented reality of finite individual egos. What is most striking about this argument is Feuerbach's transformation of the Hegelian conception of the absolute as a dynamic dialectical unity within differentiation into a dualistic "either/or" between sensuous individuality and rational, undifferentiated unity. This was clearly expressed in Feuerbach's formulation of Hegelian ethics in terms of a categorical imperative: Act according to what you are in thought.[202] The incarnation of the absolute in human culture, the transition from nature to culture, demanded, in Feuerbach's view, the elimination of the individual, who was inextricably bound to the realm of sensuality. The desire for unconditional unity and decisiveness that Feuerbach described as the primary motivation for his switch from theology to philosophy was thus also mirrored in his philosophical interpretation of Hegel. The standpoint of the autonomous subject was conceived not as a necessary Moment within the dialectical unity of spirit but as a mere residue of that sensuous immediacy, that unmediated otherness which had to be eliminated before the Kingdom of the Idea could be established on earth.

Feuerbach appears to have been self-consciously aware of his inability to provide an adequate account in his dissertation of the reconciliation of the individual and the universal. At least he noted in a letter to a Professor Harless at Erlangen that he had failed to demonstrate clearly the necessary development from self-consciousness to the universality of thought.[203] But this weakness was not merely due to intellectual immaturity or a lack of philosophical acumen. Feuerbach clearly did not believe that the standpoint of absolute Reason was simply a self-comprehension of the development from the immediacy of sensuous perception to the subject–object dualism of self-consciousness. Hegel's idea of Reason was not the fulfillment of this development but its antithesis. Both Feuerbach's reasons for holding this position and the manner in which he hoped to resolve the difficulties it created were revealed in his *Thoughts.*

We have already noted that Feuerbach's total rejection of Christianity as the religion of the pure self led him to view the historical development of western culture as a process of decline, as an accelerating "fall" away from the truth of "the universal, the whole, the truly real and essential."[204] His historical optimism was based not on a recognition of the progressive realization of Reason in history but on the belief that western man's historical experience had finally led to a dead end of total skepticism and ontological insecurity from which he could be rescued only by a recognition of the unity, universality, and reality of Reason. But if history could no longer be construed as the progressive revelation and actualization of Reason, where was contemporary man to find his saving comprehension of the unity of Reason and reality? In the *Thoughts,* Feuerbach gave an answer to this question that was to prove decisive for his future development: in nature. Nature was no longer simply identified with the sphere of individuality and finitude, but described as a living unified organism, a dynamic totality, in which the truth of Reason – the absorption of the finite in the infinite, the dissolution of the individual in the universal – was implicitly and eternally present and actual. One might almost say that Feuerbach had redefined the Hegelian absolute as "nature comprehended" rather than "history comprehended."[205]

Feuerbach's new orientation toward nature was expressed in his virtual obsession with the themes of death and love. A recognition and acceptance of the fact that the complete and final death of every individual existence was a natural necessity, Feuerbach insisted, was the starting point for the actualization of Reason in human consciousness. The free and conscious dissolution of the individual subjective ego in the spiritual activity of ethics, religion, and philosophy was nothing more than a "remembrance," a "restoration," a "coming to consciousness" of the "unconscious, involuntary" absorption of every individual being in the infinite totality of the natural cosmos.[206] "Natural death," Feuerbach claimed, "like your thoughtful surrender to, and absorption in, God has one common root and source – the original, essential, preconscious and supraconscious submergence and dissolution in God."[207] Death was the supreme revelation of the inescapable finitude of all *Dasein*. Every individual being was merely the embodiment of its negations, of the limitations and differentiations that separated it in space and time from other individual beings. As the universal principle of negation, death was not merely the end, but the very essence of individual existence; life itself was a constant dying, a continuous process of negation:

> The things and essences that exist outside you, that you differentiate from yourself and do not recognize as identical with your I or self . . . are all limitations, points of negation of your self. As much and as long as other things exist outside you, so much and so long you are not . . . Every tree, every wall, every table against which you strike is at the same time your death, the limit and the end of your existence. In order to make your end present to yourself, you do not first have to visit the graveyard; every snuffbox outside you can make you aware of the coffin of your ego. Every jab in the ribs, every pressure, every collision is a living Memento Mori; the whole of nature is a graveyard of your individuality.[208]

The external "necessity" of the process of negation in nature was transformed into the "free deed" of "inner negation" in man's cultural or spiritual activity. The same "universal spiritual will" revealed itself in the negation of individuality in both nature and culture, but in culture, or the universal consciousness of the human species, this "will" became conscious of itself, attained self-realization.[209] For Feuerbach the constant negation of individuality in both nature and spirit was at the same time an affirmation of the universal, of the infinite activity of life and spirit; dissolution was also "absorption." "Only the shell of death is hard," he insisted, "the kernel is sweet."[210] In death nature revealed itself to be "thoroughly mystical."[211]

This "mystical," "sweet kernel" of death was described by Feuerbach as the infinite activity of love. What appeared to the existing individual as the destructive murderous lust of nature or as the suffering of self-renunciation demanded by culture was actually – that is, from a supraindividual perspective – the "all-consuming," "self-dissolving," "pure activity" of love.[212] Love was not an activity of peaceful reconciliation between the individual and the totality, but a raging, sacrificial "fire" in which all individuality was destroyed. It would be absurd, Feuerbach claimed, to define love as an attribute of the individual subject; individuality and love were antitheses. The individual person as an individual person could not love because the very essence of the act of love was a dissolution of all singularity and particularity:

Insofar as you love, you are no longer there in the relationships and connections with things and people in and through which you previously existed and which alone make up your individual existence. You are no longer there in your particular interests, in your affairs, in the many objects in which you previously were; you are only in the one who is the object of your love. Everything outside this object is vanity, is nothing; that solid ground on which you otherwise stood has been pulled out from under your feet, you stand on the boundary of complete annihilation, you have sunk down into the ungrounded abyss.[213]

This "ungrounded abyss," this pure nothingness, this absolute negation of individual particularity, however, was at the same time the fullness of being. In the act of love, the individual was absorbed completely in "God," whom Feuerbach defined in terms of love as "both subject and substantive," that is, as the "pure" infinite activity of love in which love and the beloved, subject and object, were one and the same.[214] It was this universal activity of love, implicit or unconscious in nature, that was made explicit, conscious, and thus "real" in Reason. Reason was nature comprehended insofar as it was love comprehended. "Just as he who has experienced love has experienced everything," Feuerbach wrote, "so he who has comprehended love has comprehended everything; comprehend love and you have comprehended God and everything."[215]

Feuerbach's rhapsodic revelation of the inner meaning of death and love was directed polemically against the absolutization of the standpoint of the existing individual in Christian culture, a standpoint in which God, nature, and spirit remained "unredeemed," that is, never lost their impenetrable "otherness." "True religion," Feuerbach claimed, could take the form only of an "authentic and complete surrender to, and absorption in, God."[216] By perceiving God in personal terms, Christianity denied the authentic religiosity, the dissolution of the individual in the universal, that the experiences of death and love made actual to man in his daily activity as a natural and cultural being. Love and death, properly understood, revealed the actual presence of the absolute (conceived as pure self-relating activity rather than as a thing or a person) in nature and culture. In the post-Christian Kingdom of the Idea, therefore, man would not seek salvation in some transcendent future realm, but "would concentrate his efforts with total heart and soul on himself, on his world, on the present."[217]

Feuerbach conceived the post-Christian cultural vision presented in the *Thoughts* as an incarnation of the "pure Logos," as an attempt to transform the abstractions of Hegelian philosophy into the "perceptual modes" of a "manifest point of view," into a religion of "the reality of the Idea and existent Reason." But like the Schellingian disciples Hegel described in his Jena notebooks, Feuerbach found that as he tried to apply and work out the implications of the Hegelian system, the system itself tended to dissolve in his hands. The antithetical conception of the relationship between individuality and totality that had characterized Feuerbach's dissertation was not overcome in the *Thoughts* but simply extended to include the realms of both nature and spirit. The dialectical mediation between the particular and the universal in the activities of both love and thought culminated in the absolute "death" of the particular and the total victory of the universal. There was no "third stage" in Feuerbach's dialectic, no resurrection or second coming of the individual as a concrete universal; the Hegelian "identity of nonidentity and identity" became simply the victory of identity over nonidentity. This "mystical" conception of the absolute, as well as the attempt to define the unity of Reason and reality primarily as a unity of Reason and nature, suggested a return to the speculative nature philosophy that Hegel had so vehemently rejected in the preface to the *Phenomenology*. Even Feuerbach's rhapsodic hortatory style was not unlike the edifying preaching against which Hegel had defined the laborious science of the concept. It is therefore not surprising that the *Thoughts* was not recognized by members of the Hegelian school as the work of a legitimate Hegelian disciple. It was treated not as an internal revision of Hegel's philosophy, but as a departure from the very essence of the Hegelian position.[218]

Feuerbach was aware that his attempt to "realize" Hegel's philosophy, to incarnate the "pure Logos" in "existence," entailed a revision of some of the basic concepts and relationships of the Hegelian system. Contemporary Hegelianism was the perspective of an academic school within Christian culture, rather than the universal perspective, the "religion," of a post-Christian "humanity," because the dualism of Christian culture was replicated within the Hegelian system itself. Feuerbach's third doubt of 1827–8 was formulated in questions about the validity of the process of reconciliation *within* the Hegelian system. "How is thought related to being, and the Logic to nature? Is the transition from the Logic to nature legitimate?" Feuerbach's answer to the latter question was no. The inner necessity of the progression from being and nothing to the "absolute and perfect Idea" within the realm of pure thought could not be carried over to the transition from the Idea to nature. What constituted the "negative" within the Idea that necessitated the transition to nature? Nature as the negation of pure thought could not be derived from pure thought itself but must be encountered as an "other" outside thought:

> The Logic goes over into nature only because the thinking subject finds – outside the Logic – nature or something immediately existing, and is compelled to acknowledge it because of its immediate, that is, its natural giveness. If nature did not exist, the Logic, this immaculate virgin, would never be able to produce it out of itself.[219]

Feuerbach's attempts to construct or describe in the *Thoughts* a pantheistic divinity, a God who was the primal unity of spirit and nature, can thus be seen not as a misinterpretation of Hegel but as an attempt to "correct" Hegel's implicit dualism. "If nature were not in God," Feuerbach claimed, "or indeed if he himself were not nature, then the impulse, the origin and occasion of activity and decision would be outside him, he would be a heteronomous spiritless being."[220] In the satirical poems or "Xenien" that formed a kind of interlude in the prose argument of the *Thoughts,* Feuerbach expressed his difference from Hegel's position quite openly. The Hegelian "concept," he claimed, could never become "flesh and blood" in the Hegelian disciple because this concept was a comprehension only of the "skeleton (*Gerippe*)" of the real world, not of the totality of "life."[221] In his critical detachment from the "Hegelian wisdom" that was satisfied with "bones alone," Feuerbach sought a philosophical grounding in the pantheistic philosophies and theologies of Giordano Bruno, Jakob Böhme, and Spinoza, the true "prophets" of the ultimate reconciliation of spirit and nature.[222]

The most important consequence of Feuerbach's demand for an authentic reconciliation of spirit and nature was what we might call his tendency to "naturalize" spirit. This tendency was most evident in his conceptions of history and ethics. "Like the organic body," Feuerbach claimed, "mankind is caught up in the constant movement, unbroken regeneration, recreation, and transformation of its members, its individuals."[223] History, as "spirit, the essence itself, as process, in action," was the arena in which individuals were constantly being absorbed into the totality, transformed from "autonomous existences" into "objects" of spirit's "consciousness."[224] Spirit itself, however, did not change or develop in time and never made itself actual in a specific period or historical community:

> Over and above the changes of eras and individuals, over the waves of the coming and the passing, consciousness itself is in peaceful identity with itself, in undivided unity and unbroken peace, a presentness present to itself; and only within this unifying, illuminating, all-encompassing unity of consciousness . . . is mankind in constant activity, movement, and development.[225]

Because Feuerbach defined time as the "furur divinus," the process of constant negation that dissolved individuals into the eternal unity of spirit, he could not develop a coherent social and political ethic. "Highest being is communal being, highest enjoyment the enjoyment and feeling of unity," Feuerbach insisted.[226] But he conceived this community solely in terms of the universal community of the "species" in the absolute unity of spirit. His earthly ethic was confined to the demand that the individual transcend himself in the self-sacrificial activity of love, and the self-overcoming process of rational thought.

By 1830, therefore, Feuerbach's particular appropriation and revision of Hegelian philosophy had led him into what appeared to be a fundamental contradiction. On the one hand, he separated the Hegelian system from its connection to Christian culture and demanded its historical actualization in a future Kingdom of the Idea. On the other hand, he conceived this Kingdom of the Idea as an absolute integration of the individual, as both a natural and a spiritual being, into a universal community of the "species" that transcended the particularities of space and time. Feuerbach himself soon became aware of this problem and in the years after 1830 turned to a study of the historical evolution of the relationship between spirit and nature. The fact of this internal contradiction in Feuerbach's cultural stance, however, is of less interest to the intellectual historian than the manner in which it arose. The development of Feuerbach's Hegelianism, for all its particular and unique qualities, revealed a pattern of historical experience and intellectual response that was shared to a lesser or greater degree by many Hegelians and eventually resulted in the division and disintegration of the Hegelian school. Feuerbach experienced the Hegelian conversion as the elevation to a state of consciousness and being which was radically separated from that of his cultural contemporaries, not as a mere comprehension of the present reality of Christian cultural consciousness. The hostility toward his Hegelian convictions that he experienced in his home and more generally in Erlangen (where the intellectual atmosphere was dominated by a combination of pietistic Fundamentalism and Romantic conservatism) made his feelings of alienation particularly acute. In response to this experience, Feuerbach interpreted the Hegelian identification of Reason and reality as the prefiguration of a future cultural order and defined his cultural vocation in terms of the activity of "realization." But this revision of Hegel's conception of the historical role of philosophy could not be accomplished, as Feuerbach soon discovered, without a revision of Hegel's whole philosophical system. Before the theory could be made into the basis for a new practice, the theory itself would have to be changed. During the 1830s, as historical developments seemed increasingly to contradict the Hegelian reconciliation of Reason and actuality, this pattern of development became more and more prevalent within the Hegelian school.

III

The reduction of the absolute to "man": the division of the school and the emergence of the Hegelian Left, 1830–1841

7

Right, Center, and Left: the division of the Hegelian school in the 1830s

During the 1830s the divergent tendencies that had emerged within the Hegelian school during the 1820s became more obvious and more extreme. But disagreements among Hegelians concerning the relationship between the science of the absolute and the existing political and religious reality produced a division of the school into opposing factions only when they evolved into divergent interpretations of the very core of the Hegelian inheritance: the dialectical identity of finite and infinite, thought and being, subject and substance, in the self-actualizing, self-comprehending, concrete totality of absolute spirit. The publication of Strauss's *Life of Jesus* in 1835–6 marked the beginning of self-conscious disagreement on this latter, more fundamental issue, and it was Strauss himself, in response to the reception of his work by other Hegelians, who first divided the school into factions of Right, Center, and Left.[1] The most dramatic and significant development in the history of Hegelianism during the 1830s was the shift from divergent interpretations of the relationship between theory and practice to conflicts over the meaning, and ultimately the validity, of Hegelian theory, the beginnings of what Marx later satirically described as the "putrescence of the absolute spirit."[2]

Rosenkranz was one of the first Hegelians to realize that the proliferation of opposing positions within Hegelianism was leading to a decomposition of Hegelianism itself. In 1840 he published a comic drama in which the problem of "succession" within the school, of finding a legitimate heir to Hegel's throne, was made the object of gentle satire and humorous caricature.[3] Immediately after Hegel's death the inner circle of his disciples had denied that a problem of "succession" existed. Hegel did not need a successor, Gans claimed, because philosophy had "completed its circle" and its future progress could be conceived only "in terms of a thoughtful working over of the material according to the method and principle that the irreplaceable deceased established with such sharpness and clarity."[4] No new emperor would succeed the philosophical Alexander, Förster asserted in his funeral oration: "The Satraps would divide the orphaned provinces among themselves."[5] Förster seemed totally unaware of the possible implications of his analogy – that the Satraps might soon be at each other's throats in a battle for the inheritance. What he had in mind was a cooperative division of labor in the epigonal tasks of interpreting, applying, defending, and spreading the Hegelian viewpoint in the various spheres of cultural life and the different academic disciplines. A few weeks after Hegel's death, Förster, Henning, Gans, Marheineke, Schulze, Michelet, Hotho, Ludwig Boumann(1801–71), and Rosenkranz formed a Society of Friends of the Deceased that undertook the preparation and publication of a complete edition of Hegel's works, including the lectures recorded by his disciples. The "word" was to replace the departed "Christ" at the center of the school. The problem of the more particular vacant throne (Hegel's chair) was resolved by the appointment of a man whom no one could possibly confuse with a new emperor – Georg Andreas Gabler – the most unoriginal, uncritical, and colorless of Hegelian exegetes.

By 1840, however, it was obvious that all efforts to contain centrifugal tendencies within a common framework had failed. In Rosenkranz's play the goddess Minerva is so perturbed by the philosophical anarchy that follows Hegel's death that she arranges a shooting contest in a meadow near Berlin in order to determine – through the decisiveness of the deed rather than the ambiguity of the word – who has the ability to penetrate the "center of speculation" and thus claim Hegel's inheritance. The solemn competition, however, soon degenerates into a farcical series of sectarian squabbles, petty protests, and arrogant withdrawals. Before a shot can be fired, two Prussian policemen brought to the scene by Leo in order to intimidate a rambunctious "enthusiast" (Ruge) and a "mob" of "Hegelings (*Hegelingen*)" scatter the whole assembly with a warning about the consequences of disorderly conduct. The upshot is that the center of speculation remains unpenetrated, the inheritance unclaimed.[6]

Philosophical and historical interest in the disintegration of the Hegelian synthesis has focused almost exclusively on one particular group that emerged out of the decomposition of the school during the late 1830s and early 1840s: the loosely connected coterie of cultural critics and self-styled "overcomers" of Hegel commonly referred to as the "young" or "Left" Hegelians. Those Hegelians who do not fit into this category (the clear majority) have usually been relegated, without closer examination of their actual positions, to a vaguely defined party of political and religious accommodationists: the "old" or "Right" Hegelians.[7] This simplified dichotomization of the conflicts within Hegelianism has produced a great deal of confusion concerning both the nature and the causes of the division of the Hegelian school.

First, it is clearly misleading to equate the opposition between accommodationists and critics with generational conflict. We have already seen that significant differences on the relationship of Reason and reality emerged among Hegel's first disciples. To label old Hegelians like Gans and Carové Right Hegelians may seem absurd, but it has been done repeatedly.[8] The major representatives of Left Hegelianism - Strauss, Bauer, Feuerbach, Ruge, Vischer, and Stirner - were, to be sure, members of the historical generation born in the first decade of the century and thus could be described, in 1840, as young Hegelians, but their most vociferous Hegelian opponents - like Rosenkranz, Schaller, and Erdmann - were members of the same generation. If one moves to an even younger Hegelian generation - Marx, Engels, and their contemporaries - a similar ideological division is discernible.[9] Because of the confusion of generational and ideological categories one can often find individuals described as old Hegelians in the secondary literature who are younger than most of the young Hegelians.[10] Generational experience and consciousness did play a role in the division of Hegelianism, but they were more important in defining the problems considered to be important than in determining the ideological position taken on these problems. An adequate description of the experiential matrix of the division of Hegelianism must therefore take into account those factors that led to divergences not only between, but also within, different generations of Hegelians.

Before such a description can be attempted, however, a preliminary clarification of the usage of the terms "Right" and "Left" within the context of Hegelianism is necessary. The confusion of generational and ideological categories has been compounded by the absence of a clear conception of the content of the ideological divisions. Our analysis of the original appropriation of Hegel's philosophy has shown that Hegelians could already be divided into accommodationists, reformers, and "revolutionaries" during the Restoration. To a certain extent the division of the 1830s was simply an explicit articulation and radicalization of the earlier differentiation. Political, social, and religious changes made the accommodationist stance appear more reactionary and gave new impetus to reformist and revolutionary tendencies. Within this framework of explanation the focus of division was the interpretation of Hegel's identification of Reason and reality. Was this identification completed, an ongoing process, or a future goal? Even if we remain within this framework our analysis up to this point would suggest the need for significant revisions of the prevailing interpretations. First, if Left Hegelianism is defined in terms of a critique of existing political and religious forms and a future-oriented demand for the actualization of philosophy, then it can be traced back to the earliest period of Hegelianism; it did not emerge for the first time in the late 1830s. Secondly, it should have already become evident that division of the school into an accommodationist Right and a radical Left is too simplistic: It ignores the moderate critics and reformers of the "Center." During the 1830s this centrist group did not disappear, but became more significant. In 1838, in fact, Michelet, himself a member of the Center, claimed that an alliance of Center and Left would constitute a majority within the school and relegate the Right to the status of outsiders.[11] Leo's notorious polemic against the "young Hegelian gang" of the same year focused its attention as much, if not more, on the Hegelian Center as on those individuals usually defined as members of the Left.[12] The reformist Center constituted a large segment of the Hegelian school during the 1830s, and the views of its members were usually more sympathetic to the Left than to the Right. The almost universal practice of identifying the Center with the Right thus obscures and distorts the character and significance of the conflicts that divided the school in the 1830s.

Recognition of the continuity and complexity of the Hegelian debate on the identity of Reason and actuality leads to an obvious question: What was new and different in the cultural stance of the Left Hegelianism articulated by Strauss, Bruno Bauer, and Feuerbach in the late 1830s? The formulation of a satisfactory answer to this question constitutes the purpose of this and the following chapters. On the most general and preliminary level, however, we can say that the defining characteristic of this "new" Left Hegelianism was the merger of the demand for the actualization of philosophy with the implicit or explicit claim that such actualization demanded a transformative revision and development of Hegelian theory. Like the actualizers of Kantian philosophy during the 1790s, the actualizers of Hegelian philosophy during the 1830s came to recognize a radical disjuncture between their philosophical presuppositions and their historical experience and historical goals. The Left Hegelians' transformation of their philosophical inheritance took the general form of a reduction of absolute spirit to human "species being" or "species consciousness," of speculative metaphysics to cultural history, anthropology, and psychology. The Left Hegelians perceived themselves not simply as midwives for the incarnation of the Hegelian Logos in the world, but as prophets of new forms of cultural integration and human freedom that would relegate Hegel's absolute spirit to a religious and metaphysical stage of human self-alienation.

The specific nature and historical significance of the Left Hegelian cultural stance developed in the writing of Strauss, Bauer, and Feuerbach in the late 1830s has been obscured and misunderstood in part because of a disregard for, or ignorance of, the historical and cultural context in which it arose. Three aspects of this context are particularly important: (1) the changes in the political and social environment of the Hegelian school during the 1830s; (2) the general evolution and division of the school as a whole in response to these changes; and (3) the emergence of contemporaneous, rival movements for cultural transformation, especially on the Right, whose viewpoints illuminate the distinctiveness of the Hegelian cultural perspective, and whose increasing social and cultural influence was a major factor in the radicalization of the prophets of the Hegelian Left.

THE POLITICAL AND SOCIAL CONTEXT

In Karl Löwith's analysis of the "revolution in nineteenth century thought" that marked the transition from Hegel to Nietzsche, the European revolutions of 1830 are described as a decisive historical turning point. "The symptomatic character of the July Revolution," he claims, "was that it showed that the chasm of the great French Revolution had closed only in outward appearance; in reality the world stood at the beginning of a whole 'Age of Revolutions' in which the masses were to win from the upper classes an independent political power." Hegel's reconciliations lost their experiential validity as his world was transformed by "democratic levelling and industrialization."[13] Löwith's analysis, however, is conducted on a level of conceptualization far too general to provide a meaningful framework for the division of Hegelianism during the 1830s. Moreover, problems connected to the emergence of mass politics and industrialization have very limited relevance to German conditions in the decade after Hegel's death. Our first task, therefore, must be to give specificity to the social and political "movement (*Bewegung*)" that changed the environment of Hegelianism after 1830.

West of the Rhine the significance of the political unrest and revolutions of 1830 seems obvious. The political changes of 1830–2 in France, England, and Belgium, claims E. J. Hobsbawm, marked the "definitive defeat of aristocratic bourgeois power," revealed the growing split between upper-middle-class constitutional liberalism and lower-middle- and working-class democratic radicalism, and signaled the entry of the working poor (whether displaced artisans or new industrial proletarians) into organized politics as a revolutionary force. Moreover, these political changes represented "the first products of a very general period of acute and widespread economic and social unrest and rapidly quickening social change"; that is, they revealed the pervasive impact of the dynamic, transformative power of industrial capitalism.[14] East of the Rhine the significance of 1830 is more difficult to define. In central Germany popular insurrections helped produce constitutional changes in Brunswick, Hesse-Kassel, Hanover, and Saxony; and southern Germany witnessed both a resurgence of moderate liberalism in the elected diets and the emergence of a significant radical republican, democratic movement outside existing political institutions. By 1834, however, Metternichian reaction had triumphed and it appeared that Germany's "July liberalism" had been an ephemeral and derivative movement. Although the political turmoil of 1830–2 was accompanied by significant social unrest, this unrest was sporadic, disorganized, and not easily connected to the fundamental economic and social forces that conditioned the course of events in France or England. To say that developments in Germany did not conform to the patterns set by France or England, however, does not tell us very much about what was actually happening in Germany. It is true that the German liberals and radicals of the early 1830s, like their predecessors of the 1790s, looked to the west for inspiration, but, as in the 1790s, this westward gaze was motivated by the experience of an indigenous social and political crisis.

In political terms this crisis can be defined most succinctly as one of bureaucratic or administrative liberalism. The liberal movement of the early 1830s, as Leonard Krieger has noted, marked a "relocation of the liberal impulse from official institutions into citizens' groups."[15] For the most part, however, this "relocation" took peculiarly traditional forms; that is, the nature of the "liberal impulse" was not itself transformed. The "citizens' groups" who demanded constitutional government in central Germany or raised the banner of further reform in the southern diets did not aim at parliamentary control of the executive power, but sought a reform of administration and law in accordance with the ideal of a *Rechtsstaat.* Their practical demands were usually restricted to the abolition of remaining legal inequality and privilege and the creation of institutional safeguards against the abuse of executive power: freedom of the press, the separation of justice from administration, trial by jury.[16]

The modest goals of the liberal movement were rooted in its social composition. Ernest Bramsted claimed that the July Revolution "aroused the German middle-class,"[17] but this is certainly misleading unless one emphasizes that the aroused middle class consisted primarily of members of the professional stratum, of bureaucrats and academics who were as opposed to the plutocracy they saw ascendent in France and England as to the privileged position of the traditional aristocracy.[18] Recognition and criticism of the bankruptcy of a bureaucratic administration that had been forced to come to terms with traditionally privileged groups and princely absolutism after 1815 came in large part from within the administrative class itself. The liberal opposition in the southern diets was composed primarily of state officials and academics.[19] The relative impotence of the liberal movement was tied to the inherent contradictions of its project of internal criticism, reform, and revitalization of administrative liberalism. As long as they lacked a significant popular base outside the state-dependent professional class, liberal reformers were constantly faced with the necessity of renewing the compromises for which they had castigated their predecessors.[20]

The crisis of bureaucratic liberalism was revealed after 1830 not only by the conflicts within the administrative class, but also by the emergence of a movement for radical political change that aimed at transformation from below rather than reform from within or above. In 1831, the *Burschenschaft* reconstituted itself as a revolutionary society, dropped its old Christian-German program, and came out in support of egalitarian democracy and republican nationalism. During the revolutions in Hanover there was a radical student insurrection at Göttingen and an attempt to establish a revolutionary commune at Osterode.[21] But the radical movement did not really get under way until the winter of 1831-2 when two Bavarian journalists, Johannes Wirth and Philipp Siebenpfeiffer, organized a network of reading societies, the Press and Fatherland Union, in order to facilitate the distribution of radical newspapers that were continually censored and confiscated by the Bavarian authorities. As long as the issue at stake appeared to be confined to freedom of the press, this association received the support of moderate liberal deputies in the southern diets. As soon as the Union took on the character of a popular political movement with a radical republican program, however, the moderate liberals disassociated themselves from it. When the radicals organized a mass demonstration of thirty thousand people at Hambach in May 1832, the split in the liberal movement between those who were ready to reject the existing historical reality for the sake of a revolutionary future and those who aimed at liberal reform within the framework of the existing constitutions had become obvious.[22]

The Hambach festival marked the culmination of the radical movement in southern Germany. The reaction came swiftly and harshly. The Confederation passed a resolution forbidding all political associations and demonstrations. Some of the leaders of the popular movement were arrested; others fled into exile in Switzerland or France. For a few months the Palatinate was placed under martial law and occupied by armed forces. In the face of these punitive measures the radicals among the student leaders made one last attempt to arouse the German people to revolution, by seizing the Hauptwache in Frankfurt. Although the students succeeded in holding this symbol of reaction for a short time, the popular revolt did not materialize. The consequence was a new series of punitive measures aimed not only at the students involved, but at the universities and student organizations in general, which recalled the worst days of the *Demagogenverfolgung* after 1819.[23]

The repression of popular radicalism was, of course, not confined to Germany. In Britain and France as well the radical democrats were viciously repressed as the bourgeois regimes consolidated their power. But in Germany the moderates shared the fate of the radicals. The reactionary measures of the Confederation were aimed as much at Karl Rotteck and Karl Welcker, the leaders of the liberal opposition in the Baden diet, as at Wirth and Siebenpfeiffer. The "Six Acts" passed by the Confederation in the summer of 1832 severely restricted the powers of the diets in the constitutional states, and the liberal press was placed under strict censorship. The press laws that had been one of the results of the liberal victory in Baden were overturned, and Rotteck and Welcker were dismissed from their academic positions. In the central states the dynastic rulers and their ministers abused the new constitutions with impunity. By 1834 the brief flowering of July liberalism had come to an end; the "movement" had been replaced by stagnation and reaction.

But the political calm that had settled over Germany by the middle of the decade was an armed peace. Conservative "reaction" had triumphed and "liberalism" waited for its next opportunity. The brief heyday of July liberalism had been based on widespread popular discontent and social unrest. The causes of this discontent and unrest did not disappear through the resolutions of the Confederation. But what were these causes? Recent historical research seems to indicate that the most obvious place to look is not the right one; that is, German society was not in the process of being radically transformed by the effects of technological innovation in key industries, new forms of industrial organization, or a rapid rise in production. In technology as well as industrial organization the first half of the century "saw, not a transformation of techniques, as in Britain, but a slow spasmodic diffusion of new methods alongside the old."[24] Even this slow and spasmodic diffusion, moreover, had hardly begun by 1830. Productivity rose slightly in relationship to population during the first half of the century but hardly enough to justify the Prussian bureaucrat Wilhelm Dieterici's claim of a "complete revolution."[25] The problem, then, is to determine what socioeconomic factors did contribute to the social dislocation obviously experienced by many intellectuals, artisans, and peasants in the early thirties.

The first and most obvious factor, as in the crisis of the 1790s, was the continuing rapid expansion of the population. The population of non-Austrian Germany increased by 38.5 percent between 1815 and 1845. The increase was most rapid in the northwestern areas, but the effect of the increase was more traumatic in the already densely populated states of the southwest, especially Baden and Württemberg. More important, perhaps, for the discontent around 1830 is the fact that the increase of population was most rapid in the years immediately following 1815. Because of this "bulge" in the population curve, "by the 1830s everywhere in Germany an unusually large 'birth cohort' was coming of age and had created an unprecedented demand for jobs."[26] The impact of population growth in the southwestern states was revealed in the wave of emigration that set in in 1830 and in attempts by the governments to impose stricter marriage laws.[27] The rate of internal migration or urbanization in Germany, however, did not increase very significantly before 1850. Most of the population increases had to be absorbed in the countryside and small villages.[28]

What distinguished the population "crisis" of the early 1830s from that of the 1790s was that it took place within the context of the structural changes that had occurred during the liberal bureaucratic reforms of the Napoleonic period: the emancipation of the peasants from manorial bonds (*Bauernbefreiung*) and the dissolution of the regulatory power of the guilds (*Gewerbefreiheit*). The actual social realization of these reforms proceeded slowly and unevenly in various parts of Germany, but a few generalizations can be made.[29]

In the Prussian provinces east of the Elbe River, the financial terms of compensation whereby the legally emancipated peasants were allowed to attain personal ownership of the land definitely favored the large landowners. Only the most prosperous peasants were able to maintain economically viable holdings. For the vast majority "emancipation" meant primarily a loss of whatever security and legal protection they had enjoyed under the old manorial system. The large landowners were now able to appropriate the small holdings of impoverished peasants with impunity. The consolidation of land into large holdings made possible the introduction of new scientific agricultural methods and thus increased productivity. The social effect of this process, however, was, on the one hand, to provide a viable economic base for the continued political and social dominance of the aristocratic landowning class and, on the other, to create a large rural proletariat of landless agricultural laborers. Already in 1826 the conservative aristocrat J. M. von Radowitz discerned the formation of a new "serfdom" based on the cash nexus rather than personal servitude.[30] In western and southern Germany the effect of emancipation was to aggravate the already serious problem of the division of land into holdings too small to provide an adequate livelihood. Although the general trends seemed diametrically opposed to developments in the northeast, the general result of rural pauperization was the same.

The social impact of the reforms of the guild system was much more complex and has been the subject of vehement historical disagreement. What is clear is that there was overcrowding, unemployment, pauperization, and an increasingly loudly voiced insecurity and anxiety in the artisan trades. A recent review of the causes of this crisis has claimed that the common practice of blaming the liberal reforms and the resulting competitive market conditions for artisan discontent is not substantiated by the evidence. Discontent was just as prevalent in those states in which the guilds still retained a great deal of their old regulatory power. The main causes of the economic crisis in the artisanate were the pressure of expanding population and the lack of new forms of economic production and employment.[31] Yet contemporary artisans blamed the governments for their plight. Discontent among the artisans thus provided another instance in which the legitimacy of the bureaucracy's claim to represent the welfare of the whole society was placed in question.

The social unrest that accompanied the political activity of the early 1830s was thus a product of population pressures within a social context in which traditional socioeconomic relationships were gradually being abandoned or were simply disintegrating, and in which viable new relationships had not yet emerged. The emigrants who left southern Germany in the early 1830s were not the industrial proletariat of a new economic system but small farmers, artisans, and shopkeepers victimized by the insecurity and declining standards of living of a transitional period; they were "a class born of rupture between the old ways and the new; between assumed, traditional patterns and new forces for which patterns had not yet emerged."[32]

As during the 1790s, the political discontent and consciousness of crisis and transition that characterized certain segments of the professional stratum during the 1830s was not simply based on their observation of social dislocation in the lower classes of society. The general structural tensions which produced that dislocation were also operative within the educated estate, and the problems of overpopulation, proletarization, and "homelessness" became very real, immediate problems for an increasing number of young intellectuals after 1830. The amateur sociologist and conservative cultural critic W. H. Riehl, writing in 1851, claimed that the 1830s witnessed the emergence of a significant intellectual proletariat in Germany. Moreover, because of their self-consciousness and inflated social expectations, this segment of the alienated was particularly visible, audible, and dangerous. "The proletariat of intellectual labor," he stated, "are the actual *ecclesia militans* of the fourth estate in Germany. They constitute the great military column of that stratum of society which has broken openly and self-consciously with the traditional social organization."[33]

The optimistic faith in upward mobility aroused by the dissolution of the old estate barriers, the general expansion of population, the growing trend among the sons of the old aristocracy to seek careers in the bureaucracy or even the church, and the apparent absence of alternatives to state service as a means of attaining social stature combined to produce a sharp rise in university enrollment during the 1820s. In the Prussian universities, the average enrollment for five semesters in 1820–2 was 3,456; by 1829–31 it had risen to 6,082. In Tübingen, there were 465 students registered in 1817–18 and 887 in 1829–30.[34] Moreover, by far the largest percentage of these students were enrolled in the traditional "bread disciplines" of law and theology. In 1830–1, 28.3 percent of the students in all German universities were in law, 38.5 percent in theology.[35] The result was that by the early 1830s there were many more graduates in law and theology than could be absorbed by the existing bureaucratic and ecclesiastical hierarchies.

In 1836, Wilhelm Dieterici published a study of the Prussian universities that showed extreme overcrowding in the traditional careers. In the years between 1832 and 1834, his statistics revealed, there were 262 candidates for every 100 positions in the church and approximately 230 for every 100 positions in the judicial or administrative bureaucracy.[36] Dieterici was optimistic despite his statistics because of his faith in the eventual ability of population growth to absorb the educated, and also because he simply could not conceive of an "overproduction" of intelligence. In Prussia, however, the number of positions did not expand in correspondence with the increase in population. In 1840 there were fewer positions in the church than there had been in 1815.[37] Moreover, in 1825 the number of positions in the bureaucracy had been trimmed down to, and fixed at, approximately 6,600. This was just at the time when the universities were experiencing a massive increase in the number of law students.[38] A contemporary observer noted in 1838 that "from all sides and in all branches of the civil service the pressure on office is so great that it is not unusual for ten or twenty men to apply for the same position."[39]

The prospect of a fully salaried, tenured position as a "councillor (*Rat*)" in the bureaucracy or a pastor in the church for a student who completed his state examinations in the late 1820s or early 1830s thus became increasingly bleak. In 1840 there were approximately 2,500 unsalaried jurists in the Prussian bureaucracy waiting for positions that would correspond to their training and qualifications.[40] The potential discontent in this educated proletariat was aggravated by the special favors given to the increasing number of aristocrats competing for appointments. Between 1820 and 1845 the number of aristocrats appointed to positions in the Prussian provincial administrations increased from one-quarter to one-third of the total, and the highest positions remained almost exclusively in the hands of the nobly born.[41] The intense competition for office also made it easier for the established elites to impose ideological criteria in the making of appointments. This factor became especially important during the reaction that set in after the student unrest of the early 1830s.

The increasing difficulty of attaining social security and prestige in the traditional state-service careers was expressed in a sharp decline in university enrollment during the 1830s. By the second half of the decade, enrollment throughout Germany had decreased by about a third from the 1830 figures. In theology the decrease was closer to 50 percent.[42] The number of students who took the *Abitur,* however, remained in step with the increase in population. The general trend during the 1830s thus indicated that the state's traditional monopoly of educated intelligence was beginning to disintegrate. The administrative class could no longer simply identify itself with the universality of *Bildung,* or Reason, and its claims to cultural hegemony were correspondingly threatened.

The situation within the intellectual estate itself thus mirrored the general social tensions evident in the relocation of the liberal impulse outside established state institutions and in the social unrest among artisans and peasants. Moreover, within the educated estate, as in the society as a whole, alienation from the established order was exacerbated by the increasingly obvious alignment of the bureaucratic cadres with political, social, and religious reaction.[43] The problems of overpopulation in the intellectual classes and structural rigidity in the existing administrative, ecclesiastical, and academic hierarchies were complicated by ideological conflict. Consciousness of historical change led many young intellectuals to demand a certain flexibility and openness to reform on the part of the state and the established church. The threat of change, however, led to a conservative ideological retrenchment on the part of the ruling elites. The fact that the state was increasingly unable to provide secure positions for its university-educated population simply made the possibility of compromise and co-option less likely.

The impact of these tensions on one particular group of intellectuals – those who had chosen to pursue academic careers – was of particular importance in the formation and growth of the Hegelian Left. The sharp decrease in university enrollment caused by overcrowding in state-service careers obviously made it much more difficult to obtain tenured academic appointments. Advancement from the status of unsalaried lecturer (*Privatdozent*) to a fully salaried chair (*Ordinarius*) was slow and difficult in the best of times. Between 1815 and 1848 the average age of *habilitation* as a *Privatdozent* was twenty-six; the average age at which the security of an *Ordinarius* was achieved was thirty-five.[44] Just as in the judicial and administrative hierarchies, there was a long wait in poverty and insecurity before one could hope to attain social and financial security. During the 1830s this situation became considerably worse. After 1830, for instance, the budget of the University of Berlin remained fixed. Any new appointment meant a general reduction in salary for everyone. At the same time the number of *Privatdozenten* increased enormously. In the late 1830s the senior faculty at Berlin protested against the making of any new appointments, while the *Privatdozenten* and associates (*Extraordinarien*) agitated for a living wage.[45] The position of *Extraordinarius* had usually entailed at least a partial salary in the past. Because of the tight financial situation, however, many of these associate professors were relegated to the status of *Privatdozenten.* In 1835, sixteen of the associate professors at Berlin received no salary whatsoever.[46] In other Prussian universities and in southern Germany the situation was very similar. In the years between 1835 and 1840 the total number of tenured positions in law, theology, and philosophy in all German universities decreased by five.[47] At the Tübingen seminary there were only two openings between 1828 and 1843, both caused by deaths.[48] At Erlangen, where Feuerbach taught as a *Privatdozent,* the theological program (and two-thirds of the students were in theology) was severely cut back in 1834.[49]

The failure to obtain secure academic positions was a significant factor in the transformation of some of the younger Hegelians (as it had been for Carové and, to a lesser extent, Gans, in the 1820s) into radical cultural critics. Even a superficial glance at the academic status of the members of the Hegelian school in 1840 is revealing. The members of the Left either were *Privatdozenten* or had chosen or been forced to leave the academic profession. For Strauss, Bauer, Ruge, Feuerbach, and Vischer, academic frustration and cultural radicalization went hand in hand. The Hegelians of the Center and Right, however, all held academic appointments on at least the associate professorial level. Rosenkranz and Erdmann, along with older Hegelians like Hinrichs, Gans, Gabler, Henning, and Marheineke, were full professors in 1840. Moreover, those Berlin Hegelians who remained underpaid associate professors virtually all had independent sources of income. Vatke married into a rich and well-established Berlin family in 1837, and Michelet, Hotho, Werder, and the Benary brothers could all count on at least some financial support from their families. Yet even this group was noticeably more liberal than the full professors of the Center, and it constituted the most critical wing of reformist Hegelianism.[50] Ideological differentiation within the Hegelian school thus conformed to differentiation in academic status, which in turn mirrored the general tensions and conflicts in German politics and society.

Decreasing enrollments at the universities, overcrowding in academic careers, and lack of independent financial income, however, do not adequately "explain" the radical cultural criticism of those younger Hegelians who constituted the new Hegelian Left. Their academic careers were cut short because they refused to conform to a political and religious system that they perceived as historically reactionary. Their views were radicalized in response to the increasing intransigence and power of the cultural opponents of the Hegelian school in the educational, ecclesiastical, and political establishment. Quite legitimately they interpreted their personal frustration as symptomatic of a general cultural crisis. The framework in which they perceived and conceptualized this personal and cultural crisis was that of their Hegelian inheritance, not, however, as it was originally formulated by Hegel, but as it had evolved in the context of the political, social, and cultural tensions of the 1830s. To put it simply, Left Hegelianism can be understood only within the context of the evolution of Hegelianism as a whole.

Right, Center, and Left

FROM DIVERGENCE TO DIVISION: THE EVOLUTION OF HEGELIANISM, 1830–1840

On June 25, 1830, students, professors, government officials, and church leaders gathered in the Grosse Aula of the University of Berlin in order to hear Hegel, in his role as rector of the university, present a Latin oration in commemoration of the three hundredth anniversary of the Augsburg Confession. Hegel used the occasion to reiterate, in a particularly dogmatic, confident, and self-congratulatory fashion, his belief in the accomplished reconciliation of religion, philosophy, and ethical community in contemporary Protestant culture and the modern Prussian state. Because the Protestant conception of God as self-conscious Reason had been recognized as the essence of human activity by the leaders of the Prussian government, historical progress could now proceed as a "peaceful evolution," without "unrest" or "rebellion." There was no legitimate basis for opposition to the existing order because this order affirmed man's freedom and universality as a self-conscious rational being.[51]

Less than six weeks later a similar assembly met in the same hall in order to celebrate the birthday of Frederick William III. Karl Gutzkow described the rather different mood evident at this occasion:

> Hundreds of students thronged behind the barrier in front of which sat the professors, the government officials, the military. The academic choir sang behind the orator Böckh . . . The crown prince smiled, but everyone who read the newspapers knew that in France a king had just been knocked off his throne. The thunder of the cannons between the Parisian barracades echoed within the auditorium. Böckh spoke about the beauties of art but this time no one paid any attention to his thoughtful comments and classical language. Hegel stood up and announced the winners of the academic competitions . . . but no one outside of the participants paid any heed. I myself heard with one ear that I had won the prize in the philosophical faculty over six competitors, and with the other about a people who had overthrown a king, about the thunder of cannons and about thousands who had fallen in battle . . . Scientific academic study lay behind me, history before me.[52]

This new consciousness of historical change and possibility, of history as something that lay "before" and was yet to be constructed, rather than as a past that could merely be comprehended, which the events of 1830 aroused in Gutzkow, was also characteristic of many members of the Hegelian school. It made Hegel's reconciliations appear more tenuous and problematical, radicalized the differences in the interpretation of his philosophy's historical role, and thus marked the transition to a new period in the history of the school.

Hegel himself, according to his son Karl, viewed the turn of events in France and Belgium with "great dismay," as a "catastrophe that appeared to shake the secure foundations of the rational state."[53] In December 1830, Hegel wrote to Göschel that the "immensity of political interests" had "swallowed everything else," and produced a "crisis in which everything that formerly was valid seems to have become problematical." Philosophy, he claimed, could not withstand "the ignorance, outrageous violence, and evil passions of this noisy dissonance" and would have to remain content with providing peace for a select "few."[54] But this bitterly pessimistic mood did not last. By the end of January 1831, Hegel was confident that the "menacing storm clouds" on Prussia's frontiers did not threaten the political system within Prussia.[55] He did not transform his philosophy into a private compensation for historical disintegration but reasserted its historical role as a reconciling power by grasping the events of 1830–1 within the established categories of his system.

The crises in France, England, and other European states, Hegel claimed, did not mark the emergence of a new epoch in history, but simply revealed that these states had not yet attained the stage of historical development actualized in Prussia. In the Catholic countries, like France, the primary source of revolutionary unrest was the unresolved tension between a reactionary religious "disposition" and the rational institutions of the modern state. The French regime had become a "fifteen-year farce" because of the disrupting presence of a religious attitude "that regarded it a matter of conscience to destroy existing institutions." Without the "emancipation of conscience" provided by Protestantism, Hegel asserted, political freedom remained "formal"; for the individual could not recognize his own freedom in the rationally articulated will of the community as long as he remained in "religious slavery."[56] In England, which did enjoy the advantages of a Protestant "disposition," the sources of the contemporary political and social crisis were rather different: the "most bizarre and haphazard anomalies and inequalities" of a legal and institutional structure that expressed the interests of the traditionally privileged classes rather than the universal principles of Reason. What was required to resolve the British crisis was a reform and codification of law in accordance with universal, rational principles and the creation of an administrative organization that would allow the government to act according to the interests and welfare of the total community.[57]

It would be misleading to describe Hegel's response to developments in France and England as simply "reactionary." He did not defend the pre-1830 regimes, but unveiled their contradictions and insisted on the need for wide-ranging social, political, and cultural reform. Yet many of Hegel's contemporaries perceived his views as reactionary because of his vehement opposition to the popular or "democratic" liberal movement that led the assault on the Restoration regimes. In Hegel's opinion, this July liberalism was a completely negative, destructive, almost anarchical force, which possessed no positive principles for political and cultural reconstruction.[58] It was a historically regressive movement with no more legitimacy than the subjective radicalism that had animated the *Burschen* after 1815. Hegel did not believe that his philosophical position was threatened by the events of 1830–1, because he was convinced that the conflicts reflected in these events had already been resolved in Prussia and could be resolved elsewhere only on the Prussian model.

Hegel's assessment of the political crisis of 1830 was not endorsed by all of his disciples. This disagreement was aroused not by Hegel's specific analysis of the causes of the crises in France and England, or even by his critique of "subjective" liberalism (which was familiar), but by his refusal to admit the possibility of any significant progress beyond the present stage of historical development. In 1830–1, Hegel's fear of revolution and violent disruption led him, as in 1819–20, to exaggerate the conservative tendencies in his philosophical position and place himself firmly on the side of the accommodationists among his disciples. But those Hegelians who had disagreed with the accommodationist position before 1830 found it even less convincing after 1830. In the context of new evidence that the negative Moment in the historical dialectic had not lost its vitality and that the "positive" affirmations of the leaders of church and state were becoming more rigid and defensively conservative, the ideology of accomplished reconciliation seemed increasingly artificial.

The social, political, and religious environment of the Hegelian school was not, of course, suddenly and radically transformed in 1830. Few Hegelians in 1831 would have agreed with the young historian Johann Gustav Droysen when he claimed that Hegel's death marked not only the end of his personal existence, but also the collapse of the cultural world that had sustained his philosophy.[59] The historical significance of the events of 1830–1 within Germany was variegated and ambiguous, more a symptomatic indication of unresolved conflicts in the existing regimes than a decisive turn in a new direction. The history of Hegelianism between 1830 and 1840 mirrored the complexity and ambiguity of its historical context. The transition from implicit divergence to explicit conflict within the school was a gradual process and accompanied by the proliferation of individual positions. It is understandable that Rosenkranz's drama of 1840 presented the school in anarchical disarray rather than divided into two clearly defined groupings. Attempts by Hegelians themselves to define the membership of various factions and the philosophical content of their opposition were confusing and often contradictory. The categories used to delineate differences were not always the same and conceptions of who belonged in the different groupings differed from writer to writer and from year to year.[60] Recent attempts to clarify the Hegelian divisions of the 1830s have focused attention on the specific theological controversies that followed the publication of Friedrich Richter's *Doctrine of the Last Things* in 1833 and Strauss's *Life of Jesus* in 1835.[61] But this focus is too narrow and is thus misleading in at least three respects. First, it ignores those Hegelians who did not participate actively in these specific debates, like Carové or Gans, and thus presents a distorted picture of both the range of opinion within the school and the depth of support for certain positions. Secondly, the one-sided emphasis on theological issues has obscured the integral connection of political-social, religious, and philosophical issues in the divisions among Hegelians, and diverted attention away from the general problems of historical transformation and cultural reconstruction that found expression in arguments over the immortality of the soul or the historicity of Christ. Finally, the relationship between the historical experience (both sociocultural and generational) and the cultural stances of different Hegelian factions or groupings has been left unexplored – as if the publication of books and reviews with opposing positions were a cause rather than an expression of divisions within the school. In what follows I try to avoid such distortion and confusions by describing the division of Hegelianism in terms of the historical evolution of the divergent stances of the 1820s within the changing historical context of the 1830s.

One of the most significant, and least examined, elements in the evolution of the Hegelian school during the 1830s is the gradual disintegration of the power and influence of the Hegelian "establishment" and the concomitant decline in the historical relevance of the accommodationist interpretation of Hegel's philosophy. That accommodationist Hegelianism was on the verge of collapse was not immediately evident during the first half of the decade. Schulze and Altenstein survived the political reaction of the early 1830s, as they had survived the similar reaction of the early 1820s, and the mutually supportive relationship between the academic leaders of the school and the Prussian Kultusministerium, one of the major foundations of the accommodationist stance, was maintained. Large numbers of Hegelians continued to enter the academic profession confident that their devotion to the science of the spirit was completely compatible with loyal service to the Prussian state and the established church.[62] As late as 1835 even Feuerbach could give serious consideration to the proposition that an accommodationist stance might not be completely hypocritical for a Hegelian within the Prussian context.[63] But Feuerbach's own situation in Erlangen also revealed the limitations of the accommodationist stance: It had little relevance for the increasing number of non-Prussian Hegelians who remained "outsiders" within their immediate cultural environments. Even in Prussia, moreover, there were indications of the imminent end of the honeymoon between the Hegelians and the established order. Gabler's appointment to Hegel's chair was delayed for almost three years by the concerted opposition of an alliance of aristocratic and academic conservatives who had the support of the crown prince.[64] After 1835, Schulze and Altenstein found it increasingly difficult to give practical expression to their intellectual sympathies. Only one Hegelian was appointed to a full professorship between 1835 and 1840, and even appointments at the associate professorial level were rare and often required accommodation to religious and political positions that were noticeably more conservative than those that had defined accommodation a decade earlier.[65] By 1840 it was obvious that Schulze and Altenstein were not authentic representatives of the "state," but members of an increasingly impotent minority within the state. As an academic power the Hegelian school was not merely on the defensive; it had begun to retreat before the aggressive assaults of its cultural opponents.

The erosion of the power and influence of the Berlin Hegelian establishment was also evident in the declining prestige and impact of the Hegelian *Jahrbücher*. "During the early 1830s," Rudolf Haym claimed, "there was no German journal that could match the *Jahrbücher für wissenschaftliche Kritik,* the party organ of Hegel and his students, in spiritual significance."[66] In 1834, Feuerbach described the Hegelian journal as "one of the most prestigious, if not the most prestigious, scientific institutions of the time."[67] But skepticism about the *Jahrbücher*'s ability to remain in touch with the times and retain its "spiritual significance" were already surfacing among members of the Hegelian school during the heyday of the journal's cultural prestige and influence. Gans and Kapp attempted, unsuccessfully, to establish new journals in which the Hegelian viewpoint could be related more directly to contemporary concerns, and Vatke, Strauss, and Droysen planned similar projects during the early 1830s.[68] After 1835 discontent with the cautious and indecisive editorial policy of the *Jahrbücher* increased, and in the summer of 1837, Arnold Ruge was able to marshall widespread support for his project of a new Hegelian journal that would act as a "contemporary hand on the clock of German intellectual life."[69] The success of Ruge's *Hallische Jahrbücher* between 1838 and 1840 was accompanied by a rapid decline in the influence and vitality of the Berlin *Jahrbücher.* Not only a growing number of critical and "progressive" Hegelians, but even the conservative officials of the Prussian state, displayed increasing discontent with the particular brand of historical accommodation preached by the Berlin Hegelian establishment. In 1839 the *Jahrbücher* almost ceased publication because of conflicts with the Prussian censorship board.[70] By 1840 it seemed that the editorial committee of the *Jahrbücher* was as uncertain as its opponents about its ability to "tell the time," and the journal simply faded into historical irrelevance during the 1840s.[71]

The Hegelians we have described as accommodationists did not all respond to the changes in their historical circumstances in the same fashion. Among the leaders of the Berlin establishment, Schulze, Marheineke, and Förster remained loyal to the principles that had defined accommodation during the 1820s. Marheineke, like Hegel, could not discern any new progressive historical principle in the 1830 revolutions, but saw in them merely another expression of the old dualism between the freedom of the individual subject and the universal truth of the objective substance (in both politics and religion), which continued to plague Catholic cultures but had been successfully resolved in Protestant states like Prussia, who "have achieved what spirit that has attained its majority can demand for itself – a religious teaching purified of all superstitions and arbitrary human additions, freedom of thought and conscience, and a political constitution organized according to these principles."[72] In his theological lectures and writings, Marheineke continued to maintain that the whole system of religious "representations" revealed in the Bible and codified in the doctrinal teachings of the Evangelical Church could be appropriated in the form of philosophical truth without compromising the legitimate demands of human freedom or sacrificing any part of the content of religious faith.[73] Förster purveyed a similar accommodationist position in the political sphere. In a series of historical studies focused on the period of eighteenth-century Enlightened absolutism, he tried to demonstrate that the Prussian monarchy had made the progressive actualization of Reason and freedom the self-conscious principle of its own historical development. Opposition to this state must thus necessarily be historically regressive.[74] For Marheineke and Förster (as for Schulze, who supported their position), the contemporary mission of philosophy was restricted to the task of theoretical comprehension.

Outside Berlin this traditional or "orthodox" version of the accommodationist stance was most vigorously defended by the Hallean philosophers Hinrichs and Schaller. Both insisted that the identity in content of religious faith and philosophical knowledge was the very heart of the Hegelian system. What was at stake in the controversies concerning the relationship between philosophy and religion during the 1830s was the validity of the Hegelian comprehension of the absolute as a concrete universal, as the reconciliation of thought and being, Reason and reality. Those thinkers who claimed that the content of the representations of the Christian faith was incompatible with Hegel's rational ontology had simply failed to penetrate the Hegelian method of dialectical mediation in which the concrete particularity of the individual was not dissolved, but comprehended and reconstituted as a Moment in the dynamic totality of the universal. Because they remained in, or had fallen back into, the bifurcated world of the finite consciousness, such critics mistakenly interpreted Hegel's description of the self-differentiating structure of Reason either as an ideal that still required actualization or as a system of abstract logical forms that had to be transcended in order to arrive at a direct apprehension of the concreteness and particularity of reality. Contemporary demands for either a reformation of philosophy that would bring thought into conformity with the reality of human experience or a reformation of the world that would bring human experience into conformity with thought were thus dismissed by Hinrichs and Schaller as products of a failure to comprehend the reconciliation accomplished in Hegel's philosophy.[75]

The orthodox accommodationists' confidence in the ability of the Hegelian method to provide a satisfactory reconciliation of the free, rational self with its contemporary cultural environment began to falter as the 1830s drew to a close. As cultural conservatives who insisted that the preservation of the universal content of religious faith and communal ethics was dependent on the preservation of the traditional "positive" forms of Christian teaching, political authority, and social organization increased their influence in both church and state, the old manner of Hegelian apologetics began to assume a critical appearance. The world that Hegel had comprehended as the actualization of Reason was no longer the world in which his disciples lived. History seemed suddenly to be moving backward, and accommodation to the existing order thus appeared increasingly incompatible with the principle of accomplished reconciliation on which their accommodationist stance had been based. All of the orthodox accommodationists tended, during the late 1830s, to be more sympathetic to critical Hegelians than to the academic apologists of the new conservative trends. Marheineke and Gans, for example, became close friends after 1835, and Förster, Schulze, Hinrichs, and Schaller all supported Ruge in his battle with the conservatives in 1838–9.[76] None of the orthodox accommodationists were defined as Right Hegelians by their contemporaries during the 1830s. This title was reserved for a more conservative group of accommodationists – Gabler, Göschel, Henning, and Conradi of the older generation and Bruno Bauer (until 1838) and Johann Eduard Erdmann of the younger – who were willing to adapt the accommodationist stance to the new political and religious environment. Although Gabler, as Hegel's "successor," and Henning, as a full professor and editor of the *Jahrbücher,* held the most important academic positions in this group, it was Göschel, the philosophizing, pietistic judge, who emerged as its most prominent and influential spokesman during the 1830s.

In Göschel's writings the interpretation of Hegel's philosophy as an ideological justification for religious and political restoration attained its most extreme form. The activity of philosophical comprehension was stripped completely of its dynamic, negative, historical function in transforming the traditional "positive" forms of religious and political consciousness into the rational forms of the philosophical *Begriff.* In Göschel's view, Hegel had simply shown that the validity of the traditional forms could be rationally demonstrated, that philosophy was in harmony with the inherited truths of Christian culture. Hegel's great accomplishment was the scientific description of the absolute as the infinite substance that knew or comprehended itself as subject, as a concrete universal, or, as Göschel liked to put it, as a "personality" or an "individual." "In the Hegelian system," he claimed, "the *individual* is the highest, the ultimate, the foundation stone of the whole building, that which is alone real and concrete."[77] But this conception of the absolute as a concrete universal was also the central truth of the Christian faith, as expressed in the doctrines of a personal God, the complete incarnation of the divine in the historical individual Jesus Christ, and the personal immortality of the individual soul; Hegel's philosophy was merely a rational expression of this prior revealed truth. Many orthodox Hegelians supported Göschel in his defense of the Hegelian conception of the absolute against the misunderstanding of Hegel's critics or the one-sided "pantheistic" interpretations of Hegelian radicals, but they were also disturbed by his method of defense.[78] For Göschel saw no contradiction between form and content in Christian religion; the Hegelian comprehension did not complete the process of reconciliation by elevating the content of faith to its proper form, but merely provided another version of the completed reconciliation. Göschel simply asserted the identity of religious and philosophical truth, and tried to "show" it through analogy.[79] He presented himself as a defender of the dialectical conception of the absolute but did not apply the dialectical method to the relationship between religion and philosophy.

The conservative implications of this philosophical position became obvious in Göschel's attempt to defend the identity of Hegelian philosophy and traditional Christian doctrine on the issue of personal immortality. The Hegelian philosophical conversion, the elevation to the realm of spiritual comprehension, was described as a rational comprehension of the traditional Christian conversion in which the individual soul became a vessel of the divine will. In both cases the incarnation of the absolute in the individual was limited by man's continued existence in a corruptible body. The consciousness of identity with the absolute was thus merely a promise of a future, more total reconciliation that would occur when the transfigured soul was reunited with a transfigured or spiritualized body in the afterlife.[80] For Göschel, the traditional Christian eschatology that postponed final reconciliation between God and man to a transcendent realm in a life after death was not destroyed by the philosophical comprehension of religious "representations" as spiritual truths, but demonstrated as a necessary implication of the idea of the absolute as a concrete universal, as the complete incarnation of the universal in the individual.

Göschel's rejection of all attempts, Christian or Hegelian, to claim the eschatological inheritance in the here and now was clearly reflected in his political viewpoint. Here he interpreted Hegel's philosophy as simply a gloss on the traditional Lutheran conception of the authoritarian "Christian" state. The freedom of the individual subject was defined as obedience to divinely constituted authority. Contemporary demands for individual freedom and equality were dismissed as expressions of the "sinfulness" of the unconverted ego whose consciousness remained bound to the corrupting desires of the flesh. The purpose of the law was to bind and discipline this ego, to impose the divine will on a fallen world.[81] The liberal element in Hegel's political theory was completely obliterated in Göschel's conservative revision; the realm of civil society was identified completely with a feudal organization of privileged estates. It is not surprising that the Hegelians' conservative opponents greeted Göschel's works with approval, and simply dismissed his Hegelianism as a self-deception.[82] By 1840, Göschel himself appeared to have come to the same conclusion; the content of his religious and political viewpoint remained the same, but he ceased his attempt to justify it with Hegelian arguments.[83]

Two other Hegelians had preceded Göschel in this rightward shift beyond the boundaries of the Hegelian school. Both Isaak Rust and Heinrich Leo responded to the political unrest of the early thirties with a sharp turn in a conservative direction. Rust described the liberal movement as "the impudent spirit of negation penetrating into politics in its most unfettered form." The negative Moment of subjective freedom in the Hegelian dialectic was now denied all historical legitimacy. It simply expressed the rebellion of the sinful ego against the divine authority of both biblical revelation and the constituted political authorities. The rationalism of the sixteenth and seventeenth centuries, the Enlightenment, and the French Revolution were all condemned as manifestations of a demonic principle. The only solution to the present crisis, in Rust's view, was a restoration of the original Lutheran definition of Christian freedom as obedience to divine authority.[84] In 1833, Rust was already recognized as one of the leaders of the fundamentalist, neo-pietist faction in Bavarian Protestantism, and he was promoted to the position of consistory councillor in order to lead the battle against the theological rationalists who still dominated the church in the Palatinate. In 1837 he was attacked as "a man of jesuitical-pietistical-mystical-theocratical tendency."[85] By 1838 most Hegelians were ready to apply a similar label to Heinrich Leo.

We have already seen that Leo's critical Hegelianism during the 1820s was characterized by a conservative defense of the traditional autonomy of corporate political, social, and cultural institutions and associations against the leveling tendencies of bureaucratic centralization and "Jacobin" democracy. At the same time, however, he had insisted that the general process of liberalization and rationalization that had begun during the Renaissance was a necessary, albeit "negative," stage in the evolution of human community from the merely "positive" or "natural" organism of traditional feudal society to the self-consciously affirmed "spiritual" organism of the modern state. After 1830, Leo, like Rust and Göschel, rejected the historical or philosophical legitimacy of the negative, liberal Moment in the Hegelian dialectical totality and simply demanded a restoration of the traditional "positive" order. The "atomistic, modern-liberal direction in politics" was rejected as a sinful deviation from the eternally valid "natural" form of social organization represented by the "systematic" and "organic" communal order of medieval Christendom and the early Protestant German principalities.[86] This shift in Leo's political viewpoint was accompanied by an equally radical change in his religious outlook. In the fall of 1832 he began to attend the pietistic study group begun in Halle by the reactionary aristocratic judge Ludwig von Gerlach and the pietist theologian August Tholuck, and in the spring of 1833 he publicly announced his conversion to a neoorthodox Protestant Fundamentalism.[87] In contrast to his earlier position – in which the authoritarian and hierarchical aspects of Roman Catholicism and Protestant neoorthodoxy had been attacked as a denial of the principle of individuality – he now insisted that unquestioning obedience to the transcendent authority of a revealed "positive" religion was the only secure foundation for a restoration of a "natural" social and political order.[88]

Eduard Gans interpreted Leo's new cultural stance not only as a rejection of Hegelianism, but as a withdrawal from contemporary history. Leo, he claimed, had shut himself off from his time, and thus condemned himself to historical irrelevance.[89] This judgment was premature. By the late 1830s it appeared that Leo, and not Gans, was in step with his time. While Gans became increasingly estranged from the established regime, Leo found himself more and more at home in it and took on the role of defender of the existing church and state. In 1838, Leo brought the whole problem of Hegelian accommodation to a head by denouncing the majority of Hegelians as religious and political subversives. The Prussianism and Protestantism of most Hegelians, he claimed, had little in common with the existing Prussian state and Protestant church. Their loyal, apparently accommodationist phraseology concealed the revolutionary claim that political and religious authority were legitimate only if they conformed to the demands of human reason. The only Hegelians whom Leo exempted from his denunciation were the conservative accommodationists Göschel, Gabler, Bauer, and Erdmann. These Right Hegelians, he felt, were more deceived than deceiving in their attempts to fight the devil on his own terms. Their hearts were in the right place, but their heads were in the wrong philosophy. In Leo's view, the Hegelian "comprehension" of Christianity implied a transformation of not only the form but also the content of the traditional faith. The individual, personal, self-conscious God of Christianity became an absolute spirit that attained personality and self-consciousness only in man; the Christian incarnation was transformed into an immanent process of human divinization; and the eschatological hope for a total reconciliation of God and man in the hereafter became a demand for the present, immanent historical incarnation of the Kingdom of God. Hegelian Christianity, Leo claimed, was in fact a new religion that threatened to "tear the people away from the basis of its morality and faith that has existed for more than a thousand years," and to lure "the children of the German nation into Satan's watchtower," where they would "die from hunger and thirst for the word of the Lord."[90]

In 1838, few Hegelians were willing to accept the revolutionary role Leo had assigned to them. In fact, those Hegelians who might have accepted this role were not really the object of Leo's attack. His aim was to unveil the implicit revolutionary content in the stance of the moderately progressive, reformist Hegelians who continued to assert their loyalty to the rational principles of the Prussian state and the absolute truth of the Christian religion. Leo's virtual identification of this reformist Hegelian Center with the Hegelian school as a whole revealed the increasing prominence of a critical, progressive interpretation of the relationship between Reason and actuality within the Hegelian school during the 1830s.

Although Eduard Gans did not participate actively in the theological controversies of the 1830s, he may still be seen as the "godfather" of the critical Hegelianism that emerged during these debates and eventually found institutional form in Ruge's *Hallische Jahrbücher.* In Gans's lectures and writings, the interpretation of the present as a Moment in the continuing progressive actualization of Reason in history found its earliest and most forceful expression. The philosophical comprehension of contemporary history, he told the students who crowded into his classes after 1830, could illuminate the future as well as the past, and thus provide an orientation for progressive political activity.[91] In contrast to Hegel and the accommodationists, Gans took an active, sympathetic interest in the post-1830 liberal movements in France, England, Belgium, and Switzerland and made every effort to arouse his Prussian contemporaries to take up the cause of liberal reform in their own country.[92] The present Prussian state, Gans claimed, was a "tutelary state" and thus a transitional form. "A tutelary state, like tutelage itself," he wrote, "can last for only a limited time." It might delay full emancipation for a time but could not deny it "in the long run."[93] In Prussia the full equality and self-governing autonomy that defined membership in an actualized ethical community was still limited to the tutorial, or administrative, classes. The task for the future was to end the minority of the "subjects" of administration and extend the actualized ethical community to the whole society.[94]

The events of 1830 did not transform Gans into a revolutionary. Although his writings and lectures were censored by the state, he insisted on the moderate and loyal nature of his demands for reform. He did not see a new principle of political organization emerging from the crisis of 1830; he simply perceived the crisis as a sign that the actualization of Reason in modern politics was still incomplete.[95] His moderate stance was evident in his judgment of the Saint-Simonians' demands for a total social and cultural transformation. He was sympathetic toward the Saint-Simonians' critique of liberalism and agreed that the unrestricted reign of competitive individualism produced political anarchy and the unconscionable exploitation of the propertyless working class by bourgeois property owners. But he disagreed with the Saint-Simonians on the solution to these problems. The abolition of the right of inheritance, of freedom of trade, and of occupational choice, he insisted, would destroy the very foundations of ethical life in the modern world. The only historically legitimate and viable ways to resolve the conflicts of bourgeois society were political integration and cultural education. Although bourgeois society was not in itself an ethical organism, as many French and British liberals mistakenly supposed, it was a necessary, though subordinate, Moment within an authentic modern political community. The primacy of the political was not conceived by Gans as the restriction of individual freedom by political coercion but as the fulfillment of individual freedom through politicization, that is, elevation to the universal. The problem of proletarization, he claimed, could be resolved according to Hegelian principles and without the restoration of medieval guilds or a socialist revolution. The working class could be elevated to full membership in the political community through legal protection of their individual rights, social legislation that alleviated their competitive disadvantage in the marketplace, and the creation of "free corporations" that would form a bridge from the particular to the universal will.[96]

Gans's rejection of the historical necessity for any fundamental change in the structure of cultural integration was also evident in his criticism of the Saint-Simonians' attempt to establish a new religion. "The spirit of Christianity," he claimed, "is not what the Saint-Simonians call pure spirit or what we would prefer to refer to as abstract spirit," but the concrete spirit "that has entered into the world, penetrated it and constructed it according to its own principle." The task of the present age was not to discover a new religious principle but to complete the historical actualization of the old. In fact, Gans claimed that immediacy of religious faith, the belief in a transcendent religious authority, was impossible for modern European man, for whom the content of faith had taken on the "earthly form" of real social, political, and cultural relationships.[97]

Therefore, despite the radicalization of Gans's consciousness of, and hope for, historical change after 1830, he remained loyal to the reformist, progressive Hegelianism he had articulated in the 1820s. He affirmed the identity of content in Christian religion and Hegelian philosophy but, unlike the accommodationists, he emphasized the crucial significance of the difference in the two forms of appropriating the same truth. Hegel was able to articulate the truth of the concrete universal in a system of scientific concepts because that truth had become actual in the historical world during the revolutionary political and cultural transformations of the modern period.[98] For Gans, Reason was actual in the present, but in a general European and epochal sense. The final stage in the process of Reason's actualization had begun during the period of the French Revolution and Napoleonic reforms, and could thus be comprehended by Hegel, but the process was not yet complete. Even in the Prussian state, which Gans, like Hegel, perceived as the purest example of the modern rational state and the destined leader of the European transformation,[99] the actuality of the concrete universal in the form of an ethical community was restricted to the "tutorial" class of administrators and educators. Hegel's comprehension of the reality of Reason in contemporary culture thus remained in a critical relationship to existing "appearances."

By the time Strauss published his *Life of Jesus* in 1835, Gans's type of reformist, future-oriented, critical Hegelianism had become the dominant cultural stance among the younger members of the school both inside and outside Prussia. Within Prussia it was represented by the untenured academics - Michelet, Werder, Hotho, Ferdinand and Agathon Benary, Wilhelm Vatke, and Arnold Ruge - and by a growing number of intellectuals on the fringes of the academic school - like the publisher Moritz Veit (1808-64), the journalists Eduard Meyen (1812-70) and Ludwig Buhl (1813-82), and gymnasium teachers like Echtermeyer, Karl Friedrich Köppen (1808-63), Adolf Stahr (1805-76), Karl Nauwerck (1810-91), and Max Stirner.[100] Rosenkranz, who was appointed to a full professorship in Königsberg in 1833, tended to waver in his position. Although he was usually counted as a member of the progressive Hegelian Center, he often shifted to a defense of orthodox accommodationists like Hinrichs, Schaller, and Marheineke when he felt that the reformist fervor of critical Hegelians threatened to undermine the fundamental principles of Hegelian philosophy.[101] Baur articulated a similarly ambiguous position, but the younger generation of Swabian Hegelians virtually all supported the progressive Hegelianism of Strauss, Märklin, Vischer, and Binder.[102] When Ruge traveled through Württemberg in the fall of 1837, he was both surprised and gratified by the widespread support for his project of a new Hegelian journal.[103] Outside these two centers of Hegelianism, the most enthusiastic and articulate proponent of critical Hegelianism between 1835 and 1840 was Karl Bayrhoffer (1812–88), a lecturer in philosophy at Marburg.[104]

In 1838, Friedrich Vischer claimed that the publication of the *Life of Jesus* had made Strauss into one of those "representative men" who crystallize the collective consciousness of their historical generation.[105] Even if we restrict the scope of Vischer's claim to the critical Hegelians, however, it possesses only a limited validity. Strauss did articulate the general position of critical Hegelianism on the problem of the relationship between the traditional forms of Christian faith and philosophical, Hegelian Christianity or "modern consciousness." In contrast to the orthodox and conservative accommodationists, he insisted that the philosophical rehabilitation of the truth of Christianity was dependent on the destruction of the "otherness," the "positivity," of its representational form. Moreover, Strauss clearly stated that contemporary Christian consciousness was still, except among a few philosophers, chained to the traditional representational form. The process of critical negation was not yet finished. Philosophy had to take on the tasks of historical-cultural criticism before it could hope to fulfill its mission of reconciliation.[106] As the cultural influence of a conservative, neoorthodox Protestantism increased during the 1830s, even fence-sitters like Baur and Rosenkranz found it difficult to disagree with the claim that religious belief in a transcendent personal God, an exclusive, absolute incarnation of God in the historical Christ, and the personal immortality of the soul after death were identical with the Hegelian comprehension of the self-consciousness, dynamic historical actualization, and immortality of the spirit.[107] But Strauss's *Life of Jesus* did not simply give expression to the theological dimension of the critical Hegelianism of his generation. It also proposed a totally immanent interpretation of the Hegelian concrete universal, a position that isolated him from other critical Hegelians between 1835 and 1838 but formed the starting point for the development of the new Hegelian Left in 1839 and 1840.

The philosophical position of the broad movement of critical Hegelianism during the mid 1830s was most clearly formulated not by Strauss but by Bayrhoffer and Michelet, who both insisted that, on the level of philosophical principle or "method," Hegel's accomplishment could experience no further historical revision or development. Hegel had fulfilled the goal of theoretical comprehension by demonstrating the dialectical identity of subject and substance, Reason and reality. There could be no more advanced theoretical or philosophical standpoint. Particular parts of the Hegelian system might require revision, but the absolute method to which those revisions would have to conform was not itself subject to revision. There could be no "construction of a new principle," Michelet insisted.[108] In one sense, therefore, the actualization of Reason had been completed; the absolute had attained the concrete reality of self-consciousness in the thought of Hegel and his disciples. If the historical process of actualization was defined as a progressive movement toward higher and more perfect states of consciousness, Bayrhoffer stated, then historical development had reached its end.[109] In another sense, however, the process of actualization had just begun. For both Bayrhoffer and Michelet perceived the achieved reconciliation between Reason and reality as a reconciliation that had still not fully penetrated the cultural world. "Life" and "science" remained in a state of contradiction. Hegel's disciples thus still had a momentous task before them, a task that Bayrhoffer described as the "reformation of the world."[110] Already, in 1831, Michelet had written: "The owl of Minerva yields to the cockcrow that announces the dawn of a new day."[111] In 1838, he explicated this statement thus: "From the side of the thinking spirit, the reconciliation has already taken place. What still remains to be done is the elevation of reality, in all of its aspects, to rationality, so that the reconciliation will be perfected in the world as well."[112] Both Bayrhoffer and Michelet perceived the task of world reformation as having two major aspects: the educational transformation of traditional religious consciousness into the freedom of philosophical comprehension and the elevation of communal relationships into conformity with the science of Reason and freedom. Through a transformation of faith into knowledge and the state into objectified Reason the old dualism of state and church would be overcome, and the concrete universal would finally attain incarnation in the world.[113]

Throughout the 1830s, the theological or religious dimension in the critical Hegelians' program for the actualization of the Idea clearly predominated over the political dimension. The leading spokesmen for the younger generation of critical Hegelians were philosophers, theologians, and literary critics, not legal and political theorists like Gans. They focused their attention on the pedagogical task of transforming the traditional religious consciousness of their contemporaries into the modern, rational self-consciousness articulated in Hegel's philosophy. But this educational mission was presented as a prerequisite for, rather than an alternative to, political reform. Gans seemed to take the transformation of Christian consciousness for granted, and concentrated his attention on the practical issue of political reform. The younger critical Hegelians, who were caught up in a polemical battle with their conservative religious opponents in the educational and ecclesiastical system, viewed the resolution of the religious question as the most pressing and immediate problem and seemed to view political reform as a historical inevitability once their educational task had been fulfilled. When the younger Hegelians addressed themselves specifically to the political issue, however, their views were virtually indistinguishable from those of Gans. The present political situation was perceived as a transitional stage in which the actualization of freedom and Reason was still "abstract," that is, limited to the tutelary classes (in Prussia),[114] or to the empty legal forms of the *Rechtsstaat* (in Württemberg).[115] Future political progress was perceived as the transformation of the abstract form of the modern state into the concrete ethical community of a genuinely representational, liberal constitutional monarchy. In politics as in religion, critical Hegelians proposed a gradual reform of the existing order from "above," rather than from "below." They did not identify themselves with any liberal movement outside the existing state structure, but counseled and predicted an absorption of the legitimate demands of post-1830 liberalism into the existing regimes through a process of internal reform. The state, they believed, would come to recognize the critical, negative Moment of subjective freedom as a necessary component of its dialectical structure and reform itself.[116]

This moderate, liberal Hegelianism reached the apex of its self-consciousness and cultural influence in 1838. In that year, Michelet and Bayrhoffer published major works in which the viewpoint of critical Hegelianism was described as the stance of the legitimate Hegelian majority, and the conservative accommodationism of Gabler, Göschel, Bauer, and Erdmann was dismissed as the minority opinion of an errant sect.[117] The new historical confidence and self-consciousness of the critical Hegelians also found expression in two journals that emerged as significant organs of Hegelianism in 1838: the *Literarische Zeitung,* edited by Eduard Meyen, and especially Ruge's and Echtermeyer's *Hallische Jahrbücher,* which rapidly became the most widely read, controversial, and influential Hegelian journal in Germany.

The American historian William Brazill has claimed that the *Hallische Jahrbücher* was founded as the organ of a "Young Hegelian party" whose aim was to "usher in the Young Hegelian apocalypse" of "anti-Christian humanism."[118] The actual facts of the matter were not quite so dramatic. There was no "Young Hegelian party" in 1838, at least not in the sense in which Brazill uses the term, that is, as synonymous with the radical Left Hegelianism that would emerge a few years later. In fact, in 1837 and 1838, Ruge used "party" as a term of abuse, to refer to the sterile dogmatism, the "sublime Brahminism," of the Berlin accommodationists.[119] "All the power of the spirit of youth," he wrote to Rosenkranz, "wants to know nothing of the concept of a school or a party."[120] Ruge did perceive his *Jahrbücher* as an expression of the consciousness of a new generation, but only in the very general sense of that broad coalition of critical Hegelians who wanted to keep Hegel's philosophy in contact with the progressive development of history. The aim of the journal, he claimed, was to "feel the life impulse" of German intellectual life and thus "embody the principle of development."[121] At its inception, the *Jahrbücher* solicited and received the support of all Hegelians except the most conservative accommodationists.

To claim that the critical Hegelianism of the *Hallische Jahrbücher* aimed at an "apocalyptic" transformation of the existing political and cultural order is to take Leo's denunciation of Ruge, Meyen, Michelet, and Bayrhoffer at face value. Ruge himself defined the original editorial policy of the *Jahrbücher* as that of "Hegelian Christians" and "orthodox Prussians."[122] In the midst of the battle with Leo and his conservative allies, Ruge did consider the possibility that the "obscurantists" might gain control of the Prussian state, but in his view it was not his own position, but theirs, that was revolutionary, as it represented "a destruction of the genuine free spirit that has its form and existence in our state and its laws."[123] Only in the spring and summer of 1839 did Ruge begin to equate "reaction" with the existing regime. Altenstein's and Schulze's continual private assurances that the state would support the critical Hegelians in their battle against political and cultural reaction had not been substantiated by practical measures. Leo and his allies continued to increase their power and influence in the educational system, the church, and the state. Ruge's repeated petitions for academic tenure went unheeded. In September 1839 he published (anonymously) his first explicit attack on the Prussian regime, and in November he withdrew his name from the list of *Privatdozenten* at Halle and went into open and full-time opposition.[124] By the summer of 1840, the *Hallische Jahrbücher* had clearly shifted to the left of the mainstream of reformist Hegelianism, although it was not until the summer of 1841 that it became an "organ" of the new Left Hegelianism of Bauer and Feuerbach.

Not all of the critical Hegelians of the 1830s, of course, joined Ruge in his shift to the left. But the number who did was significant enough to indicate that the process of differentiation within the school had entered a new phase. After 1840, the major division within the school was no longer between accommodationists and critical reformers, but between critical reformers and the new radicals. Moreover, this division was based not on differing interpretations of the relationship between Christian religion and philosophical *Wissenschaft,* or between Hegel's conception of the modern state and the existing political regime, but on fundamental conflicts over the viability of Hegel's philosophical accomplishment. The new Hegelian Left denied the absolute claims of Hegelian "method" or "principle" and relegated Hegel, together with Christianity and the tutelary state, to the old regime of dualism and heteronomy. They thus changed the whole focus of the debate over the Hegelian inheritance. The primary issue was no longer whether one group or another could rightfully claim the Hegelian inheritance, but whether the Hegelian inheritance was worth claiming. The moderate reformist Hegelians maintained their control of the academic school and their status as official spokesmen for Hegelian philosophy after 1840.[125] In the eyes of the Left Hegelians, however, the moderates had chosen to take their stand with a dying culture and had become the sterile caretakers of a metaphysical system that had lost its ability to reconcile man with his historical world. The Left Hegelians withdrew from the school and academic life and sought their historical identity as the vanguard of a post-Hegelian cultural order that was yet to be born.

There are significant similarities between the Left Hegelianism of Ruge, Strauss, Feuerbach, Bruno Bauer, and other young Hegelians that emerged during the late 1830s and the earlier forms of Hegelian radicalism articulated in the Restoration writings of Carové and Feuerbach. But there were also major differences between these two historical stages of Left Hegelianism, differences as obvious as the differences between the Feuerbach of the *Thoughts on Death and Immortality* (1830) and the Feuerbach of *The Essence of Christianity* (1841). During the early and mid-1830s, Feuerbach, as we shall see in some detail in Chapter 10, abandoned his earlier stance and struggled with the problem of establishing a new philosophical foundation for the task of cultural reconstruction. Old Left Hegelianism, however, did not disappear during the 1830s. It continued to be represented by Carové, whose faith in an imminent breakthrough to the final reconciliation of God and man was regenerated by the revolutions of 1830, and by three younger cultural prophets on the fringes of the Hegelian school: Friedrich Richter, August Cieszkowski (1812-94), and Moses Hess (1812-75). A brief survey of their positions will help clarify what precisely was new in the Left Hegelianism of the late 1830s.

It would be misleading to describe Carové, Richter, Cieszkowski, and Hess as members of a faction or party within the Hegelian school. They developed their views independently, without any consciousness of working within a radical Hegelian tradition, and had no discernible influence on, or personal contact with, one another. What they did have in common was their situation as "outsiders," in relationship both to the academic school and to the existing German political and cultural communities. Carové continued to live the life of a "free-floating" cosmopolitan journalist and free-lance author, constantly on the move between France and Germany. His contact with the Hegelian school was limited to the occasional articles he submitted to Hegelian journals.[126] Hess, whose first book, *The Sacred History of Mankind,* was published anonymously in 1837, was the self-educated, rebellious son of a successful Rhenish Jewish merchant. He had no connections with other Hegelians until the late 1830s and was never a part of the German academic world. Neither Hess nor Carové defined himself as a Hegelian (Hess even referred to himself as a "disciple of Spinoza");[127] and they did not perceive their writings as contributions to the specific controversies that absorbed the energies of the school during the 1830s. Their criticism of the accommodationist and critical, reformist forms of Hegelianism was implicit rather than explicit, but the general structure of their viewpoints was remarkably similar to the more explicitly Hegelian cultural radicalism of Cieszkowski and Richter.

Cieszkowski and Richter did have close personal and intellectual contact with other Hegelians and formulated their words as responses to questions raised by the debates within the school. Richter, whom we have already encountered in the role of Rosenkranz's personal gadfly at Halle in 1829–30, published in 1833 two books on the doctrine of immortality that attacked the reformist and accommodationist interpretations of the relationship between Christian "representation" and philosophical concept;[128] and Cieszkowski, a student and personal friend of Karl Ludwig Michelet, conceived his *Prolegomena to Historiosophy* (1838) as a radical resolution of the problems regarding the relationship between theory and practice raised by the critical Hegelians' notions of the "actualization" of philosophy. But both Richter and Cieszkowski felt as uprooted and homeless in the historical-cultural world of the 1830s as Carové or Hess. That Cieszkowski, a Catholic Polish aristocrat who had been forced into political exile because of his participation in the Polish revolt of 1830–1, would find it difficult to accept the Hegelian claim of a completed reconciliation of Reason and reality, even in principle, is hardly surprising.[129] It was virtually inevitable that he would perceive the Hegelian concrete universal as an abstraction or an ideal in relation to his own historical experience. Richter, in contrast, was both Prussian and Protestant, and the experiential origins of his homelessness are thus more revealing of the general tensions between Hegelianism and its cultural environment.

Rosenkranz described Richter's father as an "original man" who had rapidly amassed a small fortune as a peasant sheep breeder in Saxony before 1815 and then, almost as rapidly, squandered it in numerous unsuccessful business ventures in Magdeburg during the postwar era.[130] After 1830 this ambitious, self-made man found himself, more often than not, confined within the walls of a debtors' prison. As the son of an "original man" who had emancipated himself from the confines of traditional society but failed to establish a secure basis for a new social identity, Richter might best be described as a social orphan. After being pampered as a musical prodigy during his childhood, he was suddenly forced to begin an apprenticeship as a pharmacist when his father's fortunes began to decline in the early 1820s. For Richter this career was not a satisfactory social vocation, but an arbitrary, stifling fate imposed by external circumstances. Contact with the young Rosenkranz convinced him that he possessed exceptional literary and intellectual abilities, and that God wanted him to develop these abilities for some vague, but exalted, historical mission. He quit his job, somehow financed two years of gymnasium study, and, in 1826, passed the entrance examination at the University of Berlin. It was in the classrooms of Hegel and Marheineke that his sense of divine calling found a definite object and took on a definite form. For Richter, the Hegelian conversion was an entry into a totally new world, radically opposed to the old world of the finite ego that had defined his previous existence. But the old world continued to exist, unredeemed, because the Hegelian transformation was purely theoretical and thus confined to a small group of philosophers. Like Feuerbach, Richter perceived this contradiction between philosophical theory and concrete historical existence, between the academic school and "humanity," as the inspiration for his own particular historical mission. As a "prophet and reformer" he would prepare the way for the historical actualization of the Kingdom of God.[131] In 1831 he began his new career by trying (unsuccessfully) to convince his fellow Magdeburgers that they had been divinely chosen to form a "resurrected city of God on earth" and thus to become the center of an epochal religious transformation.[132] Undaunted by this initial failure he moved on to Breslau, where for the next two years he continued his philosophical and theological studies and eked out a precarious existence as a tutor in the households of Silesian aristocrats - an experience, he later claimed, that radicalized his consciousness of the vast gap between Hegelian theory and contemporary cultural existence.[133] When the acquisition (through marriage) of a small publishing firm in Breslau in 1833 allowed him to devote all of his time and energy to his prophetic mission, however, he insisted that his conception of cultural transformation was in complete harmony with the spirit of the Prussian state and a "genuine" Christianity, and he pleaded and hoped for official support, and even subsidization, for his activities.[134] Such hopes were quickly dashed. His writings were condemned by both Hegelian and non-Hegelian academics as expressions of an anti-Christian pantheism, and Altenstein informed him that he could never expect to be considered for any appointment in Prussia unless he recanted his views.[135] This rejection by the academic world and the state was paralleled by public indifference. The weekly journal, *Der Prophet,* with which Richter hoped to bring his message to the general public attracted less than one hundred subscribers. By 1835, Richter had become a rather pathetic figure – a penniless, itinerant, unrecognized prophet, hounded by creditors, harrassed by censors, rejected and ridiculed even by those initiates into the new world whom he claimed to represent, an exile within his own country.

It was from this experience of exile or homelessness within the historical present that the Left Hegelianism of Richter, Carové, Hess, and Cieszkowski gained its common structure. Their starting point was an analysis of the present as a period of unresolved antithesis between the subjective finite ego and natural, social, and religious totality, as the culminating crisis of the historical stage of bifurcation in the evolution of mankind toward collective divinization.[136] There were, to be sure, significant differences in emphasis in their individual analyses of the general crises of bifurcation, especially on the level of communal relationships. Carové and Richter continued to perceive the external aspects of a genuine social community in terms of legal equality, a representative political constitution, and rational administration.[137] In this sense they might be described as moderate liberals. Hess and Cieszkowski, on the other hand, were much more sensitive to the class divisions and social anarchy produced by capitalist modes of production and exchange. Hess even claimed that the antithesis between individual and society was inextricably connected to the institution of private property. The abolition of traditional forms of social privilege and political authority would have to be followed by an abolition of the privileges and arbitrary power of private ownership of capital before the individual could hope to attain his essence as a social being.[138] But the significance of these differences can easily be exaggerated, for Carové, Richter, Cieszkowski, and Hess all believed that social and political relationships were dependent on, and a manifestation of, a more fundamental relationship between the human and the divine. In collective, cultural terms, the essential element in the crisis of bifurcation was the separation of church and state, the transcendent and the immanent cultural identity, religion and politics. It was the estrangement of man from God, and thus from his own essence as an infinite being, that defined the sickness of the age.[139]

The description of the present as an age of bifurcation implied and produced a significant revision of the Hegelian philosophy of history. The era of synthesis and reconciliation was displaced from the present into the future, and the whole Christian-German era was transformed into a mere transitional and preparatory stage in mankind's salvational history. The dialectical self-development and self-actualization of the absolute was simplified into a three-stage process in which the present moment marked the transition from the second to the third stage, from antithesis to synthesis, from contradiction to reconciliation, from, in Hess's terms, the Kingdom of the "Son" to the "New Jerusalem" of the Holy Spirit.[140] Both Hegelian philosophy and the traditional forms of Christian religion were relegated to the "old" world of dualism and heteronomy. The Hegelian system did represent a scientific comprehension and thus a final appropriation or actualization of the principle of Christian culture as it had evolved from the decline of the ancient world to the present day, but this historical role also defined its historical limitations. The transition to the future world of absolute reconciliation would be marked by a historical transcendence of both Christianity and Hegel. Yet Carové, Richter, Hess, and Cieszkowski also all described the culture of the future as a fulfillment of the Christian promise and, either implicitly (Carové, Hess) or explicitly (Richter, Cieszkowski), as an actualization of Hegelian philosophy.[141] Unlike the critical reformist Hegelians, however, they viewed this process of actualization not as a mere application and popularization of established principle, but as a dialectical process of negation and affirmation in which the principle itself would be transformed. This viewpoint was most clearly expressed in the writings of Richter and Cieszkowski.

Richter's writings, which, like those of the young Feuerbach, focused their cultural criticism on an analysis of the Christian doctrine of immortality, were dominated by two major concerns. First, he insisted that the Hegelian comprehension of traditional Christian "representations" destroyed the historical validity of those representations. To perceive the absolute as a personal transcendent being, the process of redemption as a series of particular miraculous acts by an individual, historical God-man, and the blessedness of salvation as an endless individual life after death was to experience the world from the standpoint of the subjective ego. Hegel's comprehension of the absolute as a self-comprehending totality, the process of redemption as the liberating labor of self-recognition and affirmation, and the blessedness of salvation as a life lived in the present eternity of the spirit presented the outlines of a world of experience radically opposed to that of Christian faith. Richter admonished Hegelians to recognize this contradiction between the representation and the concept, cease their futile attempts at accommodation, and engage in the necessary historical task of critically dismantling the old world.[142] At the same time, however, Richter asserted that the new world of Hegelian philosophy remained a world of theory and thus ultimately esoteric, "transcendent," historically impotent. Its separation from the concrete reality of historical and natural existence mirrored the dualistic structure of the Christian culture that it comprehended. Philosophical comprehension, he claimed, could never in itself provide the blessedness of absolute reconciliation; it was merely one Moment "within the sphere of the absolute," which encompassed "an absolute practice as much as an absolute knowledge," and thus subordinated philosophy to religion.[143] For Richter, religion was not synonymous with faith in representations; it was not simply a lower form of knowledge, but "the whole sphere of the spiritual, divine-human life," the "life sphere" in which "one lives speculatively, and like Christ, combines the clarity of thought with the purity of the deed."[144] The actualization of Hegelian philosophy thus entailed the negation of its one-sided theoretical character, of its limitations as merely philosophy, and its transformation into a self-comprehending absolute practice, into a religious "life." Richter, like Carové, Hess, and Cieszkowski, conceived the future cultural community as a universal terrestrial church in which the absolute content of Christian representations would be appropriated and made actual not only theoretically in the minds of an academic school, but both practically and theoretically in the concrete ethical interaction of the total human community, in the social or communal activity of love.[145]

Cieszkowski's *Prolegomena* also presented the historical actualization of Hegel's theoretical reconciliation of Reason and reality as the transition to a new and higher principle: the union of theory and practice in "absolute activity."[146] In the Hegelian philosophical universe the identity of theory and practice, Reason and reality, could be experienced only retroactively, as the contemplative comprehension of a completed practice. The absolute identity of Reason and reality thus remained theoretical, ideal, not "absolutely the absolute."[147] In his daily practical activity man remained a subjective ego at the mercy of powers he could not control. It was only after he left this world and entered the transcendent realm of pure theory that he could comprehend it as the self-objectification of absolute spirit, as the realm of freedom rather than necessity. In the future "synthetic" age, Cieszkowski claimed, this separation of thought and being would be overcome, as absolute theoretical knowledge became the informing immanent self-consciousness of "absolute, practical, social activity and life in the state."[148] Like Richter, he argued that Reason and philosophy represented a subordinate Moment in the total structure of the absolute spirit; the final all-encompassing stage was that of "absolute will." It was only when the actualization of the absolute became the freely, self-consciously willed "deed" of man that the incarnation of the divine in the human would be finally accomplished.[149] It is important to emphasize, as Cieszkowski is often perceived as a precursor of Marx, that his conception of the unity of theory and practice in social activity was presented in religious terms, as the self-conscious identification of man's self-determination with God's will.[150] Like Richter, Carové, and Hess he saw the transition to the millennium as a peaceful religious reformation, and defined the millennial community as a "divine-human" community, or universal "church."[151]

It was this interpretation of the past, present, and future in terms of the dialectical relationship between God and man, the transcendent and the immanent, that made the old Left Hegelians *old* Hegelians.[152] They interpreted the evolution of mankind as a "sacred" history, as the self-revelation of God through the divinization of man, as the dramatic story of the *reconciliation* between the divine and the human. Psychological and social bifurcation was perceived as a *manifestation* of the estrangement of man from God; it could be resolved only by a religious transformation that would evercome that estrangement. Carové, Richter, Hess, and Cieszkowski affirmed the absolute truth content of both Christian faith and Hegelian philosophy. Like Hegel, they asserted that the form of faith was inadequate to this content, but in opposition to Hegel they also insisted that the form of speculative thought was inadequate to the truth of absolute spirit. The identical "subject-object" of history remained absolute spirit; man could become the subject and object of his own history, the free self-conscious maker of his own world, only by identifying himself with the absolute, by knowing the divine Reason as his own reason, and by "living" the divine will as his own will, by making God's kingdom his own world. To criticize thinkers like Cieszkowski for their failure to define a specific historical group as the agent of the hoped-for cultural transformation is thus to misunderstand or reject the basic premise of their position. Mere "finite" social, political, or pedagogical activity could never transform the world in the radical fashion they envisioned. History was not a finite secular process of human self-realization, but the sacred process of God's self-actualization in man.

That Carové, Richter, and Cieszkowski would not welcome the Left Hegelians of the late 1830s as companions in arms is therefore quite understandable, for these new Left Hegelians denied what the old Left Hegelians had presupposed. They no longer sought to reconcile God and man, the transcendent and the immanent, but defined the problem of salvation, the actualization of essence in existence, in totally immanent, human terms. This secular "humanist" starting point – the rejection not only of the separation of the immanent and the transcendent, but of the reality of the transcendent – distinguished the new Left Hegelians from the old Left Hegelians and all other members of the Hegelian school. From the "anthropological" perspective that emerged in the writings of Strauss, Bauer, and Feuerbach around 1840, the old divisions within the Hegelian school between a Right, Center, and Left interpretation of the historical relationship between the immanent and the transcendent appeared as divisions within a limited "dualistic" cultural perspective that had lost its historical viability. To put it simply, for the new Left Hegelians the experiential reality of the "death of God" had placed the problems of human liberation and cultural reform in a totally new context, a context that was no longer compatible with the categories, the method, and the "principle" of the Hegelian system.

In 1841, Bruno Bauer presented his immanent interpretation or reduction of the Hegelian absolute in the guise of an anti-Hegelian polemic by a conservative defender of the established church and state, and thus gave expression to one of the least-known or examined aspects of the disintegration of Hegelianism.[153] For Bauer, Strauss, Feuerbach, and Ruge were not the first German intellectuals to interpret the Hegelian system in a totally immanent sense; Hegel's conservative opponents had articulated such an interpretation since the late 1820s.[154] For these conservatives, the emergence of the new Left Hegelianism in the late 1830s was a historical validation of their conviction that Hegel's reconciliation of the divine and the human, theology and philosophy, faith and knowledge, had been either a self-deception or a self-conscious deception from the very beginning. The real content of the Hegelian absolute spirit was simply the human spirit; the reconciliation between God and man was nothing more than an illegitimate attempt to put man in God's place. The conservatives' insistence on the revolutionary religious and political implications of Hegel's philosophy might best be described as a self-fulfilling prophecy. For it was the growing power of the conservatives in both church and state that made Hegel's reconciliations appear more and more like self-deception or hypocrisy to some of the younger members of the Hegelian school. Until the late 1830s, Hegelians, for all their inner differences, were united in rejecting the revolutionary identity that the conservatives continually tried to thrust upon them. The new Left Hegelians, however, accepted this identity and defined the contemporary cultural conflict as a radical opposition between theology and philosophy, religious and secular culture, Christianity and a post-Christian world view. The emergence of this new Left Hegelianism therefore cannot be described simply in relation to the divisions within the school; it was inextricably connected, in both an ideological and an experiential sense, to the evolution of the conservative opposition to Hegelianism in general.

THE FUNDAMENTALIST OPPOSITION: FROM PIETISTIC INWARDNESS TO CULTURAL RESTORATIONISM

David Friedrich Strauss began his reply to Ernst Hengstenberg's denunciation of the *Life of Jesus* in the *Evangelische Kirchenzeitung* by admitting that he welcomed a confrontation with a viewpoint so straightforward and decisive in a time when spiritual trends in Germany were generally characterized by ambiguity and confusion. "At least here one knows with what one is dealing and what one must look out for," he wrote.[155] This statement echoed Hengstenberg's own description of the *Life of Jesus* as "one of the most gratifying appearances in the sphere of contemporary theological literature."[156] The Antichrist hidden in the deceptive conciliatory garb of Hegelian Christianity had finally dared to show his true colors. Hengstenberg warned Strauss that salvation could be attained only through a self-transcending religious conversion: "Our reason is blind as our will is dead – only regeneration can bring light and life."[157] Strauss responded with the claim that Hengstenberg could come to see the light and enter the stream of contemporary history only by undergoing a philosophical "rebirth" from "abstract to concrete thinking."[158] These very parallels in the stances of Strauss and Hengstenberg were, of course, a source of division rather than reconciliation. Strauss saw no possibility for real communication or mutual understanding between modern philosophical self-consciousness and a viewpoint that denied all the "needs" of contemporary man.[159] Hengstenberg made no attempt to assess the validity of Strauss's arguments, but simply denounced his whole standpoint as an expression of rebellion against divine authority.[160]

Strauss was wrong, however, in thinking that the cultural stances of critical Hegelians and pietistic Fundamentalists were responses to totally different human needs. The very virulence of the opposition between the two groups was based on the fact that they represented mutually exclusive responses to a common cultural experience. A number of individuals - Leo, Rust, and Göschel among the Hegelians, Richard Rothe among the Fundamentalists - switched from one camp to the other during the 1830s.[161] The leaders of the Fundamentalist opposition to the Hegelian school in Prussia, northern Bavaria, and Württemberg, moreover, were academics of the same historical generation as the Hegelian Left. A brief description of the experience and thought of the Fundamentalists can thus provide insight into the general cultural context in which the Left Hegelian stance was formulated and may also help clarify the specific nature of their particular response to a shared generational experience.

The parallels in the historical experience of the Left Hegelians and their cultural opponents would undoubtedly seem more obvious if the evolution of a restorationist Fundamentalism could be described as a product of the disintegration of the Historical School or of Schleiermacher's reconciling theological vision. The battle between the Fundamentalists and Hegelians during the 1830s and 1840s could then be seen as evolving directly out of the conflict between Hegel and the Historical School during the 1820s. There is some evidence for such an attractively symmetrical conceptualization. There were connecting links, both personal and ideological, between the members of the Historical School and the Fundamentalists of the 1830s and 1840s, and the arguments between Hegelians and Fundamentalists often appeared to duplicate the ideological debates of the 1820s. The formative historical experience of the Fundamentalists during the Restoration, however, cannot be equated with an initiation into the *Weltanschauung* of Schleiermacher and the Historical School. The decisive historical experience of the Left Hegelians' cultural opponents was participation in what is generally described as the "second stage" or the "blooming" of the evangelical or pietistic "awakening (*Erweckungsbewegung*)."[162] This *Erweckungsbewegung* of the 1820s manifested itself in slightly different ways in different areas of Germany because of variations in political, social, and religious traditions and organization. For the purpose of our theme, it is most important to describe its nature and impact in those areas in which the "awakened" were in direct contact with the members of the Hegelian school: Berlin and Halle in Prussia, northern Bavaria, and Württemberg.

The distinctive feature of the religious awakening of the 1820s was that the impulse for religious renewal came from within the ecclesiastical establishment, from students and professors of theology at the universities. This revivalism from "above" was in sharp contrast to the two main types of pietistic revival that had characterized the late eighteenth and early nineteenth centuries: the spontaneous creation of lay devotional groups or conventicles that emphasized the inner experience of spiritual conversion and saw themselves as a chosen "brotherhood" of genuine Christians, and the millenarian or chiliastic movements that originated in the lower-class artisanate and peasantry in response to the social and political disorientation of the Napoleonic wars and the subsequent bureaucratic reforms. Both these types of religious revival could be described as expressions of opposition to, and discontent with, the established orthodoxy of the state churches. In very different ways they represented a demand for liberation - either the liberation of subjective experience from the deadening weight of an arid orthodoxy or, in the chiliastic movements in south Germany, a more radical liberation of the collective brotherhood of the saints from an oppressive cultural order. The emphasis in the awakening of the 1820s, however, was on the control and discipline of subjective religious experience by orthodox dogma, and the total subjection of the individual to divinely constituted authority in church and state.[163]

The development of traditional pietism into conservative Fundamentalism was most clearly revealed in the history of the awakening in Berlin. The first evidence of a religious revival within the ruling elites was the formation of a number of devotional circles composed of young aristocratic military cadets and law students in the years immediately following the wars of liberation.[164] These young Junkers had experienced the war against Napoleon as a kind of Christian-German crusade against French rationalism and liberalism and were convinced that the reconstruction of Prussia should be based on a religious as well as a political renovation. In the years between 1814 and 1816 many of them were attracted to the experiential, communitarian Christianity expounded in Schleiermacher's sermons. Schleiermacher's reconciling vision of the unity of subjective experience and traditional faith, however, did not provide a lasting solution to their religious needs. They turned instead to the simple message of repentance and faith preached by the leaders of the congregations of pietistic artisans in Berlin. By 1820 this aristocratic pietism had become a powerful and visible force in the Prussian capital. Many of the "converted" attained influential positions in the military and in the judicial and administrative bureaucracy. The sympathy and support of the crown prince and Princess Wilhelmine (the wife of the king's younger brother) gave them a strong voice at the center of political power.[165]

This growth of a Fundamentalist pietism among the members of the Prussian aristocracy was paralleled by a similar development within the nonaristocratic segment of the *Gebildete Stand.* Schleiermacher himself, of course, had a great deal of sympathy for the traditional pietism that emphasized subjective religious experience and the unity of the Christian brotherhood. He often invited the leaders of pietist congregations to preach in his pulpit and had helped bring the pietist theologian August Neander (1789–1850) to Berlin in 1813. The early 1820s, however, saw the emergence at the University of Berlin of a new group of younger pietist theologians who were closely tied to the awakening in the aristocratic circles. The leading members of this group were August Tholuck (1799–1877), Ernst Hengstenberg (1802–69), and Johannes Wichern (1806–81). Like their aristocratic counterparts, these young theologians were dissatisfied with the liberal and rational elements in Schleiermacher's theology. Hengstenberg claimed that Schleiermacher could not still his longing for a religious faith "that was built on an objective basis."[166]

It was the alliance of academic theologians and aristocratic officers, bureaucrats, and landowners that determined the specific character of the Prussian awakening of the 1820s. Both groups met for weekly devotional "hours" at the home of Baron von Kottwitz, one of the patriarchs of Berlin pietism. They provided each other with mutual support: The aristocrats used their power to secure appointments and promotions for the academics; the academics, in turn, supported the reactionary feudal politics of the aristocrats. Personal friendships and marriages bound the two groups together. Hengstenberg became engaged to the daughter of an East Prussian Junker in 1826. By 1828 he had received a full professorship at the University of Berlin, largely through the influence of his well-placed friends.[167] The alliance between the old Prussian aristocracy and Fundamentalist Christian theology represented a counterpart to the alliance between the rational reforming bureaucrats of the Hardenberg party and Hegelian philosophy. During the 1820s, the latter alliance remained the dominant force in the Prussian government. The pious aristocrats were leaders of the "feudal" opposition to the bureaucratic reformers; the pious academics were leaders of the opposition to Hegelian influence in the Prussian educational system. It is revealing that the *Erweckungsbewegung* attained cultural hegemony in the rural villages and country estates where the Junkers retained control of ecclesiastical patronage. Here the convergence of religious pietism and reactionary politics was only too obvious.[168]

In cities like Berlin and Halle, however, this convergence was not immediately evident. The search for an experiential, "living" faith united groups with different confessional backgrounds (even Catholics participated in the Berlin awakening) and academics with divergent theological viewpoints. August Tholuck looked back on the early 1820s as a "beautiful time of youth dominated by its first love, when the consciousness of unity far outweighed the consciousness of the divisions within the Church of Christ."[169] Significant political differences between aristocrats who desired a return to the Lutheran "authoritarian state (*Obrigkeitsstaat*)" and an aristocratically dominated "estates society (*Ständesstaat*)" and bureaucrats and academics who supported the Stein program of cultural reconstruction were pushed into the background by common opposition to the dominant Hegelian ideology. Political differences also failed to develop into rigid party conflicts because of the overwhelming emphasis on subjective religious experience that united the "awakened" during the 1820s. This amorphous coalition of divergent tendencies was perhaps best exemplified in the devotional meetings held in the home of Friedrich Karl von Savigny, where Catholics and Protestants, aristocratic reactionaries and bureaucratic and academic members of the Historical School, were equally welcome.[170]

By 1827 both confessional and political differences had become more obvious. That these differences had not yet hardened into party lines, however, was revealed in the founding of the *Evangelische Kirchenzeitung* in the spring of that year. Hengstenberg was appointed editor, and conservative aristocrats like Ludwig von Gerlach and Otto von Gerlach were its most important backers. The advertisement for the paper, however, strongly denied that it would function as the organ of a particular party. "The *Evangelische Kirchenzeitung,*" Hengstenberg claimed, "will demonstrate that the strength of conviction that the gospel demands of its disciples is compatible with love and tolerance."[171] Many of Hengstenberg's contemporaries welcomed the new paper as an organ for the views of "awakened" evangelical Christians throughout Germany, and as an antithesis to the recently founded Hegelian *Jahrbücher.* Schleiermacher and the Schleiermacherian or "mediating" theologians in Bonn and Göttingen originally supported the paper, as did representatives of traditional pietism like August Neander. Hengstenberg's polemical editorial stance, however, soon destroyed this broad coalition of theological anti-Hegelianism. For Hengstenberg's Fundamentalism, his belief in the absolute depravity of natural man and his demand for total surrender to unquestioned doctrinal authority, was basically incompatible with the emphasis on subjective experience and the deemphasis of doctrinal differences shared by Schleiermacher and the traditional pietists. By 1830, this disagreement had developed into an open conflict.[172]

Some of the most enthusiastic responses to the founding of the *Evangelische Kirchenzeitung* came from pietist groups in northern Bavaria and Württemberg. The evolution of the *Erweckungsbewegung* in these areas paralleled the developments in Prussia, with one major difference – the absence of the politically reactionary aristocratic component. The leadership of the awakening in both Bavaria and Württemberg was virtually monopolized by young university-trained pastors and academics. The formative religious experiences of these young men – Adolf von Harless (1806–79), Theodor Löhe (1808–72), Johannes Hofmann (1810–77), and Friedrich Julius Stahl (1802–61) in Bavaria and Ludwig Hofacker (1798–1828), Wilhelm Hofacker (1805–48), Sixt Kapff (1805–79), Albert Knapp (1798–1864), Christoph Gottlieb Barth (1799–1862), and Wilhelm Hoffmann (1806–73) in Württemberg – were remarkably similar. The original stages of their search for a "living" faith were characterized by an absorption in the undogmatic experiential Christianity described in Schleiermacher's *Speeches* or the speculative Christian mysticism that Schelling expounded at the University of Erlangen between 1820 and 1827. Like their Prussian counterparts, however, the south Germans finally found the kind of absolute religious assurance they desired in a conversion to a Fundamentalist pietistic Christianity. In Bavaria the revivalist preacher Christian Krafft (1784–1845), who was called to Erlangen in 1824, had a decisive impact on the "salvation" of many theology students. In Württemberg the Fundamentalist revival was initiated by the preaching of Ludwig Hofacker in 1823. In the five years before his death in 1828, Hofacker was able to establish his reputation as the most influential evangelist in the history of Württemberg Protestantism.[173]

A comparison of Hofacker's evangelistic message and Hengstenberg's description of the genuine road to salvation reveals the character of the experience of religious conversion that bound the Fundamentalists of the younger generation together. Like the Hegelians, both Hofacker and Hengstenberg began their search for religious assurance with the conviction that the Christian message as expounded by the traditional theologians of both the rationalist and the orthodox schools had lost its existential power and historical relevance. The "question of salvation," not the learned exegesis of dogma and inherited tradition, was to be placed at the center of Christian theology.[174] Salvation, however, could never arise from human effort. The presupposition of salvation was recognition of one's own total depravity and sinfulness. The blood of Christ had atoned for human sin, but the free gift of grace could be received only in a state of absolute self-surrender to God and blind faith in the Christian promise. Both Hengstenberg and Hofacker vehemently denied that philosophy could provide any aid in reconciling man and God. The errors and terrors of subjectivity could not be overcome through reason, but only through faith. It is significant, however, that Hengstenberg and Hofacker also rejected the religious "feeling" of communion with God as a sufficient assurance of salvation. Like the Hegelians, they sought for a more certain, "objective" basis for religious or ontological security. The Fundamentalists, however, found this certainty not in the "science" of absolute knowledge but in submission to the absolute, literal truth of the biblical revelation. The intellectual obscurantism so prevalent in the writings of the Fundamentalists, moreover, was almost inevitably combined with a strict puritanical ethics. The sexual and material demands of unregenerate natural man could not be reconciled or harmonized with the divine will, but had to be disciplined and denied in order to allow a complete surrender of the self to transcendent authority.[175]

The revolutions of 1830 marked a significant turning point in the history of the *Erweckungsbewegung.* The Fundamentalists, like many members of the Hegelian school, perceived the political changes and accompanying ideological conflicts as signs of an epochal cultural transition. The cosmic drama of sin and salvation was connected to the movement of history. Hengstenberg saw the revolutions as a "crass violation of divine law . . . that God could not leave unpunished."[176] Intellectual hubris and sensual indulgence had taken on historical, collective form in the liberal movement. The forces of sin and the forces of Christian righteousness were now clearly divided into opposing historical "parties" locked in battle for the control of European culture. The development of a similar transformation of the inner battle between sinful human nature and divine authority into a historical battle between the sinners and the saved was evident in the articles of *Der Christenbote,* the journal founded by the Württemberg Fundamentalists in 1831.[177] In both south and north Germany the Fundamentalists interpreted the battle between Christian and anti-Christian forces as a prophetic indication of the imminence of the Last Judgment and the Second Coming. "The hope of the *regnum gloriae,*" wrote Hengstenberg in 1832, "has increasingly become a necessary prerequisite for living, and only insofar as I view the contemporary cultural conflict as a precursor of its coming, can I, on occasion, view it with joy."[178] The Fundamentalists' conviction that they were participating in contemporary cultural conflicts as the agents of God's judgment reached its height in the battle against Strauss's biblical criticism in 1835 and 1836. "It has now become clearly evident," Sixt Kapff wrote in 1836, "that our time is characterized by the increasingly obvious formation of two fundamental parties, Christians and anti-Christians." This development left no historical place for reconcilers or fence-sitters. "One must choose a party," Kapff insisted.[179] Hengstenberg expressed a similar conviction in the same year:

> Two peoples exist in the body of our time and only two. Their opposition to one another will become increasingly more intense and exclusive. Infidelity will gradually divest itself of any remnants of faith, just as faith will purge the remnants of infidelity from itself. This process will be an incalculable blessing.[180]

The impact of this perception of epochal cultural change and cultural conflict was revealed in significant modifications in both the theological and the political stances of the Fundamentalists. In theology, the early 1830s witnessed a significant increase in the authoritarian tendencies already present in the religious experience of some of the younger "awakened" intellectuals during the 1820s. The invisible ecumenical brotherhood of "awakened" believers was not an adequate basis for fighting the cultural battles of the age. The community of the "saved" should take the form of a visible, unified, militant church. Such a militant unity could be based only on total obedience and conformity to unquestioned authority. For Hengstenberg and the Bavarian Fundamentalists this search for authority led to a neoorthodox confessionalism, a commitment to the absolute truth of the Augsburg Confession and the original doctrines of sixteenth-century Lutheranism. This neoorthodox Fundamentalism was most powerful in Bavaria, where its proponents gained control of the theological faculty at Erlangen and the Protestant church organization by the mid-1830s. The aim of Hengstenberg and his Prussian friends was also to gain control of the established church and the university, not to establish a separatist church or sectarian group. The desire for doctrinal purity was connected to the desire for ecclesiastical power. In Württemberg the new emphasis on authority was most evident in ecclesiastical politics. Unlike the traditional conventicles that had been indifferent to the established state church, or the separatist movements that had opposed it, the young Fundamentalists sought to spread their gospel by means of the established ecclesiastical institutions. The faith of the "saved" was to be fortified and protected not only by the authority of the Bible but also by the authority of the church.[181]

A similar emphasis on authority and similar attempts to gain control of existing authority were evident in the political stance of the Fundamentalists after 1830. All Fundamentalists equated liberal opposition to established political authority with sinful rebellion against divinely ordained order. The Bavarian political theorist Friedrich Julius Stahl expressed the political stance of the Fundamentalists most clearly in 1833:

> There can be no reconciliation, no middle ground, between absolutely opposed principles. Either all order and authority is determined by man and serves his purposes, or it is determined by God in order to fulfill his will. There is no bond between legitimacy and the sovereignty of the people, faith and infidelity, truth and error.[182]

In Prussia the impact of the 1830 revolutions helped cement the alliance of Fundamentalist theology and the political and social views of the reactionary aristocracy. Ludwig von Gerlach's diatribes against the apostasy of liberalism and declarations of the inseparability of Christian faith from an authoritarian state and corporate society were prominently featured in the *Evangelische Kirchenzeitung*.[183] In Württemberg, the pietists also departed from their traditional stance as "the quiet ones in the country (*Die Stillen im Lande*)." They attacked the participants in the Hambach festival with as much virulence as they brought to their attack on theological liberals.[184] After 1830, moreover, the Württemberg pietists consciously sought the support of the king and the established authorities for their Bible-distributing societies and charitable organizations, which, they claimed, aimed at "the maintenance of order, peace, and quiet" among the king's subjects.[185]

It would be misleading, however, to interpret the Fundamentalists' emphasis on established authority in both ecclesiastical and political affairs after 1830 as simply an accommodation to the existing order. In both Prussia and Württemberg, the religious stance of the Fundamentalists was more "conservative" than that of the established church. What they desired was ecclesiastical reform that would strip the church of its liberal and rational elements. In a sense their stance was parallel to that of the Hegelian Center whose religious views were more liberal and rational than those of the established hierarchy but who also hoped for a transformation from within that would make Hegelian Christianity and Christianity synonymous. Similar comparisons can be drawn in the political sphere. The Fundamentalist conception of the Christian state was not synonymous with the established order during the 1830s. In Prussia especially, Hengstenberg and his aristocratic friends were in conscious opposition to the policies of the more liberal elements in the state bureaucracy. Stahl's conception of the unity of legitimacy and faith in a "Christian State" was in a sense an "ideal" that had not yet been fully realized. Adherents to the Hegelian Center also did not view their conception of the rational state simply as a comprehension of the existing order, but as a future goal. Both groups, however, were able to combine their dissatisfactions with a faith that the implicit tendencies within the established ecclesiastical and political order were moving toward a fulfillment of their own cultural ideal. In 1838 Ruge and Leo could attack each other as revolutionaries and view their diametrically opposed positions as defenses of the Prussian state and the established church.

These parallels, moreover, were grounded in a fundamental similarity in the experiences of the two groups. The experience of both groups during the Restoration was characterized by decisive conversions that gave them the conviction of identity with the ultimate ground of historical reality. The consciousness of epochal historical change that followed the revolutions of 1830 made the relationship of this conversion experience to the existing cultural environment problematical. In both groups, demands arose for the cultural realization of the ideal that had been inwardly appropriated in the conversion experience. In north Germany the Fundamentalists battled for the institutionalization of their cultural ideology in a "Christian State." In Württemberg, the 1830s witnessed an equally noticeable change in the stance of the pietists. The concern for the inner transformation of individuals was transformed into a conscious attempt to establish the Kingdom of God in Württemberg.[186] The Hegelians, on the other hand, saw their main task as bringing about the perfected actualization of Reason and freedom in their cultural environment. Both groups, moreover, were especially concerned with the control of educational institutions. In their roles as academics they saw the universities as primary instruments for cultural renewal.

It is not surprising, therefore, that the Fundamentalists and the younger members of the Hegelian school saw each other as cultural rivals engaged in a battle of epochal significance whose outcome would determine the character of the future cultural order and the ultimate fate of mankind. The Hegelians acted in the confidence that the evolution of the world spirit was on their side; the Fundamentalists saw themselves as instruments of the controlling will of a transcendent God. In this context conflicts over university appointments and promotions took on world-historical significance for the members of both groups. In the Protestant areas of south Germany the balance of power in the universities and ecclesiastical organizations had clearly shifted in favor of the Fundamentalists by the mid-1830s. In Erlangen, Harless,

Löhe, and Stahl had all become full professors by 1836. Feuerbach, who had habilitated as a *Privatdozent* in 1828, never had a hope for any kind of promotion. In Württemberg, the dismissal of Strauss from his position as teaching fellow (*Repetent*) in 1835 was followed by a general campaign against Hegelianism in the church, the seminary, and the university. Whereas some of Strauss's Hegelian friends, like Märklin, were eventually forced to resign their ecclesiastical offices, their Fundamentalist contemporaries rapidly gained control of the consistory in Stuttgart and the seminary in Tübingen.[187]

In Prussia, the battle between Fundamentalists and Hegelians for control of the universities and thus for the position of cultural leadership was particularly virulent and intense during the 1830s because the parties were so evenly balanced. The polemical conflict between Ruge and Leo in 1838 seemed to indicate a virtual stalemate. Within the next two years it became rapidly obvious, however, that the favor of the Fundamentalists' patrons, the crown prince and his aristocratic pietistic camarilla, carried more weight than the favor of Altenstein and Schulze. When both Altenstein and Frederick William III died in the spring of 1840 it was clear that the special relationship between the Hegelian school and the Prussian state was at an end. The new king, Frederick William IV, began his reign by granting amnesty to political prisoners and promising greater participation of the people in public life – both through freedom of the press and through the creation of a centralized assembly of estates. Some Hegelians, most notably Friedrich Köppen and Bruno Bauer, published ringing manifestos in 1840 advising the new king to bring Prussia back to its world-historical mission as the leader of mankind toward a community of actualized Reason and freedom.[188] Köppen and Bauer, like other Hegelians, however, had little faith in the ability or willingness of Frederick William IV to accede to their demands. During the 1830s the new king – then the crown prince – had been one of the most powerful opponents of the Hegelian school and Altenstein's educational policies. Like the Hegelians, Frederick William IV was an ideologue filled with a sense of historical mission. But the ideology that he hoped to actualize in his realm was that of the "Christian state" as expounded by the more conservative members of the Historical School and the Fundamentalists of the *Evangelische Kirchenzeitung*. His amnesty had been aimed at liberating the old heroes of the Christian-German wing of the *Burschenschaften* – Ernst Moritz Arndt and Friedrich Ludwig Jahn. His "liberalization" of public life was merely an attempt to replace the rational absolutism of the bureaucratic state with a political community in which the king ruled by divine right in harmony with a loyal *Volk* organized according to the corporate structure of the old regime. His educational policy soon became obvious. A well-known representative of the conservative faction in the bureaucracy, Johann Friedrich Eichhorn, was appointed to Altenstein's position. Stahl was given the chair in political philosophy vacated by the death of Gans, and Schelling was lured to Berlin with a huge salary in the hope that he would be able to expunge the "dragon's seed" of Hegelian rationalism from the minds of Prussian youth.[189]

The specific political and administrative changes in Prussia in 1840–1 gave dramatic expression to the general change in the political and cultural environment of the Hegelian school that had occurred during the 1830s and thus helped the Left Hegelians, at least in Prussia, to crystallize their critical viewpoints into a historical *Weltanschauung* diametrically opposed to the reigning ideology of the Christian state. This process of crystallization was most evident in Arnold Ruge's attempt to transform the *Hallische Jahrbücher* into the organ of a unified Left Hegelian party in 1841 and 1842. But the deaths of Altenstein and Frederick William III should not be conceived as the "cause" of the emergence of Left Hegelianism. Strauss and Feuerbach, the two major original theoreticians of the Left Hegelian position, were not directly affected by the events in Prussia, and even Ruge and Bruno Bauer had made the decisive shift to cultural opposition before the spring of 1840. Moreover, Ruge's attempt to transform the theological and philosophical criticism of Strauss, Bauer, and Feuerbach into a unified program for historical change had very limited success and collapsed by the fall of 1842. Although the major Left Hegelian thinkers were agreed in their immanent historical definitions of the problems of human self-alienation and cultural bifurcation, and thus in their opposition to the transcendent or "theological" resolutions of the Fundamentalists, they were not in agreement in their views on the particular character of this immanent human dilemma or on its possible resolution. The chapters that follow attempt to trace the origins and the development of the Left Hegelianism of Strauss, Bauer, and Feuerbach up to 1841, and thus reveal both the nature and the cause of their unity and diversity as prophets of a post-Christian and post-Hegelian cultural order.

8

Strauss and the principle of immanence

In later years, Strauss looked back on the *Life of Jesus* as not only his most famous or notorious work but also his best book. Among all his writings, he felt, it was the one that could be described as a truly inspired work. "In his youthful survey of the state of knowledge in his discipline," Strauss wrote, "the author, with the instinct of a person who is destined to lead the race one step forward, had come upon the crucial problem of his time, taken it into his innermost self, and thus provided it with the warmth and life that made it into a fertile seed for a new scholarly life."[1] The "crucial problem" was, of course, the relationship between faith and knowledge, religion and philosophy, between the world view of traditional Christianity appropriated in faith and expressed in symbolic or "representational" form and the world view of "modern consciousness" acquired through experience and reason and expressed in the form of philosophical knowledge. It was a problem that concerned the very foundations, the presuppositions, of human activity and cultural organization. During the three years following his departure for Berlin in November 1831, Strauss devoted all his intellectual energy to a simultaneous study of both sides of this problem, and in the summer of 1835 he presented his contemporaries with the two thick volumes that proposed a new model of reconciliation between the past and the present, between traditional Christian culture and modern consciousness.

Strauss's desire to study in Berlin was based on his felt need for "oral instruction, from either the master or one of his students," in order "to penetrate fully into this [the Hegelian] system."[2] He arrived in Berlin the week before Hegel's sudden death. After hearing two of Hegel's lectures and paying a brief social call on the "master," therefore, Strauss was forced to rely on the wisdom of the disciples. He attended Henning's lectures on logic and metaphysics and Marheineke's on philosophical theology. His closest ties, however, were to the younger group of Hegelian *Privatdozenten* and associate professors: Michelet, Hotho, Agathon Benary, and especially Wilhelm Vatke. Like Strauss, Vatke was a theologian, and, like Strauss, he was deeply concerned with the relationship between Hegelian philosophy and the "representational" expressions of Christian truth in the biblical narrative. Their close personal friendship, which Strauss considered the most positive gain from his Berlin experience, was apparently based on intellectual agreement. On all the "fundamental issues," Strauss claimed, he and Vatke were of "one mind."[3]

Strauss did not find himself of "one mind," however, with the official line in Hegelian theology expounded in the lectures of Marheineke. Marheineke, he asserted, was "only a dogmatic, not a dialectical spirit." In his exposition of the identity of religion and philosophy he emphasized only the "positive Moment" of achieved reconciliation and pushed the "equally true negative Moment" into the background.[4] In a retrospective reflection of 1837, Strauss gave a fuller account of this discontent with the official Hegelian theology that he had felt in 1832. What Marheineke, and people like Gabler and Göschel, had failed to realize, Strauss claimed, was that a whole phenomenology existed between the positive dogma or historical fact and the final elevation to the *Begriff*. One could not simply move from the *Vorstellung* to the *Begriff* in a "pistol shot." Such an "easy" solution was what Hegel had found most unsatisfactory in Schelling's position. Marheineke's theology gave the impression that the Hegelian elevation marked no progress at all, but simply brought the theologian back to his starting point – chained to the positive dogmas of Christian orthodoxy. The emphasis on the reaffirmation of Christian truth, on the result of the Hegelian phenomenology, might have been a proper stance in a revolutionary age, but after fifteen years of Restoration such an emphasis could lead only to a smug self-satisfaction and an illusory sense of easy peace.[5] In 1836, Strauss explained his concern for the "negative Moment" in this fashion:

> A demonstration of the positive unity of knowledge and faith not only is superfluous at this time, but can only, if the positive is emphasized at the expense of the negative, be described as a contribution to the self-deception of the age. At this moment what really matters is that we are forced to remember that the unity with the old faith that our time enjoys is mediated through a negation of that faith, that there is a great chasm, a deep ditch filled with the dragons and monsters of doubt and despair, over which faith had to build a bridge before it arrived at its present standpoint.[6]

If the identity between faith and knowledge was to be maintained, the solidity of the mediating bridge over the critical stage of negation would have to be clearly demonstrated.

During his year in Berlin, Strauss also became increasingly aware that the difficulties involved in the identity of faith and knowledge were particularly connected to the nature of the Christian representation that was to be elevated to the status of the concept. The terminology of representation and concept had been borrowed from Hegel's general epistemological and logical analysis and simply applied to the theological problem. But the teachings of the Christian church were not simply representational expressions of philosophical truth; they claimed to be descriptions of historical fact. Was the historical narrative an essential part of the philosophical truth of Christianity, or was the historicity of the Christian faith simply a part of its representational form? This question was ignored by Marheineke and other Hegelian theologians. In his review of Rosenkranz's *Encyclopedia* in May 1832, Strauss attributed this blind spot to their one-sided philosophical perspective. Strauss accepted the basic position that philosophy and theology should eventually lead to the same truth, but he insisted that their methods of arriving there were different. The theologian had to begin with the positive material of the Christian faith, the biblical texts and the church dogmas, and work "upward" through a process of negative mediation or criticism until he arrived at the concept. The philosopher, on the other hand, began with the conceptual truth and interpreted the Christian representations from this elevated perspective. Rosenkranz had taken this latter stance, and he wound up deducing the historical necessity of all biblical events, including miracles. For Strauss, the absurdity of such conclusions led to a questioning of the validity of the method that led to them. The raw material of the biblical narrative would have to be subjected to a sophisticated process of distillation before the identity of theology and philosophy could be convincingly demonstrated. Otherwise one would be forced to believe in the historical truth of the most unbelievable kinds of events on the basis of the most rational of modern philosophies.[7]

Strauss's dissatisfaction with the way the problem of historical criticism was treated in the Hegelian school led to a growing interest in Schleiermacher's theology during his year at Berlin. He displayed a great admiration for Schleiermacher's dialectical skill and critical insights into the contradictions in the biblical narrative. But just as the identity of faith and reason could not be adequately demonstrated from a one-sided philosophical position, the results of a one-sided theological perspective were also inadequate. Because Schleiermacher did not have the fearless confidence in an ultimate identity that was provided by the philosophical perspective, his critical stance was not applied to the crucial areas in which it threatened to dissolve the very basis of the Christian faith. This self-imposed limitation was particularly evident in his attitude toward the historical reality of the incarnation of the divine in the person of Jesus Christ. Strauss claimed that Schleiermacher had drawn a "holy circle" around this problem.[8]

Such "holy circles" were unnecessary, however, for a scholar who possessed the philosophical perspective of absolute Reason. By February 1832, Strauss had decided that any attempt to resolve the problematic relationship between faith and knowledge would have to begin with an analysis of the relationship between the Jesus of the Gospels and the Christ of philosophy. He outlined his conception of the manner in which this task should be approached in a letter to Märklin. He would begin with a simple description of the life and work of Jesus as it was portrayed in the Gospel narratives and the tradition of the Christian church. This would be followed by an uninhibited criticism of the historical credibility of the biblical narratives. Finally, the eternal truths of Christianity would be resurrected from the historical ruins of the "negative Moment." Unlike Schleiermacher, Strauss could be ruthless in his historical criticism because he was confident that the eternal truths could be salvaged no matter how much the criticism might destroy. But, unlike the Hegelian theologians, Strauss would follow the empirical historical method and would accept the identity of religion and philosophy only after the *Vorstellung* had been subjected to the full brunt of negative criticism, not in blind disregard of the contradictions contained within the historical record.[9]

Strauss originally planned to present his conception of the life of Jesus in a series of lectures when he returned to Tübingen as a teaching fellow in the summer of 1832. He soon discovered, as in fact he had anticipated, that the faculty at Tübingen was not ready to accept the validity of either his extreme historical criticism or the Hegelian rehabilitation that would take away its sting. When he tried to demonstrate to his students during one of his classes in the summer of 1832 that the Christian incarnation could be grasped as a philosophical truth, he was severely reprimanded for misleading the students.[10] After this experience he restricted his attempts to integrate philosophy and theology to private study and writing. His teaching efforts were concentrated solely on the philosophical sphere. He wrote to Binder that this restriction corresponded to his own immediate needs:

> In my theology, philosophy plays such a commanding role that my theological viewpoint can be perfected only by a more thorough understanding of philosophy. I want to accomplish this task now without external disturbances and in utter disregard of whether it leads me back to theology or not . . . What interests me in theology is offensive, and what is not offensive has no attraction for me.[11]

Strauss's concentration on the philosophical dimension of the religion/philosophy problematic lasted until the summer of 1833. For three semesters he lectured on philosophy (the history of philosophy, logic, and ethical philosophy) at the university (that is, not at the seminary). Contemporary accounts and the manuscript notebooks that have been preserved indicate that Strauss defined his philosophical task simply in terms of the reproduction and exegesis of the Hegelian system.[12] He made no attempt to develop his own positions but identified philosophy itself with Hegel's philosophy, and insisted that the history of philosophy had attained its self-comprehending completion in Hegel's systematic articulation of the dialectical unity of thought and being in absolute spirit. Moreover, Strauss's lectures on logic clearly revealed that he conceived the Hegelian accomplishment in terms of a reconciliation of the transcendent and the immanent, of God and man. The Hegelian logic, he claimed, grasped and systematically articulated God's self-comprehension. To enter the Hegelian logic was to be initiated into the "Holy of Holies," to experience an "intellectual second birth" in which knowledge of God became identical with knowledge of oneself as a thinking, spiritual being.[13]

Despite the sensational success of his philosophical lectures,[14] however, Strauss was not completely happy in this exile from his chosen vocation as a theologian. He felt that he had nothing new to offer in philosophy. If he was destined to make any impact on his culture, it was in that "offensive" area where theology and philosophy met. On February 8, 1833, he wrote to Georgii that despite the "external successes" of his philosophical endeavors he had been unable to find "inner calm and peace."[15] In the fall of 1833 he stopped lecturing and devoted himself completely to the solution of his theological questions. He became totally absorbed in problems relating to the historical criticism of the biblical texts. In a review that he published in the *Jahrbücher für wissenschaftliche Kritik* in November 1834, he revealed his conception of the importance of such scholarly tasks. The historical critic, he claimed, was a major participant in the great work of "the education of humanity from the letter to the spirit."[16] This work also provided Strauss with inner satisfaction. In August 1835, in the midst of the publication of the second volume of the *Life of Jesus,* Strauss informed Georgii: "I still enjoy the satisfaction of having worked myself out of an intellectual and emotional decay, even despair, and into a healthier state through this work."[17] Unfortunately, many of Strauss's contemporaries thought that the work was more likely to cause despair than to heal it. When he wrote this letter, he had already been forced to resign from his teaching position at Tübingen.

It is ironical that Strauss gained his reputation as a nihilistic destroyer of the traditional faith through the publication of a book that originated in his own profound need to demonstrate the identity of content in Christian faith and philosophical knowledge. Although Strauss was convinced that the "identity philosophy" expounded by the Berlin Hegelians was blindly affirmative and conservative rather than critical and dialectical, and thus unsatisfactory in its results as well as its methods, he still insisted on his deep veneration for "the most sublime of all religions."[18] In the conclusion of the *Life of Jesus* he claimed that "Christianity [was] identical with the deepest philosophical truth."[19] The only way of saving the "eternal truths" of the Christian faith, however, was through radical surgery; their connection to a series of supernatural historical events had to be severed.

Strauss always insisted that the problem and the presuppositions of the *Life of Jesus* were Hegelian in origin.[20] It was his philosophical training, he wrote in the preface, that had given him the "inner liberation of feeling and thinking from religious and dogmatic prejudices."[21] The content of the *Life of Jesus,* however, was not primarily philosophical. More than fourteen hundred of its fifteen hundred pages were devoted to a systematic analysis of the historical credibility of the four Gospels – the historical sources for the Christian view of Jesus Christ, his life and significance. Strauss was convinced that the philosopher and the Christian theologian should ultimately arrive at the same truth – the philosopher through the a priori method of Reason, the theologian through the empirical criticism of the sources of the Christian faith. For Strauss the philosophical end of this identity had been accomplished in Hegelian philosophy. The task that was yet to be satisfactorily completed was the revision of the critical method of theological exegesis in a manner that would allow the religious *Vorstellung* to be reconciled with the philosophical *Begriff* in an unforced identity. The revision in critical method that Strauss proposed as being most clearly suited to bringing about this desired identity was the unfettered application of the concept of myth to the historical interpretation of the biblical accounts. The simple identification of supernatural history and philosophical concept was unacceptable. Only if this supernatural history was interpreted as myth could the identity of religious and philosophical truth be clearly demonstrated.

The use of the concept of myth in the interpretation of the historical accounts of the Bible did not begin with Strauss. As he openly admitted in his introduction, both his definition and his use of myth were based on a well-developed and widespread tradition in German biblical scholarship. On the basis of the works of his predecessors, Strauss defined myth as the description of an event or an idea in the sensuous, concrete form of a "story" or historical narrative.[22] These myths were not fables created by individuals but the "unconscious" work of the "collective individual of the whole society."[23] They were symbolic expressions of a community's understanding of its own experience. During the late eighteenth and early nineteenth centuries the mythical explanation had been used for the interpretation of increasingly large sections of the Old Testament and for some aspects of the New Testament. What was new in Strauss's approach was the application of the mythical method of interpretation to the whole historical narrative on which the Christian religion was based.

For Strauss, as for most of his predecessors in mythical exegesis, the expression mode of myth was related to a specific stage of cultural development. Strauss tended to describe this stage as that of the "oriental mind" - a phrase denoting a primitive stage of historical consciousness in which psychological states were personified as objective beings, in which no differentiation was made between illusion and reality, poetic and rational truth. It was a stage of consciousness open to miraculous explanations, willing to attribute the occurrence of the unusual to supernatural causes. This mythical stage was in sharp contrast to what Strauss referred to as modern, critical, "scientific (*wissenschaftlich*)" consciousness, which viewed nature and history as a "compact tissue of finite effects and causes" and sharply differentiated subjective interpretation from objective reality.[24]

The application of the concept of myth to the New Testament narratives was a means of making the biblical history understandable. The orthodox stance that simply accepted the biblical accounts as an accurate description of supernatural events was offensive to modern scientific consciousness. The rationalist or naturalist stance, which accepted the historical accuracy of the biblical histories but tried to explain the miraculous events in terms of rational or natural causes, was also inadequate, however. In order to transform the allegedly supernatural events into natural events the theologians of this latter school had been forced into the most fantastic kinds of speculations concerning the effects of thunderstorms and earthquakes, or dreams and somnambulist states.[25] The mythical approach, however, focused on the historical documents as expressions of subjective states, of a communal consciousness, rather than as descriptions of an external series of historical events. Through the use of mythical interpretation the historian could transport himself back to the consciousness of the early Christian church, and from this perspective the difficulties and contradictions within the biblical accounts could be resolved:

One must imagine a young church, which honors its founder with greater enthusiasm the more unexpectedly and tragically he is torn from his apparent destiny, a church filled with a mass of new ideas that were to transform a world, a church of Orientals, of primarily uneducated people, who thus could not appropriate and express these ideas in the abstract forms of reason and concept, but only in the concrete form of the imagination, as images and stories. From this perspective one will understand that what must arise under such circumstances did in fact arise - a series of sacred stories through which the whole mass of new ideas stimulated by Jesus and old ideas that were transferred on to him were brought to expression as single moments in his life.[26]

On the basis of this general perspective, Strauss proceeded to a detailed critical analysis of the "events" of Jesus' life. In each case his methods and his results were the same. He began by comparing the accounts given in the four Gospels and then proceeded to show how both the orthodox supernaturalist and the rationalist explanations were unsatisfactory. The biblical accounts became meaningful and understandable only if they were viewed as myths - as sacred stories created by the original Christian community in response to the combined impact of the actions and teachings of Jesus and the messianic expectations of the Jewish tradition. The mythical viewpoint, Strauss claimed, preserved the meaning, the Idea, of the biblical events, while sacrificing their status as historical facts.[27]

Strauss's attack on the historical foundations of the Christian faith was not meant as a denial of the historical existence of the man Jesus of Nazareth or as an assertion that all the events recorded in the four Gospels did not occur or could not have occurred. As Strauss explained to Binder, his "critical negation was relevant to the fact only in the form in which it has been handed down to us. It is not meant as a denial of everything factual, but as a demonstration that we have no reliable factual knowledge."[28] Strauss was concerned to show that one could not get from the Jesus of history to the savior of the Christian religion on the basis of historical knowledge. The biblical accounts did not provide a credible description of a series of supernatural events. Strauss was convinced that the truth of Christianity lay in the Idea and not in the historical fact. The facts of history were neither for nor against, but irrelevant to, Christian truth. At the same time, Strauss was intent on destroying the credibility of the factual account. For as long as man clung to the possibility that his faith was securely based on biblical history, he would not be challenged to move on from the letter to the spirit. "I can perceive no resurrection of the Idea," Strauss wrote to Karl Daub in August 1835, "if history is not first demolished."[29]

In recent reinterpretations of Strauss's theological significance, Karl Barth and some of his students have pointed out that Strauss was the first nineteenth-century theologian (and perhaps the only one besides Kierkegaard) who clearly saw, and tried to make others see, the huge hiatus between the Jesus of history, insofar as man can know him, and the Christ of faith.[30] Unlike Kierkegaard, however, Strauss did not think that the existence of this gap demanded a leap into faith for the attainment of ontological security. He concluded instead that the historical event was not an essential part of Christianity. In order to attain a satisfactory ontological identity man did not have to surrender himself blindly to the "absurdity" of the miracle of the historical incarnation, but should clarify his metaphysical understanding and find Christ and salvation again in the philosophical *Begriff*.

Strauss's whole stance, in fact, was based on the conception of religion as cognitive activity – as a type of knowledge – that was already evident in his dissertation of 1831. In the explanatory additions that he included in the revised versions of the *Life of Jesus* he defined religion "as the perception of truth, not in the form of an idea, which is the philosophical perception, but invested with imagery."[31] Religious consciousness was thus made synonymous with mythical expression, and both were relegated to the status of a kind of vulgar metaphysics, or the metaphysics of an immature or primitive cultural stage. Religious myths contained within them profound metaphysical ideas. But these ideas were not clearly understood by the collective group that was the myth-creating subject. The ideas were personified, transformed into sacred stories, made into "objective" realities that existed outside man's consciousness. In Hegelian terms, the "oriental" myth-creating mentality was not able to distinguish between the form and the content of myth, but identified the particular historical concrete form in which it represented the truth to itself with the actual content of that truth. The mythical form thus hid, veiled, distorted. For Hegel the concrete form of the Christian representation was an important element of the absolute truth that philosophy was to comprehend. The truth had to express itself in the real, in "myths and symbols, representations and finite relationships in general," before it could be grasped.[32] Myths were an "unveiling" as well as a "veiling" of the truth. The mythical form was thus synonymous with the experiential, concrete historical basis of all self-comprehension. By defining the concrete representations of religious myth as a primitive form of knowledge, therefore, Strauss implicitly denied the validity of the religious experience of the absolute identity of the individual and the divine. He saw his work not as an interpretative unveiling of the experiential truth of the Christian religious experience but as a destructive criticism of the religious form of knowledge.

Simply to show that the biblical histories were actually myths, therefore, did not immediately make the Christian message existentially relevant to modern man. Unlike many twentieth-century theologians, Strauss did not believe that the mythical interpretation of the biblical record could in itself reveal the eternal truths of the Christian faith. In the *Life of Jesus,* the application of the concept of myth served a primarily negative function – the destruction of the credibility of the supernatural history of the Gospels. As Strauss stated at the conclusion of his critical section, the result of his investigation had apparently been

> the annihilation of everything that the Christian believes about Jesus . . . The infinitely precious possession of truth and life on which humanity has nourished itself for eighteen centuries seems irretrievably dissipated, the most sublime leveled with the dust, God divested of his grace, man of his dignity, and the tie between heaven and earth broken.[33]

The mythological interpretation had made the accounts of the Gospels historically understandable, but had robbed them of their existential saving power. But the end of the critical section was not the end of the book. To see Strauss primarily as a historical critic rather than as a theologian interested in the existential question of salvation is certainly misleading.[34] For Strauss saw his historical criticism of the Gospels, his analysis of the sacred history as a culture-bound myth, as the groundwork on which the truths of Christianity could be saved for eternity and modern consciousness. Philosophy would give back what historical criticism had taken away.

The "concluding dissertation" in which Strauss hoped to rehabilitate the eternal truths from the carnage left by historical criticism was constructed in such a way as to form a parallel to the introduction of his work. In the introduction, Strauss had described how his mythical interpretation was the historical outcome of the tradition of exegetical theology. In the conclusion he tried to show that the Hegelian rehabilitation was the resolution of a parallel development in philosophical theology. In the introduction the word *Wissenschaft* had been used to denote the methods and presuppositions of modern critical scholarship. In the conclusion, *Wissenschaft* denoted the perspective of Hegelian philosophy. By using the same word for both the critical and the philosophical aspects of his analysis, Strauss expressed his faith in the ultimate identity of their results. In a more personal sense, this parallel demonstrated that the two professional ideals he had absorbed from Baur and Hegel, the critical scholar and the speculative thinker, could also be combined in the task of reconciling the Christian faith with modern consciousness.

The specific task of the "concluding dissertation" was to reveal how the eternal truth of the Christian incarnation could be saved once the historical life of Jesus had been demolished. The true philosophical meaning of the Christian incarnation, Strauss claimed, was the essential unity of the human and divine nature, of the finite and the infinite, as spirit: "The infinite spirit is real only when it discloses itself in finite spirits, as the finite spirit is true only when it merges itself into the infinite. The true and real existence of spirit, therefore ... is the God-man." This "truth" appeared in history when man was mature enough to receive it. But because the manner in which truth presented itself to the "popular mind" was in the form of religion, the idea of the union of man and God in spirit first appeared in history as "a fact obvious to the sense," as a "human individual who [was] recognized as the visible god."[35]

But this philosophical interpretation of the Christian doctrine could not function as a proof for the historical veracity of the biblical accounts. The union of the divine and the human in a single historical individual was simply the manner in which this truth appeared to the popular uneducated consciousness at a particular point in time: The historical incarnation of God in Jesus Christ was not a necessary part of the eternal truth. "General propositions on the unity of the divine and human nature," Strauss claimed, "do not in the least serve to explain the appearance of a person in whom this unity existed individually." Such an individual incarnation was simply "not the mode in which the Idea realizes itself." But the fact that the unity of the infinite spirit and man in one individual was an offense to reason did not mean that the Idea of the incarnation was simply a Kantian moral ideal without historical reality. The Idea realized itself "among a multiplicity of exemplars that reciprocally complete each other." In order to raise the *Vorstellung* of the Christian incarnation to the philosophical *Begriff* one merely had to substitute the idea of humanity for the historical Christ. Man could find salvation by participation in the "divinely human life of the species." Out of the destruction of the historical Christ arose the vision of a community of God-men: "Is not the Idea of the unity of the divine and human natures a real one in a far higher sense," Strauss asked, "when I regard the whole race of mankind as its realization than when I single out only one man as such a realization?"[36]

Strauss thus reconstructed the identity of content in religion and philosophy by subjecting both poles of the Hegelian conception to significant revision. His historical criticism of biblical history separated the particular, historical aspects of the Christian representation of the incarnation from its absolute content. Stripped of its obsolete mythical husk, the Christian truth was reduced to the absorption of the individual in the species through the progressive historical actualization of the "idea of humanity." But in his attempt to reconcile the content of Christian faith with the content of modern philosophical knowledge, Strauss also reduced the Hegelian comprehension of the reconciliation of man and God in the concrete universality of absolute spirit to a theoretical recognition of the ultimate unity of all finite individuals in the infinite spirit of the human "race." By denying the reality of the religious experience of the incarnation of the universal in the concrete historical individual, Strauss also denied the Hegelian claim that a philosophical comprehension of that experience accomplished the ultimate reconciliation of the individual and the absolute. Although Strauss continued to describe the content of both Christianity and Hegelian philosophy as a union of the transcendent and the immanent, the divine and the human, he had, in fact, defined this union in totally immanent terms. The divine or "infinite" attributes of the God-man Jesus Christ were displaced onto the "idea of humanity"; the self-revelation and self-actualization of the absolute in history became the secular process of man's recognition and actualization of his essence as a human being.

Strauss's position in the *Life of Jesus* also clearly implied that the process of actualization had not been completed. The representations and organization of Christian culture were not an adequate objectification of the "idea of humanity"; the process of historical actualization would not be complete until "the whole race of mankind" had recognized and affirmed, in theory and practice, its spiritual unity. Strauss conceived the historical evolution of mankind not as a completed incarnation of spirit in the world, but as an ongoing process of immanent "spiritualization." The transition from myth to self-conscious knowledge paralleled "the increasing, almost incredible, domination of man over nature . . . the irresistible force of ideas to which no unintelligent matter, whatever its magnitude, can oppose any enduring resistance." This irresistible power of the spirit, however, was most clearly evident on the level of communal relationships. The "main element" in the eternal truth of the Christian religion, he claimed, was the principle "that the negation of the merely natural and sensual life, which is itself the negation of the spirit (the negation of the negation, therefore), is the sole way to true spiritual life." The attainment of the "true spiritual life" of the actualized "idea of humanity" entailed not only a liberation from the authority of objectified, concrete religious "representations" but also a liberation from individual subjectivity and the sensual corruptions of the flesh. Only in spiritual unity with the species could man attain a "sinless existence." "Pollution cleaves to the individual only," Strauss stated, "and does not touch the race or its history."[37]

Although Strauss did not specify the political implications of his reconstructed identity of the finite and the infinite in the *Life of Jesus* or in his other published writings from this period, a letter that he wrote in the summer of 1834 reveals the general outlines of his position. In the dimension of communal organization the relationship between the religious representation and the philosophical concept was expressed in terms of the relationship between state and church. According to the Hegelian perspective, Strauss wrote, "The purpose of the church, the development of the highest consciousness of spirit about itself, is also the highest purpose of the state." For the state, "grasped according to its genuine concept," was not "merely an institution for the protection of persons and property," but rather an institution "for the common realization of the totality, spiritual as well as material, of mankind's interests." Both the state and the church thus had an essentially immanent purpose: the actualization of the idea of humanity. But if the "state satisfied all human interests," was a church still necessary? Strauss claimed that it was. As a cultural institution whose activities were focused on educating man to a theoretical self-understanding of his own nature as a universal spiritual being, the church represented the collective self-consciousness of man's social and political practice. Moreover, Strauss did not think that the contemporary state, as a particular, historically individualized community, was a perfected "realization of the concept of the state." In this context the church represented the higher community of a unified humanity that had yet to be politically realized. In 1834–5, Strauss did not yet believe that secular educational institutions like the universities could adequately take over the functions of the church. The majority of contemporary Germans were still incapable of appropriating the philosophical understanding that would make the traditional faith superfluous. But the self-consciousness of mankind as a unified "race" must be universal; it could not be confined to an educated elite. The crucial problem of the contemporary historical period concerned the ability of the church to retain its cultural universality and at the same time accept the historical necessity of the transition from faith to knowledge.[38] It was this problem to which Strauss addressed himself in the concluding comments of the *Life of Jesus.*

In the preface to the *Life of Jesus,* Strauss stated that his book was intended for his theological colleagues, not for the unlearned laity. But the results of his study obviously raised the question of the proper relationship between the philosophical theologian and the community of believers. The gap between the viewpoints of these two parties had been widened considerably by Strauss's reconstruction of the identity between religion and philosophy. Strauss stated the differences baldly:

> The church refers her Christology to an individual who existed historically at a certain period; the speculative theologian to an idea that attains existence only through the totality of individuals. By the church the evangelical narratives are perceived as history; by the critical theologian they are regarded for the most part as mere myths.[39]

Although he continued to maintain that "the distinction [was] one of form merely and [did] not affect the substance," he also admitted that there was a "marked difference" between statements based on historical events and those based on philosophical truths.[40] The practical options open to the speculative theologian remained those that Strauss had discussed with Märklin in 1831. Strauss still felt that the philosophically liberated preacher could honestly continue to speak to his congregation in the form of the *Vorstellung* and try to emphasize the spiritual rather than the historical significance of the Christian myths. Strauss concluded the book, however, not with a homily on identity but with a statement of the difficulties of reconciliation, and admitted that the speculative theologian might well be forced to leave the ministerial profession. He found consolation, however, in the recognition that these difficulties were not of his own making: "This collision is not the effect of the curiosity of the individual; it is necessarily introduced by the progress of time and the development of Christian theology. It surprises and masters the individual without his being able to guard himself from it."[41]

Strauss's theological opponents did not find his statement about the irresistible forces of history very convincing; they viewed his work and the stir it created as owing more to the "curiosity of the individual." In fact, they had made this decision even before the second volume, with the "concluding dissertation," had been published. The Württemberg Study Council (*Studienrat*), encouraged by the more conservative theological professors at Tübingen and a vociferous group of Fundamentalists, presented a report to the government which claimed that Strauss's continued presence at Tübingen could only produce unbelieving and hypocritical ecclesiastics and shatter the public trust in the school. Before the end of July, Strauss had been relieved of his duties as a teaching fellow and appointed to a new position as the teacher of classical languages in the lyceum at Ludwigsburg.[42]

The impact of Strauss's book, however, could not be as easily controlled as his personal contact with young theology students. Strauss soon found himself in the center of a mushrooming controversy, both scholarly and journalistic, which had begun immediately after the publication of the first volume of the *Life of Jesus.* In the preface to the second volume, written in October, Strauss could already comment on three significant responses to his work. By the following spring the controversy had spread from Württemberg to all of Germany. For a while the Prussian government even considered including Strauss's work within a general ban on the writings of the Young Germans.[43] Strauss was, of course, well aware that his theological standpoint was "offensive" to many of his contemporaries. He was prepared to receive condemnation from the religious restorationists like Hengstenberg and the Württemberg Fundamentalists and strong opposition from those theological positions - orthodox supernaturalism and rationalism - that had been severely criticized in the *Life*. It was only the extent and ferocity of this opposition - one of his former professors at Tübingen described him as the contemporary Judas Iscariot[44] - that surprised and dismayed him. At the same time, Strauss had written the *Life of Jesus* with the conviction that he was simply drawing out the implications of the two trends in German intellectual life that could be properly described as *wissenschaftlich:* critical historical theology and speculative philosophy. Moreover, he had seen his resolution of the problematic relationship between faith and knowledge not as a capricious subjective opinion but as an expression of the historical consciousness of many of his contemporaries, especially the younger generation of Hegelian theologians like Vatke in Berlin or his friends Märklin, Binder, and Vischer in Württemberg. In the controversial aftermath of the publication of the *Life of Jesus,* however, Strauss soon found himself in a position of isolation. The battle lines of the polemical controversy that followed the publication were drawn not between the proponents of *Wissenschaft* and the defenders of the traditional faith, but - at least so it seemed - between Strauss and the rest of the world.

Strauss became aware of the totality of his isolation when his closest personal friends failed to rally to his support. In September 1835 he wrote to Binder that he experienced "hours and days" when his usually strong faith in himself became "small and weak" and he needed "to find support for his own consciousness in that of another person."[45] Although Strauss's old classmates did not break off their personal relationships with him, they did not provide him with the kind of supportive assurance he desired. He tended to attribute their actions to their external situations; defense of Strauss could easily lead to loss of their jobs. But after a few months the continued silence of his friends began to get under his skin: "I have often been extremely irritated by my isolated position and become angry with my friends for suddenly deserting the cart, which we had pulled together for such a long time, as soon as the issue became an earnest one."[46] Strauss's Berlin comrade Wilhelm Vatke was included within the category of deserters. In 1835, Vatke had published a study of the Old Testament that seemed to parallel Strauss's work. Vatke also tried to bring the *Vorstellung* closer to the *Begriff* by interpreting most of Old Testament history as myth.[47] But though Hengstenberg was quite ready to place Vatke and Strauss in the same category, Vatke himself declined such intellectual comradeship. He refused to draw Strauss's implication that the resurrection of the Idea demanded the absolute demolition of supernatural history, and he did not agree with the application of mythical interpretation to the New Testament. Vatke viewed these differences as matters of principle; Strauss saw them as a tactful compromise, as a rather devious personal expression of the Hegelian principle of the "cunning of reason."[48] In September 1836, Strauss wrote to Vatke of his disappointment in not having received even one letter of sympathy or support during his time of persecution.[49]

The ambiguous stance taken by Ferdinand Christian Baur in the *Life of Jesus* controversy also irritated and disappointed Strauss. Strauss considered Baur his intellectual "father" as well as his teacher and mentor in the area of historical criticism and mythical interpretation, and he was obviously anxious to receive his approval and support. During the first months of the controversy, Strauss thought that Baur was essentially on his side. They discussed some of the methodological problems contained in the *Life,* and Strauss included clarifications of the issues raised by Baur in the second edition, published in the fall of 1836. But when Hengstenberg attacked the work of both Strauss and Baur as attempts to destroy the Christian faith, Baur went to great lengths to disassociate himself from his student and to emphasize the "positive" nature of his own historical criticism in comparison to Strauss's destructive negativism. Strauss described this denial as his "most distressing" experience in the whole *Life of Jesus* controversy.[50] A few months later, however, the friendship was renewed. Baur encouraged Strauss in the latter's polemic against the orthodox supernaturalist theologians, and Strauss immediately grasped the opportunity for reconciliation. On September 12, 1837, he wrote to Baur: "I always think with the greatest joy of the hours that you were able to devote to me. In my present situation it is a priceless treasure to find once again, among so many repulsive contacts, the one friendly fatherly hand."[51] But the reconciliation was only temporary, and the intellectual and psychological tensions between the two men continued. Baur continued to emphasize that historical criticism should be "positive" and that the idea of the incarnation was based on the real individual incarnation of God in the historical Christ. Strauss, however, remained convinced that Baur's critical work led to the same negative conclusions as his own. The differences between them were differences in the courage to face the implications of their scholarship. As late as 1847, Strauss insisted that, despite Baur's attempts to disown him, he remained Baur's legitimate son.[52]

Strauss's conflicts with Baur and Vatke expressed a general disagreement with the whole critical Center of the Hegelian school. The critical Hegelians, unlike Göschel, Gabler, and Bruno Bauer, were willing to accept Strauss's emphasis on the critical negation of the form of the "representation" as a prerequisite for the ultimate appropriation of the absolute content of Christian truth in the form of the concept. But they were not willing to follow Strauss in identifying the incarnation of the absolute in a particular historical individual with the religious "form." The Hegelian *Aufhebung,* they insisted, would have to include a demonstration of the historical reality of the incarnation. Ruge, for example, perceived Strauss's interpretation of the historical incarnation as an "allegory of humanity" as a fundamental rejection of the core of Hegel's philosophy: the unity of the finite individual and the infinite universal in the concrete universality of absolute spirit. Strauss had denied the reality of the Hegelian experience of living in eternity, in the fullness of the spirit, in the here and now.[53] Rosenkranz claimed that "Strauss holds to the standpoint of immanence so exclusively that he allows . . . the determination of transcendance to vanish completely."[54]

Despite his own apparent isolation and the disappointing reactions of those people from whom he had expected support, Strauss did not waver in his original position throughout the first two years of the *Life of Jesus* controversy. He was convinced that the basis of his disagreement with scholars like Vatke and Baur was psychological, not "scientific." Their own investigations and philosophical speculations led inevitably to his position, but they were afraid of accepting and stating the implications of their work.[55] He found no convincing reason for changing his own stance. The second edition of the *Life of Jesus* appeared in 1836 with clarifying additions but no substantial changes, and in the winter of 1836–7, Strauss prepared a detailed answer to his critics. In the spring of 1837 he published three volumes of *Polemical Treatises* that contained his analysis of virtually every theological stance that had been represented in the attacks on his book. His basic position was revealed most clearly, however, in his discussions of the Hegelian school and the representatives of historical criticism and in his analysis of the relationship between his work and the general process of cultural change.

In response to criticism of his *Life of Jesus* by members of the Hegelian school, Strauss defended his position against the viewpoints of both the Right and the Center. By attempting to deduce the historical truth of the biblical accounts as a philosophical necessity, the Right – represented in this instance by Bruno Bauer and Göschel – had failed to take the "negative Moment" that separated the *Vorstellung* and the *Begriff* into account.[56] The Center was characterized by its insistence on the identity of historical fact and philosophical concept on the single issue of the incarnation. On this issue, Strauss was willing to make a slight compromise. He admitted that if it could be historically proven that the Gospel of John was a credible eyewitness account, one might be justified in describing Jesus as the man in whom the unity of the infinite and finite had been more perfectly expressed than in any other man in history. But this was a quantitative rather than a qualitative distinction. Strauss continued to insist that the perfected unity of the finite and infinite could be attributed only to the whole of humanity, not to a single individual, and that the truth of this idea was completely independent of whatever history could tell us about Jesus.[57] On the basis of his continued insistence on the principle that the eternal truths of Christianity were not dependent on the historical truth of the individual incarnation described in the Bible, Strauss placed himself alone in the Hegelian Left.

This isolation from the other members of the Hegelian school, however, did not mean that Strauss was willing to renounce the legitimacy of his own claims to be a Hegelian. Through a careful analysis of the relevant passages in Hegel's *Phenomenology* and *Lectures on the Philosophy of Religion,* Strauss tried to show that his own position was compatible with the general principles of Hegel's conception of the relationship between the religious *Vorstellung* and the philosophical *Begriff.* At the same time, however, Strauss admitted that he could prove only a general compatibility. "Hegel was personally no friend of historical criticism," he wrote, and would not have greeted the *Life of Jesus* as "an expression of his meaning." In some passages, Hegel clearly indicated that he considered the historicity of Christ as a part of the content, not merely the form, of religious truth. There was an "undeniable vagueness" in Hegel's Christology that revealed "all of the ambiguity of the concept of *Aufhebung*." But Strauss attributed this vagueness and ambiguity to Hegel's personal attitudes rather than his philosophical principle. During his later years, Hegel had pushed the "negative Moment" in the dialectical relationship between faith and knowledge into the background and emphasized the "positive Moment" of reconciliation. He had become a philosopher of the Restoration, rather than of revolution, of reconciliation rather than negation and antithesis. He did not want to be disturbed in his achieved peace and would have reacted negatively to any attempt to reopen the whole problem of the nature of the philosophical *Aufhebung.*[58] But Strauss insisted that the Hegelian reconciliation would remain vague and unconvincing as long as the relationship between the "representation" and historical truth was not clarified. By clarifying this relationship he had reconstituted the Hegelian reconciliation for his own age. Strauss could maintain his claim that he remained a loyal Hegelian, however, only by ignoring those passages in which Hegel attacked the method of critical reflective history on the basis of philosophical principle, that is, as a "subjective" method that failed to comprehend the reality of the spirit in history and thus transformed the self-revelation of the absolute into a tissue of "subjective fancies."[59]

Strauss's attitude toward the historical theologians of the critical school had also become more complex by 1837. He now gave more attention to specific problems of external criticism that could lead to a change in his rejection of the historical credibility of parts of the Gospel narratives. But, whatever the mixture of myth and history contained in the Gospel accounts, Strauss still insisted on the principle that the concept of myth could be applied to the whole of biblical history and that historical exegesis could never prove the supernatural character of the biblical events. "The essential thing in Christianity," he reiterated, "is . . . the Idea and its eternal realization in humanity."[60]

The criticism of Strauss's work did not all emanate from the theological faculties in German universities, and in the *Polemical Treatises,* Strauss felt compelled to clarify his standpoint regarding the relationship between his work and the moral and religious values of his cultural environment. He presented this clarification in a critique of the conservative cultural critic Wolfgang Menzel.[61] Menzel, Strauss claimed, would have liked "to muzzle the spirit of the times and drag it, beat it, and kick it back to the abandoned altars" of the past. His value structure of absolute obedience to authority in religion, morals, and politics, however, could not be forced upon a generation living in a period of historical transition characterized by doubt and uncertainty. Modern consciousness had devoured all "solid objective determinations" and rightly so. Man was not destined to be enchained to external authority. Strauss's work was in part a contribution to this liberating critical task of destruction. But destruction was not the sole aim of his work nor the destiny of the age. The universal truths of faith and morality would be established on a new basis, as subjective spiritual values. A new culture would emerge, Strauss claimed, out of the "spirit," which "would henceforth not recognize anything that was not its own creation."[62]

The *Polemical Treatises* thus represented a reaffirmation of the basic positions Strauss had taken in the *Life of Jesus.* He was still convinced that his conception of the relationship between the Christian *Vorstellung* and the philosophical *Begriff* was valid, and he remained confident that the general thrust of his work was in conformity with a general process of cultural liberation through the spiritualization or inner, rational appropriation of cultural values. Within a year, however, his confidence had begun to waver. The year between the spring of 1837 and the spring of 1838 was a period of intellectual doubt and emotional crisis for Strauss. By the spring of 1838 he was ready to make significant concessions to both his *wissenschaftlich* opponents and the general values of his cultural environment.

For purposes of analysis, Strauss's crisis can be divided into three major components. The most obvious factor was the career or vocational problem that had arisen after his dismissal from his academic post at Tübingen in 1835. Strauss was not ready to accept the position of Latin instructor in the Ludwigsburg lyceum as his lifetime occupation. He had only ten students, and he complained that the smallness of their numbers was not in inverse proportion to their intelligence.[63] His search for an academic appointment had begun almost immediately after leaving Tübingen. By the fall of 1836, however, his hopes for an academic appointment – he had been in correspondence with Heidelberg, Giessen, and Zürich – had been temporarily dashed. In September he wrote to the king of Württemberg for a clarification of his future prospects for a position within the Württemberg ecclesiastical or educational system. The reply to his inquiry stated that the best he could hope for was a gymnasium professorship.[64]

The excellent sales of the *Life of Jesus,* however, gave Strauss a temporary economic security, and in October 1836 he moved to Stuttgart to begin a life as a free-lance author and independent scholar. The work on the *Polemical Treatises* absorbed most of his time and energy during the winter. It was only after he had completed this work that his need for a secure or "fixed" position and for the intellectual collegiality of academic life became acute. He later wrote that he was suddenly filled with "terror" at the prospect of an insecure and isolated life as a "free" intellectual.[65]

The problem of finding a secure social position was transformed into a career crisis by Strauss's increasing lack of confidence in, and commitment to, his chosen calling as a scholar and theologian. On May 7, 1837, he wrote to Rapp that the life of *Wissenschaft* had become dry and sterile for him. The theological problems that had absorbed his energies were no longer interesting, and he felt the need to escape "from this whole sphere."[66] In the following November he lamented the lack of any meaningful goal for his activity, and as his thirtieth birthday approached in January 1838, he expressed his deep fear of falling into a purposeless existence.[67] The disintegration of Strauss's commitment to *Wissenschaft* and enthusiastic absorption in the Idea had led in fact to a disintegration of his sense of identity, as the following quotation from a letter of February 7, 1838, makes very clear:

> A person of my constitution must actually be possessed (*besessen*) in order to be happy. For a number of years I was possessed by a specific *wissenschaftlich* idea. Now that this has disintegrated, my inner self is empty, and outside it a number of spirits battle to determine who shall enter. But they are all too weak in comparison to the former occupant, and so none enters and my inner self remains empty.[68]

At Easter 1838, Strauss claimed that the specific problems of scholarship had faded into insignificance as he addressed himself to the more immediately important task of "coming to terms with life."[69]

The third factor in Strauss's crisis of 1837–8 was a growing consciousness of the disturbing power of his instinctual or natural desires. Strauss himself was well aware that the disintegration of his scholarly identity and commitment to things of the spirit was closely connected to the resurgence of his erotic impulses. The process of sublimation had broken down, the "negation of the negation" was no longer a convincingly meaning-giving solution to the problems of "life." In a poem entitled "Easter Monday" he tried to describe how his winter of scholarly peace had suddenly been disturbed by the sensuous vitality of spring.[70] In a letter to Rapp he identified this springtime force with an "adventure" with a naive young country girl that had "broken the ice" and left him without "solid ground" to stand on.[71] Two subsequent "adventures" – one with a Tübingen innkeeper's daughter and one with an operatic star in Stuttgart – kept Strauss in a disturbed and restless state for almost a year.[72]

Strauss's emotional turmoil was also revealed in the less explicitly sexual desire for social companionship, for recognition as a person with normal human "feelings," and for the cultural consolations provided by poetry, art, and music. He began to participate in the social and cultural life in Stuttgart, attended the theater and the opera, and even began to write poetry again. His letters to his friends are filled with pleas to be treated as a man of feeling and emotional sensitivity, not only an intellect concerned solely with the *Begriff.*[73] In the spring of 1838 he published a biographical study of Justinus Kerner in which he recounted his youthful romantic enthusiasms. This essay, he admitted, was consciously aimed at destroying the popular conception of his own nature as that of an "abstraction of unbelief."[74]

Strauss's attempts to "come to terms with life" by constructing a more satisfying equilibrium between intellect and feeling within his experience, however, were unsuccessful. The stirrings of April among his dried tubers had proven to be an unsettling disturbance rather than the wellsprings of a new life. He soon discovered that he was inept in love, in poetic creativity, and in social life. On February 28, 1838, he wrote to Vischer that he could write volumes about "the suffering of a person, who, by nature socially inept and educated in a monastery, could fall in love only with actresses or innkeepers' daughters, because his only feminine contacts were with these kinds of women."[75] At Easter 1838, he wrote to Märklin:

> For some time now I have been so satiated with my present mode of existence, especially as my present lack of position, my isolation from any institution or group, has made it particularly perceptible, that the phrase "No dog would want to live like this" has actually become my morning and evening prayer. This mood has grown to such dimensions that it makes me incapable of work and locks me out from all society.[76]

The only way out of his depression that he could conceive was a commitment to a new scholarly project that would channel his disturbing instinctual energies back into spiritual work.

It is within this context of personal crisis, isolation, and depression that the compromises of Strauss's third edition of the *Life of Jesus* must be understood. Already, on December 9, 1837, he had written to Rapp that he no longer possessed the "pathos" of conviction that was ready to battle for principle. "As far as I am concerned," he claimed, "the world can believe everything it wants to, and I myself am ready, if it is necessary, to believe much that is unbelievable."[77] The virtually unanimous scholarly rejection of the validity of his attack on the historical credibility of the biblical accounts had led to doubts about his former skepticism. These doubts were expressed in a major concession to the biblical scholars in the third edition. Strauss now claimed that he did not have sufficient evidence to disprove the historical credibility of the Gospel of John. This crack in his former conception was a major compromise; Strauss later saw it as a virtual destruction of the original work.[78] If the Gospel of John was a credible historical account, it became possible to argue that the Jesus of history and the Christ of religion were synonymous. The concession to the biblical scholars was thus tied to a major concession to the philosophical theologians on the issue of the incarnation. In the new edition, Christ was described as "the man in whose self-consciousness the union of the human and the divine first appeared with an energy that thrust back to an infinitesimal minimum within the whole range of his mind and life all restraint upon this union; who to this extent stands unique and unrivaled in world history." Strauss would still not concede that the realization of the idea of the incarnation was completed in Jesus' life. The "religious consciousness that was first achieved and expressed in Christ" was still subject to "purification and further development in the progressive advance of the human spirit."[79] Despite the qualifications, however, the concession was major. The Idea was once again tied to the historical fact.

The scholarly concessions of the third edition of the *Life of Jesus* were expressed in more popular form in the essay "The Transitory and the Permanent Aspects of Christianity," which was published in a literary journal in the summer of 1838. This essay, Strauss later admitted, revealed his desire to build a bridge over the "chasm" that the *Life of Jesus* had created between him and "more or less believing general humanity."[80] Within the essay itself he expressed his fear that the scholarly interpretation of Christianity might become totally divorced from general cultural attitudes. In a popular style of question and answer that was quite different from the scholarly prose of the *Life of Jesus,* Strauss tried to differentiate the mythical and merely historical from the permanently meaningful aspects of all the major Christian doctrines. The results did not reveal any radical reconversion to the traditional faith. Strauss continued to describe the miracles of the New Testament as mythical constructions, and the meanings ascribed to events like the resurrection or doctrines like the atonement were in terms of universal aspects of an immanent human experience. The forgiveness of sins, Strauss claimed, was simply the religious name for the human freedom that was attained through spiritual elevation to the Idea of humanity.[81] On two crucial issues, however, Strauss did make a great effort to reconcile his position with the feelings of his cultural contemporaries. He allowed the possibility of a personal immortality after death,[82] and he brought the historical Jesus back to the center of the Christian faith.

As in the third edition of the *Life of Jesus,* Strauss described the historical Jesus as the most perfect incarnation of the union of the divine and the human who had existed in history. The Christ of the Christian faith, he claimed, was "a historical, not a mythical Christ, an individual, not a mere symbol." Strauss thus assured his readers that they need have "no fear that Christ might be lost if much of what was formerly called Christianity had to be abandoned." And Strauss now even claimed that the faith in the historical Christ was the basis of the Christian experience: "If Christ remains for us, and if he remains as the highest that we can recognize or conceive in the religious sphere, as that person without whose presence no perfect piety is possible, then what we have through him is still the essence of Christianity."[83]

In the introduction to this essay of reconciliation, Strauss had claimed that he was incapable of making himself believe in anything merely to attain "peace for [himself] and reconciliation with others."[84] Within a year, however, he was ready to describe this essay as a pragmatic compromise with an "idiotic consciousness" and to take a stance that insisted on the radical separation of modern consciousness from the traditional faith.

In the middle of June 1838, at a time when Strauss's feeling of inner emptiness and aimlessness was reaching the breaking point, he made one final desperate attempt to obtain an academic position. The chair in New Testament studies at Zürich had become vacant, and Strauss wrote a pleading letter to the rector asking for consideration. He pointed to the major concessions in the third edition of the *Life of Jesus* as a sign of his conciliatory stance and claimed that he required some kind of secure position for his own "spiritual survival." "I cannot endure such a life, without immediate scholarly stimulation and activity," he wrote; "it cripples me."[85] At first, Strauss was very pessimistic about his chances, but the Zürich faculty displayed a keen interest in his candidacy, and by the fall serious negotiations were in progress. In February 1839, Strauss finally received the official offer of a full professorship in theology. Within a month, however, Strauss's original pessimism proved to have been justified. His appointment had become a passionately contested symbolic issue in the religious and political struggle between the recently installed liberal reformist government and the vested political and religious interests threatened by liberal reform. Popular opinion was aroused against the appointment, and after a series of stormy meetings on March 18–20, 1839, the Great Council of the city of Zürich bowed to popular pressure and placed the newly appointed professor on retirement at half salary.[86]

The Zürich experience had a decisive influence on Strauss's attitude toward the Christian community and toward the doctrinal symbols and ecclesiastical institutions that bound that community together. By the time of his "retirement" he had already become indifferent to the outcome of the battle over his appointment. He had regained his confidence in his former position and its relevance to modern culture, he had begun a large new work on the scale of the *Life of Jesus,* and he had recovered his feeling of solidarity with those of his contemporaries who really mattered – the emancipated minds of the invisible church of the future.

The first signs of a change in Strauss's mood became evident in the fall of 1838. In September he made a journey down the Rhine, visiting scholars and students at universities like Heidelberg and Bonn. He was surprised and pleased by the "widespread support of [his] person and cause by respected scholars."[87] At the same time he finally received the public support of such friends in Württemberg as Vischer and Märklin.[88] The backing of the increasingly radical *Hallische Jahrbücher* renewed his confidence in the seminal importance of his own work for the younger generation. He supported the *Jahrbücher* as a journal that was liberated from the "authority and cant" of the old Hegelians.[89] It marked the recognition of the "spirit of a progressing age" among a large number of his intellectual contemporaries.[90]

The feeling of identity within a progressive group was complemented by a new sense of inner identity. The inner emptiness was filled with a new "scientific" idea. The possibility of taking up the duties of a Christian theologian at Zürich encouraged Strauss to revive an old plan to write a historical and philosophical analysis of Christian doctrine. By December 1838 he was already deeply absorbed in his research and working on a comparative study of Schleiermacher and Daub for the *Hallische Jahrbücher.* Strauss's new sense of purpose was revealed in a letter to Rapp on December 20, 1838: "Now I realize that I am still a theologian and that not everything in this area has become indifferent to me . . . You were right, old friend! Only work could cure me!"[91]

The essay on Schleiermacher and Daub, which began to appear in the *Jahrbücher* in January 1839, revealed Strauss's reaffirmation of the critical positions he had held in 1835. Once again he criticized Schleiermacher for refusing to extend the razor edge of his critical acumen to the historical Christ out of fear of destroying the last historical grounds for the traditional faith. The Hegelian Daub was criticized for his a priori deduction of the historical truth of the *Vorstellung* from the philosophical truth of the *Begriff.* He ignored the "negative Moment" of the critical "process of dissolution."[92] Thus both aspects of *Wissenschaft* to which Strauss had made concessions since 1835 were once again placed in critical perspective.

At the same time, Strauss displayed an increasingly radical disregard for the necessity of compromise with the general Christian community. He denied Schleiermacher's claim to have constructed a theology that was not separated from the common Christian experience. Schleiermacher's validation of Christian doctrine through inner experience would always and only be an intellectual's viewpoint. The masses would continue to believe in authority and tradition. Thus, Schleiermacher's attempt to subject theology to the service of the church must ultimately fail. The theologian was forced to ignore the church and its needs if he desired to retain his intellectual integrity.[93]

Strauss's confidence in his position was displayed in his reactions to the crucial turning points in the Zürich affair in March 1839. On March 1 he published an "open letter (*Sendschreiben*)" in which he defended his views. Although he made a few left-handed attempts to be diplomatic, he certainly did not bend his knees before the will of the church authorities and the aroused populace. It seems quite obvious that the pamphlet could only have harmed his cause. He separated himself from the church and its leaders by the constant use of "you" and "us" and insinuated rather strongly that the "aroused masses" were swine unworthy of his intellectual pearls.[94] Strauss's other alleged attempt to further his own cause in this affair – the republication of the essays "The Transitory and the Permanent Aspects of Christianity" and "Justinus Kerner" in a pamphlet entitled *Two Leaflets of Peace* – revealed a similar self-confident and condescending attitude. The introduction to the *Two Leaflets,* in fact, was exactly the opposite of an attempt at reconciliation. Strauss claimed that he felt it necessary to reprint the old essays for diplomatic reasons, but then proceeded to describe the publication as a futile attempt to gain the good will of those weak and uneducated people who still required some historical basis for their faith. He openly stated that he now considered his former attempt at reconciliation theologically and philosophically worthless.[95]

Strauss's attitude toward his religious opponents in Zürich was intimately connected to a renewed assurance that his own position was in tune with the times, that he was a spokesman for the progressive spirit in the present and the culture of the future. In the *Sendschreiben* he compared the reaction of the Zürich pastors to his own position to the envious fear of medieval craftsmen whose skills had been made obsolete by modern industry. The relationship between him and his opponents was like that between Gutenberg and the scribes or like that between the steamboat and the sailboat.[96] In the introduction to the *Two Leaflets,* Strauss defined the principle that he represented as an immanent spiritualized "Christianity," that is, the Idea of the incarnation generalized to refer to all humanity. For orthodox Christians the incarnation remained a "transcendent" Idea, a supernatural historical event. If Christianity itself was defined in terms of this position, then

Strauss admitted that his own stance was not Christian. But if Christianity was defined simply as a belief in the reality of the incarnation, then his own stance and the viewpoint of modern consciousness were more "Christian" than traditional Christianity.[97]

The unsuccessful outcome of the Zürich affair increased Strauss's confidence in his own position. The controversy had drawn the lines of battle more clearly, and he now felt that he was not alone on the "modern" side of the lines. "I no longer feel so isolated," he wrote to Georgii's wife, "and there is little danger that I will give up or become tired."[98] His physical drives now left him in peace, and he was no longer bothered by the disturbing problems of "coming to terms with life."[99] Moreover, the controversy had finally expunged the desire for an academic appointment from his consciousness. He now realized that he would never find the freedom and peace he needed to develop and articulate his ideas in an academic context.[100] The Zürich affair, in fact, had been a "healthy crisis," a tremendous revivifying liberation from the burdens of compromise:

> "Now it is decided! Now it is good!" I cry with Wallenstein. Decided, namely, that we can expect no support for our cause from the visible church. Thus all compromises and negotiations must be ended, and we must forge straight ahead, placing our sole hope in the still invisible church of the future.[101]

This "invisible church of the future," Strauss now insisted, would be not a historical actualization of the content of Christian culture in a new form, but a total negation of both the form and content of Christianity. On November 3, 1839, he wrote to Märklin:

> Any attempt to salvage or philosophically justify the Christian dogmas is idle affectation on our part. Not one religious feeling or perception that we possess can be naturally clothed in Christian form . . . Whoever and whatever Christ may have been in himself is completely irrelevant to our religion; because we do not recognize any savior outside of ourselves, we no longer require an oracle.[102]

This uncompromising radical stance in relationship to the forces that represented the traditional faith was expressed in formal retractions of the compromises Strauss had made in 1837 and 1838. In August 1839 he withdrew his concession to the historical theologians regarding the historical credibility of the Gospel of John and returned to his original position regarding the necessity for a demolition of historical fact as a presupposition for the resurrection of the Idea.[103] In the fourth edition of the *Life of Jesus,* published in 1840, Strauss purified his work of all the "corruptions" of the third edition that had destroyed the unity of his original conception.[104] By the time this fourth edition was at the presses, however, the first volume of Strauss's *The Christian Faith in Its*

Historical Development and Battle with Modern Science was already in print; and this work represented not only a return to the position of 1835 but a definite step beyond that position toward a more radical cultural stance.

Strauss had conceived the plan for a large work on Christian doctrine as early as 1831. The three basic elements of such a work, he had written to Georgii, were already historically "given": the traditional doctrines of the Christian faith as they had been formulated by the early Christian church, the critical negation of the validity of these doctrines by the rationalistic and pantheistic philosophy of the seventeenth and eighteenth centuries, and the reconciliation of the objective doctrines and subjective rationality in Hegel's speculative idealism.[105] The *Life of Jesus* had been conceived as a kind of prolegomena to this larger work. The result of his own historical criticism, Strauss claimed, had been to transform the biblical history into a "mental product," into doctrines unsupported by historical proof. If the teachings of the faith were to be appropriated as a "thoroughly tested and constituted science," this dogma would in turn have to be subjected to criticism. In 1835, Strauss claimed that this dogmatic criticism would have to "be made the subject of a separate work," and he offered his "concluding dissertation" merely as a preliminary sketch of the results of such a study.[106] Strauss's *Christian Faith* can thus be seen as a greatly expanded version of the concluding pages of the *Life of Jesus.* His general methodological principle had not changed. "The true criticism of dogma is its history," he wrote.[107] But by 1840, Strauss's conception of the results of this historical-critical process had undergone significant revision.

The process of criticism culminated no longer in a final reconciliation of philosophical knowledge and Christian faith, but in their total separation. Strauss looked back with sarcasm on his earlier belief in the Hegelian conception of identity of content in the different forms of philosophy and religion:

> The Hegelian system was trumpeted as the child of peace, and the promise of the beginning of a new order of things, of a time in which the wolves would live besides the lambs . . . Worldly-wisdom, that proud pagan, submitted meekly to baptism and presented a Christian confession of faith, and faith took no offense at this action.[108]

Young scholars – like the young Strauss – had been able to fill their heads with religious doubts in the full assurance that they possessed the magic formula that would ultimately dissolve these doubts. But by 1840 this magic formula had lost its experiential power. In fact, Strauss now saw the earlier reconciliation as a temporary and illusory truce. The proponents of traditional orthodoxy and the Fundamentalist pietists had never participated in the Hegelian reconciliation. The bridge over the vast chasm between faith and knowledge had been flimsy from the beginning and had now collapsed completely.

The main foundation of this bridge had been the Hegelian conception of the relationship between *Vorstellung* and *Begriff* as different forms of comprehension of the same substantial content. Strauss now claimed that Hegel's affirmation of this unity of content in the specific case of religion and philosophy contradicted his general practice of viewing the popular sensuous consciousness as an inferior form of comprehension and his constant translation of the Christian doctrines into the "higher" form of their speculative truth.[109] In his general contention that religion and modern philosophy were different in content as well as form, Strauss agreed with the contemporary works of Ludwig Feuerbach. But Strauss rejected Feuerbach's criteria for such a differentiation. Feuerbach had claimed that religion and philosophy were related to basically different human needs; religion was practical and emotional, philosophy objective and theoretical. But Strauss insisted that religion and philosophy arose from the same basic needs and had the same aims. For Strauss the drive for knowledge of self and universe could not be differentiated from the "practical" need for ontological security or spiritual "satisfaction (*Befriedigung*)." The differences between religion and philosophy, faith and knowledge, were differences between stages in cultural development. Religion and philosophy were modes of attaining knowledge and spiritual identity that expressed different levels of man's self-consciousness of his own essence and his relation to the ultimate meaning of the universe.[110] The central theme of *The Christian Faith* was the description of the development of man from Christian consciousness to "modern" consciousness as a radically liberating transition that entailed a fundamental change in *both* the content *and* the form of human knowledge and experience.

The fundamental criteria that Strauss used to differentiate Christian culture from modern consciousness were those of transcendence and immanence (*Jenseits* and *Diesseits*). The Christian faith represented a primitive stage of human self-consciousness (in his more polemical moments, Strauss called it the "idiot consciousness")[111] in which man perceived his own essence as an objective, external fact revealed to him by a transcendent god. In this stage man was alienated from his own nature; he viewed his own essential humanity as a personal being (Christ) who was essentially different from man.[112] The way in which spiritual satisfaction or ontological identity was attained at this stage of cultural development was through "faith," through a blind surrender of the human self to an objectified, transcendentalized "other."[113] For Strauss, therefore, the Christian model of cultural integration was one in which man was alienated from his own essence and dependent on an authority outside himself.

The transition to modern consciousness was characterized by the human appropriation of the alienated, objectified "truth" of the Christian doctrines. But in this process of appropriation – which was historically represented by the immanent, spiritual interpretation of Christian dogma in Hegelian philosophy – the content of the religious world view was changed. By tearing God from the heavens, by applying the predicates of the incarnate divinity to all humanity, by asserting the autonomy and self-determination of man, modern consciousness had destroyed the self-alienation, the heteronomy and the transcendence that were the essential content of Christian consciousness. In modern philosophy the "revelation" of religion was recognized as a self-objectification of the human essence; the transcendence of divinity was understood as a mythical human creation. But as soon as the immanent human meaning of the *Vorstellung* was understood, the *Vorstellung* became superfluous and dissolved into nothing. "As man recognizes his own laws in the biblical revelation," Strauss wrote, ". . . he extends his hand to the *Doppelgänger* of his mirror-image, and this image disappears as it returns into himself."[114] In Christian culture man had looked to transcendent aid for his salvation:

> As long as man is alienated from himself, or has not become conscious of and learned to control the spirit in himself, he will not be able to find the source of his actions and his circumstances within himself, but only in the sphere where he has transferred his spirit, namely, outside himself. Just as he has been made guilty through an external (*fremden*) act, so he believes that he can attain righteousness and blessedness only through an action that comes from outside him.

The self-determining, self-affirming man of modern consciousness, however, no longer needed the "grace" of God or the external action of Christ's atonement. Man was responsible for his own salvation, and he could find it only by recognizing his own essence as spirit, and thus uniting himself with the Idea of humanity.[115]

At times, Strauss appeared to believe that the destruction of the illusions of Christian transcendence would produce a radical practical transformation of collective human existence:

> This earth will no longer be a vale of misery through which man must wander in order to attain the external goal of a future heavenly existence. The riches of the divine power of life, which is inherent in every moment of earthly life, are to be appropriated and realized here and now.[116]

But Strauss's conception of this immanent realization of the Idea of humanity, of the overcoming of human self-alienation, was strictly a spiritual one. He still insisted that man could find true liberation and genuine fulfillment only in the realm of the spirit. In order to become one with humanity, man must deny his sensuous, particular, individual self. Spiritualization was synonymous with humanism. Strauss thought that the general process of cultural integration in the "new" post-Christian culture would be accomplished through a gradual process of education rather than through religious conversion. It was in the schools rather than in the churches that modern man would learn that he was a "real participant in the divine life of the Idea." The Moment of negation, the denial of individual selfishness and instinctual indulgence, was still necessary, but it would become less tortuous and traumatic in the self-determining spiritualization process of education.[117] The climax of this process would be the recognition of one's unity with the infinite Idea of humanity, the genuine reappropriation of the Christian doctrine of eschatological fulfillment. Immortality would be recognized as man's "inner universality, his power to raise himself above all finitude to the realm of the Idea."[118]

Strauss's conception of the "modern" model of cultural integration as an immanent spiritual process was set in direct opposition to the Christian viewpoint. His conception of the communal order that would express the modern consciousness was also set in direct opposition to the Christian church. The coexistence of church and state in the old culture represented the dualism of man's self-alienated existence. The new consciousness of immanent self-realization, however, would find its institutional form in what Strauss called the "humanity state (*Humanitätsstaat*)," a unified communal order in which all the former tasks of the church would be absorbed by the secular state. "No peace will be found," Strauss asserted, "until eternity is fully absorbed into time, piety has been completely taken up into morality, and the church has been absorbed into the state."[119] But his new communal order could be "unified" only at the top, within the ruling intellectual elite. For Strauss's new cultural stance of 1840 implied a radical division between the mass of the uneducated people and the educated elite.

The conception of the identity of content in the different modes of *Vorstellung* and *Begriff* had previously provided Strauss with a means for reconciling his own intellectual position with the consciousness of the general community. His rejection of this identity on the theological level also entailed its rejection on the level of communal relationships. The Zürich affair had given the final blow to Strauss's conception of a unified community. He now found his communal identity in his identification with the invisible church of the philosophically enlightened. The cultural standpoint of modern consciousness was set not only against the Christian culture of a previous era but against "popular" consciousness. The task of overcoming self-alienation could be performed only by philosophical understanding, and modern consciousness was thus possible only for the educated.[120] There were no bridges over the chasm between faith and knowledge, and Strauss openly stated that the unalienated existence of the spiritually liberated modern man must place him in a situation of "alienation" from the majority of his cultural contemporaries:

> He who does not have the spirit within himself has it outside himself . . .; he who cannot determine his own existence looks for determination through authority; he who is not ripe for Reason remains dependent on revelation . . . There have been enough false attempts at reconciliation; only a separation of opposites can lead to further progress.[121]

Strauss's concluding statement concerning the proper relationship between the theologian and the church in 1840 was radically different from his statements of 1831 and 1835. The theologian's primary contemporary task was to dismantle the faith as gently as possible. But this dismantling, demythologizing process was really relevant only to the consciousness of the educated elite. The study of theology was self-destructive, a process of liberation from the material being studied. Theology had become a sphinx that disappeared as soon as its riddle was solved.[122] Thus a serious study of theology could no longer lead to service in the church. Theological understanding made a person totally incompetent for an ecclesiastical career – only religious "idiots" would be able to fill the pulpits in the modern world. With a bitter "plague on your house," Strauss withdrew from his cultural inheritance as well as from the vocation that was meant to purvey that inheritance. But what he proposed in its stead was both vague and restricted. Instead of the transcendent consolations of faith, he offered immanent human realization through educational elevation to the Idea of humanity. Instead of the community of believers, he offered the spiritual communion of intellectually liberated philosophers and scholars. From the very beginning of his intellectual career, Strauss had defined religious faith as a popular form of theology, as a mode of knowledge rather than a mode of historical practice, a way of life. His alternative to Christian culture possessed the same intellectual focus. The "realization" of the Idea of humanity was conceived as an intellectual, educational, theoretical process. But concrete natural and social existence remained untransformed by this process. Only those individuals with the money, leisure, and self-discipline required for the elevation above natural desires and material needs could hope to enter the secular cathedral of the new humanistic culture. The separation of historical reality from the Idea, which had informed Strauss's critical method in his studies of Christian theology, also informed his vision of the future.

In November 1839, when Strauss was just beginning to write the first volume of *The Christian Faith,* he warned Märklin that they had better not remain ensconced in their former Hegelian illusions, or they would soon be criticized by the more radical younger generation as well as by the representatives of the orthodox faith.[123] Despite the radical anti-Christian stance of *The Christian Faith,* however, Strauss was unable to avoid such criticism from the Left. By the time the second volume of *The Christian Faith* was published he was being described as a historical fossil who had been overcome by the more radical religious criticism of Bauer and Feuerbach. The *Hallische Jahrbücher* supported Bauer and Feuerbach against Strauss, and in 1841, Strauss severed his relationship with the journal because of what he described as unbearable insults and condescension.[124]

In retrospect, Strauss tended to see himself as the father of the radical critique of Christianity who had been devoured by his sons, or as a Columbus, followed by an Amerigo Vespucci who had the arrogance to name the new land after himself.[125] In a sense, Strauss was right. His fundamental position – that the self-alienated transcendent world view of Christianity had become historically obsolete and should and would be replaced by a totally immanent model of cultural integration – was the starting point and common basis of the cultural stance of the Hegelian Left. But it was *only* the starting point. Strauss remained within the "spiritual" confines of the Hegelian cultural model and never developed a clear theory of social and political practice or collective historical change. In 1843, Strauss himself wrote to Vischer that his silence was based on a conviction of his increasing irrelevance. "I no longer have anything to say to the age," he admitted.[126]

9

Bruno Bauer and the reduction of absolute spirit to human self-consciousness

Among the younger members of the Hegelian school during the 1830s it was Bruno Bauer whose scholarly interests and intellectual concerns most closely paralleled those of Strauss. Bauer, like Strauss, was a philosophical theologian and biblical scholar whose writings focused on the problem of defining the relationship between the historical truth, the representational form, and the universal, philosophically comprehensible, absolute content of the biblical revelation. Moreover, Bauer's successive attempts to construct a satisfactory resolution for this problem corresponded to the general stages in Strauss's development. Bauer began his intellectual career with the firm conviction that the Hegelian doctrine of the identity of content in the different forms of the religious *Vorstellung* and the philosophical *Begriff* provided a secure basis for the reconciliation of the orthodox Christian faith with modern philosophical consciousness. Between 1835 and 1838 he tried to revise and reconstruct the Hegelian identity of religion and philosophy in a manner that would take the historical criticism of the biblical writings into account. Like Strauss, however, Bauer abandoned this attempt to reconstruct the Hegelian identity in 1839–41 and asserted the absolute opposition of modern philosophical consciousness to both the form and the content of traditional Christian culture. Finally, Bauer, like Strauss, defined the model of cultural integration for the future, post-Christian era in totally immanent terms, not as the reconciliation of God and man in an actualized Kingdom of God on earth, but as the reconciliation of man with his universal human essence in a "state of humanity."

Despite their common interests and the parallels in their personal development, however, Strauss and Bauer perceived their cultural stances as mutually antagonistic in both major stages of their reinterpretation and revision of their common Hegelian inheritance. In

1835–6 they each viewed the standpoint of the other as an expression of the problem that needed to be resolved. Bauer criticized the *Life of Jesus* as a symptomatic expression of the historical stage of one-sided subjective negation, which would inevitably have to give way to a reaffirmation of the objective reality of the absolute in history.[1] Strauss, in turn, interpreted Bauer's criticism as a reactionary attempt to simply reaffirm the position whose inadequacy had been the starting point of his investigations.[2] In 1842, however, Bauer attacked the radical solution of Strauss's *Christian Faith* as "inconsequential, half-hearted, wavering, and inconclusive." Strauss's version of anti-Christian humanism, he claimed, remained ensconced in the "theological" perspective of Christian culture and did not reveal "the faintest idea of the present task and goal of criticism."[3] Strauss made no effort to respond to this criticism but simply concluded that Bauer was a "scoundrel in every possible respect."[4]

Strauss's contemptuous dismissal of Bauer's criticism in both 1835–6 and the early 1840s was undoubtedly influenced by the attitude of arrogant condescension with which that criticism was expressed. In the "reconstruction" or "rehabilitation" phase of their parallel development, Bauer was more conservative that Strauss; during the "transformation" phase he was more radical. In both instances, however, he presented his own position as a selfless articulation of irresistible world-historical forces. Bauer's cultural stances in both the mid-1830s and the early 1840s were expressions of a supraindividual experience, but the specific determinants of this "universality" were not so much "world historical" as Prussian. Bauer's radical conversion from conservative Hegelian accommodationism to critical extremism on the Hegelian Left was intimately connected to the changing relationship between the Hegelian school and the Prussian state. His original identification with the existing order was more total than Strauss's, and his eventual disinheritance was more traumatic and more complete. This chapter attempts to show how this more radical experience of cultural disinheritance also produced a more radical vision of cultural liberation.

Bauer's earliest extant writings – reviews published in the Hegelian *Jahrbücher* and August Tholuck's *Litterarischer Anzeiger* – date from 1834. By this time, Bauer had already completed his university studies and begun an academic career as a *Privatdozent* in the theological faculty at the University of Berlin. The formative sociocultural and intellectual experiences of this twenty-five-year-old Hegelian theologian must be reconstructed from the barest skeleton of biographical facts. Although the evidence is far too meager to provide a convincing inner history of Bauer's path to Hegel, it does suggest a pattern of development similar to that of other Hegelians of his historical generation.[5]

Bauer was born on September 6, 1809, in the town of Eisenberg in the small Thuringian duchy of Saxony-Altenburg. He was the eldest son of a skilled artisan, a porcelain painter, whose income was dependent on the needs of the ducal court. The sociocultural roots of both his mother's and his father's families were in the world of the state-dependent *Kleinbürgertum* of the prerevolutionary petty Saxon principalities. In 1815, however, Bauer's father grasped at an opportunity to escape this confined and disintegrating world and accepted a position as the director of painting in a state-owned factory in Charlottenburg near Berlin, which manufactured the "hygienic china (*Sanitätsgeschirr*)" - perhaps more aptly described as bathroom fixtures - for the residences of the Prussian kings. The social and financial security Bauer's father had hoped to attain in his new sphere of activity eluded him, and he increasingly transferred his ambitions to his sickly, but intellectually gifted, eldest son. He was determined that Bruno should become a minister in the Prussian church. The cost of the gymnasium and university education that was the prerequisite for such a career was not easy for the Bauer family to bear. Bruno could never forget that his own opportunities grew out of his family's sacrifices.[6] The experience of being the embodiment of his family's hopes and ambitions helped produce Bauer's lifelong conviction of having been chosen for some special historical mission, but it also saddled him with a sense of guilt as he increasingly defined his mission in a manner his parents could not completely understand or wholeheartedly approve. The dilemma is familiar: The educational process that was to prepare Bauer to fulfill his father's ambitions estranged him from his father's world. This tension was most obvious in the sphere of religion and was first clearly expressed in 1832-4, after the completion of Bauer's university studies, when he chose, against his father's wishes, to pursue an academic rather than an ecclesiastical career. But the tension was never resolved with a clean break, for Bauer never found a permanent cultural "home" to replace the family he had left behind.

The spiritual pilgrimage that culminated in Bauer's Hegelian conversion conforms to a familiar pattern. Raised in a strictly orthodox and pious (though not pietistic) home, he experienced his first religious doubts when his original naive faith in the absolute transcendent truth of biblical Christianity was confronted by the world views of neoclassical humanism and Romantic aestheticism during his gymnasium years.[7] By the time he matriculated in the theological faculty at the University of Berlin in 1828 his religious views had become "indecisive" and he began an active search for a scholarly method that could provide a secure, objective grounding for his wavering faith. Like so many of his contemporaries he found that Schleiermacher's attempt to base religious assurance on subjective feeling did not provide an adequate ontological security. The "liberal crisis," he felt, could be resolved only by a rehabilitation of the "dogma," of the positive content of Christian revelation. Hegel's "positive method" of speculative comprehension, however, "captivated" him almost immediately. He felt completely "at home (*heimisch*)" in Hegel's philosophy because it appeared simply as a "clarification" of his original faith.[8] During his first semesters, Bauer appears to have taken a special interest in Hegelian aesthetics. He attended Hotho's as well as Hegel's lectures, and in the summer of 1829 he was awarded the essay prize in the philosophical faculty for a paper in which Kant's aesthetic theory was criticized from the Hegelian perspective.[9] But his interests soon focused more exclusively on the philosophical theology of Hegel and Marheineke.

During the winter of 1831–2, Marheineke is reported to have countered Wilhelm Vatke's praise of Strauss with the claim that Bauer was the most promising theologian of the younger generation. "He will accomplish great things," he prophesied.[10] Marheineke's inclination to rank Bauer above Strauss was undoubtedly connected to Bauer's accommodationist tendency to emphasize the positive rather than the negative Moment in the Hegelian rehabilitation of Christian dogma and history. In fact, Bauer's conservative tendencies were so obvious that he succeeded in gaining both Marheineke's and Hengstenberg's support when he applied for lecturing privileges in the theological faculty in 1834.[11] But it would be very misleading to describe Bauer as a "Hengstenbergian" in 1834. Bauer's earliest published writings – even those published in Tholuck's pietistic journal – clearly show that he was convinced that the truth of the positive content of Christian history and dogma could be demonstrated only by the speculative method of Hegelian philosophy.

The reviews that Bauer published in 1834 and 1835 were overwhelmingly concerned with the defense of the validity of the Hegelian method of speculative comprehension against the one-sided and thus ultimately false perspectives of reflective rationalism and orthodox supernaturalism. He paid little attention to the specific arguments of the exegetical and historical studies he was asked to review but judged them simply in terms of their epistemological presuppositions. His arguments generally followed the well-developed pattern already established by Hegelian theologians like Marheineke and Daub. Both the rationalists and the supernaturalists were accused of representing, or rather misrepresenting, the truth of the Christian revelation from the distorting perspective of the subjective ego. The rationalists dismissed the objective, divine content of Christian history because it was in apparent contradiction with the rational understanding of the finite human subject. The supernaturalists defended the divine content of Christianity, but as an arbitrary and thus ultimately incomprehensible revelation of a transcendent, personal, infinite ego. Only speculative science could overcome the alienation of the human subject from the absolute content of Christian revelation. "Science," Bauer claimed, "recognizes in the appearance the objectification of the concept, and as this recognition, science is nothing more than a remembrance of this objectification."[12] The Hegelian philosopher did not impose a subjective structure on the object of his investigation but simply recognized and reconstructed the dynamic inner structure of the objective content itself.

Bauer's defense of the Hegelian absolute method defined him as an orthodox Hegelian epigone. What was striking and unusual in his earliest writings was his insistent claim that every detail of the biblical letter could be demonstrated as historically true through the activity of Hegelian comprehension. The apparent contradictions of the biblical record were a product of faulty epistemology. From the perspective of the self-remembering absolute these contradictions appeared as Moments in the dynamic "unity of the Idea."[13] The goal of biblical exegesis, Bauer insisted, was to show "the unity of the Idea in the separation of its Moments as it is described in the Old Testament and then its unmediated unity as portrayed in the New Testament."[14] "The totality of the Holy Scriptures," he wrote, "in itself represents the totality of the System."[15] And Bauer was certainly convinced that the historicity of the incarnation of God in Jesus Christ was a necessary Moment in this "System": "Because the ideal Messiah is a necessary expression of the Idea, so is the historical Messiah. Both are inextricably one, because it belongs to the essence of the Idea that it reveal itself in history."[16]

Although Bauer's reviews focused on the methodological problems of biblical exegesis, they also had a broader, less academic dimension. He described the reconciling comprehension of the historical past as a religious experience: "For the Idea finds itself again in history, and the objective writing of history is nothing but the blessedness of this reappropriation in the Kingdom of God."[17] The achievement of an objective historical method was inextricably connected to the entry into the Kingdom of God on earth, to what Bauer described as the conversion from "individuality" to "personality." Man became an individual through the act of self-consciousness whereby he separated himself from the "otherness" of the world that transcended his finite ego. But this act of separation produced an isolated ego, an "abstract man" alienated from the concrete content of life, a subject without "substance." The finite self-consciousness of "individuality" could be transformed into the concrete universality of "personality" only through an elevation to identity with the "absolute personality of God" in speculative thought. The achievement of "personality" was a product of the Hegelian conversion experience, which was itself merely a comprehension, a making explicit, of the Christian incarnation, the historical actualization of the infinite spirit in the concrete individual.[18] In defending the historical truth of the biblical revelation, Bauer was also defending the historical reality of his own "blessedness," the validity of the ontological security he had gained through his Hegelian conversion. His aim was to secure the Hegelian claim that "human self-consciousness knows itself as an individual and is not dissolved, but is elevated to the consciousness of God in that God himself had actualized his eternal consciousness in individual human consciousness."[19]

In 1840, Bauer described the impact of Strauss's *Life of Jesus* on his original Hegelian cultural stance with the critical distance gained from a new perspective:

Like immortal gods the disciples lived with patriarchal calm in the Kingdom of the Idea that their master had left behind as his inheritance. The chiliasts' dreams of eschatological fulfillment appeared finally to have been realized when the lightning of reflection struck in the Kingdom of the blessed. The blow was so unexpected that the representatives of scientific criticism in Berlin appointed a reviewer for Strauss's book who still lived most securely in the dream of the unity of the Idea and immediate reality (or more specifically, the world of empirical consciousness) and who even wanted to perpetuate this dream in a new journal.[20]

This quotation appears to indicate that Bauer's response to the problem raised by Strauss's work was a simple reaffirmation of his previous positions, a continuation in the old dream. This is not entirely true. Bauer did not simply ignore the attack on the historical credibility of the Bible expressed in the works of Strauss and Wilhelm Vatke (whose study on the Old Testament was more directly related to Bauer's scholarly interests). He saw this criticism rather as the beginning of a new phase in the evolution of speculative theology, in which the historical truth of the biblical revelation would become the central issue. For Hegel and Marheineke the problems of historical criticism had remained outside the purview of speculation; Strauss and Vatke had placed them in the center of the process of reconciling faith and knowledge, religion and philosophy. The historical critics had "called forth a contradiction within the general consciousness of the school and thus provided it with a new beginning in its history."[21]

For Bauer, therefore, the work of Strauss and Vatke pointed to a new stage of consciousness and gave him a new sense of purpose. The epigonal task of defending the Hegelian position against the attacks of non-Hegelians was replaced by the epochal task of reworking the Hegelian vision in such a way that it would overcome the contradictions of a new age. Bauer's attempt to fulfill this task can be analyzed as the combination of three simultaneous efforts. First of all, he tried to clarify and define the nature and historical significance of the general crisis in consciousness represented by the emergence of historical criticism of the biblical revelation within the Hegelian school. Secondly, he sketched out the general guidelines for a solution to this crisis and tried to persuade his contemporary speculative theologians to engage in a collective effort of reinterpreting the biblical revelation in such a way as to reestablish the unity of faith and knowledge at a new and higher level of consciousness. These aims were expressed in the *Zeitschrift für spekulative Theologie,* which Bauer edited from 1836 to 1838. Finally, Bauer began work on a general study of the whole biblical revelation that would overcome the criticisms of Vatke and Strauss and demonstrate that if the biblical account was viewed in terms of the dynamic development of its separate Moments, it could be understood as a philosophically necessary and thus historically true manifestation of the development of absolute spirit. The first part of this work, *The Religion of the Old Testament in the Historical Development of Its Principles,* was published in two volumes in 1838.

Bauer's initial response to the attack on the historical credibility of the biblical revelation was to try to place the critics and their criticism within the perspective of general historical trends. Strauss's claim that the resurrection of the eternal philosophical meaning of the Christian teaching could arise only from a destruction of the supernatural history of the Scriptures was the culmination of a rebellion of man's subjective rationality against the authority of the transcendent religious "object" that had begun in the eighteenth century. The mythical interpretation of the biblical accounts represented man's attempt to overcome his estrangement from a transcendent god separated from human consciousness. Strauss's work was historically necessary in that it fearlessly "developed the critical principles to their universal consequences."[22] The divine revelation was seen as a creation of collective human consciousness. But Bauer denied that this viewpoint satisfactorily solved the problem of the dualism between human subjectivity and divine revelation. It represented, in fact, a simple negation, a total denial of the divine content of biblical history. The "object" had been not reconciled with the subject, but simply dissolved in it. Strauss's critique of the Gospels expressed the final stage of the liberation of finite human self-consciousness from the "unconscious" or "immediate" unity of finite and infinite in the religious consciousness of medieval Christendom. But this liberation was also a separation of man from God, of human subjectivity from the original subject – object unity, and was thus not a satisfactory resolution of man's religious quest but simply the preparatory stage for a new, "higher," self-conscious unity of the finite and infinite.[23] In fact, Bauer described Strauss's stance as an expression of the "general guilt" and "sin" of modern consciousness.[24] For "sin" was defined as the subjective denial of the reality of God and the attempt to place the finite subject in God's place.[25]

What differentiated Strauss's standpoint from the tradition of rational criticism, however, was his claim that a rejection of the historical reality of the biblical revelation was necessary for the resurrection of the philosophical truth of the Christian teaching. Strauss had thus brought critical negation into the sphere of speculative philosophy. The absolute contradiction between finite and infinite that defined the "sin" of modern consciousness had "been driven into the clarity and determination of the philosophical sphere."[26] For Bauer this absorption of the problems of historical criticism within the philosophical sphere was extremely important, because it meant that the solution for these problems would have to be a philosophical one. "Because the letter has experienced a critical death within the sphere of philosophy," he claimed, "then it will also be resurrected here; the passion week of the letter will be followed by its Easter, when it will arise again in the body."[27]

The major problems raised by Strauss's work, according to Bauer, could not be resolved through historical investigations that might invalidate his criticisms of the credibility of the Gospels as historical documents. The major issue was a philosophical one. Strauss had denied the credibility of the Gospels because of his philosophical presupposition that the absolute Idea could not have had that kind of history.[28] His claim that the biblical accounts were replete with absurdities and contradictions was a philosophical, not a historical, claim. If it could be demonstrated that the difficulties in the historical record were in fact understandable and necessary aspects of the evolution of the absolute Idea, if the biblical history could be understood as a succession of temporal stages that were objectified Moments of the eternal evolution of absolute spirit, then the spirit would recognize itself again in the divine revelation and the minor problems of historical criticism would soon lose their importance. And, in fact, Bauer was convinced that a philosophical demonstration of the truth of the biblical history was possible. Strauss and Vatke had simply not tried hard enough. "This conclusion," Bauer claimed, "of declaring the object impossible because of a few historical difficulties, looks too much like a flight from the problem for criticism to be satisfied with it."[29]

Bauer's refusal to accept the validity of Strauss's position was based on his conviction that Strauss's work expressed a fundamental denial of the identity of finite human consciousness and absolute spirit that was the core of the Hegelian vision. Strauss's unwillingness to believe in the historical reality of the incarnation of the divine in a historical individual represented a denial of the reality of the Hegelian conversion from "individuality" to "personality." If finite subjective consciousness could not, in fact, attain identity with the infinite self-consciousness of the absolute spirit, then the Hegelian claims for absolute knowledge were shattered. How could the speculative philosopher hope to understand and recognize the "objectifications" or "appearances" of spirit in historical reality if it was impossible to gain the perspective of the spirit that had objectified itself? Moreover, Strauss's standpoint appeared to deny the essential nature of the Hegelian absolute as a comprehended dialectical process. The eternal truths of Hegelian philosophy were not mere abstractions that could be separated from historical reality, but "concrete" ideas that contained their dialectical history within themselves as comprehended Moments of a dynamic process. More particularly, Bauer insisted that there was no way one could arrive at the comprehended history of the *Begriff* without having first gone through the stage of historical objectification. If the self-conscious union of finite and infinite spirit in contemporary philosophy was the necessary culmination of the development of the absolute spirit, then the historical externalization of that union was also philosophically necessary.[30] Bauer thus accused Strauss of abandoning the fundamental perspective of Hegelian philosophy.

"It is in the best interests of science (*Wissenschaft*)," Bauer wrote, "to have the negation expressed in its most extreme and perfect form, for only the most profound and concentrated denial can form the concluding transition to affirmation."[31] It was Strauss's historical "right" and justification to have expressed this stage of negation and denial in the evolution of the spirit. By doing so, however, he had merely articulated a crisis, not solved it. The task that Bauer set for himself and speculative theology in general was to move on to the next stage, the stage of affirmation and reconciliation. The Straussian criticism would be "taken up" into a new unity, the historical truth of the Scriptures would be demonstrated as philosophically necessary. Bauer vehemently denied the insinuations in Strauss's *Polemical Treatises* that his own stance simply represented a reactionary affirmation of the old identity that had broken down. The stage of affirmation would be a new reconciliation arising from "the self-determination of free thinking."[32] Because of his continued faith in the validity of the basic Hegelian identity of philosophical truth and historical reality, moreover, Bauer was supremely confident concerning the ultimate results of his efforts. In the letter to Altenstein in which he asked for permission to publish a new journal that would provide a vehicle for the collective efforts of contemporary theologians interested in working toward the new stage of affirmation, Bauer confessed: "I live and die in the faith that if contemporary developments are led by science (*Wissenschaft*), they will progress toward a recognition of the absolute truth of the orthodox faith."[33] And in the first issue of the journal he wrote:

> Of this the editor is certain, that the acceptance of the positive even in the detail of its accidents can be reconciled with the absolute prerogatives of self-consciousness, and that the positive faith will necessarily penetrate into the new heaven of modern self-consciousness as that which is eternally new.[34]

Although Bauer's contemporaries immediately viewed the *Zeitschrift für spekulative Theologie* as the organ of a specific wing within the Hegelian school – its major contributors were Marheineke, Daub, Göschel, Gabler, Erdmann, and Schaller – Bauer himself conceived the journal as an inclusive expression of the contemporary stage in theological development. The journal opened its pages to all areas of theological study, not only speculative philosophy of religion and philosophical dogmatics, but also biblical exegesis and historical criticism. Strauss's *Life of Jesus* had brought the problems of textual interpretation and historical criticism into the realm of speculative theological interpretation; it was thus "in the nature of things" that a scholarly vehicle should be established in which theologians could relate their various investigations to the central problems of the age.[35] Bauer also insisted that the *Zeitschrift* welcomed contributions from every contemporary theological perspective. The viewpoints of rationalist and orthodox theologians would be treated not as antagonistic to the Hegelian standpoint but as Moments within the dialectical unity of speculative theology. "While rationalism has defended the freedom of the subject, and supernaturalism the reality of the object," Bauer asserted, "the scientific viewpoint (*Wissenschaft*) feels no need to oppose these tendencies in an abstract manner, for they both fuse in the culminating point of speculative theology."[36] The problem with the standpoints of the critical rationalists and the orthodox supernaturalists was that they attempted to resolve the dualism between finite and infinite by denying the reality of either the former or the latter dimension. But such a one-sided viewpoint could lead only to pyrrhic victories. The suppressed aspect of the dualism would always return to disturb the peace. The only way out of this impasse was to rise to a state of consciousness in which the contradictions within religious consciousness were not denied but mediated or reconciled within a dialectical unity:

> It is absolutely impossible to avoid the penetrating elements of modern culture, and only that form of consciousness will be able to overcome the contradiction which recognizes this contradiction as the *inner contradiction of the total consciousness of the present,* and thus leads it back into the unity of consciousness and allows it to be dissolved there.[37]

Bauer's essays and reviews in the *Zeitschrift für spekulative Theologie* displayed a persistent attempt to persuade the representatives of the nonspeculative poles of theological interpretation that the presupposition for resolving the present cultural crisis of alienation between man and God was a recognition that everyone was equally guilty. "The present confusion cannot be resolved," Bauer claimed, "until every party recognizes its own guilt and takes its part of the collective guilt of modern consciousness upon itself."[38] Though Bauer directed his criticisms at both the rationalists and the supernaturalists, he definitely displayed a more positive attitude toward the stance of the orthodox theologians. He found less to condemn in the work of Hengstenberg than in the work of Strauss or Vatke. The defenders of the orthodox position might be misguided in their methods, but Bauer, after all, was also engaged in an attempt to construct a new apologia for the orthodox faith. What he criticized in Hengstenberg was the inability to accept the historical necessity and justification of the stage of critical negation, the futile attempt to suppress completely the rebellion of subjective consciousness.[39] A genuine, secure, convincing defense of the Christian faith must be based on an acceptance of the necessary historical liberation of human subjectivity and a reconciliation with the absolute "prerogatives" of human self-consciousness.

While Bauer was engaged in the task of trying to persuade theologians of different views to accept their necessary role in the contemporary cultural crisis, he was also writing the work that he believed would demonstrate the validity of the program he had outlined for the resolution of that crisis. In the long theoretical introduction of *The Religion of the Old Testament,* Bauer gave his systematic response to the problems raised by the Straussian criticism of the biblical history as subjectively created myth. He analyzed and modified the method and content of speculative philosophy of religion in such a way that the historical criticism of the Scriptures became a necessary part of its task, and he reconstructed the evolutionary stages of the progress of religious consciousness so that the peculiarities of the Christian religion as a historical "revelation" would be philosophically justified.

Bauer defined his task as "the constructive analysis (*Darstellung*) of the historical evolution of revelation."[40] His purpose was to describe a particular segment of religious history, to portray the concept of religion as it appeared historically in the national consciousness of the Hebrews, in the self-consciousness of Christ, and in the "representations (*Vorstellungen*)" of the first Christians. But this historical stage of "revealed religion" in the general history of religious development was also a definite stage in the logical, dialectical development of the concept or *Begriff* of religion. A knowledge of this *Begriff*, that is, a knowledge of speculative philosophy of religion, was thus the necessary presupposition for an understanding of the history of revealed religion. Whereas the philosophy of religion constructed the dynamic evolution of the concept of religion in the eternal forms of philosophical thought, the task of biblical theology was to "recognize" the "historical objectification" of that *Begriff* in such a way that the unity of the concept and its historical appearance would be "scientifically" demonstrated.[41]

If such a demonstration was to be convincing, the contradictions and apparent absurdities that the historical critics had found in the biblical texts would have to be revealed as necessary aspects of the evolution of the relationship between divine consciousness and human consciousness, the infinite and the finite spirit, during the historical stage of religious revelation. Hegel had "comprehended" the empirical history of religious evolution as a historical expression of the concept of religion in a general sense, but he had never attempted to provide a philosophical justification for the special character of biblical religion as a stage of religion as revelation. Bauer's attempt to develop the "idea of revelation" as a specific stage in religious development is one of the most obscure pieces of writing in the whole corpus of the Hegelian school. Most scholars have found the task of deciphering his argument simply too arduous.[42] But the theoretical reconstruction of the Hegelian philosophy of religion in the introduction of *The Religion of the Old Testament* represented Bauer's solution to what he considered an epochal crisis in the contemporary religious consciousness of man. Some understanding of its basic argument is essential for a historical comprehension of his subsequent development.

The general form of the relationship between God and man that characterized the historical stage of religion as revelation, Bauer stated, was the form of "proclamation (*Bekanntmachung*)." The subjective spirit, or man, was treated as a purely passive receptacle to whom an account of divine truth was given as an external fact. But this relationship between man and God in the form of revelation involved a fundamental self-contradiction. Man was asked to accept an account of divine purpose as something totally outside himself rather than as his own self-determination. In order to be able to appropriate the content of this revelation of divine purpose, however, man must already have been aware of the nature of the divine will, must have been able to recognize an authentic revelation when it was proclaimed to him. Such a recognition of the divine purpose of revelation could not be obtained through the passive consciousness of immediate vision but demanded what Bauer called "mediation" or the active participation of human consciousness.[43] There was also a further contradiction in the form of revelation. The proclamation of divine will appeared as a historical account. But the basis of historical development was human self-consciousness and freedom. By demanding that man receive the divine truth as a historical account in which human self-consciousness did not participate, the religious revelation became "a violent jerk (*Rück*) in the process of the spirit and imposed itself on self-consciousness from the outside as an impenetrable other (*das Andere*)."[44] The fundamental contradiction in the form of religion as revelation, therefore, was that divine truth appeared in the form of self-consciousness and at the same time was proclaimed as something totally external to self-consciousness.

The same contradiction was evident within the content of biblical revelation. The divine revelation was to be accepted as absolute truth, and yet it developed in a series of limited historical stages or Moments. Each stage displayed the limitations of the earlier stage, and yet each proclamation of God's purpose was to be accepted as eternally valid. The infinity of the claims of revealed religion was thus continually in contradiction with the finite historical expression of those claims.[45]

It was the recognition of these contradictions within the religious consciousness of the stage of revealed religion, Bauer claimed, that led to the historically justified rebellion of subjective consciousness against the "otherness" of the divine revelation. This alienation of the human subject from the divine "object," which had culminated in the work of Strauss, was both a liberation of human self-consciousness and a necessary stage toward a new and genuine reconciliation of the divine and the human that would not deny, but affirm, the freedom of human self-consciousness. Subjective spirit, Bauer claimed, "cannot recognize any absolute object and is obligated in its freedom to surrender itself only to that power in which it can recognize itself and its own free power."[46] This ultimate and genuine reconciliation of the divine and the human was attained by an elevation to the perspective of the absolute spirit in philosophical knowledge, and it was only from this perspective that man could recognize the historical stage of revelation as a necessary stage in his religious development. A rehabilitation of the necessary truth of biblical history thus had to begin with a demonstration that the religious relationship defined as revelation was also a necessary epistemological and logical stage in the dynamic unity of the religious concept (*Begriff*).

Hegel had defined the epistemological stages within the religious concept as a development from an immediate unconscious unity of the subjective and objective in feeling, through the stage of representational thinking in which a consciousness of the separation of the subject from the object became evident, to a final self-conscious unity of subjective spirit and objective spirit in philosophical knowledge. Bauer modified this triadic development by dividing the stage of immediate unity into two phases, feeling and contemplation (*Anschauung*).[47] In "feeling" the human self experienced the identity with the divine as an infinite expansion of its own self. In "contemplation," however, the relationship between the human self and God took the form of myth or symbol. This stage of contemplation remained within the general category of immediate unity because the particularity of the symbol was not differentiated from the universality of its content. The sensuous image itself was seen as the absolute truth. The union of the self with God in the epistemological stage of contemplation thus demanded a total surrender of the subjective freedom of the self to an external "object."[48]

The significance of the evolution to the epistemological stage of representational thinking or *Vorstellung* was that the immediate unity of self and God, which characterized the previous stages, was broken. The relationship between the human self and the divine spirit became a self-conscious relationship. Self-consciousness was possible only with the recognition of, and separation from, an "other." The epistemological stage of *Vorstellung*, Bauer claimed, represented a recognition of this separation by both God and man. God expressed his self-conscious separation from man by proclaiming his own purpose in the form of a historical revelation that man was to accept as the authentic expression of absolute truth. On man's side, therefore, the relationship to God could not simply take the form of unconscious surrender. Man was required to engage in a continual activity of relating the particulars of the historical account of the revelation to the divine truth which that revelation was supposed to represent. This continual movement of the human spirit from the particular to the universal, from the sensuous image to the purpose expressed in that image, was the essential aspect of representational thinking.[49] It was only with the historical appearance of this kind of relationship, in which God and man appeared to each other as something other than themselves, Bauer claimed, that one could begin to speak of a genuine religious relationship. For it was only with the development of the self-conscious separation of God and man that the problem of reconciliation, the religious problem of salvation, became a determining factor in the historical process.

The intellectual effort that Bauer invested in modifying the Hegelian conception of the dialectical stages within the concept of religion had a very specific purpose. The religious stage of contemplation, in which the relationship between man and God was expressed in the form of myth, was separated from the stage of *Vorstellung* that characterized biblical religion, and thus the mythical interpretation was virtually eliminated as a proper tool for interpreting biblical history. In Bauer's analysis the epistemological stage of representational thinking in the development of the concept of religion corresponded exactly to the historical stage of religious evolution that he had defined as revelation. By redefining the Hegelian viewpoint in this fashion, Bauer hoped not only to make Strauss's method irrelevant for the material of biblical history, but also to preserve the special place of biblical religion within the historical evolution of man's religious consciousness. The nonbiblical religions that expressed the relationship between man and God in terms of myth or symbol were relegated to an earlier historical phase and a "lower" stage of epistemological development.[50]

Bauer believed that his definition of the historical stage of religion as revelation and his description of the corresponding epistemological stage of representational thinking had provided the basis for a demonstration that the historical truth of the biblical accounts was philosophically necessary. The contradictions within the biblical narratives were contradictions inherent to the historical form of religion as revelation, and this historical form was a necessary objectification of a specific epistemological stage in the relationship between finite and infinite spirit. But it is important to emphasize that Bauer conceived the relationship between man and God in biblical religion as a stage of self-contradiction within the development of absolute spirit. Biblical religion or revealed religion was not the final stage of religious consciousness, just as the epistemological stage of representational thinking was not the ultimate form of knowledge. The alienation between man and

God, the epistemological contradiction between subject and object, could be overcome only at a higher stage of consciousness. This "higher" stage was, of course, the stage of speculative knowledge in which the relationship between God and man, infinite and finite, was seen as an internal relationship within the unity of absolute spirit.[51] Bauer's position was thus radically different from that of the orthodox apologists who tried to describe biblical or revealed religion as the eternally valid form of the religious relationship, as the relationship between man and God that had to be accepted for all time, and not just understood as a necessary historical stage in man's development.

At the same time, Bauer's basic standpoint in *The Religion of the Old Testament* was obviously more "orthodox" than Strauss's position in the *Life of Jesus*. Bauer affirmed the historical truth of the biblical accounts. Unlike Strauss, he insisted that the historicity of the biblical *Vorstellung* could not be separated from its philosophical truth. In his conception of the content of this philosophical truth, moreover, Bauer was also more orthodox than Strauss. He saw the evolution of absolute spirit not as a dialectical relationship between finite, individual, human consciousness and the consciousness of the species, but as a relationship between man and God. For Bauer the Hegelian reconciliation was a union of transcendence and immanence, not just an immanent identity between individual man and his spiritual essence as a "species being.[52] Because of the use of the protean term "spirit" to describe the realm of universality in both positions, the distinctions were not always crystal clear, but Bauer obviously thought that the difference between his own position and that of Strauss was crucial. He insisted that the infinite spirit with which man was reconciled in speculative thought was an "objective" spirit, not just an abstract idea of humanity. The idea of humanity could not be completely realized in a single individual, but Bauer was convinced that a single historical individual could attain unity with the eternal divine spirit. Man could attain genuine immortality in his present life: he could rise to the perspective of absolute spirit in which his knowledge of himself was identical with knowledge of God. This completed unity of finite and infinite spirit. Bauer felt, was the core of the Hegelian experience and the only secure foundation for its claim to absolute knowledge.[53]

When he wrote the introduction to the second volume of *The Religion of the Old Testament* in September 1838, Bauer was still convinced that he was simply acting as the channel for the expression of absolute truth. He denied vehemently that his own position represented the position of a party or school. His scholarly ego, he claimed, had been completely surrendered to "the power of the universal spirit." His "faithful service" to the cause of the ultimate reconciliation of the contradictions of contemporary religious consciousness was based on the "firm assurance" that his efforts "would not disappear into the void."[54] This reaffirmation of his former position was made in the face of growing evidence that the spirit was in no hurry to go on to the next stage of reconciliation. Neither the orthodox theologians nor the rationalist critics had shown any desire to accept their part in the collective guilt of the age. The *Zeitschrift für spekulative Theologie* was finally forced to cease publication in 1838, having failed to attract even one hundred subscribers.[55] But Bauer saw these difficulties as a period of purgation and testing that would make the ultimate reconciliation all the more secure when it finally came.[56] The demonstration of the validity of his faith that the present contradictions between orthodoxists and rationalists were merely dialectical "determinations" within the unity of absolute spirit was not dependent on his own individual efforts. History would prove him right; the future was on his side.[57]

The only detailed and systematic study of Bauer's theological views before 1839 has argued that the stimulus for his attempts to modify and reformulate the Hegelian philosophy of religion in such a way that it would rehabilitate the literal truth of the biblical accounts was strictly scholarly and intellectual. Bauer was simply interested in providing a satisfactory solution to problems in biblical interpretation raised by the works of Strauss and Vatke.[58] It is easy to see how such a thoroughly academic interpretation could arise. There is virtually no evidence concerning Bauer's inner experience or his social-political attitudes during this period,[59] and the obscurity of his prose might seem to indicate that the problems with which he was concerned were esoteric, far-removed from the existential questions of everyday life. Yet there is a great deal of internal evidence in Bauer's scholarly work which indicates that the questions stimulating his scholarly activity were not academic or esoteric. We have already noted that he continually related the specific issue of the relationship between the literal historical truth of the Scriptures and the eternal philosphical truth of the Hegelian concept to the fundamental doctrines of the Hegelian system. From Bauer's standpoint the separation of fact from Idea in Strauss's critique of the Gospels threatened the fundamental Hegelian claim that the elevation to the realm of absolute spirit was a comprehending reconciliation with historical reality, not a flight into an abstract harmony. The denial of the historical reality of the incarnation in a single individual, Bauer felt, was a denial of the validity of the experience of union with infinite spirit, of present eternity, that had been gained through the Hegelian speculative elevation or conversion.

Bauer interpreted the problems raised in the works of Strauss and Vatke as intellectual problems, as problems of philosophical knowledge. But for Bauer, as for Strauss and the other Hegelians, such problems of philosophical comprehension were profoundly existential problems; it was through knowledge that they had gained ontological identity, spiritual satisfaction. "People may say that thought lacks the warmth of life," Bauer observed, "but one must reply that thought also has its inner experiences and needs to be experienced." It would require a "history of the self," Bauer claimed, to demonstrate the existential meaning of speculative thought. The presupposition of the experience of elevation to self-conscious spirit was the alienated existence of the individual, isolated, finite self.[60] This life in finitude was a life of suffering, of meaninglessness and emptiness. In speculative thought, however, the self was "raised into a sphere into which those sufferings do not reach, where they are overpowered; as infinite self man overcomes his sufferings while standing in the midst of them."[61] This experience of elevation to the sphere of the infinite was "most profound" and "full of life," Bauer claimed, "because the spirit that now knows itself as a Moment in the divine life remembers in what total opposition he stood to God while he was still a reflective individual."[62]

For Bauer, therefore, the real meaning of the Hegelian elevation to union with the divine spirit was its ability to reconcile the self with the suffering and alienation of its finite historical existence. Strauss's separation of historical fact from eternal philosophical truth was an expression of a general separation of historical existence from the experience of absolute spiritual unity. The culminating vision was no longer a reconciliation in which finite suffering was remembered as a Moment within the total evolution of spirit, but a separate sphere of harmony, an abstract vision of unity set against the realities of historical life. Strauss, Bauer thought, had destroyed the Hegelian theodicy, not only for the general history of mankind, but for the history of the individual self.

The ontological identity that Bauer had found in Hegelian metaphysics was also the basis for his communal identity. The sphere of social life was a sphere in which men related to each other as finite concrete individuals; it was the sphere in which the sufferings of finitude were most acutely manifest in the continuous collision of individual egos. It was a "foolishness of mere reflective understanding," he claimed, for man to expect to achieve a genuine consciousness of being "at home" in the immanent realm of finite communal relationships. "In the world of the finite and the appearance one can discover no central artery on which one might sail through happily."[63] Only the comprehension of the immanent as a Moment within the totality of the absolute could reconcile man with the inadequacies of his finite existence. In 1838, Bauer still found a satisfactory compensation for his concrete immanent sufferings in his "faithful service" to "the power of the universal spirit." In the years that followed, however, the compensatory reconciling power of absolute knowledge rapidly lost its experiential validity. Within the span of three years, Bauer went through a process of radicalization, an experience of disinheritance and liberation from his Hegelian inheritance and its cultural context, that had extended over more than a decade in Strauss's development. By 1841, Bauer was ready to dismiss the Hegelian elevation to absolute spirit as an illusory compensation for the inadequacies of finite existence and proclaim the necessity for an immanent resolution of man's immanent suffering.

The first indication of a change in Bauer's cultural stance was a marked increase in the intensity of his opposition to the orthodox and Fundamentalist apologists of the Christian faith. His attempt to persuade the orthodox apologists to accept the validity of his own analysis by emphasizing the common concern of both speculative and orthodox theology in defending the literal historical truth of the biblical Scriptures had not had the desired results. Hengstenberg had seen Bauer's conciliatory efforts simply as a sign of weakness, an admission of the bankruptcy of Hegelian theology, and had invited him to abandon the speculative standpoint and return to the traditional faith.[64] The Hegelians of the Center and Left, like Michelet, Ruge, and Strauss, thought that Bauer had already implicitly joined the Fundamentalists, and they viewed his attempts to provide a philosophical demonstration of the historical truth of "events" like the virgin birth as obscurantist sophistry.[65] The passages in Bauer's works in which the Hegelian reconciliation of God and man in absolute spirit was described as a higher stage of consciousness that reconciled the contradictions of the biblical stage of revealed religion were ignored by the critical Hegelians and exaggerated by the orthodox.

A gradual shift toward a more positive evaluation of the critical stance was revealed in Bauer's reviews in the *Jahrbücher für wissenschaftliche Kritik* in the winter and spring of 1839. Bauer had always viewed subjective, rational criticism of the orthodox faith as a necessary stage in the development of the spirit. But between 1835 and 1838 he had equated this stage of the "negation" with the sinful denial of the reality of God. He now emphasized the positive, liberating aspects of the rational criticism of the Enlightenment. The autonomy of the human spirit that the rationalists had defended against the authority of the traditional faith was described no longer as a state of sin but as the "necessary means of salvation," as the absolute foundation on which a genuine reconciliation of the divine and the human would have to be based.[66] In March, Bauer attacked the orthodox conception of philosophy as a handmaiden of faith. The traditional faith would have to be destroyed before the rehabilitation of its eternal content in philosophical knowledge could be accomplished. "He whose faith has not been shattered by skepticism, he who has not experienced the uncertainty of doubt," Bauer claimed, "will never attain true knowledge and will not even experience the need for such knowledge."[67] The orthodox belief in the transcendent personal God of the biblical revelation, which Bauer had previously related positively to his own attempts to save the "object," was not ridiculed as an irrational devotion to an empty abstraction. Theology would be able to reconcile contemporary man with God only if it abandoned the obsolete conceptions of the traditional faith and "descended" to the "clear world of self-consciousness."[68]

Bauer's new emphasis on the positive, liberating aspects of the stage of "negation" in the dialectical progress of absolute spirit to self-conscious unity could be compared to Strauss's stance in the early 1830s. But while Bauer, like Strauss, thought that the resurrection of the eternal truths of Christianity could occur only after the destruction of the orthodox position, he disagreed with Strauss in continuing to believe that the resurrection would include the "letter" of biblical history. One might interpret his emphasis on the legitimacy of the critical negation as simply a clarification of his position in the light of the misunderstandings of both the orthodox apologists and the Hegelian Center. That the shift in emphasis was more than a mere clarification of his former position, however, was revealed in a change in the general tone and style of Bauer's writing. His long, convoluted, obscure, conciliatory sentences gave way to a more direct, terse prose punctuated by exclamation and question marks. He began to parody and satirize the mentality of the orthodox theologians. He described them as senile old men who could be revitalized only by the "energetic freshness of the negation." He complained about the difficulty of staying awake while reading their boring repetitions of obsolete arguments.[69]

In his program for the *Zeitschrift für spekulative Theologie,* Bauer had rejected a polemical stance because of his conception of all competing theological viewpoints as Moments within the dynamic unity of speculative theology. The conciliatory nature of this stance was most strikingly expressed in his attempts to bring Hengstenberg's orthodox defense of the literal truth of the biblical revelation into harmony with his own position. By April 1839, however, he had come to see the divergent theological trends of his time as contradictory standpoints and had accepted the necessity of polemical conflict. This new stance was expressed in a pamphlet in which he attacked Hengstenberg's conception of the unity of the Old Testament. The basic argument of this pamphlet was not new. Bauer had always claimed that Hengstenberg's view of the Old Testament as an abstract unity could not account for its contradictions – which had to be seen as Moments in the evolution of the relationship between finite and infinite spirit.[70] What was new was the forcefulness and even recklessness of the polemic against Hengstenberg's "shortsighted theological apologetics."[71] Bauer claimed that he had tried for eight years to establish a state of peace and reconciliation between Hengstenberg's orthodox position and his own speculative standpoint, but he had finally decided that the two positions were incompatible. This decision gave him a tremendous sense of inner freedom and allowed him to participate in the spiritual development of an age "that will have nothing to do with indecision." Bauer claimed that his attack on Hengstenberg aimed "to show what hour the clock has struck."[72] The new crisis of the age was defined by the battle between an irrational affirmation of the orthodox standpoint and the free appropriation of the truth of Christianity in Hegelian speculation. Once again, Bauer was convinced that the present was an epochal moment in human history. But this time he defined it not in terms of reconciliation, but as a decisive imminent victory of Hegelian Christianity over the "shortsighted apologetics" of the Fundamentalists. History, he claimed, "no longer progresses at a slow pace."[73]

During the same month in which Bauer published his attack on Hengstenberg he submitted his candidacy for an opening in the theological faculty at Bonn. Although he had published extensively and could count on the enthusiastic recommendations of Marheineke, Schulze, and Altenstein, he was still an unsalaried, impoverished *Privatdozent.* His academic frustration cannot be attributed simply to the general problems of decreasing enrollments and overcrowding in academic careers. The promotion of Vatke to an associate professorship in 1837 had aroused tremendous opposition among the Fundamentalist theologians and their conservative supporters in the bureaucracy and at the court.[74] Altenstein could not hope to impose another Hegelian on the theological faculty in the foreseeable future. Marheineke later claimed that "complete mediocrities" were promoted ahead of Bauer because of their conformity to the increasingly dominant Fundamentalist theology.[75] The transition from reconciliation to hostility in Bauer's attitude toward Hengstenberg and his followers was thus related to the growing power of the conservative party in the Prussian administration and expressed the tensions that this development created in Bauer's academic situation.

These tensions were not alleviated by Bauer's transfer to Bonn in September 1839. The theological faculty in Bonn was completely dominated by conservative students of Schleiermacher, who had immediately lodged a protest with Altenstein when they discovered that a Hegelian had been recommended for the vacancy in their faculty.[76] Although the faculty finally allowed Bauer to register as a *Privatdozent* on November 2, 1839, they never had any intention of recommending him for a tenured position. By the spring of 1840, Bauer's career difficulties had reached a stage of crisis. His financial straits forced him to sell the personal scholarly library he had accumulated in Berlin and placed him in the humiliating position of being the only one of the editors of Hegel's works to ask Frau Hegel for remuneration for his work.[77] At the same time, he felt that the authorities in Berlin were either unable or unwilling to change his status. He became disgusted with the obsequious, and apparently futile, petitioning his insecure status seemed to demand, and in March 1840, he solemnly burned his correspondence with Altenstein and Schulze.[78] In April his brother Edgar informed him that Schulze had admitted that Bauer had "no prospects" for promotion in the immediate future.[79] When Altenstein and then Frederick William III died in the following months, Bauer's last slim hopes for academic success within the Prussian university system vanished, and he expressed his readiness to abandon the academic world and become a free-lance writer and independent cultural critic.[80]

In June of 1839, Marheineke expressed concern that the continued frustration of Bauer's academic ambitions might dampen his scholarly enthusiasm and cause him to lose courage and confidence in his abilities.[81] But Bauer himself perceived his academic tribulations, not as a judgment of his personal abilities, but as a sign that he had been chosen for a special historical mission. "It is exactly in my suffering," he wrote to Marx in March 1840, "that I become increasingly conscious of my calling, and I am happy because I am approaching ever closer to that calling and being educated for it."[82] The move from Berlin to Bonn had given him a new perspective on the tensions in his academic situation. In Berlin he had constantly labored under pressure to accommodate his views to the wishes of his father, his academic mentors in the Hegelian school, and the established church and the state. The removal from Berlin was experienced as a release from the inhibiting effect of these pressures. "At that moment in which I was, for the first time, thrown into a strange world," Bauer wrote to his brother Edgar on November 5, 1839, "... I was suddenly able inwardly to develop my position to a new decisiveness, to a decisiveness that is diametrically opposed to all of my previous presuppositions."[83] During his first year in Bonn, Bauer's new "decisiveness" was most clearly evident in two areas: in his conceptions of the relationship between theology and philosophy and in his view of the relationship between philosophical science and the contemporary Prussian state. In Berlin the Left Hegelian opposition to orthodox Christianity and the established state had "the appearance of an extreme," but from his isolated position in Bonn, Bauer began to view this extreme as the only valid stance for a disciple of philosophical *Wissenschaft* in the contemporary world.[84]

Bauer's attack on Hengstenberg had revealed his growing consciousness of the irreconcilable antagonism between Fundamentalist and Hegelian theology. During his first months in Bonn, this consciousness was transformed into a conviction that Hegelian theology was a contradiction in terms. The fundamental antagonism of the age was not between different forms of Christian theology but between theology and philosophy, faith and *Wissenschaft.* In February 1840, Edgar Bauer had abandoned his theological studies at the University of Berlin, and in the ensuing conflict with his father, he had used Bruno's experience as a demonstration of the historical bankruptcy of the Christian faith. "Bruno no longer believes in anything," he had asserted.[85] Bauer, however, was not willing to agree completely with this characterization of his own position. He confessed that there was still a residual element of faith battling with the growing power of philosophy in his mind; at least he was not yet able to regard the Christian faith as something totally alien. He thus found it impossible simply to abandon his theological vocation for a secular career. "Theology has become so much a part of my life," he wrote, "that whatever I do with myself I do with theology; that is, I wash the dirt off myself as I clean up in theology. When I am finished I will be completely pure."[86] In another letter, Bauer described theology as the hell through which he had to pass in order to penetrate to the pure heavenly air of *Wissenschaft.*[87] During the winter of 1839–40, Bauer increasingly perceived his own development as a manifestation of the historical process of self-criticism and self-purification in which theology was transformed into philosophy. He would not resign from the theological faculty because he was convinced that the critical destruction of, and liberation from, theological consciousness was a consequence of the necessary inner development and self comprehension of theology.

Between 1835 and 1838, Bauer had insisted that the problems concerning the relationship between the religious *Vorstellung* and the philosophical *Begriff* raised by Strauss's critique of the historical credibility of the Gospels could be resolved through a reaffirmation, clearer understanding, and detailed application of the Hegelian method of philosophical comprehension. As he became more and more convinced of the antagonistic relationship between theology and philosophy, however, his faith in the reconciling power of the Hegelian method began to disintegrate. In December 1839 he urged Marx to work on a revision of Hegel's *Logic* because he felt that his own discontent with the Hegelian conception of the identical content in religious faith and philosophical knowledge was related to unresolved problems in the very "essence" of the Hegelian system.[88] At this time, Bauer himself was editing the revised edition of Hegel's *Lectures on the Philosophy of Religion,* a responsibility that had been delegated to him by Marheineke. He included his "clarification" of the stages of religious evolution in the new edition, and some Hegelians accused him of revising Hegel's work in a Right Hegelian direction.[89] Bauer vehemently denied this change. His concerns in editing the Hegelian text, he claimed, had been "purely theoretical" and without "party sympathy." The reason he gave for this "fundamental indifference" to his task was a significant revelation of his new standpoint. On rereading the Hegelian lectures he had found not a convincing reconciliation of faith and knowledge, but a welter of contradictions. His primary editorial responsibility, he claimed, was to maintain the role of a detached historical scholar and allow both Hegel's affirmations of orthodox doctrine and his philosophical transformations of that doctrine to stand in their unresolved tension.[90] By the spring of 1840, Bauer was convinced that the tensions between Christian religion and modern *Wissenschaft* had not been and could not be resolved on the basis of Hegel's own methodological principles, but he had not yet clearly formulated a post-Hegelian standpoint from which they could be resolved. It was not until August that he could write: "I have found the point to which I merely have to connect the threads in order to bring everything into order."[91]

The transitional stage of unresolved tension in Bauer's evolving conception of the relationship between the Christian revelation and philosophical *Wissenschaft* was expressed in the major theological work that he wrote in the winter of 1839–40 and sent to the publisher in the spring: *Critique of the Gospel of John.* In a formal sense this study of the Johannine Gospel represented the third volume of the philosophical reconstruction of revealed religion that Bauer had begun in 1835. By 1839–40, however, the presuppositions with which Bauer approached his material had undergone a drastic change. His original plan for the sequel to *The Religion of the Old Testament* had been to study the Hebraic consciousness in the centuries before Christ, in order to show how the Jews were prepared to receive the revelation of the incarnate God as a *Vorstellung* that could be meaningfully related to their subjective consciousness. He had now decided, however, that the historical reality of the union of the human and the divine in Christ's self-consciousness and activity had been so distorted and overlaid by the reflective judgments and historically limited interpretations of this reality by Christ's followers (including the writers of the four Gospels) that his first task would have to be a critical analysis of the credibility of the historical sources on which contemporary Christian theologians based their Christological doctrines.[92]

This new approach entailed an entirely new method. In his earlier writings, Bauer had simply accepted the given content of the biblical writings as the historical fact that the philosophical theologian was required to "remember," as the reality of the dialectically self-developing absolute Idea. In the *Critique of the Gospel of John,* however, Bauer claimed that the letter of the Scriptures hid more than it revealed; it was a "fetter" on the spirit.[93] Before the reality of the past could be comprehended by the philosopher, it would have to be discovered by the historical critic. Bauer's application of the methods of historical criticism to the Johannine Gospel, however, led him to the conclusion that this biblical text could provide no historical reality for the contemporary philosopher; it was not a credible historical account of the reality of Christ's consciousness or activity but a secondary, reflective interpretation composed by a theologian whose outlook was determined by the historically limited dualistic consciousness of a Christian community existing in a precarious antagonistic relationship to the rest of the world. The content of the fourth Gospel was neither objective history nor a myth created by the collective unconscious of the early church, but pragmatic theological apologetics.[94]

Unlike Strauss in 1835, however, Bauer in the spring of 1840 was not yet prepared to claim that a resurrection of the Idea demanded a destruction of the historicity of the Christian incarnation. The reality of the genuine historical Christ, the true revelation of the identity of the divine and the human, he suggested, would eventually be recovered from secondary theological distortion through a historical criticism of the synoptic Gospels. He did not reduce the Christian incarnation to a subjective representation of the Idea of humanity but continued to insist that the historical reality of the union of the divine and the human in Jesus Christ was the prerequisite for the philosophical appropriation of this absolute truth in the present. The ultimate goal of historical criticism remained the reconciliation of finite self-consciousness with absolute self-consciousness. The "spiritual fire" of criticism was directed at the distortions of Christian theology, not the reality of the Christian truth. The dualistic preconceptions of the theological perspective were opposed to the absolute content of the Christian revelation. "The self-consciousness of absolute spirit" would "perfect and complete the remembrance of its historical revelation" only after the limitations of Christian theology had been comprehended and thus dissolved by philosophical *Wissenschaft.*[95]

A few months after the completion of his *Critique of the Gospel of John,* Bauer published a pamphlet – *The Prussian Evangelical State Church and Science* – in which he made an attempt to relate his new theological, or rather antitheological, stance to the contemporary cultural and political situation. During the winter of 1839–40 he had become convinced that his personal academic frustrations were a sign of the general tension between the liberating mission of philosophical *Wissenschaft* and the policies of the existing state. In a letter to Marx on March 1, he described the Prussian administration as a "Chinese police system" engaged in a futile attempt to repress the inevitable evolution of "decisive contradictions" between theological and scientific consciousness. If philosophical science was to remain true to its own principle and fulfill its historical mission, it would have to emancipate itself from inhibiting dependence on a repressive and sophistical state and "lead the battle" against theological consciousness.[96] If the state continued its present policy of repressive accommodation or decided to ally itself with the Fundamentalists, the contemporary tensions would inevitably evolve into a cultural crisis of revolutionary proportions. "The catastrophe will be terrible and will become immense," Bauer wrote to Marx in April, "and I would even be inclined to say that it will become more terrible and more immense than that which marked the entry of Christianity into the world."[97]

In *The Prussian Evangelical State Church,* Bauer insisted that a revolutionary confrontation between the proponents of philosophical *Wissenschaft* and the Prussian state was still avoidable. In fact, such a confrontation could occur only if the state denied its own inner principle and tried to halt or even reverse the progressive historical actualization of Reason and freedom in the immanent ethical relationships of communal life. Philosophical *Wissenschaft* was simply the self-conscious comprehension of the actual historical process in which the state as "the divinity and perfected organization of the immanent (*Diesseits*)" absorbed "the powers of the transcendent into itself and consumed them."[98] The critical dissolution of theology as an autonomous form of knowledge (i.e., a knowledge of the transcendent) through the immanent appropriation of its content in philosophical *Wissenschaft* corresponded to the historical emergence of the state as "that form of spiritual life in which the form of the visible church has been dissolved."[99] Because the state was no longer simply a "finite institution" but "the only form in which the infinity of Reason and freedom, the highest goods of the human spirit, exist in reality," the church had become historically superfluous, a mere empty form or "ghost (*Gespenst*)" whose content or "life" had been absorbed, dissolved, "taken up" into the state.[100] The dialectical historical relationship between finite and infinite spirit thus no longer took the form of an external relationship between state and church, but had become an internal relationship within the divine-human totality of the state itself. The absolute content of the Christian faith – "self-renunciation and the resurrection of the spirit through faith in the Idea" – had become historically actual as the "religious" Moment within the secular community.[101] Philosophical *Wissenschaft* was the self-comprehension of the reality of secular salvation in the modern state.

Bauer's cultural stance in this pamphlet was that of a particularly belligerent critical Hegelian. Like Ruge in 1838, he presented his position as an expression of the "Protestant" principle and as a defense of the historical actuality of the modern Prussian state. He claimed that the transformation of the Prussian state into a genuine ethical community, into the all-encompassing form of "spiritual life" in which the "visible church" had been "dissolved," had been historically accomplished in the legal and institutional reforms of the Napoleonic period. Those elements within the Prussian administration and university system that were trying to subordinate the state to the church and *Wissenschaft* to theology were described not as apologists for the existing order but as revolutionary cultural restorationists living under the illusion that they could reverse the process of historical development. As he had defended the historical reality of the Christian incarnation against the self-deceiving distortions of Christian theology in his critical study of the Gospel of John, so he defended, in *The Prussian Evangelical State Church,* the historical reality of the modern Prussian state against the self-deceiving distortions of the self-styled apologists of the existing order. Bauer claimed that his own position stood "firmly" on the "highest law of the state." He proposed not a transformation of existing reality but a self-conscious recognition and affirmation of that reality.[102]

By the summer of 1840, however, Bauer's definition of this contemporary historical "reality" was no longer compatible with the Hegelian reconciliation of church and state, theology and philosophy. Such reconciliations were relegated to the category of self-deceiving illusions. The old Hegelian accommodationists had been unable or unwilling to recognize that a reconciliation with historical reality demanded a radical destruction of the regressive historical forms of ecclesiastical organization and theological consciousness. Bauer thus made a radical distinction between contemporary historical reality and the representations of that reality in the consciousness of the majority of his cultural contemporaries. Everyone, except Bauer himself, was still enchained by the empty forms of a bygone era of cultural development. There can be little doubt that Bauer did not really expect the newly installed Prussian king, Frederick William IV, to heed his advice, break through these empty forms, and recognize Bauer's version of philosophical *Wissenschaft* as the theoretical self-consciousness of the existing Prussian state. But even if the the state betrayed its own inner principle, and condemned him as a revolutionary and a heretic, the superannuated consciousness of an obsolete culture could not ultimately triumph over historical reality. "In the end it will be seen who has chosen correctly," he wrote. "We stand firm and await the outcome."[103]

As it became increasingly obvious that the new administration was not about to be converted to Bauer's conception of the reality of the Prussian state, however, Bauer did not "remain firm and await the outcome." During the fall and winter of 1840–1 his cultural stance evolved through a new phase of radicalization that included a fundamental, reductive reinterpretation of his Hegelian inheritance. By the spring of 1841, Bauer had emerged, along with Ruge, as a leading spokesman of the Left Hegelian opposition to the Prussian state and Christian culture.

The shift in Bauer's position was evident, first of all, in the emergence of a new attitude toward the whole problem of his academic promotion. Despite his repeated earlier assertions that he would never again stoop to petitioning the Berlin authorities for academic recognition, he renewed his efforts to obtain a tenured position in the fall of 1840. The motivation for this change in tactics was revealed when Bauer returned to Berlin in October and discussed his academic situation with Eichhorn, Schulze, and other members of the administration. What he sought was not a reconciliation, but a confrontation with the new regime. He did not plead for financial security and personal recognition but demanded public recognition or rejection of the principle that he represented. The government was to be forced to take a principled stand that would reveal its position in the contemporary cultural conflict between scientific and theological consciousness. When Eichhorn offered Bauer a research stipend, Bauer perceived and rejected it as a bribe and returned to Bonn, where he continued his aggressive campaign to transform his personal academic fate into a public expression of the contemporary cultural crisis.[104] He tried to persuade his colleagues in the theological faculty to prepare a position paper on his theological viewpoint for Eichhorn, even though he was well aware that their judgment would be unremittingly hostile. At the same time he fed inside information to Arnold Ruge for articles that attacked the reactionary views of the Bonn theologians and the equivocations of the ministry in Berlin.[105] Throughout the spring of 1841, however, both the faculty and the ministry continued to perceive Bauer's situation in personal rather than world-historical terms. When the church historian at Bonn died in May 1841, Eichhorn and Schulze advised Bauer to lecture in ecclesiastical history and apply for the vacant post. Bauer refused. Any indication that he was motivated by personal academic ambition would compromise his position. "It is my duty," he wrote to Edgar, "to do what I can. I must allow things to develop to the final question of whether the principle I teach is the correct development of theology."[106]

By the spring of 1841, Bauer was clearly convinced that the existing regime could not recognize the validity of his "principle" without destroying itself. The reconciliation of philosophical *Wissenschaft* and the contemporary historical community could be accomplished only through a revolutionary transformation of the existing order. In an article published in Ruge's *Jahrbücher* in June 1841, Bauer analyzed the contemporary Prussian state as a peculiarly modern, transitional form of the "Christian state," in which the external tension between church and state, which had characterized the Middle Ages, had been transformed into an internal contradiction within the state itself. The continuing vitality of the church and the theological world view in contemporary Prussia, he now claimed, was due to the fact that state had not fully appropriated and actualized the universal content of the traditional faith – the identity of the finite and infinite spirit – in its immanent organization and communal consciousness. The concrete universality of a genuine ethical community was still an "abstract postulate"; it had not yet been recognized and actualized as "the deed of the spirit and the determination of self-consciousness."[107] Traditional Christian theology, of course, denied the possibility of an immanent historical salvation and thus construed the existing imperfections and contradictions in the communal order as evidence of a permanent universal condition that justified its own belief in the necessity of a transcendent solution. The proponents of philosophical *Wissenschaft* recognized the same imperfections in contemporary political organization and consciousness but defined them as the historically determined contradictions of a particular stage in human development and pressed for their immanent resolution. The state, which had destroyed the autonomy of the church and subordinated its institutions and doctrines to its own absolute will, Bauer claimed, now feared and resisted the further development of its own principle – the transformation of absolute monarchy into a truly universal ethical community. It supported the church and its theologians as a means of repressing the political and intellectual forces of historical progress. It betrayed its own principle in order to prevent the revolutionary actualization of its own principle.[108]

The task of philosophical *Wissenschaft* within the cultural context of the Christian state, according to Bauer, was twofold. First, it must above all keep itself "pure." "Now and in the immediate future," he wrote to Ruge on April 16, 1841, "*Wissenschaft* must make sure that its categories and evolution are kept free of any infection from earlier representations. The break must be clean and absolute."[109] All cultural and political phenomena in the Christian state were corrupted by the distorted principles of Christian theology. If philosophy was to emancipate man from this total system of deception and repression it must first of all keep itself free from any compromise with this system. This task of self-criticism and purification, however, was inextricably connected to the task of critically demolishing the presuppositions of the existing culture. To free oneself from the Christian state was to unveil its self-deceptions and contradictions and thus destroy its historical legitimacy. On a number of occasions in the spring of 1841, Bauer compared the theoretical criticism of the established order in church and state to a revolutionary terror. "The terrorism of true theory will clear the field," he wrote to Marx on March 28,[110] and three days later he added, "Theory is now the most effective practice and we cannot yet predict in what a great manner it can become practical."[111] Particular "practical" reforms were impractical if the whole system was rotten to the core. "These nests must all be swept clean . . . ," Bauer wrote to Ruge on June 20; "one must channel one's anger and passion into work and chase the dogs out of the temples, even if the temples become mausoleums in the process. Better than dog kennels! New temples will replace them."[112] In August he reiterated his confidence in the revolutionary consequences of a "pure" theoretical terrorism. "They all howl about revolution here," he told Ruge; "like dogs they sense the approach of a thunderstorm. These rotten nests must be exterminated."[113]

In the summer of 1841, Bauer's theoretical terrorism finally goaded Eichhorn into the kind of public, principled confrontation that Bauer desired. In August, Eichhorn asked the theological faculties of the six Prussian universities to present their general opinion of Bauer's theological writings and to answer the specific question whether he should be allowed to teach theology at a Prussian university. Eichhorn had already clearly made up his own mind when he sent out his memorandum, but the process dragged on until March 29, 1842, when Bauer's teaching license was officially rescinded. Bauer made every effort to transform the decision over his academic fate into a public trial that would reveal the reactionary nature of the existing regime, and to ensure that the decision would be negative. "My blasphemous spirit would be satisfied only if I were given the authority of a professorship to teach publicly the system of atheism," he wrote to Ruge on December 6, 1841.[114] and a few months later he asserted: "I will not be satisfied until I have blown all the theological faculties sky high."[115]

Bauer vehemently rejected any insinuation that his opposition to the existing cultural order could have been mollified by a different decision by the Prussian government in 1842.[116] In fact this whole line of argument seemed nonsensical to him. By the spring of 1841 he had clearly and openly committed himself to a cultural principle that was diametrically opposed to the existing cultural order. He had liberated himself from the existing culture before the caretakers of that culture had officially disinherited him. Bauer's academic frustrations undoubtedly played an important role in the radicalization of his cultural stance between 1838 and 1840. But these frustrations were not so much the result of his personal defects as a scholar as a consequence of significant changes in his cultural environment. In a sense he was right in viewing his own experience as a representative experience, in identifying the "good cause of freedom" with his "personal affair."[117] Bauer's intellectual development might have been very different if he had received a salaried academic appointment during the mid- or late-1830s. By 1841, however, the possibility of accommodation between Bauer and his cultural environment had become extremely unlikely. He was able to accept this disinheritance from the existing culture because of his total commitment to an alternative cultural order. His uncompromising belligerence toward the established authorities even before he had been dismissed from his position was grounded in his confidence that the cultural principle he espoused would be historically realized in the near future. This confidence, in turn, was sustained by his sense of solidarity with the vanguard of the widespread opposition to the Christian state of Frederick William IV – the Left Hegelians.

In the fall of 1839, Arnold Ruge had still described Bauer as part of the "reactionary" party in contemporary theology.[118] In 1840, however, very favorable reviews of Bauer's *Dr. Hengstenberg* and *The Prussian Evangelical State Church* appeared in the *Hallische Jahrbücher,* and by November, Bauer's commitment to the progressive evolution of freedom and Reason was regarded as an established fact.[119] In the spring of 1841, Bauer himself described the Left Hegelians as the authentic interpreters of the Hegelian vision for the new age.[120] He stopped writing reviews for the *Jahrbücher für wissenschaftliche Kritik* and became a regular contributor to Ruge's journal. Between the spring of 1841 and the summer of 1842, Bauer's writings, along with those of Ludwig Feuerbach, were clearly perceived by himself and by other Hegelians as the major theoretical articulations of a Left Hegelian ideology, and Bauer's academic "trial" became the focus of the Left Hegelian confrontation with the Prussian state. Like Strauss in 1839–40, Bauer in 1840–41 was inspired to develop his position into an uncompromising opposition to Christian culture by his consciousness of participating in and representing an irresistible collective revolutionary movement whose ultimate triumph was imminent. He became increasingly convinced that the present was a moment of epochal historical change in which anyone who made even the smallest compromise with the existing culture would be swept aside or devoured by the revolutionary process. He reminded Ruge of the fate of Danton and Camille Desmoulins and insisted: "In our case the process will proceed with an equally violent rapidity."[121]

Bauer's total opposition to the established culture did not represent merely a tactical shift in response to the increasing conservatism of that culture. The criteria by which he judged his cultural environment had also changed. The new tactics were inextricably connected to new philosophical assumptions, to a new "principle." The nature of this new principle was first clearly articulated in Bauer's *Critique of the Synoptic Gospels,* which he presented to Eichhorn and the educated public as the final resolution of the issues raised by Strauss's historical criticism of the Christian revelation in the New Testament Gospels. Bauer's Right Hegelian resolution of the apparent contradiction between the "positivity" of the biblical letter and the freedom of the modern scientific spirit was based on a critique of Strauss's methodological and philosophical assumptions and a reaffirmation of the Hegelian method of absolute knowledge. The literal truth of the biblical revelation, he had claimed, could be resurrected only if the letter was comprehended or "remembered" as a necessary stage in the self-determination of absolute spirit. Bauer's Left Hegelian resolution of the tensions between the letter and the spirit was also first articulated as a critique of Strauss's methodological assumptions, but in this case his critique was based on a radically immanent reinterpretation of the Hegelian method of absolute knowledge. "I always experience a philosophical paroxysm," he wrote to Ruge in April 1841, "when I read these tirades about the absolute spirit, world spirit, etc. The substance (by which even Strauss is still much too captivated) and its mysteriousness must be completely overcome."[122]

Between 1835 and 1839, Bauer had rejected Strauss's mythical interpretation of the sacred history because it implied a radical negation of the absolute content – the union of the divine and the human in a concrete, self-conscious person – of the Christian revelation. In his *Critique of the Synoptic Gospels,* Bauer dismissed Strauss's mythical interpretation as "the mysterious fog of the tradition hypothesis" in which the "religious" form of the relationship between the free self-determination of human subjectivity and the absolute "Substance" (in this case, the Idea of humanity) was not destroyed or overcome but merely reconstructed within the context of an immanent interpretation of man's historical evolution.[123] One might say that Bauer now viewed Strauss's standpoint as the theoretical correlate to the stage of historical development represented by the merely formal or "abstract" absorption of the church into the state during the Prussian reform movement. The content of the Christian revelation no longer was perceived as the description of a relationship between God and man, the transcendent and the immanent, but was defined as the relationship between the universal and the individual within the realm of immanent human relationships. At the same time, however, this universal Moment within the realm of immanence had "not yet arrived at the real and rational determination of universality, which can be achieved only in the singularity and infinity of self-consciousness."[124] As long as the Idea of humanity was not fully appropriated as the determination of self-consciousness, it remained, in a sense, "transcendent"; that is, it took the form of an absolute "substance" to which human subjectivity or self-consciousness had to submit. Just as Bauer described the contemporary Prussian state as the last and final form of the Christian state, so he described Strauss's theological standpoint as the last and final form of Christian apologetics.

Strauss's writings, Bauer claimed, described both the content and the form of the biblical accounts as an unmediated manifestation of the unconscious powers of inherited communal traditions or myths in the early Christian church. Such an interpretation remained "mysterious" because it attributed the universal content of Christian history to arbitrary (i.e., philosophically incomprehensible) forces outside the self-consciousness of the individual Christian writers. Strauss had revived the orthodox theory of inspiration in a new, secular form. The unconscious forces of communal myth, Bauer insisted, had no hands to write, no sense of composition, and no judgment for discerning the relative importance of different facts in a narrative account; only the self-conscious subject possessed these qualities. In the accounts of the four Gospels the absolute "substance" of communal myth was "mediated" or transformed by human self-consciousness and reconstructed as a self-determination of the subject. It was this transformation of substance into subject that represented the absolute content of the Christian revelation and differentiated it from the preceding tradition. The four evangelists were not merely mouthpieces of an unconscious tradition, but world-historical individuals "who gave the world a new principle and devoted themselves to its development."[125]

In one rather important sense, Bauer's method of biblical interpretation had the same implications as Strauss's mythical interpretation. Like Strauss, Bauer denied that the four Gospels provided accurate historical accounts of the life and self-consciousness of the historical individual Jesus Christ: "Everything that constitutes the historical Christ, what is said of him, what we know of him, belongs to the world of representation, more particularly of Christian representation. But this information has absolutely nothing to do with a person who belongs to the real world."[126] In 1840, Bauer had suggested that the synoptic Gospels might contain the unmediated genuine history of Christ's self-consciousness and activity, which had been distorted by the reflective mediations of the Gospel of John. In 1841, however, he claimed that all four Gospels had the same "theological" character. The Christ of the Gospels was a creation and manifestation of human self-consciousness at a particular stage of its historical evolution. The religious relationship between the individual subject and the revelation of the absolute identity of God and man in Christ was reduced to the relationship between the subject as a particular individual and its essence as universal, self-determining spirit.

In opposition to Strauss, however, Bauer insisted, as he had in 1838, on the significance of the distinction between the mythical and representational stages in the development of religious self-consciousness. Strauss's failure to grasp this distinction was intimately connected to his perception of the immanent absolute – the Idea of humanity – as a static universal "substance" immediately revealed or "given" in Christian myth, and not as a universal activity in which the "substance" of humanity was recognized and appropriated as a self-determination of the subject, as a Moment in the infinite activity of self-consciousness. Strauss, Bauer claimed, simply did not understand the dynamic dialectical structure of the human spirit, and thus could not explain the emergence of the Christian form of religious self-consciousness as a philosophical necessity. It was Strauss's philosophical inadequacy, his inability to grasp the nature of self-conscious spirit, his reversion to an immanent form of the pantheistic heresy ("the substance is the absolute"), that led him to seek for the causes of the Christian revelation in the "mysterious" forces of an unconscious communal tradition.[127] Once the Idea of humanity was grasped as the infinite activity of self-consciousness, however, the mystery of Christianity was dissipated and man could understand his Christian past as a stage in the self-determination of his own spirit:

> As spirit, however, and as the religious spirit, it [self-consciousness] is movement and the drive to differentiate itself from its own universality. It must differentiate itself from this universality so that it can relate to it as a real consciousness. And who can bring about this differentiation and real creation? Who else but itself: But it does not, in this creative moment know that it is itself the essential creativity; *we* know it as such, but it itself does not. As religious self-consciousness it is grasped most profoundly by the content, cannot live without it, and without its continuous description and production, for it possesses in this activity the experience of its own determination. But as religious consciousness it perceives itself at the same time in complete differentiation from its own essential content, and as soon as it has developed it, and in the same moment that it develops and describes it, this essential content becomes for it a reality that exists for itself, above and outside religious consciousness, as the absolute and its history.[128]

Once the Christian representations were grasped as the "determination, the work, and the revelation of self-consciousness," Bauer proclaimed, the positive authority, the "transcendence" of the letter, was finally overcome.[129] The long struggle for mediation and reconciliation between the objective, positive letter and the freedom of the human subject, which characterized the whole history of Christian theology, finally reached its conclusion in the liberating recognition that the letter was simply a self-objectification of the subject. The tension between the letter and the spirit did not express a tension between God and man, the transcendent and the immanent, but a tension between human self-consciousness and its own alienated universality. Once this relationship was comprehended, man was freed from the sufferings of religious consciousness:

Oh, from what misery, from what involuntary lies, does criticism liberate us! Do not say that we speak like Pharisees! No, we speak like men who once again feel themselves to be men and breathe free air, after having been chained to the letter for millenia, and having played with their chains like slaves! To be free, means to be ethical (*sittlich*)![130]

To recognize the chains of the transcendent as self-imposed chains was to dissolve them. Theoretical comprehension was at the same time practical liberation.

A few months after he published the first volume of his *Critique of the Synoptic Gospels,* Bauer presented his philosophy of immanent self-consciousness to the public, through the indirect means of a conservative denunciation of Hegel's system, as the true inner meaning of Hegel's philosophy of absolute spirit. Although Hegel's philosophy had been perceived by many of his students as "a mirror of orthodoxy," Bauer insisted that it was actually a "system of atheism."[131] Previous misconceptions and distortions of Hegel's meaning were based on an inability to break through the esoteric husk of Hegel's metaphorical, theological, and metaphysical terminology – the use of terms like "God," "absolute spirit," "world spirit," "objective universal," and so on, which appeared to denote an absolute power, a universal "substance" that transcended human self-consciousness and merely actualized itself *in* human self-consciousness – and grasp the implications of his conception of the dialectical relationship between substance and subject. In Hegel, Bauer asserted, the subordination of human self-consciousness to the absolute "substance" or objective universal was merely a limited stage – the stage of the "religious relationship" – in the evolution of human self-consciousness:

The substance is merely the momentary fire in which the self sacrifices its finitude and limitation. The conclusion of the movement is not the substance, but the self-consciousness, which actually posits itself as the infinite and appropriates the universality of the substance as its own essence.[132]

The human ego (*das Ich*) as the activity of self-consciousness, Bauer claimed, was "the genuine substance." The religious relationship as a "substantiality relationship" or a relationship between God and man was actually nothing more than the "inner relationship of self-consciousness to itself."[133] Philosophical theory recognized the self-duplicating nature of the religious relationship and thus absorbed or appropriated the "substance" or God as a self-determination of self-consciousness. "God is dead for philosophy," Bauer proclaimed, "and only the ego as self-consciousness . . . only the ego lives, creates, works, and is everything."[134] The inner meaning of Hegel's conception of the actualization of the absolute spirit in the world was that "self-consciousness is the only power in the world and in history, and history has no other meaning than the becoming and development of self-consciousness."[135]

The philosophy of self-consciousness in Bauer's view was not simply a contemplative theory, a passive comprehension of the human essence, but an active practical actualization of that essence. Hegel's purpose, he wrote, was "the destruction of the established world. His theory was practice in itself, and thus the most dangerous, all-encompassing, and destructive form of practice. It was the revolution itself."[136] When man came to know the "established," the "positive," in religion and politics as the self-determination of his own freedom, he would no longer endure "servitude and tutelage" but instead "attack and shatter the established relations without compunction."[137] Philosophy did not merely elevate the content of Christian culture to a new form; the emergence of a new form was also the emergence of a new content. Christian culture was characterized by the domination of the "substance" over the subject, or man's self-alienated objectified universality over his creative freedom; and this perverted structure of domination was expressed in the "external statutes" of communal life. "Knowledge, however, is free and liberates the spirit," Bauer wrote, "and its determinations transform the previous content into a new form and, through this transformation, also into a new content, namely, into the laws of freedom and self-consciousness." Theoretical criticism made a radical distinction between what "is" and what "must be" and thus led necessarily to the "deed" and "practical opposition."[138]

Bauer's Left Hegelian, immanent interpretation or reduction of Hegel's philosophy of absolute spirit differed from that of Strauss in a number of significant ways. Bauer defined the human essence or man's "species being" (which he, like Strauss, perceived as the "true" content of both the Christian incarnation and the Hegelian absolute) as the *activity* of self-consciousness, that is, as the dialectical process in which the human spirit created, or objectified itself in, a succession of self-limiting cultural worlds (specific value systems with corresponding institutional forms) and finally came to recognize these worlds as self-objectifications, as historical Moments in the process of its own self-determination and actualization. This view was more "radical" than Strauss's interpretation of the Hegelian absolute as the Idea of humanity in two major ways. First, Bauer insisted that the emancipation of philosophical *Wissenschaft* from Christian theology and the emancipation of the state from the church involved a revolutionary transformation of the total system, the "world" of Christian culture, including its politics and its *Wissenschaft*. "L'infame is immortal," he wrote to Feuerbach in March 1842, "if it is not demolished in politics and law,"[139] and in his critique of Strauss he constantly reiterated that the religious form of consciousness would remain "immortal" as long as philosophy continued to define itself as a knowledge of man's essence as a universal, objective "substance" rather than as a self-comprehension of the "infinite" self-determining activity of the human spirit or "self-consciousness."[140] Unlike Strauss, therefore, Bauer claimed that the destruction of theological consciousness implied a destruction of the existing forms of political or communal life and the transformation of philosophy from the esoteric knowledge of a universal substance by an invisible church of the scientific and cultural elite into the self-consciousness of a new form of collective life.

It would be more accurate to say form*s* of collective life. For Bauer the essence of man was the activity of making cultural forms, of constructing meaningful cultural worlds, of value creation, of self-objectification. To actualize one's human essence was to engage in this activity in full self-conscious knowledge of one's own creative powers and responsibilities. No particular form or objectification, of course, could perfectly embody the human essence. Every objectification was a limitation. But this did not mean, as Strauss had contended, that the essence of humanity could never be actualized in a particular individual or cultural community. If the human essence was defined as "self-consciousness" rather than as an objective "substance," as the activity of creating cultural forms in the full knowledge that they were free creations rather than as an idea of a perfected humanity that could be only approximated in any particular and thus limited cultural form, then the actualization of the universal in the individual was not only possible but historically necessary. Bauer was thus more radical than Strauss not only in his revolutionary opposition to the structure of domination or unfreedom that was embodied in every aspect of the existing Christian culture, but also in his conception of the future as the emancipation of man from all objective universals, whether religious or secular – as an era in which man would become the free maker of his own history, in which self-objectification would be synonymous no longer with self-alienation and surrender to the reified activity of an absolute substance, but with the infinite process of self-determination.

In two important aspects of his cultural stance, however, Bauer was in essential agreement with Strauss. Like Strauss, he perceived human liberation as the incorporation of the empirical finite individual into the spiritual universality of the species, even though he defined this universality in personal and active terms as "self-consciousness" and the "ego." The death of the empirical ego was a prerequisite for its resurrection as a Moment in the self-determination of the universal ego, the spiritual essence of humanity. Secondly, Bauer, like Strauss, contended that the world of nature, including man's instinctual impulses and material needs, attained its true reality only when it was incorporated into the world of human culture as a self-determination of spirit. For both Bauer and Strauss man was essentially a cultural or spiritual being and the "world" was the world as defined and determined by man's cultural activity. In this sense they remained more loyal to their Hegelian inheritance than they perhaps realized. For Feuerbach, however, the absorption of nature into culture, the realm of the senses and desires into the realm of spiritual activity, was a problem rather than a presupposition, and the attempt to resolve this problem led him to a more radical critique and revision of the Hegelian system than either Strauss or Bauer had envisioned.

10

Feuerbach and the reduction of absolute spirit to human "species being"

Ludwig Feuerbach's *The Essence of Christianity* was published in the same year (1841) as the second volume of Strauss's *Christian Faith* and the first two volumes of Bauer's *Critique of the Synoptic Gospels*, and like these two contemporaneous studies its aim was to reveal Christian theology and religious consciousness as the psychological and historical culmination of human self-alienation. It was not surprising, therefore, that Feuerbach, Strauss, and Bauer were often grouped together by contemporary observers as a Left Hegelian atheistic trio. Feuerbach, however, resisted the identification of his standpoint with those of Strauss and Bauer. His own critique of Christian religion and culture, he insisted, went beyond their works in at least two significant respects.

The object of Bauer's and Strauss's criticism, Feuerbach claimed, was biblical and dogmatic theology, the "theoretical" objectifications of Christian religious experience; their analysis did not penetrate beyond historical forms to the religious experience expressed in those forms. "The main object of my inquiry," he wrote, "is Christianity, is religion, as it is constituted in its *immediacy* by the *objectification* of the essence of man."[1] This differentiation, however, was misleading. Bauer and Strauss were also concerned with the religious experience embodied in Christian "representations" and also analyzed religious consciousness in terms of the objectification and self-alienation of "the essence of man." The distinctiveness of Feuerbach's viewpoint lay in his conception of human essence, of man's "species being." It was not his "humanism," his reduction of theology and metaphysics to "anthropology," that made him unique among the Left Hegelians, but his "sensualism," "naturalism," or "materialism," his attempt to ground man's autonomy and universality as a "species being" in the concrete reality of his natural, sensuous, "immediate" existence.

The second factor that distinguished him from Bauer and Strauss, Feuerbach believed, was his critical dissection and transcendence of

Hegelian metaphysics. Because Strauss and Bauer had not penetrated to the experiential source of religious self-alienation, they had failed to grasp the theological presuppositions of Hegel's philosophy. Their discontents with the philosophy of the absolute were not developed into a clear break with their philosophical inheritance.[2] As Engels noted many years later, it was Feuerbach who broke the "spell" of the "system" among Hegel's radical disciples and consciously joined the emancipation from Christian culture to an emancipation from the whole tradition of speculative idealism and "classical" German philosophy.[3]

In 1843, Feuerbach summarized his spiritual itinerary in one short sentence: "God was my first, Reason my second, and Man my third and last thought."[4] This development from theology, to philosophy, to "anthropology" roughly paralleled Feuerbach's personal evolution from theology student, to Hegelian academic, to independent intellectual and cultural critic. But this simplistic schema obscures more than it illuminates. Our previous analysis of Feuerbach's Hegel reception and transition from theology to philosophy has indicated how misleading it would be to describe his second phase as simply Hegelian or "philosophical." If labels must be affixed, then the Feuerbach of 1830 might best be described as an idiosyncratic cultural prophet of the old Hegelian Left. He was a member of the Left in the sense that he interpreted the philosophy of absolute spirit as a radical negation of the presuppositions of Christian culture (subjective egoism, the dualism of spirit and nature, the separation of the transcendent and the immanent), and defined his historical task as the actualization of the Hegelian absolute in a post-Christian cultural order, the Kingdom of the Idea. Feuerbach's position was idiosyncratic because he sought the implicit concrete basis for the historical actualization of Reason in a post-Christian culture in the existential reality of the individual's absorption (in love and death) in the dynamic totality of the natural cosmos.

The "Hegelianism" that was the starting point of Feuerbach's development after 1830 was thus distinguished by a peculiar combination of prophetic anti-Christian radicalism and an unhistorical, almost mystical pantheism. His transition from this position to the anthropological standpoint of *The Essence of Christianity* can best be understood as a process of self-clarification and self-criticism in the context of a changing historical experience, a process that divides into two phases. Between 1830 and his withdrawal from the academic world in 1837, Feuerbach temporarily abandoned the prophetic activism of the *Thoughts* and devoted himself to a critical appraisal and historical reconstruction of the evolution of the philosophical standpoint he had hoped would provide the foundation for a new religious consciousness and cultural community. His systematic and historical analysis of the presuppositions of modern philosophy led to a critique of the mystical pantheism espoused in the *Thoughts* and an explicit defense of Hegel's dialectical conception of the identity of spirit and nature. But Feuerbach's apparent return to a more orthodox Hegelian position was misleading, for his recognition that the actualization of the absolute could not be accomplished through a regression to pre-Hegelian conceptions also laid the foundations for a new, more radical critique of both Christianity and Hegelian philosophy in the years between 1838 and 1841.

During the early 1830s, Feuerbach was forced to come to terms with the gap between his vision of imminent cultural transformation and the recalcitrant actuality of his historical environment, between his prophetic calling and the necessity of historical survival. He later described these years as an "abominably dismal period," a time "in which public life was so poisoned and befouled that the only way of preserving one's freedom of spirit and one's health was to abandon all government service, every public function, even that of university instructor."[5] Feuerbach's separation from the public world of the state-service class, however, was as much an external necessity as an inner choice. It was only after his third application for a salaried professorship at Erlangen was rejected in 1837 that he finally decided to withdraw from academia and become an independent intellectual. In retrospect he perceived this break with the established culture as the end of a frustrating conflict between his "innermost desires" and "external necessity," and the beginning of a "new period" in his development.[6]

The faculty at Erlangen, it must be remembered, provided the theological leadership for the Fundamentalist "awakening" among Bavarian Protestants during the 1820s and 1830s. In philosophy it was dominated by the specifically anti-Hegelian speculative theism of Schelling's more conservative followers. Feuerbach's belligerent and reckless articulation of a prophetic and specifically antitheological version of Hegelianism in 1829–30 isolated him from the rest of the faculty and virtually closed the door to academic promotion. By the summer of 1831 he had begun to consider alternate careers, and in the spring of 1832 he decided that the only way to resolve the conflict between his intellectual convictions and his cultural environment was emigration. His first choice was Paris – the historical home of the anti-Christian Enlightenment. If Paris was not the New Jerusalem, at least it would provide an atmosphere where one could live in the present as a citizen of the future. He moved to Frankfurt, spent the summer studying

French, planned a career as a literary critic or political journalist, and sent his dissertation to Victor Cousin – but it all came to nought.[7] His father was already supporting two of his sons in Paris and could not afford the expense of a third foreign dependent. A salaried position in the French capital was also not obtainable. Feuerbach was thus forced to return to the inhospitable atmosphere of Erlangen in the fall of 1832, but he remained determined not to follow his older brother's advice and "conform in everything in which everyone must now conform" in order to obtain a secure position.[8] He continued to hope that somewhere, if not in Germany or France, perhaps in the United States, a position could be found that would not require dishonest conformity to the values of Christian culture.

Two events in the spring of 1833 brought a new intensity to Feuerbach's search for a secure position: the death of his father and the beginning of his courtship with Bertha Löw. Despite the intellectual disagreements and personal tensions between Feuerbach and his father, Anselm Feuerbach had been his son's most influential and concerned advocate in the search for an academic job and had been more than willing to provide for Feuerbach's daily needs, either in Erlangen or, when Erlangen became unbearable, at his home in Ansbach. The desire to marry and establish an independent household, moreover, brought the problem of gaining some form of financial security to a head.

Between 1833 and 1835, Feuerbach focused his search for an academic position on the Prussian university system. In the fall of 1833 he sent his recently published *History of Modern Philosophy* to Gans, Altenstein, and Henning in Berlin. Gans responded with effusive praise for Feuerbach's work and encouraged him to bring his intellectual energy and enthusiasm to the increasingly sterile philosophical atmosphere in Berlin. But he admitted that Feuerbach, regardless of his qualifications, could not expect to receive an offer of a tenured appointment in the immediate future.[9] Altenstein was also complimentary regarding Feuerbach's scholarship and pessimistic about his chances for a salaried position.[10] Feuerbach was clearly gratified and encouraged by the Berliners' praise of his work. He joined the Society for Scientific Criticism and accepted Henning's invitation to review a series of books on the history of philosophy, including Hegel's posthumously published *Lectures*, for the *Jahrbücher*. Although he described the Berlin Hegelians as "slaves of a great mind," he preferred their company to that of self-styled "original" thinkers who were simply "asses on their own account."[11] On March 26, 1835, he wrote to Johannes Schulze that he considered Prussia "my second, my spiritual, my true fatherland," and that he could think of no "greater happiness" than "to find an ethical position in a state where the speculative intellect has created a permanent existence for itself, where the individual does not feel isolated and rejected in his work, but can comprehend himself as a member of a cooperative totality engaged in a common task."[12]

Feuerbach's rapprochement with the Hegelian school's academic establishment in 1834 and 1835 was more than a tactical ploy for obtaining a job or the expression of a psychological need for membership in "a cooperative totality engaged in a common task." His experience of the "pietistic flood"[13] that engulfed Erlangen after 1830 produced a noticeable shift in his cultural stance, a shift that was most clearly evident in his growing critical detachment from the mystical pantheistic religiosity that had pervaded his *Thoughts.* The contemporary form of Christian "barbarism," he soon realized, was inwardly connected to the philosophy of speculative mysticism to which he had temporarily surrendered in his attempts to transcend the apparent dualism between spirit and nature in Hegelian philosophy. The reactionary political and religious implications of Schelling's philosophy of absolute identity were expressed for Feuerbach in the work of Friedrich Julius Stahl, who had been appointed to a full professorship at Erlangen in 1834 and promptly proceeded to fill "the pietistic cesspools of the university with his excrement," to great popular acclaim.[14] Feuerbach's return to what appeared to be a more orthodox form of Hegelianism constituted an attempt to clarify the philosophical foundations for a critique of this perverted expression of the actualization of speculative philosophy in a popular religiosity. At the same time, he gained a new regard for the Prussian Hegelians' bureaucratic connections and detachment from popular pressures. "Only that Reason which has the advantage of an official position," he wrote to his friend Christian Kapp, "can have an impact on men; for Reason in and for itself, without this accreditation, is impotent."[15] Yet Feuerbach's rapprochement with academic Hegelianism never became a wholehearted alliance. He did not abjure his earlier "doubts" nor deny his prophetic cultural calling. He merely recognized that his first attempt to resolve those doubts and fulfill that calling had been misconceived.

The critical component in Feuerbach's new "accommodationism" was revealed in 1835 when Henning asked him to write a review of Stahl's book on the history of Christian law for the *Jahrbücher*. This assignment forced Feuerbach to make a difficult decision. If he published an honest, and thus devastating, critique of Stahl's work and its philosophical presuppositions, any hope he might still entertain for an academic appointment in Bavaria would have to be given up. He expressed his personal anguish in his letters to his fiancée. Should he compromise his intellectual integrity in order to gain the financial security that would allow them to get married?[16] But there was also a chance that a brilliant and incisive critique of Stahl would bring new recognition from Berlin and open up the possibility of a career in Prussia. When Feuerbach finally wrote the review, however, he alienated the Prussian Hegelians as well as his Bavarian colleagues. Not only did he attack Stahl's attempt to justify religious obscurantism and feudal-authoritarian politics with speculative principles drawn from Schelling's philosophy, but he claimed that the Christian religion itself was incompatible with both genuine philosophical *Wissenschaft* and the legal and political institutions of the modern state. His criticism was thus applicable not only to Stahl and other conservative Schellingians, but also to most of the Prussian Hegelians. When his manuscript arrived in Berlin it was severely censored, and Henning wrote Feuerbach a critical schoolmasterly letter pointing out the un-Hegelian nature of a cultural stance based on a life-and-death struggle between Christianity and the ethical community that philosophy comprehended as the actuality of Reason.[17]

This clear revelation of the immense gap that still separated Feuerbach's views from those of the Hegelian academic establishment constituted the final blow to his hope that Prussia might provide a cultural environment where he would be able to think and act as a member of a "cooperative totality." He was now convinced that the only way to obtain an academic position in Germany was to veil one's philosophical convictions in Christian garb. An academic career and loyalty to the principle of Reason could not be reconciled. In order to get a job, he claimed, "one must now sacrifice that which alone gives value to man."[18] After a careful inventory of his own and Bertha's financial assets, Feuerbach finally decided to withdraw from the academic world in the summer of 1837. Bertha had inherited a share in a porcelain factory on the country estate of Bruckberg near Ansbach. The profits from the factory, Feuerbach's small inheritance, and the royalties from his writings allowed a modest independent existence. On November 12, 1837, he and Bertha Löw were married. At the same time he severed his connection with the Berlin *Jahrbücher* and accepted Arnold Ruge's invitation to become a contributor to the *Hallische Jahrbücher*.

The tensions that characterized Feuerbach's relationship to his cultural environment and the Hegelian school between 1830 and 1837 were expressed in theoretical form in his published writings. In part they were expressed indirectly – by what he did not say. The connection between his "head" and his "hand," he claimed, was often broken by the necessity of taking public, and specifically academic, opinion into consideration.[19] He deleted all direct attacks on Christianity from his writings and later complained that he had been forced to "swallow" his best ideas.[20] But this self-censorship was not based only on "external necessity." Feuerbach turned to historical scholarship and sought official academic validation of his work in the early thirties because of an inner need to discipline and "transcend" the subjective longings and resentments that had led him astray in 1830. "The paradoxical aphorism of our life," he wrote in 1834, "loses its fragmentary significance, and gains sense and meaning, only when it is read in connection with the great text of the past."[21] The character of Feuerbach's major writings between 1833 and 1837 – besides two volumes in the history of philosophy, he published an extended defense of Hegel against the criticism of Karl Friedrich Bachmann – seems to indicate an epigonal, past-oriented cultural consciousness. But Feuerbach perceived his turn to the past as a self-discipline and self-comprehension that would provide a secure, "objective" basis for a turn to the future. The creation of a new world, the transformation of philosophical theory into cultural practice, could not be achieved until philosophy had clarified its presuppositions and completed its historical development. "Although detached from the superficial hurly-burly of contemporary life," Feuerbach wrote, "the historian cultivates the earth of the present."[22]

Feuerbach's conviction of the contemporary relevance of his historical studies was based on the Hegelian claim that the individual Moments in the systematic totality of scientific truth were articulated and developed in the temporal progression of the history of philosophy. Feuerbach was concerned not with the learned compilation and description of historical philosophical texts, but with the internal "appropriation (*Aneignung*)" of the stages of historical development as present moments in the self-comprehension of absolute spirit. "The history of philosophy," he wrote in 1835, "is therefore concerned not with the past but with the present, with what is still living." The "essential elements" of philosophical systems were retained in the "more developed" systems that succeeded them. "The study of the history of philosophy," he insisted, "is thus the study of philosophy itself."[23] His only criticism of Hegel's reconstruction of the history of philosophy in the *Lectures* was that it stressed the historical succession of previous systems more than the simultaneity of their essential elements in the present "Idea of truth." The present significance of particular historical moments in the development of the Idea was therefore not always obvious, and the misconception that these earlier moments had simply been left behind rather than *aufgehoben* in the construction of the

Hegelian system could easily arise.[24] In his contemporaneous unpublished lectures on the history of philosophy, however, Feuerbach extended this apparently modest criticism of Hegel's method of "successive" development one step further. Hegel pushed the "idea of unity" too much into the "background," Feuerbach claimed. Although it was "necessary" for "us" as individual thinking beings that the absolute unity appear in successive moments, the purpose of philosophical "science" was to "destroy succession" in "the idea of unity," for it was only in the destruction of the particularity of the individual Moments in the eternal presence of the totality that man could achieve peace and satisfaction.[25]

The philosophical viewpoints or systems of the past, Feuerbach insisted, could not be appropriated as necessary Moments in the eternal "Idea of truth" in their historical entirety, but only in their "essence." The first task of the historian of philosophy must be a critical differentiation of essence from appearance, the spirit from the letter, in a particular historical text. The similarity between this methodological position and Strauss's attitude toward the texts of biblical history is striking. Like Strauss, Feuerbach claimed that the resurrection of the spirit could emerge only from the critical destruction of the historical letter. Moreover, Feuerbach also specifically differentiated his position from the Right Hegelian historical method as articulated in Johann E. Erdmann's history of philosophy. Erdmann had tried to deduce the historical necessity of the letter from the necessary stages in the development of the Idea.[26] Feuerbach reversed this procedure. If the *Aufhebung* of the past in the "living present" was to be convincing, the contradictions of the letter would have to be taken seriously and subjected to systematic critical analysis. The historian had to work through, in fact "live" through, the stages of philosophical development, and thus appropriate the essence of each stage, before he could claim the result of the development, the concrete "Idea of truth," as his own truth.[27]

Parallels between Strauss's and Feuerbach's position during the early 1830s can also be discerned on another level. Strauss had criticized Right Hegelian theologians like Marheineke for not taking the negative Moment of empirical historical particularity seriously enough. They had simply affirmed the final Moment of complete reconciliation and ignored the critical dialectical process embodied and thus eternally present in this "conclusion." From Feuerbach's perspective, the "negative Moment" that had to be remembered and taken seriously was defined as "empiricism" or "nature." His dissatisfaction with the orthodox Hegelianism of the "school" was formulated in terms of the need to provide a convincing "vindication" of "empiricism." "Only then will philosophy arrive at a better time," he claimed, "when it no longer leaves empiricism outside itself, but penetrates and vindicates it."[28]

Feuerbach's attempts to vindicate empiricism were complicated by the very general definition he gave to empiricism. He was not merely a professional philosopher concerned with epistemological questions but also, and primarily, a cultural critic and historical prophet.[29] His *History* began with a broad characterization of the evolution of spirit from Classical to Christian and finally to Modern culture. The task of modern philosophy was a historical, cultural task: the overcoming of the "bifurcation of spirit and matter, God and the world," which characterized Christian culture.[30] The vindication of empiricism was synonymous with the reconciliation of the abstract, subjective Christian ego and the objective reality of "matter," "nature," the "flesh," and the "world." Moreover, Feuerbach also claimed that the reconciliation of spirit and nature was inextricably connected to the emancipation of Reason, of self-determining thought, from the authority of the supernatural, from the dogmas of faith. Once the world was recognized and affirmed as the immanent reality of the absolute, a transcendent God became superfluous. Dualism and heteronomy were correlative phenomena. Feuerbach's wide-ranging definition of the tasks of modern philosophy often produced a terminological vagueness that does not make for easy reading. But this apparent lack of conceptual clarity and rigor should not be seen as a confusion, for it expressed quite clearly the sweeping historical tasks and purposes that Feuerbach attached to the philosophical vocation in the modern world.

In true Hegelian fashion, Feuerbach conceived the progress of modern philosophy as a dialectical development in which the end was implicit in the beginning. His divergence from the orthodox Hegelian position, however, was evident in the particular way he defined this beginning. Both Hegel and Erdmann had described Descartes as the "founder" of modern philosophy because it was Descartes who had first articulated – albeit in an abstract, undeveloped, and thus ultimately one-sided form – the principle of self-determining, self-conscious spirit.[31] Feuerbach criticized this position because it did not give adequate consideration to the genesis of Descartes's standpoint. The "first real beginning of modern philosophy," the decisive break with Christian dualism and spiritualism, he insisted, should be traced back to the identification of the divine spirit with the natural and human world in the pantheistic philosophies of Bruno, Cardano, Telesius, and other thinkers of the Italian Renaissance.[32] The evolution of modern consciousness was defined as a process of critical reflection on, and self-conscious appropriation of, this beginning, as the transformation of the implicit, immediate identity of spirit and nature to an explicit, mediated identity of spirit and nature, as a movement from "unconscious pantheism" to "pantheism become conscious of itself" or speculative idealism.[33] The first Moment in this process of critical mediation was represented by the empiricist and materialist philosophies of Bacon, Hobbes, and Gassendi, in which spirit articulated its emancipation from transcendent authority by "emptying," or externalizing, itself in the immanent material world of sensuous experience. This negation of the supernatural, however, was also a negation of spirit or thinking activity that was now conceived as dependent on nature, on the authority of the senses. Descartes's significance in the history of modern thought lay in his recognition of the inadequacy of the empiricist and materialist positions and his attempt to define the spiritual ground for sensuous experience and the natural world in the self-differentiating activity of thought. The philosophy of Descartes constituted the Moment of separation between spirit and nature within the immanent perspective of modern consciousness, and thus set the stage for the reconciliation of spirit and nature in the philosophies of Spinoza, Leibniz, and the speculative idealists.[34]

Two aspects of Feuerbach's reconstruction of the historical development of modern philosophy deserve special emphasis. First, he insisted that empiricist and materialist philosophy constituted a necessary, essential Moment in the emancipation of Reason from the authority of faith and the bifurcations of Christian consciousness. Philosophy could not fulfill its historical task as long as it refused to recognize the legitimacy of empiricism and the reality of the material world. At the same time, however, Feuerbach continued to define empiricism and materialism as *only* a Moment within the self-development of the absolute identity of spirit and nature:

> Empiricism and materialism constitute the period in the life cycle of the thinking spirit that corresponds to the stage in the life cycle of the individual in which he throws himself down from the heights of his first subjective ideals – which were not based on experience or constructive thought – into the stream of sensuous life. Only that idealism which is constructed after the return from the self-dispersal of this period of experience is a genuine concentration of the spirit, a mature thoughtfulness, and thus a proven, self-assured idealism.[35]

Feuerbach thus had no intention of elevating empiricism to the status of a philosophical alternative to Hegelian "idealism"; he merely insisted that empiricism must be taken seriously if the idealist resolution was to attain demonstrable certainty and self-assurance. However, Feuerbach's reconstruction of the historical development of modern philosophy did not reach beyond the early eighteenth century (Leibniz and Bayle), and the projected idealist resolution of the spirit/nature dichotomy was never systematically or historically "demonstrated." Feuerbach's assertions of loyalty to Hegelian idealism during the early 1830s were grounded not so much in the demonstrated validity of the Hegelian resolution of the tasks of modern philosophy as in a conviction of the superiority of the Hegelian resolution to existing alternatives.

The manner in which Feuerbach construed and defended the "idealist" vindication of nature in Hegel's philosophy of identity was most clearly expressed in his critique of Bachmann's *Anti-Hegel.* Bachmann had claimed that Hegel's doctrine of the identity of spirit and nature was a purely formal, abstract assertion that stood in sharp contradiction to his conception of the natural, empirical world as the negative "other" of spirit. Feuerbach, however, insisted that this contradiction was a product of a fundamental misunderstanding of Hegel's dialectical conception of the unity of thought and being, Reason and reality. Bachmann had ignored the Hegelian distinction between appearance and reality, existence and being, and interpreted the doctrine of identity as a simple congruence between sensuous perception and the rational concept. The dynamic, critical quality of the Hegelian theory of identity was totally lost in this misconception. Nature as it existed in the external, sensuous form of existing "appearances" was rational in the sense that it was an objectification of spirit, but it was spirit in a form that did not adequately express its essence, reality, or "being." In the active, critical process of philosophical comprehension, however, the arbitrary external form of the appearance was stripped away and nature revealed itself as identical with the concept. Nature became the embodiment, the reality, of spirit through a process of critical negation in which its essence was differentiated from its existence, its reality from its appearance. If the philosophical concept was understood simply as a generalization abstracted from empirical particulars (as Feuerbach interpreted the empiricist position), then nature would remain forever alienated from the thinking spirit. For the empiricist, nature was an external, dead, ultimately unknowable "matter." Nature could be vindicated, penetrated, reconciled with spirit, only if it was grasped in its essence, as the reality of Reason. Empiricism could be vindicated only through a process of critical negation in which it was absorbed into the more comprehensive perspective of idealism.[36]

Feuerbach employed a similar pattern of argument in describing the relationship between body and mind, flesh and spirit, in man. The individual existing person, human "being-there (*Dasein*)" in the body and in the world of other bodies, corresponded to the "appearance form" of sensuous perception. In the activity of thinking, however, the individual existed as an "organ" of the infinite spirit that was independent of his finite empirical existence. The empiricists' claim that thought was dependent on sensuous perception, that mind was dependent on the body, was just as misleading as the claim that universals were mere abstractions from empirical particulars. The fact that a child existed as a finite, particular body before it became a self-conscious human being demonstrated the validity of the idealist position. Before coming to self-consciousness the child existed as a human being only implicitly, in itself, and for others, primarily its parents. The child actualized its potentiality, became a "real" human being, moreover, through the mediation of the consciousness of other human beings. The transformation of *Dasein* into humanity was dependent on the activity of human "species consciousness," on the universal spirit.[37]

For Feuerbach the statements "nature is spirit" or "man is spirit" meant that it was the essence of nature and of man as a part of nature to become spirit. They constituted descriptions of a dynamic process in which the subject was transformed into, was actualized in, the predicate. It was only in temporal "appearance" that existence preceded essence, that the actualization of what man and nature were in "truth" came at the end of a process of emancipation from and sublimation of the sensuous particularity of *Dasein.* From the standpoint of self-conscious Reason, the spiritual essences of both man and nature were comprehended as the informing power, the purpose and the inherent meaning and structure of the world of sensuous particularity. It was only by becoming spirit that nature and man as a part of nature could be liberated from their opposition to, alienation from, and external subjugation by the abstract spirituality of the subjective ego.[38] The spiritualization of nature was at the same time the affirmation and vindication of nature. "Duty commands indulgence," Feuerbach claimed, "not renunciation."[39] Sexual desire was not a mere lust of the flesh, an "illegitimate child" of "nature" that opposed the unity of humanity in spirit, but the "legitimate daughter of philosophy," the incarnation of spirit in the world.[40]

By 1835, therefore, Feuerbach's reexamination of his philosophical inheritance had led him back to the position he had held before 1830. The infinity, universality, and unity of Reason were implicit in nature and human *Dasein*, and became explicit and actual in the activity of thought. But the philosophical comprehension and thus "actualization" of the identity of nature and spirit, Feuerbach claimed, presupposed an original absolute identity prior to both nature and human thinking. "The self-consciousness of God," he wrote in his critique of Bachmann, "is thus the absolute beginning from which nature and humanity arose, just as the absolute Idea is the ground of being and essence."[41] This position, however, still left unresolved the question that had determined Feuerbach's conception of his cultural calling in 1828, the question of the collective, historical, cultural actualization of the philosophically comprehended identity of nature and spirit. He continued to believe that the historical actualization of philosophical principle, the incarnation of the Idea in a Kingdom, demanded the transformation of philosophy into a religion:

> Whatever enters into the world as a new principle must at the same time express itself as a religious principle. Only thus does it strike the world with the force of a shattering and fearsome thunderbolt. Only thus can it become the general concern of the world, controlling the emotional and moral disposition of men.[42]

His first attempt to transform the Hegelian Idea into a religious world view, however, was now recognized as a failure. The undialectical mystical pantheism of the *Thoughts* constituted a regression to the beginnings, rather than an actualization of the culminating fulfillment, of modern philosophy. However, as Feuerbach reexamined and clarified his philosophical position in the early thirties, and reaffirmed the validity of the dialectical reconciliation of spirit and nature in the comprehending process of speculative thought, he became increasingly pessimistic about the possibility of a religious reformation emerging from Hegelian principles. By 1834–5 it seemed that he was ready to resign himself to the possibility that the present immortality of identification with absolute spirit could be attained only by a philosophical elite, that the actualization of a true, universal humanity was a privilege of the select few who actually lived as thinking spirits, as philosophers and writers.[43] It was this historical pessimism that motivated Feuerbach's attempts at accommodation with the academic world and the Hegelian school. Identification with the philosophical elite seemed the only alternative to total cultural isolation. In many ways, Feuerbach's dilemma between 1830 and 1837 paralleled that of the young Hegel during the 1790s. Feuerbach's original aim was to actualize the principles of his philosophical inheritance in the form of a historical *Volksreligion*. In his attempts to accomplish this task, however, he became increasingly aware that his philosophical commitments resisted historical actualization. Like Hegel, moreover, Feuerbach eventually resolved this dilemma by means of a fundamental critique and reformation of the philosophical principles that had originally defined his calling. But Feuerbach's path toward resolution diverged radically from Hegel's.

Instead of identifying himself with the historical present and taking up a career as an academic philosopher, Feuerbach found his new perspective through a radical separation from contemporary culture and a rejection of the academic world.

The first three years of Feuerbach's self-imposed exile from the present in the bucolic atmosphere of Bruckberg were the most creative and productive years of his life. It was during this period that he connected his critical analysis of the nature and presuppositions of Christian faith and culture to a fundamental transformation of his philosophical inheritance, and formulated the distinctive "anthropological" position that had such a liberating effect on his intellectual contemporaries. His new perspective was first clearly and convincingly articulated in *The Essence of Christianity,* which was completed in 1840 and published in 1841. In the preface, Feuerbach stated that the book "epitomized," "amplified," and "explicated" the occasional, aphoristic, polemical thoughts and Christianity, religion, theology, and speculative philosophy that were scattered throughout his previous books and articles.[44] But *The Essence of Christianity* was more than a collection or summary of Feuerbach's previously stated opinions. Although the work was unsystematic, repetitious, and rhetorical, it achieved the undeniably exciting and epiphanylike quality of a unified vision that resolved old problems by viewing them in a new perspective. With the revolutionary simplicity of a new philosophical Copernicus, Feuerbach exploded "the old metaphysical standpoint of the absolute" by unveiling the "secret" of religion, theology, and speculative philosophy as the self-alienation, reification, and mystification of the essential powers of the concrete human subject, man in nature. The ultimate identity of spirit and nature was to be found not in the actualization of "the self-consciousness of God" in nature and humanity, but in the self-actualization and self-comprehension of man as both a natural and spiritual being.

Feuerbach was quite ready to admit that his breakthrough to this "anthropological" perspective was connected to his social experience and social position. "More than man himself is aware," he commented in 1838, "his class and his profession influence his way of thinking, his inner life, his faith." Inevitably and unconsciously the individual tended to conform his opinions to his "office (*Amt*)."[45] During his student years, Feuerbach had perceived the academic office as peculiarly universal, as a cultural position in which the individual was transformed into an "organ" of the totality of scientific knowledge. As late as 1834–5 he was willing to concede the compatibility between his philosophical calling and an academic career within the "cooperative totality" of the Hegelian school. By 1838, however, he was convinced that the office of university professor and the philosophical vocation could not be reconciled. Appointment to an academic office presupposed and demanded conformity to the self-deceptions of a particular social class within a particular historical culture. The achievement of a truly universal, human perspective required a total break with the academic world and the specific social and cultural limitations it embodied and articulated. "Philosophy is essentially free spirit," Feuerbach claimed, "and thus the privilege only of free men."[46] He even insisted on his independence from all institutional or party connections in his relationship to the Left Hegelians. Although he contributed to the *Hallische Jahrbücher,* and was ready to defend the Left Hegelians as the only genuine philosophers of his age, he refused to make any binding commitments to either Ruge's journal or the Left Hegelian "party." He persistently rejected Ruge's and Bauer's invitations to join the "brethren" in Dresden or on the Rhine. His isolation in the "woods" of Bruckberg, he claimed, was the experiential basis of his philosophical commitment to the universally human. "I am . . . something," he wrote to Kapp in 1840, "as long as I am nothing."[47]

Feuerbach believed that his apparent isolation in Bruckberg not only gave him the intellectual freedom from social and cultural presuppositions demanded by his philosophical vocation, but also opened up realms of experience that were closed to the academic philosopher and radical urban journalist. In a retrospective comment in 1860 he interpreted his opposition to Hegel in terms of the differences in their "external fates." Hegel's conception of man and nature as objectifications of the absolute spirit expressed his social and cultural position as an "absolute professor" ruling the world from his lectern. The actuality of the natural, empirical world did not enter the classroom, and the problem of dealing with the "other self" as a real, existing individual was relegated to the state. In Bruckberg, however, the world of nature and concrete human relationships was the unavoidable actuality of the philosopher's experience and a constant, living negation of the pretensions of the absolute spirit.[48]

The shift in philosophical perspective that followed Feuerbach's break with the intellectual "estate" of the established culture was clearly articulated in the opening pages of *The Essence of Christianity.* The defining characteristic of man, Feuerbach claimed, was self-consciousness. Man was "a being to whom his species, his essential nature, is an object of thought."[49] In contrast to animals, man possessed both an inner and an outer life, an individual and an "essential" or "infinite" consciousness. Insofar as man was conscious of his own essential nature as a human being, the separation and limitations of individual finitude were overcome. Man was both "I" and "thou"; he could "put himself in the place of another."[50] Up to this point, Feuerbach's analysis was not fundamentally different from the position of his 1828 dissertation. What was new in 1841 was the definition of man's "essential nature." In 1828 it had been defined as "Reason," and man's elevation from individuality to universality had been described as an elevation to union with absolute Reason. In the *Essence*, however, Feuerbach defined human nature as "Reason, Will, Affection." This trinity did not consist of attributes or faculties that connected man to some infinite entity, some absolute outside himself, but was in itself the absolute nature, the "essence," of man. "Man exists to think, love and will," Feuerbach insisted.[51] The dichotomies of universal and particular, infinite and finite, thus did not represent an antithesis of Reason and feeling, of the absolute spirit and the natural man, but were "nothing else than the antithesis between human nature in general and the human individual."[52]

The central element of Feuerbach's new cultural stance was the transformation of the absolute from spirit or Reason into "man." "Man cannot get beyond his true nature," Feuerbach insisted.[53] To conceive of an absolute spirit or a transcendent God that was somehow above, beyond, or apart from human nature required an extrahuman perspective and was thus simply not possible for man. Yet religion, theology, and speculative philosophy were based on the presupposition of such an extrahuman perspective from which human nature could be viewed as in some way faulty, defective, limited. One of Feuerbach's primary objectives in *The Essence of Christianity* was to demonstrate that the alleged universal "objects" to which man related in religion and theology were illusions. These "objects" were "nothing else than the subject's own nature taken objectively"; they were "objectifications" of man's own essential nature as a rational, emotive, and volitional being.[54] Feuerbach's criticism of the viewpoint of religion and theology was based on a conception of *Wissenschaft* or philosophy that revealed his own emancipation from the speculative metaphysic of absolute idealism. In 1841, as in 1828, he described Christian religion and modern philosophy as antithetical world views. But by 1841, Feuerbach's definition of philosophy had undergone a radical transformation.

Feuerbach's criticisms of Hegel between 1828 and 1838 were "internal" criticisms; they were grounded in a philosophical viewpoint that remained within the general context of speculative idealism. The unity of thought and being, "subject" and "substance," in the dynamic "becoming" of absolute spirit was the unquestioned presupposition on which Feuerbach based his prophetic hopes for an incarnation of the spirit in life, his historical attempts to reappropriate the past, and his epistemological attempts to "vindicate" nature. In fact, this speculative standpoint was viewed as synonymous with philosophy itself. After the early 1830s, however, Feuerbach recognized that the viewpoint of absolute idealism was not a particular possession of Hegel. Hegel's philosophy was the culmination, the perfected systematic expression, of speculative philosophy in general.[55] Feuerbach's criticism of Hegel's predecessors and rivals in the speculative tradition, especially Schelling and his followers, thus revealed the embryo of his criticism of Hegel himself. His statement in 1838 that there was "an essential difference between philosophy and speculation" led directly to the critique of Hegel's "speculation" in 1839.[56]

Feuerbach's critique of the speculative standpoint was grounded in his earlier criticism of Christian religion and theology. The focus of that criticism had been his claim that Christian religious consciousness conceived the absolute as a subjective individual ego, as an absolute transcendent personality that governed history and nature from above like an arbitrary despot. Theology had tried to give conceptual form to the concrete images and representations of religious imagination and feeling, and as early as 1835, Feuerbach had claimed that the speculative theism of Stahl and other Schellingeans remained caught in the theological perspective.[57] In 1837, Feuerbach added a further element to his description of the theological standpoint: It was essentially "practical," originating in finite human needs and desires.[58] To perceive God as an individual, personal being was to bring him into a meaningful relationship to the particular personal needs and wishes of the individual human subject. Speculative theism, like Christian religion and theology, was thus an "ideological" system: It presented the projected image of finite human need as an objective, infinite truth.

Between 1828 and 1838, Feuerbach saw the alternative to this subjective, practical, and ideological standpoint in Hegel's objective, scientific comprehension of the absolute as the self-determining, necessary structure of Reason. If the absolute was comprehended as the infinite unity of Reason, then man, insofar as he was a rational being, could elevate himself to the status of a transparent organ of the absolute. He could free himself from the needs and desires of finite subjectivity and know the absolute on its own terms. In his study of Leibniz, Feuerbach called this the "theoretical" in contrast to the "practical" standpoint. In thinking activity the object of consciousness was not a projection of subjective need, but the real universal substance: The absolute was understood from the standpoint of the absolute, "for itself" and thus "objectively."[59]

Feuerbach was not averse to calling his philosophical viewpoint "pantheism" as long as the identity of the universal and the particular, spirit and nature, was defined as an identity in "essence," not a simple congruency between the empirical appearance and the speculative *Begriff*. This "pantheism" was especially attacked by Schelling, Baader, Anton Günther, and other speculative theists as a species of self-worship, as a projection of the thinking self into the place of the infinite transcendent God. In his extensive critique of the speculative theists in 1838, Feuerbach reversed the charges. The personal God of the speculative theists was simply a projection, an "objectification," of their own "shallow" and "egoistic" selves.[60] Moreover, because this self-projection was not understood as a self-projection, it was transformed into a self-alienation. The projected self was perceived as an "objective" absolute personality; it became the creative source of the projecting self. The human was unconsciously made into the divine, and then the human was consciously perceived as secondary, as derivative from the divine.[61]

Feuerbach was particularly critical of the self-projecting stance of the speculative theists because of what he called their "positivism." The self-divinization of the speculative theists was a divinization of the impenetrable immediacy of the individual ego; they elevated the particular individual to a higher status than that of the universal essence of man as spirit. But the explanatory model of self-objectification and self-alienation could also be applied to the pantheistic view, and Feuerbach admitted that Hegel himself was not entirely free of the "intoxicated," self-alienating, mystical speculation that characterized the philosophy of his day.[62]

It was on the basis of his insight into the self-objectifying, self-alienating process of speculative thinking that Feuerbach was able to unify and transform his former "doubts" into an emancipation from the Hegelian system. These "doubts" had become an often-repeated group of internal criticisms between 1828 and 1838. By 1838, Feuerbach had come to realize that the problems of the historical relativism of Hegel's system, of its relationship to Christian culture, and of the "vindication" of the empirical world all centered on the question of the incarnation of the absolute in the world, the infinite in the finite. Unlike Bauer and Strauss, however, Feuerbach approached this question not through an analysis of the historical Christ, but through an analysis of the historical Hegel.

"It is a speculative superstition to believe in a real incarnation of philosophy in a determinate historical appearance," Feuerbach claimed in 1838.[63] The Hegelian school was obviously guilty of such "speculative superstition." Was this weakness inherent in the Hegelian philosophy? Feuerbach thought it was. Hegel had overemphasized historical succession in his description of the Moments of Reason's self-actualization and self-determination. As a result, the concluding Moment of absolute self-comprehending unity was conceived as a particular stage in historical time. Feuerbach criticized this claim as part of an untenable belief in the possibility of the incarnation of the infinite in the finite, the absolute in the individual. The *deus terminus* stood as "watchman at the entrance of the world." "Reason . . . knows nothing of the real absolute incarnation of the species in a definite individuality," Feuerbach insisted; ". . . what once enters into time and space must conform to the laws of time and space."[64] Like Strauss's rejection of the Christian incarnation in 1835, Feuerbach's rejection of the incarnation of infinite Reason in any historical individual marked a radical break with Hegel's ontology. Reason was conceived no longer as a transcendent, suprahuman power that gave itself actuality, determinate form, in the evolution of human existence and self-consciousness, but simply as the immanent telos of human existence and self-consciousness. The goal of history was not the reconciliation between God and man, but the actualization and self-comprehension of man's essential capacities and powers, his "species being." Moreover, like Strauss, Feuerbach claimed that this process of human self-actualization and self-knowledge could be conceived only as a collective act, as the act of a "we" rather than an "I." Was the actualization of human essence in a single historical individual possible? Feuerbach answered with a quotation from Goethe: "Only the totality of men . . . live the human."[65]

Hegel had been a finite, mortal human being. His philosophy could express no more than he was; his system was merely his own thinking objectified in philosophical language, not thinking itself, or spirit in its own self-determining objectivity. The "necessary" stages of the *Logic* were not mediations within the absolute spirit itself, but "a mediation through language between thinking insofar as it is mine, and thinking insofar as it is his."[66] The self-determination of the *Begriff* in the system was a "formal" activity, not a creation out of nothing, but a development of Hegel's thoughts in such a way that they could become communicable, that they could be appropriated by another. Philosophy did not "give" any objective "Reason" to a person, but presupposed a common possession of the ability to think logically. Philosophical expression in a logical system of concepts was an aspect of the self's drive to have itself affirmed by another, to break through the limitations of its own subjectivity. But no "thing" was expressed in philosophical language. It was merely an objectification of the thinking of a philosopher. It could "have the significance only of a means."[67]

The most perfect means of communicating thought, Feuerbach claimed, was a system in which the end was implicit in the beginning. The process of explication then became a process of revelation. Like other means of communication, philosophical system building was an art: "The system maker is the artist; the history of philosophical systems is the picture gallery – the *Pinakothek* – of Reason."[68] Hegel was the "most perfect philosophical artist," but this strength was also his great weakness. Both for Hegel and for his disciples the true nature of the system as a "means" of communication had been forgotten, or denied, and the system was perceived as Reason itself. The expression of thought for others was transformed into thought itself, the means was "idolized," the form made into essence. The Hegelian system thus became the total self-alienation of human Reason.[69]

By critically unveiling the system of absolute idealism as a self-alienation of Reason, as an expression of thought rather than thought itself, Feuerbach asserted the priority of thinking to the Hegelian "objectification" and thus provided a justification for an independent critical attitude toward Hegelian philosophy. The system began with the concept of "pure being," which allegedly contained the whole system within itself in implicit, undifferentiated form. But why should one accept this premise, this "beginning"? Why could one not simply state that "pure being" was an abstraction that corresponded to nothing real, that only the concrete individual was real? The Hegelian system began with a denial of sensuous reality. Absolute idealism did not begin in a dialogue between the speculative and the empirical viewpoints but presupposed the absolute truth of the speculative position. The dialectic thus became an internal monologue by the speculative thinker. The conclusion of the system – the absolute identity of real and ideal in absolute spirit – was accepted on faith, not based on a convincing refutation of the empirical position. The logical development whereby the incorporation of the real world within the all-encompassing spirit was "demonstrated" was not in "earnest"; it was a mere formal game. For Hegel the unity of subject and object in absolute spirit was an "immediate" truth, an unquestioned presupposition. It was only in his explication that this truth appeared as the "end," as the conclusion of a logical process.[70]

The reason that the Kingdom of the Idea could not be established, that "empiricism" could not be vindicated, from a standpoint within the

Hegelian system was that the system had never taken the reality of immediate sensual existence seriously. The contradictions between thought and being, spirit and nature, remained contradictions within thought, within spirit. Nature never received an independent status; it was reconciled only as the thought of the "otherness" of thought.[71] The victor was predetermined. Hegelian philosophy was uncritical and dogmatic in relationship to its origins in the contradictions of real existence. It was formally critical but not genetically critical. Hegelian philosophy was a "rational mysticism" that was not exempt from the "vanity" of all mystifying speculation that objectified human processes into metaphysical entities and claimed a perspective outside man and nature.[72]

When Feuerbach was negotiating with his publisher about the publication of the book that eventually appeared as *The Essence of Christianity*, he considered giving it the title "Know Thyself."[73] This title expressed his feeling that the main task of contemporary philosophy was the destruction of the illusions that alienated man from his own nature. Philosophy was to become "sober" after its "intoxicating" period of speculative mysticism. A new Copernican revolution in philosophical thinking based on an affirmation of the validity of the human or anthropological perspective would demonstrate that "the simplest views and reasons are the only true views and reasons."[74] The speculative distinction between "reason (*Vernunft*)" and "understanding (*Verstand*)" was "adapted to the justification of every absurdity."[75] Any claim to a philosophical perspective outside healthy common sense (*der gesunde Menschenverstand*) was illusory "transcendentalism."[76]

The illusory nature of speculative philosophy lay in its objectification of human processes as transcendent entities. The critical destruction of the illusions of speculation thus also revealed their psychological or anthropological truth. The negation of self-alienation was a "positive" negation; it "preserved" the truths of speculative philosophy by appropriating the anthropological essence of its mystical objectifications.[77] The new definitions that Feuerbach gave to *Wissenschaft* and spirit revealed the positive, preserving character of his criticism.

Man was defined by his ability to possess self-conscious knowledge of his own essence, to know himself as a "species being." It was this self-consciousness that made him capable of "science (*Wissenschaft*)": "Only a being to whom his own nature is an object of thought can make the essential nature of other things or other beings an object of thought."[78] Insofar as he had attained the standpoint of the species, man was capable of objective, "scientific," or "theoretical" knowledge; he could perceive the objects of his experience as they existed "in themselves."[79]

But the truths of science were human truths; they were validated by human consensus, not by transcendent guarantee:

That which I think according to the standard of the species I think as man in general only can think if he thinks normally . . . That is true which agrees with the nature of the species; that is false which contradicts it. There is no other rule of truth.[80]

The "truth" of the metaphysical doctrine of the evolution of absolute spirit through self-differentiation and objectification to self-conscious unity was revealed as, or reduced to, a psychological truth. Man came to consciousness of his own humanity, Feuerbach claimed, through the agency of other men, through human society. It was only through consciousness of himself that man could comprehend nature or the objective world as something different from himself:

A man existing absolutely alone would lose himself without any sense of his individuality in the ocean of nature; he would comprehend neither himself as man nor nature as nature. The first object of man is man. The sense of nature, which opens to us the consciousness of the world as a world, is a later product; for it arises through the distinction of man from himself.[81]

Thus, as in his earlier writings, Feuerbach perceived the existence of nature for man as a stage within the evolution of consciousness. But in 1841 he rejected the Hegelian notion that this psychological fact meant that the existence of nature was *dependent* on consciousness. Such an absurd conclusion could arise only if the psychological process was projected onto an infinite metaphysical spirit that had to create or "posit" the world in order to come to self-consciousness.

It was in his perception of nature and the empirical world that Feuerbach's break with his speculative inheritance was most obvious. To destroy the illusions of Hegelian speculation meant, for Feuerbach, to vindicate the independence, the reality, of the natural world.[82] Spirit could not exist without nature, because spirit or self-consciousness defined itself in relation to nature. Without nature, "personality, individuality, consciousness" were "nothing." Without "body" there was "no spirit."[83] But Feuerbach had not become a "vulgar empiricist." The attempt to make the human spirit totally derivative from, dependent on, the "facts" of nature represented a "servility of the spirit."[84] In a sense, Feuerbach admitted to a dualistic viewpoint, a dualism of spirit and flesh, freedom and "sexuality."[85] But this dualism was unified in the human existence through which it was defined. The essence of man was "species consciousness" or "spirit," but man could come to self-consciousness and "species consciousness" only if he recognized the reality of his corporeal natural existence. If human nature was defined in terms of a reciprocal relationship between nature and spirit, philosophy – the activity of understanding the nature of man and the world – must begin in a dialogue with its antithesis, sensuous perception. Man could elevate himself to the sphere of theoretical understanding only if he took empirical reality "seriously." Thus, Feuerbach claimed that the definition of the "essence" of religious consciousness should be based on a "genetic" and "empirical" study of religious phenomena.[86] Man could liberate himself from religious illusions only if he understood the origin of those illusions in his actual human experience.

The outlines of Feuerbach's analysis of Christianity and religion in general in *The Essence of Christianity* are well known and do not require a detailed explication here. What is important for our theme is to see how Feuerbach "resolved" the contradictions of Christian consciousness with the aid of his inversion of Hegelian categories and how he related this resolution to the problems of cultural change with which he had been grappling for over a decade.

In religion, as in speculative metaphysics, man projected "his being into objectivity" and then subordinated himself as an "object" to this "projected image of himself."[87] But the speculative philosophy of Hegel was a self-projection of man as a thinking being. In Feuerbach's protean terminology the mere fact of self-projection often defined the nature of the religious relationship. But in contrast to the self-alienation of the speculative philosopher, Feuerbach also recognized a more original or basic religious experience in which God was defined as a "being of the heart," in which the "essence" of religion lay in a "projection of man's essential nature as an emotional and sensuous being, governed and made happy only by images."[88]

Because the essential content of religion was defined as emotional, moral, and imaginative, Feuerbach saw Christology as the central doctrine of the Christian church. Christ was a "person," the divinization of the concrete individual; he was an "image" of God, the divinization of the imagination; he was the expression of universal love, the divinization of man's moral nature; he was the passive suffering God, the divinization of human sensitivity and feeling.[89] In one sense, this projection of human qualities on an objective divine being constituted an alienation of man from his own nature: "To enrich God, man must become poor; that God may be all, man must become nothing."[90] But because this self-alienation was an imaginative, emotional experience, it was not perceived as a self-alienation. In feeling and imagination, Feuerbach claimed, the distinction between subjective and objective was not made. The religious man did not view the projection of his own qualities on a personal God as a self-alienation because he enjoyed and received back what he had renounced "in an incomparably higher and fuller measure" by identifying himself with his projected image, with God.[91] Religious experience thus also constituted a self-affirmation, an affirmation of the absolute, "divine" nature of human qualities: "In the religious systole man propels his own nature from himself, he throws himself outward; in the religious diastole he receives the rejected nature into his heart again."[92]

The origins of the religious projection were man's subjective, "practical," needs and desires. "The end of religion," Feuerbach claimed, "is the welfare, the salvation, the ultimate felicity of man."[93] In the imaginative identification with the divine in religious experience, man freed himself from the limitations of his individual existence. The performance of miracles expressed the essentially wish-fulfilling character of the projected God.[94] Christ's greatest miracle – the redemption of man from his sins – freed man from "the conditions to which virtue is united in the natural course of things,"[95] from his moral obligations as a sexual and communal being.[96]

The wish-fulfilling character of the religious self-projection was described by Feuerbach as "the dream of waking consciousness." In dreams man perceived the "spontaneous action" of his "own mind" as an action that impinged upon him from "without"; emotions were transformed into "events."[97] The passive subordination to the objectification of the subjective wish was what Feuerbach defined as "faith." But this form in which the wish-fulfillment was experienced contradicted its content. Religious symbols, like the images of human dreams, contained not only a self-affirming psychological or anthropological element but also a self-denying "pathological" element.[98] The Christian teaching of the unity of the individual and the species in self-sacrificing love was expressed in the form of a personal God of love to whom man was to devote his total being. The unity of mankind in an ethical community of love was transformed into a particular unity with a personal "external" being, an "outward fact."[99] In faith, therefore, Feuerbach saw "a malignant principle." Man's relationship to his own nature in the form of "faith" transformed the religious experience from an affirmation of human nature into a pathological denial of human nature.[100]

The contradictions within the religious experience were thus "explained" as necessary aspects of man's relationship to his own nature in the form of "faith." The primary emphasis in *The Essence of Christianity* was on an analysis of man's consciousness in the age of "faith," on the "pure," original Christianity of the Middle Ages. But Feuerbach did not conceive his book as a contribution to the historical study of medieval Christendom; it was meant to have a practical contemporary effect.[101] These contemporary aims were clearly evident in the evolutionary perspective in which he placed his analysis of Christianity.

Much like Strauss, Feuerbach described the imaginative, emotional, self-projecting consciousness of medieval Christianity as the consciousness of a "primitive," "oriental" stage in the evolution of human culture.[102] It was the earliest form of self-knowledge, which preceded philosophical understanding "in the history of the race as also in that of the individual."[103] For the child, or primitive man, moral laws were efficacious only as divine commandments. The child was necessarily determined in his actions from without. To have his own essential nature work on him with the irresistible powers of feeling and imagination was beneficial and even necessary. While religion remained on the level of the subject-object unity of sensuous "immediacy," it was not in contradiction with philosophical understanding, but a necessary stage toward a more self-conscious and mature self-knowledge.[104]

The naive, childlike stage of Christian culture had begun to disintegrate in the Renaissance and Reformation. As more and more of man's secular activity was emancipated from religious tutelage, Christianity became less and less a religion "of the heart" and was transformed into a theological religion. Man's alienation from his own nature now became most evident in the theoretical realm, in the conflict between faith and reason. Theological reflection destroyed the unconscious unity of subjective and objective in religion. Historical "proofs" and rational "demonstrations" could not rehabilitate the former "immediate" feeling of identity between man and his projected essence.[105] Hegel's speculative metaphysics represented the culmination of the theological attempt to salvage the transcendent "objectivity," the content of the traditional faith. Hegel's vision of the union of finite and infinite was the ultimate self-projection of human nature into a transcendent "other." Hegel's *Logic* merely expressed in concepts what religion had invested "with imagination";[106] it was only "a consistent carrying out, a completion of a religious truth."[107] The destruction of the self-alienating mysticism of speculative philosophy thus represented man's final liberation from religious consciousness, his reappropriation of his own essential nature.

Feuerbach was convinced that the present was the "necessary turning point in history" in which man had finally come to the realization that the "consciousness of God was nothing less than the consciousness of the species."[108] Philosophy had ceased to be simply a rationalized version of Christian consciousness and had become the great instrument of liberation, the destroyer of the illusions that alienated man from himself. Unlike Strauss, however, Feuerbach did not think that the new culture would be defined simply by philosophical knowledge, and, unlike Bauer, he did not interpret the leap into the future as a liberation of human "self-consciousness" from all cultural objectifications. The return of man to himself, the reappropriation of human nature, meant that man was to establish a new cultural order in which he would affirm his own nature as a rational, emotional, and volitional being.

The old order had been characterized by man's projections of his own essence into a transcendent heaven. The new order would be characterized by man's realization of his own essence in an "earthly heaven." The means by which the New Jerusalem would be established was "culture" or "cultivation (*Bildung*)."[109] Feuerbach's continual use of the word *Bildung* to describe the defining characteristic of the new order was an expression of a vision of cultural liberation that would include the whole man, and not just the human spirit. Insofar as man was a self-conscious rational being, of course, "culture" was a spiritual or theoretical activity. "Culture, in general," Feuerbach wrote, "is nothing else than the exaltation of the individual above his subjectivity to objective universal ideas, to the contemplation of the world."[110] The Christian religion provided an illusory compensation for individual subjectivity through an imaginary union with an omniscient God. In "culture" the subjective deficiencies of the individual were overcome through a progressive elevation to "species consciousness." In the new order man could attain "objective" knowledge, a knowledge without illusions.[111]

But the victory of human *Bildung* over religious self-alienation also had an ethical significance. In Christianity the ethical imperfections of the subjective ego were viewed as determining the human condition. Man's estrangement from a genuine community, his separation from the rest of humanity, his inability to achieve "wholeness," was overcome only in an illusory fashion, through an imaginary supernatural salvation.[112] From the standpoint of human *Bildung*, however, the ethical incompleteness of man could be overcome through the incarnation of "species consciousness" in the real community of men, through friendship and love. Salvation from the finitude of the subjective ego came through the "species," which the individual encountered as the other man or the other woman. "Only community constitutes humanity," Feuerbach insisted, and the individual became a participant in community through the consciousness "that the thou belongs to the perfection of the I, that men are required to constitute humanity."[113] For the individual "I," the "thou" was the Christ who mediated between the individual and the universality of the species. The central ethical principle of the new cultural order would be *Homo homini Deus est.* "This is the axis," Feuerbach claimed, "on which revolves the history of the world."[114]

The theoretical destruction of the illusions of Christian religion and speculative philosophy would not in itself bring about the historical actualization of the New Jerusalem. The notion that salvation was a free gift of grace passively received was a part of the old Christian order. "Culture overcomes the limits of sensuous consciousness and life by real activity," Feuerbach stated.[115] The successful creation of an earthly heaven required that the relationship of the individual to the universal be transformed from the passive relationship of prayer to the active one of creative labor. Commitment to the fulfillment of one's humanity through creative labor was based on the destruction of the wish-fulfilling illusions of Christianity, on an acceptance of the limited "conditionality" of a world in which every effect had a natural cause and every aim required a corresponding operation for its fulfillment. The undeluded man of the post-Christian era would transform his "attainable wishes" into "objects of real activity."[116]

For Feuerbach, the motivating impulse of the self-alienating projections of Christian consciousness – the need to find compensation for the poverty and imperfection of individual existence – remained in the new order as the driving impulse of *Bildung.* The "sense of poverty" was the "impulse to all culture."[117] Theoretical science, ethical community, and creative labor were all expressions of man's striving to actualize his essence, his "species being," in real life. The attainment of "species being" was an overcoming of subjective individuality; *Bildung* required "the northern principle of self-renunciation."[118] But this self-renunciation was not the same as the self-renunciation demanded by Christianity. The compensation for renunciation was not a transcendent illusion but the appropriation of one's essential humanity.

If culture was activity with a purpose, Feuerbach claimed, it could also, in a sense, be described as a new "religion." What Feuerbach meant by this statement was that in order to attain the practical realization of his "species being," man must have that "species being" as the aim of his activity, and "he who has an aim . . . has *eo ipso* a religion."[119] All aspects of life that expressed man's activity as a "species being" were "sacred": marriage, love, friendship, labor, knowledge. "The idea of activity, of making, of creation is in itself a divine idea," Feuerbach claimed. In the activity of *Bildung* man was creating himself, transforming his existence into his essence. Such labor was a "joyful activity," for it was "in accordance with our own nature."[120] "Religion" was universal in the sense that "every man must place before himself a God."[121] But the God that man placed before himself in the post-Christian world was "man," not as an objectified transcendent being who demanded passive subordination, but as his own essential nature that required practical realization.

As Feuerbach wrote *The Essence of Christianity,* therefore, he appeared supremely confident that his critical unveiling of the human, "anthropological" content of the transcendent objects of religious feeling and imagination, theological reflection and philosophical speculation, provided the long-sought-for "positive" foundation for the historical emergence of a post-Christian cultural community in which dualism and heteronomy would finally be abolished, and man would become the autonomous maker of his own history, the subject and object of his own theory and practice. By comprehending the hidden content of the religious image, theological dogma, and metaphysical Idea as the essential nature of human existence, as man's "species being," Feuerbach contended, he was not simply creating another philosophical theory of man. The human essence that was the object of anthropological knowledge was not an abstraction, an object or determination of pure thought, but the self-comprehension of the real, sensuous, practical existence of human beings in nature and history. The new theory was not divorced from "practice," from the desires, feelings, and needs of the "heart," but was this practice, or existential being, comprehended, raised to self-consciousness. Thus, Feuerbach claimed that his anthropological theory was not just scientific knowledge, an objective, demythologized, critical understanding of the empirically real, but also "religion," or, we might say, "ideology." But this positive humanism, this religion without self-alienation in which the comprehended essence of man's concrete existence would become the object of his theory and practice, was not systematically elaborated in *The Essence of Christianity.* Thus it was not always obvious what Feuerbach meant when he claimed that man's universal essence, his "species being," *was* his concrete, practical existence, that "species consciousness" was nothing more than the self-conscious awareness of the nature of sensuous human being-in-the-world, or that the particular could be grasped as the universal, nature as spirit, without transcending the realm of the particular and nature. In fact, the positive appropriation and articulation of the real, natural, human kernel of Hegel's metaphysical "concrete universal" turned out to be a much more problematic and complex operation than Feuerbach's optimistic and rhetorical "inversions" had originally indicated. As Feuerbach focused on the systematic explication of the positive content of the "new philosophy" that was also "religion," of the theory that was at the same time "an autonomous deed of mankind,"[122] in the years after 1841, it became increasingly clear that his anthropological reduction of Christian religion, theology, and metaphysics had not dissolved the contradictions of all previous historical experience and thought, but rather had reconstituted these contradictions in a new form. In this experience of disillusionment that turned the proffered solution into a new problematic, Feuerbach was not alone. His fate was exemplary of the movement of Left Hegelian humanism as a whole.

Epilogue: beyond "man" – the rise and fall of Left Hegelian humanism

During the summer and fall of 1841 the general principles of philosophical, dialectical humanism that had been developed in the critical writings of Strauss, Bauer, and Feuerbach between 1835 and 1841 were tenuously and temporarily consolidated into the collective ideology of a small but vociferous group of philosophic radicals – the Left Hegelian "movement" or "party." Although this Left Hegelian movement has attracted an enormous amount of scholarly attention because of its significance in the early intellectual development of Marx and Engels, it was an ephemeral historical phenomenon. Not only for Marx and Engels, but also for thinkers like Bauer and Feuerbach, who have so often been fixated in, retrospectively defined by, their Left Hegelian stance, the Left Hegelian movement was a crucial but limited and passing historical Moment that came to an end in the spring of 1843 when the repressive censorship policy of the Prussian government forced the two major journalistic organs, and only significant organizational focal points of the movement – Ruge's *Jahrbücher* and the *Rheinische Zeitung* – to cease publication. The revolutionary hope that had sustained and unified the Left Hegelian movement, despite internal tensions, throughout 1842 was revealed, by the actual course of historical events, as a self-deceiving illusion. Out of this disillusioning revelation emerged a new period of reassessment, self-criticism, division, and reconstruction.

If Left Hegelianism is placed in context and viewed from a historical perspective, its development divides quite obviously into three major phases. This particular account of Hegelianism has culminated in the first phase of Left Hegelianism: the genesis of its theoretical foundations in the humanist inversions of Hegelian metaphysics in the critical writings of Strauss, Bauer, and Feuerbach. An equally detailed description of the second and third phases, of the Moment of ideological consolidation and attempted historical actualization and the Moment of division, disintegration, and reconstruction, must be postponed to a future study. At this point I would simply like to sketch the general trajectory of Left Hegelian humanism after 1841 from the perspective of the dominant themes and problems of this study.

The emergence of Left Hegelian humanism as the ideology of a distinguishable "party" or intellectual faction first became historically evident in a shift to the left of the editorial policy of the *Hallische Jahrbücher*. From the time Ruge first openly condemned the "hierarchical," "Romantic," and "Catholic" elements in the Prussian administration during the fall of 1839 until he was forced to change his base of operations from Halle to Dresden because of the threat of Prussian censorship in June 1841, the criticism of the political and cultural policies of the established regime articulated in the leading articles of the *Jahrbücher* was marked by a steadily increasing virulence and belligerence. But this opposition to the existing Prussian regime remained a loyal opposition and was formulated within the philosophical and historical framework of the liberal Hegelian Center. The reactionary policies of the government were denounced for their divergence from the authentic inner "spirit" of Prussian political development and the Protestant tradition. Between 1839 and 1841 the oppositional stance of the *Jahrbücher* could be summarized in two demands: (1) that the state consciously recognize and reappropriate the Hegelian Idea of concrete freedom as the basis and telos of its historical development; and (2) that it engage in a progressive actualization of this principle through a political policy of reform that would transform the tutelary state into the genuine ethical community of a liberal constitutional monarchy and a cultural policy that would recognize the free development of Hegelian *Wissenschaft* as the highest form of Protestant Christianity.

By the summer of 1841, however, Ruge had become convinced that the "Christian state" of Frederick William IV could and would never accede to these demands and reform itself from within. After the *Jahrbücher* emigrated from Prussia and became the *Deutsche Jahrbücher*, however, its editorial stance became rapidly identified with a total opposition to the existing political and cultural system theoretically grounded in the atheistic humanism of Bauer and Feuerbach. As the *Jahrbücher* became more radical, however, its intellectual base became increasingly narrow. The majority of reformist, liberal Hegelians, including the *Jahrbücher*'s coeditor Theodor Echtermeyer, resisted Ruge's shift to the left and withdrew their support.[1] These "defections" involved not only the moderate Prussian academics like Michelet, Hotho, Werder, the Benary brothers, Vatke, Rosenkranz, Hinrichs, and Schaller, but virtually the whole Swabian contingent of the school, including Strauss and Vischer. When most censorship restrictions were lifted in Prussia on December 24, 1841, the *Deutsche Jahrbücher* entered the ensuing ideological fray as the organ of a relatively small group of nonacademic Prussian intellectuals. Although occasional articles by moderate Prussian academics and Swabian Hegelians continued to appear in the *Jahrbücher* until it ceased publication in January 1843, they no longer set the tone of the journal.

The most prominent figures in the Left Hegelian movement of 1841–3 were Ruge, Bauer, and Feuerbach. Although Ruge was not an original or systematic theorist, or even a particulary trenchant critic, his wide-ranging interests, journalistic and organizational talents, political passion, and enormous energy made him into a representative figure and leader of this phase of Left Hegelianism. Journalistic criticism, in which Left Hegelian principles were propagated in sloganlike fashion and applied to contemporary, especially political, issues, rather than large-scale treatises devoted to the construction and clarification of principles, was the characteristic mode of expression during this phase. In fact, the history of Left Hegelianism in 1841 and 1842 can almost be written as a history of the journals in which they had a predominant influence: Ruge's *Jahrbücher;* the *Rheinische Zeitung,* edited first by Rutenberg and then by Marx; the liberal *Leipziger Allgemeine Zeitung*, which opened its columns to the radical Berlin Hegelians in 1841–2; and the short-lived *Athenäum* and *Patriot.* The troops of the Left Hegelian movement were not scholars and philosophers but journalists, free-lance authors, and coffeehouse intellectuals like Eduard Meyen, Ludwig Buhl, Adolf Rutenberg, Friedrich Köppen, Karl Nauwerck, and Edgar Bauer, whose relationship to the state was largely negative (evasion of censorship and avoidance of the police) and who lived on the margins of respectable middle-class society. In Berlin, Left Hegelian humanism emerged, in the summer and fall of 1841, as the ideology of a coterie of *Weinstube* literati within the subculture of the city's intellectual proletariat, a group that called itself The Free (*Die Freien*) and was described by the Prussian police as "literati who make a vocation out of journalism and political argument."[2] But it would be misleading to reduce the Left Hegelian movement to journalistic manipulation, popularization, and vulgarization of inherited ideas and ideals. As the intellectual itineraries of not only Bauer and Feuerbach, but also Marx, Engels, Hess, and Stirner, attest, it was also a crucial historical test of the new humanist ideology and thus a major presupposition for the critical revisions and creative reconstructions that followed.

For Bauer and Feuerbach the two years of the Left Hegelian movement were an exhilarating and demanding time. After years of relative obscurity they suddenly found themselves in the public eye as intellectual mentors of a party of radical, atheistic "Jacobins." Bauer and Feuerbach, Ruge claimed in the fall of 1841, had raised the banner of "the Mountain" on German soil.[3] In contrast to Hegel, their historical moment seemed to have arrived almost simultaneously with their breakthrough to a new intellectual principle. Neither Bauer nor Feuerbach repudiated the historical role that was thrust upon them, although Feuerbach did not revel in it quite as much as Bauer. Both focused their intellectual energies on the needs and problems of Left Hegelian humanism as a historical movement – the translation of the new principles into an ideology that could have a broad public impact (a new version of the old Hegelian problem of a *Volksreligion*), the application of the new principles to the process of political reform and/or revolution, and the general relationship between theoretical principle and concrete activity or "practice." It is important to emphasize, because Bauer and Feuerbach are so often seen as proponents of opposing idealist and materialist versions of Left Hegelian humanism, that in 1841 and 1842 they saw themselves as participants in a common movement. Bauer greeted Feuerbach as a fellow "apostle" of the new humanism and as a "brother" in the battle against the "infamy" of Christian religion and politics.[4] Feuerbach also stressed his identity or "communality (*Gemeinsamkeit*)" with the other Left Hegelians and decried petty quarrels among individuals committed to the same cause. "What stupidity," he wrote to Ruge in 1842, "to forfeit the only means – the impression of compact unity – through which the world and its rulers might be impressed."[5] An examination of the common perspectives that made this consciousness of identity between Bauer and Feuerbach possible illuminates the core of Left Hegelian ideology in the second phase of its development.

Up to 1841, Bauer and Feuerbach had developed and articulated their new humanist perspective in the indirect fashion of a critical negation and inversion of Christian religion, theology, and speculative philosophy. They continued to emphasize the historical importance of the critical destruction of inherited illusions after 1841. "Only he who has the courage to be absolutely negative also has the power to create something new," Feuerbach claimed.[6] The positive affirmation of "man" as "man's highest being" presupposed "the renunciation of a God who is other than man." Atheism and humanism were correlative terms.[7] Similarly, Bauer continued to call for a ruthless criticism of all forms of religious and theological self-alienation. "The inner core, the essence of the matter, must be unveiled," he insisted; "the depth of the spirit must be torn open so that mankind will know where it stands, so that our essence, which has been taken away from us . . . once again returns to us as our true, pure essence, develops within us, and finally makes us free."[8] At the same time, it is clear that after 1841, Bauer and Feuerbach conceived their primary task as the positive articulation and explication of the "truths" of human "species being" and "species consciousness" that had emerged from their critical destruction of the illusions of religion and philosophy. "Not the idea," Feuerbach claimed, "but the working out of the idea makes the man."[9] What this "working out" implied was a demonstration that the new theory was not *just* theory, an abstract philosophical construction, but a convincing and inclusive self-comprehension of man's actual, concrete activity as a historico-cultural (for Bauer) and a natural (for Feuerbach) being.

Between 1841 and 1843, Feuerbach was obviously more troubled by the complexity and difficulty of this task of positive construction than Bauer. Although Bauer's reconstruction of human history as a completely secular, immanent development toward the freedom and unity of "self-consciousness" was sketchy at best, he confidently proclaimed, in July 1842, that he had spoken the "decisive word" that allowed contemporary men to appropriate fully their essential human nature. The crisis of "principle" or "theory" had been resolved; the task that remained was "practical recognition."[10] Feuerbach agreed that what was needed was the "decisive word": "We must concentrate into one ultimate principle, one ultimate word, what we wish to be; only thus can we sanctify our life and determine its direction."[11] Although he occasionally indicated that this word was simply "man,"[12] he was not as confident as Bauer that the new humanism had been formulated in a convincing fashion. His relative detachment from the Prussian Hegelians' journalistic campaigns was grounded in a concern that the desire for immediate political impact might be premature. The first goal must be clarity and decisiveness in matters of fundamental principle. Once this was achieved, "everything else will eventually follow on its own."[13]

Feuerbach's hesitations regarding the political tactics of the Prussian Left Hegelians, however, should not be construed as a disinterest in politics or a rejection of the significance of political practice in the creation of a new "human" culture. Like Bauer, Ruge, and other Left Hegelians, Feuerbach saw politics or the state as the realm in which man produced the perfected objectification of his essential nature, his "species being." "The true state is the unlimited, infinite, true, perfect, and whole man," he claimed. "It is primarily the state in which man emerges as man; the state in which the man who relates himself to himself is the self-determining, absolute man."[14] In politics man self-consciously made his own essence the object of his activity, produced himself as his own god. In this sense, politics was the historical form of the new "religion" of anthropotheism.

The politics of the Left Hegelian movement of 1841–3 had two major dimensions. First, the Left Hegelians demanded the emancipation of the state from the church, the creation of a completely secular, immanent human community. This demand corresponded to the humanist reduction in its most general form. Man was henceforth to seek his salvation, achieve reconciliation with himself as a universal being, within the structure of his this-worldly communal activity and relationships. However, the Left Hegelians also claimed that the creation of a secular state necessarily implied a radical change of traditional political forms. Hierarchical authority and legal privilege were expressions of the self-alienation and fragmentation of Christian religious consciousness. A "true" and "free" state would take the form of an egalitarian, democratic republic in which everyone would recognize and live the communal will as his own will. Only a state that was a real "communal being (*Gemeinwesen*)," Feuerbach insisted, could make heaven superfluous, by abolishing the need for heaven.[15]

How was such a state to be created? This question leads to the central problematic of the Left Hegelian movement. Bauer, Ruge, Feuerbach, and the other Left Hegelians believed that the humanistic inversion of Hegelian metaphysics preserved the real, immanent content of the Hegelian dialectic. Their theories of "man" and "state" were to be conceived not as mere abstractions, but as true self-comprehensions of the real structure of human activity and consciousness previously veiled by the self-alienating forms of religious faith and philosophical speculation. Because theory was the comprehension of concrete existence, practice made self-aware, their primary "political" task was defined as public enlightenment, as the destruction of illusions and critical unveiling of the real human needs and interests previously hidden and distorted by these illusions. It is misguided to accuse the Left Hegelians of transforming the Hegelian dialectic into an abstract "antithetic" between a moral ideal and existing reality.[16] Their negation was not of "reality" but of the illusions that hid reality from their contemporaries. In this sence, Marx's well-known statement from 1843 can stand as a representative expression of the Left Hegelians' conception of the relationship between theory and practice:

> The reform of consciousness consists *only* in enabling the world to clarify its consciousness, in waking it from its dreams about itself, in explaining to it the meaning of its actions . . . We can therefore encapsulate the tendency of our journal in one word: self-comprehension (critical philosophy) of the age con-

cerning its own struggles and desires . . . It is a matter of confession, no more. To have its sins forgiven, mankind has only to declare them for what they really are.[17]

The problem with this conception of the relationship between theory and practice was not that it was undialectical, but that it was proved false by historical developments. The "age" and the "people" did not recognize their struggles and desires in Left Hegelian ideology. The revolutionary confidence of the Left Hegelian movement of 1841–3 was sustained by the belief that the new humanism simply brought to consciousness the actual movement of history and the real desires and needs of the "people." In order to understand how this belief arose and why it eventually disintegrated, we must turn to the "experiential matrix" of the Left Hegelian movement.

The historical emergence of the Left Hegelian movement is usually interpreted as a direct response to the reactionary social, political, and cultural policies of the regime of Frederick William IV.[18] This view, however, is much too mechanical and arbitrary. The specific events in Prussia during the early 1840s had such a profound impact on the consciousness of Left Hegelians because they crystallized general and long-term social, political, and cultural tensions in an extreme form. The three major dimensions of these tensions have already been described in Chapters 1, 3, and 7. The Prussian "crisis" of the early 1840s was first of all, and most obviously, a political crisis in which the tutelary role of the bureaucratic state was challenged by a movement for liberal constitutional reform both within the administrative classes themselves and among the recently emerged capitalist bourgeoisie of the Rhineland and East Prussia. The conflicts within the administration helped dispel the last vestiges of the Hegelian myth of the "universal class," and the external liberal movement aroused a belief among many Left Hegelians that they were in the midst of a general process of political transformation.[19]

The second major factor in the Prussian crisis of the early 1840s was the pauperization and proletarization of increasingly large numbers of rural and urban artisans and laborers and of university-educated youth. The combination of the legal and demographic changes analyzed in Chapter 7, with the expansion of unrestricted market relations and technological innovation and new forms of industrial organization in key industries like metallurgy and textiles had created a vast, mobile, visible "mass" of the economically destitute, socially disinherited, and politically "homeless" in German society.[20] Hegel, Gans, and Carové had already been aware of pauperization and social alienation as significant, troubling side effects of the freedoms of civil society, but it was only in the 1840s that the "social question" moved into the center of intellectual and public concern, and presented the historical possibility – which could be conceived as either a threat or a hope – of a total negation of the existing system, in both its reactionary and its liberal aspects, in the name of more inclusive forms of social and political community. Proletarization and social disinheritance were not only crucial components of the experiential matrix of Left Hegelians; they also defined their historical task: to educate the disinherited to a consciousness of their freedom, to transform the passive victims of historical change into the active subjects of their own history. The major aim of Left Hegelian journalism – the preeminent form of their revolutionary activity – was not simply to articulate the particular interests of "youth" or the "people," but to transform the consciousness of these "masses" into the self-consciousness of a revolutionary, "human" subject. It was the failure of this theoretical practice of cultural education that turned the external repression of Left Hegelian journals in 1843 into an internal crisis of historical consciousness and confidence for the Left Hegelian movement.

The emphasis on theoretical practice, on the transformation of consciousness, in Left Hegelian ideology revealed that for the Left Hegelians of 1841–2 the most significant dimension of the Prussian crisis was the crisis of cultural values, the conflict over the fundamental presuppositions of communal life. The regime of Frederick William IV had connected its restorationist social and political policy to an attempt to impose a specific form of Christian "disposition (*Gesinnung*)" on those groups most directly involved in the education of public consciousness: clergy, teachers, professors, writers, and journalists. As Eichhorn stated in 1842, the cultural policy of the new regime was "not neutral, but partisan, totally partisan."[21] The Left Hegelian opposition to the government thus also took the form of cultural opposition. It was on this level that the gap between the Left Hegelians and various liberal, reformist groups was most obvious. The Left Hegelians aimed at a "total" revolution, a transformation of the system, the framework, of communal relationships. For all their emphasis on focusing public attention on political issues, the Left Hegelians were more concerned with the presuppositions of political life than with specific political changes. What was at stake was not simply the redress of particular grievances but the liberation of "man" from the millennial suffering of self-alienation. The indeterminate character of this Left Hegelian humanism became obvious as the exhilarating consciousness of imminent historical transformation dissipated in 1843 and individual Left Hegelians were forced to reconsider, revise, and define more precisely their conceptions of human essence and of the historical process through which this human essence would become a historical actuality. The pattern should by now be familiar. As the project of making philosophy worldly and the world philosophical shattered against the resistance of the "world," philosophy or theory was revised in ways that, it was hoped, would reconstitute the original project in a realistic manner and make its fulfillment not only possible, but inevitable.

Preliminary indications of some of the conflicts that would tear apart the Left Hegelian movement after 1843 were already evident in 1842 as both Marx and Ruge expressed increasing dismay with the recklessly belligerent, self-indulgent writing and bohemian antics of The Free.[22] After the suppression of the *Deutsche Jahrbücher* and *Rheinische Zeitung* in the spring of 1843, Ruge, Marx, Engels, and Hess went into exile in the hope of realizing one of the recurring dreams of the Left Hegelian movement – the alliance of the French "heart" and the German "head" in an international revolutionary movement – while Feuerbach and the Berliners, who remained in Germany, went into a kind of internal exile as they became increasingly pessimistic about the possibilities of an alliance between critical theory and the contemporary interests and needs of the "masses." Collaboration within both groups, however, lasted hardly a year, and Feuerbach continued to follow his own path in critical detachment from both. By the end of 1844, Left Hegelianism had disintegrated completely as a coherent movement. The methods of ideological analysis and critique were now focused primarily on polemical battles among the former comrades-in-arms, as each accused the others of remaining captive to the "religious" or "theological" illusions of the philosophical humanism of 1842. When read together, however, these polemics reveal a general process of self-criticism and self-clarification among all of the major theorists and leaders of the Left Hegelian movement.

The internal critical assessment of the historical failure of the Left Hegelian movement focused first of all on the illusions of political emancipation. By 1844, Bauer viewed his former beliefs in politics as the primary means for man's self-liberation and in the state as the actualization of the human essence as the sign of an incomplete liberation from the presuppositions of the old order. Not only a specific form of politics, but "the whole political essence," was in contradiction with genuine human liberation.[23] Why? Because political liberation and integration necessarily remained abstract. The freedom and universality of the citizen were illusions that merely hid, protected, and sustained the actual enslavement and isolation of the individual ego in the competitive mechanism of "mass" society. The "world form" that was the true goal of critical theory, Bauer insisted, was not merely legal and political, but "social."[24] In thus shifting the locus of human emancipation from the political to the social dimension, Bauer echoed Marx's indirect self-criticism (articulated in a critique of Bauer)[25] and expressed a general trend among the former German "Jacobins." In 1841, Stirner identified the actualization of man as a free and universal being with the creation of a "true state."[26] In 1845 he attacked political emancipation as the epitome of self-alienation, as the surrender of the individual's concrete freedom and power to a hypostatized abstraction.[27] After 1843, Feuerbach dropped all mention of a new "religious" politics from his writings, and he referred to himself as a "communist" on a number of occasions in 1844 and 1845.[28]

The critical unveiling of political emancipation as a secular duplication of religious self-alienation did not, of course, necessarily imply commitment to some form of socialist or communist ideology. In fact, Bauer and Stirner specifically rejected all contemporary forms of socialism and communism as secular religions that demanded the dissolution of concrete individual existence in the "higher" substance of "society" or the "proletariat."[29] What the common critique of political illusions did reveal was a shared recognition that freedom and community were "real" only if they were embodied or lived in the actual concrete relationships of individually existing human beings. The disillusionment with political emancipation was a part of a more general disillusionment with the whole doctrine of human essence on which the movement of Left Hegelian humanism had been grounded. The final phase of Left Hegelianism should be seen not as a developmental sequence from one thinker to another in which individual positions were *aufgehoben* in higher syntheses, but as the contemporaneous construction of alternative positions from a common starting point: the reduction of "man" to "real existing active men."[30] Moreover, it was not only this "existential" ontology that was shared by Marx, Feuerbach, Bauer, and Stirner around 1845. Although they all accused each other of regressing to the abstract and undialectical positions of traditional metaphysical idealism or materialism, they all laid claim to the dialectical inheritance. The existential reductions of 1844–5, like the earlier humanist reductions, were presented as positive appropriations of the real content of Hegel's self-actualizing, self-comprehending, and self-sufficient concrete universal. Even Stirner's heaven-storming nihilism did not relinquish this redemptive core of the Hegelian project.

Although Feuerbach was so often fixated and criticized as the representative theorist of Left Hegelian humanism by his Left Hegelian contemporaries, he actually inaugurated the self-critical development beyond this humanism with his "Principles of the Philosophy of the

Future" in 1843. In a retrospective analysis of 1846, Feuerbach noted that his first formulations of the anthropological principle during the early 1840s had still been "haunted by abstract rational being, by the being of philosophy as distinct from the actual sensuous existence of nature and man."[31] Between 1843 and 1846, Feuerbach attempted to "fill in the last pores in the human head in which the divine ghosts have always nested," and insisted that only sensuous being, that is, concrete, individual, existing being, was "real."[32] Real being, he claimed, was "that which cannot be verbalized (*das Unsagbare*)":

> Where words cease, life begins and being reveals its secret. If, therefore, non-verbality is the same as irrationality, then all existence is irrational, because it is always and forever *this* existence. But irrational it is not. Existence has meaning and reason in itself, without being verbalized.[33]

This "meaning and reason" within the sensuous and concrete was described by Feuerbach as a dialectical relationship between passive perception and active desire, feeling and need, being-for-self and being-for-others. Sensuous being was necessarily, he contended, an active relationship, a sensuous interaction between subject and object, between "I" and "thou." The "reality" of the Hegelian subject–object identity was to be construed not as the mutual identity of individuals in some higher human "essence," but simply as the totality of the actual sensuous relationships of man as a suffering, "needy," desiring being – as, to echo Marx's famous phrase, the ensemble of sensuous relationships.[34]

Marx's own process of reconstruction after 1843 was grounded on the Feuerbachian premise that only the concrete and sensuous was real, but Marx defined concrete being as productive activity, as "making" rather than feeling and desiring. On this foundation, of course, he was able to reconstruct the Hegelian concrete universal in social and historical terms, a goal that always eluded Feuerbach. Feuerbach was well aware that the complete actualization of human potentialities in the totality of sensuous relationships required a transformation of objective social and political conditions, but he remained vague and abstract in his analysis of the practical transformations that would bring an end to sensual poverty and sensual repression. As Marx Wartofsky has recently pointed out, however, Marx and Engels remained abstract and vague in the area where Feuerbach's analysis was concrete and dialectical: the "psychology and phenomenology of conscious experience."[35] The numerous twentieth-century attempts to enrich Marxian social and economic theory with a more systematic and concrete psychology, as well as recent reexaminations of the relationship between

Marx's conception of socioeconomic practice and the "natural life foundations of society,"[36] indicate the extent to which the Feuerbach–Marx relationship is a living, unresolved problem.

It is not usually recognized to what extent the development of Bauer's critical theory after 1843 was also grounded in a critical reduction of the illusions of human essence to the concrete relationships of human existence. His historical and intellectual reputation has never recovered from the denunciation of his viewpoint as subjective idealism and transcendent spiritualism by Marx and Engels in 1845.[37] But Bauer consistently repudiated all forms of spiritualism and abstract idealism, and even described his theory of the free, self-actualizing, self-comprehending activity of "self-consciousness" as "the truth of materialism."[38] Self-consciousness was "real" only in the constant, concrete, historical activity of objectification and dissolution of social and cultural forms or modes of life. Bauer insisted that his critical theory was not a new "gospel" or "religion," a resting place for the disinherited psyche, but simply a comprehension of man's total responsibility for his existence.[39] The only absolute for Bauer was the constant present activity of actualizing and comprehending the infinite possibilities of human existence. The source of Bauer's divergence from Marx was not a regression to some pre-Hegelian form of subjective idealism, but a different experience of, and perspective on, the revolutionary possibilities within the contemporary historical situation. From the "parochial" perspective of Berlin, the belief in the proletariat as a collective historical subject that embodied the revolutionary negation of human self-alienation seemed like a wish-fulfilling fantasy.[40] In Bauer's view the actual tendencies of the present pointed toward the creation of a totally administered, one-dimensional, "mass" society in which the critical, self-transcending freedom of the theorist could find no material allies. In such a situation the task of critical theory was not to flatter the masses but to "keep the gates of the future open" by rejecting all forms of co-optation.[41] Yet Bauer also insisted that such negative dialectics was a positive, communal activity. In the act of negation, in the refusal to be defined and determined by any particular form of human association or collective commitment, the concrete, existing individual lived the life of the universal and was absorbed into the historical community of free men.

In their own particular and rather different ways, therefore, Bauer, Feuerbach, and Marx responded to their common disillusionment with Left Hegelian philosophical humanism by attempting to construct or reveal the identity of individual and communal being within the dialectical structure of concrete human existence. Stirner's unique role in the disintegration of Left Hegelian humanism was defined by his apparent rejection of this identity. With an almost obsessive, monomaniacal insistency, Stirner developed the process of ideological critique and "desacralization" to its most extreme form and drew from the liberation of concrete being from the self-alienating mystifications of Christian culture the conclusions that the other Left Hegelians had been trying desperately to avoid. The emancipation of real existence from determination by an alien, abstract essence, he insisted, culminated in the liberation of the individual ego from all communal ties. Yet the nihilism of Stirner's "unique one (*der Einzige*)" was not as nihilistic or as unique as it first appeared. Stirner's solution to the bifurcation of essence and existence and the self-alienating subordination of existence to the illusions of essence was conceived and articulated within the framework of the dialectical tradition, and his book culminated with the claim that the qualities and powers that men had formerly projected onto the alien "spooks" of "God," "Spirit," "Reason," "Man," "Society," "State," and so on, could now be finally and fully appropriated and concretely lived by the sovereign individual ego – the indefinable, finite, transitory, creative, and dissolving "act" at the center of everyone's constantly changing, unique world of natural, social, and cultural relationships.[42] Moreover, Stirner, like Nietzsche, conceived the emergence of the sovereign individual who was the self-sufficient, self-affirming master of his own world as the highest product and imminent telos of world history and psychological development, as the "laughing heir" of the millennial labors and sufferings of mankind.[43]

Stirner's belligerent and rhetorical affirmation that the ephemeral present existence of the continually self-creating and self-consuming individual ego was the only "absolute" reality in a universe finally stripped of the last illusions of the sacred has usually been understood and dismissed as a purely subjective, ideal or imaginary, and thus ultimately impotent, self-deluding, and self-defeating resolution of the historical dilemma of human self-alienation. This viewpoint is misleading, however, because it distorts the nature of Stirner's cultural stance and thus misses its historical significance. Like Bauer and Feuerbach, Stirner focused his critical analysis on the problem of psychic liberation from the self-created fetishes that denied man's freedom to define his identity or essence and veiled his responsibility for all meaning, coherence, and value in the world. But Stirner, like Bauer and Feuerbach, was acutely aware that the transformation of consciousness remained an ideal without content as long as the objective conditions of human activity remained untransformed. The self could not live as the master and playful consumer of its world as long as the regulation of individual actions and the ownership of material things lay in the hands of "others" – the clergy, the government, and the capitalists. A denial of the sacred character of political obligation or property rights did not in itself transform the world into "my own"; property and power had to be "taken."[44] The act of taking, or conquest, however, was necessarily a collective act; the real political and socioeconomic forces that oppressed and impoverished the self could not be destroyed by the individual on his own, but only in concert or "union" with others. Stirner thus affirmed that self-liberation involved not only a reinterpretation of the world, a new "philosophy," but also a practical transformation of the world.

Unlike Marx and Engels, and like Bauer and Feuerbach, Stirner examined the dialectical relationship between the transformation of consciousness and the transformation of conditions primarily from the subjective side of the relationship. But the basic dilemma was common to all of Hegel's radical heirs during the mid-1840s. The insistence that the self could discover and appropriate the autonomy and wholeness it had for so long projected onto some alien essence in the concrete reality of its finite activity and consciousness seemed a hollow and impotent claim in the face of the overwhelming "objective" powers of the state and the capitalist economy. Self-liberation and self-affirmation could become "real" only through a revolutionary destruction of the conditions and powers that inhibited and prevented their concrete historical actualization. The tasks of revolution, however, demanded self-renunciation, devotion to a common goal, commitment to suprapersonal values, belief in an objective meaning in history – that is, a denial of precisely those values of individual autonomy, self-expression, and self-enjoyment that constituted the goal of a revolution which would finally "make an end" to the historical pathology of self-alienation. Self-liberation and the liberation of the world seemed to be both inextricably connected and inevitably in opposition to each other. The dilemma should not be unfamiliar to those who seek some enlightenment regarding man's fate and man's hope within the various contemporary strands of dialectical thought – all of which can trace at least one branch of their historical roots to the apparently parochial, yet strangely paradigmatic, situation and consciousness of a small group of culturally disinherited, alienated intellectuals in early nineteenth-century Germany.

Notes

Introduction

1. The "classic" statements of these two perspectives on the fate of thought and life "after Hegel," both originally published in 1941, are Karl Löwith, *From Hegel to Nietzsche: The Revolution in Nineteenth-Century Thought*, trans. David E. Green (Garden City, N.Y., 1967); and Herbert Marcuse, *Reason and Revolution: Hegel and the Rise of Social Theory*, 3rd ed. (Boston, 1960).
2. The "Hegel to Marx" paradigm has, for obvious reasons, dominated most previous analyses of Hegelianism after Hegel, though these analyses have been confined to the "young" or "Left" Hegelians rather than the movement as a whole, and have usually tended simply to repeat or amplify Marx's and Engels's own critique of their intellectual mentors in *The Holy Family* and *The German Ideology*. From this perspective, D. Koigen, *Zur Vorgeschichte des modernen philosophischen Sozialismus in Deutschland: Zur Geschichte der Philosophie und Sozialphilosophie dus Junghegelianismus* (Bern, 1901); Sidney Hook, *From Hegel to Marx: Studies in the Intellectual Development of Karl Marx* (New York, 1936); Auguste Cornu, *Karl Marx et Friedrich Engels: leur vie et leur oeuvre*, 4 vols. (Paris, 1955–70); and David McLellan, *The Young Hegelians and Karl Marx* (London and Toronto, 1969), are particularly noteworthy. In recent years there has been a noticeable tendency to reopen the debate between Marx and Left Hegelians like Bauer, Feuerbach, and Stirner for purposes of an internal critique of Marxism, or a reevaluation of what might have been lost in Marx's critical transcendence of his Hegelian heritage. This tendency is evident in McLellan, but more striking in Alfred Schmidt, *Emanzipatorische Sinnlichkeit: Ludwig Feuerbachs anthropologischer Materialismus* (Munich, 1973); Lothar Koch, *Humanistischer Atheismus und gesellschaftliches Engagement: Bruno Bauers Kritische Kritik* (Stuttgart, 1971); John Carroll, *Break-Out from the Crystal Palace: The Anarcho-psychological Critique: Stirner, Nietzsche, Dostoevsky* (London, 1974); and the special triple issue of the *Philosophical Forum* 8, nos. 2–4 (1978), edited by Marx Wartofsky and Hans-Martin Sass.
3. Aside from the critical analysis of the Hegelians' eschatological, allegedly "totalitarian" politics in Jürgen Gebhardt, *Politik und Eschatologie: Studien zur Geschichte der Hegelschen Schule in den Jahren 1830–1840* (Munich, 1963), one can find brief analyses of some early Hegelians' philosophies of religion in Hans-Martin Sass, *Untersuchungen zur Religionsphilosophie in der Hegelschule, 1830–1850* (Münster, 1963), and Peter Cornehl, *Die Zukunft der Versöhnung: Eschatologie und Emanzipation in der Aufklärung, bei Hegel und in der Hegelschen*

Schule (Göttingen, 1971). The relevant chapters in Nicholas Lobkowicz, *Theory and Practice: History of a Concept from Aristotle to Marx* (Notre Dame, Ind., 1967), follow Gebhardt very closely. The most distinguished modern study of the Hegelian phenomenon that does not follow the "Hegel to Marx" paradigm is Horst Stuke, *Philosophie der Tat: Studien zur 'Verwirklichung der Philosophie' bei den Junghegelianern und wahren Sozialisten* (Stuttgart, 1963), but Stuke's analysis is focused on the theory/practice problematic in Bauer, Hess, and Cieszkowski during the early 1840s. William Brazill's *The Young Hegelians* (New Haven and London, 1970) is little more than a series of biographical accounts of Strauss, Feuerbach, Vischer, Bauer, Stirner, and Ruge, and its treatment of the Hegelian school and its divisions repeats tired and misleading clichés.

4. See for example Jean-Paul Sartre, *Search for a Method,* trans. Hazel Barnes (New York, 1968); or the work of Jürgen Habermas and the original members of the "Frankfurt School."

5. The role of Hegelianism in the historical development of the concept of ideology is described in Hans Barth, *Wahrheit und Ideologie,* 2nd ed. (Zürich and Stuttgart, 1961), pp. 61 ff.; and George Lichtheim, *The Concept of Ideology and Other Essays* (New York, 1967), pp. 11–22.

6. "Differenz des Fichteschen und Schellingschen Systems der Philosophie" (1801) in G. W. F. Hegel, *Werke,* ed. E. Moldenhauer and K. Michel, 20 vols. (Frankfurt, 1969–72), II, 22.

7. *Hegel's Philosophy of Right,* ed. and trans. T. M. Knox (New York, 1967), p. 11.

1. The origins of the Hegelian project

1. Karl Rosenkranz, *G. W. F. Hegels Leben* (Berlin, 1844), pp. 141–2. This remains the basic biography, although it should now be supplemented by Gustav E. Müller, *Hegel: Denkgeschichte eines Lebendigen* (Berlin, 1959); Franz Wiedmann, *G. W. F. Hegel* (Hamburg, 1965); and the useful English introduction by Walter Kaufmann: *Hegel: A Reinterpretation* (Garden City, N.Y., 1965).

2. Friedhelm Nicolin, *Hegel, 1770–1970* (Stuttgart, 1970), p. 51; Franz Nauen, *Revolution, Idealism and Human Freedom: Schelling, Hölderlin and Hegel and the Crisis of Early German Idealism* (The Hague, 1971), p. 2. For a recent mistaken view of the social status of Hegel's father see H. S. Harris, *Hegel's Development: Toward the Sunlight, 1770–1801* (Oxford, 1971), p. 1.

3. For a concise, comparative summary of this often-analyzed process see Peter Lundgren, "Gegensatz und Verschmelzung von 'alter' und 'neuer' Bürokratie im Ancien Regime: Ein Vergleich von Frankreich und Preussen," in Hans-Ulrich Wehler, ed., *Sozialgeschichte Heute: Festschrift für Hans Rosenberg* (Göttingen, 1974), pp. 104–18. There is a brief introduction to the history of the educated estate in W. H. Bruford, *Germany in the Eighteenth Century: The Social Background of the Literary Revival* (Cambridge, 1935), pp. 235–69. An important phase in its later development is analyzed in Fritz K. Ringer, *The Decline of the German Mandarins: The German Academic Community, 1890–1933* (Cambridge, Mass., 1969).

4. Mack Walker, *German Home Towns: Community, State and General Estate, 1648–1871* (Ithaca, N.Y., 1971), pp. 119–33. See also Leonard Krieger, *The German Idea of Freedom: History of a Political Tradition* (Boston, 1957), pp. 34–45; and Reinhart Koselleck, *Preussen zwischen Reform und Revolution: Allgemeines*

Landrecht, Verwaltung und soziale Bewegung von 1791 bis 1848 (Stuttgart, 1967), pp. 78–115.

5. *Home Towns,* p. 129.

6. There is a brilliant summary of these overlapping tensions in Krieger, *Idea,* p. 8.

7. Rudolf Vierhaus, "Ständewesen und Staatsverwaltung in Deutschland im späteren 18. Jahrhundert," in R. Vierhaus and M. Botzenhart, eds., *Dauer und Wandel in der Geschichte: Aspekte Europäischer Vergangenheit* (Münster, 1966), pp. 337–60; Hans Rosenberg, *Bureaucracy, Aristocracy and Autocracy: The Prussian Experience, 1660–1815* (Boston, 1966), pp. 137–201.

8. *Bureaucracy,* p. 163.

9. Koselleck, *Preussen,* pp. 90–5; Klaus Epstein, *The Genesis of German Conservatism* (Princeton, N.J., 1966), pp. 372–87; Rosenberg, *Bureaucracy,* pp. 190–1.

10. Erwin Hölzle, *Das Alte Recht und die Revolution: Eine politische Geschichte Württembergs in der Revolutionszeit, 1789–1850* (Munich and Berlin, 1931), pp. 3–4, 33–44.

11. Walter Grube, *Der Stuttgarter Landtag, 1457–1957* (Stuttgart, 1957), pp. 427–9; F. L. Carsten, *Princes and Parliaments in Germany* (Oxford, 1959), pp. 140–4.

12. Hölzle, *Alte Recht,* pp. 13–15.

13. Martin Hasselhorn, *Der altwürttembergische Pfarrstand im 18. Jahrhundert* (Stuttgart, 1958), pp. 1–23; Heinrich Hermelink, *Geschichte der evangelischen Kirche in Württemberg von der Reformation bis zur Gegenwart* (Stuttgart and Tübingen, 1949), pp. 85–96.

14. Hölzle, *Alte Recht,* pp. 26–32; Otto Hammer, *Schwäbisches Beamtentum* (Stuttgart, 1923).

15. Hasselhorn, *Pfarrstand,* pp. 39–44, 50–5; Hermelink, *Geschichte,* pp. 97–103.

16. Hans-Martin Decker-Hauff, "Die geistige Führungsschichte in Württemberg," in Günther Franz, ed., *Beamtentum und Pfarrerstand, 1400–1800* (Limburg am Lahn, 1972), pp. 65–70; Hasselhorn, *Pfarrstand,* pp. 26, 63.

17. Hasselhorn, *Pfarrstand,* pp. 29–30, 33–4.

18. Julius Klaiber, *Hölderlin, Hegel und Schelling in ihren schwäbischen Jugendjahren* (Stuttgart, 1877), p. 13.

19. Nicolin, *Hegel,* pp. 29–36; Klaiber, *Hölderlin,* pp. 106–8.

20. Decker-Hauff, "Die geistige Führungsschichte," p. 64.

21. Hasselhorn, *Pfarrstand,* pp. 25, 26, 34–5.

22. On the "ideological" nature of Hellenic neo-humanism see Hans Gerth, *Die sozialgeschichtliche Lage der bürgerlichen Intelligenz um die Wende des 18. Jahrhunderts: Ein Beitrag zur Geschichte des Frühliberalismus* (Frankfurt, 1935), p. 62; Ringer, *Decline,* pp. 18–21; Rosenberg, *Bureaucracy,* pp. 182–92; and W. H. Bruford, *Culture and Society in Classical Weimar* (Cambridge, 1962), passim.

23. Hasselhorn, *Pfarrstand,* pp. 46–7.

24. See Alexandra Schlingensiepen-Pogge, *Das Sozialethos der lutherischen Aufklärungstheologie am Vorabend der industriellen Revolution* (Göttingen, 1967); Karl Aner, *Die Theologie der Lessingzeit* (Halle, 1929).

25. Epstein, *Genesis,* pp. 41–4, 52–3; Krieger, *Idea,* pp. 21 ff.

26. Hölzle, *Alte Recht,* pp. 44–54; Adolf Wohlwill, *Weltbürgertum und Vaterlandsliebe der Schwaben* (Hamburg, 1875), pp. 1 21.

27. Albrecht Ritschl, *Geschichte des Pietismus in der lutherischen Kirche des 17.*

und 18. Jahrhunderts, 3 vols. (Bonn, 1886), III, 19.
28. Hartmut Lehmann, *Pietismus und weltliche Ordnung in Württemberg vom 17. bis zum 20. Jahrhundert* (Stuttgart, 1969), pp. 66 ff. See also Harmelink, *Geschichte,* pp. 153–260.
29. The arguments and evidence on this issue are summarized in Martin Brecht and Jörg Sandberger, "Hegel's Begegnung mit der Theologie im Tübinger Stift," *Hegel-Studien* 5 (1969):48–81.
30. Hölzle, *Alte Recht,* pp. 56–8.
31. For the role of the ducal Rentkammer in attempts at administrative reform during the last decades of the century see Heinrich Scheel, *Süddeutsche Jakobiner:Klassenkämpfe und republikanische Bestrebungen im deutschen Süden Ende des 18. Jahrhunderts* (Berlin, 1962), pp. 38–9.
32. Hasselhorn, *Pfarrstand,* pp. 64–5.
33. Lehmann, *Pietismus,* pp. 135–51.
34. Grube, *Landtag,* p. 449; Hölzle, *Alte Recht,* pp. 58–84.
35. For Prussia see Krieger, *Idea,* pp. 43–4; and Rosenberg, *Bureaucracy,* pp. 175–201. A general overview of the polarization of political attitudes within the intellectual classes during the last decades of the century can be found in Fritz Valjavec, *Die Entstehung der politischen Strömungen in Deutschland, 1770–1815* (Munich, 1951), pp. 13–145.
36. Wilhelm Abel, *Geschichte der deutschen Landwirtschaft vom frühen Mittelalter bis zum 19. Jahrhundert* (Stuttgart, 1962), p. 252; Paul Mombert, *Bevölkerungslehre* (Jena, 1929), pp. 96–7; Erich Keyser, *Bevölkerungsgeschichte Deutschlands* (Leipzig, 1938), p. 301.
37. Mombert, *Bevölkerungslehre,* pp. 100–1, 108, 151–3; Henri Brunschwig, *La crise de l'Etat prussien à la fin du xviii*[e] *siècle et la genèse de la mentalité romantique* (Paris, 1947), p. 122.
38. Max Müller, *Die Auswanderung der Württemberger nach Westpreussen und dem Netzegau, 1776–1786* (Stuttgart, 1935), esp. pp. 70–2.
39. See especially Otto Büsch, *Militärsystem und Sozialleben im Alten Preussen, 1713–1807* (Berlin, 1962); and Gerth, *Lage,* pp. 6–15.
40. Scheel, *Jakobiner,* pp. 38–9.
41. Hasselhorn, *Pfarrstand,* pp. 34–5, 54. See also Paul Schwarz, *Die Gelehrtenschulen Preussens unter dem Oberschulkollegium,* 2 vols. (Berlin, 1910), I, 70–1; and Brunschwig, *Crise,* pp. 147–75.
42. Gerth, *Lage,* pp. 80–95; Franz Neumann, *Der Hofmeister: Ein Beitrag zur Geschichte der Erziehung im achtzehnten Jahrhundert* (Halle, 1930), pp. 48–72.
43. Bruford, *Germany,* p. 290.
44. This does not mean, of course, that the Romantic ideology of the 1790s can be reduced to, and dismissed as, an irrational leap out of social frustration – a position argued, or rather rhetorically declaimed, by Brunschwig in his *Crise,* esp. pp. 217 ff.
45. Gustav Lang, *Geschichte der Stuttgarter Gelehrtenschule von ihren ersten Anfängen bis zum Jahre 1806* (Stuttgart, 1928), pp. 249–64.
46. "Ueber die Religion der Griechen und Römer," in G. W. F. Hegel, *Dokumente zu Hegel's Entwicklung,* ed. J. Hoffmeister (Stuttgart, 1936), pp. 43–8.
47. "Tagebuch," in Hegel, *Dokumente,* pp. 13, 22–3, 27, 37.
48. "Ueber die Religion," p. 47; "Rede beim Abgang vom Gymnasium," in Hegel, *Dokumente,* p. 52.
49. "Ueber die Religion," pp. 47–8.

50. "Ueber einige charakteristische Unterschiede der alten Dichter (von den neueren)," in Hegel, *Dokumente*, pp. 48–50.

2. Revolution and Romanticism

1. *Phänomenologie des Geistes*, in Hegel, *Werke*, ed. Moldenhauer and Michel, III, 18.
2. Schelling to Hegel, Feb. 4, 1795, in G. W. F. Hegel, *Briefe von und an Hegel*, ed. J. Hoffmeister, 4 vols. (Hamburg, 1952–60), I, 21. These volumes cited hereafter as *Briefe (Hegel)*.
3. Dieter Henrich, "Leutwein über Hegel: Ein Dokument zu Hegel's Biographie," *Hegel-Studien* 3 (1965):55; Harris, *Hegel's Development*, pp. 58–70.
4. Richard Samuel, *Die poetische Staats- und Geschichtsauffassung Friedrich von Hardenbergs* (Frankfurt, 1925), pp. 64–89; Roy C. Shelton, *The Young Hölderlin* (Bern and Frankfurt, 1973), pp. 107–18; Ernst Behler, *Friedrich Schlegel* (Hamburg, 1966), pp. 20–9; Rudolf Haym, *Wilhelm von Humboldt, Lebensbild und Charakteristik* (Berlin, 1856), pp. 32–66.
5. Heinrich Leube, *Das Tübinger Stift, 1770–1950* (Stuttgart, 1954), pp. 115–39; Harris, *Hegel's Development*, pp. 97, 116; Friedrich Hölderlin, *Sämtliche Werke*, ed. F. Beissner and A. Beck, 7 vols. in 14 pts. (Stuttgart, 1946–77), VI, pt. 1, 77. See also Pierre Bertaux, *Hölderlin und die französische Revolution* (Frankfurt, 1969), pp. 49–63; and Walter Betzendörfer, *Hölderlins Studienjahre im Tübinger Stift* (Heilbronn, 1922).
6. *The Philosophy of History*, trans. J. Sibree (New York, 1956), p. 447.
7. Jan. 1795, in *Briefe (Hegel)*, I, 18. See also Hölderlin to Hegel, July 10, 1794, in *Briefe (Hegel)*, I, 9.
8. *Hyperion, or the Hermit in Greece*, trans. W. Trask (New York, 1965), p. 108.
9. *Briefe (Hegel)*, I, 24. See also F. W. J. von Schelling, *Vom Ich als Prinzip der Philosophie oder das Unbedingte im menschlichen Wissen* (1795), in F. W. J. von Schelling *Sämmtliche Werke*, ed. K. F. A. Schelling, 14 vols. in 2 ser. (Stuttgart, 1856–61), I, pt. 1, 157.
10. Aug. 1794, in Friedrich Schlegel, *Friedrich Schlegel und Novalis: Biographie einer Romantiker Freundschaft in ihren Briefen*, ed. M. Preitz (Darmstadt, 1957), pp. 51–3.
11. "Volksreligion und Christentum: Fragmente" (1793), in G. W. F. Hegel, *Hegel's Theologische Jugendschriften*, ed. H. Nohl (Tübingen, 1907), pp. 20, 27.
12. May 18/19, 1794, in Barthold Georg Niebuhr, *Die Briefe Barthold Georg Niebuhrs*, ed. D. Gerhard and W. Norvin (Berlin, 1926), I, 27. See also Schlegel, *Friedrich Schlegel und Novalis*, p. 53; Hölderlin, *Hyperion*, p. 44; and Alexander Hollerbach, *Der Rechtsgedanke bei Schelling* (Frankfurt, 1957), pp. 84–5.
13. Hegel to Schelling, Apr. 16, 1795, in *Briefe (Hegel)*, I, 23.
14. Letter to his brother, Jan. 1, 1799, in Hölderlin *Werke*, VI, p. 1, 303–4.
15. Schelling to Hegel, Feb. 4, 1795, in *Briefe (Hegel)*, I, 21. See also F. D. E. Schleiermacher, *Aus Schleiermachers Leben in Briefen*, ed. L. Jonas and W. Dilthey, 4 vols. (Berlin, 1858–63), I, 70, IV, 45; and Friedrich Schlegel, *Friedrich Schlegels Briefe an seinem Bruder August Wilhelm*, ed. O. Walzel (Berlin, 1890), p. 127.
16. *Briefe (Hegel)*, I, 14.
17. Letter to Baggesen, Apr. 1795, in J. G. Fichte, *Briefwechsel*, ed. H. Schulz, 2 vols. (Leipzig, 1925), I, 449–50.

18. *Abhandlungen zur Erläuterung des Idealismus der Wissenschaftslehre,* in Schelling, *Werke,* I, pt. 1, 409.
19. *Schlegels Briefe an seinem Bruder,* pp. 111, 416. See also Schleiermacher, *Aus Schleiermachers Leben,* III, 103.
20. *Briefe (Hegel),* I, 22.
21. *Philosophische Briefe über Dogmatismus und Kritizismus* (1795), in Schelling, *Werke,* I, pt. 1, 318.
22. *Vom Ich als Prinzip der Philosophie,* p. 176.
23. Ibid., p. 199.
24. *Neue Deduktion des Naturrechts* (1796), in Schelling, *Werke,* I, pt. 1, 247–8.
25. Novalis, "Philosophische Studien" (1795–6), in Novalis, *Schriften,* ed. P. Kluckhohn, 4 vols (Leipzig [1929]), II, 159–60; Dieter Henrich, *Hegel im Kontext* (Frankfurt, 1967), pp. 21–2.
26. "The Positivity of the Christian Religion" (1795–6), in G. W. F. Hegel, *On Christianity: Early Theological Writings,* trans. T. M. Knox (New York, 1961), pp. 69, 71.
27. Schleiermacher's early fragments are printed in the appendix of Wilhelm Dilthey, *Leben Schleiermachers* (Berlin, 1870). See also Harris, *Hegel's Development,* pp. 258–70.
28. See E. M. Butler, *The Tyranny of Greece over Germany* (Cambridge, 1935), chaps. 1–6; Henry Hatfield, *Aesthetic Paganism in German Literature* (Cambridge, Mass., 1964), esp. pp. 166–211; Werner Weiland, *Der junge Friedrich Schlegel oder die Revolution in der Frühromantik* (Stuttgart, 1968), pp. 26–52; and J. Glenn Gray, *Hegel and Greek Thought* (New York, 1968), chap. 4.
29. "Positivity," p. 154.
30. Friedrich Schiller, *On the Aesthetic Education of Man: In a Series of Letters,* trans. R. Snell (New York, 1971), letters 16 and 27. For a recent analysis of Schiller's relationship to Hegel and Hölderlin see Jacques Taminaux, *La Nostalgie de la Grece à l'aube de l'idéalisme Allemand* (The Hague, 1967). For the Schiller/Schlegel relationship see R. Brinkmann, "Romantische Dichtungstheorie in Fr. Schlegels Frühschriften und Schillers Begriffe des Naiven und Sentimentalischen," *Deutsche Vierteljahresschrift für Literatur und Geistesgeschichte* 32 (1958):344–71.
31. See Otto Pöggeler, "Hegel der Verfasser des ältesten Systemprogramms des deutschen Idealismus," *Hegel-Studien,* supp. 4: *Hegel-Tage Urbino, 1965* (Bonn, 1969), pp. 17–32.
32. G. W. F. Hegel, "Das älteste Systemprogramm des deutschen Idealismus," in Hegel, *Werke,* ed. Moldenhauer and Michel, I, 234–6.
33. Novalis, "Randbemerkungen zu Fr. Schlegels 'Ideen'," in Novalis, *Schriften,* III, 364.
34. Friedrich Schlegel, *Friedrich Schlegel, 1794–1802: Seine Prosäische Jugendschriften,* ed. J. Minor, 2 vols. (Vienna, 1882), II, 306, 324, 338–40; F. D. E. Schleiermacher, *On Religion: Speeches to Its Cultured Despisers,* trans. J. Oman (New York, 1958), p. 43; Schleiermacher, *Aus Schleiermachers Leben,* III, 8.
35. *Darstellung meines Systems der Philosophie,* in Schelling, *Werke,* I, pt. 4, 129.
36. "Fragment of a System" (1800), in Hegel, *On Christianity,* p. 312.
37. See Brunschwig, *Crise,* pp. 270–301.
38. *Dialogue on Poetry and Literary Aphorisms,* trans. and ed. E. Behler and R. Struc (University Park, Pa., 1968), p. 150.

39. "Fragment of a System," p. 313.
40. *On Religion,* p. 36.
41. Ibid., speeches 1 and 5.
42. *Schlegel und Novalis,* p. 130; Novalis, *Schriften,* II, 20, IV, 239. See also Bertaux, *Hölderlin,* pp. 64–84.
43. *Von der Weltseele* (1798), in Schelling, *Werke,* I, pt. 2, 345 ff. See also Joseph L. Esposito, *Schelling's Idealism and Philosophy of Nature* (London, 1977), chaps. 3–5.
44. *System des transcendentalen Idealismus* (1800), in Schelling, *Werke,* I, pt. 3, 339 ff.
45. *On University Studies,* ed. N. Guterman (Athens, Ohio, 1966), p. 8.
46. *System des transcendentalen Idealismus,* p. 627.
47. *Dialogue on Poetry,* pp. 53–5; *Schlegel, 1794–1802,* II, 293, 294, 303. See also Novalis, *Schriften,* II, 26; Hölderlin, *Werke,* IV, pt. 1, 275–81.
48. *Dialogue on Poetry,* pp. 140, 145, 155. See also Hans Eichner, *Friedrich Schlegel* (New York, 1970), pp. 58 ff.
49. *Dialogue on Poetry,* pp. 81–2, 156–7.
50. *Soliloquies,* ed. and trans. H. L. Fries (Chicago, 1957), p. 31.
51. Schlegel, *Schlegel, 1794–1802,* II, 289, 291, 294.
52. "The Spirit of Christianity and Its Fate," in Hegel, *On Christianity,* pp. 241, 247. For general discussions of the Romantic love ethic see Ricarda Huch, *Die Romantik: Blütezeit, Ausbreitung und Verfall* (Tübingen, 1951), pp. 227–52; and Paul Kluckhohn, *Die Auffassung der Liebe in der Literatur des 18, Jahrhunderts und in der deutschen Romantik* (Halle, 1931).
53. "The Spirit of Christianity," pp. 278–9, 300–1.
54. *On University Studies,* pp. 104, 114.
55. *Soliloquies,* p. 59.
56. Novalis, *Schriften,* II, 49–52; Schlegel, *Schlegel, 1794–1802,* II, 236, 268.
57. See Georg Lukács, *The Young Hegel: Studies in the Relations between Dialectics and Economics,* trans. R. Livingstone (Cambridge, Mass., 1976), esp. pp. 130 ff.
58. "The German Constitution," in G. W. F. Hegel, *Hegel's Political Writings,* trans. T. M. Knox (Oxford, 1964), pp. 162, 198, 203 ff.
59. Ibid., pp. 147, 154, 163, 234. There is a good commentary on this work in Shlomo Avineri, *Hegel's Theory of the Modern State* (Cambridge, 1972), pp. 34–62.
60. "The German Constitution," p. 145.
61. *Dialogue on Poetry,* p. 151.
62. Ibid., p. 144.
63. Novalis, *Schriften,* II, 274, 281; Schelling, *On University Studies,* pp. 108–9.
64. Schelling, *On University Studies,* p. 106; Schlegel, *Dialogue on Poetry,* pp. 60, 74.
65. "The Spirit of Christianity," p. 273.
66. "Das achtzehnte Jahrhundert," in Wilhelm von Humboldt, *Gesammelte Schriften,* 17 vols. (Berlin, 1903), II, 14.
67. Novalis, *Schriften,* II, 63–84; Schelling, *On University Studies,* p. 83.
68. *Dialogue on Poetry,* p. 88.
69. *On University Studies,* p. 69.
70. Schlegel, *Schlegel, 1794–1802,* II, 215.

3. The reconciliation of Reason and reality

1. See Paul G. Klussmann, "Ludwig Tieck," in B. v. Wiese, ed., *Deutsche Dichter des 19, Jahrunderts* (Berlin, 1969), esp. pp. 15–22; and Hans-Jörg Sandkühler, *Freiheit und Wirklichkeit: Zur Dialektik von Politik und Philosophie bei F. W. J. Schelling* (Frankfurt, 1968), chaps. 3–4.
2. A richly detailed, though conservatively skewed, account of the administrative and institutional reconstruction in all the German states after 1800 can be found in Ernst Rudolf Huber, *Deutsche Verfassungsgeschichte seit 1789,* 4 vols. (Stuttgart, 1957–69), I, 95 ff. See also Hajo Holborn, *A History of Modern Germany, 1648–1840* (New York, 1964), pp. 355–422.
3. "Fragment of a System," pp. 313–19.
4. Hegel to Schelling, Nov. 2, 1800, in *Briefe (Hegel),* I, 59–60.
5. "Differenz des Fichteschen und Schellingschen Systems der Philosophie," pp. 20–1.
6. Hegel first sketched out the general outlines of this position in his Jena lectures of 1804–5. See G. W. F. Hegel, *Jenenser Logik, Metaphysik und Naturphilosophie,* ed. G. Lasson (Leipzig, 1923), pp. 1–186; and also Marcuse, *Reason and Revolution,* pp. 62–73.
7. *Phänomenologie,* p. 591.
8. Ibid., p. 19.
9. *Faith and Knowledge,* trans. and ed. W. Cerf and H. S. Harris (Albany, 1977), p. 56.
10. *Phänomenologie,* pp. 16–17, 19–20.
11. *Natural Law,* trans. T. M. Knox (Philadelphia, 1975), pp. 98–115. See also Marcuse, *Reason and Revolution,* pp. 56–61; and Raymond Plant, *Hegel* (Bloomington, Ind., 1973), pp. 89–96.
12. *Jenaer Realphilosophie,* ed. J. Hoffmeister (Hamburg, 1967), pp. 232–3, 242–63.
13. *Briefe (Hegel),* I, 235.
14. Ibid., pp. 253–4.
15. F. D. E. Schleiermacher, "Brouillon zur Ethik," in F. D. E. Schleiermacher, *Werke: Auswahl in vier Bänden,* ed. O. Braun and J. Bauer (Leipzig, 1913), II, 106. This volume cited hereafter as Braun, *Ethik.*
16. *Christmas Eve: Dialogue on the Incarnation,* ed. and trans. T. N. Tice (Richmond, Va., 1967), pp. 36, 40, 45, and esp. 83–4.
17. Richard R. Niebuhr, *Schleiermacher on Christ and Religion: A New Introduction* (New York, 1964), pp. 34–40, 72–134; Yorick Spiegel, *Theologie der bürgerlichen Gesellschaft: Sozialphilosophie und Glaubenslehre bei Friedrich Schleiermacher* (Munich, 1968), pp. 21–64.
18. *Aus Schleiermachers Leben,* II, 62–63. For Schleiermacher's social theory during his Halle years see Braun, *Ethik,* pp. 106–49, 166–7, 236–9, 333–47.
19. See Johannes Bauer, *Schleiermacher als patriotischer Prediger* (Giessen, 1908); and Franz Kade, *Schleiermachers Anteil an der Entwicklung des preussischen Bildungswesens von 1808–1818* (Leipzig, 1925).
20. Hegel to Niethammer, Feb. 11, 1808, in *Briefe (Hegel),* I, 218–19. See also ibid., I, 120, 137.
21. Ibid., I, 137–8, 185, 197–8. See also Avineri, *Hegel's Theory,* pp. 62–72; and Wilhelm R. Beyer, *Zwischen Phänomenologie und Logik: Hegel als Redakteur der Bamberger Zeitung* (Frankfurt, 1955).

22. Hegel to Niethammer, May 21, 1813, in *Briefe (Hegel),* II, 6.
23. See especially his attack on the historically regressive opposition of the Württemberg estates to the administrative liberalism and rationalism of the monarch in "Proceedings of the Estates Assembly in the Kingdom of Württemberg, 1815–1816," in Hegel, *Hegel's Political Writings,* pp. 246–94.
24. Koselleck, *Preussen,* pp. 278–9.
25. Humboldt's constitutional plans are contained in his "Denkschrift über Preussens ständische Verfassung," in Humboldt, *Schriften,* XII, 225–96. There is a discussion of the "fall" of the Humboldt party within the bureaucracy in Walter Simon, *The Failure of the Prussian Reform Movement, 1807–1819* (Ithaca, N.Y., 1955), pp. 197 ff., but with a rather exaggerated emphasis on purely personal factors.
26. Max Lenz, *Geschichte der königlichen Friedrich-Wilhelms-Universität zu Berlin,* 4 vols. (Halle, 1910–18), II, pt. 1, 39.
27. "Der Hegelianismus in Preussen," ed. Helmut Diwald, *Zeitschrift für Religions- und Geistesgeschichte* 10 (1958):55–7.
28. See his letter to the king, Feb. 20, 1818, printed in Lenz, *Geschichte,* IV, 334–5; and a letter to Hardenberg on June 10, 1822, printed in *Hegel in Berichten seiner Zeitgenossen,* ed. Günther Nicolin (Hamburg, 1970), p. 241.
29. "Rede zum Antritt des Philosophischen Lehramts an der Universität Berlin," in G. W. F. Hegel, *Berliner Schriften, 1818–1831,* ed. J. Hoffmeister (Hamburg, 1956), pp. 3–4.
30. *Sämtliche Werke,* 54 vols. (Leipzig, 1867–90), LI/LII, 588.
31. For the conflict between Hegelians and the Prussian Academy see Johannes Hoffmeister's notes in *Briefe (Hegel),* II, 397 ff., 440 ff., 448 ff. For Hegel's conception of the *Jahrbücher* as a weapon to defeat the Historical School see J. L. Döderlein, "Regest eines Briefs von Hegel an Niethammer," *Hegel-Jahrbuch* 13 (1978):75–6.
32. Lenz, *Geschichte,* II, pt. 1, 85–7, 173–5.
33. *Philosophy of Right,* pp. 6 ff.
34. Lenz, *Geschichte,* II, pt. 1, 110.
35. Ernst Simon, *Ranke und Hegel* (Munich and Berlin, 1928), pp. 112–14. See also Christoph Albrecht, *Schleiermachers Liturgik* (Göttingen, 1963), pp. 136–61.
36. *Philosophy of Right,* pp. 160–1.
37. Ibid., pp. 12–13.
38. Ibid., pp. 17, 135–6, 141, 270–1, 274.
39. "Rede zum Antritt," pp. 8–9.
40. "Vorrede zu Hinrichs Religionsphilosophie" (1822), in Hegel, *Werke,* ed. Moldenhauer and Michel, XI, 42–67.
41. See his comments to his colleagues Sack and DeWette in *Aus Schleiermachers Lebel,* IV, 306, 309.
42. *The Christian Faith,* trans. H. R. Mackintosh and J. S. Stewart, 2 vols. (New York, 1963), I, 18–20.
43. *On Religion,* p. 145 (addition to the 1821 ed.).
44. *Aus Schleiermachers Leben,* IV, 272; Adolf Stoll, *Friedrich Karl von Savigny: Professorenjahren in Berlin* (Berlin, 1929), p. 288.
45. This is essentially the position of Marcuse on Hegel and Spiegel on Schleiermacher.
46. See Schleiermacher's "Ueber den Beruf des Staates zu Erziehung" (1814),

in F. D. E. Schleiermacher, *Sämtliche Werke,* 32 vols. in 3 ser. (Berlin, 1835–64), 3rd ser., III, 227–51.
47. Quoted in Franz Schnabel, *Deutsche Geschichte im 19. Jahrhundert.* 2nd ed., 4 vols. (Freiburg, 1947–9), II, 373.
48. Rosenberg, *Bureaucracy,* chap. 8; Willard R. Fann, "The Rise of the Prussian Ministry, 1806–1827," in Wehler, *Sozialgeschichte Heute,* pp. 119–29.
49. Koselleck, *Preussen,* p. 153.
50. Mack Walker, "Home Towns and State Administrators: South German Politics, 1815–1830," *Political Science Quarterly* 82 (1967):35–60.
51. *Nürnberger Schriften,* ed. J. Hoffmeister (Leipzig, 1938), pp. 305, 309, 311.
52. *The Christian Faith,* I, 76.
53. *Enzyklopädie der philosophischen Wissenschaften im Grundrisse* (1830), in Hegel, *Werke,* ed. Moldenhauer and Michel, X, 393.
54. *Briefe (Hegel),* II, 89. On the nature of the Hegelian "supersession" of religion by philosophy see Emil Fackenheim, *The Religious Dimension in Hegel's Thought* (Boston, 1967); and Darrel E. Christenson, ed., *Hegel and the Philosophy of Religion* (The Hague, 1970).
55. *Enzyklopädie* (1830), pp. 353–65.
56. Spiegel, *Theologie,* p. 231; Löwith, *From Hegel to Nietzsche,* pp. 29–49.
57. The term is taken, of course, from M. H. Abrams's brilliant, comparative study of Romanticism: *Natural Supernaturalism: Tradition and Revolt in Romantic Literature* (New York, 1971).

4. Hegel and Hegelianism

1. *Phänomenologie,* p. 66.
2. Ibid., p. 20.
3. In a speech at a party given by his disciples, according to a report of Varnhagen von Ense: *Briefwechsel zwischen Karl Rosenkranz und Varnhagen von Ense,* ed. A. Warda (Königsberg, 1926), p. 90.
4. "Aphorismen aus Hegel's Wastebook" (1803–6), in Hegel, *Werke,* ed. Moldenhauer and Michel, II, 548.
5. *Briefe (Hegel),* II, 98; "Aphorismen," pp. 551, 542; *Phänomenologie,* pp. 14–18, 65.
6. "Maximen des Journals der deutschen Literatur" (1807), in Hegel, *Werke,* ed. Moldenhauer and Michel, II, 572–3.
7. *Briefe (Hegel),* I, 138–9, 314–5.
8. "Maximen," pp. 568–74; "Ueber die Einrichtung einer kritischen Zeitschrift der Literatur," in Hegel, *Werke,* ed. Moldenhauer and Michel, XI, 31–41.
9. Hegel admonished his students never to refer to his philosophy as "Hegel's" philosophy. See his letter to Hinrichs in 1819: *Briefe (Hegel),* II, 215–16.
10. Cited in *Hegel in Berichten,* pp. 322–3. Hegel's conception of the dialectical relationship between intellectual elite and cultural community is very close to Gramsci's conception of "organic" intellectuals. See Antonio Gramsci, *Selections from the Prison Notebooks,* ed. Q. Hoare and G. N. Smith (New York, 1971), pp. 5 ff.
11. Hegel to v. Raumer, Aug. 2, 1816, in *Briefe (Hegel),* II, 100–1.

12. Karl Ludwig Michelet, *Wahrheit aus meinem Leben* (Berlin, 1884), pp. 624–5; Hegel to Hinrichs, Nov. 1819, in *Briefe (Hegel)*, II, 222–3.
13. *Vorlesungen über die Philosophie der Religion*, in Hegel, *Werke*, ed. Moldenhauer and Michel, XVII, 343.
14. Rosenkranz admonished his contemporaries to respect the individuality of Hegelians as early as 1834: *Hegel: Sendschreiben an den Hofrath und Professor der Philosophie Herrn Dr. Carl Friedrich Bachmann in Jena* (Königsberg, 1834), pp. 133–4. One modern scholar has taken this advice more literally than it was intended and denied the label "Hegelian" to even the most orthodox Hegelians. See Falk Wagner's essays on Marheineke and Rosenkranz in *Neue Zeitschrift für systematische Theologie und Religionsphilosophie* 10 (1968):44–88; 12 (1970):313–37.
15. Hegel to v. Raumer, Aug. 2, 1816, in *Briefe (Hegel)*, II, 99.
16. Ibid.
17. Hegel to Fromann, Apr. 14, 1816, in *Briefe (Hegel)*, II, 73.
18. Hegel to v. Thaden, in *Briefe (Hegel)*, II, 139.
19. For some judgments from the late 1820s see *Hegel in Berichten*, pp. 375–9, 421–2.
20. Schelver to Hegel, Jan. 1807, in *Briefe (Hegel)*, I, 139.
21. See Heinrich Hotho, *Vorstudien für Leben und Kunst* (Stuttgart, 1835), p. 386.
22. This phrase was used by the writer Karl Gutzkow to describe his own transformation from a "theologizing Paul into a philosophizing Saul." See Gutzkow, "Das Kastanienwäldchen in Berlin," in Karl Gutzkow, *Ausgewählte Werke*, ed. H. H. Houben, 12 vols. (Leipzig, 1908), XII, 36, 42–3.
23. *Briefe* (Hegel), I, 77, 83, 95–101, 149, 226–7.
24. Heinz Kimmerle, "Dokumente zu Hegels Jenaer Dozententätigkeit (1801–1807)." *Hegel-Studien* 4 (1967):53–4.
25. "Bericht Gablers über Hegel" (1840), in Kimmerle, "Dokumente," pp. 67–8, 70.
26. Rosenkranz, *Hegels Leben*, pp. 214–15.
27. *Briefe (Hegel)*, I, 426.
28. G. Nicolin, ed., "Zwei unbekannte Briefe von Hegel aus dem Jahre 1807," *Hegel-Studien* 4 (1967):101–7.
29. "Bericht Gablers," p. 69.
30. Karl Länig, "Die pädagogische Jahre Hegels in Nürnberg," in W. R. Beyer, K. Länig, and K. Goldmann, *Georg Wilhelm Friedrich Hegel in Nürnberg, 1808–1816* (Nürnberg, 1966), pp. 17–37; *Hegel in Berichten*, pp. 114–16, 128–30, 136.
31. After a few years as tutor to Schiller's sons, Gabler began a career as a gymnasium professor in Ansbach and Bayreuth. His *Lehrbuch der philosophischen Propädeutik als Einleitung zur Wissenschaft* (Erlangen, 1827), a popular introduction to Hegel's system, was very favorably received by Hegel, and Gabler was appointed to Hegel's chair in 1835.
32. "System der Wissenschaft, von G. W. Fr. Hegel," *Heidelbergische Jahrbücher* 3, no. 1 (1810):146–8.
33. *Ueber Philosophie und ihre Geschichte* (Jena, 1811), p. 77.
34. Hegel to v. Ghert, Oct. 15, 1810, in *Briefe (Hegel)*, I, 330.
35. *Ueber die Philosophie meiner Zeit: Zur Vermittlung* (Jena, 1816), pp. 1, 233–51, 304–14.
36. *Ueber Geschichte der Philosophie* (Jena, 1820), pp. 106–8.

37. *System der Logik: Ein Handbuch zum Selbststudium* (Leipzig, 1828), pp. vi–ix and passim.
38. See especially Christian H. Weisse, *Ueber den gegenwärtigen Standpunkt der philosophischen Wissenschaft in besonderer Beziehung auf Hegels System* (Leipzig, 1829); Immanuel H. Fichte, *Beiträge zur Charakteristik der neueren Philosophie* (Sulzbach, 1829); and Johann G. F. Billroth, *Beiträge zur wissenschaftlichen Kritik der herrschenden Theologie* (Leipzig, 1831).
39. Karl Ludwig Michelet, *Geschichte der letzten Systeme der Philosophie in Deutschland von Kant bis Hegel,* 2 vols. (Berlin, 1837–8), II, 630 ff.
40. v. Ghert to Hegel, Mar. 1, 1816, in *Briefe (Hegel),* II, 246.
41. *Briefe (Hegel),* II, 69–71; A. V. N. van Woerden, "Das konfessionale Element in van Gherts Hegel-Rezeption," *Hegel-Jahrbuch* (1972), pp. 11–14; Wim van Dooren, "Eine frühe Hegel-Diskussion in Holland," *Hegel-Studien* 11 (1976):211–17.
42. *Briefe (Hegel),* II, 158–9, III, 117–18, 233–34, 313–14, 433–35.
43. A good selection of opinions from the faculties at Heidelberg and Berlin can be found in *Hegel in Berichten,* pp. 120–7.
44. *Briefe (Hegel),* I, 102, 139–40.
45. *Aus Schellings Leben in Briefen,* ed. G. L. Plitt, 3 vols. (Leipzig, 1869), II, 143–4.
46. Ibid., p. 128.
47. *Hegel in Berichten,* pp. 120, 122, 125–6.
48. "Maximen," p. 571.
49. *Briefe (Hegel),* I, 307.
50. See his letter to Hegel in *Hegel (Briefe),* I, 223.
51. See Albert Sonnenschein, *Görres, Windischmann und Deutinger als christliche Philosophen* (Bochum, 1938), pp. 7–35.
52. *Briefe (Hegel),* III, 27.
53. *Judas Ischariot, oder das Böse im Verhältniss zum Guten,* 2 vols. (Heidelberg, 1816–18), I, ix.
54. v. Thaden to Hegel, Aug. 8, 1821, in *Briefe (Hegel),* II, 278–82. Paulus's critical review of Hegel's *Philosophy of Right* is reprinted in G. W. F. Hegel, *Vorlesungen über Rechtsphilosophie,* ed. Karl-Heinz Ilting, 4 vols. (Stuttgart and Bad Cannstatt, 1973–6), I, 359–76.
55. Dec. 17, 1817, in *Briefe (Hegel),* II, 171–2. Niethammer was responding to Hegel's article on the Württemberg estates.
56. Evidence for Hegel's growing impact on students between 1816 and 1822–3 can be found in Friedhelm Nicolin, "Hegel als Professor in Heidelberg: Aus den Akten der philosophischen Fakultät, 1816–1818" *Hegel-Studien* 2 (1963):71–98; Otto Pöggeler, "Hegel and Heidelberg," *Hegel-Studien* 6 (1971):65–133; Lenz, *Geschichte,* II, pt. 1, 204–7; and *Hegel in Berichten,* pp. 139 ff.
57. "Die Heidelberger Niederschrift der Einleitung," in G. W. F. Hegel, *System und Geschichte der Philosophie,* ed. J. Hoffmeister, 2 vols. (Hamburg, 1940), I, 3–4.
58. *Hegels Leben,* p. 338.
59. Eduard Gans, *Rückblicke auf Personen und Zustände* (Berlin, 1836), pp. 215–56; Fritz Schlawe, "Die Berliner Jahrbücher für wissenschaftliche Kritik: Ein Beitrag zur Geschichte des Hegelianismus," *Zeitschrift für Religions- und Geistesgeschichte* 11 (1959):240–58.

60. The phrase is Gans's. See his *Vermischte Schriften, juristischen, historischen, staatswissenschaflichen und ästhetischen Inhalts,* 2 vols. (Berlin, 1834), II, 249–50.
61. Rosenkranz, *Hegel: Sendschreiben,* p. 132.
62. *Hegel in Berichten,* pp. 300–3, 391–4, 451–4; Robert Klein, *Heinrich Theodor Rötschers Leben und Wirken* (Berlin, 1919), pp. 19–20; Rosenkranz, *Hegels Leben,* pp. 352–62.
63. Hegel to Gabler, Mar. 4, 1828, in *Briefe (Hegel),* III, 224–5. Hegel's praise of Göschel can be found in the Jahrbücher für wissenschaftliche Kritik (1829), cols. 789–816, 833–5. See also Gebhardt, *Politik und Eschatologie,* pp. 54–61.
64. "Grabrede," *Hegel in Berichten,* p. 476.
65. "Trauerrede," *Hegel in Berichten,* p. 474.
66. Ibid., pp. 474–5.
67. Förster, "Grabrede," p. 477; Marheineke, "Trauerrede," p. 474.
68. Förster, "Grabrede," p. 477.
69. "Vorrede zu Hinrichs Religionsphilosophie," p. 44; letter to Windischmann, May 27, 1810, in *Briefe (Hegel),* I, 314–15.
70. *Aphorismen über Nichtwissen und absolutes Wissen im Verhältnisse zur christlichen Glaubenserkenntnis* (Berlin, 1829), p. 160.
71. *Briefe (Hegel),* III, 29.
72. *Kritische Erläuterungen des Hegelschen Systems* (Königsberg, 1840), p. 354.
73. "Bericht Gablers," pp. 65–73.
74. Karl Rosenkranz, *Von Magdeburg bis Königsberg* (Berlin, 1873), pp. 291, 381; Michelet, *Wahrheit aus meinem Leben,* pp. 59–61; Arnold Ruge, *Aus früherer Zeit,* 4 vols. (Berlin, 1862–7), IV, 7 ff.; David Friedrich Strauss, "Christian Märklin: Ein Lebens- und Charakterbild aus der Gegenwart" (1851), in David Friedrich Strauss, *Gesammelte Schriften,* ed. E. Zeller, 12 vols. (Bonn, 1876–8), X, 223–4; Ludwig Feuerbach, *Briefwechsel und Nachlass,* ed. and intro. by Karl Grün, 2 vols. (Leipzig and Heidelberg, 1874), I, 386–7; Friedrich Theodor Vischer, "Mein Lebensgang," in Friedrich Theodor Vischer, *Altes und Neues,* 3 vols. (Stuttgart, 1882), III, 266 ff.
75. *Christus und die Weltgeschichte, oder Sokrates und die Wissenschaft: Bruchstücke einer Theodicee der Wirklichkeit oder Stimme eines Predigers in der Wüste* (Heidelberg, 1823), p. x.
76. *Vorstudien,* p. 381.
77. Quoted in Heinrich Benecke, *Wilhelm Vatke in seinem Leben und seinen Schriften* (Bonn, 1883), pp. 47–8.
78. *Wahrheit aus meinem Leben,* p. 61.
79. *Kritische Erläuterungen,* p. 354.
80. *Christus und die Weltgeschichte,* p. 361.
81. *Vorstudien,* p. 392.
82. *Wahrheit aus meinem Leben,* p. 61.
83. *Briefe (Hegel),* III, 153.
84. "Ueber den Standpunkt der Philosophie und die Bedeutung ihres Studiums in gegenwärtiger Zeit" (1819), *Neue Berliner Monatsschrift für Philosophie, Geschichte, Literatur und Kunst* (1821), pt. 1, p. 139.
85. Quoted in Benecke, *Vatke,* p. 48.
86. *Wahrheit aus meinem Leben,* p. 60.

5. Hegelian politics during the Restoration

1. Heinrich Heine, *Sämtliche Werke,* ed. O. Walzel, 10 vols. (Leipzig, 1911–15), IX, 484, VII, 344, X, 171.

2. Karl-Heinz Ilting, "Einleitung" to Hegel, *Vorlesungen über Rechtsphilosophie* I, 25 ff. See also Rolf P. Horstmann, "Ist Hegel's Rechtsphilosophie, das Produkt der politischen Anpassung eines Liberalen?" *Hegel-Studien* 9 (1974):244–52; and Rolf Hocevar, *Hegel und der preussischer Staat* (Munich, 1973), pp. 80–116.

3. Ilting, "Einleitung," pp. 83–6, 88–93.

4. "Vorrede" to G. W. F. Hegel, *Werke*, ed. P. Marheineke et al., 18 vols. (Berlin, 1832–45), XIII: *Grundlinien der Philosophie des Rechts*, pp. ix–x.

5. Hegel to Niethammer, June 9, 1821, in *Briefe (Hegel)*, II, 272.

6. *Briefe (Hegel)*, II, 263, 305; Rosenkranz, *Hegels Leben*, pp. 336–7.

7. See E. Weil, *Hegel et l'état* (Paris, 1950), pp. 11 ff.; Joachim Ritter, *Hegel und die französische Revolution* (Frankfurt, 1965), p. 79; and Avineri, *Hegel's Theory*, p. 116.

8. For Heine's interpretation of Hegel see Paul Konrad Kurz, *Künstler, Tribun, Apostel: Heinrich Heine's Aufassung vom Beruf des Dichters* (Munich, 1967), pp. 68–81; and Georg Lukács, *Deutsche Realisten des 19. Jahrhunderts* (Berlin, 1952), pp. 108 ff. Recent discussion of the possible revolutionary implications of Hegel's doctrine of the absolute spirit can be found in Michael Theunissen, *Hegel's Lehre vom absoluten Geist als theologisch-politischer Traktat* (Berlin, 1970); and Herbert Scheit, *Geist und Gemeinde: Zum Verhältnis von Religion und Politik bei Hegel* (Munich and Salzburg, 1973).

9. On Heine's contact with the more radical forms of Jewish Hegelianism, see Hanns Günther Reissner, *Eduard Gans: Ein Leben im Vormärz* (Tübingen, 1965), pp. 83 ff.

10. Manfred Riedel, "Hegel und Gans," in H. Braun and M. Riedel, eds., *Natur und Geschichte: Karl Löwith zum 70. Geburtstag* (Stuttgart, 1967), p. 258.

11. "Die Heidelberger Niederschrift," pp. 3–4.

12. Hegel to v. Raumer, Aug. 2, 1816, in *Briefe (Hegel)*, II, 101.

13. Biographical data can be found on Schulze in Conrad Varrentrapp, *Johannes Schulze und das höhere preussische Unterrichtswesen in seiner Zeit* (Leipzig, 1889); on Henning in *Allgemeine Deutsche Biographie*, XI, 777–8, and Lenz, *Geschichte*, II, pt. 1, 56–8; on Förster in *Allgemeine Deutsche Biographie*, VII, 185–9, Friedrich Förster, "Aus der Knabenzeit," in Friedrich Förster, *Kunst und Leben: Aus Friedrich Försters Nachlass*, ed. Hermann Kletke (Berlin, 1873), pp. 1–163, and Ernst Förster, *Aus der Jugendzeit*, ed. K. v. Binzer (Stuttgart and Berlin, 1887); on Leo in Heinrich Leo, *Meine Jugendzeit* (Gotha, 1880), and Paul Krägelin, *Heinrich Leo* (Leipzig, 1908).

14. Varrentrapp, *Schulze*, pp. 24–60, 66–76. Schulze's nationalist pedagogical hopes are most clearly articulated in his *Aufruf an die deutsche Jünglinge* (Jena, 1808).

15. Johannes Schulze, *Predigten* (Leipzig, 1810); Johannes Schulze, *Reden über die christliche Religion* (Halle, 1811).

16. Varrentrapp, *Schulze*, pp. 153, 159–61.

17. Cited in Varrentrapp, *Schulze*, p. 160, from Johann Schulze, *Zwei Reden geweiht den widergebornen Hessen* (Hanau, 1813).

18. Varrentrapp, *Schulze*, pp. 174–178ff.

19. Lenz, *Geschichte*, II, pt. 1, 56–7.

20. A good selection can be found in Max Mendheim, ed., *Lyriker und Epiker der klassischen Periode*, pt. 3 (Stuttgart, n.d.), pp. 325–35.

21. Förster's disillusionment is clearly expressed in "Blücher schreibt nach Wien" (1815), in Mendheim, *Lyriker und Epiker*, pt. 3, p. 335.

22. "Vorrede" to Friedrich Förster, ed., *Beiträge zur neueren Kriegsgeschichte*, 2

vols. (Berlin, 1816), I, xiii. See also Friedrich Förster, *Von der Begeisterung des preussischen Volkes im Jahre 1813 als Vertheidigung unseres Glaubens* (Berlin, 1816), esp. pp. 7, 9, 12.

23. Cited in Krieger, *Idea,* p. 219. Henning made his contribution to the constitutional movement by translating Thomas Jefferson's *Handbook of Parliamentary Procedure* into German.

24. Cited in Krieger, *Idea,* p. 217.

25. *Briefe (Hegel),* II, 468–71 (Hoffmeister's notes).

26. Lenz, *Geschichte,* II, pt. 1, 58; *Briefe (Hegel),* II, 482.

27. *Meine Jugendzeit,* pp. 49, 54–5, 73–4, 89–90, 100–4.

28. Ibid., p. 100.

29. Ibid., pp. 194–204.

30. Ibid., p. 153.

31. Ibid., pp. 220–30.

32. Heinrich Leo, *Die Hegelingen: Actenstücke und Belege zu der s. g. Denunciation der ewigen Wahrheit,* 2nd ed. (Halle, 1839), p. 52; Leo, *Meine Jugendzeit,* pp. 232–3.

33. *Ueber die Verfassung der freien lombardischen Städte im Mittelalter* (Rudolstadt, 1820), pp. xi–xii.

34. Ibid., p. xviii.

35. Leo to J. Böhmer, Mar. 15, 1823, in Johannes F. Böhmer, *Leben, Briefe und kleinere Schriften,* ed. J. Janssen, 3 vols. (Freiburg im Breisgau, 1868), I, 86.

36. Biographical data on Carové can be found in *Allgemeine Deutsche Biographie,* IV, 7–8; and there are autobiographical accounts in Friedhelm Nicolin, "Hegel als Professor in Heidelberg," pp. 87–91, and Friedrich Wilhelm Carové, *Ueber alleinseligmachende Kirche,* 2 vols. (Frankfurt and Göttingen, 1826–7), II, xiii–xv.

37. Carové's contributions to various Romantic journals and collections of poetry during this period are discussed in Albert Schürmann, *Friedrich Wilhelm Carové: Sein Werk als Beitrag zur Kritik an Staat und Kirche im frühliberalen Hegelianismus* (Bochum, 1971), pp. 13–18.

38. Eduard Dietz, *Die deutsche Burschenschaft in Heidelberg: Ein Beitrag zur Kulturgeschichte deutscher Universitäten* (Heidelberg, 1895), pp. 14–23.

39. "Ansichten der Kunst des deutschen Mittelalters," in E. v. Groote, F. W. Carové, et al., eds., *Zeit und Kunst: altteutsche* (Cologne, 1822), pp. 55, 93–5. This is a new edition of an anthology originally published in 1816.

40. See especially "Meine Kindheit" and "Herbstklage" in Groote, Carové, et al., *Zeit und Kunst,* pp. 333–4, 336.

41. Siegfried Ucko, "Geistesgeschichtliche Grundlagen der Wissenschaft des Judentums (Motive des Kulturvereins vom Jahre 1819)," *Zeitschrift für die Geschichte der Juden in Deutschland* 5 (1935):3–4.

42. Ismar Freund, "Die deutsche Judenfrage vor 100 Jahren," *Zeitschrift für die Geschichte der Juden in Deutschland* 5 (1935):34–5; Reissner, *Gans,* pp. 56–7.

43. Reissner, *Gans,* pp. 14–25.

44. Ucko, "Grundlagen," pp. 3–4.

45. Reissner, *Gans,* pp. 50–1, 59–83.

46. Michael Meyer, *The Origins of the Modern Jew: Jewish Identity and European Culture in Germany, 1749–1824* (Detroit, 1967), pp. 139–43; Jacob Katz, *Out of the Ghetto: The Social Background of Jewish Emancipation, 1770–1870* (Cambridge, Mass., 1973), pp. 200 ff.

47. H. G. Reissner, "Rebellious Dilemma: The Case Histories of Eduard Gans and Some of His Partisans," *Leo Baeck Institute Year Book* 17 (1972):179–93.

48. Gans's reply to Rühs is printed in Ludwig Geiger, "Aus Eduard Gans' Frühzeit (1817)," *Zeitschrift für die Geschichte der Juden in Deutschland* 5 (1892):93–6.

49. Saint-Marc-Girardin, "Erinnerungen an Eduard Gans," *Zeitung für die Elegante Welt*, no. 14–16 (Jan. 21, 1840), p. 57.

50. Erich Landsberg, *Geschichte der deutschen Rechtswissenschaft* (Munich and Leipzig, 1910), III, pt. 2, 69–88. Gans's own appreciation of Thibaut can be found in his *Das Erbrecht in weltgeschichtlicher Entwicklung*, 4 vols. (Berlin, 1824–35), I (1824), pp. xix–xx.

51. *Ueber Römisches Obligationsrecht, insbesondere über die Lehre von den Innominatcontracten und dem jus poenitendi* (Heidelberg, 1819); *Scholien zum Gajus* (Berlin, 1821).

52. Lenz, *Geschichte*, II, pt. 1, 218–19.

53. *Scholien zum Gajus*, pp. vii–viii.

54. "Die juristische Fakultät an das Ministerium," Apr. 4, 1820, in Lenz, *Geschichte*, IV, 449; Gans to Altenstein, May 3, 1821, in Lenz, *Geschichte*, IV, 452.

55. *Erbrecht*, I, xvi.

56. Varrentrapp, *Schulze*, p. 432.

57. Ibid., p. 433.

58. Ibid., p. 431.

59. Franz Rosenzweig, *Hegel und der Staat*, 2 vols. (Munich and Berlin, 1920), II, 169.

60. Varrentrapp, *Schulze*, pp. 432–3.

61. Schulze's educational philosophy during the 1820s was clearly articulated in his review of Friedrich Thiersch's *Ueber gelehrte Schulen* in the *Jahrbücher für wissenschaftliche Kritik* (1827), cols. 86–107.

62. Ernst Förster, *Aus der Jugendzeit*, p. 168.

63. One of the most dramatic of these conversions was that of Gustav Asverus (1798–1843), who had been one of the major opponents of Carové's Hegelianism in Heidelberg. See Paul Wentzcke, "Ein Schüler Hegels aus der Frühzeit der Burschenschaft: Gustav Asverus in Heidelberg, Berlin und Jena," *Quellen und Darstellungen der Geschichte der Burschenschaft und der deutschen Einheitsbewegung*, V, (Heidelberg, 1920), 93–132.

64. Hegel, *Berliner Schriften*, pp. 598–9.

65. Ilting, "Einleitung," pp. 51–5.

66. Ernst Förster, *Aus der Jugendzeit*, 170–4.

67. "Vorwort," *Neue Berliner Monatsschrift* (1821), pt. 1, p. 2.

68. "Ueber das Verhältnis der Philosophie zu den positiven Wissenschaften überhaupt und insbesondere zur Rechtswissenschaft als auf historische Grundlage ruhend," *Neue Berliner Monatsschrift* (1821), pt. 5, p. 1.

69. "Die Romantische Kunst," *Neue Berliner Monatsschrift* (1821), pt. 2, p. 199.

70. "Ein Märchen," *Neue Berliner Monatsschrift* (1821), pt. 1, p. 27.

71. Förster, "Die Romantische Kunst," pp. 185–6; Leopold Henning, "Zur Verständigung über das gegenwärtige Zeitalter," *Neue Berliner Monatsschrift* (1821), pt. 1, p. 242.

72. "Zur Verständigung," p. 242.

73. "Die Romantische Kunst," p. 184.
74. "Zur Verständigung," pp. 291, 293.
75. *Der Feldmarschall Fürst von Blücher von Wahlstatt und seine Umgebungen* (Leipzig, 1821), p. vii. For Henning's new positive evaluation of Napoleon see *Briefe (Hegel),* III, 365.
76. "Ueber das Verhältnis," p. 22.
77. "Zur Verständigung," pp. 230–6; "Ueber das Verhältnis," pp. 5–9.
78. "Ueber das Verhältnis," p. 106.
79. See his *Principien der Ethik in historischer Entwicklung* (Berlin, 1824), esp. pp. xiii, 194 ff. Even Hinrichs found Henning too uncritical; see Hinrichs to Hegel, Aug. 1826, in *Briefe (Hegel),* III, 132.
80. *Jahrbücher für wissenschaftliche Kritik* (1827), cols. 1592, 1588. Henning never wavered from this position; see his *Zur Verständigung über die preussische Verfassungsfrage* (Berlin, 1845), pp. 41–2.
81. *Vertraute Briefe über Preussens Hauptstadt* (Stuttgart and Leipzig, 1837), pp. 96–7; Rosenkranz, *Von Magdeburg bis Königsberg,* pp. 185–9, 212–13.
82. *Briefe (Hegel),* II, 470–1; *Neue Berliner Monatsschrift* (1821), pt. 2, pp. 345–6.
83. *Neue Berliner Monatsschrift* (1821), pt. 1, pp. 210–11, 432–3, pt. 2, pp. 249–54.
84. Ibid., pt. 1, p. 32.
85. "Die Gratulanten," *Neue Berliner Monatsschrift* (1821), pt. 2, p. 479.
86. *Hegel in Berichten,* pp. 416, 662.
87. "Der neue Herkules," *Hegel in Berichten,* pp. 305–8.
88. "Grabrede," p. 477.
89. J. Saling, *Die Gerechtigkeit in ihrer geschichtlichen Entwicklung* (Berlin, 1827); Karl Ludwig Michelet, *Das System der philosophischen Moral mit Rücksicht auf die juridische Imputation der Geschichte der Moral und das christliche Moralprinzip* (Berlin, 1828).
90. Julius F. H. Abegg, *Encyclopädie und Methodologie der Rechtswissenschaft im Grundrisse* (Königsberg, 1823); Johann F. G. Eiselen, *Handbuch des Systems der Staatswissenschaften* (Breslau, 1828); Konrad Moritz Besser, *System des Naturrechts* (Halle and Leipzig, 1830).
91. *Grundbegriff preussischer Staats- und Rechtsgeschichte als Einleitung in die Wissenschaft des preussischen Rechts* (Berlin, 1829), pp. xvi, 97–100, 403–4, 702. See also Michelet, *Geschichte der letzten Systeme,* II, 665–6.
92. Leo to Perthes, June 12, 1824, in Dieter Gebhard, "Zur Geschichte der historischen Schule: Drei Briefe von Ranke und Heinrich Leo," *Historische Zeitschrift* 132 (1925):105.
93. *Entwicklung der Verfassung der lombardischen Städte bis zu der Ankunft Kaiser Friedrichs I in Italien* (Hamburg, 1824), pp. 69–70.
94. "Vorrede" to Heinrich Leo, ed., *Die Briefe des Florentinischen Kanzlers und Geschichtsschreibers Niccolo di Bernardo dei Machiavelli an seine Freunde, aus dem Italienischen übersetzt von Heinrich Leo* (Berlin, 1826), pp. v–vii. For a detailed discussion of the Ranke-Leo controversy see George Iggers, *The German Conception of History: The National Tradition of Historical Thought from Herder to the Present* (Middletown, Conn., 1968), pp. 67–9; Simon, *Ranke und Hegel,* pp. 93–101; and above all Kurt Mautz, "Leo und Ranke," *Deutsche Vierteljahresschrift für Literaturwissenschaft und Geistesgeschichte* 27 (1953):207–35.
95. *Jahrbücher für wissenschaftliche Kritik* (1827), col. 355.

96. Ibid., cols. 365–6.
97. *Vorlesungen über die Geschichte des jüdischen Staates* (Berlin, 1828), pp. 56–62.
98. Ibid., p. 5.
99. Letter to Heinrich Ranke, Apr. 16, 1828, in Ranke, *Werke,* LIII/LIV, 196.
100. *Vorlesungen,* p. v.
101. *Jahrbücher für wissenschaftliche Kritik* (1829), pt. 2, col. 551.
102. Ibid., pp. 551, 555.
103. He was especially drawn to the "individualism" of the Italian Renaissance. See his *Geschichte der italienischen Staaten,* 5 vols. (Hamburg, 1829–32), I, 33–40, 469, II, 129.
104. *Lehrbuch der Geschichte des Mittelalters,* 2 vols. (Halle, 1830), I, 171.
105. Leo to Hegel, Dec. 20, 1827, in *Briefe (Hegel),* III, 213.
106. Ibid., p. 214; *Die Hegelingen* (1838), pp. 93–5.
107. Leo to Altenstein, Nov. 24, 1827, in Lenz, *Geschichte,* IV, 495.
108. These addresses are printed in S. Rubaschoff, "Erstlinge der Entjudung," *Der Jüdische Wille* 1 (1918–19):36–41, 108–21, 193–203.
109. Address of Apr. 28, 1822, in Rubaschoff, "Erstlinge," p. 110.
110. Immanuel Wolf (Wohlwill), "Ueber den Begriff einer Wissenschaft des Judenthums," *Zeitschrift für die Wissenschaft des Judenthms* 1 (1822–3):3.
111. Address of Apr. 28, 1822, in Rubaschoff, "Erstlinge," p. 110.
112. Address of Oct. 28, 1821, in Rubaschoff, "Erstlinge," pp. 39, 38, 42.
113. Address of May 4, 1823, in Rubaschoff, "Erstlinge," pp. 198, 195.
114. Ibid., p. 198.
115. Address of Apr. 28, 1822, in Rubaschoff, "Erstlinge," p. 111.
116. Reissner, *Gans,* p. 92.
117. Ibid., pp. 83–102.
118. Albert R. Friedlander, "The Moser-Wohlwill Correspondence," *Leo Baeck Institute Year Book* 11 (1966):289, 292, 296–7.
119. *Erbrecht,* I, xiii, xxxix, xli.
120. Gans's attack on the Historical School for its "emigration" to the Middle Ages runs through all of his writings but is most succinctly summarized in "Ueber das Studium des Römischen Rechts," in Eduard Gans, *System des Römischen Civilrechts im Grundrisse* (Berlin, 1827), pp. 155–74.
121. As Gans admitted in his *Erbrecht,* I, xiii.
122. Schulze to Altenstein, Nov. 12, 1823, in Lenz, *Geschichte,* IV, 457; Hegel to Windischmann, Apr. 11, 1824, in *Briefe* (*Hegel*), III, 41.
123. Cousin to Hegel, Dec. 13, 1825, in *Briefe* (*Hegel*), III, 99–100.
124. Reissner, *Gans,* 108–9.
125. Gans's year in Paris is described in his memoir "Paris im Jahre 1825," *Rückblicke auf Personen und Zustände,* pp. 1–47.
126. "Naturrecht, Vorlesungsnachschrift," (1828–9), in Eduard Gans, *Philosophische Schriften,* ed. Horst Schröder (Glashütten in Taunus, 1971), p. 149.
127. From a transcript of a meeting of the association on Dec. 22, 1821, printed in Ucko, "Grundlagen," p. 19.
128. From a conversation recorded in Felix Eberty, *Jugenderinnerungen eines alten Berliners* (Berlin, 1925), p. 89.
129. Eduard Gans, "Die Stiftung der Jahrbücher für wissenschaftliche Kritik," in *Rückblicke auf Personen und Zustände,* pp. 234–5, 253–5.
130. *Hallische Jahrbücher,* no. 113 (1840), p. 901.

131. Ruge, *Aus früherer Zeit,* IV, 431.
132. "Naturrecht," p. 44.
133. Ibid., pp. 111, 119, 122–3.
134. Ibid., p. 135.
135. Ibid., pp. 136–7.
136. Ibid., p. 140.
137. "Geschichte der neuesten Zeit von 1789 an, in besonderer Beziehung auf öffentliches Recht," cited from the lecture notes of Felix Mendelssohn-Bartholdy in Reissner, *Gans,* p. 126.
138. Saint-Marc-Girardin, "Erinnerungen an Eduard Gans," pp. 57–8.
139. *Entwurf einer Burschenschafts-Ordnung und Versuch einer Begründung derselben* (Eisenach, 1818), p. 55.
140. Ibid., p. 56.
141. Ibid., pp. 67, 70.
142. Shlomo Avineri, "A Note on Hegel's View on Jewish Emancipation," *Jewish Social Studies* 25 (1963): 148–51. Carové's specific statements about Jews and foreigners are in *Entwurf,* pp. 196–7.
143. *Entwurf,* p. 10.
144. Ibid., p. 140.
145. Ibid., p. 59.
146. Cited in *Hegel in Berichten,* p. 180.
147. Dietz, *Die deutsche Burschenschaft,* pp. 24–5; Wentzcke, "Ein Schüler Hegels," pp. 97–106.
148. *Ueber die Ermordung Kotzebues* (Eisenach, 1819), pp. 7, 14.
149. *Briefe (Hegel),* II, 455–68.
150. From an unpublished letter cited in Schürmann, *Carové,* p. 31.
151. "Ueber die Stellung das Naturrechts im absoluten Idealismus und seine Bedeutung für gegenwärtige Zeit," *Neue Berliner Monatsschrift* (1821), pt. 1, pp. 377–8.
152. *Ueber alleinseligmachende Kirche,* I, xii–xiii.
153. "Die Formen der Authorität in der Geschichte" (1823), in Friedrich Wilhelm Carové, *Kosmorama: Eine Reihe von Studien zur Orientierung in Natur, Geschichte, Staat, Philosophie und Religion* (Frankfurt, 1831), p. 126.
154. *Ueber das Recht, die Weise und die wichtigsten Gegenstände der öffenlichen Beurtheilung mit stäter Beziehung auf die neueste Zeit* (Trier, 1825), p. v–vi; *Ueber alleinseligmachende Kirche,* I, vi.
155. *Ueber das Recht,* pp. 131–5.
156. Ibid., p. 136.
157. "Die Formen der Authorität," p. 127.
158. *Ueber alleinseligmachende Kirche,* I, 175–6; II, 358–9; *Ueber das Recht,* pp. 138–9.
159. "Frankreich und Deutschland," *Neue Berliner Monatsschrift* 2 (1821): 125–34; *Religion und Philosophie in Frankreich: Eine Folge von Abhandlungen aus dem französischen übersetzt und eingeleitet* (Göttingen, 1827).
160. *Ueber das Recht,* pp. 47, 49–50, 137; *Ueber alleinseligmachende Kirche,* I, xiv–xv.
161. *Ueber das Recht,* p. 48.
162. From an unpublished letter to Büchner, Nov. 21, 1836, cited in Schurmann, *Carové,* p. 38.

6. Christian religion and Hegelian philosophy

1. *Vorlesungen über die Philosophie der Religion,* XVI, 62, 63.
2. "Vorrede zu Hinrichs Religionsphilosophie," pp. 62, 63.
3. Biographical information on Daub and Marheineke has been drawn from *Realencyklopädie für Protestantische Theologie und Kirche,* 3rd ed., 24 vols. (1896–1913), IV, 496–502, XII, 304–9; and *Allgemeine Deutsche Biographie,* IV, 768, XX, 338–40.
4. *Predigten nach Kantischen Grundsätzen* (Königsberg, 1794), "Vorrede" (unpaginated), 207–8, 268–9.
5. *Lehrbuch der Katechetik* (Frankfurt, 1801), esp. pp. 402 ff. Daub's self-criticism is contained in his *Judas Ischariot,* I, x–xi.
6. The shift to Schelling was evident in his *Theologumena: sive doctrinae de religione christiana, ex natura Dei perspecta, repetendae, capita potiora* (Heidelberg, 1806). See Wilhelm Hermann, *Die speculative Theologie in ihrer Entwicklung durch Daub* (Hamburg, 1847), pp. 32–3; and Karl Rosenkranz, *Erinnerungen an Karl Daub* (Berlin, 1837), pp. 7–11.
7. *Realencyklopädie für Protestantische Theologie und Kirche,* XII, 304–5. His teacher was Christoph Friedrich Ammon, a major representative of the rationalist school in German Protestant theology.
8. *Christliche Predigten zur Belebung des Gefühls fürs Schöne und Heilige, nebst einer Abhandlung* (Erlangen, 1805), pp. 29–30, 50–7.
9. *Allgemeine Darstellung des Theologischen Geistes der kirchlichen Verfassung und kanonischen Rechtswissenschaft in Beziehung auf die Moral des Christenthums und die ethische Denkart des Mittelalters* (Nürnberg, 1806), pp. xiii, xiv.
10. Rosenkranz, *Erinnerungen,* pp. 3–5.
11. Heinrich Hermelink, *Das Christenthum in der Menschheitsgeschichte von der französischen Revolution bis zur Gegenwart,* 2 vols. (Stuttgart, 1951), I, 338–9.
12. *Einleitung in das Studium der christlichen Dogmatik aus dem Standpunkte der Religion* (Heidelberg, 1810), pp. iv–vii, 364.
13. Ibid., pp. 358–9.
14. Ibid., pp. 354–7.
15. *Christliche Symbolik, oder historischkritische und dogmatischkomparative Darstellung des Katholischen, Luterischen, Reformirten und Socianischen Lehrbegriffs* (Heidelberg, 1810), esp. pp. 29–30.
16. *Predigten vor den verschiedenen Gemeinden in Berlin* (Berlin, 1814), pp. iv–v; *Geschichte der teutschen Reformation,* 2 vols. (Berlin, 1816), I, xxxi–xxii.
17. *Die Grundlehren der christlichen Dogmatik* (Berlin, 1819), p. v.
18. *Judas Ischariot,* I, 136–246.
19. Rosenkranz, *Erinnerungen,* p. 14; Daub to Hegel, Mar. 18, 1821, in *Briefe (Hegel),* II, 235–6.
20. Rothe to his father, Jan. 24, 1819, in Friedrich Nippold, *Richard Rothe: Ein christliches Lebensbild,* 2 vols. (Wittenberg, 1873), I, 118.
21. Daub to Hegel, Sept. 19, 1821, in *Briefe (Hegel),* II, 291.
22. The essays were collected, in 1833, into Daub's *Die Dogmatische Theologie jetziger Zeit oder die Selbstsucht in der Wissenschaft des Glaubens und ihrer Artikel* (Heidelberg, 1833).
23. *Grundlehren* (1819), pp. 16–19.
24. *Die Grundlehren der christlichen Dogmatik als Wissenschaft* (Berlin, 1827), pp. xxxii, 44, 66.

25. For his early support of a state-controlled church, see his *Geschichte der teutschen Reformation* (1816), I, xviii. His opposition to Schleiermacher in the battle over the Prussian liturgy is articulated in *Ueber die wahre Stelle des liturgischen Rechts im evangelischen Kirchenregiment* (Berlin, 1825).
26. *Grundlehren* (1827), pp. 384–7.
27. Ibid., pp. 13, 18, 67.
28. Cornehl, *Die Zunkunft der Versöhnung,* p. 169.
29. *Phänomenologie,* pp. 545 ff., esp. 557–62; *Vorlesungen über die Philosophie der Religion,* XVI, 139 ff.
30. See especially *Betrachtungen über das Leben und die Lehre des Welterlösers: Zur häuslichen Erbauung* (Berlin, 1823); and *Predigten der häuslichen Frömmigkeit* (Berlin, 1826).
31. Heinrich Schmeider, *Karl Friedrich Göschel* (Berlin, 1863), pp. 37–43.
32. *Aphorismen,* p. vii.
33. Ibid., p. 97.
34. Ibid., p. 23. Göschel's sympathy for the pietists is clearly expressed in his *Cäcilius und Octavius, oder Gespräche über die vornehmsten Einwendungen gegen die christliche Wahrheit* (Berlin, 1828), a dialogue between a pietist and a philosopher that was introduced by the pietist theologian Friedrich Tholuck. See also Göschel's letter to Hegel, Oct. 4, 1829, in *Briefe (Hegel),* III. 283.
35. The relevant works are Kasimir Conradi, *Selbstbewusstsein und Offenbarung, oder Entwicklung des religiösen Bewusstseins* (Mainz, 1831); and Isaak Rust, *Philosophie und Christenthum, oder Wissen und Glauben* (Mannheim, 1825).
36. *Philosophie und Christenthum,* p. 357.
37. Ibid., p. 358. See also ibid., pp. 353–4.
38. For Rust's biography see *Realencyklopädie für Protestantische Theologie und Kirche,* XVII, 262–5; for Conradi's see *Allgemeine Deutsche Biographie,* IV, 441.
39. *Jahrbücher für wissenschaftliche Kritik* (1827), cols. 1044–78; Rosenkranz, *Kritische Erläuterungen,* pp. 251–9.
40. *Briefe (Hegel),* II, 157–9, 230–2, 278–9.
41. For Hinrichs's biography see *Allgemeine Deutsche Biographie,* XII, 462; and Rosenkranz, *Von Magdeburg bis Königsberg,* 280–1. For Kapp's see the introduction by his son August Kapp to Ludwig Feuerbach, *Briefwechsel zwischen Ludwig Feuerbach und Christian Kapp, 1832 bis 1848* (Leipzig, 1876), pp. 5–12.
42. Hinrichs to Hegel, Jan. 25, 1822, in *Briefe (Hegel),* II, 300.
43. This was Hinrichs's original choice for a title, but it was abandoned because it appeared too dangerously revealing of the actual content of the book. See Hinrichs to Hegel, Oct. 13, 1821, in *Briefe (Hegel),* II, 297; Hegel to Hinrichs, Apr. 7, 1821, in ibid., p. 256.
44. Rosenkranz, *Von Magdeburg bis Königsberg,* p. 283.
45. Hermann F. W. Hinrichs, *Die Religion im inneren Verhältnisse zur Wissenschaft* (Heidelberg, 1822), pp. 204–25.
46. Hegel to Hinrichs, Apr. 7, 1821, in *Briefe (Hegel),* II, 254.
47. *Briefe (Hegel),* III, 20–1, 74–5; Rosenkranz, *Von Magdeburg bis Königsberg,* p. 280.
48. Rosenkranz, *Von Magdeburg bis Königsberg,* pp. 285–7.
49. *Grundlinien der Philosophie der Logik als Versuch einer wissenschaftlichen Umgestaltung ihrer bisherigen Principien* (Halle, 1826). See especially the "Vorerinnerung," pp. iv ff.

50. *Christus und die Weltgeschichte,* p. x.
51. Ibid., p. viii.
52. Ibid., p. 361.
53. Ibid., p. 2.
54. Ibid., pp. lxx, 367 ff.
55. Ibid., p. xlvii.
56. "Dr. Christian Kapp und seine literarischen Leistungen," in Ludwig Feuerbach, *Gesammelte Werke,* ed. W. Schuffenhauer, 10 vols. to date (Berlin, 1967–), IX, 67.
57. *Von Magdeburg bis Königsberg,* pp. viii, 183.
58. Ibid., p. 465.
59. Rosenkranz to Varnhagen von Ense, Oct. 19, 1837, in Karl Rosenkranz, *Briefwechsel zwischen Karl Rosenkranz und Varnhagen von Ense,* ed. A. Warda (Königsberg, 1926), p. 58.
60. *Von Magdeburg bis Königsberg,* p. 437.
61. Ibid., p. 396.
62. Michelet, *Wahrheit aus meinem Leben,* pp. 18–21.
63. Besides the state-service class (from which most Hegelians came), this would include the Jews (the Benary brothers and Gottfried Bernhardy) and the merchant-manufacturers with supralocal connections (Werder and Stieglitz).
64. *Von Magdeburg bis Königsberg,* pp. 76, 88, 396.
65. Ibid., pp. 188–91.
66. Ibid., pp. 109–11, 73–4.
67. Ibid., p. 108.
68. Ibid., pp. 147–8.
69. Ibid., p. 153.
70. Ibid., pp. 212–13.
71. "Die Mystik" (1826), in Karl Rosenkranz, *Studien,* 5 vols. (Leipzig, 1842–8), V, 78–9, 82, 98.
72. Ibid., p. 99.
73. *Von Magdeburg bis Königsberg,* p. 276; see also Karl Rosenkranz, *Kritik der Schleiermacherschen Glaubenslehre* (Königsberg, 1836), pp. vi–vii.
74. *Von Magdeburg bis Königsberg,* pp. 296–7, 38–1.
75. Ibid., p. 381.
76. *Geschichte der deutschen Poesie im Mittelalter* (Halle, 1830), p. 28.
77. "Einleitung über den Roman," in Karl Rosenkranz, *Aesthetische und poetische Mittheilungen* (Magdeburg, 1827), p. 37.
78. *Geschichte der deutschen Poesie,* p. viii.
79. Ibid., pp. 3–4.
80. *Das Heldenbuch und die Nibelungen: Grundriss zu Vorlesungen* (Halle, 1829), p. 77.
81. *Geschichte der deutschen Poesie,* p. 4.
82. *Ueber den Titurel und Dante's Komödie mit einer Vorerinnerung über die Bildung der geistlichen Ritterorden* (Halle and Leipzig, 1829), pp. 3–5.
83. *Geschichte der deutschen Poesie,* pp. 27–9, 619–20.
84. *Ueber den Titurel,* pp. 35–7.
85. *Geschichte der deutschen Poesie,* pp. 28–9, 619–20.
86. Rosenkranz, *Von Magdeburg bis Königsberg,* pp. 413 ff.
87. Ibid., p. 422.
88. Ibid., p. 416.

89. *Der Zweifel am Glauben: Kritik der Schriften: De Tribus Imposteribus* (Halle and Leipzig, 1830), pp. 1–24.
90. *Jahrbücher für wissenschaftliche Kritik* (1830), cols. 848–9, 867–9, 887.
91. *Encyklopädie der theologischen Wissenschaften* (Halle, 1831), p. ix.
92. Ibid., pp. xxxiv, 3.
93. Joachim Mehlhausen, *Dialektik, Selbstbewusstsein und Offenbarung: Die Grundlagen der spekulativen Orthodoxie Bruno Bauers in ihrer Zusammenhang mit der Geschichte der theologischen Hegelschule* (Bonn, 1965), pp. 112–16.
94. "Rosenkranz: Encyklopädie der theologischen Wissenschaften," in David Friedrich Strauss, *Charakteristiken und Kritiken: Eine Sammlung zerstreuter Aufsätze aus den Gebieten der Theologie, Anthropologie und Aesthetik* (Leipzig, 1839), p. 224. The review was originally published in the Hegelian *Jahrbücher* in 1832.
95. *Ausgewählte Briefe von David Friedrich Strauss,* ed. E. Zeller (Bonn, 1895), pp. 7–8.
96. "Christian Märklin," esp. chaps. 2–4.
97. Emmanuel Hirsch, *Geschichte der neuern evangelischen Theologie,* 5 vols. (Gütersloh, 1949–54), V, 71 ff. Strauss later wrote an extensive critique of this position in his *Streitschriften zur Vertheidigung meiner Schrift über das Leben Jesu und zur Charakteristik der gegenwärtigen Theologie,* 3 vols in 1 (Tübingen, 1837), I, 1–182.
98. "Christian Märklin," pp. 179–80.
99. "Mein Lebensgang," in Vischer, *Altes und Neues,* III, 250–1, 254.
100. "Christian Märklin," p. 184.
101. "Zum Andenken an meine Mutter," in Strauss, *Gesammelte Schriften,* I, 90–1.
102. Ibid., p. 99.
103. Letter to Rapp, Apr. 10, 1841, in Strauss, *Ausgewählte Briefe,* p. 101.
104. Vischer, "Mein Lebesgang," pp. 261–2; Strauss, "Christian Märklin," p. 206.
105. Friedrich Theodor Vischer, "Dr. Strauss und die Wirtemberger" (1838), in Friedrich Theodor Vischer, *Kritische Gänge,* 2 vols. (Tübingen, 1844), I, 92.
106. David Friedrich Strauss, "Literarische Denkwürdigkeiten" (1866–72), in Strauss, *Gesammelte Schriften,* I, 8; H. Traub, "Die Stiftsakten über David Friedrich Strauss," *Blätter für württembergische Kirchengeschichte, Neue Folge* 27 (1923):52, 54. See also Theobald Ziegler, *David Friedrich Strauss,* 2 vols. (Strassburg, 1908), I, 62.
107. "Justinus Kerner" (1839), in Strauss, *Gesammelte Schriften,* I, 129.
108. Ibid., pp. 125, 130.
109. Ibid., p. 131.
110. *Symbolik und Mythologie oder die Naturreligion des Alterthums,* 2 vols. (Stuttgart, 1824–5), esp. I, v–xii. See also Peter C. Hodgson, *The Formation of Historical Theology: A Study of Ferdinand Christian Baur* (New York, 1966), pp. 13–15, 97–8.
111. Hodgson, *Formation,* p. 14.
112. For this reason, Müller's argument about Baur's decisive influence on Strauss's later theories of myth is unconvincing. See Gotthold Müller, *Identität und Immanenz: Zur Genese der Theologie von David Friedrich Strauss* (Zürich, 1968), pp. 175–96.
113. Strauss, "Christian Märklin," pp. 223–4.
114. Strauss, *Streitschriften,* III, 57; Vischer, "Mein Lebensgang," 273–4.

115. Traub, "Die Stiftsakten über David Friedrich Strauss," pp. 50–1, 55. See also Gotthold Müller, "David Friedrich Strauss als Prediger und Katechet," *Monatsschrift für Pastoraltheologie* 53 (1964):502–10.
116. *Ausgewählte Briefe,* p. 2.
117. Ibid.
118. The sermon is printed in Ziegler, *Strauss,* I, 63–9.
119. Strauss to Märklin, Dec. 26, 1830, in Strauss, *Ausgewählte Briefe,* pp. 3–6.
120. MSS in the Schiller National-Museum, Marbach, Strauss-Märklin Correspondence, no. 20311.
121. Letter from Mar. 18, 1831, in Theobald Ziegler, "Zur Biographie von David Friedrich Strauss," *Deutsche Revue* 30, no. 2 (1905):199.
122. Strauss to Märklin, June 27, 1831, MSS in the Schiller National-Museum, Marbach, Strauss-Märklin Correspondence, no. 20311.
123. *Briefe von David Friedrich Strauss an L. Georgii,* ed. Heinrich Maier (Tübingen, 1912), p. 4.
124. "Die Lehre von der Wiederbringung aller Dinge in ihrer religionsgeschichtlichen Entwicklung," in Müller, *Identität und Immanenz,* pp. 50–82. Cited hereafter as Strauss, "Lehre."
125. Strauss, "Lehre," p. 50.
126. Ibid., p. 82.
127. Ibid., pp. 50, 82.
128. Müller, *Identität und Immanenz,* pp. 89 ff.
129. Strauss, "Lehre," pp. 75–80.
130. Ibid., p. 81.
131. Ibid., p. 82.
132. Ibid., p. 81.
133. Ibid., p. 82.
134. Ibid., p. 67.
135. *Ausgewählte Briefe,* p. 7.
136. "Aus dem Nachlass: Feuerbach's Verhältniss zu Hegel" (1840), in Feuerbach, *Briefwechsel und Nachlass,* I, 388.
137. Letter to Ludwig Noack, 1846, cited in Karl Grün's introduction to Feuerbach, *Briefwechsel und Nachlass,* I, 10. The debate over Feuerbach's early religiosity is summarized in Uwe Schott, *Die Jugendentwicklung Ludwig Feuerbachs bis zum Fakultätswechsel 1825* (Göttingen, 1973), pp. 14–20. The main issue in this debate is whether Feuerbach's pre-Hegelian religious standpoint can be described as "mystical."
138. Letter to Noack, 1846, in Feuerbach, *Briefwechsel und Nachlass,* I, 10.
139. "Aus dem Nachlass," p. 387.
140. The standard work on Feuerbach's father is Gustav Radbruch, *Paul Johann Anselm Feuerbach: Ein Juristenleben,* 2nd ed. (Göttingen, 1957); but I have also found Richard Hartmann, *P. J. A. Feuerbach's Politische und Strafrechtliche Grundanschauungen* (Berlin, 1961), and Eberhard Kipper, *Johann Paul Anselm Feuerbach: Sein Leben als Denker* (Köln, 1969), useful.
141. Radbruch, *Feuerbach,* pp. 102 ff.; Ludwig Feuerbach, "Paul Johann Anselm Feuerbach und seine Söhne," in Feuerbach, *Gesammelte Werke,* X, 327–9. This edition cited hereafter as *Werke* (Schuffenhauer).
142. Radbruch, *Feuerbach,* pp. 137–41; Kipper, *Feuerbach,* 127–39.
143. Radbruch, *Feuerbach,* pp. 142–4.
144. Theodor Spoerri, *Genie und Krankheit. Eine psychopathologische Unter-*

suchung der Familie Feuerbach (Basel, 1952), pp. 37–44, 47–56; Richard Steer, "Zum Ursprung der Religionskritik von Ludwig Feuerbach," *Jahrbuch für christliche Sozialwissenschaften* 9 (1968):49–50; Henriette Feuerbach, *Anselm Feuerbachs Leben, Briefe und Gedichte* (Braunschweig, 1853), p. 15.
145. Cited from an unpublished letter in Schott, *Jugendentwicklung*, p. 25.
146. Schott, *Jugendentwicklung*, p. 24, n. 21.
147. His admiration for his father is clearly evident in a letter to his mother from Aug. 1821, in *Sämtliche Werke*, ed. Hans-Martin Sass, 13 vols. (Stuttgart, 1964), XII, 216. This edition cited hereafter as *Werke* (Sass).
148. Schott, *Jugendentwicklung*, pp. 24–6.
149. The view that the early Feuerbach was a mystic is advanced without any concrete evidence by R. Lorenz, "Zum Ursprung der Religionstheorie Ludwig Feuerbachs," *Evangelische Theologie* 17 (1957):171–88; and Johannes Wallmann, "Ludwig Feuerbach und die theologische Tradition," *Zeitschrift für Theologie und Kirche* 67 (1970):56–86. Both writers project Feuerbach's position in 1830 back into the possible implications he may have drawn from some of his readings.
150. Cited from a school report by Schott, *Jugendentwicklung*, p. 33.
151. Letter from Aug. 1821, in *Werke* (Sass), XII, 216–17.
152. "Fragmente zur Charakteristik meines philosophischen Entwicklungsgangs," in *Werke* (Sass), II, 381–2.
153. Letter to Noack, 1846, in Feuerbach, *Briefwechsel und Nachlass*, I, 12.
154. Schott, *Jugendentwicklung*, pp. 30–1.
155. Ibid., p. 33.
156. Ibid., pp. 37–70; letter to Noack, 1846, in Feuerbach, *Briefwechsel und Nachlass*, I, 11.
157. *Werke* (Sass), XII, 215.
158. Ibid., pp. 218–22.
159. Ibid., pp. 218.
160. J. P. A. Feuerbach to Paulus, Feb. 24, 1823, in K. A. Reichlin-Meldegg, *H. E. G. Paulus und seine Zeit*, 2 vols. (Stuttgart, 1853), II, 154; J. P. A. Feuerbach to Ludwig Feuerbach, June 16, 1823, in *Werke* (Sass), XII, 217.
161. Letter to his father, fall 1823, in *Werke* (Sass), XII, 223–6.
162. Letter to Karl Daub, Aug. 1824, in Carlo Ascheri, "Ein unbekannter Brief von Ludwig Feuerbach an Karl Daub," in H. Braun and M. Riedel, eds., *Natur und Geschichte: Karl Löwith zum 70. Geburtstag* (Stuttgart, 1967), p. 450.
163. Letter to Noack, 1846, in Feuerbach, *Briefwechsel und Nachlass*, I, 16.
164. Letter to his father, fall 1823, in *Werke* (Sass), XII, 224.
165. Letter to Noack, 1846, in Feuerbach, *Briefwechsel und Nachlass*, I, 15.
166. Letter to his father, May 24, 1824, in *Werke* (Sass), XII, 231.
167. Feuerbach to Daub, Aug. 1824, in Ascheri, "Ein unbekannter Brief," p. 450.
168. "Aus dem Nachlass," p. 387.
169. Feuerbach to Daub, Aug. 1824, in Ascheri, "Ein unbekannter Brief," p. 450.
170. Ibid., p. 451.
171. Feuerbach to Daub, Jan. 29, 1825, in *Werke* (Sass), XII, 236–40.
172. Feuerbach to his father, Mar. 22, 1825, in *Werke* (Sass), XII, 243.
173. Ibid., p. 244.
174. Feuerbach to Daub, Jan. 29, 1825, in *Werke* (Sass), XII, 239.

175. W. Kohl to Feuerbach, Feb. 6, 1825, in *Werke* (Sass), XII, 241.
176. Feuerbach to his brother Eduard, late fall 1828, in *Werke* (Sass), XII, 253.
177. Feuerbach to his mother, Oct. 2, 1824, in *Werke* (Sass), XII, 236.
178. Feuerbach to his father, Mar. 22, 1825, in *Werke* (Sass), XII, 244.
179. J. P. A. Feuerbach to Ludwig Feuerbach, Apr. 20, 1825, in *Werke* (Sass), XII, 250–1.
180. The death of Maximilian I of Bavaria led to a cancellation of Feuerbach's academic stipend, and his father refused further support.
181. "Fragmente" p. 362.
182. "Aus dem Nachlass," p. 389.
183. J. P. A. Feuerbach to Anselm Feuerbach, Dec. 1828, quoted in Wilhelm Bolin, "Biographische Einleitung," in *Werke* (Sass), XII, 19–20.
184. "Fragmente," pp. 362–4.
185. Michael von Gagern, *Ludwig Feuerbach* (Munich and Salzburg, 1970), pp. 57–8.
186. "Fragmente," p. 363.
187. Ibid.
188. Feuerbach to Hegel, Nov. 22, 1828, in Ludwig Feuerbach, *Kleine Schriften*, ed. Karl Löwith (Frankfurt, 1966), p. 11.
189. Ibid., p. 12.
190. *Gedanken uber Tod und Unsterblichkeit aus dem Papieren eines Denkers, nebst einen Anhang theologisch-satyrischen Xenien,* in *Werke* (Sass), XI, 78–84.
191. Ibid., pp. 84–8.
192. Feuerbach to Hegel, Nov. 22, 1828, in Feuerbach, *Kleine Schriften,* pp. 8–10.
193. Ibid., p. 10.
194. Ibid., p. 9.
195. Ibid., p. 11.
196. *Gedanken,* pp. 182–3.
197. "Ueber die Vernunft" (1828), in Ludwig Feuerbach, *Werke,* ed. Erich Thies, 6 vols. (Frankfurt, 1975 ff.), I, 48.
198. Ibid., p. 18.
199. Ibid., p. 48.
200. Ibid., p. 35.
201. Ibid., pp. 17 ff., 28–32, 39.
202. Ibid., p. 50.
203. *Briefwechsel und Nachlass,* I, 201–5.
204. *Gedanken,* p. 84.
205. See Peter Cornehl, "Feuerbach und die Naturphilosophie: Zur Genese der Anthropologie und Religionskritik des jungen Feuerbach," *Neue Zeitschrift für systematische Theologie und Religionsphilosophie* 11 (1969):37–93. Cornehl sees Feuerbach's turn to nature as a product of the "influence" of Schellingian "nature philosophy" and a misunderstanding of Hegel, rather than a product of historical experience and a revision of Hegel.
206. *Gedanken,* pp. 95–6.
207. Ibid., p. 95.
208. Ibid., p. 106.
209. Ibid., p. 212.
210. Ibid., p. 94.
211. Ibid., p. 96.

212. Ibid., p. 93.
213. Ibid., p. 37.
214. Ibid., p. 113.
215. Ibid., p. 104.
216. Ibid., p. 90.
217. "Fragmente," p. 367.
218. Johann Eduard Erdmann, *A History of Philosophy, trans. W. S. Hough,* 3 vols. (London, 1890–2), III, 58–9.
219. "Fragmente," pp. 362–3.
220. *Gedanken,* p. 100.
221. Ibid., p. 203.
222. Ibid.
223. Ibid., p. 219.
224. Ibid., p. 218.
225. Ibid., p. 220.
226. Ibid., p. 79.

7. Right, Center, and Left

1. *Streitschriften,* III, 95 ff.
2. "Die Deutsche Ideologie," in Karl Marx and Friedrich Engels, *Historisch-kritische Gesamtausgabe,* ed. D. Riazonov, 11 vols. in 3 ser. (Frankfurt, 1927–32), pt. 1, vol. V, p. 8. This edition cited hereafter as *MEGA.*
3. *Das Centrum der Speculation: Eine Komödie* (Königsberg, 1840).
4. "Nekrolog von G. W. F. Hegel," in Gans, *Vermischte Schriften,* II, 251–2.
5. "Gabrede," p. 477.
6. *Das Centrum der Speculation,* pp. 81–98.
7. A particularly blatant recent example of this practice can be found in Brazill, *The Young Hegelians,* p. 50.
8. The West German political theorist Hermann Lübbe has taken advantage of this confusion of categories in his attempt to rehabilitate the Right Hegelians as moderate political liberals. Both Gans and Carové play a crucial role in the argument of his "Die politische Theorie der Hegelschen Rechten," in Hermann Lübbe, *Politische Philosophie in Deutschland: Studien zu ihrer Geschichte* (Basel and Stuttgart, 1963). For critiques of Lübbe's methods see Wilhelm Raimund Beyer, *Hegel-Bilder: Kritik der Hegel-Deutungen* (Berlin, 1964), pp. 52ff.; and George Lichtheim, *From Marx to Hegel* (New York, 1971), pp. 56–7.
9. Right Hegelians of Marx's and Engels's generation would include Constantin Rössler (1820–96), H. B. Oppenheim (1819–80), Moritz Carrière (1817–95), and Constantin Frantz (1817–91), all of whom were much more concerned with the "social question" than members of older generations of Hegelians.
10. Löwith, *From Hegel to Nietzsche,* pp. 50–62.
11. *Geschichte der letzten Systeme,* II, 659.
12. *Die Hegelingen.* Aside from Ruge, Leo directed his ire particularly at Michelet, Karl Bayrhoffer, and Eduard Meyen.
13. Löwith, *From Hegel to Nietzsche,* pp. 25–6.
14. Eric. J. Hobsbawm, *The Age of Revolution, 1789–1848* (New York, 1964), pp. 139, 145.

15. *Idea*, p. 278.
16. Ibid., p. 300. The fullest account of the events of the German revolutions of 1830 is in Heinrich von Treitschke, *Hisotry of Germany in the Nineteenth Century*, trans. E. Paul and C. Paul, 6 vols. (New York, 1919), vol. V. See also Huber, *Verfassungsgeschichte*, II, 30–46.
17. *Aristocracy and the Middle-Classes in Germany: Social Types in German Literature, 1830–1900*, rev. ed. (Chicago and London, 1964), p. 43.
18. Heinrich Heffter, *Die deutsche Selbstverwaltung im* 19. *Jahrhundert: Geschichte der Ideen und Institutionen* (Stuttgart, 1950), p. 168.
19. Werner Conze, ed., *Staat und Gesellschaft im deutschen Vormärz* (Stuttgart, 1962), pp. 134, 146, 227–8.
20. See for example, Heffter's discussion of the fate of Baden liberal leader Ludwig Winter in his *Selbstverwaltung*, p. 172.
21. Treitschke, *History*, V, 184.
22. For a good recent discussion of the Hambachers and their significance for the development of south German liberalism see Fritz Trautz, "Das Hambacher Fest und der Südwestdeutsche Frühliberalismus," *Heidelberger Jahrbücher* 2 (1958):14–52.
23. Huber, *Verfassungsgeschichte*, II, 151–84.
24. David S. Landes, *The Unbound Prometheus: Technological Change and Industrial Development in Western Europe from 1750 to the Present* (Cambridge, 1969), p. 174.
25. Quoted in Donald Rohr, *The Origins of Social Liberalism in Germany* (Chicago and London, 1963), p. 12.
26. Ibid., p. 19.
27. Mack Walker, *Germany and the Emigration, 1816–1885* (Cambridge, Mass., 1964), chap. 2.
28. Rohr, *Origins*, pp. 15–16.
29. Two standard accounts that provide a good survey of the variety of conditions are Heinrich Bechtel, *Wirtschaftsgeschichte Deutschlands im 19. und 20. Jahrhundert* (Munich, 1956), pp. 195–247; and Friedrich Lütge, *Deutsche Sozial- und Wirtschaftsgeschichte: Ein Ueberblick*, 3rd ed., rev. and exp. (Berlin and Heidelberg, 1966), pp. 431–50.
30. Quoted in Werner Conze, "Vom 'Pöbel' zum 'Proletariat,' sozialgeschichtliche Voraussetzungen für den Sozialismus in Deutschland," *Vierteljahresschrift für Sozial- und Wirtschaftsgeschichte* 41 (1954):342, n. 19.
31. Friedrich-Wilhelm Henning, "Die Einführung der Gewerbefreiheit und ihre Auswirkung auf das Handwerk in Deutschland," in Wilhelm Abel et al., eds., *Handwerksgeschichte in neuer Sicht* (Göttingen, 1970), pp. 142–72. See also Wolfram Fischer, "Soziale Unterschichtungen im Zeitalter der Frühindustrialisierung," *International Review of Social History* 8 (1963):414–35.
32. Walker, *Germany and the Emigration*, p. 53.
33. *Die bürgerliche Gesellschaft* (Stuttgart and Tübingen, 1851), p. 299.
34. Johannes Conrad, *The German Universities for the Last Fifty Years*, trans. John Hutchison (Glasgow, 1885), pp. 14–15.
35. Ibid., p. 71.
36. *Geschichtliche und statistiche Nachrichten über die Universitäten im preussischen Staat* (Berlin, 1836), pp. 117, 126.
37. Conrad, *Universities*, p. 88.
38. Koselleck, *Preussen*, p. 438.

39. Clemens Theodor Perthes, *Der Staatsdienst in Preussen* (Hamburg, 1838), p. 54.
40. Koselleck, *Preussen,* p. 439.
41. Ibid., p. 436.
42. Conrad, *Universities,* pp. 14–15, 74.
43. For a brilliant analysis of this development see Koselleck, *Preussen,* pt. 3, chap. 2.
44. Alexander Busch, *Die Geschichte der Privatdozenten: Eine soziologische Studie zur grossbetrieblichen Entwicklung der deutschen Universitäten* (Stuttgart, 1959), pp. 46–7.
45. Lenz, *Geschichte,* II, pt. 1, 407–25.
46. Ibid., p. 410, n. 3.
47. Conrad, *Universities,* p. 193.
48. Karl Klüpfel, *Geschichte und Beschreibung der Universität Tübingen* (Tübingen, 1849), pp. 403–25.
49. Theodor Kolde, *Die Universität Erlangen unter das Hause Wittelsbach, 1810–1890* (Erlangen and Leipzig, 1910), p. 335.
50. See Eric J. C. Hahn, "The Junior Faculty in 'Revolt': Reform Plans for the Berlin University in 1848," *American Historical Review* 82 (1977):880, where Hotho, Vatke, the Benary brothers, and Michelet are described as "Left-Hegelians."
51. "Rede bei der dritten Säkularfeier der Uebergabe der Augsburgischen Konfession," in Hegel, *Berliner Schriften, 1818–1831,* pp. 28–55, and esp. 51, 53, 55.
52. "Vergangenheit und Gegenwart, 1830–1838," in Karl Gutzkow, *Werke,* ed. P. Müller, 4 vols. (Leipzig and Vienna, 1912), pp. 153–4.
53. *Leben und Erinnerungen* (Leipzig, 1900), p. 15.
54. *Briefe (Hegel),* III, 323.
55. Hegel to Schulz, in *Briefe (Hegel),* III, 333.
56. *Vorlesungen über die Philosophie der Geschichte,* in Hegel, *Werke,* ed. Moldenhauer and Michel, XII, 534–5.
57. "The English Reform Bill," in Hegel, *Hegel's Political Writings,* pp. 295–6, 300, 325, 330.
58. *Vorlesungen über die Philosophie der Geschichte,* p. 534.
59. Droysen to Ludwig Moser, Nov. 29, 1831, cited in *Hegel in Berichten,* p. 490.
60. See, for example, Strauss, *Streitschriften,* III, 95 ff.; Michelet, *Geschichte der letzten Systeme,* II, 654–9; and Karl Theodor Bayrhoffer, *Die Idee und Geschichte der Philosophie* (Marburg, 1838), pp. 490–2. Reactions against the tendency toward party labeling can be found in Rosenkranz, *Kritische Erläuterungen,* pp. vii–xxxvi; and in H. W. F. Hinrichs, "Die Fragen der Gegenwart und Prof. Michelet's Geschichte der letzten Systeme," *Hallische Jahrbücher* (1839), pp. 457 ff.
61. Gebhardt, *Politik und Eschatologie,* chap. 5; Sass, *Untersuchungen zur Religionsphilosophie,* pp. 192 ff.; Cornehl, *Die Zukunft der Versöhnung,* pp. 260 ff.
62. Lenz, *Geschichte,* II, pt. 1, 484.
63. Feuerbach to Johannes Schulze, Mar. 26, 1835, in Adolph Kohut, *Ludwig Feuerbach: Sein Leben und seine Werke* (Leipzig, 1909), p. 114.
64. Lenz, *Geschichte,* II, pt. 1.
65. The one Hegelian to receive a tenured appointment was Johann Eduard

Erdmann, one of the most conservative Hegelians of the younger generation. See Hermann Glockner, *Johann Eduard Erdmann* (Stuttgart, 1932), pp. 37 ff. The difficulties that Vatke experienced in attaining an associate professorship at Berlin are detailed in Benecke, *Vatke,* pp. 160, 258 ff., 270–1.

66. *Das Leben Max Dunckers* (Berlin, 1891), p. 25.

67. Feuerbach to Kapp, May 16, 1834, in Feuerbach, *Briefwechsel zwischen Ludwig Feuerbach und Christian Kapp,* p. 49.

68. Reissner, *Gans* pp. 138 ff.; August Kapp, "Einleitung" to Feuerbach, *Briefwechsel zwischen Ludwig Feuerbach und Christian Kapp,* pp. 12 ff.; *Hegel in Berichten,* pp. 431, 666; Benecke, *Vatke,* pp. 78–9.

69. *Aus früherer Zeit,* IV, 458.

70. Schlawe, "Die Berliner Jahrbücher," p. 348.

71. Ibid., pp. 351–6.

72. *Geschichte der teutschen Reformation,* 2nd ed., 4 vols. (Berlin, 1831–4), I, xxxv.

73. See, for example, his reiteration of these positions in *Einleitung in die öffentlichen Vorlesungen über die Bedeutung der Hegelschen Philosophie in der christlichen Theologie: Nebst einen Separatvotum ueber B. Bauer's kritik der evangelischen Geschichte* (Berlin, 1842).

74. *Friedrich Wilhelm I, König von Preussen,* 5 vols. (Potsdam, 1834–5), I, 2–3; *Die Höfe und Cabinette Europas im achtzehnten Jahrhundert,* 3 vols. (Potsdam, 1836–9), I, xi.

75. H. F. W. Hinrichs, *Die Genesis des Wissens: Erster Metaphysischer Teil* (Heidelberg, 1835), pp. iii–iii; Julius Schaller, *Die Philosophie unserer Zeit: Zur Apologie und Erläuterung des Hegelschen Systems* (Leipzig, 1837), passim.

76. Schlawe, "Die Berliner Jahrbücher," p. 347; Friedrich Förster, "Noch ein Denunciat der Hegelschen Philosophie," *Hallische Jahrbücher* (1839), p. 392.

77. Review of Richter's *Die neue Unsterblichkeitslehre,* in *Jahrbücher für wissenschaftliche Kritik* (1834), col. 11.

78. See Hinrichs in the *Jahrbücher für wissenschaftliche Kritik* (1836), cols. 497 ff.; and Rosenkranz in his *Kritische Erläuterungen,* pp. 348 ff.

79. This method was especially evident in his *Von den Beweisen für die Unsterblichkeit der menschlichen Seele im Lichte der spekulativen Philosophie* (Berlin, 1835), pp. 153 ff.

80. Ibid., pp. 204, 252–8.

81. Karl F. Göschel, *Zerstreute Blätter aus den Hand- und Hülfsakten eines Juristen: Wissenschaftliches und Geschichtliches aus der Theorie und Praxis oder aus der Lehre und dem Leben des Rechts,* 3 vols. (Erfurt and Schleusingen, 1832–7), I, 38–40, 82–5, 139–49, II, 107–11, 482–6.

82. See, for example, the response to his political writings by the conservative editors of *Die Evangelische Kirchenzeitung,* no. 11 (1833), cols. 91 ff.

83. Schmieder, *Göschel,* pp. 43 ff., 57 ff.

84. *Stimmen der Reformation und der Reformatoren an die Fürsten und Völker dieser Zeit* (Erlangen, 1832), pp. v–ciii.

85. *Realencyklopädie für Protestantische Theologie und Kirche,* XVII, 264.

86. Leo to Raumer, Jan. 1, 1831, in Friedrich von Raumer, *Lebenserinnerungen und Briefwechsel,* 2 vols. (Leipzig, 1861), II, 321–3. See also Heinrich Leo, *Studien und Skizzen zu einer Naturlehre des Staates* (Halle, 1833), pp. 1–24.

87. Krägelin, *Heinrich Leo,* pp. 84–5.

88. Hans-Joachim Schoeps, *Das Andere Preussen: Konservative Gestalten und Probleme im Zeitalter Friedrich Wilhelms IV,* 3rd ed. (Berlin, 1964), pp. 221–3.
89. Review of Leo's *Studien und Skizzen,* in Gans, *Vermischte Schriften,* II, 221–3.
90. *Die Hegelingen* (1838), pp. 43–4.
91. "Vorlesungen über die Geschichte der letzten fünfzig Jahre," *Historisches Taschenbuch* 4 (1833):285–92.
92. *Rückblicke auf Personen und Zustände,* pp. 48 ff., 176 ff., 257 ff.
93. *Beiträge zur Revision der preussischen Gesetzgebung* (Berlin, 1830–2), p. 471.
94. Ibid., pp. 10–17, 365–76, 468–77.
95. See especially his introductory lecture to a course on "Deutsches Staatsrecht," printed in Gans, *Philosophische Schriften,* pp. 157–81.
96. "Paris im Jahre 1830," pp. 97–101.
97. Ibid., pp. 93–4.
98. Ibid., p. 93.
99. Gans, *Beiträge,* pp. 7, 470.
100. The widespread support of Gans's position among the younger Berlin Hegelians is noted in Michelet, *Wahrheit aus meinem Leben,* pp. 286–7. See also Moritz Veit, *Saint-Simon und der Saintsimonismus: Allgemeiner Völkerbund und ewiger Frieden* (Leipzig, 1834), pp. 276–82; and Helmut Hirsch, "Karl Friedrich Köppen: Der Intimste Berliner Freund Marxens," *International Review of Social History* 1 (1936):313 ff.
101. See for example the introductions to his *Kritik der Schleiermacherschen Glaubenslehre* and *Psychologie, oder die Wissenschaft vom subjektiven Geist* (Königsberg, 1837). Rosenkranz defended himself against the charge that he lacked any decisive convictions in the introduction to his *Kritische Erläuterungen.*
102. Most of the younger Swabian Hegelians, in fact, first learned their Hegel from Strauss. See Eduard Zeller, *David Friedrich Strauss in seinem Leben und seinen Schriften* (Bonn, 1874), pp. 30 ff.
103. Ruge to Rosenkranz, Dec. 16, 1837, in Arnold Ruge, *Briefwechsel und Tagebuchblätter aus den Jahren 1825–1880,* ed. Paul Nerrlich, 2 vols. (Berlin, 1886), I, 96–7. See aslo Hermann Fischer, "Die Hallischen Jahrbücher und die Schwaben," *Württembergische Vierteljahreshefte für Landesgeschichte, Neue Folge* 25 (1916):558 71.
104. Bayrhoffer's critical Hegelianism was first clearly evident in his *Die Idee des Christenthums im Verhältnisse zu den Zeitgegensätzen der Theologie: Eine speculative Kritik* (Marburg, 1836).
105. "Dr. Strauss und die Wirtemberger," p. 3.
106. See the detailed discussion in Chap. 8.
107. See Rosenkranz, *Kritische Erläuterungen,* pp. 348 ff.; and Ferdinand Christian Baur, *Die Christliche Gnosis, oder die christliche Religionsphilosophie in ihrer geschichtlichen Entwicklung* (Tübingen, 1835), pp. 715 ff.
108. *Geschichte der letzten Systeme,* II, 610.
109. *Idee und Geschichte,* pp. vii, 400–2.
110. Ibid., p. 420.
111. *Jahrbücher für wissenschaftliche Kritik* (1831), pt. 1, col. 697.
112. *Geschichte der letzten Systeme,* II, 800.
113. Karl Theodor Bayrhoffer, *Das Verhältnis des Staats zur Kirche* (Leipzig, 1838), pp. 12 ff.

114. Even Rosenkranz held to this position. See his "Deutschland, Preussen und die Wissenschaft im Herbst 1839," in Rosenkranz, *Studien,* V: *Reden und Abhandlungen* (1848), pp. 18 ff.
115. Christian Märklin, *Ueber die Reform des protestantischen Kirchenwesens mit besonderer Rücksicht auf die protestantische Kirche in Württemberg* (Tübingen, 1833), pp. 37–42.
116. [Ludwig Buhl], *Hegel's Lehre vom Staat und seine Philosphie der Geschichte in ihren Hauptresultaten* (Berlin, 1837), pp. 23 ff.; Michelet, *Geschichte der letzten Systeme,* II, 622–3; Bayrhoffer, *Idee und Geschichte,* pp. 417–18; Eduard Meyen, *Heinrich Leo, der verhallerte Pietist: Ein Literaturbrief allen Schülern Hegels gewidmet* (Leipzig, 1839), pp. 13, 36–7.
117. Bayrhoffer, *Idee und Geschichte,* p. 490; Michelet, *Geschichte der letzten Systeme,* II, 658.
118. *The Young Hegelians,* pp. 73–5, 233.
119. *Aus früherer Zeit,* IV, 462.
120. Ruge to Rosenkranz, Dec. 16, 1837, in Ruge, *Briefwechsel und Tagebuchblätter,* I, 97.
121. *Aus früherer Zeit,* IV, 472.
122. Ibid., p. 484.
123. *Preussen und die Reaction: Zur Geschichte unserer Zeit* (Leipzig, 1838), p. 112.
124. "Karl Streckfuss und das Preussenthum," *Hallische Jahrbücher* (Nov. 1839), cols. 2089 ff. See also Walter Neher, *Arnold Ruge als Politiker und politischer Schriftsteller* (Heidelberg, 1933), pp. 54 ff.; and Hans Rosenberg, "Arnold Ruge und die 'Hallischen Jahrbücher,'" *Archiv für Kulturgeschichte* 20 (1930):295–6.
125. Lübbe, "Die politische Theorie der Hegelschen Rechten," pp. 30–2.
126. Carové's cultural viewpoint did not change in any significant way after 1830, but the revolutionary upheavals of 1830 and the emergence of Messianic sects like the Saint-Simonians inflated his hopes for an imminent historical actualization of the Kingdom of God. See especially Friedrich Wilhelm Carové, *Rückblick auf die Ursachen der französischen Revolution und Andeutung ihrer Welthistorischen Bestimmung* (Hanau, 1834), pp. 114–86; and Friedrich Wilhelm Carové, *Die letzten Dinge des römischen Katholicismus in Deutschland* (Leipzig, 1832), pp. vi–ix.
127. *Die heilige Geschichte der Menschheit,* von einem Jünger Spinoza's (Stuttgart, 1837).
128. Friedrich Richter, *Die Lehre von den letzten Dingen,* I: *Eine wissenschaftliche Kritik aus dem Standpunct der Religion unternommen* (Breslau, 1833); Friedrich Richter, *Die neue Unsterblichkeitslehre: Gespräch einer Abendgesellschaft* (Breslau, 1833).
129. For Cieszkowski's biography see Walter Kühne, *Graf August Cieszkowski: Ein Schüler Hegels und des deutschen Geistes* (Leipzig, 1838).
130. *Von Magdeburg bis Königsberg,* pp. 413–15.
131. Friedrich Richter, *Die Lehre von den letzten Dingen,* II: *Die Lehre von jüngsten Tage, Dogma und Kritik* (Berlin, 1844), pp. 202–3. Pp. 199–260 of this work contain Richter's autobiography and general reflections on his prophetic career.
132. *Magdeburg, die wieder-emporgerichtete Stadt Gottes auf Erden: Denkschrift zur zweiten Seculärfeier der Zerstörung Magdeburgs* (Zerbst, 1831).
133. *Lehre von den letzten Dingen,* II, 204.

134. Ibid., pp. 213–14.
135. Ibid., p. 241.
136. Hess, *Geschichte,* pp. 287 ff.; Richter, *Lehre von den letzten Dingen,* I, 12–14, 91.
137. Carové, *Rückblick,* pp. ix–xvii; Richter, *Lehre von den letzten Dingen,* II, 218–38 (reprint of an article written in 1833).
138. Hess, *Geschichte,* pp. 259 ff., 303 ff.
139. Ibid., pp. 234, 337–9; Stuke, *Philosophie der Tat,* pp. 109–10.
140. Hess, *Geschichte,* pp. 71 ff., 139 ff.; August Cieszkowski, *Prolegomena zur Historiosophie* (Berlin, 1838), pp. 24–5.
141. Hess, *Geschichte,* p. 187; Cieszkowski, *Prolegomena,* pp. 29–3, 85, 114, 124, 130; Richter, *Lehre von den letzten Dingen,* I, 27.
142. *Lehre von den letzten Dingen,* I, 7–9.
143. Ibid., p. 19–20.
144. Ibid., p. 27.
145. Ibid., p. 39–40.
146. *Prolegomena,* p. 11.
147. Ibid., p. 103.
148. Ibid., p. 112.
149. Ibid., pp. 118 ff.
150. Ibid., pp. 20–1.
151. Stuke, *Philosophie der Tat,* p. 108.
152. Both Richter and Cieszkowski rejected the Left Hegelian movement of the 1840s. See Cieszkowski, *Gott und Palingenesie* (Berlin, 1842), p. 11; and Richter, *Lehre von den letzten Dingen,* II, 258.
153. *Die Posaune des jüngsten Gerichts über Hegel den Atheisten und Antichristen: Ein Ultimatum* (Leipzig, 1841).
154. Udo Köster, *Literarischer Radikalismus: Zeitbewusstsein und Geschichtsphilosophie in der Entwicklung vom Jungen Deutschland zur Hegelschen Linken* (Frankfurt, 1972), pp. 66–71.
155. *Streitschriften,* III, 7.
156. *Evangelische Kirchenzeitung* (1836), p. 382.
157. Ibid., p. 385.
158. *Streitschriften,* III, 23.
159. Ibid., III, 7.
160. *Evangelische Kirchenzeitung* (1836), p. 284.
161. Rothe's "return" to Hegelianism after fifteen years in the Fundamentalist camp was expressed in his *Die Anfänge der christlichen Kirche und Verfassung: Ein geschichtlicher Versuch* (Wittenberg, 1837).
162. Karl Müller, *Die religiöse Erweckung in Württemberg am Anfang des 19. Jahrhunderts* (Tübingen, 1925), pp. 1–9, 28–39; Walter Wendland, "Studien zur Erweckungsbewegung in Berlin (1810–1830)," *Jahrbuch der Brandenburgische Kirchengeschichte* 19 (1924):6–10, 21–6.
163. Wendland, "Studien," p. 25; Fritz Fischer, "Der deutsche Protestantismus und die Politik im 19. Jahrhundert," *Historische Zeitschrift* 170 (1951):481–3; Lehmann, *Pietismus,* pp. 188 ff.
164. Fritz Fischer, *Moritz August von Bethmann-Hollweg und der Protestantismus* (Berlin, 1938), pp. 68–111; Wendland, "Studien," pp. 22–6.
165. Wendland, "Studien," pp. 57–61.
166. Letter to his father, Easter 1825, quoted in Johannes Bachmann, *Ernst*

Wilhelm Hengstenberg: Sein Leben und Wirken, 3 vols. (Gütersloh, 1876–92), I, 107–8.
167. Bachmann, *Hengstenberg,* I, 278 ff.
168. For a general discussion of the alliance between Fundamentalist theology and reactionary politics in pre-1848 Prussia, see Robert M. Bigler, *The Politics of German Protestantism: The Rise of the Protestant Church Elite in Prussia, 1815–1848* (Berkeley, 1972), pp. 76–155.
169. Quoted in Bachmann, *Hengstenberg,* I, 189.
170. Fischer, *Bethmann-Hollweg,* pp. 58–9.
171. Quoted in Bachmann, *Hengstenberg,* II, 93.
172. Nathanael Bonwetsch, "Die Anfänge der 'Evangelischen Kirchenzeitung': Ein Beitrag zur Geschichte des religiösen und kirchlichen Lebens im 19. Jahrhundert," in *Geschichtliche Studien: Albert Hauck zum 70. Geburtstage* (Leipzig, 1916), pp. 286–99.
173. Georg Merz, *Das Bayerische Luthertum* (Munich, 1955), pp. 19–28; Müller, *Die religiöse Erweckung,* pp. 9–26.
174. Bachmann, *Hengstenberg,* III, 7.
175. Ibid., I, 170, 228–32; Hermelink, *Geschichte,* pp. 362–70.
176. Letter to his father, Aug. 22, 1830, quoted in Bachmann, *Hengstenberg,* II, 286.
177. Harmelink, *Geschichte,* 377–79.
178. Hengstenberg to L. v. Gerlach, July 27, 1832, quoted in Bachmann, *Hengstenberg,* II, 327.
179. *Die Zukunft des Herrn* (Stuttgart, 1836), p. 67.
180. *Evangelische Kirchenzeitung* (1836), p. 44.
181. Merz, *Bayerische Luthertum,* pp. 21–5; Emmanuel Hirsch, *Geschichte der neuern evangelischen Theologie,* V, 118–30, 170–90; Lehmann, *Pietismus,* pp. 203–5.
182. *Philosophie des Rechts nach geschichtlicher Ansicht,* II: *Christliche Rechts- und Staatslehre,* 2 pts. (Heidelberg, 1833–7), pt. 1, p. vi.
183. Bachmann, *Hengstenberg,* II, 287–99.
184. Lehmann, *Pietismus,* p. 194.
185. Ibid., p. 204.
186. Ibid., p. 203.
187. Hermelink, *Geschichte,* pp. 379–86; Lehmann, *Pietismus,* pp. 207–12.
188. Karl Friedrich Köppen, *Friedrich der Grosse und seine Widersacher: Eine Jubelschrift* (Leipzig, 1840); [Bruno Bauer], *Die evangelische Landeskirche Preussens und die Wissenschaft* (Leipzig, 1840).
189. Cited in Gustav Mayer, "Die Anfänge des politischen Radikalismus im vormärzlichen Preussen," *Zeitschrift für Politik* 6 (1913):16.

8. Strauss and the principle of immanence

1. "Literarische Denkwürdigkeiten," p. 4.
2. Strauss to Binder, Mar. 18, 1831, in Ziegler, "Zur Biographie von David Friedrich Strauss," p. 199.
3. Strauss to Georgii, Mar. 11, 1832, in Strauss, *Briefe von David Friedrich Strauss an L. Georgii,* p. 5. Strauss's Hegelian contacts in Berlin are described in Benecke, *Vatke,* pp. 71–80.

4. Strauss to Georgii, Mar. 11, 1832, in Strauss, *Briefe von David Friedrich Strauss an L. Georgii,* p. 6.
5. *Streitschriften,* III, 58–60, 65–8.
6. Strauss to Käferle, Jan. 17, 1836, in Strauss, *Ausgewählte Briefe,* p. 18.
7. *Charakteristiken und Kritiken,* pp. 213–34.
8. Strauss to Märklin, Feb. 6, 1832, in Strauss, *Ausgewählte Briefe,* p. 14.
9. Ibid., pp. 12–13.
10. Traub, "Die Stiftsakten über David Friedrich Strauss," p. 56.
11. Letter of Jan. 5, 1833, in Ziegler, "Zur Biographie von David Friedrich Strauss," p. 343.
12. Zeller, *Strauss,* p. 30; David Friedrich Strauss, "Vorlesungen über die Geschichte der Philosophie," MSS in Tübingen Universitätsbibliothek, Strauss Nachlass, Sig. MH II 127, pp. 23–44, 377–456. See also Jörg F. Sandberger, *David Fr. Strauss als theologischer Hegelianer: Mit unveröffentlichten Briefen* (Göttingen, 1972), pp. 66–72.
13. "Vorlesungen über Logik und Metaphysik," MSS in Tübingen Universitätsbibliothek, Strauss Nachlass, Sig. Mh II 128, p. 4.
14. Ziegler, *Strauss,* I, 116.
15. *Briefe von David Friedrich Strauss an L. Georgii,* p. 7.
16. *Charakteristiken und Kritiken,* p. 285.
17. *Briefe von David Friedrich Strauss an L. Georgii,* p. 11.
18. *Das Leben Jesu kritisch bearbeitet,* 2 vols. (Tübingen, 1835–6), II, 687.
19. Ibid.
20. See his later comment in *Die Halben und die Ganzen: Eine Streitschrift* (Berlin, 1865), p. 42.
21. *Leben Jesu* (1835–6), I, vi.
22. Ibid., p. 29.
23. Ibid., p. 74.
24. *Leben Jesu,* 2nd ed. (1837), I, 86–7.
25. *Leben Jesu* (1835–6), I, 37.
26. Ibid., pp. 71–2.
27. Ibid., II, 274.
28. Letter of May 12, 1836, in Ziegler, "Zur Biographie von David Friedrich Strauss," p. 350.
29. The letter is printed in Ziegler, *Strauss,* II, 767–8.
30. Karl Barth, *Protestant Thought from Rousseau to Ritschl,* trans. Brian Cozens (New York, 1959), pp. 362–89; Ernst Wolf, "Die Verlegenheit der Theologie: David Friedrich Strauss und die Bibelkritik," in E. Wolf and W. Matthias, eds., *Libertas Christiana: Festschrift für Friedrich Delekat* (Munich, 1957), pp. 219–39.
31. *Leben Jesu* (1837), I, 87–8.
32. G. W. F. Hegel, *Einleitung in die Geschichte der Philosophie,* 3rd ed., ed. J. Hoffmeister and F. Nicolin (Hamburg, 1959), p. 55.
33. *Leben Jesu* (1835–6), II, 686.
34. This is the viewpoint of Günther Backhaus, *Kerygma und Mythos bei David Friedrich Strauss und Rudolf Bultmann* (Hamburg, 1956), esp. pp. 79–82, as well as of Christian Hartlich and Walter Sachs, *Der Ursprung des Mythosbegriffs in der modernen Bibelwissenschaft* (Tübingen, 1952), pp. 134–47.
35. *Leben Jesu* (1835–6), II, 729–30, 732.
36. Ibid., pp. 733–4.
37. Ibid., pp. 735, 737.

38. Strauss to M. Fraas, June 4, 1834, in Sandberger, *Strauss,* pp. 226–9.
39. *Leben Jesu* (1835–6), II, 740.
40. Ibid., pp. 740, 743.
41. Ibid., p. 744.
42. Ziegler, *Strauss,* I, 178–95; Adolph Hausrath, *David Friedrich Strauss und die Theologie seiner Zeit,* 2 vols. (Heidelberg, 1876–8), I, 174–84.
43. Hausrath, *Strauss,* I, 192.
44. C. A. Eschenmayer, *Der Ischariotismus unserer Tage: Eine Zugabe zu den jüngst erschienen Werke, Das Leben Jesu von Strauss* (Tübingen, 1835).
45. Ziegler, "Zur Biographie von David Friedrich Strauss," p. 347.
46. Strauss to Binder, May 12, 1836, in ibid., p. 351.
47. *Die biblische Theologie,* I: *Die Religion des Alten Testaments nach den kanonischen Büchern* (Berlin, 1835), esp. pp. v–viii, 19–20.
48. Strauss to Vatke, Jan. 17, 1836, in Benecke, *Vatke,* pp. 183–4.
49. Benecke, *Vatke,* pp. 260–3.
50. Strauss to Baur, Aug. 19, 1836, in Ernst Barnikol, "Der Briefwechsel zwischen Strauss und Baur," *Zeitschrift für kirchengeschichte* 78, no. 1 (1962):89.
51. Ibid., p. 101.
52. Strauss to Zeller, Feb. 1, 1847, in Wilhelm Lang, "Ferdinand Baur und David Friedrich Strauss," *Preussische Jahrbücher* 161 (1915):131.
53. Ruge, "Strauss und seine Gegner," *Blätter für literarische Unterhaltung* (June 12, 1837), p. 657.
54. *Kritische Erläuterungen,* p. xx.
55. Strauss leveled the same accusation against De Wette in the *Jahrbücher für wissenschaftliche Kritik* (1837), pt. 1, cols. 17–18.
56. Strauss, *Streitschriften,* III, 95–120.
57. Ibid., pp. 120–6.
58. Ibid., pp. 60–94.
59. See the discussion in Sandberger, *Strauss,* pp. 154–5.
60. *Streitschriften,* III, 160.
61. Menzel, who, like Heinrich Leo, had gained a reputation as a "liberal" because of his opposition to bureaucratic hierarchy in the 1820s, had, like Leo, switched to the camp of the conservative Fundamentalists after the revolutions of 1830. For a fuller discussion of Menzel see my dissertation: "The Innocence of the Self: Cultural Disinheritance and Cultural Liberation in the Experience and Thought of the Young Germans and Young Hegelians" (Harvard University, 1973), pp. 198 ff., 401 ff.
62. *Streitschriften,* II, 181–6.
63. Strauss to Hermann Zeller, Jan. 30, 1838, in David Friedrich Strauss, "Ein unbekannter Brief von David Friedrich Strauss aus dem Jahre 1838," ed. Walter Hagen, *Ludwigsburger Geschichtsblätter* (1964), p. 364.
64. Ziegler, *Strauss,* I, 228–34.
65. "Literarische Denkwürdigkeiten," p. 13.
66. *Ausgewählte Briefe,* p. 36.
67. Strauss to Rapp, Jan. 10, 1838, in ibid., pp. 49–50.
68. Strauss to Rapp, Feb. 7, 1838, in Strauss, *Ausgewählte Briefe,* p. 51.
69. Strauss to Märklin, in Strauss, *Ausgewählte Briefe,* p. 63.
70. *Gesammelte Schriften,* XII, 11–13.
71. Strauss to Rapp, May 7, 1837, in Strauss, *Ausgewählte Briefe,* p. 36.
72. *Ausgewählte Briefe,* pp. 33–4, 35–6, 42–3, 49–50.

73. See especially the letter to Rapp, Apr. 5, 1838, in Strauss, *Ausgewählte Briefe,* pp. 60–2.
74. Ibid., p. 62.
75. *Briefwechsel zwischen Strauss und Vischer,* ed. A. Rapp, 2 vols. (Stuttgart, 1952–3), I, 51.
76. *Ausgewählte Briefe,* p. 63.
77. Strauss to Rapp, Dec. 9, 1837, in Strauss, *Ausgewählte Briefe,* p. 48.
78. "Literarische Denkwürdigkeiten," p. 5.
79. *Leben Jesu,* 3rd ed. (1838), I, 778.
80. "Literarische Denkwürdigkeiten," p. 13.
81. "Vergängliches und Bleibendes im Christenthum," *Der Freihafen: Galerie von Unterhaltungsbildern aus den Kreisen der Literatur, Gesellschaft und Wissenschaft* 1, no. 3 (1838):16.
82. See the discussion in Cornehl, *Die Zukunft der Versöhnung,* pp. 241–6.
83. "Vergängliches und Bleibendes," p. 48.
84. Ibid., p. 1.
85. Strauss to Professor Hitzig, June 14, 1838, in Hausrath, *Strauss,* vol. I, appendixes, p. 18.
86. The fullest account of the Zürich affair is in Hausrath, *Strauss,* I, 331–423.
87. Strauss to Frau Georgii, Apr. 9, 1839, in Strauss, *Briefe von David Friedrich Strauss an L. Georgii,* p. 28. See also Strauss, *Briefwechsel zwischen Vischer und Strauss,* I, 69.
88. Vischer's article "Dr. Strauss und die Wirtemberger" began to appear in serial form in the *Hallische Jahrbücher* in the summer of 1838. Märklin entered into a public denunciation of Strauss's opponents in *Darstellung und Kritik des modernen Pietismus* (Stuttgart, 1839). See also Gustav Binder, *Der Pietismus und die Moderne Bildung: Sendschreiben an den Herrn Herausgeber des Christenboten* (Stuttgart, 1838).
89. Strauss to Georgii, Dec. 24, 1838, in Strauss, *Briefe von David Friedrich Strauss an L. Georgii,* p. 25.
90. Strauss to Zeller, Jan. 8, 1839, in Strauss, *Ausgewählte Briefe,* p. 75. In the fall of 1838, Ruge asserted that the "Straussian Criticism" was the center of contemporary theological development. See his *Pruessen und die Reaction,* p. 112.
91. *Ausgewählte Briefe,* p. 74.
92. "Schleiermacher und Daub," in Strauss, *Charakteristiken und Kritiken,* p. 208.
93. Ibid., p. 52.
94. *Sendschreiben an die hochgeachtete Herren: Bürgermeister Hirzel, Professor Orelli und Professor Hitzig in Zürich* (Zürich, 1839), pp. 13, 22.
95. *Zwei friedliche Blätter* (Altona, 1839), pp. v, ix–x.
96. *Senschreiben,* pp. 9–10, 22–3.
97. *Zwei friedliche Blätter,* pp. xxx–xxxiii.
98. *Briefe von David Friedrich Strauss an L. Georgii,* p. 28.
99. Strauss to Rapp, June 17, 1839, in Strauss, *Ausgewählte Briefe,* p. 90.
100. Ibid., p. 89.
101. Strauss to H. Kern, Aug. 26, 2839, MSS in Tübingen Universitätsbibliothek, Strauss Nachlass, letters to H. Kern (copies), Sign. Md 887/3, no. 6.

102. MSS in Schiller National-Museum, Marbach, Strauss-Märklin Correspondence, no. 20336.
103. In the "Vorrede" to *Charakteristiken und Kritiken,* pp. v, vii.
104. "Vorrede" to *Leben Jesu,* 4th ed. (1840), I, ix–x.
105. Strauss to Georgii, Jan. 1, 1831, in Strauss, *Briefe von David Friedrich Strauss an L. Georgii,* p. 4.
106. *Leben Jesu* (1835–6), II, 688.
107. *Die christliche Glaubenslehre in ihrer geschichtlichen Entwicklung und im Kampfe mit der modernen Wissenschaft,* 2 vols. (Tübingen, 1840–1), I, 71.
108. Ibid., I, 1–2.
109. Ibid., pp. 12–13.
110. Ibid., pp. 17–19, 22–3.
111. Ibid., II, 625.
112. Ibid., I, 75.
113. Ibid., p. 282.
114. Ibid., p. 355.
115. Ibid., II, 75.
116. Ibid., I, 68.
117. Ibid., II, 495–7.
118. Ibid., p. 737.
119. Ibid., p. 618.
120. Ibid., I, 340, 355.
121. Ibid., pp. 355–6.
122. Ibid., II, 626, n. 17.
123. MSS in Schiller National-Museum, Marbach, Strauss-Märklin Correspondence, no. 20336.
124. *Briefe von David Friedrich Strauss an L. Georgii,* p. 39; *Briefwechsel zwischen Vischer und Strauss,* I, 95, 105.
125. "Literarische Denkwürdigkeiten," p. 14; "Berliner Art (Br. Bauer.)," in Strauss, *Gesammelte Schriften,* XII, 28.
126. *Briefwechsel zwischen Vischer und Strauss,* I, 131.

9. Bruno Bauer

1. *Jahrbücher für wissenschaftliche Kritik* (1835), pt. 2, cols. 879 ff.
2. He referred to Bauer's review as pure "shamelessness" (*Unverschämtheit*) in a letter to Baur, May 1, 1836, in Barnikol, "Der Briefwechsel zwischen Strauss und Baur," p. 83.
3. *Deutsche Jahrbücher für Wissenschaft und Kunst* (July 1842), col. 671.
4. Strauss to H. Kern, June 13, 1843, MSS in Tübingen Universitätsbibliothek, Strauss Nachlass, letters to Kern (copies), Sig. Md 887/3, no. 10.
5. When not otherwise noted, the biographical information on Bauer has been taken from E. Schläger, "Bruno Bauer und seine Werke," *Schmeitzner's Internationale Monatsschrift* 1 (1882):377–380; and Dieter Hertz-Eichenrode, *Der Junghegelianer Bruno Bauer im Vormärz* (Berlin, 1959), pp. 8–10.
6. See the discussion of Bauer's unpublished familial correspondence in Ernst Barnikol, *Bruno Bauer: Studien und Materialien,* ed. Peter Reimer and Hans-Martin Sass (Assen, 1972), pp. 6–20.
7. Bruno Bauer, "Die humanistische Bildung der Deutschen in der zweiten

Hälfte des 18. Jahrhunderts," *Vierteljahrsschrift für Volkswirtschaft, Politik und Kulturgeschichte* 59 (1878):44–6.

8. "Curriculum Vitae" (1839), in Barnikol, *Bauer*, pp. 516–17.
9. Hegel's comments on the essay are printed in Hegel, *Berliner Schriften*, p. 672.
10. Quoted in Benecke, *Vatke*, p. 74.
11. Barnikol, *Bauer*, pp. 22–3.
12. *Jahrbücher für wissenschaftliche Kritik* (1835), pt. 1, col. 848.
13. Ibid. (1834), pt. 1, col. 650.
14. Ibid. See also *Litterarischer Anzeiger für christliche Theologie und Wissenschaft* (1834), no. 79, p. 630, (1835), no. 38, pp. 303–4.
15. *Jahrbücher für wissenschaftliche Kritik* (1834), pt. 2, col. 328.
16. *Litterarischer Anzeiger* (1835), no. 49, p. 389.
17. *Jahrbücher für wissenschaftliche Kritik* (1835), pt. 2, col. 88.
18. Ibid., col. 70.
19. Ibid. (1834), pt. 2, col. 814.
20. *Die evangelische Landeskirche*, pp. 2–3.
21. B. Bauer to F. C. Baur, Jan. 3, 1836, MSS in Tübingen Universitätsbibliothek, Baur Nachlass, Sig. Md 750 I, 2.
22. *Jahrbücher für wissenschaftliche Kritik* (1835), pt. 2, col. 883.
23. Ibid., col. 886.
24. Ibid., cols. 86, 886–8.
25. *Zeitschrift für spekulative Theologie* 2, no. 2 (1836):441.
26. *Jahrbücher für wissenschaftliche Kritik* (1835), pt. 2, col. 886.
27. Ibid.
28. Ibid., col. 888.
29. Ibid., col. 892.
30. Ibid. (1838), pt. 1, cols. 827–9.
31. Ibid. (1935), pt. 2, col. 912.
32. Ibid. (1838), pt. 1, col. 823.
33. Bauer to Altenstein, May 21, 1836, quoted in Hertz-Eichenrode, *Bruno Bauer im Vormärz*, p. 19.
34. *Zeitschrift für spekulative Theologie* 1, no. 1 (1836):140.
35. Ibid., Ankündigung, p. 1.
36. Ibid., Ankündigung, p. 3.
37. Ibid., pp. 141–2. Bauer's italics.
38. Ibid., p. 176.
39. Ibid. 2, no. 2 (1837):441–2.
40. *Die Religion des Alten Testaments in der geschichtlichen Entwicklung ihrer Principien dargestellt*, 2 vols. (Berlin, 1838), I, xvi.
41. Ibid., pp. xvii, xcv–xcvi.
42. The only work that has attempted a detailed analysis of Bauer's theological position during his Right Hegelian period is the extremely abstract theological dissertation by Joachim Mehlhausen: *Dialektik, Selbstbewusstsein und Offenbarung.*
43. *Die Religion des Alten Testaments*, I, xxi.
44. Ibid., p. xxii.
45. Ibid., pp. xxiii–xxiv.
46. Ibid., p. xxv.

47. This modification of the Hegelian schema was first pointed out by Mehlhausen, *Dialektik, Selbstbewusstsein und Offenbarung,* pp. 237–50.
48. *Die Religion des Alten Testaments,* I, xxxii–xxxvi.
49. Ibid., p. xl.
50. Ibid., pp. lxvii–lxxix.
51. Ibid., pp. xlvii–xlviii.
52. Ibid., p. xlix.
53. *Jahrbücher für wissenschaftliche Kritik* (1836), pt. 1, col. 704.
54. *Die Religion des Alten Testaments,* II, xviii.
55. Hertz-Eichenrode, *Bruno Bauer im Vormärz,* p. 22; Mehlhausen, *Dialektik, Selbstbewusstsein und Offenbarung,* pp. 55–6.
56. *Jahrbücher für wissenschaftliche Kritik* (1837), pt. 2, col. 9.
57. *Die Religion des Alten Testaments,* II, ix.
58. Mehlhausen, *Dialektik, Selbstbewusstsein und Offenbarung,* pp. 312–14.
59. We know only that he frequented the salon of Bettina von Arnim and that he was a leading member of the Hegelian discussion group known as the Doktorklub. No specific ideological tendencies can be deduced from his contacts with either of these groups. See Hertz-Eichenrode, *Bruno Bauer im Vormärz,* pp. 30–1. The claim by Jürgen Kempski in "Ueber Bruno Bauer: Eine Studie zum Ausgang des Hegelianismus," *Archiv für Philosophie* 11 (1961–2):116, that Bauer's membership in the Doktorklub marked a decisive turn toward an atheistic position is totally unfounded.
60. *Die Religion des Alten Testaments,* I, xlix.
61. Ibid., II, 497.
62. Ibid., I, xlix.
63. Ibid., II, 497.
64. *Evangelische Kirchenzeitung* (1836), p. 21.
65. Michelet, *Geschichte der letzten Systeme,* II, 646; Strauss, *Streitschriften,* III, 104 ff.
66. *Jahrbücher für wissenschaftliche Kritik* (1839), pt. 1, col. 263.
67. Ibid., col. 325.
68. Ibid., cols. 89, 349.
69. Ibid., cols. 349–50.
70. *Zeitschrift für spekulative Theologie* 2, no. 2 (1837):439–66; *Die Religion des Alten Testaments,* I, 140, 257, II, 129–32, 268–70.
71. Bruno Bauer, *Herr Dr. Hengstenberg: Kritische Briefe über den Gegensatz des Gesetzes und des Evangelium* (Berlin, 1839), p. 2.
72. Ibid., p. 6.
73. Ibid., p. 129.
74. Benecke, *Vatke,* pp. 258 ff.
75. *Gutachten der evangelisch-theologischen Facultäten der Königlich preussischen Universitäten über den Licentiaten Bruno Bauer in Beziehung auf dessen Kritik der evangelischen Geschichte der Synoptiker* (Berlin, 1842), p. 29.
76. O. Ritschl, *Die evangelisch-theologische Facultät zu Bonn in dem ersten Jahrhundert ihrer Geschichte, 1819–1919* (Bonn, 1919), p. 20.
77. B. Bauer to E. Bauer, Mar. 15, 1840, in Bruno Bauer, *Briefwechsel zwischen Bruno Bauer und Edgar Bauer während der Jahre 1839–1842* (Charlottenburg, 1844), p. 51.
78. B. Bauer to E. Bauer, Mar. 31, 1840, in B. Bauer, *Briefwechsel zwischen Bruno Bauer und Edgar Bauer,* p. 59.

79. E. Bauer to B. Bauer, Apr. 21, 1840, in B. Bauer, *Briefwechsel zwischen Bruno Bauer und Edgar Bauer,* p. 65.
80. B. Bauer to E. Bauer, June 21, 1840, in B. Bauer, *Briefwechsel zwischen Bruno Bauer und Edgar Bauer,* pp. 87–8.
81. Marheineke to Altenstein, June 16, 1840, in Barnikol, *Bauer,* p. 463.
82. Bauer to Marx, Mar. 40, 1840, in *MEGA,* pt. 1, vol. I, sec. 2, p. 240.
83. B. Bauer to E. Bauer, Nov. 4, 1839, in B. Bauer, *Briefwechsel zwischen Bruno Bauer und Edgar Bauer,* p. 12.
84. B. Bauer to E. Bauer, Mar. 15, 1840, in B. Bauer, *Briefwechsel zwischen Bruno Bauer und Edgar Bauer,* pp. 49–50.
85. B. Bauer to E. Bauer, Jan. 20, 1840, in B. Bauer, *Briefwechsel zwischen Bruno Bauer und Edgar Bauer,* p. 31.
86. B. Bauer to E. Bauer, Jan. 5, 1840. This passage was deleted by the Prussian censors from the 1844 edition of the *Briefwechsel zwischen Bruno Bauer und Edgar Bauer* and printed by Bauer in the *Allgemeine Literatur-Zeitung* 1, no. 6 (1844):41.
87. B. Bauer to E. Bauer, Jan. 20, 1840, in B. Bauer, *Briefwechsel zwischen Bruno Bauer und Edgar Bauer,* p. 37.
88. Bauer to Marx, Dec. 11, 1839, in *MEGA,* pt. 1, vol. I, sec. 2, p. 235.
89. B. Bauer to E. Bauer, Mar. 15, 1841, in B. Bauer, *Briefwechsel zwischen Bruno Bauer und Edgar Bauer,* p. 49.
90. Ibid., pp. 49–50.
91. B. Bauer to E. Bauer, Aug. 7, 1840, in B. Bauer, *Briefwechsel zwischen Bruno Bauer und Edgar Bauer,* p. 104.
92. Bruno Bauer, *Kritik der evangelischen Geschichte des Johannes* (Bremen, 1840), pp. vi–xii.
93. Ibid., pp. vi–xiii.
94. Ibid., pp. 56–7, 89, 94, 101.
95. Ibid., pp. 182–3.
96. Bauer to Marx, Mar. 1, 1840, in *MEGA,* pt. 1, vol. I, sec. 2, p. 237.
97. Bauer to Marx, Apr. 5, 1840, in *MEGA,* pt. 1, vol. I, sec. 2, p. 241.
98. *Die evangelische Landeskirche,* p. 80.
99. Ibid., p. 65.
100. Ibid., p. 104.
101. Ibid., p. 59.
102. Ibid., pp. 135–6.
103. Ibid., p. 136.
104. Hertz-Eichenrode, *Bauer,* pp. 75–6; Barnikol, *Bauer,* pp. 136–56.
105. Ruge began to present Bauer's case to the public as a reflection of the contemporary cultural crisis in the spring of 1841. See *Hallische Jahrbücher* (1841), cols. 363–4, 423–4, 427–8.
106. B. Bauer to E. Bauer, May 6, 1841, in B. Bauer, *Briefwechsel zwischen Bruno Bauer und Edgar Bauer,* p. 137.
107. "Die christliche Staat und unsere Zeit," in Bruno Bauer, *Feldzüge der reinen Kritik,* ed. and epilogue by Hans-Martin Sass (Frankfurt, 1968), p. 32.
108. Ibid., pp. 36–7.
109. Bauer to Ruge, Apr. 16, 1841, in Barnikol, *Bauer,* p. 51.
110. Bauer to Marx, Mar. 28, 1841, in *MEGA,* pt. 1, vol. I, sec. 2, 247.
111. Bauer to Marx, Mar. 31, 1841, in *MEGA,* pt. 1, vol. I, sec. 2, 250.
112. Bauer to Ruge, June 20, 1841, in Barnikol, *Bauer,* p. 54.

113. Bauer to Ruge, Aug. 17, 1841, in Barnikol, *Bauer,* p. 54.
114. Bauer to Ruge, Dec. 6, 1841, in *MEGA,* pt. 1, vol. I, sec. 2, p. 264.
115. Bauer to Ruge, Mar. 1, 1842, MSS Sächsische Landesbibliothek, Dresden, Sig. h 46 I, no. 12.
116. *Die Gute Sache der Freiheit und meine eigene Angelegenheit* (Zürich and Winterthur, 1842), p. 234.
117. As he did in the title of his analysis of the controversy over his appointment: *Die Gute Sache der Freiheit und meine eigene Angelegenheit.*
118. Ruge to Rosenkranz, Oct. 2, 1839, in Ruge, *Briefwechsel und Tagebuchblätter,* I, 181.
119. *Hallische Jahrbücher* (1840), col. 2206.
120. *Posaune,* p. 13.
121. Bauer to Ruge, Oct. 19, 1841, in Barnikol, *Bauer,* p. 57.
122. Bauer to Ruge, Apr. 16, 1841, in Barnikol, *Bauer,* p. 51.
123. *Kritik der evangelischen Geschichte der Synoptiker,* 3 vols. (Leipzig and Braunschweig, 1841–2), I, v, III, 199.
124. Ibid., I, vi.
125. Ibid., p. 409.
126. Ibid., III, 308.
127. Ibid., I, 82. See also ibid., II, 157.
128. Ibid., I, vi.
129. Ibid., p. xx.
130. Ibid., p. 311.
131. *Posaune,* p. 163.
132. Ibid., pp. 64–5.
133. Ibid., p. 48.
134. Ibid., p. 77.
135. Ibid., p. 70.
136. Ibid., p. 81.
137. Ibid., p. 83.
138. Ibid., p. 82.
139. Bauer to Feuerbach, Mar. 10, 1842, in Hans-Martin Sass, "Bruno Bauer's Idee der 'Rheinischen Zeitung,'" *Zeitschrift für Religions- und Geistesgeschichte* 19 (1967):322.
140. *Die Gute Sache,* pp. 117–22.

10. Feuerbach

1. *Das Wesen des Christentums,* in *Werke* (Schuffenhauer), V, 23 (translated as *The Essence of Christianity* by George Eliot [reprint, New York, 1957], p. xlii). English citation given hereafter in parentheses.
2. "Zur Beurteilung der Schrift 'Das Wesen des Christentums,'" in *Werke* (Schuffenhauer), IX, 229–30; letters to Arnold Ruge from 1841 and 1842 in *Werke* (Sass), XIII, 387–8, 391, 393.
3. *Ludwig Feuerbach and the Outcome of Classical German Philosophy,* trans. C. P. Dutt (New York, 1941), p. 18.
4. "Fragmente," p. 388.
5. *Lectures on the Essence of Religion,* trans. Ralph Manheim (New York, 1967), p. 3.
6. Feuerbach to C. Kapp, Jan. 14, 1835, in *Werke* (Sass), XII, 284.

7. Feuerbach to Friedrich Feuerbach, Mar. 12, 1832, in *Werke* (Sass), XII, 256–7.
8. Eduard Feuerbach to Ludwig Feuerbach, Sept. 23, 1832, in *Werke* (Sass), XII, 260.
9. Gans to Feuerbach, Oct. 11, 1833, and Jan. 4, 1834, in Feuerbach, *Briefwechsel und Nachlass,* I, 235, 236–7.
10. Altenstein to Feuerbach, Oct. 13, 1833, in Feuerbach, *Briefwechsel und Nachlass,* I, 235–6.
11. Feuerbach to C. Kapp, Jan. 14, 1835, in *Werke* (Sass), XII, 284.
12. Kohut, *Feuerbach,* p. 114.
13. Feuerbach to C. Kapp, Feb. 3, 1835, in *Werke* (Sass), XII, 292.
14. Feuerbach to C. Kapp, Jan. 13, 1835, in *Werke* (Sass), XII, 284.
15. Feuerbach to C. Kapp, Feb. 3, 1835, in *Werke* (Sass), XII, 292.
16. Feuerbach to B. Löw, Feb. 3, 6, and 12, 1835, in *Werke* (Sass), XII, 286–8.
17. Henning to Feuerbach, Apr. 17, 1835, in Feuerbach, *Briefwechsel und Nachlass,* I, 241–4.
18. Feuerbach to B. Löw, Apr. 1836, in *Werke* (Sass), XII, 305.
19. Feuerbach to Kapp, Feb. 3, 1840, in *Werke* (Sass), XIII, 30.
20. *Lectures on the Essence of Religion,* p. 6; Feuerbach to Kapp, Nov. 1840, in *Werke* (Sass), XIII, 51.
21. *Abelard und Heloise: Der Schriftsteller und der Mensch: Humoristischphilosophischen Aphorismen,* in *Werke* (Sass), I, 288.
22. Review of Erdmann, *Versuch einer wissenschaftliche Darstellung der Geschichte der neueren Philosophie,* in *Werke* (Schuffenhauer), VIII, 128.
23. Review of Hegel, *Vorlesungen über die Geschichte der Philosophie,* in *Werke* (Schuffenhauer), VIII, 50.
24. Ibid., p. 46.
25. *Vorlesungen über die Geschichte der neueren Philosophie,* ed. C. Ascheri and E. Thies (Darmstadt, 1974), pp. 182–3.
26. Johann Eduard Erdmann, *Versuch einer wissenschaftlichen Darstellung der Geschichte der neueren Philosophie* (Riga and Dorpat, 1834), I, pt. 1, vii.
27. Review of Erdmann, in *Werke* (Schuffenhauer), VIII, 130; "Brief an C. Riedel," in *Werke* (Sass), II, 395–6.
28. Feuerbach to C. Kapp, June 17, 1835, in *Werke* (Sass), XII, 294.
29. This does not mean that Feuerbach should not be taken seriously as a philosopher. Marx Wartofsky's *Feuerbach* (Cambridge, 1977), a very detailed and closely argued study, rehabilitates Feuerbach as an acute analyst of the process of human belief and concept formation, as a dialectical phenomenologist of human consciousness whose work is very relevant to contemporary philosophical concerns.
30. *Geschichte der neuern Philosophie von Bacon von Verulam bis Benedikt Spinoza,* in *Werke* (Schuffenhauer), II, 11.
31. G. W. F. Hegel, *Vorlesungen über die Geschichte der Philosophie,* in Hegel, *Werke,* ed. Moldenhauer and Michel, XX, 123.
32. Ibid., p. 34.
33. *Vorlesungen über die Geschichte der neueren Philosophie,* p. 141.
34. Ibid., pp. 294 ff.
35. Ibid., p. 102.
36. "Kritik des 'Anti-Hegels,'" in *Werke* (Schuffenhauer), VIII, 79–83.
37. Ibid., pp. 102–4, 106.

38. Ibid., pp. 107–8.
39. "Fragmente," p. 371.
40. Ibid.
41. Review of Rosenkranz, *Sendschreiben an C. F. Bachmann,* in *Werke* (Schuffenhauer), VIII, 12.
42. *Geschichte der neuern Philosophie von Bacon von Verulam bis Benedikt Spinoza,* p. 26.
43. *Abalard und Heloise,* pp. 309–23, 343.
44. *Das Wesen des Christentums,* p. 3.
45. *Pierre Bayle: Ein Beitrag zur Geschichte der Philosophie und Menschheit,* in *Werke* (Schuffenhauer), IV, 27.
46. "Der wahre Gesichtspunkt aus welchem der 'Leo-Hegelsche Streit' beurteilt werden muss," in *Werke* (Schuffenhauer), VIII, 210.
47. Feuerbach to C. Kapp, Nov. 6, 1840, in *Werke* (Sass), XIII, 47.
48. Feuerbach to W. Bolin, Oct. 20, 1860, in *Werke* (Sass), XIII, 246.
49. *Das Wesen des Christentums,* p. 28 (1).
50. Ibid., p. 29 (2).
51. Ibid., pp. 30–1 (3).
52. Ibid., p. 48 (14).
53. Ibid., p. 43 (11).
54. Ibid., p. 46 (12).
55. "Aus dem Nachlass," p. 389.
56. "Zur Kritik der 'positiven Philosophie,'" in *Werke* (Schuffenhauer), VIII, 182.
57. "'Die Philosophie des Rechts nach geschichtlicher Ansicht,' von Friedr. Jul. Stahl," in *Werke* (Schuffenhauer), VIII, 25–31.
58. *Geschichte der neuern Philosophie: Darstellung, Entwicklung und Kritik der Leibnizischen Philosophie,* in *Werke* (Schuffenhauer), III, 112–19.
59. Ibid., pp. 119–20.
60. "Zur Kritik der 'positiven Philosophie,'" p. 193.
61. Ibid., pp. 197–98, 202.
62. Ibid., p. 207.
63. Ibid.
64. "Zur Kritik der Hegelschen Philosophie," in *Werke* (Schuffenhauer), IX, 20.
65. Ibid.
66. Ibid., p. 28.
67. Ibid., p. 31.
68. Ibid., p. 33.
69. Ibid., pp. 33–5.
70. Ibid., p. 40.
71. Ibid., pp. 42–4.
72. Ibid., p. 53.
73. Feuerbach to O. Wigand, Jan. 5, 1841, in *Werke* (Sass), XIII, 55.
74. "Zur Kritik der 'positiven Philosophie,'" p. 207.
75. *Das Wesen des Christentums,* p. 388 (233).
76. Ibid., p. 52 (16).
77. Ibid., pp. 75 ff. (33 ff.).
78. Ibid., p. 28 (2).
79. Ibid., pp. 77–8 (34–5).

80. Ibid., p. 277 (158).
81. Ibid., pp. 165–6 (82–3).
82. Ibid., pp. 170 ff. (87 ff.).
83. Ibid., p. 177 (91).
84. "Zur Kritik des Empirismus," in *Werke* (Schuffenhauer), VIII, 155.
85. *Das Wesen des Christentums,* p. 176 (91).
86. Feuerbach to O. Wigand, Jan. 5, 1841, in *Werke* (Sass), XIII, 55.
87. *Das Wesen des Christentums,* pp. 70–2 (29–30).
88. Ibid., pp. 153–4 (75).
89. Ibid., pp. 154–5, 117–20 (75–6, 59–61).
90. Ibid., p. 65 (26).
91. Ibid.
92. Ibid., p. 73 (31).
93. Ibid., p. 316 (185).
94. "Ueber das Wunder," in *Werke* (Schuffenhauer), VIII, 293–340.
95. *Das Wesen des Christentums,* p. 252 (143).
96. Ibid., pp. 264–6, 293–4 (151–2, 170).
97. Ibid., pp. 346–7 (204–5).
98. Ibid., pp. 173–4 (89).
99. Ibid., p. 411 (248).
100. Ibid., pp. 418, 334–5 (252, 197).
101. Feuerbach to O. Wigand, Jan. 5, 1841, in *Werke* (Sass), XIII, 55.
102. *Das Wesen des Christentums,* pp. 116, 212–13, 443–4 (58, 116, 270).
103. Ibid., pp. 46–7 (13).
104. Ibid., pp. 353–4 (208).
105. Ibid., pp. 335–7 (197–8).
106. Ibid., p. 377 (226).
107. Ibid., p. 384 (230).
108. Ibid., p. 443 (270).
109. Ibid., pp. 236–7, 363–5 (132–3, 216–17).
110. Ibid., p. 236 (132).
111. Ibid., pp. 237–8, 267–9 (133, 152–3).
112. Ibid., pp. 270–5 (155–7).
113. Ibid., pp. 277, 273 (158, 155).
114. Ibid., p. 444 (271).
115. Ibid., pp. 363–4 (216).
116. Ibid., p. 222 (123).
117. Ibid., p. 364 (217).
118. Ibid., p. 236 (132).
119. Ibid., p. 130 (64).
120. Ibid., p. 364 (217).
121. Ibid., p. 130 (64).
122. "Vorläufige Thesen zur Reformation der Philosophie," in *Werke* (Schuffenhauer), IX, 263.

Epilogue

1. Fritz Schlawe, "Die junghegelische Publizistik," *Die Welt als Geschichte* 20 (1960):33; Heinz Kornetzki, "Die revolutionär-dialektischen Entwicklung in den Hallischen Jahrbücher: Eine Untersuchung der Quellen des Sozialismus

in der linkshegelianische Zeitschrift des 19. Jahrhunderts" (doctoral diss., Munich, 1955), pp. 78–94. Echtermeyer's defection is described in Adolf Stahr, "Theodor Echtermeyer: Ein Denkstein," in Adolf Stahr, *Kleine Schriften zur Literatur und Kunst* (Berlin, 1871), pp. 416–22.

2. Cited in Mayer, "Die Anfänge des politischen Radikalismus im vormärzlichen Preussen," p. 43.

3. Ruge to Stahr, Sept. 8, 1841, in Ruge, *Briefwechsel und Tagebuchblätter,* I, 239.

4. Bauer to Feuerbach, Mar. 10, 1842, in Sass, "Bruno Bauer's Idee der 'Rheinischen Zeitung,'" pp. 321–2.

5. Nov. 8, 1842, in *Werke* (Sass), XIII, 404.

6. "Notwendigkeit einer Veränderung," in Ludwig Feuerbach, *Kleine Schriften,* ed. Karl Löwith (Frankfurt, 1966), p. 221.

7. Ibid., p. 225; "Vorläufige Thesen," p. 256.

8. *Die Gute Sache,* p. 209.

9. Feuerbach to C. Kapp, Dec. 30, 1842, in *Werke* (Sass), XIII, 115.

10. Review of Ammon's *Leben Jesu* in Arnold Ruge, ed. *Anekdota zur neuesten deutschen Philosophie und Publizistik,* 2 vols. (Zürich and Winterthur, 1843), II, 164; review of Strauss's *Leben Jesu* (4th ed.) in *Deutsche Jahrbücher* (July 1842), p. 667.

11. "Notwendigkeit einer Veränderung," p. 225.

12. "Vorlige Thesen," pp. 260–1.

13. Feuerbach to Ruge, Dec. 20, 1841, in *Werke* (Sass), XIII, 389.

14. "Notwendigkeit einer Veränderung," p. 226.

15. Ibid., pp. 234–5. See also Bruno Bauer, "Die Zersplitterung der Parteien in Frankreich," *Rheinische Zeitung* (Jan. 27, 1842), supp.

16. See McLellan, *Young Hegelians,* pp. 18–19; and Hans-Martin Sass, "Die Emanzipation des Dialektikbegriffs von Karl Marx aus der Interpretation, die Bruno Bauer und die 'Freien' der Hegelschen Dialektik gaben," *Hegel Jahrbuch* (1975), pp. 554–67.

17. Marx to Ruge, Sept. 1843, in *Deutsch-Französische Jahrbücher* 1–2 (1844):39–40.

18. See McLellan, *Young Hegelians,* pp. 15–17.

19. Koselleck, *Preussen,* pt. 3; John R. Gillis, *The Prussian Bureaucracy in Crisis, 1840–1860: Origins of an Administrative Ethos* (Stanford, 1971), pp. 22–84.

20. Rohr, *Origins,* pp. 50–77; Conze, "Vom 'Pöbel' zum 'Proletariat,'" pp. 333–64; Frederick D. Marquardt, "Pauperismus in Germany during the Vormärz," *Central European History* 2 (1969):85–8.

21. Cited in Lenz, *Geschichte,* II, pt. 2, 39.

22. Marx to Ruge, Nov., 30, 1842, in *MEGA,* pt. 1, vol. I, sec. 2, p. 285; Ruge to K. Fleischer, Dec. 12, 1842, in Ruge, *Briefwechsel und Tagebuchblätter,* I, 287.

23. "Was ist jetzt Gegenstand der Kritik?" in Bauer, *Feldzüge der reinen Kritik,* p. 206.

24. "Neueste Schriften über die Judenfrage," *Allgemeine Literaturzeitung* 4 (Mar. 1844):15.

25. "Zur Judenfrage," *Deutsch-Französische Jahrbücher* 1–2 (1844):182–214.

26. "Deutschlands Beruf in der Gegenwart, von Theodor Rohmer," *Die Eisenbahn: Ein Unterhaltungsblatt für die gebildete Welt,* no. 78 (Dec. 30, 1841), pp. 310–11.

27. *Der Einzige und sein Eigenthum* (Leipzig, 1845), pp. 131–2.

28. "Ueber das 'Wesen des Christenthums' in Beziehung auf den 'Einzigen und sein Eigenthum,'" in *Werke* (Schuffenhauer), IX, 432–3; "Fragmente," p. 381.
29. Bruno Bauer, "Die Gattung und die Masse," in Bauer, *Feldzüge der reinen Kritik,* pp. 214–18, 221–2; Max Stirner, *Der Einzige,* pp. 153 ff.
30. Karl Marx, "The German Ideology," in Karl Marx, *Writings of the Young Marx on Philosophy and Society,* trans. and ed. L. Easton and K. Guddat (Garden City, N.Y., 1967), p. 417.
31. "Vorwort" (1846), in *Werke* (Schuffenhauer), X, 188.
32. Feuerbach to Georg Herwegh, Nov. 25, 1845, in Marcel Herwegh and Victor Fleury, "Briefwechsel Georg und Emma Herweghs und Ludwig Feuerbach," *Nord und Süd: Eine deutsche Monatsschrift* 128 (1909):31.
33. "Grundsätze der Philosophie der Zukunft," in *Werke* (Schuffenhauer), IX, 308.
34. For Feuerbach's theory of sensualism see, aside from the "Grundsätze," his "Wider den Dualismus von Leib und Seele, Fleisch und Geist," in *Werke* (Schuffenhauer), X, 122–50; and the already cited "Ueber das 'Wesen des Christenthums' in Beziehung auf den 'Einzigen und sein Eigenthum.'"
35. *Feuerbach,* p. 225.
36. Schmidt, *Emanzipatorische Sinnlichkeit,* p. 40. See also Hermann Lübbe and Hans-Martin Sass, eds., *Atheismus in der Diskussion: Kontroversen über Ludwig Feuerbach* (Munich, 1975).
37. See Karl Marx and Friedrich Engels, "Die Heilige Familie, oder Kritik der kritischen Kritik: Gegen Bruno Bauer und Consorten," in *MEGA,* pt. 1, vol. 3, esp. p. 179.
38. *Das Entdeckte Christenthum: Eine Erinnerung an das achtzehnte Jahrhundert und ein Beitrag zur Krise des Neunzehnten* (Zurich and Winterthur, 1843), reprinted in Ernst Barnikol, ed., *Das Entdeckte Christenthum im Vormärz* (Jena, 1927), p. 160.
39. "Charakteristik Ludwig Feuerbachs," *Wigands Vierteljahresschrift* 3 (1845): 106.
40. "Die Gattung und die Masse," p. 213; "Charakteristik Ludwig Feuerbachs," pp. 138–43.
41. "Neueste Schriften über die Judenfrage," p. 10.
42. *Der Einzige,* pp. 426 ff.
43. Ibid., p. 286. See Friedrich Nietzsche, *The Genealogy of Morals,* Second Essay, no. 2.
44. *Der Einzige,* pp. 333–43.

Bibliography

This bibliography is restricted to a listing of materials directly relevant to the historical reconstruction of Hegelianism in the period before 1840. It makes no attempt to provide even a selective list of exegetical and critical works crucial for the internal comprehension of Hegel's thought. My own critical comments on major historiographical issues can be found in the text and notes. Secondary works that contain significant primary material not published elsewhere are followed by an asterisk. English translations are listed separately except where their contents correspond exactly to items listed in the original language. The bibliography does not include standard reference works or items of peripheral relevance to the main theme that were cited in the notes for purposes of illustration or comparison.

Primary sources

MANUSCRIPT MATERIALS

Sächsische Landesbibliothek, Dresden. 18 letters of Bruno Bauer to Arnold Ruge. Sig. h 46 I, nos. 4-21.
Schiller National-Museum, Marbach. Strauss-Märklin Correspondence. Nos. 20306 ff.
Universitätsbibliothek, Tübingen. Baur Nachlass. Letter of Bruno Bauer to F. C. Baur, Jan. 3, 1836. Sig. Md 750 I, 2.
Universitätsbibliothek, Tübingen. Strauss Nachlass. Student notebooks (Vorlesungsnachschriften) of lectures given in 1832-3 (Sig. Mh II 127 and Mh II 128) and letters to Heinrich Kern [Copies] (Sig. Md 887/3).

JOURNALS AND NEWSPAPERS

Allgemeine Literaturzeitung, 1844.
Blätter für literarische Unterhaltung, 1830-8.
Der Christenbote, 1831-8.
Deutsche Jahrbücher für Wissenschaft und Kunst, July 1841-Jan. 1843.
Deutsch-Französische Jahrbücher, 1844.

Die Evangelische Kirchenzeitung, 1833–8.
Hallische Jahrbücher für deutsche Wissenschaft und Kunst, 1838–41.
Jahrbücher für wissenschaftliche Kritik, 1827–46.
Literarische Zeitung, 1838.
Litterarischer Anzeiger für christliche Theologie und Wissenschaft überhaupt, 1834–5.
Morgenblatt für gebildete Stände: Literaturblatt, 1835–6.
Neue Berliner Monatschrift für Philosophie, Geschichte, Literatur und Kunst, 1821.
Rheinische Zeitung für Politik, Handel und Gewerbe, 1842.
Zeitschrift für spekulative Theologie, 1836.
Zeitschrift für die Wissenschaft des Judenthums, 1822–3.

PUBLISHED WORKS OF HEGEL, THE HEGELIAN SCHOOL, AND THEIR CONTEMPORARIES

Abegg, Julius F. G. *Encyclopädie und Methodologie der Rechtswissenschaft im Grundrisse.* Königsberg, 1823.
Bachmann, Karl Friedrich. *Anti-Hegel: Antwort an Herrn Professor Rosenkranz.* Jena, 1835.
System der Logik: Ein Handbuch zum Selbststudium. Leipzig, 1828.
"System der Wissenschaft, von G. W. Fr. Hegel." *Heidelbergische Jahrbücher* 3, no. 1 (1810):145–63, 193–209.
Ueber Geschichte der Philosophie. Jena, 1820.
Ueber Hegels System und die Notwendigkeit einer nochmaligen Umgestaltung der Philosophie. Leipzig, 1833.
Ueber die Philosophie meiner Zeit: Zur Vermittlung. Jena, 1816.
Ueber Philosophie und ihre Geschichte. Jena, 1811.
Bauer, Bruno. *Briefwechsel zwischen Bruno Bauer und Edgar Bauer während der Jahre 1839–1842.* Charlottenburg, 1844.
"Charakteristik Ludwig Feuerbachs." *Wigands Vierteljahresschrift* 3 (1845): 86–146.
Das Entdeckte Christenthum: Eine Erinnerung an das achtzehnte Jahrhundert und ein Beitrag zur Krise des Neunzehnten. Zürich and Winterthur, 1843. Reprinted in Ernst Barnikol, ed., *Das Entdeckte Christenthum im Vormärz.* Jena, 1927.
Feldzüge der reinen Kritik. Ed. and epilogue by Hans-Martin Sass. Frankfurt, 1968.
Die Gute Sache der Freiheit und meine eigene Angelegenheit. Zürich and Winterthur, 1842.
Herr Dr. Hengstenberg: Kritische Briefe über den Gegensatz des Gesetzes und des Evangelium. Berlin, 1839.
"Die humanistische Bildung der Deutschen in der zweiten Hälfte des 18. Jahrhunderts." *Vierteljahrsschrift für Volkswirtschaft, Politik und Kulturgeschichte* 59 (1878).
Kritik der evangelischen Geschichte des Johannes. Bremen, 1840.
Kritik der evangelischen Geschichte der Synoptiker. Vols. 1–2. Leipzig, 1841. Vol. 3: *Kritik der evangelischen Geschichte der Synoptiker und des Johannes.* Braunschweig, 1842.
Die Religion des Alten Testaments in der geschichtlichen Entwicklung ihrer Principion dargestellt. 2 vols. Berlin, 1838.

Bibliography

[Bauer, Bruno.] *Die evangelische Landeskirche Preussens und die Wissenschaft.* Leipzig, 1840.

Die Posaune des jüngsten Gerichts über Hegel den Atheisten und Antichristen: Ein Ultimatum. Leipzig, 1841.

Baur, Ferdinand Christian. *Die christliche Gnosis, oder die christliche Religionsphilosophie in ihrer geschichtlichen Entwicklung.* Tübingen, 1835.

Symbolik und Mythologie, oder die Naturreligion des Alterthums. 2 vols. Stuttgart, 1824–5.

Bayrhoffer, Karl Theodor. *Die Grundprobleme der Metaphysik.* Marburg, 1835.

Die Idee des Christenthums im Verhältnisse zu den Zeitgegensätzen der Theologie: Eine speculative Kritik. Marburg, 1836.

Die Idee und Geschichte der Philosophie. Marburg, 1838.

Das Verhältnis des Staats zur Kirche. Leipzig, 1838.

Besser, Karl Moritz. *System des Naturrechts.* Halle and Leipzig, 1830.

Billroth, Johann G. F. *Beiträge zur wissenschaftlichen Kritik der herrschenden Theologie.* Leipzig, 1831.

Vorlesungen über Religionsphilosophie. Ed. by J. E. Erdmann. Leipzig, 1837.

Binder, Gustav. *Der Pietismus und die moderne Bildung: Sendschreiben an den Herrn Herausgeber des Christenboten.* Stuttgart, 1838.

Böhmer, Johannes F. *Leben, Briefe und kleinere Schriften.* Ed. by J. Janssen. 3 vols. Frieburg im Breisgau, 1868.

Buhl, Ludwig. *Der Beruf der Preussischen Presse.* Berlin, 1842.

[Buhl, Ludwig.] *Hegel's Lehre vom Staat und seine Philosophie der Geschichte in ihren Hauptresultaten.* Berlin, 1837.

Carové, Friedrich Wilhelm. *Entwurf einer Burschenschafts-Ordnung und Versuch einer Begründung derselben.* Eisenach, 1818.

Kosmorama: Eine Reihe von Studien zur Orientierung in Natur, Geschichte, Staat, Philosophie und Religion. Frankfurt, 1831.

Die letzten Dinge des römischen Katholicismus in Deutschland. Leipzig, 1832.

Der Messianismus, die neuen Templar und einige andere merkwürdige Erscheinungen auf dem Gebiete der Religion und Philosophie in Frankreich nebst einer Uebersicht des gegenwärtigen Zuständes der Philosophie in Italien. Liepzig, 1834.

Neorama. 3 vols. Leipzig, 1838.

Religion und Philosophie in Frankreich: Eine Folge von Abhandlungen aus dem französischen übersetzt und eingeleitet. Göttingen, 1827.

Rückblick auf die Ursachen der französischen Revolution und Andeutung ihrer Welthistorischen Bestimmung. Hanau, 1834.

Der Saint-Simonismus und die neuere französische Philosophie. Leipzig, 1831.

Ueber alleinseligmachende Kirche. 2 vols. Frankfurt and Göttingen, 1826–7.

Ueber das Recht, die Weise und die wichtigsten Gegenstände der öffentlichen Beurtheilung mit stäter Beziehung auf die neueste Zeit. Trier, 1825.

Ueber die Ermordung Kotzebues. Eisenach, 1819.

Ueber Frankreich, Italien und Spanien von Fievée, Stendhal und Rotalde. Leipzig, 1831.

Cieszkowski, August. *Gott und Palingenesie.* Berlin, 1842.

Prolegomena zur Historiosophie. Berlin, 1838.

Conradi, Kasimir. *Christus in der Gegenwart, Vergangenheit und Zukunft: Drei Abhandlungen als Beiträge zur richtigen Auffassung des Begriffs der Persönlichkeit.* Mainz, 1839.

Selbstbewusstsein und Offenbarung, oder die Entwicklung des religiösen Bewusstseins. Mainz, 1831.
Unsterblichkeit und Ewiges Leben: Versuch einer Entwicklung des Unsterblichkeitsbegriffs der menschlichen Seele. Mainz, 1837.

Daub, Karl. *Die dogmatische Theologie jetziger Zeit oder die Selbstsucht in der Wissenschaft des Glaubens und ihrer Artikel.* Heidelberg, 1833.
Einleitung in das Studium der christlichen Dogmatik aus dem Standpunkte der Religion. Heidelberg, 1810.
Judas Ischariot, oder das Böse im Verhältnis zum Guten. 2 vols. Heidelberg, 1816–18.
Lehrbuch der Katechetik. Frankfurt, 1801.
Predigten nach Kantischen Grundsätzen. Königsberg, 1794.
Theologumena: sive doctrinae de religione christiana, ex nautra Dei perspecta, repetendae, capita potiora. Heidelberg, 1806.

Eiselen, Johann F. G. *Handbuch des Systems der Staatswissenschaften.* Breslau, 1828.

Engels, Friedrich. *Ludwig Feuerbach and the Outcome of Classical German Philosophy.* Trans. by C. P. Dutt. New York, 1941.

Erdmann, Johann Eduard. *A History of Philosophy.* Trans. by W. S. Hough. 3 vols. London, 1890–2.
Leib und Seele nach ihrem Begriff und ihrem Verhältnis zu einander. Halle, 1837.
Versuch einer wissenschaftlichen Darstellung der Geschichte der neueren Philosophie. Riga and Dorpat, 1834.

Eschenmayer, C. A. *Der Ischariotismus unserer Tage: Eine Zugabe zu den jüngst erschienen Werke, Das Leben Jesu von Strauss.* Tübingen, 1835.

Feuerbach, Henriette. *Anselm Feuerbachs Leben, Briefe und Gedichte.* Braunschweig, 1853.

Feuerbach, Ludwig. *Briefwechsel und Nachlass.* Ed. and intro. by Karl Grün. 2 vols. Leipzig and Heidelberg, 1874.
Briefwechsel zwischen Ludwig Feuerbach und Christian Kapp, 1832 bis 1848. Ed. by A. Kapp. Leipzig, 1876.
"Drei unveröffentlichte Briefe Ludwig Feuerbachs." *Menschheitsziele: Monatsrundschau für wissenschaftliche begründete Weltanschauung und Gesellschaftsreform* 1, no. 3 (1908):90–1.
Einleitung in die Logik und Metaphysik. Ed. by C. Ascheri and E. Thies. Darmstadt, 1975.
The Essence of Christianity. Trans. by George Eliot. Reprint. New York, 1957.
Gesammelte Werke. Ed. by Werner Schuffenhauer. 10 vols. to date. Berlin, 1967–.
Kleine Schriften. Ed. by Karl Löwith. Frankfurt, 1966.
Lectures on the Essence of Religion. Trans. by Ralph Manheim. New York, 1967.
Sämtliche Werke. Ed. by Hans-Martin Sass. 13 vols. Stuttgart, 1964. Vols. I–X of this edition are a reprint of *Sämtliche Werke,* ed. by Wilhelm Bolin and Friedrich Jodl (Stuttgart, 1903–11). Vols. XII–XIII are a slightly revised and expanded reedition of *Ausgewählte Briefe von und an Ludwig Feuerbach,* ed. by Wilhelm Bolin. Leipzig, 1904.
"Unveröffentliche Briefe Ludwig Feuerbachs an seine Brüder Anselm und Fritz," *Menschheitsziele: Monatsrundschau für wissenschaftliche begründete Weltanschauung und Gesellschaftsreform* 1, no. 12 (1908):14–17.

Vorlesungen über die Geschichte der neueren Philosophie. Ed. by C. Ascheri and E. Thies. Darmstadt, 1974.
Werke. Ed. by Erich Thiess. 6 vols. Frankfurt, 1975 ff.
Feuerbach, Ludwig, ed. *Anselm Ritter von Feuerbachs Leben und Wirken.* 2 vols. Leipzig, 1852.
Fichte, Immanuel H. *Beiträge zur Charakteristik der neueren Philosophie.* Sulzbach, 1829.
Fichte, Johann Gottlieb. *Briefwechsel.* Ed. by Hans Schulz. 2 vols. Leipzig, 1925.
Förster, Ernst. *Aus der Jugendzeit.* Ed. by K. von Binzer. Berlin and Stuttgart, 1887.
Förster, Friedrich. *Der Feldmarschall Fürst von Blücher von Wahlstaat und seine Umgebungen.* Leipzig, 1821.
Friedrichs des Grossen Jugendjahre: Bildung und Geist. Berlin, 1823.
Friedrich Wilhelm I, König von Preussen. 5 vols. Potsdam, 1834–5.
Die Höfe und Cabinette Europas im achtzehnten Jahrhundert. 3 vols. Potsdam, 1836–9.
Kunst und Leben: Aus Friedrich Försters Nachlass. Ed. by Hermann Kletke. Berlin, 1873.
Von der Begeisterung des preussischen Volkes im Jahre 1813 als Vertheidigung unsers Glaubens. Berlin, 1816.
Förster, Friedrich C., ed. *Beiträge zur neueren Kriegsgeschichte.* 2 vols. Berlin, 1816.
Gabler, Georg Andreas. *Die Hegelsche Philosophie: Beiträge zur ihrer richtigeren Beurtheilung und Würdigung.* Berlin, 1843.
Lehrbuch der philosophischen Propädeutik als Einleitung zur Wissenschaft. Erlangen, 1827.
De Verae philosophiae erga religionem christianem pietate. Berlin, 1836.
Gans, Eduard. *Beiträge zur Revision der preussischen Gesetzgebung.* Berlin, 1830–2.
Das Erbrecht in weltgeschichtlicher Entwicklung. 4 vols. Berlin and Stuttgart, 1824–35.
Philosophische Schriften. Ed. by Horst Schröder. Glashütten im Taunus, 1971.
Rückblicke auf Personen und Zustände. Berlin, 1836.
Scholien zum Gajus. Berlin, 1821.
System des Römischen Civilrechts im Grundrisse. Berlin, 1827.
Ueber Römisches Obligationsrecht, insbesondere über die Lehre von den Innominatcontracten und dem jus poenitendi. Heidelberg, 1819.
Vermischte Schriften, juristischen, historischen, staatswissenschaftlichen und ästhetischen Inhalts. 2 vols. Berlin, 1834.
"Vorlesungen über die Geschichte der letzten fünfzig Jahre." *Historisches Taschenbuch* 4 (1833):285–326.
Göschel, Karl Friedrich. *Aphorismen über Nichtwissen und absolutes Wissen im Verhältnisse zur christlichen Glaubenserkenntnis.* Berlin, 1829.
Beiträge zur spekulativen Philosophie von Gott und dem Menschen und von dem Gott-Menschen mit Rücksicht auf Dr. D. F. Strauss' Christologie. Berlin, 1838.
Cäcilius und Octavius, oder Gespräche über die vornehmsten Einwendungen gegen die christliche Wahrheit. Berlin, 1828.
Hegel und seine Zeit, mit Rücksicht auf Göthe. Berlin, 1832.
Der Monismus des Gedankens: Zur Apologie der gegenwärtigen Philosophie. Naumburg, 1832.

Von den Beweisen für die Unsterblichkeit der menschlichen Seele im Lichte der spekulativen Philosophie. Berlin, 1835.

Zerstreute Blätter aus den Hand- und Hülfsakten eines Juristen: Wissenschaftliches und Geschichtliches aus der Theorie und Praxis oder aus der Lehre und dem Leben des Rechts. 3 vols. Erfurt and Schleusingen, 1832–7.

Gutachten der Evangelisch-theologischen Facultäten der Königlich Preussischen Universitäten über den Licentiaten Bruno Bauer in Beziehung auf dessen Kritik der evangelischen Geschichte der Synoptiker. Berlin, 1842.

Gutzkow, Karl. *Ausgewählte Werke.* Ed. by H. H. Houben. 12 vols. Leipzig, 1908.

Werke. Ed. by P. Müller. 4 vols. Leipzig and Vienna, 1912.

Hegel, Georg Wilhelm Friedrich. *Berliner Schriften, 1818–1831.* Ed. by J. Hoffmeister. Hamburg, 1956.

Briefe von und an Hegel. Ed. by J. Hoffmeister. 4 vols. Hamburg, 1952–60.

Dokumente zu Hegel's Entwicklung. Ed. by J. Hoffmeister. Stuttgart, 1936.

Einleitung in die Geschichte der Philosophie. 3rd ed. Ed. by J. Hoffmeister and G. Nicolin. Hamburg, 1959.

Erste Druckschriften. Ed. by G. Lasson. Hamburg, 1928.

Faith and Knowledge. Trans. and ed. by W. Cerf and H. S. Harris. Albany, 1977.

Hegel's Philosophy of Right. Ed. and trans. T. M. Knox. New York, 1967.

Hegel's Political Writings. Trans. T. M. Knox. Oxford, 1964.

Hegel's Theologische Jugendschriften. Ed. by Hermann Nohl. Tübingen, 1907.

Jenaer Realphilosophie. Ed. by J. Hoffmeister. Hamburg, 1967.

Jenenser Logik, Metaphysik und Naturphilosophie. Ed. by G. Lasson. Leipzig, 1923.

Natural Law. Trans. by T. M. Knox. Philadelphia, 1975.

Nürnberger Schriften. Ed. by J. Hoffmeister. Leipzig, 1938.

On Christianity: Early Theological Writings. Trans. by T. M. Knox. New York, 1961.

The Philosophy of History. Trans. by J. Sibree. New York, 1956.

System und Geschichte der Philosophie. Ed. by J. Hoffmeister. 2 vols. Hamburg, 1940.

Vorlesungen über Rechtsphilosophie. Ed. by Karl-Heinz Ilting. 4 vols. Stuttgart and Bad Cannstatt, 1973–6.

Werke. Ed. by P. Marheineke et al. 18 vols. Berlin, 1832–45.

Werke. Ed. by E. Moldenhauer and K. M. Michel. 20 vols. Frankfurt, 1969–72.

Hegel in Berichten seiner Zeitgenossen. Ed. by G. Nicolin. Hamburg, 1970.

Hegeling, A. [pseud.] *Heinrich Leo vor Gericht: Dramatische Scene aus dem Leben gegriffen.* Leipzig, 1838.

Die Hegelsche Linke. Ed. by K. Löwith. Stuttgart, 1962.

Die Hegelsche Rechte. Ed. by H. Lübbe. Stuttgart, 1962.

Heine, Heinrich. *Sämtliche Werke.* Ed. by O. Walzel. 10 vols. Leipzig, 1911–15.

Henning, Leopold. *Einleitung zu öffentlichen Vorlesungen über Göthe's Farbenlehre.* Berlin, 1822.

Principien der Ethik in historischer Entwicklung. Berlin, 1824.

Zur Verständigung über die preussische Verfassungsfrage. Berlin, 1845.

[Hess, Moses.] *Die heilige Geschichte der Menschheit.* Stuttgart, 1837.

Hinrichs, Hermann F. W. *Aesthetische Vorlesungen über Göthe's Faust als Beitrag zur Anerkennung wissenschaftlicher Kunstbeurtheilung.* Halle, 1825.

Die Genesis des Wissens: Erster Metaphysischer Teil. Heidelberg, 1835.
Grundlinien der Philosophie der Logik als Versuch einer wissenschaftlichen Umgestaltung ihrer bisherigen Principien. Halle, 1826.
Politische Vorlesungen. 2 vols. Halle, 1843.
Die Religion im inneren Verhältnisse zur Wissenschaft. Heidelberg, 1822.
Schiller's Dictungen. 2 vols. Leipzig, 1837–9.
Hölderlin, Friedrich. *Hyperion, or the Hermit in Greece.* Trans. by W. Trask. New York, 1965.
Sämtliche Werke. Ed. by F. Beissner and A. Beck. 7 vols. in 14 pts. Stuttgart, 1946–1977.
Hotho, Heinrich Gustav. *Vorstudien für Leben und Kunst.* Stuttgart, 1835.
Humboldt, Wilhelm von. *Gesammelte Schriften.* 17 vols. Berlin, 1903.
Kapff, Sixt. *Die Zukunft des Herrn.* Stuttgart, 1836.
Kapp, Christian. *Christus und die Weltgeschichte, oder Sokrates und die Wissenschaft: Brüchstücke einer Theodicee der Wirklichkeit oder Stimme eines Predigers in der Wüste.* Heidelberg, 1823.
Das concrete Allgemeine der Weltgeschichte. Erlangen, 1826.
Ueber den Ursprung der Menschen und Völker nach der mosaischen Genesis. Nürnberg, 1829.
Köppen, Karl Friedrich. *Friedrich der Grosse und seine Widersacher: Eine Jubelschrift.* Leipzig, 1840.
Leo, Heinrich, ed. *Die Briefe des Florentinischen Kanzlers und Geschichtsschreibers Niccolo di Bernardo dei Machiavelli an seine Freunde, aus dem Italienischen übersetzt von Heinrich Leo.* Berlin, 1826.
Entwicklung der Verfassung der lombardischen Städte bis zu der Ankunft Kaiser Friedrichs I in Italien. Hamburg, 1824.
Geschichte der italienischen Staaten. 5 vols. Hamburg, 1829–32.
"Der Hegelianismus in Preussen." Ed. by H. Diwald. *Zeitschrift für Religions- und Geistesgeschichte* 10 (1958):51–60.
Die Hegelingen: Actenstücke und Belege zu der s. g. Denunciation der ewigen Wahrheit. Halle, 1838. 2nd ed. Halle, 1839.
Herr Dr. Diesterweg und die deutschen Universitäten. Leipzig, 1836.
Lehrbuch der Geschichte des Mittelalters. 2 vols. Halle, 1830.
Meine Jugendzeit. Gotha, 1880.
Sendschreiben an J. Görres. Halle, 1838.
Studien und Skizzen zu einer Naturlehre des Staates. Halle, 1833.
Ueber die Verfassung der freien lombardischen Städte im Mittelalter. Rudolstadt, 1820.
Ueber Odins Verehrung in Deutschland. Erlangen, 1822.
Von der Entstehung und Bedeutung der deutschen Herzogsämter nach Karl dem Grossen. Berlin, 1827.
Vorlesungen über die Geschichte des jüdischen Staates. Berlin, 1828.
Marheineke, Philipp K. *Allgemeine Darstellung des Theologischen Geistes der kirchlichen Verfassung und kanonischen Rechtswissenschaft in Beziehung auf die Moral des Christenthums und die ethische Denkart des Mittelalters.* Nürnberg, 1806.
Betrachtungen über das Leben und die Lehre des Welterlösers: Zur häuslichen Erbauung. Berlin, 1823.
Christliche Predigten zur Belebung des Gefühls fürs Schöne und Heilige, nebst einer Abhandlung. Erlangen, 1805.

Christliche Symbolik, oder historischkritische und dogmatischkomparative Darstellung des Katholischen, Luterischen, Reformirten und Socianischen Lehrbegriffs. Heidelberg, 1810.
Einleitung in die öffentliche Vorlesungen über die Bedeutung der Hegelschen Philosophie in der christlichen Theologie: Nebst einen Separatvotum ueber B. Bauer's Kritik der evangelischen Geschichte. Berlin, 1842.
Entwurf der praktischen Theologie. Berlin, 1837.
Geschichte der teutschen Reformation. 2 vols. Berlin, 1816. 2nd ed. 4 vols. Berlin, 1831-4.
Grundlegung der Homiletik in einigen Vorlesungen über den wahren Charakter eines Protestantischen Geistlichen. Hamburg, 1811.
Die Grundlehren der christlichen Dogmatik. Berlin, 1819.
Die Grundlehren der christlichen Dogmatik als Wissenschaft. Berlin, 1827.
Lehrbuch des christlichen Glaubens und Lebens für denkende Christen. 2nd ed. Berlin, 1836.
Predigten der häuslichen Frömmigkeit. Berlin, 1826.
Predigten vor den verschiedenen Gemeinden in Berlin. Berlin, 1814.
Ueber die wahre Stelle des liturgischen Rechts im evangelischen Kirchenregiment. Berlin, 1825.
Märklin, Christian. *Darstellung und Kritik des modernen Pietismus.* Stuttgart, 1839.
Die spekulative Theologie und die evangelische Kirche. Stuttgart, 1840.
Ueber die Nothwendigkeit einer umfassenden Volksbildung und Erziehung mit besonderer Rücksicht auf vaterländische Zustände. Stuttgart, 1836.
Ueber die Reform des protestantischen Kirchenwesens mit besonderer Rücksicht auf die protestantische Kirche in Württemberg. Tübingen, 1833.
Marx, Karl. *Writings of the Young Marx on Philosophy and Society.* Trans. and ed. by L. Easton and K. Guddat. Garden City, N.Y., 1967.
Marx, Karl and Engels, Friedrich. *Historisch-kritisch Gesamtausgabe.* Ed. by D. Riazonov. 11 vols. in 3 ser. Frankfurt, 1927-32.
Matthias, Konrad, G. W. *Die Idee der Freiheit im Individuum, im Staate und in der Kirche.* Marburg, 1834.
Matthies, Conrad Stephan. *Propadeutik der Neutestamentlichen Theologie.* Griefswald, 1836.
Meyen, Eduard. *Heinrich Leo, der verhallerte Pietist: Ein Literaturbrief allen Schülern Hegels gewidmet.* Leipzig, 1839.
Michelet, Karl Ludwig. *Geschichte der letzten Systeme der Philosophie in Deutschland von Kant bis Hegel.* 2 vols. Berlin, 1837-8.
Das System der philosophischen Moral mit Rücksicht auf die juridische Imputation der Geschichte der Moral und das christliche Moralprinzip. Berlin, 1828.
Wahrheit aus meinem Leben. Berlin, 1884.
Mussmann, Johann Georg. *Grundriss der allgemeinen Geschichte der christlichen Philosophie.* Halle, 1830.
Lehrbuch der Seelenwissenschaft oder rationalen und empirischen Psychologie. Berlin, 1827.
Niebuhr, Barthold Georg. *Die Briefe Barthold Georg Niebuhrs.* Ed. by D. Gerhard and W. Norvin. Berlin, 1926.
Novalis. *Schriften.* Ed. by P. Kluckhohn. Leipzig [1929].
Ranke, Leopold von. *Sämtliche Werke.* 54 vols. Leipzig, 1867-90.

Raumer, Friedrich von. *Lebenserinnerungen und Briefwechsel.* 2 vols. Leipzig, 1861.
Richter, Friedrich. *Geschichte des deutschen Freiheitskrieges vom Jahre 1813 bis zum Jahre 1815.* 4 vols. Berlin, 1840-1.
Die Lehre von den letzten Dingen. Vol. I: *Eine wissenschaftliche Kritik aus dem Standpunct der Religion unternommen.* Breslau, 1833. Vol. II: *Die Lehre von jüngsten Tage, Dogma und Kritik.* Berlin, 1844.
Magdeburg, die wieder-emporgerichtete Stadt Gottes auf Erden: Denkschrift zur zweiten Seculärfeier der Zerstörung Magdeburgs. Zerbst, 1831.
Die neue Unsterblichkeitslehre: Gespräch einer Abendgesellschaft. Breslau, 1833.
Rosenkranz, Karl. *Aesthetische und poetische Mittheilungen.* Magdeburg, 1827.
"Alphabetische Bibliographie der Hegel'schen Schule." *Der Gedanke* 1 (1860-1):77-80, 183-4, 256-64.
Briefwechsel zwischen Karl Rosenkranz und Varnhagen von Ense. Ed. by A. Warda. Königsberg, 1926.
Das Centrum der Speculation: Eine Komödie. Königsberg, 1840.
Encyklopädie der theologischen Wissenschaften. Halle, 1831.
Erinnerungen an Karl Daub. Berlin, 1837.
Geschichte der deutschen Poesie im Mittelalter. Halle, 1830.
G. W. F. Hegels Leben. Berlin, 1844.
Hegel: Sendschrieben an den Hofrath und Professor der Philosophie Herrn Dr. Carl Friedrich Bachmann in Jena. Königsberg, 1834.
Das Heldenbuch und die Nibelungen: Grundriss zu Vorlesungen. Halle, 1829.
Kritik der Schleiermacherschen Glaubenslehre. Königsberg, 1836.
Kritische Erläuterungen des Hegelschen Systems. Königsberg, 1840.
Psychologie, oder die Wissenschaft vom subjectiven Geist. Königsberg, 1837.
Studien. 5 vols. Leipzig, 1842-8.
Ueber den Titurel und Dante's Komödie mit einer Vorerinnerung über die Bildung der geistlichen Ritterorden. Halle and Leipzig, 1829.
Von Magdeburg bis Königsberg. Berlin, 1873.
Der Zweifel am Glauben: Kritik der Schriften: De Tribus Imposteribus. Halle and Leipzig, 1830.
Rothe, Richard. *Die Anfänge der christlichen Kirche und Verfassung: Ein geschichtlicher Versuch.* Wittenberg, 1837.
Rötscher, Heinrich Theodor. *Aristophanes und sein Zeitalter: Eine philologisch-philosophische Abhandlung zum Alterthumsforschung.* Berlin, 1827.
Ruge, Arnold, ed. *Anekdota zur neuesten deutschen Philosophie und Publizistik.* 2 vols. Zürich and Winterthur, 1843.
Aus früherer Zeit. 4 vols. Berlin, 1862-7.
Briefwechsel und Tagebuchblätter aus den Jahren 1825-1880. Ed. by P. Nerrlich. 2 vols. Berlin, 1886.
Preussen und die Reaction: Zur Geschichte unserer Zeit. Leipzig, 1838.
Zwei Jahre in Paris: Studien und Erinnerungen. 2 vols. Leipzig, 1846.
Rust, Isaak. *Philosophie und Christenthum, oder Wissen und Glauben.* Mannheim, 1825.
Stimmen der Reformation und der Reformatoren an die Fürsten und Völker dieser Zeit. Erlangen, 1832.
Saint-Marc-Girardin. "Erinnerungen an Eduard Gans." *Zeitung für die Elegante Welt* no. 14-16 (Jan 21, 1840), pp. 53-64.
Saling, J. *Die Gerechtigkeit in ihrer geschichtlichen Entwicklung.* Berlin, 1827.

Schaller, Julius. *Der historische Christus und die Philosophie: Kritik der Grundidee des Werks Das Leben Jesu von Dr. David F. Strauss.* Leipzig, 1838.
Die Philosophie unserer Zeit: Zur Apologie und Erläuterung des Hegelschen Systems. Leipzig, 1837.
Schelling, Friedrich Wilhelm Joseph von. *Aus Schellings Leben in Briefen.* Ed. by G. L. Plitt. 3 vols. Leipzig, 1869.
Briefe und Dokumente. Ed. by H. Fuhrmans. 3 vols. Bonn, 1962–75.
On University Studies. Ed. by N. Guterman. Athens, Ohio, 1966.
Sämmtliche Werke. Ed. by K. F. A. Schelling. 14 vols. in 2 ser. Stuttgart, 1856–61.
Schiller, Friedrich. *On the Aesthetic Education of Man: In a Series of Letters.* Trans. by R. Snell. New York, 1971.
Schlegel, Friedrich. *Dialogue on Poetry and Literary Aphorisms.* Trans. and ed. by E. Behler and R. Struc. University Park, Pa., 1968.
Friedrich Schlegel, 1794–1802: Seine Prosäische Jugendschriften. Ed. by J. Minor. 2 vols. Vienna, 1882.
Friedrich Schlegels Briefe an seinem Bruder August Wilhelm. Ed. by O. Walzel. Berlin, 1890.
Friedrich Schlegel und Novalis: Biographie einer Romantiker Freundschraft in ihren Briefen. Ed. by M. Preitz. Darmstadt, 1957.
Kritische Friedrich Schlegel Ausgabe. Ed. by E. Behler, J. Anstett, and H. Eichner. 16 vols. to date. Munich, 1957–.
Schleiermacher, Friedrich Daniel Ernst. *Aus Schleiermachers Leben in Briefen.* Ed. by L. Jonas and W. Dilthey. 4 vols. Berlin, 1858–63.
The Christian Faith. Trans. by H. R. Mackintosh and J. S. Stewart. 2 vols. New York, 1963.
Christmas Eve: Dialogue on the Incarnation. Ed. and trans. by T. Tice. Richmond, Va., 1967.
On Religion: Speeches to Its Cultured Despisers. Trans. by J. Oman. New York, 1958.
Sämtliche Werke. 32 vols. in 3 ser. Berlin, 1835–64.
Soliloquies. Ed. and trans. by H. Friess. Chicago, 1957.
Werke: Auswahl in vier Bänden. Ed. by O. Braun and J. Bauer. Leipzig, 1913.
Schulze, Johannes. *Aufruf an die deutsche Jünglinge.* Jena, 1808.
Predigten. Leipzig, 1810.
Reden über die christliche Religion. Halle, 1811.
Sietze, Karl F. F. *Grundbegriff preussischer Staats- und Rechtsgeschichte als Einleitung in die Wissenschaft des preussischen Rechts.* Berlin, 1829.
Stahl, Friedrich Julius. *Philosophie des Rechts nach geschichtlicher Ansicht.* Vol. II: *Christliche Rechts- und Staatslehre.* 2 pts. Heidelberg, 1833–7.
Stieglitz, Heinrich. *Eine Selbstbiographie.* Ed. by L. Curtze. Gotha, 1865.
Stirner, Max [pseud.] "Deutschlands Beruf in der Gegenwart, von Theodor Rohmer." *Die Eisenbahn: Ein Unterhaltungsblatt für die gebildete Welt,* no. 77 (Dec. 18, 1841), pp. 307–8, no. 78 (Dec. 30, 1841), pp. 310–12.
Der Einzige und sein Eigenthum. Leipzig, 1845.
Strauss, David Friedrich. *Ausgewählte Briefe von David Friedrich Strauss.* Ed. by E. Zeller. Bonn, 1895.
Briefe an seine Tochter nebst Briefen seiner Mutter an ihn selbst. N.p., 1921.
Briefe von David Friedrich Strauss an L. Georgii. Ed. by H. Maier. Tübingen, 1912.

Briefwechsel zwischen Strauss und Vischer. Ed. by A. Rapp. 2 vols. Stuttgart, 1952–3.
Charakteristiken und Kritiken: Eine Sammlung zerstreuter Aufsätze aus den Gebieten der Theologie, Anthropologie und Aesthetik. Leipzig, 1839.
Die christliche Glaubenslehre in ihrer geschichtlichen Entwicklung und im Kampfe mit der modernen Wissenschaft. 2 vols. Tübingen, 1840–1.
"Ein unbekannter Brief von David Friedrich Strauss aus dem Jahre 1838." Ed. by Walter Hagen. *Ludwigsburger Geschichtsblätter* (1964), pp. 363–5.
Gesammelte Schriften. Ed. by E. Zeller. 12 vols. Bonn, 1876–8.
Die Halben und die Ganzen: Eine Streitschrift. Berlin, 1865.
Das Leben Jesu kritisch bearbeitet. 2 vols. Tübingen, 1835–6. 2nd ed. 1837. 3rd ed. 1838. 4th ed. 1840.
Sendschreiben an die hochgeachtete Herren: Bürgermeister Hirzel, Professor Orelli und Professor Hitzig in Zürich. Zürich, 1839.
Streitschriften zur Vertheidigung meiner Schrift über das Leben Jesu und zur Charakteristik der gegenwärtigen Theologie. 3 vols. in 1. Tübingen, 1837.
"Vergängliches und Bleibendes im Christenthum." *Der Freihafen: Galerie von Unterhaltungsbildern aus den Kreisen der Literatur, Gesellschaft und Wissenschaft* 1, no. 3 (1838):1–48.
Zwei friedliche Blätter. Altona, 1839.
Vatke, Wilhelm. *Die biblische Theologie.* Vol. I: *Die Religion des Alten Testaments nach den kanonischen Büchern.* Berlin, 1835.
Veit, Moritz. *Saint-Simon und der Saintsimonismus: Allgemeiner Völkerbund und ewiger Frieden.* Leipzig, 1834.
Vertraute Briefe über Preussens Hauptstadt. Stuttgart and Leipzig, 1837.
Vischer, Friedrich Theodor. *Altes und Neues.* 3 vols. Stuttgart, 1882.
Kritische Gänge. 2 vols. Tübingen, 1844.
Weisse, Christian. *Ueber den gegenwärtigen Standpunkt der philosophischen Wissenschaft in besonderer Beziehung auf Hegels System.* Leipzig, 1829.
Zeit und Kunst: altteutsche. Ed. by E. v. Groote, F. W. Carové, et al. Köln, 1822.

Secondary sources

CRITICAL AND HISTORICAL STUDIES ON HEGEL, HEGELIANS, AND HEGELIANISM

Ascheri, Carlo. "Ein unbekannter Brief von Ludwig Feuerbach an Karl Daub," in H. Braun and M. Riedel, eds., *Natur und Geschichte: Karl Löwith zum 70. Geburtstag*, pp. 441–53. Stuttgart, 1967.*
Arvon, Henri. *Ludwig Feuerbach ou la transformation du sacré.* Paris, 1957.
Avineri, Shlomo. *Hegel's Theory of the Modern State.* Cambridge, 1972.
"A Note on Hegel's Views on Jewish Emancipation." *Jewish Social Studies* 25 (1963):145–51.
Backhaus, Gunther. *Kerygma und Mythos bei David Friedrich Strauss und Rudolf Bultmann.* Hamburg, 1956.
Barnikol, Ernst. "Der Briefwechsel zwischen Strauss und Baur." *Zeitschrift für Kirchengeschichte* 78, no. 1 (1962):74–125.*
Bruno Bauer: Studien und Materialien. Ed. by P. Reimer and H. M. Sass. Assen, 1972.*
"Bruno Bauer's frühe Grundthese von der Entstehung des Christenthums." *Theologische Jahrbücher* (1956), pp. 87–8.*

"Bruno Bauer's Kampf gegen Religion und Christenthum und die Spaltung der vormärzlichen preussischen Opposition." *Zeitschrift für Kirchengeschichte* 46 (1917):1–34.
Barth, Hans. *Wahrheit und Ideologie.* 2nd ed. Zürich and Stuttgart, 1961.
Barth, Karl. *Protestant Thought from Rousseau to Ritschl.* Trans. by Brian Cozens. New York, 1959.
Benecke, Heinrich. *Wilhelm Vatke in seinem Leben und seinen Schriften.* Bonn, 1883.*
Benz, Ernst. "Hegel's Religionsphilosophie und die Linkshegelianer." *Zeitschrift für Religions- und Geistesgeschichte* 7 (1955):247–70.
Bergh van Eysinga, B. A. van den. "Aus einer unveröffentlichten Biographie von Bruno Bauer." *Annali Feltrinelli* (1963), pp. 329–86.
Beyer, Wilhelm R. "Gans' Vorrede zur Hegelschen Rechtsphilosophie." *Archiv für Rechts- und Sozialphilosophie* 45 (1959):257–73.
Hegel-Bilder: Kritik der Hegel-Deutungen. Berlin, 1964.
Zwischen Phänomenologie und Logik: Hegel als Redakteur der Bamberger Zeitung. Frankfurt, 1955.
Beyer, Wilhelm R.; Länig, K.; and K. Goldmann. *Georg Wilhelm Friedrich Hegel in Nürnberg, 1808–1816.* Nürnberg, 1966.
Bockmühl, Klaus E. *Leiblichkeit und Gesellschaft: Studien zur Religionskritik und Anthropologie im Frühwerk von Ludwig Feuerbach und Karl Marx.* Göttingen, 1961.
Bolin, Wilhelm. *Ludwig Feuerbach: Sein Wirken und seien Zeitgenossen.* Stuttgart, 1891.*
Braun, Hans-Jürg. *Ludwig Feuerbachs Lehre vom Menschen.* Stuttgart and Bad Cannstatt, 1971.
Die Religionsphilosophie Ludwig Feuerbachs. Stuttgart and Bad Cannstatt, 1972.
Brazill, William. *The Young Hegelians.* New Haven and London, 1970.
Brecht, Martin and Sandberger, Jörg. "Hegel's Begegnung mit der Theologie im Tübinger Stift." *Hegel-Studien* (1969):48–81.
Christenson, Darrel E., ed. *Hegel and the Philosophy of Religion.* The Hague, 1970.
Cornehl, Peter. "Feuerbach und die Naturphilosophie: Zur Genese der Anthropologie und Religionskritik des jungen Feuerbach." *Neue Zeitschrift für systematische Theologie und Religionsphilosophie* 11 (1969):37–93.
Die Zukunft der Versöhnung: Eschatologie und Emanzipation in der Aufklärung, bei Hegel und in der Hegelschen Schule. Göttingen, 1971.
Cornu, Auguste. *Karl Marx et Friedrich Engels: leur vie et leur oeuvre.* 4 vols. Paris, 1955–70.
Cromwell, Richard S. *David Friedrich Strauss and His Place in Modern Thought.* Fairlawn, N.J., 1974.
Deutsche Zeitschrift für Philosophie 20, no. 9 (1972). Special issue on Feuerbach.
Dicke, Gerd. *Der Identitätsgedanke bei Feuerbach und Marx.* Köln, 1960.
Döderlein, J. L. "Regest eines Briefs von Hegel an Niethammer." *Hegel-Studien* 13 (1978):74–6.*
Dooren, Wim van. "Eine frühe Hegel-Diskussion in Holland." *Hegel-Studien* 11 (1976):211–17.
Dupre, Louis. *The Philosophical Foundations of Marxism.* New York and Chicago, 1966.
Eberty, Felix. *Jugenderinnerungen eines alten Berliners.* Berlin, 1925.

Eck, Else von. *Die Literaturkritik in den Hallischen und Deutschen Jahrbüchern (1838-1842).* Berlin, 1926.
Fackenheim, Emil. *The Religious Dimension in Hegel's Thought.* Boston, 1967.
Fischer, Hermann. "Die Hallischen Jahrbücher und die Schwaben." *Württembergische Vierteljahreshefte für Landesgeschichte, Neue Folge* 25 (1916):558-71.
Friedländer, Albert R. "The Wohlwill-Moser Correspondence." *Leo Baeck Institute Yearbook* 11 (1966):262-99.*
Gagern, Michael von. *Ludwig Feuerbach.* Munich and Salzburg, 1970.
Gebhard, Dieter. "Zur Geschichte der historischen Schule: Drei Briefe von Ranke und Heinrich Leo." *Historische Zeitschrift* 132 (1925):94-105.*
Gebhardt, Jürgen. *Politik und Eschatologie: Studien zur Geschichte der Hegelschen Schule in den Jahren 1830-1840.* Munich, 1963.
Geiger, Ludwig. "Aus Eduard Gans' Frühzeit (1817)." *Zeitschrift für die Geschichte der Juden in Deutschland* 5 (1892):91-8.*
Glockner, Hermann. *Johann Eduard Erdmann.* Stuttgart, 1932.
Gray, J. Glenn. *Hegel and Greek Thought.* New York, 1968.
Hahn, Erich J. C. "The Junior Faculty in 'Revolt': Reform Plans for the Berlin University in 1848." *American Historical Review* 82 (1977):875-95.
Harris, H. S. *Hegel's Development: Toward the Sunlight, 1770-1801.* Oxford, 1971.
Harris, Horton. *David Friedrich Strauss and His Theology.* Cambridge, 1973.
Hartlich, Christian and Sachs, Walter. *Der Ursprung des Mythosbegriffs in der modernen Bibelwissenschaft.* Tübingen, 1952.
Hausrath, Adolph. *David Friedrich Strauss und die Theologie seiner Zeit.* 2 vols. Heidelberg, 1876-8.*
Hegel, Karl. *Leben und Erinnerungen.* Leipzig, 1900.
Henrich, Dieter. *Hegel im Kontext.* Frankfurt, 1967.
"Leutwein über Hegel: Ein Dokument zu Hegel's Biographie." *Hegel-Studien* 3 (1965):39-77.*
Hermann, Wilhelm. *Die speculative Theologie in ihrer Entwicklung durch Daub.* Hamburg, 1847.
Hertz-Eichenrode, Dieter. *Der Junghegelianer Bruno Bauer im Vormärz.* Berlin, 1959.
"'Massenpsychologie' bei den Junghegelianern." *International Review of Social History* 7 (1962):231-59.
Herwegh, Marcel and Fleury, Victor. "Briefwechsel Georg und Emma Herweghs und Ludwig Feuerbach." *Nord und Süd: Eine deutsche Monatsschrift* 128 (1909):25-47, 260-75, 489-500; 129 (1909):146-57.*
Hirsch, Helmut. "Karl Friedrich Köppen: Der intimste Berliner Freund Marxens." *International Review of Social History* 1 (1936):311-70.
Hocevar, Rolf. *Hegel und der preussischer Staat.* Munich, 1973.
Hodgson, Peter C. *The Formation of Historical Theology: A Study of Ferdinand Christian Baur.* New York, 1966.
Hook, Sidney. *From Hegel to Marx: Studies in the Intellectual Development of Karl Marx.* New York, 1936.
Horstmann, Rolf P. "Ist Hegel's Rechtsphilosophie das Produkt der politischen Anpassung eines Liberalen?" *Hegel-Studien* 9 (1974):244-52.
Jacobson, Max. "Zur Geschichte der Hegelschen Philosophie an der preussischen Universitäten in der Zeit von 1838 bis 1860." *Deutsche Revue* 30 (1905):118-23.

Jaeschke, Walter. "Feuerbach Redivivus." *Hegel-Studien* 13 (1978):199–237.
Jessin, I. M. *Die materialistische Philosophie Ludwig Feuerbachs.* Berlin, 1956.
Jung, G. "H. F. W. Hinrichs." *Geistige Arbeit* 2, no. 18 (1935): n.p.
Kamenka, Eugene. *The Philosophy of Ludwig Feuerbach.* New York, 1970.
Kaufmann, Walter. *Hegel: A Reinterpretation.* Garden City, N.Y., 1965.
Kegel, Martin. *Bruno Bauer's Uebergang von der Hegelschen Rechten zum Radikalismus.* Erlangen, 1908.
Bruno Bauer und seine Theorien über die Entstehung des Christenthums. Leipzig, 1908.
Kelly, George Armstrong. *Hegel's Retreat from Eleusis: Studies in Political Thought.* Princeton, 1978.
Kempski, Jürgen. "Ueber Bruno Bauer: Eine Studie zum Ausgang des Hegelianismus." *Archiv für Philosophie* 11 (1961–2):223–45.
Kimmerle, H. "Dokumente zu Hegels Jenaer Dozententätigkeit (1801–1807)," *Hegel-Studien* 4 (1967):21–99.*
Klaiber, Julius. *Hölderlin, Hegel und Schelling in ihren schwäbischen Jugendjahren.* Stuttgart, 1877.
Klein, Robert. *Heinrich Theodor Rötschers Leben und Wirken.* Berlin, 1919.
Klimkeit, Hans-Joachim. *Das Wunderverständnis Ludwig Feuerbachs in religionsphenomenologischer Sicht.* Bonn, 1965.
Koch, Lothar. *Humanistischer Atheismus und gesellschaftliches Engagement: Bruno Bauers Kritische Kritik.* Stuttgart, 1971.
Kohut, Adolph. *David Friedrich Strauss als Denker und Erzieher.* Leipzig, 1908.
Ludwig Feuerbach: Sein Leben und seine Werke. Leipzig, 1909.*
Koigen, David. *Zur Vorgeschichte des modernen philosophischen Sozialismus in Deutschland: Zur Geschichte der Philosophie und Sozialphilosophie des Junghegelianismus.* Bern, 1901.
Kornetzki, Heinz. "Die revolutionär-dialektischen Entwicklung in den Hallischen Jahrbücher: Eine Untersuchung der Quellen des Sozialismus in der linkshegelianischen Zeitschrift des 19. Jahrhunderts." Doctoral dissertation. Munich, 1955.
Köster, Udo. *Literarischer Radikalismus: Zeitbewusstsein und Geschichtsphilosophie in der Entwicklung vom Jungen Deutschland zur Hegelschen Linken.* Frankfurt, 1972.
Krägelin, Paul. *Heinrich Leo.* Leipzig, 1908.
Kühne, Walter. *Graf August Cieszkowski: Ein Schüler Hegels und des deutschen Geistes.* Leipzig, 1938.
Lang, Wilhelm. "Ferdinand Baur und David Friedrich Strauss." *Preussische Jahrbücher* 160 (1915):474–504; 161 (1915):123–44.*
Lévy, Albert. *David-Frédéric Strauss, la vie et l'oeuvre.* Paris, 1910.
La Philosophie de Feuerbach et son influence sur la litterature allemande. Paris, 1904.
Lichtheim, George. *From Marx to Hegel.* New York, 1971.
The Concept of Ideology and Other Essays. New York, 1967.
Lobkowicz, Nicholas. *Theory and Practice: History of a Concept from Aristotle to Marx.* Notre Dame, Ind., 1967.
Lorenz, R. "Zum Ursprung der Religionstheorie Ludwig Feuerbachs." *Evangelische Theologie* 17 (1957):171–88.
Löwith, Karl. *From Hegel to Nietzsche: The Revolution in Nineteenth-Century Thought.* Trans. by David E. Green. Garden City, N.Y., 1967.

"Ludwig Feuerbach und der Ausgang der klassischen deutschen Philosophie." *Logos* 17 (1928):323–47.
Lübbe, Hermann. *Politische Philosophie in Deutschland: Studien zu ihrer Geschichte.* Basel and Stuttgart, 1963.
Lübbe, Hermann and Sass, Hans-Martin, eds. *Atheismus in der Diskussion: Kontroversen über Ludwig Feuerbach.* Munich, 1975.
Lukács, Georg. *The Young Hegel: Studies in the Relations between Dialectics and Economics.* Trans. by R. Livingstone. Cambridge, Mass., 1976.
Lutz, Rolland, R. "The 'New Left' in Restoration Germany." *Journal of the History of Ideas* 31 (1970):235–52.
McLellan, David. *The Young Hegelians and Karl Marx.* London and Toronto, 1969.
Maier, Heinrich. *An der Grenze der Philosophie: Melancthon, Lavater, David Friedrich Strauss.* Tübingen, 1909.
Marcuse, Herbert. *Reason and Revolution: Hegel and the Rise of Social Theory.* 3rd ed. Boston, 1960.
Mautz, Kurt. "Leo und Ranke." *Deutsche Vierteljahresschrift für Literaturwissenschaft und Geistesgeschichte* 27 (1953):207–35.
Mayer, Gustav. "Die Anfänge des politischen Radikalismus im vormärzlichen Preussen." *Zeitschrift für Politik* 6 (1913):1–113.*
"Die Junghegelianer und der preussische Staat." *Historische Zeitschrift* 121 (1920):413–40.
Maync, Harry. "David Friedrich Strauss und Eduard Mörike: Zwölf ungedruckte Briefe." *Deutsche Rundschau* 115 (1903):94–117.*
Mehlhausen, Joachim. *Dialektik, Selbstbewusstsein und Offenbarung: Die Grundlagen der spekulativen Orthodoxie Bruno Bauers in ihrer Zusammenhang mit der Geschichte der theologischen Hegelschule.* Bonn, 1965.
Metzke, Erwin. *Karl Rosenkranz und Hegel: Ein Beitrag zur Geschichte der Philosophie des sogenannten Hegelianismus im 19, Jarhhundert.* Leipzig, 1929.
Meyer von Bargholz, Hermann. "Der Ursprung des Mythosbegriffs in der modernen Bibelwissenschaft." Doctoral dissertation. Tübingen, 1951.
Moog, Willy. *Hegel und die Hegelsche Schule.* Munich, 1930.
Müller, Gotthold. "David Friedrich Strauss als Prediger und Catechet." *Monatsschrfit für Pastoraltheologie* 53 (1964):502–10; 54 (1965):33–9.
Identität und Immanenz: Zur Genese der Theologie von David Friedrich Strauss. Zürich, 1968.*
Müller, Gustav. "Die Entwicklung der Religionsphilosophie in der Hegelschen Schule." *Zeitschrift für philosophische Forschung* 4 (1950):347–76.
Hegel: Denkgeschichte eines Lebendigen. Berlin, 1959.
Nauen, Franz. *Revolution, Idealism and Human Freedom: Schelling, Hölderlin and Hegel and the Crisis of Early German Idealism.* The Hague, 1971.
Neher, Walter. *Arnold Ruge als Politiker und politischer Schriftsteller.* Heidelberg, 1933.
Nicolin, Friedhelm. *Hegel, 1770–1970.* Stuttgart, 1970.
"Hegel als Professor in Heidelberg: Aus den Akten der philosophischen Fakultät, 1816–1818." *Hegel-Studien* 2 (1963):71–98.*
Nicolin, G., ed. "Zwei unbekannte Briefe von Hegel aus dem Jahre 1807." *Hegel-Studien* 4 (1967):101–7.*
Nippold, Friedrich. *Richard Rothe: Ein christliches Lebensbild.* 2 vols. Wittenberg, 1873.*

Nüdling, Gregor. *Ludwig Feuerbachs Religionsphilosophie: Die Auflösung der Theologie in Anthropologie.* Paderborn, 1961.
Pepperle, Ingrid. *Junghegelianische Geschichtsphilosophie und Kunsttheorie.* Berlin, 1978.
The Philosophical Forum 8, no. 2-4 (1978). Special issue on the Left Hegelians and Marx.
Plant, Raymond. *Hegel.* Bloomington, Ind., 1973.
Pöggeler, Otto. "Hegel der Verfasser des ältesten Systemprogramms des deutschen Idealismus." *Hegel-Studien,* supp. 4: *Hegel-Tage Urbino, 1965,* pp. 17-32. Bonn, 1969.
"Hegel und Heidelberg." *Hegel-Studien* 6 (1971):65-133.
Rawidowicz, Simon. *Ludwig Feuerbachs Philosophie: Ursprung und Schicksal.* Berlin, 1931.
Reissner, Hanns Günther. *Eduard Gans: Ein Leben im Vormärz.* Tübingen, 1965.
"Rebellious Dilemma: The Case Histories of Eduard Gans and Some of His Partisans." *Leo Baeck Institute Yearbook* 17 (1972):179-93.
Revue Internationale de Philosophie 26, no. 101 (1972). Special Feuerbach issue.
Riedel, Manfred. "Hegel und Gans," in H. Braun and M. Riedel, eds., *Natur und Geschichte: Karl Löwith zum 70. Geburtstag,* pp. 257-73. Stuttgart, 1967.
Ritter, Joachim. *Hegel und die französische Revolution.* Frankfurt, 1965.
Rosen, Zvi. *Bruno Bauer and Karl Marx: The Influence of Bruno Bauer on Marx's Thought.* The Hague, 1977.
"The Radicalism of a Young Hegelian: Bruno Bauer." *Review of Politics* 33 (1971):377-404.
Rosenberg, Hans. "Arnold Ruge und die 'Hallische Jahrbücher.'" *Archiv für Kulturgeschichte* 20 (1930):281-308.
Rosenzweig, Franz. *Hegel und der Staat.* 2 vols. Munich and Berlin, 1920.
Rotenstreich, Nathan. "Hegel's Image of Judaism." *Jewish Social Studies* 15 (1953):33-52.
Rubaschoff, S. "Erstlinge der Entjudung." *Der Jüdische Wille* (1918-19):36-41, 108-21, 193-203.*
Sandberger, Jörg F. *David Fr. Strauss als theologischer Hegelianer: Mit unveröffentlichten Briefen.* Göttingen, 1972.*
Sass, Hans-Martin. "Bruno Bauer's Idee der 'Rheinischen Zeitung.'" *Zeitschrift für Religions- und Geistesgeschichte* 19 (1967):321-32.*
"Die Emanzipation des Dialektikbegriffs von Karl Marx aus der Interpretation, die Bruno Bauer und die 'Freien' der Hegelschen Dialektik gaben." *Hegel-Jahrbuch* (1975), pp. 554-60.
Untersuchungen zur Religionsphilosophie in der Hegelschule, 1830-1850. Münster, 1963.
Scheit, Herbert. *Geist und Gemeinde: Zum Verhältnis von Religion und Politik bei Hegel.* Munich and Salzburg, 1973.
Schilling, Werner. *Feuerbach und die Religion.* Munich, 1957.
Schlawe, Fritz. "Die Berliner Jahrbücher für wissenschaftliche Kritik: Ein Beitrag zur Geschichte des Hegelianismus." *Zeitschrift für Religions- und Geistesgeschichte* 11 (1959):240-58, 343-56.
Friedrich Theodor Vischer. Stuttgart, 1959.
"Die junghegelsche Publizistik." *Die Welt als Geschichte* 20 (1960):30-50.
Schmidt, Alfred. *Emanzipatorische Sinnlichkeit: Ludwig Feuerbachs anthropologischer Materialismus.* Munich, 1973.

Schmieder, Heinrich. *Karl Friedrich Göschel.* Berlin, 1863.
Schott, Uwe. *Die Jugendentwicklung Ludwig Feuerbachs bis zum Fakultätswechsel 1825.* Göttingen, 1973.*
Schröder, Horst. "Zum Gedenken an Eduard Gans." *Staat und Recht* 13 (1964):1413–24.
Schuffenhauer, Werner. *Feuerbach und der junge Marx: Zur Entstehungsgeschichte der marxistischen Weltanschauung.* Berlin, 1965.
Schürmann, Albert. *Friedrich Wilhelm Carové: Sein Werk als Beitrag zur Kritik an Staat und Kirche im frühliberalen Hegelianismus.* Bochum, 1971.
Silberner, Edmund. *Moses Hess: Geschichte seines Lebens.* Leiden, 1966.
Simon, Ernst. *Ranke und Hegel.* Munich and Berlin, 1928.
Spoerri, Theodor. *Genie und Krankheit: Eine psychopathologische Untersuchung der Familie Feuerbach.* Basel, 1952.
Stähler, Wilhelm. *Zur Unsterblichkeitsproblematik in Hegels Nachfolge.* Münster, 1928.
Stahr, Adolf. "Theodor Echtermeyer: Ein Denkstein," in Adolf Stahr, *Kleine Schriften zur Literatur und Kunst.* Berlin, 1871.
Steer, Richard. "Zum Ursprung der Religionskritik von Ludwig Feuerbach." *Jahrbuch für christliche Sozialwissenschaften* 9 (1968):43–71.
Steussloff, Hans. "Die Religionskritik von David Friedrich Strauss (1808–1874)." *Deutsche Zeitschrift für Philosophie* 10 (1962):744–57.
Strauss, Herbert. "Zur sozial- und ideengeschichtlichen Einordnung Arnold Ruges." *Schweitzer Beiträge zur Allgemeinen Geschichte* 12 (1954):162–73.
Stuke, Horst. *Philosophie der Tat: Studien zur 'Verwirklichung der Philosophie' bei den Junghegelianern und wahren Sozialisten.* Stuttgart, 1963.
Taminaux, Jacques. *La Nostalgie de la Grece à l'aube de l'idéalisme Allemand.* The Hague, 1967.
Taylor, Charles. *Hegel.* Cambridge, 1975.
Theunissen, Michael. *Hegel's Lehre vom absoluten Geist als theologisch-politischer Traktat.* Berlin, 1970.
Thies, Erich, ed. *Ludwig Feuerbach.* Darmstadt, 1976.
Traub, H. "Die Stiftsakten über David Friedrich Strauss." *Blätter für württembergische Kirchengeschichte, Neue Folge* (27 (1923):48–64.*
Ucko, Siegfried. "Geistesgeschichtliche Grundlagen der Wissenschaft des Judentums (Motive des Kulturvereins vom Jahre 1819)." *Zeitschrift für die Geschichte der Juden in Deutschland* 5 (1935):1–34.*
Varrentrapp, C. *Johannes Schulze und das höhere preussische Unterrichtswesen in seiner Zeit.* Leipzig, 1889.
Wagner, Falk. "Der Gedanke der Persönlichkeit Gottes bei Philipp Marheineke." *Neue Zeitschrift für systematische Theologie und Religionsgeschichte* 10 (1968): 44–88.
"Zur pseudoproduktivität von Missverständnissen in der Hegelschule: der Gedanke der Persönlichkeit Gottes bei K. Rosenkranz und K. L. Michelet." *Neue Zeitschrift für systematische Theologie und Religionsphilosophie* 12 (1970): 313–37.
Wallmann, Johannes. "Ludwig Feuerbach und die theologische Tradition." *Zeitschrift für Theologie und Kirche* 67 (1970):56–86.
Wartofsky, Marx W. *Feuerbach.* Cambridge, 1977.
Weil, E. *Hegel et l'état.* Paris, 1950.
Wentzcke, Paul. "Ein Schüler Hegels aus der Frühzeit der Burschenschaft:

Gustav Asverus in Heidelberg, Berlin und Jena," in *Quellen und Darstellungen der Geschichte der Burschenschaft und der deutschen Einheitsbewegung,* V, 93–132. Heidelberg, 1920.
Weser, H. A. *Frueds und Feuerbachs Religionskritik.* Leipzig, 1936.
Wiedmann, Franz. *G. W. F. Hegel.* Hamburg, 1965.
Woerden, A. V. N. van. "Das konfessionale Element in Van Gherts Hegel-Rezeption." *Hegel-Jahrbuch* (1972), pp. 11–14.
Wolf, Ernst. "Die Verlegenheit der Theologie: David Friedrich Strauss und die Bibelkritik," in E. Wolf and W. Matthias, eds., *Libertas Christiana: Festschrift für Friedrich Delekat,* pp. 219–39. Munich, 1957.
Xhaufflaire, Marcel. *Feuerbach et la Théologie de Sécularisation.* Paris, 1970.
Zeller, Eduard. *David Friedrich Strauss in seinem Leben und seinen Schriften.* Bonn, 1874.
Ziegler, Theobald. *David Friedrich Strauss.* 2 vols. Strassburg, 1908.*
"Zur Biographie von David Friedrich Strauss." *Deutsche Revue* 30, no. 2 (1905):196–208, 342–51, no. 3 (1905):99–108.*

OTHER WORKS IN POLITICAL, SOCIAL, RELIGIOUS, AND INTELLECTUAL HISTORY

Abel, Wilhelm. *Geschichte der deutschen Landwirtschaft vom frühen Mittelalter bis zum 19. Jahrhundert.* Stuttgart, 1962.
Abrams, M. H. *Natural Supernaturalism: Tradition and Revolt in Romantic Literature.* New York, 1971.
Albrecht, Christoph. *Schleiermachers Liturgik.* Göttingen, 1963.
Aner, Karl. *Die Theologie der Lessingzeit.* Halle, 1929.
Ayconberry, P. and Droz, J. "Structures sociales et courants idéologique dans l'Allemagne prérévolutionnaire, 1835–1847." *Annali Feltrinelli* 6 (1963): 164–236.
Bachmann, Johannes. *Ernst Wilhelm Hengstenberg: Sein Leben und Wirken.* 3 vols. Gütersloh, 1876–92.*
Bauer, Johannes. *Schleiermacher als patriotischer Prediger.* Giessen, 1908.
Bechtel, Heinrich. *Wirtschaftsgeschichte Deutschlands im 19. und 20. Jahrhundert.* Munich, 1956.
Behler, Ernst. *Friedrich Schlegel.* Hamburg, 1966.
Bertaux, Pierre. *Hölderlin und die französische Revolution.* Frankfurt, 1969.
Betzendörfer, Walter. *Hölderlins Studienjahre im Tübinger Stift.* Heilbronn, 1922.
Bigler, Robert M. *The Politics of German Protestantism: The Rise of the Protestant Church Elite in Prussia, 1815–1848.* Berkeley, 1972.
Bonwetsch, Nathaniel. "Die Anfänge der 'Evangelischen Kirchenzeitung': Ein Beitrag zur Geschichte des religiösen und kirchlichen Lebens im 19. Jahrhundert," in *Geschichtliche Studien: Albert Hauck zum 70. Geburtstage,* pp. 286–99. Leipzig, 1916.
Bramsted, Ernest K. *Aristocracy and the Middle-Classes in Germany: Social Types in German Literature, 1830–1900.* Rev. ed. Chicago and London, 1964.
Brinkmann, R. "Romantische Dichtungstheorie in Fr. Schlegels Frühschriften und Schillers Begriffe des Naiven und Sentimentalischen." *Deutsche Vierteljahresschrift für Literatur und Geistesgeschichte* 32 (1958):344–71.
Bruford, Walter H. *Culture and Society in Classical Weimar.* Cambridge, 1962.

Germany in the Eighteenth Century: The Social Background of the Literary Revival. Cambridge, 1935.

Brunschwig, Henri. *La crise de l'Etat prussien à la fin du xviiie siècle et la genèse de la mentalité romantique.* Paris, 1947.

Busch, Alexander. *Die Geschichte der Privatdozenten: Eine soziologische Studie zur grossbetrieblichen Entwicklung der deutschen Universitäten.* Stuttgart, 1959.

Büsch, Otto. *Militärsystem und Sozialleben im Alten Preussen, 1713–1807.* Berlin, 1962.

Butler, E. M. *The Tyranny of Greece over Germany.* Cambridge, 1935.

Carsten, F. L. *Princes and Parliaments in Germany.* Oxford, 1959.

Conrad, Johannes. *The German Universities for the Last Fifty Years.* Trans. by J. Hutchison. Glasgow, 1885.

Conze, Werner. "Vom 'Pöbel' zum 'Proletariat,' Sozialgeschichtliche Voraussetzungen für den Sozialismus in Deutschland." *Vierteljahresschrift für Sozial- und Wirtschaftsgeschichte* 41 (1954):333–64.

Conze, Werner, ed. *Staat und Gesellschaft im deutschen Vormärz.* Stuttgart, 1962.

Dieterici, Wilhelm. *Geschichtliche und statistische Nachrichten über die Universitäten im preussischen Staat.* Berlin, 1836.

Dietz, Eduard. *Die deutsche Burschenschaft in Heidelberg: Ein Beitrag zur Kulturgeschichte deutscher Universitäten.* Heidelberg, 1895.

Dilthey, Wilhelm. *Leben Schleiermachers.* Berlin, 1870.*

Eichner, Hans. *Friedrich Schlegel.* New York, 1970.

Epstein, Klaus. *The Genesis of German Conservatism.* Princeton, N.J., 1966.

Esposito, Joseph L. *Schelling's Idealism and Philosophy of Nature.* London, 1977.

Fischer, Fritz. "Der deutsche Protestantismus und die Politik im 19. Jahrhundert." *Historische Zeitschrift* 170 (1951):473–518.

Moritz August von Bethmann-Hollweg und der Protestantismus. Berlin, 1938.

Fischer, Wolfram. "Soziale Unterschichtungen im Zeitalter der Frühindustrialisierung." *International Review of Social History* 8 (1963):414–35.

Franz, Günther, ed. *Beamtentum und Pfarrerstand, 1400–1800.* Limburg im Lahn, 1972.

Freund, Ismar. "Die deutsche Judenfrage vor 100 Jahren." *Zeitschrift für die Geschichte der Juden in Deutschland* 5 (1935):34–42.

Gerth, Hans. *Die sozialgeschichtliche Lage der bürgerlichen Intelligenz um die Wende des 18. Jahrhunderts: Ein Beitrag zur Geschichte des Frühliberalismus.* Frankfurt, 1935.

Gillis, John R. *The Prussian Bureaucracy in Crisis, 1840–1860: Origins of an Administrative Ethos.* Stanford, 1971.

Grube, Walter. *Der Stuttgarter Landtag, 1457–1957.* Stuttgart, 1957.

Hammer, Otto. *Schwäbisches Beamtentum.* Stuttgart, 1923.

Hartmann, Richard, *P. J. A. Feuerbach's Politische und Strafrechtliche Grundanschauungen.* Berlin, 1961.

Hasselhorn, Martin. *Der altwürttembergische Pfarrstand im 18. Jahrhundert.* Stuttgart, 1958.

Hatfield, Henry. *Aesthetic Paganism in German Literature.* Cambridge, Mass., 1964.

Haym, Rudolf. *Das Leben Max Dunckers.* Berlin, 1891.

Wilhelm von Humboldt, Lebensbild und Charakteristik. Berlin, 1856.

Heffter, Heinrich. *Die deutsche Selbstverwaltung im 19. Jahrhundert: Geschichte der Ideen und Institutionen.* Stuttgart, 1950.

Henning, Friedrich-Wilhelm. "Die Einführung der Gewerbefreihet und ihre Auswirkung auf das Handwerk in Deutschland," in Wilhelm Abel et al., eds., *Handwerksgeschichte in neuer Sicht,* pp. 142–72. Göttingen, 1970.
Hermelink, Heinrich. *Das Christenthum in der Menschheitsgeschichte von der französischen Revolution bis zur Gegenwart.* 2 vols. Stuttgart, 1951.
Geschichte der evangelischen Kirche in Württemberg von der Reformation bis zur Gegenwart. Stuttgart and Tübingen, 1949.
Hirsch, Emmanuel. *Geschichte der neuern evangelischen Theologie.* 5 vols. Gütersloh, 1949–54.
Hobsbawm, E. J. *The Age of Revolution, 1789–1848.* New York, 1964.
Holborn, Hajo. *A History of Modern Germany, 1648–1840.* New York. 1964.
Hollerbach, Alexander. *Der Rechtsgedanke bei Schelling.* Frankfurt, 1957.
Hölze, Erwin. *Das Alte Recht und die Revolution: Eine politische Geschichte Württembergs in der Revolutionszeit, 1789–1850.* Munich and Berlin, 1931.
Huber, Ernst Rudolf. *Deutsche Verfassungsgeschichte seit 1789.* 4 vols. Stuttgart, 1957–69.
Huch, Ricarda. *Die Romantik: Blütezeit, Ausbreitung und Verfall.* Tübingen, 1951.
Iggers, George G. *The German Conception of History: The National Tradition of Historical Thought from Herder to the Present.* Middletown, Conn., 1968.
Kade, Franz. *Schleiermachers Anteil an der Entwicklung des preussischen Bildungswesens von 1808–1818.* Leipzig, 1925.
Katz, Jacob. *Out of the Ghetto: The Social Background of Jewish Emancipation, 1770–1870.* Cambridge, Mass., 1973.
Keyser, Erich. *Bevölkerungsgeschichte Deutschlands.* Leipzig, 1938.
Kipper, Eberhard. *Johann Paul Anselm Feuerbach: Sein Leben als Denker.* Köln, 1969.
Kluckhohn, Paul. *Die Auffassung der Liebe in der Literatur des 18. Jahrhunderts und in der deutschen Romantik.* Halle, 1931.
Klüpfel, Karl. *Geschichte und Beschreibung der Universität Tübingen.* Tübingen, 1849.
Kolde, Theodor. *Die Universität Erlangen unter das Hause Wittelsbach, 1810–1890.* Erlangen and Leipzig, 1910.
Koselleck, Reinhart. *Preussen zwischen Reform und Revolution: Allgemeines Landrecht, Verwaltung und soziale Bewegung von 1791 bis 1848.* Stuttgart, 1967.
Krieger, Leonard. *The German Idea of Freedom: History of a Political Tradition.* Boston, 1957.
Kurz, Paul Konrad. *Künstler, Tribun, Apostel: Heinrich Heine's Auffassung vom Beruf des Dichters.* Munich, 1967.
Landes, David S. *The Unbound Prometheus: Technological Change and Industrial Development in Western Europe from 1750 to the Present.* Cambridge, 1969.
Landsberg, Erich. *Geschichte der deutschen Rechtswissenschaft.* Munich and Leipzig, 1910.
Lang, Gustav. *Geschichte der Stuttgarter Gelehrtenschule von ihren ersten Anfängen bis zum Jahre 1806.* Stuttgart, 1928.
Lehmann, Harmut. *Pietismus und weltliche Ordnung in Württemberg vom 17. bis zum 20. Jahrhundert.* Stuttgart, 1969.
Lenz, Max. *Geschichte der königlichen Friedrich-Wilhelms-Universität zu Berlin.* 4 vols. Halle, 1910–18.
Leube, Heinrich. *Das Tübinger Stift, 1770–1950.* Stuttgart, 1954.

Lukács, Georg. *Deutsche Realisten des 19. Jahrhunderts.* Berlin, 1952.
Lütge, Friedrich. *Deutsche Sozial- und Wirtschaftsgeschichte: Ein Ueberblick.* 3rd ed., rev. and exp. Berlin and Heidelberg, 1966.
Marquardt, Frederick D. "Pauperismus in Germany during the Vormärz." *Central European History* 2 (1969):76–88.
Masur, Gerhard. *Friedrich Julius Stahl: Geschichte seines Lebens.* Berlin, 1930.
Merz, Georg. *Das Bayerische Luthertum.* Munich, 1955.
Meyer, Michael A. *The Origins of the Modern Jew: Jewish Identity and European Culture in Germany, 1749–1824.* Detroit, 1967.
Mombert, Paul. *Bevölkerungslehre.* Jena, 1929.
Müller, Karl. *Die religiöse Erweckung in Württemberg am Anfang des 19. Jahrhunderts.* Tübingen, 1925.
Müller, Max. *Die Auswanderung der Württemberger nach Westpreussen und dem Netzegau, 1776–1786.* Stuttgart, 1935.
Neumann, Franz. *Der Hofmeister: Ein Beitrag zur Geschichte der Erziehung im achtzehnten Jahrhundert.* Halle, 1930.
Niebuhr, Richard R. *Schleiermacher on Christ and Religion: A New Introduction.* New York, 1964.
Perthes, Clemens Theodor. *Der Staatsdienst in Preussen.* Hamburg, 1838.
Radbruch, Gustav. *Paul Johann Anselm Feuerbach: Ein Juristenleben.* 2nd ed. Göttingen, 1957.
Reichlin-Meldegg, K. A. *H. E. G. Paulus und seine Zeit.* 2 vols. Stuttgart, 1853.*
Riehl, W. H. *Die bürgerliche Gesellschaft.* Stuttgart and Tübingen, 1851.
Ringer, Fritz K. *The Decline of the German Mandarins: The German Academic Community, 1890–1933.* Cambridge, Mass., 1969.
Ritschl, Albrecht. *Geschichte des Pietismus in der lutherischen Kirche des 17. und 18. Jahrhunderts.* 3 vols. Bonn, 1886.
Ritschl, O. *Die evanlgelisch-theologische Facultät zu Bonn in dem ersten Jahrhundert ihrer Geschichte, 1819–1919.* Bonn, 1919.
Rohr, Donald. *The Origins of Social Liberalism in Germany.* Chicago and London, 1963.
Rosenberg, Hans. *Bureaucracy, Aristocracy and Autocracy: The Prussian Experience, 1660–1815.* Boston, 1966.
Samuel, Richard. *Die poetische Staats- und Geschichtsauffasung Friedrich von Hardenbergs.* Frankfurt, 1925.
Sandkühler, Hans-Jörg. *Freiheit und Wirklichkeit: Zur Dialektik von Politik und Philosophie bei F. W. J. Schelling.* Frankfurt, 1968.
Scheel, Heinrich. *Süddeutsche Jakobiner: Klassenkämpfe und republikanische Bestrebungen im deutschen Süden ende des 18. Jahrhunderts.* Berlin, 1962.
Schlingensiepen-Pogge, Alexandra. *Das Sozialethos der lutherischen Aufklärungstheologie am Vorabend der industriellen Revolution.* Göttingen, 1967.
Schnabel, Franz. *Deutsche Geschichte im 19. Jahrhundert.* 2nd ed. 4 vols. Freiburg, 1947–9.
Schoeps, Hans-Joachim. *Das Andere Preussen: Konservative Gestalten und Probleme im Zeitalter Friedrich Wilhelms IV.* 3rd ed. Berlin, 1964.
Schulin, Ernst. "Ranke's erstes Buch." *Historische Zeitschrift* 203 (1967):587–93.
Schwarz, Paul. *Die Gelehrtenschulen Preussens unter dem Oberschulkollegium.* 2 vols. Berlin, 1910.
Shelton, Roy C. *The Young Hölderlin.* Bern and Frankfurt, 1973.

Simon, Walter. *The Failure of the Prussian Reform Movement, 1807–1819*. Ithaca, N.Y., 1955.
Sonnenschein, Albert. *Görres, Windischmann und Deutinger als christliche Philosophen*. Bochum, 1838.
Spiegel, Yorick. *Theologie der bürgerlichen Gesellschaft: Sozialphilosophie und Glaubenslehre bei Friedrich Schleiermacher*. Munich, 1968.
Stoll, Adolf. *Friedrich Karl von Savigny: Professorenjahren in Berlin*. Berlin, 1929.
Strauss, Herbert. "Pre-emancipation Prussian Policies towards the Jews, 1815–1847." *Leo Baeck Institute Yearbook* 11 (1966):107–36.
Trautz, Fritz. "Das Hambacher Fest und der Südwestdeutsche Frühliberalismus." *Heidelberger Jahrbücher* 2 (1958):14–52.
Treitschke, Heinrich von. *History of Germany in the Nineteenth Century*. Trans. by E. Paul and C. Paul. 6 vols. New York, 1919.
Valjavec, Fritz. *Die Entstehung der politischen Strömungen in Deutschland, 1770–1815*. Munich, 1951.
Vierhaus, Rudolf. "Ständewesen und Staatsverwaltung in Deutschland im späteren 18. Jahrhundert," in R. Vierhaus and M. Botzenhart, eds., *Dauer und Wandel in der Geschichte: Aspekte Europäischer Vergangenheit*, pp. 337–60. Münster, 1966.
Walker, Mack. *German Home Towns: Community, State and General Estate, 1648–1871*. Ithaca, N.Y., 1971.
Germany and the Emigration, 1816–1885. Cambridge, Mass., 1964.
"Home Towns and State Administrators: South German Politics, 1815–1830." *Political Science Quarterly* 82 (1967):35–60.
Wehler, Hans-Ulrich, ed. *Sozialgeschichte Heute: Festschrift für Hans Rosenberg*. Göttingen, 1974.
Weiland, Werner. *Der junge Friedrich Schlegel oder die Revolution in der Frühromantik*. Stuttgart, 1968.
Wendland, Walter. "Studien zur Erweckungsbewegung in Berlin (1810–1830)." *Jahrbuch der Brandenburgischen Kirchengeschichte* 19 (1924):5–77.
Wohlwill, Adolf. *Weltbürgertum und Vaterlandsliebe der Schwaben*. Hamburg, 1875.

Index

Index

Index